Your All-in-One Resource

On the CD that accompanies this book, you'll find additional resources to extend your learning.

The reference library includes the following fully searchable titles:

- *Microsoft Computer Dictionary*, 5th ed.
- *First Look 2007 Microsoft Office System* by Katherine Murray
- Windows Vista Product Guide

Also provided are a sample chapter and poster from *Look Both Ways: Help Protect Your Family on the Internet* by Linda Criddle.

The CD interface has a new look. You can use the tabs for an assortment of tasks:

- Check for book updates (if you have Internet access)
- Install the book's sample files
- Find links to helpful tools and resources
- Go online for product support or CD support
- Send us feedback

The following screen shot gives you a glimpse of the new interface.

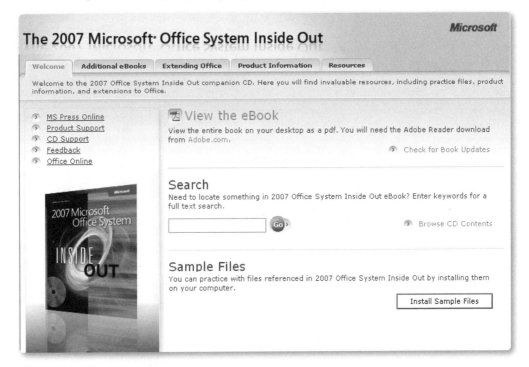

Microsoft

Microsoft® Office Excel® 2007 Inside Out

Mark Dodge
Craig Stinson

PUBLISHED BY
Microsoft Press
A Division of Microsoft Corporation
One Microsoft Way
Redmond, Washington 98052-6399

Library of Congress Control Number: 2006937709

Printed and bound in the United States of America.

2 3 4 5 6 7 8 9   QWT   2 1 0 9 8 7

Distributed in Canada by H.B. Fenn and Company Ltd.

A CIP catalogue record for this book is available from the British Library.

Microsoft Press books are available through booksellers and distributors worldwide. For further information about international editions, contact your local Microsoft Corporation office or contact Microsoft Press International directly at fax (425) 936-7329. Visit our Web site at www.microsoft.com/mspress. Send comments to mspinput@microsoft.com.

Microsoft, Microsoft Press, Access, Active Accessibility, ActiveX, AutoSum, Calibri, Cambria, Excel, IntelliMouse, Internet Explorer, MSDN, MS-DOS, MSN, Outlook, PivotChart, PivotTable, PowerPoint, SharePoint, SQL Server, Visual Basic, Windows, Windows Live, Windows Server, and Windows Vista are either registered trademarks or trademarks of Microsoft Corporation in the United States and/or other countries. Other product and company names mentioned herein may be the trademarks of their respective owners.

The example companies, organizations, products, domain names, e-mail addresses, logos, people, places, and events depicted herein are fictitious. No association with any real company, organization, product, domain name, e-mail address, logo, person, place, or event is intended or should be inferred.

This book expresses the author's views and opinions. The information contained in this book is provided without any express, statutory, or implied warranties. Neither the authors, Microsoft Corporation, nor its resellers, or distributors will be held liable for any damages caused or alleged to be caused either directly or indirectly by this book.

Acquisitions Editor: Juliana Aldous Atkinson
Developmental Editor: Sandra Haynes
Project Editor: Melissa von Tschudi-Sutton
Project Management: Publishing.com
Compositor: Curtis Philips

Technical Reviewer: Rozanne Whalen
Copy Editor: Kim Wimpsett
Proofreader: Andrea Fox
Indexer: Wright Information Indexing Services

Body Part No. X12-65192

In memory of

Regina Dodge

&

Leroy W. Southers, Jr.

Contents at a Glance

Table of Contents

What do you think of this book? We want to hear from you!

Microsoft is interested in hearing your feedback so we can continually improve our books and learning resources for you. To participate in a brief online survey, please visit:

www.microsoft.com/learning/booksurvey/

Part 5: Creating Formulas and Performing Data Analysis....... 425

Part 6: Creating Charts 613

What do you think of this book? We want to hear from you!

Microsoft is interested in hearing your feedback so we can continually improve our books and learning resources for you. To participate in a brief online survey, please visit:

www.microsoft.com/learning/booksurvey/

Acknowledgments

There is an old joke where a guy is beating himself on the head with a hammer. When asked why, he says "because it feels so good when I stop." We all can relate to this at times on book projects like this one, but when we get around to writing these acknowledgments, the beatings have subsided and the good feelings are already flowing. However, the hammer was soft and merciful during this particular project, due in large part to the efforts of a great team. Without them, we'd be lucky to publish a blog.

Thanks to Lucinda Rowley for presiding over the smoothly operating machine that is Microsoft Press, and thanks once again to Sandra Haynes for her masterful steerage of the good ship Inside Out. This book could never have existed without the patient and steady guidance of Curtis Philips of Publishing.com, as well as the unflinching eyes of Melissa von Tschudi-Sutton, Rozanne Murphy Whalen, Kim Wimpsett, and Andrea Fox. Sincere thanks to all those who had a hand in this (and related) endeavors, including but not limited to Juliana Aldous Atkinson, Linda Engelman, Bill Teel, Asa Noriega, Claudette Moore, Jensen Harris, John Pierce, and Sondra Scott. And a special serving of applause to Reed Jacobson and Gini Courter.

Musical props go to that woman who forced Mark to endure piano lessons at age 8, serving to "tune the instrument" for the next 46 years of a very musical life. Thanks, Mom.

About the CD

 The companion CD that ships with this book contains many tools and resources to help you get the most out of your Inside Out book.

What's on the CD

Your Inside Out CD includes the following:

- **Sample files** Click the Browse Sample Files link on the Welcome page to browse the sample files and resources referenced in the book.

- **Additional eBooks** In this section you'll find the following resources:
  - *Microsoft Computer Dictionary*, Fifth Edition
  - *First Look 2007 Microsoft Office System* (Katherine Murray, 2006)
  - Sample chapter and poster from *Look Both Ways: Help Protect Your Family on the Internet* (Linda Criddle, 2007)
  - Windows Vista Product Guide

- **Extending Office** Here you'll find links to Microsoft and other third-party tools that will help you get the most out of your software experience.

- **Resources** In this section, you'll find links to white papers, users assistance articles, product support information, insider blogs, tools, and much more.

System Requirements

The following are the minimum system requirements necessary to run the CD:

- Microsoft Windows Vista, Windows XP with Service Pack (SP) 2, Windows Server 2003 with SP1, or newer operating system

- 500 megahertz (MHz) processor or higher

- 2 gigabytes (GB) storage space (a portion of this disk space will be freed after installation if the original download package is removed from the hard drive)

- 256 megabytes (MB) RAM

- CD-ROM or DVD-ROM drive

- 1024×768 or higher resolution monitor

- Microsoft Windows or Windows Vista–compatible sound card and speakers

- Microsoft Internet Explorer 6 or newer

- Microsoft Mouse or compatible pointing device

> **Note**
> An Internet connection is necessary to access the hyperlinks on the companion CD. Connect time charges may apply.

Support Information

Every effort has been made to ensure the accuracy of the contents of the book and of this CD. As corrections or changes are collected, they will be added to a Microsoft Knowledge Base article. Microsoft Press provides support for books and companion CDs at the following Web site: *http://www.microsoft.com/learning/support/books/*.

If you have comments, questions, or ideas regarding the book or this CD, or questions that are not answered by visiting the site above, please send them via e-mail to *mspinput@microsoft.com*.

You can also click the Feedback or CD Support links on the Welcome page. Please note that Microsoft software product support is not offered through the above addresses.

If your question is about the software, and not about the content of this book, please visit the Microsoft Help and Support page or the Microsoft Knowledge Base at *http://support.microsoft.com*.

In the United States, Microsoft software product support issues not covered by the Microsoft Knowledge Base are addressed by Microsoft Product Support Services. Location-specific software support options are available from *http://support.microsoft.com/gp/selfoverview/*.

Microsoft Press provides corrections for books through the World Wide Web at *http://www.microsoft.com/mspress/support/*. To connect directly to the Microsoft Press Knowledge Base and enter a query regarding a question or issue that you may have, go to *http://www.microsoft.com/mspress/support/search.htm*.

> **Note**
> This companion CD relies on scripting for some interface enhancements. If scripting is disabled or unavailable in your browser, follow these steps to run the CD:
> 1. From My Computer, double-click the drive that contains this companion CD.
> 2. Open the Webfiles folder.
> 3. Double-click Welcome.htm to open the CD in your default browser.

Conventions and Features Used in This Book

This book uses special text and design conventions to make it easier for you to find the information you need.

Text Conventions

Convention	Meaning
Abbreviated commands for navigating the Ribbon	For your convenience, this book uses abbreviated commands. For example, "Click Home, Insert, Insert Cells" means that you should click the Home tab on the Ribbon, then click the Insert button, and finally click the Insert Cells command.
Boldface type	**Boldface** type is used to indicate text that you type.
Initial Capital Letters	The first letters of the names of tabs, dialog boxes, dialog box elements, and commands are capitalized. Example: the Save As dialog box.
Italicized type	*Italicized* type is used to indicate new terms.
Plus sign (+) in text	Keyboard shortcuts are indicated by a plus sign (+) separating two key names. For example, Ctrl+Alt+Delete means that you press the Ctrl, Alt, and Delete keys at the same time.

Design Conventions

INSIDE OUT This Statement Illustrates an Example of an "Inside Out" Heading

These are the book's signature tips. In these tips, you'll get the straight scoop on what's going on with the software—inside information about why a feature works the way it does. You'll also find handy workarounds to deal with software problems.

Sidebars

Sidebars provide helpful hints, timesaving tricks, or alternative procedures related to the task being discussed.

TROUBLESHOOTING

This statement illustrates an example of a "Troubleshooting" problem statement.

Look for these sidebars to find solutions to common problems you might encounter. Troubleshooting sidebars appear next to related information in the chapters. You can also use "Index to Troubleshooting Topics" at the back of the book to look up problems by topic.

Cross-references point you to other locations in the book that offer additional information about the topic being discussed.

CAUTION!

Cautions identify potential problems that you should look out for when you're completing a task or problems that you must address before you can complete a task.

Note

Notes offer additional information related to the task being discussed.

When an example has a related file that is included on the companion CD, this icon appears in the margin. You can use these files to follow along with the book's examples.

PART 1
Examining the Excel Environment

What's New in Microsoft Office Excel 2007

In 1962, Thomas Kuhn wrote *The Structure of Scientific Revolution*, the book that gave birth to the concept of the "paradigm shift." His premise was that scientific advancement is not evolutionary but rather "a series of peaceful interludes punctuated by intellectually violent revolutions." No mere software upgrade can hope to rise to the level of world-changing paradigms such as agriculture or movable type, but in the Microsoft Office universe, Microsoft Office Excel 2007 comes pretty close.

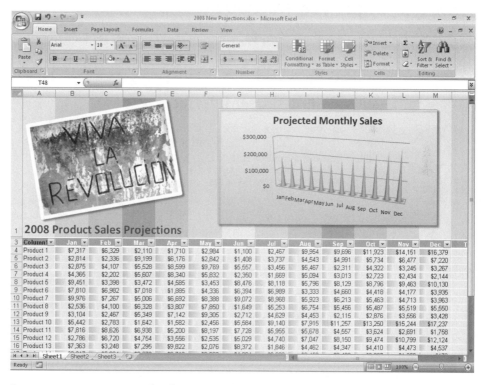

Sometimes new versions of software just don't seem compelling enough for you to take the upgrade plunge. You wonder how many more big leaps can really be made in usability and functionality. Excel has certainly evolved into a "mature" program. This release is definitely flashy, but it is nonetheless much more than just a cosmetic change.

This time, the cosmetics are simply a clue to the fundamental change in thinking that appears to have taken place. The new "results-oriented user interface" puts almost everything Office Excel 2007 can do out in the open, making more accessible many of the features that had previously been buried deep in menus and dialog boxes. Toolbars are passé; now there's the "Ribbon," a monolithic, dynamic tabbed bar that not only replaces 20-odd toolbars but also replaces the familiar multilevel menu structure with task-structured tabs and galleries.

Despite the radical change in appearance, the spreadsheet still works like a spreadsheet should; most of the previous version's tools and functions continue to work as expected, or even better. And if you have developed a vocabulary of keyboard command shortcuts to save time and clicks, the same keys will continue to perform the same actions. There are some differences and a few new procedures to learn, but initial challenges aside, we're sure that after you get used to working with the new interface, you won't miss the "old Excel." The following sections offer an overview of the new features you'll find in Excel 2007.

New and Improved for 2007

First, we'll highlight the new features in the 2007 release of Microsoft Office and Excel, and later, we'll talk about features that have been "retired" from the program and summarize the features that will be new to you if you skipped the last upgrade.

Results-Oriented User Interface

Microsoft Office
Button

The most obvious change in Excel 2007 is the way it looks and operates, as you can see in Figure 1-1. The familiar toolbars and menu bar are essentially gone, replaced by a single toolbar and a new "dashboard" called the Ribbon, with a task-oriented structure and easily recognizable tools. Most of the old menus have been reborn as tabs, except for the old File menu, which is now a big round button with the Microsoft Office logo on it, called the Microsoft Office Button. While you are working, you'll see applicable tools in context, showing you only the tools you need for the current task. For example, when you select a chart, the Chart Tools collection of contextual tabs appears on the Ribbon. And when you right-click pretty much anywhere on a worksheet, a context-sensitive menu of applicable commands appears as it has in past releases, but if appropriate, a floating toolbar also appears containing pertinent buttons.

For more information, see "Exploring the Ribbon" on page 30; also see Chapter 3, "Custom-Tailoring the Excel Workspace."

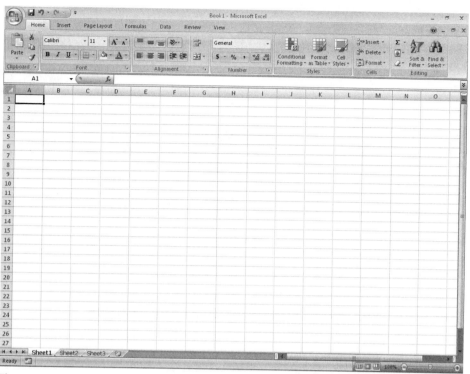

Figure 1-1 Excel 2007 looks and operates differently than previous versions. For example, the big orb with the Microsoft Office logo in the upper-left corner replaces the File menu.

Graphic Enhancements

Excel has improved greatly over the years as a platform for graphics and design, and this release includes a few subtle enhancements. Microsoft has folded the old Insert Diagram and Organization Chart features into a much more robust SmartArt feature. You display the SmartArt gallery shown in Figure 1-2 by clicking the SmartArt button on the Insert tab on the Ribbon. All the familiar devices such as Venn diagrams and flow charts are there, but now they sport a more sophisticated look. Other features with updated graphics include conditional formatting, shapes, charting, and the new document themes and cell styles.

For more information about graphic tools including SmartArt, see Chapter 10, "Creating Spiffy Graphics."

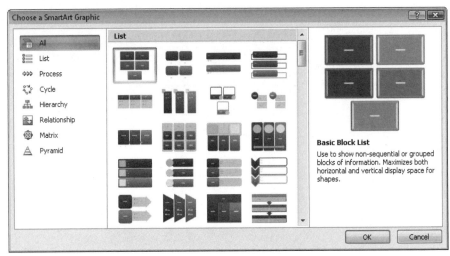

Figure 1-2 The SmartArt gallery gives a clue to the kind of visual enhancements added in Excel 2007.

Improved Formatting and Output Tools

Microsoft has built a lot more intelligence into the formatting features of Excel. Managing printed headers and footers is now easier using the new Page Layout view. And the new themes feature makes it possible to define distinctive color and font combinations that you can share with other Microsoft Office 2007 programs, making it easier to create a consistent look among your various electronic and paper-based communications materials. Many of the new formatting features such as cell styles come with palettes of presets, and you see live previews without actually having to apply any formats. Figure 1-3 shows the Color Scales palette of conditional formatting being used to find an appropriate preset to apply to a data table. Simply resting the pointer on the items in the palette causes Excel to change the selected area in the worksheet (or object), showing you what will happen when and if you click.

Page Layout View

Now you can see exactly what's going to happen when you print—at all times, if you like. Unlike Print Preview, Page Layout view is really more than a view; it's a working mode with rulers and page previews in which you have full editing functionality and control over the appearance of your documents, as you can see in Figure 1-4. If you create a lot of worksheets destined for publication, this might become your view of choice.

For more information about themes, cell styles, and other formatting features, see Chapter 9, Worksheet-Formatting Techniques." For more about output options, including Page Layout view, see Chapter 11, "Printing and Presenting."

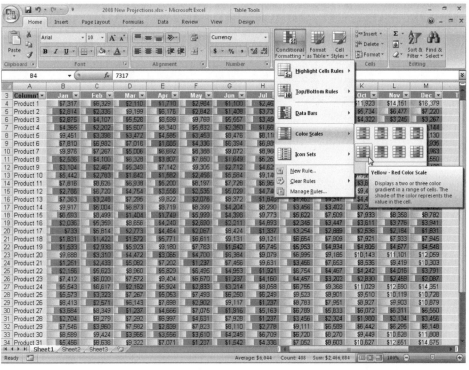

Figure 1-3 Rest the pointer on most palettes to see live previews of the effects on selected cells or objects.

New Templates

Excel now ships with a few more built-in templates for popular uses such as balance sheets and expense reports, but the real news is the enhanced New Workbook dialog box that gives you access to a vast library at Microsoft Office Online. Dozens of templates are available, addressing tasks ranging from the commonplace to the esoteric, such as a Bathroom Remodel Cost Calculator and two Baseball Scorecards—with and without pitch count.

For more information about using templates, see Chapter 9.

Updated Conditional-Formatting Features

Conditional formatting is almost like a new feature. It has been around for a while, but this enhancement makes it much more accessible and compelling. You can add visual impact using gradients and data bars to call out trends and thresholds, providing instantly understandable visual cues directly in cells. You can use conditionally triggered icon sets to add graphic elements that help call attention to extreme values in cells, as shown in Figure 1-5.

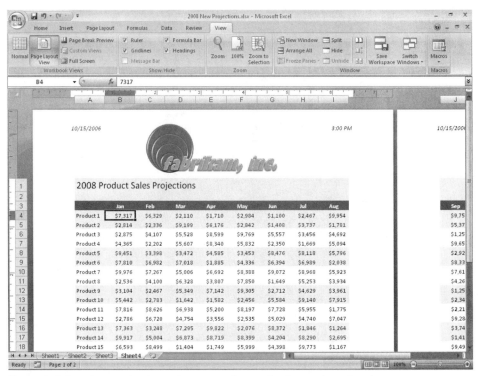

Figure 1-4 Page Layout view is a welcome new feature for fine-tuning printed output.

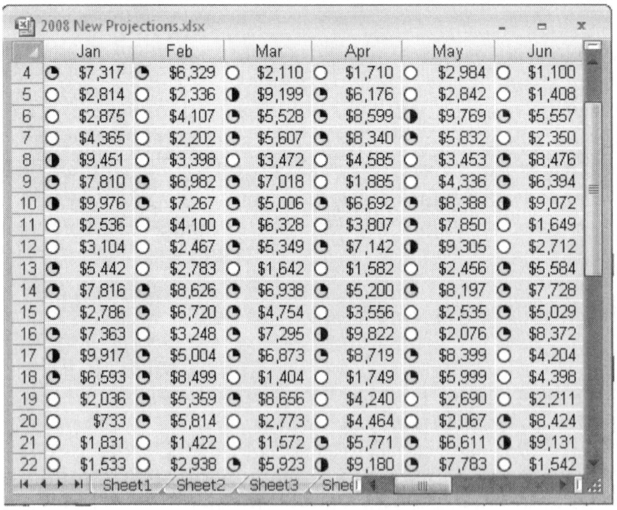

	Jan		Feb		Mar		Apr		May		Jun
4	$7,317		$6,329		$2,110		$1,710		$2,984		$1,100
5	$2,814		$2,336		$9,199		$6,176		$2,842		$1,408
6	$2,875		$4,107		$5,528		$8,599		$9,769		$5,557
7	$4,365		$2,202		$5,607		$8,340		$5,832		$2,350
8	$9,451		$3,398		$3,472		$4,585		$3,453		$8,476
9	$7,810		$6,982		$7,018		$1,885		$4,336		$6,394
10	$9,976		$7,267		$5,006		$6,692		$8,388		$9,072
11	$2,536		$4,100		$6,328		$3,807		$7,850		$1,649
12	$3,104		$2,467		$5,349		$7,142		$9,305		$2,712
13	$5,442		$2,783		$1,642		$1,582		$2,456		$5,584
14	$7,816		$8,626		$6,938		$5,200		$8,197		$7,728
15	$2,786		$6,720		$4,754		$3,556		$2,535		$5,029
16	$7,363		$3,248		$7,295		$9,822		$2,076		$8,372
17	$9,917		$5,004		$6,873		$8,719		$8,399		$4,204
18	$6,593		$8,499		$1,404		$1,749		$5,999		$4,398
19	$2,036		$5,359		$8,656		$4,240		$2,690		$2,211
20	$733		$5,814		$2,773		$4,464		$2,067		$8,424
21	$1,831		$1,422		$1,572		$5,771		$6,611		$9,131
22	$1,533		$2,938		$5,923		$9,180		$7,783		$1,542

Figure 1-5 Icon sets give you quick visual clues about relative values within tables of data.

For more information, see "Formatting Conditionally" on page 284.

Increased Capacity and Speed

The new XML file format and other internal improvements give Excel 2007 greatly increased capacities in just about every specification, such as spreadsheets that can hold more than 1 million rows of data and 64 levels of nesting in formulas. If your computer hardware supports it, you'll get built-in support for dual processors and multi-threaded chipsets. You probably didn't even know you used to be limited to a mere 4,000 formats in a workbook, but those days are gone; you can now pack up to 64,000 formats into a single workbook. (And what must such a workbook look like?) Here are the most compelling speed and capacity improvements in Excel 2007:

- The total number of available columns in Excel is now 16,384 (was 256).

- The total number of available rows in Excel is now 1,048,576 (was 65,536).

- The total amount of computer memory that Excel can use is now the maximum allowed by Microsoft Windows (was 1 megabyte).

- The number of unique colors allowed in a single workbook is now 4.3 billion (was 56).

- The number of conditional format conditions on a cell is now limited only by available memory (was 3).

- The number of levels of sorting you can perform on a range or table is now 64 (was 3).

- The number of items allowed in the Filter drop-down list is now 10,000 (was 1,000).

- The total number of unique cell formats in a workbook is now 64,000 (was 4,000)

- The maximum number of characters allowed in formulas is now 8,000 (was 1,000).

- The number of levels of nesting that Excel allows in formulas is now 64 (was 7).

- The maximum number of arguments allowed to a function in now 255 (was 30).

- The maximum number of items returned by the Find command is now 2 billion (was 64,000).

- The number of rows allowed in a PivotTable is now 1 million (was 64,000).

- The number of columns allowed in a PivotTable is now 16,000 (was 255).

- The maximum number of unique items within a single PivotTable field is now 1 million (was 32,000).

- The maximum length of the MDX name for a PivotTable item, the string length for a relational Pivot Table, the caption length, and field label length is now 32,000 (was 255).

- The number of fields that a single PivotTable can have is now 16,000 (was 255).

- The number of array formulas that can refer to another worksheet is now limited only by available memory (was 65,000).

- Excel now doesn't have any limit to the number of rows that you can refer to in an array formula (was 64,000).

- The number of categories allowed for custom functions is now 255 (was 32).

- Excel now supports dual processors and multithreaded chipsets.

Better and Easier Tables

What used to be referred to as *list management* in Excel has metamorphosed into a more robust table feature, incorporating PivotTable-like intelligence with easier formatting and editing. When you create a table, Excel automatically labels column headings and creates filtering controls, so you can quickly and easily focus on table rows of interest. A new Table Styles gallery puts dozens of well-designed formatting configurations at your disposal, providing easy experimentation and modification. Column headings in long tables stay in view as you scroll down the page (as shown in Figure 1-5), and tables are dynamic, so when you add rows or columns, Excel extends the formatting along with the appropriate formulas and filters.

With structured referencing, you can create formulas that cite table elements using column and row labels and special code characters. And the new Remove Duplicates feature in Excel 2007 also makes it easy to flag and remove duplicate entries. You could do this in earlier versions of Excel, but the functionality was hard to find and hard to use. Now the command is right there on the Ribbon.

For more information about tables, see Chapter 21, "Managing Information in Tables." For information about structured references, see "Using Structured References" on page 454.

Improved PivotTables and PivotCharts

Can such a seemingly simple feature as the ability to undo the changes made to a Pivot-Table change your life? Well, it might if you work with a lot of PivotTables. This addition plus a few key improvements to PivotTable filtering, design, and layout add up to an easier PivotTable lifestyle. And, the greatly improved appearance of the charting features trickle down so you can create more compelling PivotCharts, as well, as shown in Figure 1-6.

For more information about PivotTables and PivotCharts, see Chapter 22, "Analyzing Data with PivotTable Reports."

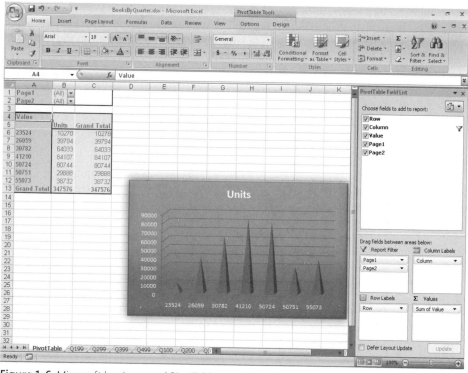

Figure 1-6 Microsoft has improved PivotTables and PivotCharts, and the new interface makes it easier to work with them.

Better Database Connectivity

Along with better PivotTables, Excel 2007 gives you more access to the kind of data that PivotTables were born to massage. Full support for SQL Server Analysis Services is now built in, which includes support for the Unified Dimensional Model (UDM), defining specific business metrics and logical constructions. This provides default fields and metadata for PivotTables, as well as support for Online Analytical Processing (OLAP) browsers and Key Performance Indicators (KPIs).

For more information about connectivity issues, see Chapter 23, "Working with External Data."

Formula AutoComplete

It was just a matter of time. Many of us have gotten accustomed to features that "auto-complete" for us; we get a drop-down list of uniform resource locators (URLs) in the Microsoft Internet Explorer Address text box as we type, Microsoft Office Word 2007 fixes common spelling errors for us (*teh* to *the*), and for a couple of releases now, Excel has had in-cell AutoComplete, offering menus of similar entries while we type columns of data. Now, typing functions in formulas is a little easier as well. When you type an equal sign followed by any letter, you get a drop-down list of functions that start with that letter, as shown in Figure 1-7. Type another letter, and the list narrows. If you have defined cell range names in your workbook, these appear in the list as well. As an added bonus, a brief description of the highlighted function appears in a floating ScreenTip. It's very handy.

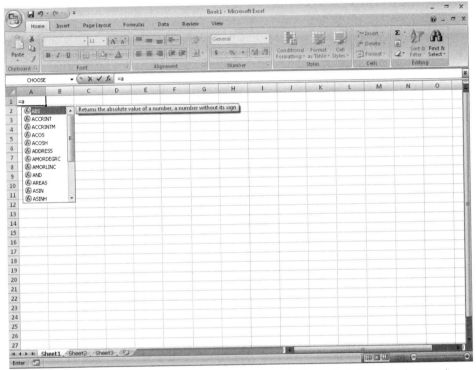

Figure 1-7 Type an equal sign and any letter (or letters) to display an AutoComplete function list with descriptive ScreenTips.

For more information about functions and AutoComplete, see Chapter 13, "Using Functions."

Tools for Creating Formulas

Besides Formula AutoComplete, Excel 2007 includes a few other niceties for your formula-building pleasure. The new formula bar is manually resizable to let you display or hide lengthy formulas, and you can enter longer formulas than ever, with more levels of nesting (parenthetical expressions within expressions). When you expand the formula bar, the worksheet cells move out of the way rather than the formula obscuring them. And Microsoft has updated the venerable cell range–naming feature to give you greater organization and editing possibilities using the new Name Manager dialog box, shown in Figure 1-8. In addition, Excel 2007 has many small improvements in the way it works internally, including improvements in subtotals and regression formulas.

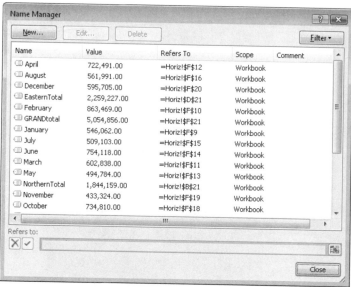

Figure 1-8 Use the Name Manager dialog box to audit and organize named ranges in your workbooks.

Built-In Analysis Toolpak Functions

The Analysis Toolpak add-in has been around for a long time. In previous editions, you had to manually enable these useful functions. However, at long last, Microsoft has fully integrated the trusty statistical functions of the add-in into the program. The odd news is that the functions now might produce slightly different results; however, the results are so insignificantly different that Microsoft says the results are nonetheless "equally correct."

For more information about using formulas and functions, see Chapter 12, "Building Formulas."

Enhanced Charting Features

Excel 2007 includes lots of new chart types, updated graphics, and a new Chart Tools set of contextual tabs that makes experimentation and modification a whole lot easier, as shown in Figure 1-9. You now have a lot more graphic flexibility with the chart elements; you can apply shadows, bevels, and most anything else you can do with other types of graphic elements. In addition, Microsoft Office PowerPoint 2007 and Office Word 2007 now use the Excel 2007 charting engine, making creating charts much easier and more powerful within those applications, as well as generally making charts in all your 2007 Microsoft Office system documents more consistent and easier to share, link, copy, and update.

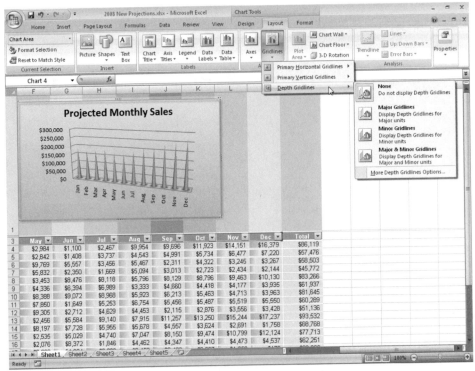

Figure 1-9 Charting is easier and flashier than ever.

For more information about charts, see Part 6, "Creating Charts."

New XLSX File Format

Although the phrase *new file format* tends to send shivers down the spines of IT profes-sionals, we have good news to report. The new Microsoft Office Open XML file formats (with the extension .xlsx in Excel) provide better integration with external data sources and result in significantly smaller file sizes. When saving Excel 2007 files that you need to share with others using previous versions of Excel, you can easily identify features that are not backward compatible in order to make any necessary modifications before saving. In addition, you can install converters that let you open and work on XLSX files in older versions of Excel without affecting any functionality specific to Excel 2007. Also, a new Compatibility mode becomes automatically active whenever you open a workbook saved in an older format. If you try to use an Excel 2007–specific feature while in Compatibility mode (which is indicated in the title bar), Excel lets you know you'll have to save the workbook in the XLSX format to preserve your changes.

For more information about file formats, see "Exploring File Management Fundamentals" on page 45.

INSIDE OUT Saving in Portable File Formats

Adobe's Portable Document Format (PDF) has historically been the most reliable format for capturing and sharing visual representations of documents across applications and computer platforms. Microsoft's XML Paper Specification (XPS) is the new kid in town with similar skills, created to take advantage of the efficiency of the XML format. Support for one or both formats is available as a separate download. On the Microsoft Web site (*www.microsoft.com*), click Downloads, and search for the Microsoft Save as PDF or XPS add-in.

Improved Sorting and Filtering

Managing large amounts of data is easier with improved sorting and filtering features. In previous versions, the Sort command allowed three levels of sorting at a time (for example, sorting by State, then by City, then by ZIP Code), but now you can specify up to 64 levels, which you can easily rearrange. The Filter feature shown in Figure 1-10 is better as well, offering the ability to make multiple selections in Filter drop-down lists, filter by color or date, filter PivotTable data, and apply custom filters to multiple items in a list.

The Remove Duplicates button (shown in Figure 1-10, in the Tools group on the Ribbon) helps make it easier to manage your database information, letting you specify in which columns to look for duplicate information.

For more information about sorting and filtering, see Chapter 21.

Collaboration Enhancements

If you have access to a server running Excel Services on Microsoft Office SharePoint Server 2007, you can save workbooks that other users can access by using Microsoft Office Excel Web Access. You also have control over which parts of the workbook are made available to these users. Excel Services makes it easy because you can upload an entire workbook and then specify both the components you want to publish and the permissions you want to grant. You can also use Excel Services with Document Management Server to establish validation actions and workflow notifications.

For more information, see Chapter 24, "Collaborating on a Network or by E-Mail."

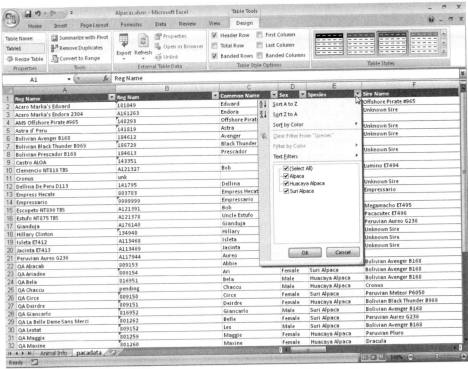

Figure 1-10 Filter is more automatic and provides more powerful filtering than ever.

Enhanced Security Features

Security is always top priority, and Microsoft has added a number of new features in Excel 2007 to help address this issue. The Trust Center is a central location where you can control how Excel responds to active content in add-ins, macros, and ActiveX controls, as well as providing control for trusted data sources. Plus, Excel now provides a Digital Signatures interface to help secure documents you share with others.

For more information, see Chapter 4, "Security and Privacy."

Retired in 2007

Software companies are reluctant to remove features from programs for fear of disrupting the workflow of customers using older versions of their programs. The most visible (and vocal) customers are large corporations with countless desktops. Nonetheless, sometimes you have to make the hard choices if features are not used often, if they cause more problems than they are worth, or if their functionality has been assimilated into a newer, better feature. Here is a list of retired (or assimilated) features:

- **The Office Assistant** The animated Help characters were, shall we say, not as popular as was hoped. Alas, poor Clippit, we hardly knew ye. Please send remembrances to the Microsoft Bob Memorial Fund for Homeless Virtual Personalities. The animated Help characters from previous editions of Office, like Rocky shown here, were distracting to some users and have been retired from this edition:

- **Natural-language formulas (NLFs)** This feature was well-intentioned but confusing and buggy, so it's gone. If you used NLFs in an existing workbook, Excel will inform you when you open it and will convert them to static cell references. Note, however, that the new structured references are better at this sort of task anyway. See "Using Structured References" on page 454.

- **Lists** At one point, Microsoft's usability studies found that making lists was one of the most common tasks mentioned by users of Excel. So Microsoft expanded on that functionality with a new tables feature.

- **Open file formats** The list of supported file formats used to be long indeed. Microsoft kept adding more formats with each edition. Many of them are no longer relevant or can be handled using another import or export method. Therefore, the following formats are no longer available in the Files Of Type list in the File Open dialog box: WK1, WK4, WJ3, WKS, WK3, WK1 FMT, WJ3 FJ3, WK3 FM3, WK1 ALL, WJ2, WQ1, WJ1, WKS, DBF 2, and Microsoft Excel Chart (.XLC).

- **Save file formats** Microsoft has also removed many outdated file formats from the Save menus, including some of its own Excel file formats. You can now use external converters in older versions of Excel to open files saved in the new Excel 2007 format, so the following save formats are no longer available: Excel 97 – Excel 2003 & 5.0/95 Workbook, Excel 3.0 Macro, Excel 2.1 Macro, Excel 4.0 Macro, Excel 2.1 Worksheet, Excel 4.0 Worksheet, Excel 3.0 Worksheet, Excel Chart (.XLC), Excel 4.0 Workbook, DBF 4, DBF 3, WK1, WK4, WKS, WK3, WK1 FMT, WK1 ALL, DBF 2, WQ1, and WK3 FM3.

- **Lotus 1-2-3 support** You might guess, judging by the file formats that are no longer available, Microsoft has finally abandoned its support for Lotus 1-2-3, but you'd be only partly right. Although you can't save or open Lotus 1-2-3 files anymore, you can still use Lotus 1-2-3 keyboard shortcuts such as pressing the slash (/) key to access the menus and then pressing "accelerator" keys to drill down the menu tree. Except, you may say, Excel doesn't really have menus anymore! Well, for accessibility's sake, these keyboard accelerators remain but are somewhat hidden. When you press the slash key, you will see KeyTips, little pop-ups containing a single letter that appear adjacent to the names of tabs and commands. This functionality replaces the little underlines you may have never noticed that appeared under the equivalent letter of each menu command in previous versions of Excel. And you can still activate what are called transition options (as in transitioning from Lotus 1-2-3 to Excel), governing the behavior of navigation keys as well as formula entry and evaluation.

● **Other** Some of the new features listed earlier in this chapter supersede old features that have undergone a major evolutionary leap; others may be similar in name but radically different procedurally. Some of the old ways of doing tasks may be gone, renamed, repurposed, or simply assimilated into the collective. Such features include charting, PivotTables, graphics in general, and toolbars. We'll go into detail on the redesign of these features in later chapters.

If You Missed the Last Upgrade . . .

Just in case you leapfrogged a software upgrade and missed the last big Microsoft Office release, here is a brief description of a few features that are essentially new to you but were actually introduced in the previous release:

● **Online assistance** In the previous release of Excel, Web-based assistance became a priority, with direct Help connections to Microsoft. The online Help system automatically looked for additional topics on the Microsoft Web site, making the system more complete and accurate. Online/offline integration was seamless—just connect to the Internet, and the Help system automatically availed itself of available online content. In addition, Microsoft added new features that control and enhance Web interactions and customer feedback. Microsoft has enhanced this online focus in Excel 2007.

● **Side-by-side comparison of worksheets** The Compare Side By Side command made it easy to scan differences between two worksheets, letting you scroll through both worksheets simultaneously to identify differences. In Excel 2007, Microsoft has transformed this command into a button named View Side By Side, but the functionality is still there.

● **Improved statistical functions** A number of the built-in statistical analysis functions became more accurate in Excel 2003; past versions of these functions had produced slightly different rounding results.

● **Task panes** Microsoft added the Research task pane, offering a wide variety of reference information and expanded resources with an Internet connection. The Research feature now lives on the Review tab on the Ribbon.

- **Collaboration** With the advent of Windows SharePoint Services (version 2), Excel 2003 provided improved support for collaborative projects. In 2007, Microsoft has made collaboration even more robust with Windows SharePoint Services (version 3).

- **Information Rights Management** The Information Rights Management (IRM) features introduced in Excel 2003 provided a measure of control over unauthorized access to your workbooks. Microsoft has updated this feature for 2007 and requires you to install a service pack (SP) upgrade to the Windows Rights Management client.

- **List management** Enhanced list management features in Excel 2003 helped ensure list integrity and made it easier to upload list ranges to Windows SharePoint Services sites. Excel 2007 discards the concept of lists and upgrades to the concept of tables.

Onward . . .

Taken together, the improvements made for the 2007 Microsoft Office system and Excel 2007 represent significant steps forward in ease of use, collaboration, and the publication of documents with visual impact. And if you skipped the last upgrade, you're really in for a treat—and a bit of re-education. Read on!

Chapter 1

Chapter 2
Exploring Excel Fundamentals

Before you can get the feel of the controls, you need to know where they are. This chapter tells you where to find the Microsoft Office Excel 2007 tools and accessories.

What Happens After You Install Excel?

This is really basic, but we have a moral obligation to briefly mention it anyway. You can start Office Excel 2007 in two principal ways:

- In Microsoft Windows, click Start, Microsoft Office Excel 2007 (or click All Programs, Microsoft Office, Microsoft Office Excel 2007).

- In Windows Explorer, double-click any Office Excel 2007 file or shortcut.

Activating Excel

Microsoft Office
Button

When you start Excel for the first time, you will be asked to register, or *activate*, the program. The easiest way to do this is by letting Excel register online, assuming your computer is connected to the Internet. (You're going to want that—we'll talk later.) Online registration is fast and painless and a lot easier than taking a postcard to the mailbox. It is also highly recommended. The Activation Wizard opens automatically when you first start the program. Alternatively, you can click Cancel and activate Excel later by clicking the Microsoft Office Button, clicking the Excel Options button, and selecting the Resources category to display the dialog box shown in Figure 2-1. You'll have to go through the completely painless activation process at some point—you can start Excel exactly 50 times without going through the activation process before the program stops being cooperative.

You may have qualms about any kind of owner registration, but with software, it's really a good idea—trust us. When you register, you'll automatically be in the loop for fixes (there will certainly be a service release or service pack available within a year or so), updates, and "special offers." Registering a garden tool, for example, may not be worth the annoyance of registering, but if you essentially get a new tool for free in a few months, you just might want to go for it. You won't see too many upgrades for weed whackers, of course, but with software you can rely on getting an upgrade at some point.

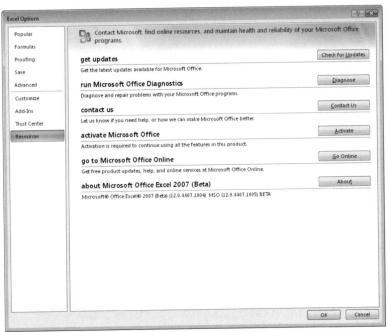

Figure 2-1 If you don't do it when you first start Excel, you can use the Excel Options dialog box to activate the program later.

Getting Updates

Microsoft service releases (SRs) begin to appear a year or so after the most recent version of the Microsoft Office system is released. Microsoft will probably always release at least one SR for each new version of Office/Excel and most likely will release more than one for releases of Windows. SRs comprise good bits of software code that replace bad bits, circumvent errors, or otherwise intercept known problems. These updates might even activate new features that were "hidden" because they were only partially implemented when the software finally had to ship.

SRs are always free, but they are not very well advertised. If your computer is connected to the Internet, the easiest way to keep your software current is to click the Check For Updates button. Click the Microsoft Office Button, and then click the Excel Options button. The Check For Updates button appears in the Resources category. Clicking this button displays the dialog box shown in Figure 2-2, where you will find links to any available updates for Microsoft products installed on your computer, including Windows.

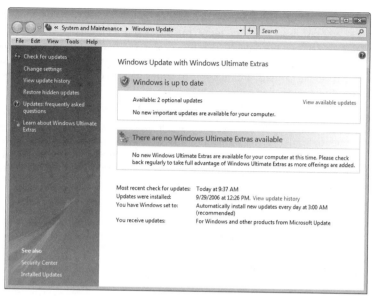

Figure 2-2 Click Check For Updates to keep your Microsoft products current.

Also in the Resources category in the Excel Options dialog box shown in Figure 2-1 is the Register button, which opens the Microsoft Office Online Web site where you can register for online services and special offers. You don't need to register to find lots of free stuff, but if you do, you'll get more options, including Microsoft Office Live, a Web hosting service. Microsoft Office Online is a sort of central clearinghouse for templates, general assistance, news, and lesser updates that might be available for individual programs or add-ins. You should definitely explore it.

Legacy of the Great Feature Wars

Software almost never ships with "showstopper" bugs anymore; rigorous beta testing generally takes care of these problems. That said, all companies routinely ship software that is riddled with bugs—it's the way of the software marketing world. Every software company is equally guilty. But why?

As the battle for market share raged among application developers in the 1980s and 1990s, the mantra among developers was "Ship, ship, ship!" They raced to see how fast they could release the next version of their products for several reasons. First, software products lived or died because of feature checklists published in major computer magazines. If the new version of your program didn't make it into, for example, the annual "Big Spreadsheet Showdown Issue," you and your development group were in deep doo-doo. So, product managers had incentive to link software development schedules with magazine publication dates. Second, most of the money earned by "mature" products such as Excel comes from upgrades, so software marketers pushed to ship new versions every year. But not only did customers have a hard time justifying the purchase of annual upgrades, developers had a hard time keeping pace. It takes time to develop ideas, write code, integrate it with existing code, and then document, design, manufacture, market, and distribute. Plus, the more "mature" a program becomes, the more complex and unpredictable it becomes. Chaos theory starts to rear its ugly head. Finally, these programs have to remain compatible with "legacy" systems; programs need to recognize their own old file formats, and features that may have been rendered essentially obsolete still have to be reconciled with new features.

Completely debugging a program as complex as Excel could take years. Some think it is impossible to absolutely eliminate all potential malfunctions in any program. Software companies determine an acceptable threshold and severity of bugs that are acceptable to ship in a "finished" product. The good news is that these leftover bugs are usually so esoteric that most folks will never have to deal with them. So, the next time someone complains about how "buggy" a particular program is, you can say with authority, "Aren't they all?"

Examining the Excel 2007 Workspace

This section will take you on a tour of not only the dashboard of Office Excel 2007 but also the trunk and the glove compartment. We might even slip on some gloves and take a peek under the floor mats.

Facts About Worksheets

Here are a few random tidbits of interesting information about the grid called the *worksheet*, shown in Figure 2-3.

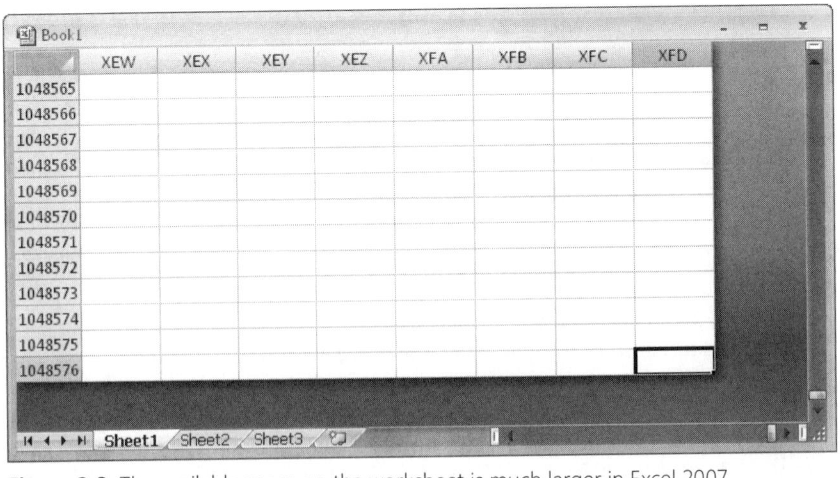

Figure 2-3 The available space on the worksheet is much larger in Excel 2007.

- Column letters range from A through XFD. (After column Z comes column AA, after column ZZ comes column AAA, and so on, up to XFD.) Row numbers range from 1 through 1,048,576.

- The currently selected cell is referred to as the *active cell*. When you select a range of cells, only the cell in the upper-left corner is considered the active cell. The reference of the active cell appears in the Name box on the left end of the formula bar.

- The headings for the columns and rows containing selected cells are highlighted, making it easier to identify the location of selected cells.

- With 16,000 columns and 1,048,576 rows, your worksheet contains more than 16 trillion individual cells. Before you try to unravel the mysteries of the universe on a single worksheet, however, remember that the number of cells you can use at a time is limited by the amount of memory your computer has. Although Excel allocates memory only to cells containing data, you might have trouble actually using *all* the cells on one worksheet, no matter how much memory you have.

Chapter 2

The Porthole Window

The workbook window is like a porthole through which you can see only a portion of a worksheet. To illustrate, suppose you were to cut a small, square hole in a piece of cardboard and place the cardboard over this page. At any given time, you could see only a portion of the page through the hole. By moving the cardboard around the page, however, you could eventually read the entire page through the window in your piece of cardboard. Viewing worksheets in Excel is much the same. You can also open another window to view different sections of the same worksheet simultaneously.

Using the Workbook Window

A new workbook, shown *floating* (that is, neither maximized nor minimized) in Figure 2-4, originally consists of three individual worksheets.

For more information about using workbooks, see Chapter 7, "How to Work a Workbook."

Workbooks are great organizational tools. For example, you can keep in the same workbook all the documents that relate to a specific project, department, or individual. Workbooks can eliminate a considerable amount of clutter on your hard disk. The more documents you have to manage, the more valuable workbooks become. You can use workbooks as a multiuser management tool. For example, you can organize worksheets in groups for individual tasks or individual users. You can also share a workbook so more than one person can work on it at the same time.

Chapter 2

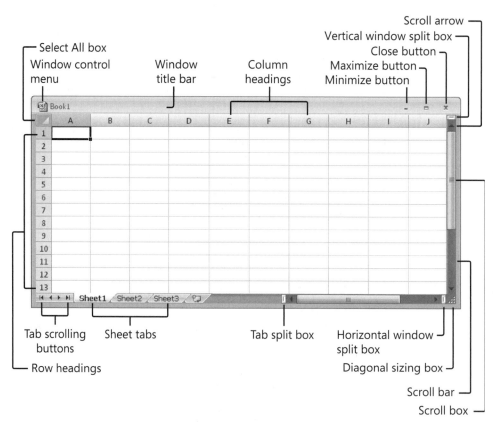

Figure 2-4 Workbooks initially comprise three worksheets.

If you routinely create folders on your hard disk to contain groups of related files, you can think of workbooks as folders where you can keep all related spreadsheets.

For more information about using and sharing workbooks, see Chapter 24, "Collaborating on a Network or by E-Mail."

The Title Bar

At the top of the Excel workspace is the *title bar*, which displays the application name along with the name of the workbook in which you are currently working. If the window is floating, as shown in Figure 2-4, the workbook name appears at the top of the window instead of at the top of the Excel workspace. (For more information about maximizing and minimizing your Excel workbook, see "Resizing the Window" on page 29.)

Getting Around in the Workbook

At the bottom of the workbook window are controls you can use to move from worksheet to worksheet in a workbook. Figure 2-5 shows these navigational controls.

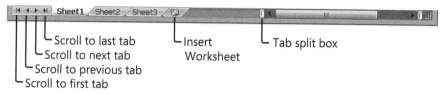

Scroll to last tab
Scroll to next tab
Scroll to previous tab
Scroll to first tab
Insert Worksheet
Tab split box

Figure 2-5 Use the workbook navigational controls to move among undisplayed worksheets.

You need the tab-scrolling buttons shown in Figure 2-5 only when your workbook contains more sheet tabs than can be displayed at once.

If You Have a Wheel Mouse

If you have one, you can use the wheel on your Microsoft IntelliMouse pointing device (or any wheel-equipped mouse) to scroll through your worksheet. Turn the wheel toward you to scroll down or away from you to scroll up. To scroll left to right, press the wheel button, and drag the mouse in the direction you want to move. (This is alternatively referred to as *panning*.) When you press the wheel button, a gray directional device appears, which is anchored to the spot where you first pressed the wheel button. The speed of panning depends on how far you drag away from the anchored directional device. As you press the button down and drag, a black arrow appears, pointing in the direction you're dragging:

You can change the default behavior of the wheel from scrolling to zooming. To do so, click the Microsoft Office Button, click Excel Options, and in the Advanced category, select the Zoom On Roll With IntelliMouse check box.

Chapter 2

For more information, see "Zooming Worksheets" on page 154.

Workbook Navigation Tips

Many features and controls can help you navigate through the rows, columns, and worksheets in a workbook. Here are the highlights:

- Use the sheet tab navigation buttons to view all the sheet tabs in your workbook; click a tab to view the contents of that worksheet.

- Drag the tab split box to the right if you want to see more sheet tabs at the expense of the horizontal scroll bar width. To return to the usual tab display, double-click the tab split bar.

- Press Ctrl+Page Down to activate the next worksheet in the workbook; press Ctrl+Page Up to activate the previous worksheet.

- Press Ctrl+Home to jump to cell A1 from anywhere on a worksheet.

- Right-click any scroll bar to display a shortcut menu dedicated to scrolling actions, as shown in Figure 2-6.

Figure 2-6 Right-click a scroll bar to display a shortcut menu of navigational commands. Only the active workbook window has scroll bars.

- Drag the scroll box (also known as the *scroll thumb*) to move around the worksheet. Click the scroll bar anywhere outside the scroll box to move one screen at a time in that direction.

- The size of the scroll box changes depending on the size of the scrollable area. For example, the scroll boxes shown in Figure 2-6 are more than half as large as the scroll bars themselves, indicating there is little more to see in the active area of the workbook—nothing, in fact, because this is a blank workbook. As you add data to more columns and rows than can appear on a single screen, the scroll boxes get proportionally smaller, giving you immediate feedback about the size of the worksheet.

- Using the scroll arrows at either end of the scroll bars, you can move through the worksheet one column or row at a time.

- The Name box at the left end of the formula bar always displays the active cell reference, regardless of where you scroll the window.

- To scroll the worksheet without changing the active cell, press Scroll Lock. For example, to scroll to the right one full screen without moving the active cell, press Scroll Lock, and then press Ctrl+Right Arrow.

> **Note**
>
> The *active area* of a worksheet is simply the rectangular area that encompasses all the data the worksheet contains. So if you have just three rows and columns of actual data in the top-left corner of the worksheet, the active area would be A1:C3. If on the same worksheet, a stray character (even a space) happens to be in cell AB1299, the active area would be A1:AB1299. On a new, blank worksheet, however, Excel considers the default active area to be roughly what you can see on the screen, even before you enter any data.

Resizing the Window

At the right end of the workbook window title bar are the Minimize, Maximize/Restore, and Close buttons. When your workbook window is maximized, the active window opens at full size in the Excel workspace.

After you maximize the window, a button with two small boxes—the Restore button—takes the place of the Maximize button. When you click the Restore button, the active window changes to a floating window.

> **INSIDE OUT**   **See More Rows on Your Screen**
>
> You can set the Windows taskbar at the bottom of the screen to automatically hide itself when not in use. Click the Windows Start button, click Control Panel, click Appearance And Personalization, and click Taskbar And Start Menu (in Windows XP, just click Taskbar And Start Menu in the Control Panel). On the Taskbar tab, select the Auto-Hide The Taskbar check box, and then click OK. Now the taskbar stays hidden and opens only when you move the pointer to the bottom of the screen.

When you click the Minimize button (the one with a small line at the bottom), the workbook collapses to a small title bar.

Minimizing workbooks is a handy way to reduce workspace clutter when you have several workbooks open at the same time. Click the Restore button on the title bar to display the workbook at its former floating size, or click the Maximize button to make the workbook fill the Excel workspace.

You can also drag the borders of a floating window to control its size. The smaller the window, the less you see of the worksheet; however, because you can open multiple windows for the same workbook, you might find it more convenient to view different parts of the workbook, or even different parts of an individual worksheet, side by side in two small windows rather than switch between worksheets or scroll back and forth in one large window.

INSIDE OUT   Microsoft and the SDI

No, we're not talking about the Strategic Defense Initiative (a.k.a. Star Wars). The single document interface (SDI) initiative that Microsoft implemented in its Office programs a couple of versions ago is, for the first time, an *option* in Office Excel 2007. Prior to SDI, regardless of the number of documents you had open, the applications were visible and available for task switching in Windows only by pressing Alt+Tab or by using the Windows taskbar. If you had three Excel worksheets open, you saw only one instance of Excel.

Microsoft's SDI initiative dictates that each document generates its own window, each of which becomes a separate item on the taskbar. Open three Excel worksheets, and you'll see three items on the taskbar. This is arguably a more realistic way to handle documents, which is why Microsoft did it in the first place. Some, however, might prefer the old method, which reduces the number of open windows on the desktop. In Excel 2007, you have the ability to choose between multiple document interface (MDI) and SDI. (By the way, you'll never see these terms used anywhere—for good reason: *Multiple* creates a single window, and *single* creates multiple windows. Geek double-speak!) To change from SDI (the default) to MDI, click the Microsoft Office Button, and then click the Excel Options button to display the dialog box of the same name. In the Personalize category, in the Top Options For Working With Excel area, clear the Show All Windows In The Taskbar check box, and then click OK to save your changes. Doing so causes only one Excel item to appear on the Windows taskbar regardless of how many workbooks you have open.

Exploring the Ribbon

After you get the raw data into Excel by whatever means, you'll be spending a lot of time using the Ribbon to massage and beautify your data. The Ribbon is one of the most ambitious user interface (UI) changes ever attempted, and it redefines the workflow in every 2007 Microsoft Office system program. You'll take a quick look here, but rest assured the Ribbon will be a hot topic throughout this book. Figure 2-7 shows the Ribbon at rest.

Figure 2-7 The Ribbon, which includes what used to be called the *menu bar,* dominates the top of the Excel window.

The Ribbon comprises a number of tabs, each containing several Ribbon groups, which in turn contain sets of related controls: commands, buttons, menus, galleries, and Dialog Box Launchers. The hierarchy within and among Ribbon tabs was designed to approximate a general "workflow" model, with the most often used features and options stacked more or less from left to right within and among tabs. For example, the Home tab contains commands you need when you create a new worksheet and start performing tasks such as cutting and pasting, formatting, and sorting. Well to the right of the Home tab, the Review tab contains commands relating to documents that are more or less complete, addressing issues such as verifying the spelling and protecting the document.

The Ribbon Speaks

For years now, many of us in the computer-book writing business have been anticipating early retirement due to the expected advent of stunningly simple user interfaces and the holy grail of "self-documenting" software. In reality, this goal has proven as elusive as the "paperless office," so we've kept as busy as ever. But this release of the 2007 Microsoft Office system represents another fine attempt at rendering our jobs obsolete. You can gain helpful information about your immediate surroundings by simply brandishing your pointer. For example, the left side of Figure 2-8 shows the ScreenTip that opens when you rest the pointer anywhere in the Number Format drop-down list. The right side of Figure 2-8 shows what happens when you click the Number Format drop-down list.

The icons representing the various options in the Number Format drop-down list shown in Figure 2-8 are another step in the right documentation direction, although further exploration might be required to discover the meaning of items such as the cryptic "12" icon for Number format. (See "Using Accounting Formats" on page 301.) And, as always, you can press F1 at any time to open the Excel Help window and gain additional insight.

> **Note**
>
> If you need to maximize your worksheet area, you can temporarily hide the Ribbon by double-clicking the active tab. Once hidden, clicking any tab puts the Ribbon back into view.

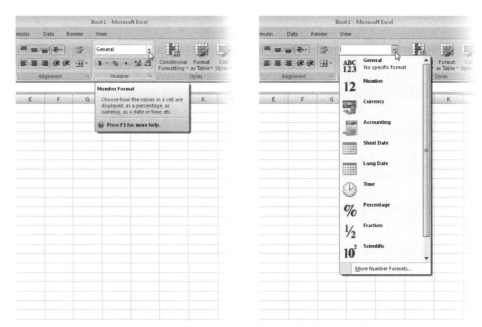

Figure 2-8 Rest your pointer on an object on the Ribbon to display an explanatory ScreenTip. Click any drop-down list on the Ribbon to display a menu, list, or gallery of options.

Drop-Down Lists and Dialog Box Launchers

The Number group on the Home tab shown in Figure 2-8 contains the aforementioned Number Format drop-down list, four regular buttons, and a menu button (the $ sign), which acts like any other button when you click the button proper, but when you click the arrow next to it, displays a drop-down list of alternate actions for that button. Anytime you see an arrow directly to the right of a button or a box on the Ribbon, clicking the arrow reveals more options. (Just to confuse the issue a bit, the Decrease Font Size button in the Font group has an identical arrow, which is actually part of the button and doesn't invoke a drop-down list.)

Many groups display a tiny button in the lower-right corner called a Dialog Box Launcher. This is a visual cue telling you there is more you can do there. When you rest the pointer on a Dialog Box Launcher, a ScreenTip opens with details about its function; click the Dialog Box Launcher to display the promised result, as shown in Figure 2-9.

Sometimes Dialog Box Launchers actually launch dialog boxes, as shown in Figure 2-9; other times clicking the Dialog Box Launcher displays a task pane on the side of the window, as shown in Figure 2-10. In the latter case, the Dialog Box Launcher button acts as a *toggle*—that is, clicking it opens the task pane, and clicking it again closes the task pane.

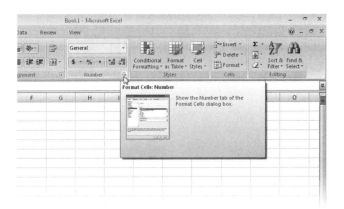

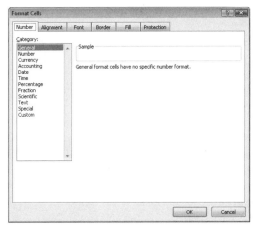

Figure 2-9 Rest the pointer on a Dialog Box Launcher button for an explanation of its function; click the button to open the corresponding dialog box.

Another way to access advanced options relegated to dialog boxes is to look for commands listed at the bottom of menus and galleries sporting an ellipsis (...). For example, at the bottom of the Number Format drop-down list shown in Figure 2-8 is a command called More Number Formats. Just like the Dialog Box Launcher, you can click this to display the Format Cells dialog box. As was the case in previous versions of Excel, an ellipsis adjacent to the name of a command indicates that clicking that command displays a dialog box with additional options rather than immediately issuing the command.

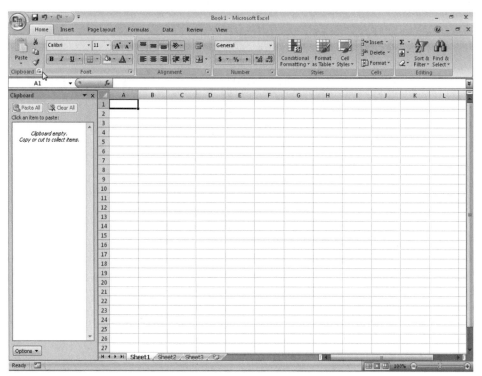

Figure 2-10 Clicking some Dialog Box Launcher buttons causes a task pane to open on the side of the window.

Galleries and Live Preview

The concept of galleries goes way back, even if the term is new to Office Excel 2007. The idea is to provide a visual clue about what's going to happen when you click something, besides just the name of a command or button. Microsoft has done this with fonts for some time now. When you click the Font menu or drop-down list, each font name appears in its own font. Excel 2007 includes a bunch of other galleries that provide similar visuals and adds nifty functionality called *live preview*. Taking the same example one step further, Figure 2-11 shows the Font drop-down list displaying the available fonts "in situ." With live preview, you simply rest the pointer on the font name to momentarily cause selected cells to display that font. (In the figure, the entire worksheet is selected.)

As you can see in Figure 2-11, perhaps Algerian isn't the best font for a table of sales totals, but it's easy to get a look at a lot of options this way. The cell contents are not affected; this is simply a way to visualize what will happen if you actually commit by clicking. Have some fun by dragging the pointer up and down the list of fonts and watching them change almost as fast as you can drag.

The Omnipotent Excel Options Dialog Box

The dialog box that opens when you click the Microsoft Office Button and then click Excel Options is probably the most important. As you can see, the Excel Options dialog box contains options that control nearly every aspect of Excel, including general settings such as how many worksheets appear in a default workbook and the name and point size of the default font:

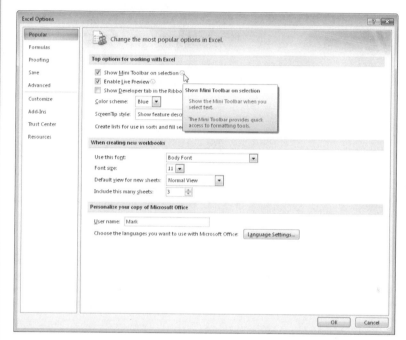

You'll see little *i* (for *information*) icons adjacent to many of the items shown in the dialog box; rest the pointer on them to display ScreenTips, as shown previously. The Excel Options dialog box also provides special settings for default file-saving formats, worksheet-level and workbook-level display settings, and many other hard-to-classify options. If you take a moment to click each tab on the left side of the dialog box and look through the options available, you'll get an idea of the scope of the program as well as the degree of control you have over your workspace. If you're unsure about what a particular setting or option does, simply click the Help button (the question mark icon) in the title bar of the dialog box to open the Help system.

Chapter 2

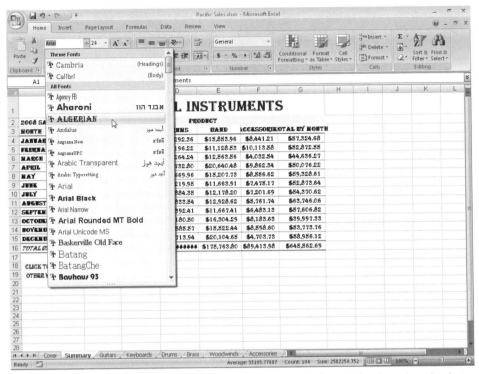

Figure 2-11 Not only are font names displayed in their respective fonts in the drop-down list, but simply resting the pointer on a font name temporarily displays that font in selected cells.

> **Note**
>
> Not all of the seemingly gallery-like items on the Ribbon exhibit this live preview behavior. For example, you might think the Number Format drop-down list would be an excellent application of live preview, but it doesn't work that way. As we explain features in detail throughout the book, we'll point out any live preview opportunities.

Introducing Contextual Tool Sets

Microsoft has been dancing with context sensitivity for several releases now. In 2000, Excel shipped with default "learning" menus and toolbars that modified themselves based on usage patterns, which turned out to be somewhat unpopular because commands would tend to "disappear" with lack of use. Some of this functionality carried through to Excel 2003, with a somewhat better implementation. The context sensitivity built into Office Excel 2007 is smarter and, best of all, does not take little-used items away like the previous approaches—in fact, the Ribbon and its normal contents remain steadfast, while additional context-triggered tools appear on Ribbon tabs that display only when needed. Figure 2-12 shows what happens when you click a chart object.

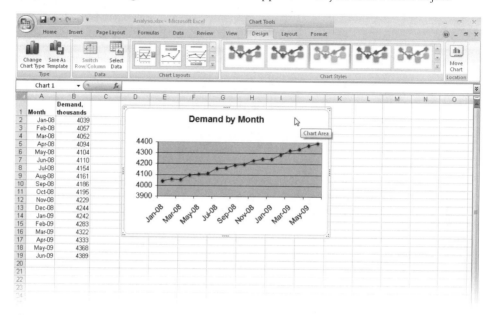

Figure 2-12 When you select an object, tabs appear containing tools that apply only to that object. Here, three tabs of chart tools appear on the Ribbon when a chart is selected.

Not only do three new tabs appear on the Ribbon in Figure 2-12—Design, Layout, and Format—you'll also see a higher-level heading, entitled Chart Tools, above the new tabs. These headings appear over sets of contextually triggered tabs to define their overall function. Chart objects are complex enough that clicking one triggers several tabs' worth of contextual tools; other objects might generate only one tab. This functionality helps reduce clutter in the interface, taking groups of task-specific tools out of the way until you need them.

Where Is the File Menu?

It's probably one of the three things you first notice once you start working with Office Excel 2007. At first, it looks like the old menus are across the top of the screen, just like before, until you start clicking and you see that no menus are dropping down. And then you notice that the "menu" names are different from what you remember. And just as you try to open one of your trusty old Excel files, it hits you—where's the File menu?

A new File menu is in town, called the Microsoft Office Button, which sports a big Microsoft Office logo. It's the big orb in the upper-left corner of the screen, as shown in Figure 2-13.

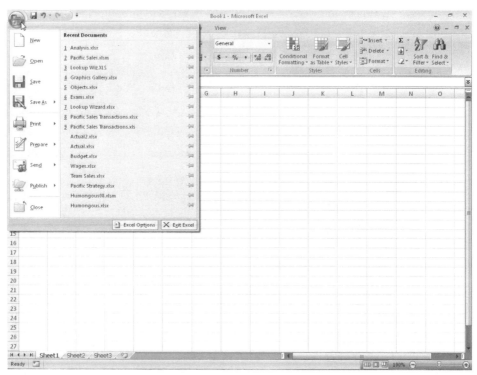

Figure 2-13 The new File menu is an orb with the 2007 Microsoft Office logo on it.

As you can see, even the one "menu" left doesn't really look much like a menu, but many of the old File menu commands are still here as clickable items on the left side of the menu. The Excel 2003 File menu used to be the longest menu in all the land! So, the new Microsoft Office Button is a definite organizational improvement.

Using the Quick Access Toolbar

It's hard not to think of the Ribbon as a toolbar, since anyone who has used Microsoft Office programs in the past 10 years or so has gotten accustomed to them and to the term. The Ribbon is not a toolbar according to Microsoft, and only one "real" toolbar is left. It's at the top of the screen, and it's now called the Quick Access Toolbar, as shown in Figure 2-14.

Figure 2-14 Meet the lone survivor of the Great Toolbar Massacre of 2006, the Quick Access Toolbar.

> **Note**
>
> To suit your work style, you can add buttons and even entire Ribbon groups to the Quick Access Toolbar. For more information, see "Customizing the Quick Access Toolbar" on page 83.

The Quick Access Toolbar is pretty much like toolbars as you knew them, with a few exceptions. You can dock it in only two locations—either above or below the Ribbon—unlike previous toolbars that could "float" over the worksheet or be docked at the top, bottom, or sides of the screen. And you cannot close or hide the Quick Access Toolbar.

INSIDE OUT   **Customizing the UI**

Some of us have spent time customizing the UI of Excel and other Microsoft Office programs by changing and adding toolbars and menus. Office Excel 2007 has only one toolbar, you cannot create new ones, and you cannot mess with the Ribbon at all. But perhaps not surprisingly, 98 percent of the Excel-using public will not miss this functionality. (This is an accurate number gleaned from usability surveys!) For those of us in the other 2 percent, we won't be getting our toolbars back, but we can still customize the Quick Access Toolbar, and for the more adventurous among us, Ribbon customization will be made possible with the help of the Microsoft Developer Network. Tweaking your UI has changed from being a procedure anyone could tackle by taking a peek "under the hood" and has moved further "behind the curtain," geared to those with a working relationship with Visual Basic for Applications (VBA). Visit MSDN.com, and check out the Ribbon tools.

Accessing Commands with the Keyboard

When you press the Alt key, Excel activates keyboard command mode and displays little pop-up labels adjacent to each tab and toolbar button, as shown at the top of Figure 2-15.

For example, after you press the Alt key to activate the pop-up labels, you can press the N key to display the Insert tab and add pop-up labels to the commands it contains. Then, press the M key—the pop-up letter adjacent to the SmartArt button—to display the SmartArt dialog box, as shown in Figure 2-15. So, instead of reaching for the mouse, simply pressing Alt, N, M gets you there. This makes for extremely fast command access after you've learned the right keys for tasks you do often.

Chapter 2

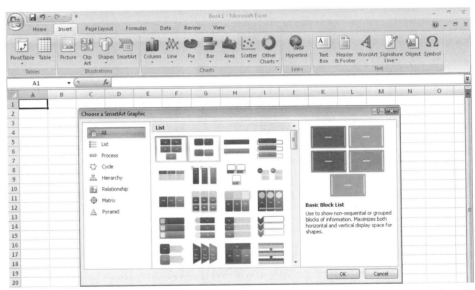

Figure 2-15 Press the Alt key to activate keyboard command mode and display pop-up labels showing you the keys you can press to activate the respective tab, button, or command.

Keyboard Command Activation Options

You can use the slash (/) key just like the Alt key to access the Excel command structure. But you can alternatively set a different key to activate menus. Click the Microsoft Office Button, click Excel Options, select the Advanced category, scroll down to the Lotus Compatibility options, and then type a different character in the Microsoft Office Excel Menu Key text box.

The Joy of Shortcut Menus

Shortcut menus contain only those commands that apply to the item indicated by the position of the pointer when you activate the menu. Shortcut menus provide a handy way to access the commands most likely to be useful at the pointer's current location and to help minimize mouse movements (which are hard on wrists!).

To access a shortcut menu, right-click. The menu opens adjacent to the pointer, as shown in Figure 2-16.

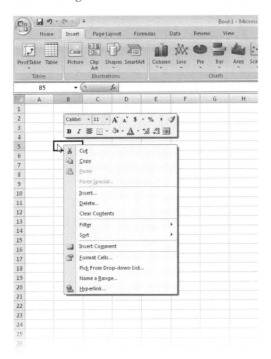

Figure 2-16 Right-clicking displays a shortcut menu.

Shortcut menus can contain many combinations of commands, depending on the position of the pointer and the type of worksheet. For example, if you display a shortcut menu when the pointer is on a cell rather than a column heading, some of the commands change to ones specific to cells rather than columns.

Belly Up to the Mini-Bar

A new feature added in Office Excel 2007 is the Mini toolbar, a small floating toolbar that opens along with the shortcut menu whenever the selected object can contain any kind of text, as you can see in Figure 2-16. You can control whether the Mini toolbar appears from the Excel Options dialog box. Click the Microsoft Office Button, click Excel Options, and in the Personalize category, select or clear the Show Mini Toolbar On Selection check box.

Meet the Formula Bar

Worksheet cells are the building blocks of Excel. They store and display the information you enter on an Excel worksheet so you can perform worksheet calculations. You can enter information directly in a cell, or you can enter information through the formula bar, as shown in Figure 2-17.

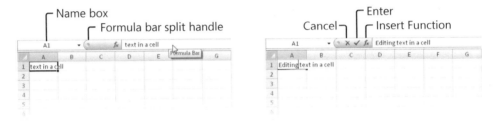

Figure 2-17 The formula bar displays the contents of the active cell.

The contents of the active cell appear in the formula bar, and the active cell address appears in the Name box at the left end of the formula bar. The formula bar split handle and the Insert Function button are always available, but the other two formula-editing buttons appear only while you are entering or editing data in a cell, as shown in Figure 2-17. Clicking the Cancel button cancels the current action in the cell and is the same as pressing the Esc key. Clicking the Enter button enters the current action in the cell and is the same as pressing the Enter key (except that pressing the Enter key also usually activates the cell directly below the active cell). You can drag the formula bar split handle to the left to make more room for formulas or to the right to increase the size of the Name box. Clicking the Insert Function button displays a dialog box that helps you construct formulas. For information about creating formulas and using the Insert Function dialog box, see Chapter 12, "Building Formulas."

Note

By default, Excel displays the formula bar in your workspace. If you prefer to hide the formula bar, click the View tab, and clear the Formula Bar check box in the Show/Hide group. To redisplay the formula bar, simply reverse this process.

A new wrinkle in Office Excel 2007 is the ability of the formula bar to expand and contract to display or hide long formulas. The formula bar split handle helps a bit, but for really long formulas the formula bar is vertically expandable, as shown in Figure 2-18. Previously, long formulas would cause the formula bar to open and obscure worksheet data, so this is a definite improvement.

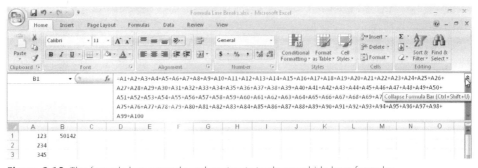

Figure 2-18 The formula bar expands and contracts to show or hide long formulas.

When you select a cell containing a long formula, you'll see only part of the formula in the formula bar. If there is more formula to be seen, Excel displays a set of up and down arrows at the right end of the formula bar, which you can use to scroll through the formula one line at a time. At the far right end of the formula bar is the Expand Formula Bar button sporting a chevron, which, when clicked, expands the formula bar. If you need to see even more of the formula, you can drag the bottom border of the formula bar as far as you need, as shown in Figure 2-18. (This particular 100-cell formula is good for illustrating the expanding formula bar, but failure to use the SUM function in this situation might get you drummed out of the Sensible Formulas Guild.) The next time you click the Expand Formula Bar chevron, the bar expands to the last size you specified.

> **Note**
>
> Functions are the Clydesdales of Excel—they do most of the heavy work. To learn all about functions, see Chapter 13, "Using Functions."

Facts About the Status Bar

The status bar, located at the bottom of the Excel window, displays information about what's happening in your workspace. For example, most of the time, Excel displays the word *Ready* at the left end of the status bar. When you type, the status bar displays the word *Enter*; when you double-click a cell that contains data, the status bar displays the word *Edit*.

Several items appear at the right end of the status bar: several buttons, a slider, and a display area for various purposes including summary information, keyboard modes, page numbers, and much more, any of which you can turn on or off. Right-click the status bar anywhere to show the Customize Status Bar shortcut menu filled with options, as shown in Figure 2-19.

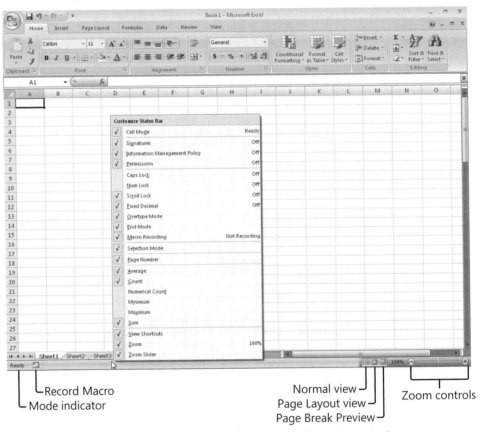

Figure 2-19 You have numerous options for displaying information on the status bar.

All the commands on the Status Bar Configuration menu with check marks adjacent to them are turned on by default. Most of the commands on this menu control the display of different types of information depending on what is selected. Cell Mode refers to the aforementioned Ready/Enter/Edit indicators when working in cells. The icon that looks like a spreadsheet with a tiny red ball shown in Figure 2-19 on the left side of the status bar is a record button for macros. The Macro Recording command controls its display. (If any macros are available, a Play arrow appears next to the icon, the display of which is controlled by the Macro Playback command.) The last three commands on the menu control the display of items on the right end of the status bar. View shortcuts are the three buttons (Normal, Page Layout View, and Page Break Preview) visible next to Zoom percentage and the Zoom slider, which also have corresponding commands controlling their display. Drag the Zoom slider to change the percentage, or click the percentage indicator to display the Zoom dialog box for more precision.

For more information about keyboard modes, see "Navigating Regions with the Keyboard" on page 126. For more about views, see Chapter 11, "Printing and Presenting."

Chapter 2

Quick Totals on the Status Bar

When you select two or more cells that contain values, Excel displays summary information using those values on the status bar:

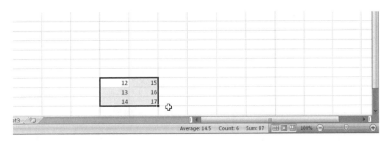

This is the AutoCalculate feature. The AutoCalculate area of the status bar usually displays the sum and average of the selected values, as well as the number of cells selected that contain any kind of data (blank cells are ignored). As you can see in Figure 2-19, additional AutoCalculate options are available, including Minimum and Maximum values in selected cells, and Numerical Count, which counts only cells containing numbers and ignores cells containing text.

Exploring File Management Fundamentals

One of the advantages of working with computers is the convenience of electronic files. In this section, we describe both the usual and unusual ways you can manage your Excel files.

Creating Workbooks

To create a new workbook, click the Microsoft Office Button, and click New to display the New Workbook dialog box, as shown in Figure 2-20. When you click Blank Workbook and press Enter (or click the Create button at the bottom of the dialog box), a fresh workbook opens. Each new workbook you create in the current Excel session is numbered sequentially: Book1, Book2, and so on.

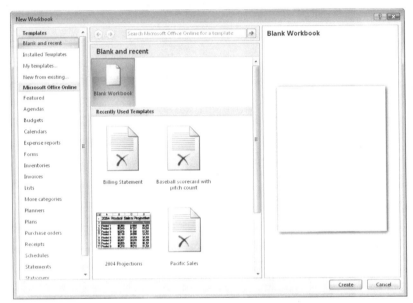

Figure 2-20 Click the Microsoft Office Button and then click New to display the New Workbook dialog box.

With the New Workbook dialog box, you can create all kinds of new workbooks from templates or existing workbooks. The category you select on the left side of the dialog box controls what appears on the right. The Blank And Recent category appears in the Templates group when you first open the dialog box. The categories on the left include the following items:

- **Blank And Recent** Clicking the Blank Workbook icon creates just that—a new, blank workbook. The Recently Used Templates area shows the last few templates you have opened.

- **My Templates** Clicking My Templates opens your own personal template treasure trove.

- **New From Existing** Clicking this icon displays the dialog box shown in Figure 2-21. This dialog box opens any existing Excel file as a template. This means two things happen differently than with the Open dialog box: First, instead of opening the actual workbook, it opens a copy of it. Second, when you save the workbook, it appends a number to the end of the file name and displays the Save As dialog box, making it virtually impossible to overwrite the original file.

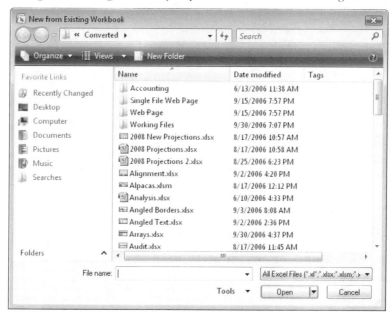

Figure 2-21 You create a copy of any file you select in the New From Existing Workbook dialog box.

- **Installed Templates** If you have used any templates, the New Workbook dialog box adds another group in the Blank And Recent area—Recently Used Templates, as shown in Figure 2-20. Selecting the Installed Templates category displays all the templates that are stored on your computer as part of your initial Excel installation, as shown in Figure 2-22.

- **Microsoft Office Online** While your computer is connected to the Internet, you can click items in the Microsoft Office Online area of the New Workbook dialog box to open the selected item or browse the Microsoft Web site for additional templates.

> **Note**
>
> You can choose whether to let the Microsoft Office Online area of the New Workbook dialog box be *active content*, which is dynamically updated via a Web connection. For more information, see "Privacy Options" on page 108.

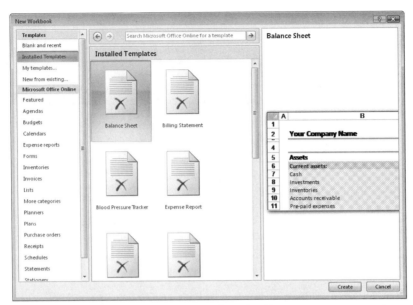

Figure 2-22 A number of templates are ready and waiting on your computer when you first install Excel.

Office Excel 2007, being more Web connected than ever, takes advantage of this by storing most templates on the Microsoft Office Online Web site, instead of putting them on your computer. This not only saves space on your hard disk but also makes it possible to offer many more templates than would be possible on CDs and makes it easy for developers to keep them up-to-date. Figure 2-23 shows just a few of the templates available in one of the categories.

Installing Your Own Templates

Installing your own templates is a great step to take with worksheets you use a lot. You can click New From Existing in the New Workbook dialog box to open any workbook as a template. Better yet, you can put any workbook in a special folder, and it automatically becomes an *installed* template. You can find this folder in the following locations:

- **Windows XP** C:\Documents and Settings\<your name>\Application Data\ Microsoft\Templates

- **Windows Vista** C:\Users\<your name>\AppData\Roaming\Microsoft\Templates

Anything you put in this folder will appear in the New dialog box, shown in Figure 2-24, which opens when you double-click the My Templates icon in the New Workbook dialog box. Great trick.

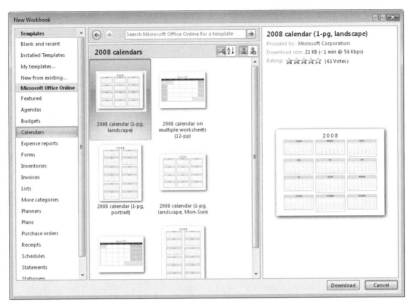

Figure 2-23 Microsoft Office Online provides a fortune in template treasures from which to choose.

INSIDE OUT Hidden Windows Folders Revealed

You will probably have to change a Windows setting to find the AppData folder (Application Data in Windows XP), because it is normally hidden. To reveal it, navigate to the folder that bears your name in Windows Explorer, as shown in the previous paths. Then from the Organize menu (the Tools menu in Windows XP), click Folder Options, and on the View tab, click Show Hidden Files And Folders. Note that <your name> is the user name you use when logging on to Windows.

Create Your Own Template Tabs

The New dialog box derives its contents from a special folder installed by the 2007 Microsoft Office system, as described in "Installing Your Own Templates" on the previous page. You can create subfolders in this special folder that become tabs in the New dialog box when they contain template files. The name of each folder becomes the title of each new tab. Figure 2-25 shows the New dialog box with a new tab, which opened after creating a folder in the Templates folder and adding an Excel template file.

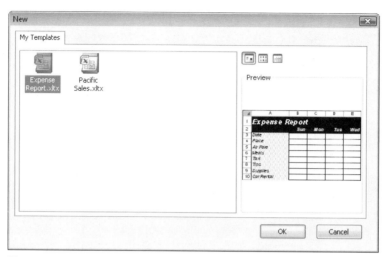

Figure 2-24 You can add your own templates to the New dialog box.

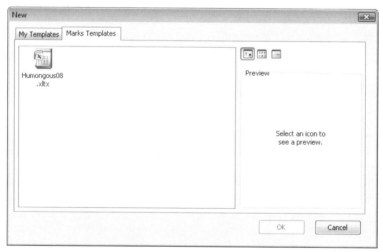

Figure 2-25 It's easy to create your own tabs in the New dialog box.

Note that in previous versions of Excel, you could put any type of Excel file into the Templates folder or any of its subfolders, and Excel would treat them all as templates. Office Excel 2007 no longer allows this—only template files show up in the New dialog box.

INSIDE OUT **Office-Wide Templates Tabs**

When you create a custom folder within the Templates folder, it is available to other 2007 Microsoft Office applications too. Your custom folder appears as a tab in the Templates dialog box of every 2007 Microsoft Office application, but only if the folder actually contains a template in that application's native format. For example, if you create an Accounting folder in the Templates folder and you copy a Microsoft Office Word 2007 document into it, the Accounting folder will appear as a tab in the Templates dialog box of Office Word 2007. If the folder contains only Excel files, the tab will not appear in Office Word 2007.

Saving Files

Arguably, the most important function of any computer application is preserving data. In Excel, you can save your files in many ways, including clicking the Save, Save As, Publish, Save Workspace, Close, and Exit commands and—the easiest way to save—clicking the Save button on the Quick Access Toolbar.

One other command that saves your workbooks is the Share Workbook command in the Changes group on the Review tab. When you click this command, you save your workbook in shared mode. Besides saving the file, this command makes the workbook available to others on a network, who can then open it and make changes of their own.

For more information, see "Sharing Workbooks on a Network" on page 790.

The first time you save a file, the Save As dialog box opens, as shown in Figure 2-26.

Note

If you use the same folder most of the time, you can specify that folder as the default location that the Open, Save, and Save As dialog boxes use when you first open them. Click the Microsoft Office Button, click Excel Options, select the Save category, and type the full path and file name for the folder you want to use in the Default File Location text box.

The Windows Vista version of the Save As dialog box has a lot more bells and whistles than previous versions. This is also true with other dialog boxes that are provided by the operating system, including Save and Open. If you haven't upgraded to Windows

Vista, you might as well. You're learning a lot of new stuff with 2007 Microsoft Office anyway, much of which was designed around Vista functionality, and the Save As dialog box is a good example. If you click the Browse Folders button, the dialog box expands to include a sophisticated new file interface that includes a number of useful Windows Vista features such as the ability to zoom the file display using a slider and the ability to customize the dialog box layout. For details, click the Help button (the question mark icon) in the Save As dialog box to display the corresponding Windows Help file.

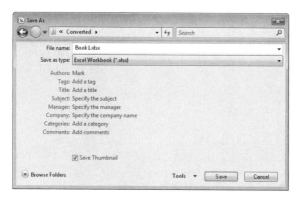

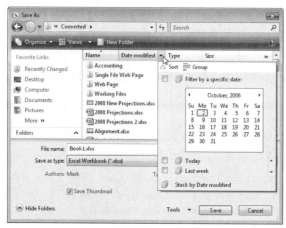

Figure 2-26 The Save As dialog box opens when you save a file for the first time.

Rules for File Naming

File names in Excel can have up to 218 characters. They can include any combination of alphanumeric characters, spaces, and the special characters, with the exception of the forward slash (/), backslash (\), greater-than sign (>), less-than sign (<), asterisk (*), question mark (?), quotation mark ("), pipe symbol (|), colon (:), and semicolon (;). Although you can use any combination of uppercase and lowercase letters, keep in mind that Excel does not distinguish case in file names. For example, to Excel the names *MYFILE*, *MyFile*, and *myfile* are identical.

How Much Disk Space Do You Need?

To ensure that a new copy of a file is properly saved before the original is deleted, Excel makes a temporary file when it saves and then deletes the original and renames the temporary file to the original name. This prevents loss of both the original and the version being saved if something goes wrong in mid-save. Because of this, you can never open, make changes to, and then save a file that is bigger than half the amount of available space on the disk being used. For example, if you are working with a file on a 1.44 megabyte (MB) floppy disk (yes, people do still use these on occasion), you cannot open, make changes to, and then save it if it is larger than approximately 720 kilobytes (KB) (which is a pretty big file). In this case, you would need to make all your changes in a copy of the workbook located on your hard disk and then save it to the floppy disk when you're finished. It's unlikely you'll run into this problem on a hard disk or CD, but if you do see symptoms of insufficient space while saving an Excel file, it might be time for a little disk cleanup or to install another disk drive.

The old familiar MS-DOS three-character file name extensions, which now come in a four-character version as well, help identify your Excel files, and they are added automatically when you save a file. Table 2-1 lists some of the Excel default extensions.

Table 2-1 The Excel Default Extensions

Document Type	Extension
Add-in	.xlam
Macro-enabled template	.xltm
Macro-enabled workbook	.xlsm
Excel binary workbook	.xlsb
XML data	.xml
XML spreadsheet 2003	.xml
Template	.xltx
Workbook	.xlsx
Workspace	.xlw

INSIDE OUT   Hidden File Name Extensions Revealed

Note that file name extensions might not appear with Windows file names, depending on your settings. To display file name extensions, click the Start button, and then click Computer (Control Panel in Windows XP). Next, click Folder Options (located on the Organize menu in Windows Vista), and on the View tab, scroll down and clear the Hide Extensions For Known File Types check box.

File Formats

In addition to providing the file name and location, you can specify a different file format in the Save As dialog box. Click the Save As Type drop-down list, which expands to reveal all the formats in which you can save your files.

The default format is Excel Workbook (XLSX), and you'll almost always use this option. If you want to export an Excel file to another program, however, you can use one of the other options to convert the file to a format that is readable by that program.

For more information about the Excel export formats, see "Importing and Exporting Files" later in this chapter on page 68.

Ensuring File Compatibility with Previous Versions of Excel

When you open a workbook in Office Excel 2007 that was created in a previous version of Excel, it automatically opens in Compatibility mode, a condition that is indicated in the Excel title bar, as shown in Figure 2-27. You can always tell by looking at the title bar whether you've converted a file to the new format.

Figure 2-27 Files created by any previous version of Excel open in Compatibility mode.

You can work normally with Compatibility mode, and when you save the file, it will remain in the old file format. If, however, you make any changes using features that are not compatible with the older version, the Excel Compatibility Checker intervenes when you save and displays a dialog box like the one in Figure 2-28.

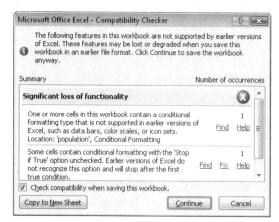

Figure 2-28 The Compatibility Checker opens when you try to save an old-format workbook containing features not supported by the older version of Excel.

INSIDE OUT   What Doesn't Work in Compatibility Mode?

When Compatibility mode is on, Excel disables a number of features that produce results that cannot be transferred to older versions of Excel. You can still click disabled commands, but when you do, Excel displays a ScreenTip explaining why you can't use it. For example, Office Excel 2007 allows 64 levels of nesting in formulas (parenthetical expressions within expressions), but previous versions allowed only 7. If you are working on a worksheet where you try to exceed the previous limitation, Excel prevents it and displays an error message:

Here are some of the things that can trigger compatibility error messages:

- A workbook contains too many rows and/or columns.
- A formula exceeds the maximum allowed number of characters.
- A formula exceeds seven nested levels.
- A formula exceeds the maximum number of arguments in a function.
- A formula contains more than 40 operands.
- A workbook contains too many cross-sheet array formulas.
- A workbook has more than 4,050 unique cell formats.
- A PivotTable field has more than 32,500 unique items.
- A PivotTable item has a string length greater than 255 characters.
- A PivotTable caption has more than 255 characters.
- A PivotTable field list has more than 1,024 fields.

In case you're wondering how to "get out of" Compatibility mode, all you have to do is save the workbook in one of the new file formats such as XLSX or XLSM and then close and reopen the new converted file you just saved.

The Compatibility Checker lets you know exactly what is causing the problem, so you can click Cancel and rework your worksheet using a different approach or save it anyway. You can click the Find or Fix links in the Compatibility Checker dialog box to highlight or correct each item that is causing compatibility problems. Clicking the Copy To New Sheet button adds a new worksheet to the current workbook entitled *Compatibility Report*, containing a copy of the information displayed in the dialog box—sort of a compatibility paper trail. If you clear the Check Compatibility When Saving This Workbook check box, this dialog box will no longer open when you save the current workbook. You might prefer this if you plan to repeatedly edit and save without updating the workbook to the new file format. But fear not, you can always look for problems at your convenience; click the Microsoft Office Button, click Prepare, and then click Run Compatibility Checker to display the same dialog box shown in Figure 2-28.

If you need to save files in other formats, the Save As Type drop-down list in the Save As dialog box includes a number of special formats you can choose, including Excel 97-2003 Workbook and Microsoft Excel 5.0/95 Workbook. Users of any of these versions of Excel can open a file saved in this format, but if someone using Excel 95 or Excel 5 saves changes to this file, any features from Excel versions 2000 through 2003, as well as the formatting, are lost. To alleviate this and other problems, you can download the Office 2007 Converter: File Format Compatibility Pack from the Office Online Web site to open and edit Excel 2007 files using earlier versions of Excel. When you use these converters, you don't have to save files in the old file format, and you don't have to upgrade the old Excel installation. You do, however, have to make sure you have the latest service pack (SP) installed. The easiest way to find the converters as well as the SPs is to press F1 to open the Excel Help window and click the File Conversion link (or type **file conversion** in the Search box). The File Conversion Help topic includes links to relevant topics containing the appropriate download locations on the Microsoft Office Online Web site.

For more information about the new, less-restrictive limitations of Excel, see "Increased Capacity and Speed" on page 9.

Understanding the "XL" Formats

Although Microsoft trimmed some of the lesser-used file formats from its list of file types, the volume of Excel 2007 file formats has swelled somewhat. Excel 2007 has 11 Excel-centric file formats; we'll explain the major differences here:

- **Excel Workbook (XLSX)** This is the new default Excel 2007 file format that is based on XML and uses ZIP compression for reduced file size and increased security. Note that unlike the default file format in previous versions of Excel (XLS), this format does not support VBA or XLM macro code.

- **Excel Macro-Enabled Workbook (XLSM)** Microsoft created a completely separate XML-based file type to be used for workbook files containing VBA or XLM macro code. This increases security by making it impossible to inject macro code into non-macro-enabled workbooks and makes for easier identification of files containing code.

- **Excel Binary Workbook (XLSB)** This is a lean and mean file format designed for the fastest possible loading and saving. It supports all the features of Office Excel 2007 and also supports macro code, but it is not XML based, does not use compression, and is less secure than XML-based formats.

- **Excel Template (XLTX)** This is the template version of the new Office Excel 2007 file format. Note that this format does not support VBA or XLM macro code.

- **Excel Macro-Enabled Template (XLTXM)** This is the template version of the Office Excel 2007 file format that does allow VBA and XLM macro code.

- **Excel 97-2003 Workbook (XLS)** This is the "legacy" file format used by previous versions of Excel.

- **Excel 97-2003 Template (XLT)** This is the "legacy" template format used by previous versions of Excel.

- **Excel Add-In (XLAM)** This is a special type of VBA-enabled workbook that can be loaded as a supplemental program in Excel.

In addition to these "XL" file types, there are two XML file types that are somewhat related. XML Spreadsheet 2003 (XML) is the previous XML file format provided as an option in Excel 2003. Another format shares the same extension but produces entirely different results: XML Data (XML) is a proprietary XML format that requires specific programmatic data maps to be present before you can even save the file. You'll know if you need it.

INSIDE OUT   What Is XML?

The new Office Excel 2007 file format is based on XML, which was created as a way for structured data to be interpreted and was originally envisioned for use on the Web. Excel 2003 introduced XML as an optional file format; the new Excel 2007 uses XML as the default format, indicated by the new file name extension .xlsx. Based on a file format specification called *SpreadsheetML*, Microsoft's implementation of XML has undergone significant improvements since being introduced. At first, the format didn't have, shall we say, sufficient language skills to interpret all of what Excel could do, including objects such as charts and graphics. The latest incarnation of SpreadsheetML can handle everything Excel can dish out and does so in a much more efficient manner than the old XLS format, resulting in significantly smaller file sizes. The new XML formats also provide improved recovery of damaged files and better overall security. And, because SpreadsheetML is part of an overall extensible Open XML format initiative coming with the 2007 Microsoft Office system, it's easier for developers to create ways to hook things together.

For some additional information about XML, see "Working with XML Files" on page 755.

Specifying the Default File Format

Usually when you save a new workbook, you'll save it in the Excel Workbook format (XLSX). You can specify a different format as the default for saving files. This might be helpful, for example, if you share files regularly with users of Excel 2003. To do so, click the Microsoft Office Button, click Excel Options, and select the Save category, shown in Figure 2-29.

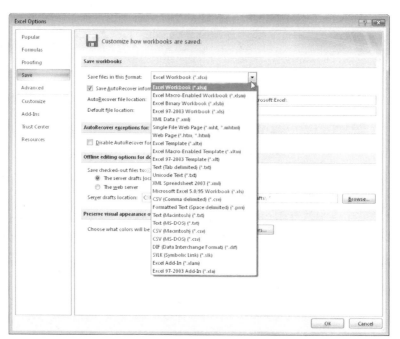

Figure 2-29 You can specify the default format to use when saving.

The Save Files In This Format drop-down list contains all the same file formats as the Save As Type drop-down list in the Save As dialog box.

Creating Automatic Backup Files

You can have Excel create a duplicate copy of your file on the same disk and in the same folder as the original, every time you save. Click the Microsoft Office Button, click Save As, click Tools at the bottom of the Save As dialog box, and click General Options to display the dialog box shown in Figure 2-30. Then select the Always Create Backup check box.

The backup file is a duplicate file that carries the same name as your original, but the name is preceded by *Backup of* and has the file name extension .xlk.

CAUTION

Keep in mind that Excel always uses an .xlk extension when creating backup files regardless of the file type. Suppose you work with a workbook named Myfile.xls as well as a template file on disk named Myfile.xlt and you select the Always Create Backup check box for both. Because only one Myfile.xlk can exist, the most recently saved file is saved as the .xlk file, and Excel overwrites the other file's backup if one exists.

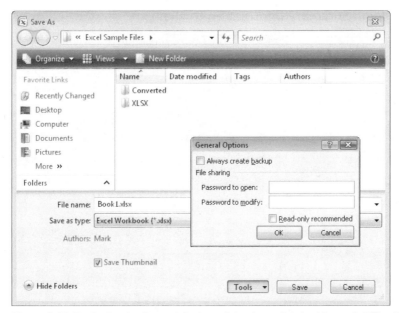

Figure 2-30 To display the General Options dialog box, click the Microsoft Office Button, click Save As, and then click Tools, General Options.

Protecting Files

You can password protect your files by using options in the General Options dialog box shown in Figure 2-30. Choose from two types of passwords: Password To Open and Password To Modify. Passwords can have up to 15 characters, and capitalization matters. Thus, if you assign the password *Secret* to a file, you can't reopen that file by typing *SECRET* or *secret*.

- **Password To Open** Excel prompts you to supply the password before reopening the file.

- **Password To Modify** Anyone can look at the file, but they need the password to open or save it.

- **Read-Only Recommended** This politely suggests that the user open the file as read-only.

INSIDE OUT   Create a Better Password

Although Microsoft has tightened the under-the-hood security measures of Excel over the years, some people delight in finding new and better ways to crack passwords. You can help by simply building better passwords. Make sure your password is eight or more characters long—the longer, the better—and try to use a healthy mix of capital and lowercase alphanumeric characters and nonalphanumeric characters.

Chapter 2

Adding Summary Information to Files

When you click the Microsoft Office Button, click Prepare, and then click Properties, Excel displays a Properties Ribbon that you use to record general information about the active workbook, as shown in Figure 2-31.

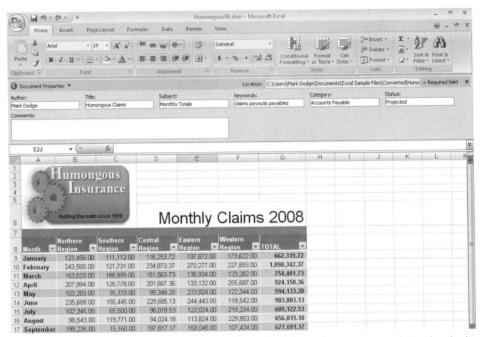

Figure 2-31 Use the Properties Ribbon to add descriptive information you can use later when looking for that needle in a file stack.

If you juggle a lot of files, getting into the habit of adding properties can make it a lot easier to find something later. This is easy to do using the Open dialog box, as shown in Figure 2-32.

Click the Microsoft Office Button, click Open, select a file, and on the Organize menu, click Properties to display a dialog box full of information. All the summary information is visible on the Details tab. You can even edit much of the Description and Origin information shown on the Details tab—simply select the value you want to change and type, as shown in Figure 2-32. Also, Windows looks at these property values when you use the Search command to locate files on your computer.

Saving the Entire Workspace

Click the View tab, and in the Window group, click Save Workspace to save a snapshot of your current Excel environment. When you save a workspace, Excel notes the locations of all the workbooks that are currently open, as well as many of the workspace settings, so you can retrieve your files and settings in the same configuration they were in when you saved. Settings that are saved with workspaces include many display and calculation settings. The default file name suggested for a workspace file is Resume.xlw, but you can rename it.

> **Note**
>
> The Save Workspace command pertains to a different universe, as compared with the Create Document Workspace command, revealed by clicking the Microsoft Office Button and then the Publish tab. A document workspace is a 2007 Microsoft Office collaboration tool for people who work on projects in teams. For more information, see "Creating a New Document Workspace" on page 816.

Chapter 2

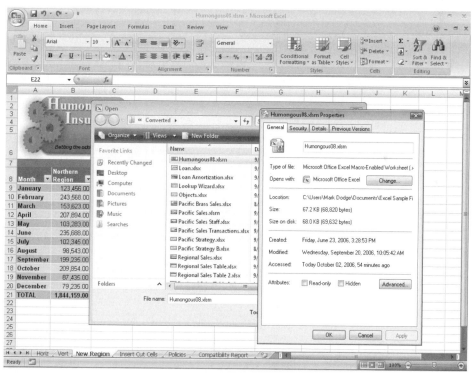

Figure 2-32 View properties about any file before you open it.

Linking Custom Properties to Cells

You can link your own custom-built properties to named cells on your worksheet. When you do, the value of the custom property becomes whatever the named cell contains and changes whenever the value in the cell changes. First you must name a cell (see "Rules for Naming" on page 445). Then open the Properties dialog box by clicking the words *Document Properties* in the title bar of the Properties Ribbon and then clicking Advanced Properties. The Custom tab in the Properties dialog box activates a Link To Content check box when a named cell is available in the workbook. When you select the Link To Content check box, the workbook's defined names appear in the Value drop-down list (whose name changes to Source when linking content), as shown in Figure 2-33.

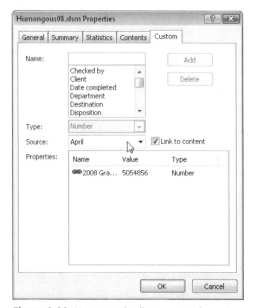

Figure 2-33 Use named cells to create dynamic properties based on worksheet cells.

Select or create a name for the custom property in the Name box. (The Type drop-down list becomes unavailable when you're linking to content.) When you've specified a Source (the named cell to which you want to link), click Add, and the custom property appears in the Properties list.

If the link is broken (the defined name is deleted, for example), the Properties dialog box stores the last value recorded for that property.

If the name defines a range of cells, only the value in the cell in the upper-left corner of the range appears as the property value.

Opening Files

Only slightly less basic than saving files is opening them. Click the Microsoft Office Button, and click Open to display the Open dialog box, shown in Figure 2-34.

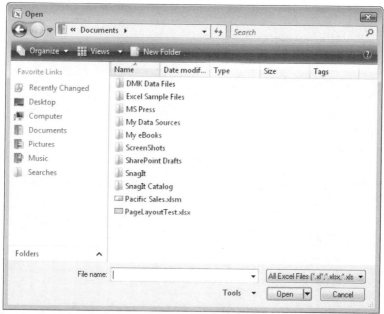

Figure 2-34 Click the arrow next to the Open button for more choices when opening documents.

Click the Favorite Links icons on the left side of the dialog box to display the corresponding files on the right side. Clicking the Documents icon displays the contents of the folder of the same name when you first open the dialog box, unless you have changed the default file location (click the Microsoft Office Button, click Excel Options, and select the Save category).

- The Recent icon lists files you have opened and folders you have navigated to, in chronological order with the latest first. This view actually displays the contents of an Application Data folder named Recent, which is populated automatically with shortcuts to the files and folders you use in the Open and Save As dialog boxes.

- The Desktop icon brings you to the top level of your computer's file system so you can click your way down through the hierarchy.

- The Documents icon displays the contents of the Documents folder.

- The Computer icon displays all storage locations available on your computer, including disks, CD and DVD drives, and shared folders.

- The Network Shortcuts icon opens files in any available locations on your network or on the Web.

- The drop-down list to the right of the File Name text box at the bottom of the Open dialog box determines which files are available for selection. The default option is All Microsoft Excel Files, which displays file names whose extensions begin with *xl*. You can display specific file types or all files by clicking the arrow to the right of the menu.

> **Note**
>
> To open several files at once, press the Ctrl key, and select each file name you want to open.

- With the Views button, you can select different ways to display files in the dialog box.

- The Tools button displays a drop-down list that contains a single command, Map Network Drive, which lets you connect to a location on your network.

> **Note**
>
> You can right-click most files listed in the Open and Save As dialog boxes to display a shortcut menu that contains commands you can use with the selected file. For example, you can delete a file displayed in the Open dialog box by using this shortcut menu.

Notice that headings appear at the top of the file list in the Open dialog box. When you click one of these headings, you sort the files in order, based on that heading. For example, if you click the Date Modified heading, you sort the files in date order. You can further refine your quest using the hidden menus adjacent to each heading. When you rest the pointer on a heading, a downward-pointing arrow appears to the right of the heading; click it to display a menu of additional options pertinent to that heading, as shown in Figure 2-35.

Each heading has its own menu of options, some of which are based on the actual files contained in the current folder. For example, when you click the menu for the Type heading, you can select from the list of file types contained in the folder.

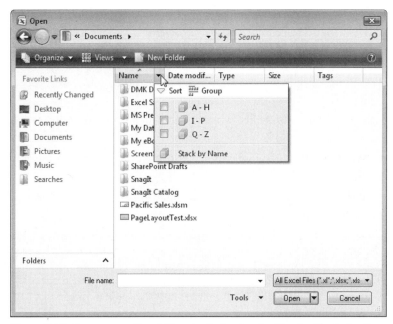

Figure 2-35 You can specify additional criteria when looking for files in the Open dialog box, using the menu buttons adjacent to each heading in the file list.

Special Ways to Open Files

To the right of Open at the bottom of the Open dialog box is a small arrow. Clicking this arrow (see Figure 2-34) displays a menu containing the following options:

- **Open Read-Only** This opens the file so you cannot save any changes made to it without renaming it.

- **Open As Copy** This creates a duplicate of the selected file, adds the words *Copy of* to the file name, and leaves the original untouched.

- **Open In Browser** This applies only to HTML documents and opens the selected file in your default Web browser.

- **Open And Repair** This is a powerful feature that you can use to try opening corrupted files. For more information, see "Recovering Corrupted Files" on the next page.

Opening Files When You Start Excel

If you have files you need to work on every day, you can store them in a special folder called XLStart. Every time you start Excel, any files in the XLStart folder automatically open.

> **Note**
>
> You can save workspace files in the XLStart folder so that all the files and the workspace setup are automatically loaded each time you start Excel. For more information about workspace files, see "Saving the Entire Workspace" earlier in this chapter on page 60.

The XLStart folder was created when you installed Excel and is located in the following place:

- **Windows XP**   C:\Documents and Settings\<your name>\Application Data\ Microsoft\Excel\XLStart

- **Windows Vista**   C:\Users\<your name>\AppData\Roaming\Microsoft\Excel\ XLStart

If you want to start Excel and simultaneously open files that are in a folder other than the XLStart folder, you can specify an alternate startup folder. Click the Microsoft Office Button, click Excel Options, select the Advanced category, and in the At Startup, Open All Files In text box under General options, type the full path of the folder. This feature is particularly useful if your computer is connected to a network and you want to open files from a shared folder.

Recovering Corrupted Files

Figure 2-34 shows the Open dialog box, where you'll find the Open Options menu (the arrow next to the Open button) containing the Open And Repair command. This command gives you a fighting chance at either repairing a corrupted file or extracting the data from it if it doesn't respond to a repair attempt. When you select a file and click the Open And Repair command, the message box shown in Figure 2-36 opens.

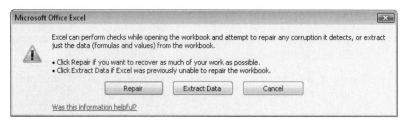

Figure 2-36 The Open And Repair command gives you a ray of hope for recovering lost data.

Try the Repair button first, and if Excel still has no luck opening the file, try the Extract Data button, which displays the message box shown in Figure 2-37.

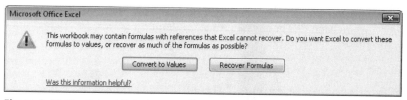

Figure 2-37 The Extract Data button offers two ways to recover your data.

You'll have to make a judgment call here—if you think your formulas will be OK after extraction, click Recover Formulas; otherwise, click Convert To Values. Recovering formulas will probably work unless the formulas include references to cells that were lost in corruption. Whatever you choose, the Extract Data feature will pull all the data from your workbook, including all worksheets and tabs, in the same order they appeared in the original file. Unfortunately, the recovery process ignores all formatting, charts, and other objects—you can recover only the actual cell contents (the important stuff).

Note that unless the part of the file that became corrupted was the part storing passwords, you probably won't be able to use this technique to retrieve data from a password-protected file.

INSIDE OUT   Recover Data Using Links

You can recover data from a corrupted workbook by using another trick. It is essentially the same trick used by the Excel Open And Repair command, but it still might be worth a try if Open And Repair fails.

First, open two new workbooks. Select cell A1 in one of the workbooks, and then press Ctrl+C to copy. Activate the second workbook, and right-click cell A1. Click Paste Special, and then click the Paste Link button. Next, click the Microsoft Office Button, click Prepare, click Edit Links To Files (you might have to scroll down to see this command), click Change Source, and locate the corrupted workbook. Click OK, and then click Close to close the Edit Links dialog box.

If luck is with you, data from cell A1 in the lost workbook will appear in cell A1, thanks to the linking formula. If it does, press F2 to activate Edit mode, and press F4 three times to change the absolute reference $A$1 to its relative form, A1. Finally, copy the formula down and across until you can see all the data you need to retrieve. Repeat for each worksheet in the workbook. You will lose the formatting and formulas, of course, and zeros will appear in every blank cell, but at least you can get at the important stuff. Although you can save this worksheet with linking formulas, you might consider converting all the formulas to their underlying values, just in case the original corrupted file has any further degradation. To do so, select all the cells containing the formulas you just created, click Ctrl+C to copy, right-click, click Paste Special, select Values, and then click OK.

For more information about document recovery, see "Recovering from Crashes" later in this chapter on page 79. For more information about passwords, see "Hiding and Protecting Workbooks" on page 175.

Importing and Exporting Files

Excel gracefully accepts proprietary data created in many other applications. Excel also makes it easy to import data from text files and helps you parse it into worksheet columns.

> **Note**
>
> Mountains of very specific, sleep-inducing technical details are available about importing and exporting files. If you need such detail for conversion issues such as transferring hundreds of macro-driven Lotus files into Excel, you should consult the Microsoft Office 2007 Resource Kit, available from Microsoft Press. Also, for information regarding sharing data with other Microsoft Office 2007 applications and working with external databases, see Chapter 31, "Using Excel Data in Word Documents," and Chapter 23, "Working with External Data."

Using the Open and Save As Commands to Import and Export Files

To import a file from another application or from an earlier version of Excel, click the Microsoft Office Button, click Open, and select the file you want to import from the list of files in the Open dialog box. To narrow the list of files and zero in on a specific file type you want to import, use the File Name drop-down list at the bottom of the Open dialog box, shown in Figure 2-38. When you choose a file type, the Open dialog box displays only files of that type in its list. Keep in mind that it is not necessary to include a file name extension when you import a file because Excel determines the format of the file by examining the file's contents, not its name.

To export an Excel file to another application or to an earlier version of Excel, click the Microsoft Office Button, and click Save As. Then select the application you're exporting to in the Save As Type drop-down list, which is similar to the File Name drop-down list shown in Figure 2-38, except it contains somewhat different format options for saving. For example, although Text Files is the only text format listed in the Open dialog box, you can save an Excel file in many different flavors of text format, including tab-delimited text, Unicode text, formatted text, and more.

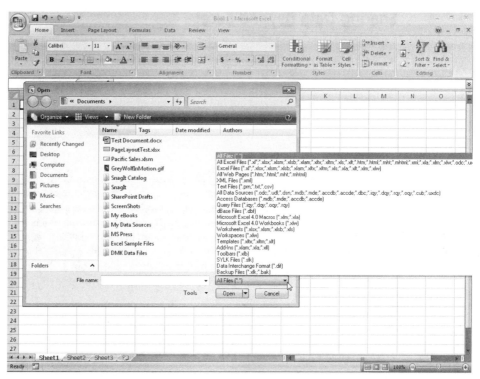

Figure 2-38 Use the File Name drop-down list to specify files created by a particular application.

Sharing Data with Excel for the Macintosh

Excel for the Macintosh since 1998 has been using the same file format as Windows versions of Excel from 97 through 2003. You can share these files with Macintosh users by simply transferring files from one computer to the other.

To save an Excel 2007 file to share with someone using the Macintosh version of Excel, click the Microsoft Office Button, click Save As, and click the Microsoft Excel 97-2003 Workbook option in the Save As Type drop-down list.

To import Macintosh files to your PC, you first need to transfer the file to your PC via a cable, a disk, a network, an e-mail, a Web site, or a tool such as MacOpener. Exporting files from a Windows version of Excel to the Macintosh version is just as easy as importing Macintosh files. Simply transfer the file from the Macintosh computer to Windows using your method of choice, and then use the Open command to load it into Excel.

Chapter 2

Sharing Data Beyond Excel

Yes, some people don't use Excel, and you might meet one someday. Seriously, plenty of reasons exist for making Excel-based data accessible outside the program, whether or not Excel is available at the destination. Posting data to a Web site or creating data sets for proprietary analysis software are two possible applications where you might want data that can fly free, independent of the Excel mother ship.

Adjusting Date Values

Although the Windows and Macintosh versions of Excel share many characteristics and capabilities, they do not use the same date system. In the Windows version of Excel, the base date is January 1, 1900. In the Macintosh version, the base date is January 2, 1904. When you transfer files either to or from the Macintosh, Excel maintains the date type by selecting or clearing the 1904 Date System option in the When Calculating This Workbook area in the Advanced category in the Excel Options dialog box. This technique is usually acceptable, but it can cause problems when a date from a Macintosh file is compared with a date from a Windows file. For this reason, we suggest you use the same date setting on all your machines.

Using Web File Formats

Two options in the Files Of Type drop-down list in the Save As dialog box produce files that you can use as Web pages: Web Page (HTM, HTML) and Single File Web Page (MHT, MHTML). They produce essentially the same result, the important difference being that the Web Page format saves not only a main HTML file but also a folder containing supporting files that must travel with the main file. As you might expect, the Single File Web Page format manages to cram it all into a single file without using the supporting folder. Single File Web Page has the advantage of being more portable, but Web Page gives you more control over individual elements. A separate cascading style sheet is created using the Web Page format, along with individual HTML files for each worksheet in the workbook. Figure 2-39 shows the contents of the supporting folder that is created after saving a seven-sheet workbook entitled *Humongous* using the Web Page file format.

If you are an HTML aficionado, you can open the supporting files in other programs. For example, if the original workbook contains any graphics, Excel saves them as separate image files (JPEG, PNG, or GIF) that you could modify with an image-editing program. Or you could change the fonts used by editing the cascading style sheet using a text editor such as Notepad. This is not the kind of work for the timid, of course. The slightest editing error in the HTML code of any of the files has the potential to render them all unusable.

Figure 2-39 The Web Page file format creates a folder full of supporting files to go with the main Web page.

Importing and Exporting Text Files

To export an Excel file as a text file, click the Microsoft Office Button, click Save As, and select one of the following eight text formats from the Save As Type drop-down list. In all of these formats, Excel saves only the current worksheet. Number formatting is preserved, but all other formatting is removed.

- **Formatted Text (Space Delimited) (*.PRN)** This creates a file in which column alignment is preserved by means of adding space characters to the data in each column so each column is always filled to its maximum width.

- **Text (Tab Delimited) (*.TXT)** This separates the cells of each row with tab characters.

- **Unicode Text (*.TXT)** This is a worldwide standard text format that stores each character as a unique number; Unicode defines a number for every character in every language and on any computer platform.

- **CSV (Comma Delimited) (*.CSV)** This separates the cells of each row with commas. Comma-delimited text files are preferable to tab-delimited files for importing into database management programs. (Many database management programs can accept either form of text file, but some accept only .csv files.) Also, many word-processing applications can use .csv files to store the information for mail merge operations.

Chapter 2

- **Text (Macintosh) (*.TXT)** This saves the current worksheet as a tab-delimited text file using the Macintosh character set.

- **Text (MS-DOS) (*.TXT)** This saves the current worksheet as a tab-delimited text file, compatible with the character-based MS-DOS interface.

- **CSV (Macintosh) (*.CSV)** This saves a comma-delimited text file using the Macintosh character set. The differences between the normal, Macintosh, and MS-DOS variants of each file type have to do only with characters that lie outside the normal 7-bit ASCII range.

- **CSV (MS-DOS) (*.CSV)** The MS-DOS options use the IBM PC extended character set. (You might see this also referred to as *OEM text*.) Select one of these options if you intend to import your text file into a non-Windows-based application.

> **Note**
>
> Office Excel 2007 uses a file format that is incompatible with previous Excel versions. And Excel 2003 shares with its predecessors (Excel 2002, Excel 2000, Excel 97) a file format that is incompatible with even older Excel versions. However, you can use the Save As command to export Excel 2007 workbooks that will play nicely with older versions of Excel, using two formats in the Save As Type list: Excel 97-2003 Workbook and Microsoft Excel 5.0/95 Workbook.
>
> If you regularly share files with colleagues using different vintages of the program, you might want to read "Ensuring File Compatibility with Previous Versions of Excel" on page 54.

Other File Formats

You can use a few other file formats, most of which you won't even need unless you have a particular program with which you want to share data. Data Interchange Format (DIF) is a legacy format that allows the specification of data in rows and columns, saves only the active worksheet, and does not process graphic content. Symbolic Link (SYLK), a format that dates back to the days of VisiCalc and Multiplan, is a sort of "rich-text format" for spreadsheets that saves only the active worksheet and does not process graphic content.

Portable Document Format (PDF) and XML Paper Specification (XPS), two formats that allow accurate visual representations of documents to be easily shared across platforms, were going to ship with the 2007 Microsoft Office system, but legal entanglements at the time of this writing have jeopardized this plan. Fear not—one or both of these formats should be downloadable from the Office Update Web site (*www.officeup-date.com*) if they are not available in your copy of Excel.

Using the Online Help System

Excel was a powerful program right out of the starting gate way back in 1985. Over the years, Excel has developed into an extremely complex and sophisticated application. It's so complex, in fact, that most people need to learn only 20 percent or so of its capabilities. Many people turn to books like this one to help them make sense of it all. But almost every Excel user turns to the Help system at some point. And after years of working out the kinks, Microsoft has made the Excel Help system less obtrusive, more comprehensive, and much easier to use.

Help on the Surface

Although the mythical, magical, space-age vision of easily understood, self-documenting software has yet to be fully realized, Excel 2007 is taking steps in the right direction. Dynamic pop-up labels called *ScreenTips* have been around for quite a while providing visual clues to elements in the interface. This time, however, many ScreenTips have increased in size considerably, containing more and better information. Simply rest the pointer on any button or command on the Ribbon or the Quick Access Toolbar to display a ScreenTip, as shown in Figure 2-40.

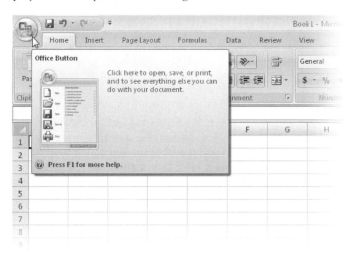

Figure 2-40 Rest the pointer on any command or button on the Ribbon or the Quick Access Toolbar to display a ScreenTip.

Help in the form of ScreenTips is also available for many items in dialog boxes such as Excel Options (to open this dialog box, click the Microsoft Office Button, and click Excel Options). In this context, look for the little *i* (for *information*) icons next to items in the dialog box, indicating more information is available. Just rest the pointer on the icon to display the ScreenTip, as shown in Figure 2-41.

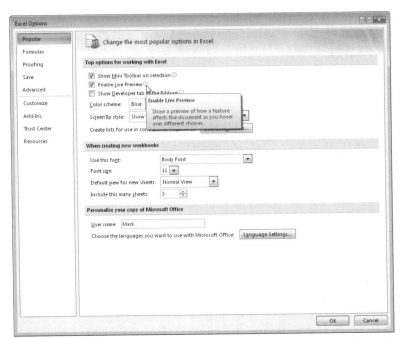

Figure 2-41 A little circle icon containing an *i* means you can see more information by simply resting the pointer on the icon.

Help In Depth

When you need more information than a ScreenTip can provide, it's time to invoke the Help dialog box. Simply click the Help button (the question mark icon) that is always available in the upper-right corner of the screen (or any dialog box) to display the Help dialog box. When you first open the dialog box, it attempts to connect to the Microsoft Office Online Web site, as shown on top in Figure 2-42. If you are connected to the Internet, the dialog box should quickly display an opening menu of topics, similar to the one shown on the bottom in Figure 2-42. As mentioned previously, one of the beauties of Web-based Help is that it can be continually updated, so it is quite possible this opening screen will change in content and appearance over time; more and more Help topics should be added as well.

As long as you have the Help dialog box open and your Internet connection remains active, Web-based Help continues to be available. In the dialog box on the top in Figure 2-42, there is a link labeled Show Me Offline Help From My Computer. If you click this link (or lose your Internet connection), Excel stops trying to connect to the Web and displays the "offline" Help system—that is, only those Help topics installed on your computer. When this happens, you'll see a slightly different opening Help screen, as shown in Figure 2-43. You can also get to this screen by clicking the "globe" menu at the bottom of the Help dialog box (that says Connected To Office Online in Figure 2-42) and clicking Show Content Only From This Computer.

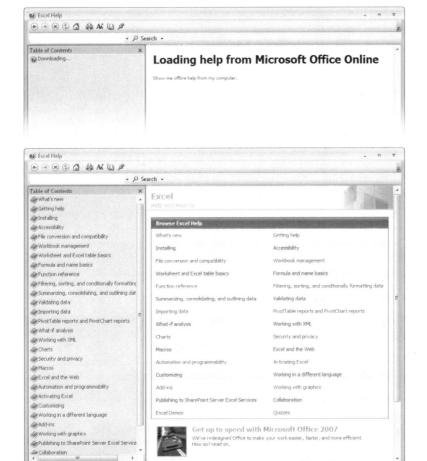

Figure 2-42 The Help dialog box attempts to connect to the Web when you first open it.

> **You can prevent Excel from automatically trying to connect to the Web using the Trust Center dialog box. See "Privacy Options" on page 108.**

You'll find that a lot of good information is available even when you're not connected to the Web, but if you can maintain a connection, you'll probably have a more satisfying experience. Plenty of "bulky" content is available on the Web that isn't feasible to ship on CD, including templates, sample files, and even interactive quizzes you can take to hone your skills.

INSIDE OUT 2007: A Help Odyssey

The implication of the term *online Help* has changed somewhat over the years. It used to mean that, in addition to the primary source of user assistance—the printed manual—how-to topics and explanations of commands and features were available right on your computer by pressing F1. What a concept! Today, the best of Help really is *online*, and an Internet connection is almost essential—preferably broadband.

Those who write user assistance topics and implement the Help system historically had to limit the amount of actual assistance they could provide, constrained by the amount of space allocated for Help files on the installation CDs (or floppy disks!). Over the past few Office releases, the need for Help files actually shipped on CD has decreased because of the new user assistance paradigm: Web-based Help. This offers tremendous advantages over "in-the-box" Help. First, instead of having to cram increasing amounts of information into decreasing amounts of CD space, keeping Help files on the Web allows virtually unlimited information to be made available. Second, it allows information to be more up-to-date, which is actually an incredible understatement.

Consider that under the old paradigm, Help content had to be written early and sent through the editorial pipeline many weeks prior to shipping the software—often before developers were finished tweaking features. (Add another month or so for printed manuals! Remember those?) With the constraints on disk space, tough decisions often were made regarding helpful topics and useful aids such as videos and presentations that would simply have to be eliminated to save room. No wonder Help systems have historically been dissed for being inaccurate and incomplete. Under the new "truly online" Help paradigm, topics that would never have made it onto the CD are instead available on the Web, and user assistance writers can update and add more Help topics, videos, presentations, and templates even after the product ships. The bottom line is that in case you haven't noticed, the 2007 Microsoft Office Help systems have been getting better, and the 2007 Microsoft Office system raises the bar once again.

You'll notice that the Help dialog box has a tiny toolbar with controls that look—and act—similarly to the controls on your Web browser's toolbar. The first two buttons are Back and Forward, which operate like their browser counterparts—they'll move you to the next or previous topic in your history list. The Stop button cuts off the data stream, in case you want to stop downloading some bulky Web content that is laboring over a slow Internet connection. The Refresh button simply reloads the current topic, which you might want to do if you clicked the Stop button in mid-download. The Home button returns you to the opening Help screen, and the Print button prints the current topic. Clicking the Change Font Size button displays a menu of text size options. The button that looks like a little book is the Hide Table Of Contents button, which controls the display of the side-navigation pane, as shown in Figure 2-44. This button is a toggle; that is, clicking it again displays the navigation pane.

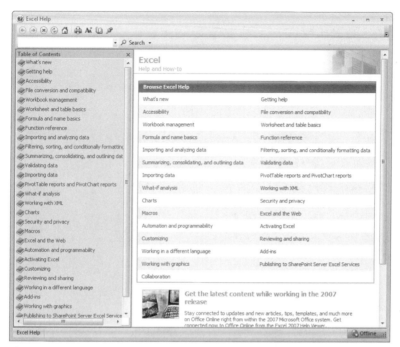

Figure 2-43 Your Help system works a bit differently if you are not connected to the Web.

The Table Of Contents pane shows you the top-level topics available. Clicking each closed book icon changes it to an open book icon and displays the topics contained beneath the main heading. If you are connected to the Internet, the list of Help topics will also include any additional topics that exist on the Microsoft Web site.

The last button on the little toolbar in the Help dialog box is Keep On Top, and it looks like a little pushpin. When it appears diagonally, as in Figure 2-44, the Help dialog box behaves like a normal window, giving way to the active window when you click outside the dialog box. You can click the pushpin button to change this behavior so that instead of giving way, it stays on top of the Excel workspace, letting you refer to Help topics while you work. This button is a toggle; its name is Not On Top in its diagonal appearance, and it changes to Keep On Top when the button appears as "looking from above." Whatever setting was active when you close the dialog box persists the next time you open it.

Note

Most dialog boxes (except the Help dialog box!) include a Help button located in the title bar (identified by a question mark icon). Clicking this button displays a Help topic describing the function of and options within that dialog box. If you click the Help button in a tabbed dialog box, you'll see information pertaining to that particular tab.

Figure 2-44 Click the Table Of Contents Button to display or hide the navigation pane.

Because so much Help content is available between the installed Help files and the vast storehouse of possibility on the Web, Microsoft decided to add some Search options to the Help dialog box, to save you some time. Figure 2-45 shows the Search menu that opens when you click the arrow next to the Search button.

The Search menu gives you a clue as to how the Help material is set up; you'll see major categories of Excel Help and Developer Reference with subcategories, all of which can change as time goes by in this "living" Help system. As you can see in Figure 2-45, you can choose between online and offline Help, subdivided into categories. This is handy when searching for Help content because hundreds of templates are available online, apparently loaded with keywords since many searches return a few Help topics scattered among pages of templates and training links. So, you might find it useful to limit your search by selecting Excel Help from the Search menu, effectively excluding templates and training from the search results.

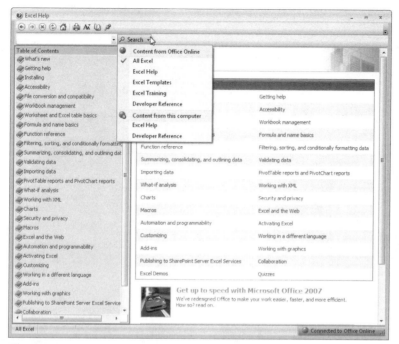

Figure 2-45 Narrow your results using the Search menu.

Recovering from Crashes

In the past, "crash recovery" largely involved an initial flurry of expletives followed by a brisk walk around the office and perhaps a couple of aspirin. Office Excel 2007 provides something beyond comfort and sympathy for digital mishaps—an actual mechanism that attempts to tuck away open files before the program comes screeching to a halt. And it works pretty well. If Excel encounters a problem, it attempts to save any files that were open at the time the problem occurred, before bad things happen to them when the program crashes and burns.

Using AutoRecover

Although Excel has greatly improved its ability to recover lost work after a crash, you should take advantage of the additional insurance provided by the AutoRecover feature.

AutoRecover is turned on by default. To turn it off, click the Microsoft Office Button, click the Excel Options button, select the Save category, and clear the Save AutoRecover Information Every check box, as shown in Figure 2-46.

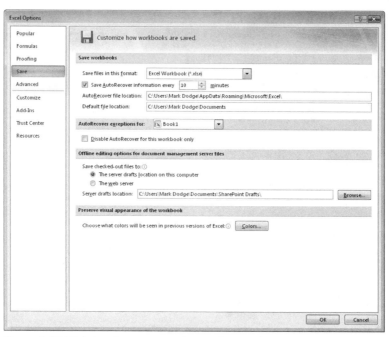

Figure 2-46 With AutoRecover, you can specify how often Excel will automatically save your work.

The AutoRecover File Location is set to a subfolder buried deep in your hard disk—this is OK, because you'll want to save the real files elsewhere rather than clutter up your working directories with recovery files. If you want, you can easily change the location. You can also choose to disable AutoRecover for specific workbooks without having to turn it off and on manually. You can use the AutoRecover Exceptions For area in the dialog box to do this. Just select a workbook in which you want AutoRecover disabled from the drop-down list displaying all the currently open workbooks, and select the Disable AutoRecover For This Workbook Only check box. You can do this separately for any open workbook.

Calling Dr. Office

Excel does its best to recover any unsaved files after a crash, and it is pretty effective. As for other issues relating to the health and well-being of your 2007 Microsoft Office installation, it's possible that other forces are at work, polluting the virtual environment. If weird and wacky things continue to happen while working in any 2007 Microsoft Office program, get a professional opinion from Dr. Office—the Microsoft Office Diagnostics program. Before you start, you'll need to be connected to the Internet, and it's always best to close other running programs first (if you can!). Then click the Windows Start button, click All Programs, click Microsoft Office, click Microsoft Office Tools, and click Microsoft Office Diagnostics. The Microsoft Office Diagnostics dialog box opens, as shown in Figure 2-47.

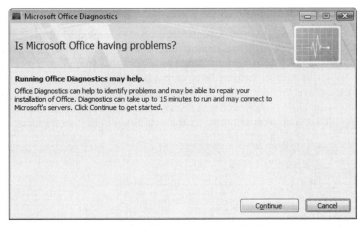

Figure 2-47 The Microsoft Office Diagnostics dialog box gives you a chance to get your ailing Office installation back in shape.

> **Note**
>
> You can also run Microsoft Office Diagnostics from within Excel. Click the Microsoft Office Button, click Excel Options, select the Resources category, click Diagnose, click Continue in the Microsoft Office Diagnostics dialog box, and then click Run Diagnostics.

The Microsoft Office Diagnostics program examines a number of things; for example, it looks for whether any programs need to be updated, looks for "known solutions," inspects your computer's memory and hard disk, examines the Setup files, and looks for evidence of compatibility issues with any other installed versions of 2007 Microsoft Office programs.

Office Diagnostics replaces (and represents an upgrade from) the Detect And Repair feature in Excel 2003.

Chapter 2

Before You Call Product Support

We encourage you to use Excel documentation, online Help, the Microsoft Excel Web site (*www.microsoft.com/excel/*), and especially *this book* to find answers to your questions before you reach for the telephone. When you have exhausted these resources, it's time to call Microsoft Product Support Services. But before you do, click the Microsoft Office Button, click Excel Options, select the Resources category, click the About button, and click the System Info button. Doing so displays a dialog box that lists your current system configuration, the applications running, some display information, and much more:

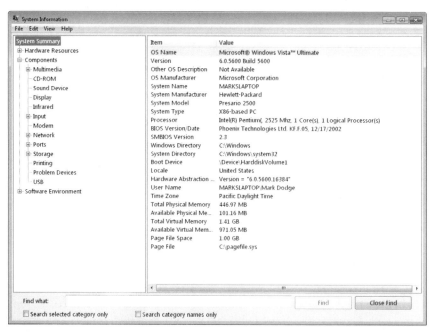

If you want, you can print the information in a report or save it as a file on disk. Then you can click Tech Support in the About Microsoft Excel dialog box to display a dialog box with information about contacting Product Support Services around the world. When you talk to Product Support Services, having the System Info report at your fingertips will assist the representative in diagnosing your problem and will save you time.

Custom-Tailoring the Excel Workspace

You needn't settle completely for the way the Microsoft Office Excel 2007 command and control system is organized. Although the Office Excel 2007 command structure is not as universally configurable as previous versions, you can still customize it for the way you work.

Customizing the Quick Access Toolbar

In previous versions of Excel, you could fill the screen with built-in and custom toolbars, docked on all four sides of the screen and floating everywhere in between. In Excel 2007, you get the Quick Access Toolbar—that's it. The good news is that Excel 2007 offers buttons for every command, plus introduces some new buttons for sets of commands called *Ribbon groups.*

Positioning the Toolbar

When you first start Excel, the Quick Access Toolbar appears above the Ribbon, as shown in Figure 3-1. You can change this so the toolbar appears below the Ribbon. Click the Customize Quick Access Toolbar button (the little arrow on the right end of the toolbar), and click Show Below The Ribbon. When you do, the name of the command changes appropriately, as shown in Figure 3-2.

Figure 3-1 The Quick Access Toolbar usually appears above the Ribbon, on the title bar.

Moving the Quick Access Toolbar below the Ribbon offers you a couple of advantages. First, it's closer to the action on the worksheet. Second, more space is available for additional tools, which we'll discuss in depth in "Adding Tools to the Toolbar." The drawback to placing the toolbar below the Ribbon is that it takes space away from the worksheet; conversely, the advantage of leaving it at the top of the screen is it can occupy unused space on the title bar.

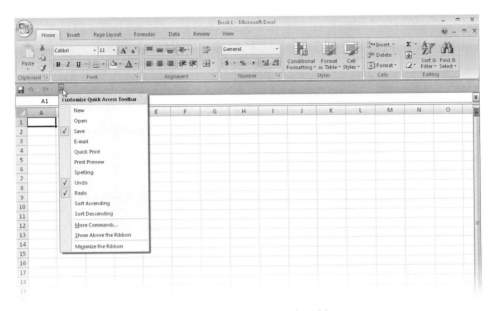

Figure 3-2 You can move the Quick Access Toolbar below the Ribbon.

Adding Tools to the Toolbar

You get three tools to start with on the Quick Access Toolbar—Save, Undo, and Repeat. These are undeniably heavily used commands, but you perform other tasks often too and might like to have them just a click away. It's easy to customize the toolbar, and you have a couple of ways to do it.

Microsoft Office
Button

> **Note**
>
> The Microsoft Office Button is not part of the Quick Access Toolbar—it stays in the upper-left corner, no matter what.

Adding Tools As You Work

If you find yourself continually returning to the same tab on the Ribbon and using a particular command, you might consider adding it to the Quick Access Toolbar. The easiest way to do this is to right-click the command to display the shortcut menu, as shown in Figure 3-3.

In Figure 3-3, we added the Switch Windows command to the Quick Access Toolbar by right-clicking the command and clicking Add To Quick Access Toolbar. A button then appears on the toolbar that looks similar to the command on the Ribbon. Each new button you add appears to the right of the previous button. Not all toolbar buttons are easy to identify, so you can always rest the pointer on a button to display a ScreenTip explaining its function, as shown at the bottom of Figure 3-3. If you add a lot of buttons, these ScreenTips are indispensable.

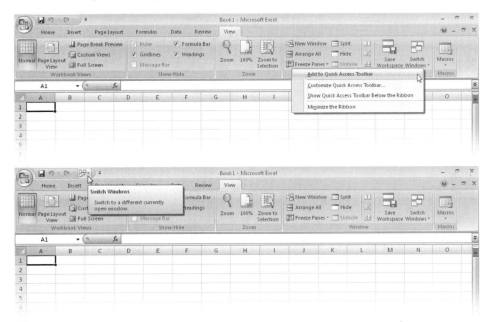

Figure 3-3 Right-click any command or group, and you can add it to the Quick Access Toolbar.

Removing Tools

You can remove tools from the Quick Access Toolbar using the same technique as you use to add them. Right-click any tool on the toolbar, and click Remove From Quick Access Toolbar.

Adding and Organizing Tools

You can add virtually any command or group to the Quick Access Toolbar using the right-click technique, but if you want to dig in and really create an organized toolbar, you'll want to use the Customize category in the Excel Options dialog box. Right-click the toolbar, and click Customize Quick Access Toolbar to open the Customize category in the Excel Options dialog box, as shown in Figure 3-4.

As you can see in Figure 3-4, the box on the right shows the buttons currently visible on the toolbar, including the Switch Windows command we added earlier. It's pretty easy to figure out how this works—just select any item on the left side, and then click the Add button to add it to the list on the right. Select any item on the right side, and click the Remove button to get rid of it; when you've selected an item, you can also click the Up and Down buttons to reposition the selected item in the list. You can always click the Reset button if you want to discard all your changes and return to the original configuration.

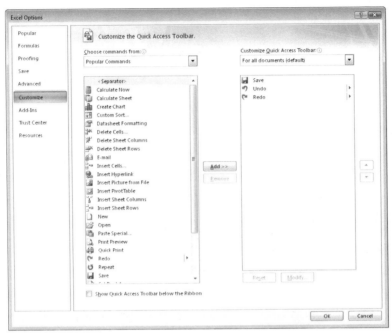

Figure 3-4 The Customize category in the Excel Options dialog box is the command center for the Quick Access Toolbar.

Notice in Figure 3-4 that <Separator> is the first item in the list on the left of the Customize category. This is the first item in each command category, and with it, you can insert small vertical bars on the Quick Access Toolbar to visually separate groups of related commands. You can add separators and move them up and down the list on the right side of the dialog box, just like commands.

When you first access the Customize category, the Choose Commands From drop-down list displays Popular Commands. Click this drop-down list to see the rest of the available options, as shown in Figure 3-5.

The items in the Choose Commands From drop-down list include an eponymous item for each of the command tabs visible on the Ribbon, plus a number of other categories that at first glance don't seem to relate to the Ribbon at all. These are categories that contain commands available on *contextual tabs*, that is, tabs that appear on the Ribbon only when an object is selected. For example, close the Excel Options dialog box, click SmartArt on the Insert tab, and then click OK. An object like the one in Figure 3-6 appears on the worksheet, and you'll see two new tabs on the Ribbon—Design and Format—under a SmartArt Tools heading. Anytime you select a SmartArt object, these tabs appear, offering relevant tools. These two tabs correspond to the two SmartArt items visible in the Choose Commands From drop-down list (shown in Figure 3-5).

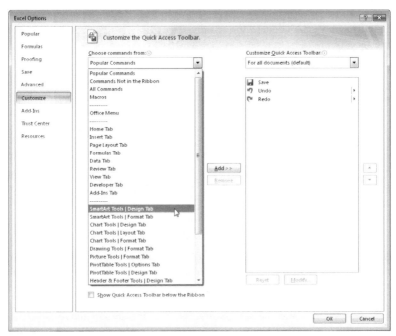

Figure 3-5 Each item in the Choose Commands From drop-down list corresponds to a tab on the Ribbon.

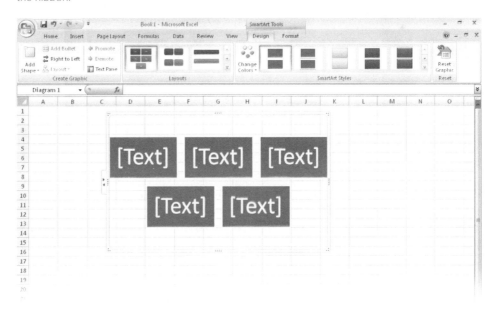

Figure 3-6 When you select an object on the worksheet, additional tabs appear that correspond to items in the Choose Commands From drop-down list.

Chapter 3

Several of these "phantom" groups appear in the Choose Commands From drop-down list, with headings such as Chart Tools, PivotTable Tools, and Drawing Tools, all of which correspond to tabs that are contextually triggered by selecting particular types of objects.

The last three items in the Choose Commands From drop-down list merit special attention. First, when you select Macros, any available macros appear, and you can assign them to buttons; you'll learn more about this later in "Creating Your Own Buttons" on page 91. Second, Commands Not In The Ribbon is handy and can be a good place to look for buttons with which to populate the Quick Access Toolbar. Finally, All Commands is especially useful if you're not sure which group a command might fall into, and it can save you a lot of clicking and scanning through lists of commands.

INSIDE OUT   Create a Mini-Ribbon

Here is a useful trick you can use if it just seems like too much bother to click those tabs all the way at the top of the Ribbon or you just want to maximize your screen space. Saving a click here and there can make quite a difference if you do a lot of repetitive work in Excel that requires constantly accessing different tabs on the Ribbon. The following illustration shows the Quick Access Toolbar with the Ribbon minimized (double-click any tab to do this) and with buttons that correspond to every group on every default tab on the Ribbon:

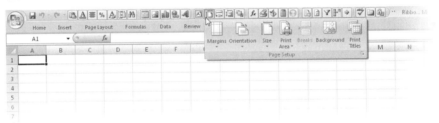

The idea here is to make available every command that is usually available on the Ribbon, without actually having to click a Ribbon tab. The toolbar shown here includes only buttons that correspond to the Ribbon groups (not the individual commands) on every tab. Notice that clicking the Page Setup button displays a drop-down list of commands identical to those in the Ribbon group of the same name on the Page Layout tab. To customize the toolbar this way, you should use the Customize category in the Excel Options dialog box. Although you can build a similar toolbar using the right-click approach, using the dialog box offers the advantage of being able to insert separators between groups of buttons.

Identifying Items in the Customize Dialog Box

Most of the items you can see in the command list on the left side of the Customize category in the Excel Options dialog box are buttons. That is, clicking the command button on the toolbar executes the associated command immediately. You'll notice that some items also have a small icon to the right of the command name in the dialog box. These are called *command modifiers*, and they tell you that although the item may still be a button, it is also something more, as detailed in Table 3-1.

Table 3-1 **Command Modifiers**

Item	Description	Image
Drop-down list	A control that displays a menu or palette from which you select an option, such as the Conditional Formatting button on the Home tab	▸
Split button	A two-part item—one side looks and acts like a button, and the other side has a small arrow that displays a drop-down list, such as the Font Color button on the Home tab	▸
Edit control	A control you can type into—for example, the Font drop-down list on the Home tab	I ▾
Ribbon group	A control that displays a palette of items, such as the "boxed" group of Font controls on the Home tab	▾

If you want a little more information about the commands in the command list, rest the pointer on any command to display a ScreenTip like the one shown in Figure 3-7.

The first part of the ScreenTip tells you where on the Ribbon the command appears. In Figure 3-7, the Accounting Number Formats button (which, as you know because of the icon to the right of the command, is a split button) appears in the Number group on the Home tab. The portion of the ScreenTip in parentheses indicates the name used to refer to the command programmatically using Visual Basic for Applications (VBA).

> For more information about VBA and creating macros, see Chapter 26, "Recording Macros."

Too Many Tools?

It is certainly possible to load more buttons onto the Quick Access Toolbar than can fit across the screen, even if you move the toolbar below the Ribbon. If this happens, a More Controls button appears at the right end of the toolbar, looking like a fast-forward button (>>). As shown in Figure 3-8, clicking More Controls displays the hidden controls on a drop-down toolbar. If you'd rather have some these overflowing controls appear on the main part of the toolbar, select the Customize category in the Excel Options dialog box, and rearrange the controls in the list using the Up and Down buttons.

Chapter 3

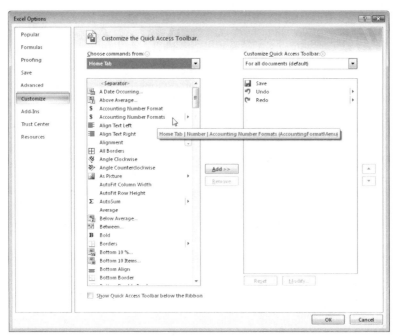

Figure 3-7 ScreenTips help you identify commands in the list.

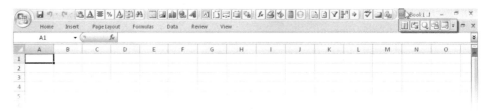

Figure 3-8 If you add more buttons than can be displayed, click the More Controls button.

Note that we collapsed the Ribbon in Figure 3-8. To do this, double-click any tab, or click Minimize The Ribbon on the Customize Quick Access Toolbar menu (refer to Figure 3-2). Click any tab again to restore the Ribbon. Also note that when the More Controls button appears, the Customize Quick Access Toolbar button (the downward-pointing arrow) that usually appears at the right side of the toolbar moves to the "overflow" area of the bar.

Creating Your Own Buttons

Right-click any button on the Ribbon, click Customize Quick Access Toolbar, and click the Choose Commands From drop-down list. You'll see a special option listed there: Macros. *Macros* are sequences of commands you can create to help perform repetitive tasks. When you select the Macros option, nothing appears on the right side of the dialog box unless a macro-enabled workbook is open and the workbook actually contains macros. All the macros available appear here. Figure 3-9 shows the Customize Quick Access Toolbar list containing a single macro that has been added to the toolbar.

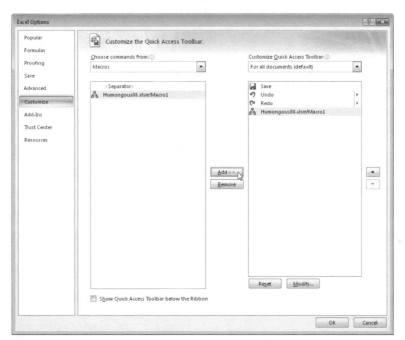

Figure 3-9 You can add custom buttons to run macros in macro-enabled workbooks.

You might notice that for the first time the Modify button below the list is active. By clicking it, you can modify the button image displayed on the toolbar, if the default image doesn't do it for you. In case you were wondering, you can modify only custom macro buttons, which is why the Modify button is not available when you select built-in commands. When you click the Modify button, the Modify Button dialog box, as shown in Figure 3-10, lets you select a different image.

For more information about macro-enabled workbooks, see "Saving Files" on page 51 and also see Chapter 26.

Figure 3-10 You can change the default button image for your custom macro-driven buttons.

INSIDE OUT **A Word About RibbonX**

Microsoft made a lot of changes in the 2007 Microsoft Office system, not least of which are the Ribbon and the new XML-based file format. Put 'em together, and what do you get? RibbonX! OK, it's not really that simple, but if you want to do some extreme customization of the new user interface (UI) that Microsoft spent so much time and energy to change, you'll need to get acquainted with the XML extensibility model called *RibbonX* that "controls the controls" of Excel 2007.

In previous versions of Excel, toolbars and menus ruled. You could easily change them, and you could create your own toolbars and menus for special purposes. But real-world observation showed that UI anarchy was the rule, not the exception. Researchers found stray toolbars littering the screens of a huge percentage of those surveyed. So, Microsoft removed most of the up-front UI-customizing tools. Now, manipulating the Ribbon is a task you can accomplish only in VBA. So if you can't make do with customizing the Quick Access Toolbar, you'll need some basic programming skills. To take the first step, you can find a bit more information in Chapter 26.

Attaching Custom Toolbar Configurations to Workbooks

Excel saves the configuration of the Quick Access Toolbar when you exit the program. You can also attach a custom configuration for the Quick Access Toolbar to a workbook. The exact configuration you specify is activated only when you open the corresponding workbook. That way, you can repurpose the Quick Access Toolbar for specific tasks that apply to specific workbooks. You can even send copies of workbooks to co-workers, and the attached toolbar configuration appears—only when that workbook is active.

If you have two workbooks open, only one of which has an attached toolbar configuration, the Quick Access Toolbar switches between configurations when you switch between workbooks. If you created attached toolbars in previous versions of Excel, this is a welcome change, because attached toolbars would persist forever unless you specifically removed them. This old behavior was part of the UI clutter problem identified by usability studies that eventually resulted in the creation of the Ribbon.

To attach a custom toolbar configuration to a workbook, right-click any button or tab, and click Customize Quick Access Toolbar. In the Excel Options dialog box, click the Customize Quick Access Toolbar drop-down list, as shown in Figure 3-11.

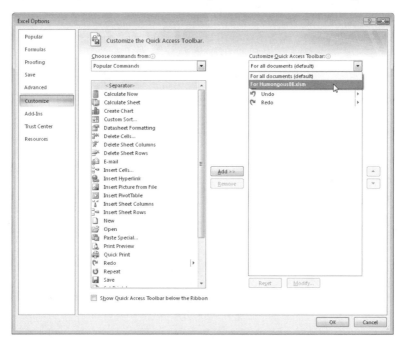

Figure 3-11 You can configure a custom version of the Quick Access Toolbar that travels with a workbook.

The drop-down list shows two items: For All Documents and For <the active workbook name>. If you select the active workbook, the command list starts out blank, and you can begin adding items from the list on the left. (Despite that the list starts out blank, the default tools—Save, Undo, Redo, and Quick Print—always appear at the left end of your custom bar.) Any commands you add to the active workbook's toolbar are relevant only to the active workbook, they will be saved with the workbook, and they will reappear on the toolbar the next time you open the workbook. To remove a custom toolbar configuration from a workbook, select its name in the Customize Quick Access Toolbar drop-down list, and click the Reset button.

INSIDE OUT   **What Happened to My Custom Toolbar?**

If you've grown accustomed to modifying toolbars and menus to suit your working preferences, many modifications are unfortunately not possible in Excel 2007 without employing VBA programming and the XML implementation called RibbonX. The good news is that any custom toolbars you created and attached to workbooks in previous versions of Excel are still accessible, though you might not think so at first glance. If you open an existing workbook with an attached toolbar, the toolbar doesn't appear on the screen. But look at the Add-Ins tab on the Ribbon. You might not have seen the Add-Ins tab before, but click this tab, and there it is—your custom toolbar, which will look something like the one shown here:

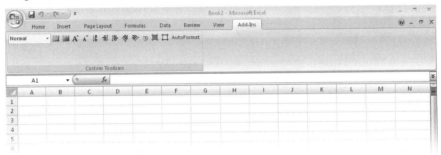

So, all your hard work creating custom toolbars is not lost—provided you attached them to workbooks. (Or find an older version of Excel, re-create them, and attach them!) After you open a workbook containing an attached toolbar, the toolbar continues to appear on the Add-Ins tab each time you start Excel. To get rid of it, right-click it, and close it using the Delete Custom Toolbar command. If the custom toolbar is the only item on the Add-Ins tab, the Add-Ins tab disappears as well. Unfortunately, you can't modify attached toolbars in Excel without working in VBA. For more information, see the sidebar "A Word About RibbonX" earlier in this chapter on page 92.

Restoring the Toolbar

Now that you've thoroughly scrambled the Quick Access Toolbar, perhaps you're experiencing a bit of remorse. Don't worry—it's easy to return it to normal.

- **Restoring the toolbar** Select Customize in the Excel Options dialog box, and click the Reset button. Click OK to confirm the restoration.

- **Removing individual buttons** Right-click the button on the Quick Access Toolbar you want to remove, and then click the Remove From Quick Access Toolbar command, as shown in Figure 3-12.

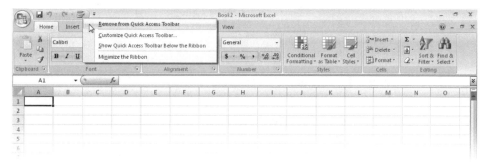

Figure 3-12 You can easily remove any button added to the Quick Access Toolbar.

Exploring Other Toolbar and Ribbon Options

The following are a few more customization options that are quite helpful. Unless otherwise noted, you can find these options by clicking the Microsoft Office Button, clicking the Excel Options button, and then selecting the Popular category.

- Show Mini Toolbar On Selection—the first option in the Popular category in the Excel Options dialog box—controls the display of the "mini-bar" whenever you right-click a cell or object where its formatting tools are applicable, as shown in Figure 3-13.

- You can select a ScreenTip scheme to customize the label that appears when you rest the pointer on any item on the toolbar or the Ribbon. You can choose to see only a small label with the name of the item, a larger ScreenTip that includes a description, or no label at all. (For more information, see "Enhancing Accessibility" on page 100.)

- By selecting the Enable Live Preview option in the Popular category, you can simply rest the pointer on many palette items to show what the effect would look like, without even clicking the item.

- Also in the Popular category, the Show Developer Tab In The Ribbon option adds a new tab with controls for creating macros and editing VBA code.

For more information about fonts and formatting and Live Preview, see Chapter 9, "Worksheet Formatting Techniques." For more information about macros and VBA, see Chapter 26.

Chapter 3

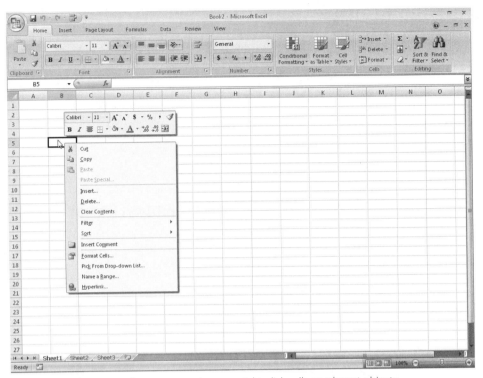

Figure 3-13 The Mini toolbar appears when you right-click cells or relevant objects.

Controlling Other Elements of the Excel 2007 Interface

In several important locations in Excel, you can control the way your worksheets appear on the screen. These include the Popular and Advanced categories in the Excel Options dialog box and the View tab on the Ribbon, as shown in Figure 3-14. Some of these options, such as Gridline Color, are self-explanatory; here we'll talk about options with "issues."

The Show/Hide group on the View tab controls the display of the formula bar as well as the appearance of gridlines, column and row headings, and more. These are the options that are most often used, which is why they appear on the Ribbon. (The Ruler option applies only in Page Layout view, and the Message Bar option becomes active only when a security alert appears.) But you'll discover more ways to tweak your UI when you click the Microsoft Office Button and then the Excel Options button.

For more about Page Layout view, see Chapter 11, "Printing and Presenting." For more about security issues, see Chapter 4, "Security and Privacy."

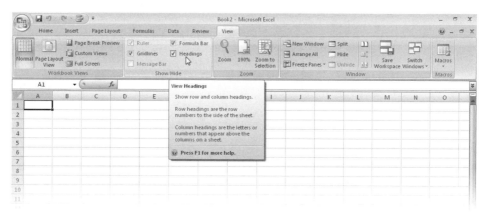

Figure 3-14 The View tab on the Ribbon contains commands you can use to control the appearance of your workbook.

The Popular category includes the Color Scheme drop-down list, which you can use to choose the overall look of the program. But the Advanced category is where most of the action is; it contains three groups of options, shown in Figure 3-15 (you'll need to scroll down a bit), that control different display behaviors for the program in general and for workbooks and worksheets in particular.

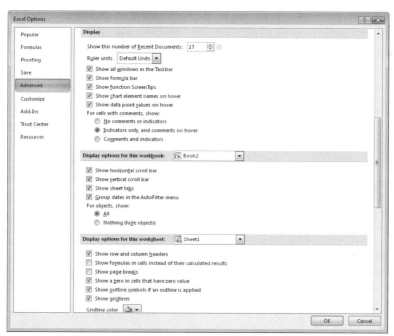

Figure 3-15 The Advanced category in the Excel Options dialog box includes a number of display options.

Chapter 3

The options you select in the Display Options For This Workbook area affect only the workbook selected in the drop-down list, which lists all the currently open workbooks; these options do not change the display of any other workbooks, and they do not affect the way the worksheets will look when you print them. Similarly, the options in the Display Options For This Worksheet area apply only to the worksheet you select in the drop-down list.

Displayed vs. Printed Gridlines and Headings

Typically, Excel displays a grid to mark the boundaries of each cell on the worksheet and also displays row and column headings. Although the grid and headings are usually helpful for selecting and navigating, you might not want them displayed all the time. To hide these items, clear the Gridlines or Headings check box on the View tab on the Ribbon.

Clearing these check boxes on the View tab removes gridlines and headings from your screen but does not affect whether they will be printed. If you want them printed but not displayed (or vice versa), click the Page Layout tab, and then in the Sheet Options group, select or clear the View and Print options under Gridlines or Headings. For convenience, both of these View options on the Page Layout tab are linked to corresponding Gridlines and Headings options on the View tab.

For more about printing a document, see Chapter 11.

Displaying Underlying Formulas

Usually when you enter a formula in a cell, you see the results of that formula, not the formula itself. Similarly, when you format a number, you no longer see the underlying (unformatted) value displayed in the cell. You can see the underlying values and formulas only by selecting individual cells and looking at the formula bar or by double-clicking the cell.

By selecting the Show Formulas In Cells Instead Of Their Calculated Results check box in the Excel Options dialog box (shown in Figure 3-15), you can display underlying values and formulas. Select a worksheet in the Display Options For This Worksheet drop-down list. As you can see in the worksheet view shown at the bottom of Figure 3-16, the underlying contents of each cell appear, as in the sum formulas in rows 6 through 10, and all the cells are left-aligned. (Excel 2007 ignores any alignment formatting when you select the Show Formulas check box.) In addition, the width of each column on the worksheet approximately doubles to accommodate the underlying formulas. (The actual width of the columns remains unchanged; columns appear wider only on the screen.) When you clear the Show Formulas check box, Excel restores all columns to their former widths.

> **Note**
> You can quickly display and hide formulas in your worksheet by pressing Ctrl+' (a single opening quote), which is located on the tilde key on most keyboards. To redisplay values, press Ctrl+' again.

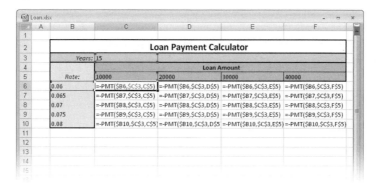

Figure 3-16 Display underlying values and formulas for easier auditing.

> **Note**
> If you click the New Window command on the View tab to create two or more windows in which to view the same workbook, you can use different display options in each window. For example, you can display formulas in one window and see the results of those formulas (the usual view) in another window.

The Show Formulas check box is particularly helpful when you need to edit a large worksheet. You can see your formulas without having to activate each cell and view its contents on the formula bar. You can also use the Show Formulas check box to document your work: After you select the Show Formulas check box, you can print your worksheet with the formulas displayed for archiving purposes.

Hiding Zeros

Usually, zeros entered in cells, or the results of formulas that produce zero values, display on your worksheet. Sometimes, especially for presentation purposes, it is helpful to eliminate the clutter of excessive zero values on a worksheet. Clearing the Show A Zero In Cells That Have Zero Value check box in the Advanced category in the Excel Options dialog box causes any such cells to appear as blank cells on the worksheet. The underlying entries are unaffected, of course. If you edit an entry or if the result of a formula changes so the cell no longer contains a zero value, the value immediately becomes visible. If the Show Formulas check box is also selected, clearing the Show A Zero check box has no effect on the display.

CAUTION

If you hide zero values, be careful when editing your worksheet. What appears to be an empty cell might actually contain a formula.

Changing the Standard Display Font

The standard display font is used not only for all text and numbers you enter in a workbook, but it also determines the font used in row and column headings. You can change this in the Popular category in the Excel Options dialog box. The default font is Body Font, which uses the font defined as such in the current theme. The new standard display font will not become active until you exit and restart Excel. The next time you start Excel, all new workbooks you create display using the new font. You can learn a lot more about formatting and themes in Chapter 9.

Enhancing Accessibility

Office Excel 2007 and all other Microsoft Office 2007 system programs now support the Microsoft Active Accessibility (MSAA) specification. This makes various accessibility aids more effective, including screen readers and screen enlargers. For more information, visit the Microsoft Accessibility Web site at *www.microsoft.com/enable/*.

The following is a list of built-in features that, either by design or by default, enhance the accessibility of Excel:

- **ScreenTips** These are the little descriptive labels that appear under toolbar buttons and Ribbon controls when you rest the pointer on them. Select one of three display options from the ScreenTip Style drop-down list in the Popular category in the Excel Options dialog box. For more information, see "Exploring Other Toolbar and Ribbon Options" on page 95.

- **Visceral feedback** The Advanced category in the Excel Options dialog box contains two options in the General group: Provide Feedback With Animation and Provide Feedback With Sound. When you insert rows or columns, instead of simply appearing, they appear with a flourish. And you'll hear sounds where you might not expect them, such as when you click the Undo or Redo button. Note that if you select the sound option, you may be prompted to download an add-in from the Microsoft Office Web site, which requires that you exit and restart Excel.

- **Function ScreenTips** This is a type of pop-up label that displays the syntax and arguments for functions as they are entered or selected on the formula bar or in cells. Select the Show Function ScreenTips check box in the Advanced category of the Excel Options dialog box in the Display area. For more information, see Chapter 13, "Using Functions."

- **Cell value AutoComplete** When entering data in a column, the AutoComplete feature automatically inserts entries in the same column that match the current entry. This option saves keystrokes, for example, when repeatedly typing the same entry. Select the Enable AutoComplete For Cell Values check box in the Editing Options area in the Advanced category in the Excel Options dialog box. For more information, see "Letting Excel Help with Typing Chores" on page 230.

- **Gridline color** You can change the color of gridlines on your worksheet. Under Display Options For This Worksheet in the Advanced category in the Excel Options dialog box, click the Gridline Color drop-down list, and then choose a color.

- **Colored sheet tabs** You can apply color to a single worksheet tab to make it easier to find a key worksheet, or you can assign different colors to each tab. Right-click the worksheet tab you want to color, point to Tab Color, and then click the color you want from the palette. For more information, see the note on page 148.

- **Keyboard shortcuts** Keyboard shortcuts give you access to any command in Excel using the keyboard. For more information, see Appendix B, "Keyboard Shortcuts."

- **Scroll and pan** If you have a Microsoft IntelliMouse pointing device, you can scroll through a worksheet by simply turning the wheel in the direction you want to scroll. If you press the wheel and drag the mouse, you can pan the worksheet in any direction.

Chapter 3

- **Zoom** You can enlarge the worksheet display up to 400 percent by using the Zoom slider in the lower-right corner of the Excel window, by using the Zoom commands on the View tab on the Ribbon, or by holding down Ctrl and turning the wheel on a Microsoft IntelliMouse pointing device.

Ease of Access in Windows Vista

Windows Vista includes a number of accessibility options referred to as the *Ease Of Access* options. You can find these on the Windows Vista Start menu by clicking Control Panel and then clicking Ease Of Access to display the dialog box shown here:

Many of these settings used to be scattered around or available only as add-ins to Windows, so these Ease Of Access options represent Microsoft's ongoing commitment to providing access to users with varying abilities. Help is available in each dialog box, which you access by clicking the little question mark icons.

Security and Privacy

In this chapter, we'll cover overall system security issues, including ways to help protect your system against malicious software and hide your personal information from unwanted scrutiny. And we'll discuss using digital signatures to both verify incoming files and certify your own outgoing files. Microsoft Office Excel 2007 has additional security features you can apply within workbooks, worksheets, and even cells. We'll discuss these features in "Protecting Worksheets" on page 156 and in "Hiding and Protecting Workbooks" on page 175.

The Trust Center

Microsoft Office
Button

Microsoft consolidated the kind of security features that are common to many 2007 Microsoft Office system programs in a dialog box it calls the Trust Center. Click the Microsoft Office Button, click Excel Options, and select the Trust Center category to display the first dialog box shown in Figure 4- 1.

This category in the Excel Options dialog box contains links to disclaimers and declarations on the Web. Click Trust Center Settings to open the second dialog box in Figure 4-1, where the security settings live.

> **Note**
>
> If you work in an organization, the Trust Center may contain default settings specified by your network administrator that you cannot (or should not) modify. Contact your friendly internal administrator for more information.

The settings you can configure within the Trust Center determine how Excel responds when you open a file with active content—that is, any external file that contains links or code used to communicate to another location on the Internet or an intranet. When you do so, Office Excel 2007 investigates several measures of trustworthiness. Rules exist by which a publisher attains Trusted status. Defined as *reputable developers*, Trusted publishers must sign their code using valid, current digital signatures that are issued by certified certificate authorities such as IntelliSafe. If you open a file that does not meet one of these criteria, a security alert appears, and you need to decide whether to run the active content anyway. But even if you add a publisher, unsigned code from that publisher will still trigger a security alert. Most of the categories in the Trust Center dialog box deal with issues that directly affect the triggering of security alerts and the ability to run active content.

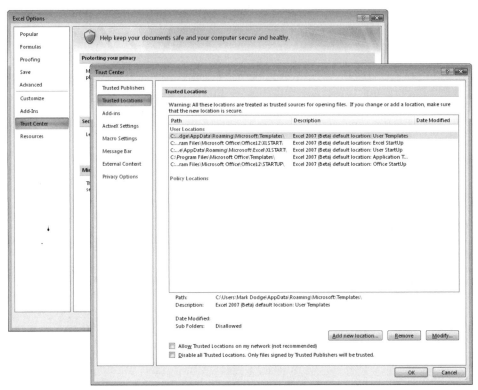

Figure 4-1 The Trust Center dialog box controls many security settings.

Excel displays security alerts in the Message Bar, which appears right under the formula bar. If you click the Options button in the Message Bar, a dialog box like the one in Figure 4-2 appears, giving you choices about the various types of active content lurking within the file.

For more information about code signing, see "Using Digital Signatures" on page 112.

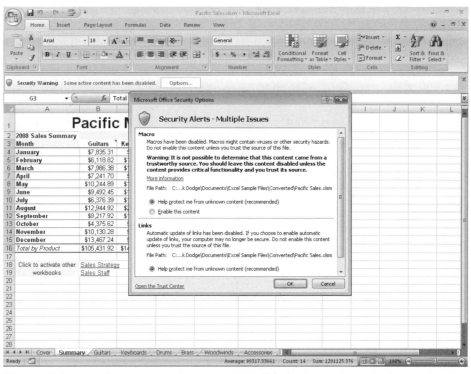

Figure 4-2 Security alerts appear in the Message Bar. Click the Options button in the Message Bar to learn more about the active content in the file.

Trusted Publishers and Locations

In this context, a publisher is any software developer, which can range in relative scale and trustworthiness from the guy in the next cubicle to Microsoft. You might know the guy next door, and you might not trust Microsoft. Whatever the case, you can apply your unique level of paranoia by adding or deleting publishers using the first two categories in the Trust Center dialog box. Excel populates the Trusted Publishers list whenever you open a macro or add-in for the first time that triggers a security alert. If you decide to enable the content, Excel adds the publisher to the list. Subsequent active content from the same publisher opens without triggering a security alert.

Trusted locations can be folders on your own hard disk or on a network; the more precise, the better. We recommend you designate trusted locations on the subfolder level—even the default Documents folder (a.k.a. The Folder Formerly Known As My Documents) is too broad, particularly if you work in a networked environment. It is better to designate subfolders of Documents—or better yet, outside the Documents folder entirely—to minimize the ease with which others can locate interesting stuff on your computer to steal or to modify. Several trusted locations are installed with Excel, such as subfolder locations of template and startup files, as shown in Figure 4-1.

Chapter 4

Add-Ins, ActiveX Settings, and Macro Settings

The Add-Ins, ActiveX Settings, and Macro Settings categories in the Trust Center, as shown in Figure 4-3, deal with blocking active content. You have only two choices for add-ins: just disable them all, or require them to be from a trusted publisher. If you decide on the latter, you can additionally disable the usual Message Bar notification when an add-in is unsigned.

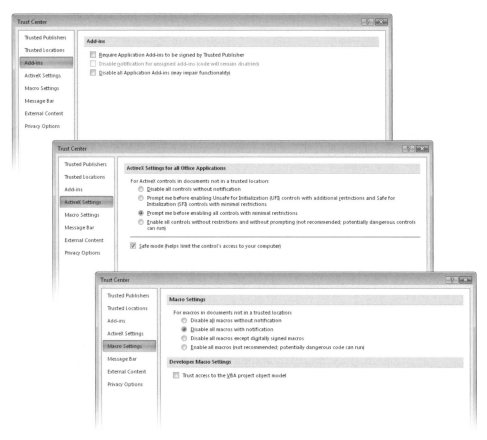

Figure 4-3 Using the options in the Add-Ins, ActiveX Settings, and Macro Settings categories, you can enable or disable most types of active content that you might encounter.

ActiveX controls are more general than add-ins, and they can be designed to run on the Web or on your computer but always within a host application. ActiveX has been the language of choice for many malicious code developers (a.k.a. *hackers*), because it allows nearly unlimited access to your computer. You should never allow ActiveX controls without restriction—the minimum protection option should be Prompt Me Before Enabling All Controls With Minimal Restrictions. The option that mentions Safe For Initialization (SFI) controls refers to a sort of internal code-signing protocol set by the developer to verify its safety. Choosing this option puts your code through a few more levels of restriction. The best solution if you want to stay safe yet you need to use certain ActiveX controls is to set up or utilize a trusted location to store the ActiveX controls you know to be safe.

INSIDE OUT   Of Web Beacons and Homograph Attacks

The word *exploits*, which used to conjure images of heroic figures and derring-do, has come to describe the actions of malicious software. *Phishing* is a rather clever type of lure used by phishers (hackers, trolling for data) to reel unsuspecting prey into their virtual creels. *Homographs* use the extended international character set to create scam Web sites with uniform resource locators (URLs) that replace one or more English-alphabet letters in the real domain names with similar ones from another language's character set. You see what you think is a trusted URL, and if you access the site, you might end up sharing information with the phishermen instead of the trusted site. Where homographs are designed to lure you in, *web beacons* might be what you "win" after you get there. These are forms of spyware that infiltrate your system and then just sit there transmitting data—beacons of information—to malicious data-mining operations. These are just a few of the many clever methods being employed to rip you off. The new Trust Center in the 2007 Office system addresses some of the grim realities of this new world of "insecurity" in which we live.

You can read more about all this in the online Help for the 2007 Office system. The easiest way to get to the relevant topics is to open the Trust Center dialog box and then click the Help button (the little question mark icon in the upper-right corner) to display a Help topic about the currently active category.

Unlike ActiveX controls, macros are application-specific, but they can be destructive when they emanate from a malicious coder. The Trust Center Macro Settings category reveals options that are similar to those of ActiveX controls, as are the recommendations. The Trust Access To The VBA Project Object Model option is for developers only but might be desired in a development environment where a shared Visual Basic for Applications project object model is not secure.

Message Bar

The Message Bar category in the Trust Center dialog box simply lets you turn off the display of security alerts in the Message Bar. It does not turn off the actual security features, just the notifications. The Message Bar is ordinarily turned on, unless you opt to disable all macros. ActiveX controls still generate their own security alerts.

External Content

External content comes in many flavors, and people can use it in many ways to implement malicious intent. The Trust Center dialog box can intercept potential problems

Chapter 4

by blocking external content such as data connections, hyperlinks, and images, all of which can contain or facilitate malicious code. Figure 4-4 shows the External Content category of the Trust Center dialog box.

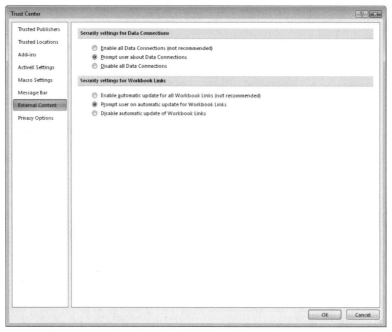

Figure 4-4 The External Content category contains settings that control data connections and links.

The real difference between the two sets of External Content options is that *data connections* are links to data from other programs such as databases while *workbook links* are external references used between Excel workbooks. If you do not control or do not have confidence in the linked or connected sources, it's best to go with the default settings, prompting you for a decision whenever external content is encountered. As with most of these Trust Center options, allowing all data connections or workbook links is not recommended.

Privacy Options

Excel 2007 includes more interactive features than ever. In fact, Excel 2007 uses the Internet behind the scenes to give you access to all the information you need at a moment's notice. Many people want to know exactly when their computer is retrieving online information, so Microsoft lets you control these interactions by clicking the Microsoft Office Button, clicking Excel Options, clicking Trust Center, and then clicking Trust Center Settings. In the Trust Center dialog box, click the Privacy Options category to display the dialog box shown in Figure 4-5.

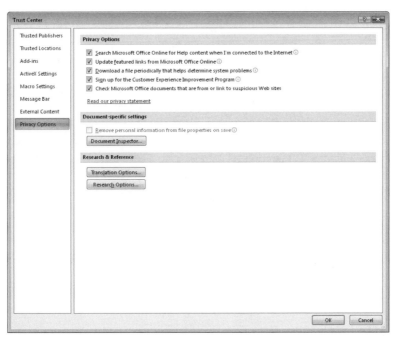

Figure 4-5 If you are uncomfortable with Excel connecting automatically to the Web, you can specify otherwise.

The first set of options you see in Figure 4-5 control whether Excel can automatically communicate and share information over the Internet under various circumstances:

- **Search Microsoft Office Online For Help Content When I'm Connected To The Internet** You might prefer to take control of Web interactions yourself, for example, if you use a dial-up Internet connection. If you clear this check box, you can still connect to the online Help content from within the Help dialog box.

- **Update Featured Links From Microsoft Office Online** This has implications similar to the previous option for those with slow Internet connections; it allows a dynamic link from the Microsoft Office Online Web site to the dialog box that appears when you click the Microsoft Office Button and click New. With this check box selected, the graphic display area toward the bottom of the New dialog box changes periodically, responding to updates posted on the Web site. When you clear this check box, this area remains static.

- **Download A File Periodically That Helps Determine System Problems** You need to decide whether to allow Microsoft to send diagnostic programs to your computer. If you worry about losing data to system crashes, you can select this check box to aid in any future system rehab and recovery efforts.

- **Sign Up For The Customer Experience Improvement Program** Over the years, Microsoft's on-site usability lab has been instrumental in helping refine products based on how people actually work. The Customer Experience Improvement

Chapter 4

Program is similar, except that instead of conducting tests in a controlled environment on the Microsoft corporate campus, data is accumulated in a collective "lab" that potentially includes your office. The usage data collected by this program is much more useful than that generated in the artificial environment of a laboratory. This program began with Excel 2003 and has been at least partially responsible for some of the many changes you see in Excel 2007. It's kind of like installing a Nielsen ratings box on your television—yes, they'll know what you're watching, but maybe the TV shows will get better.

- **Check Microsoft Office Documents That Are From Or Link To Suspicious Web Sites** This option turns on what Microsoft calls *spoofed Web site detection*. This refers to a homograph-type phishing scheme using Web domain names that closely resemble trusted sites. It's often hard to tell the difference with the naked eye, so you can let Excel do it for you. (See the sidebar "Of Web Beacons and Homograph Attacks" on page 107.)

For all these privacy issues, Microsoft won't collect any personal information and promises that participants will remain completely anonymous. You might want to return to the Excel Options dialog box and read the linked information in the Trust Center category before deciding whether to select these check boxes.

File Security

Legions of hackers are seemingly willing to go to any length to gain bragging rights by creating viruses, breaking firewalls, and thwarting password protection. Excel has always had security features, but Office Excel 2007 has added a couple of new features to help make your workbooks a little more secure.

For more about workbook security, see "Hiding and Protecting Workbooks" on page 175.

Removing Personal Information from Your Workbooks

It is increasingly important to keep track of the information you send over the Internet or share with others. Identity theft is a growing problem, and it's important to make sure you don't leave helpful tidbits of information lying around for others to abuse. Although it's up to you to make sure you're not giving away personal information in your worksheets (your password-protected worksheets, of course!), information also lives in places you might not think to look. Excel 2007 includes the new Document Inspector that is designed to look in all the nooks and crannies for you. Click the Microsoft Office Button, click Prepare, and then click Inspect Document to display the dialog box shown in Figure 4-6. (You can also access the Document Inspector by clicking the button of the same name located in the Privacy Options category in the Trust Center dialog box.)

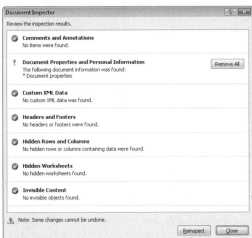

Figure 4-6 The Document Inspector examines the hidden places in your workbooks where personal data can hide.

As you can see in Figure 4-6, data can hide in many places. The Document Inspector looks in them all and reports on what it finds, as shown on the dialog box on the bottom of Figure 4-6. You can then click any Remove All buttons that appear or close the dialog box and edit the area in question. Most of these items will usually be perfectly benign, of course. You probably wouldn't want to purge your headers and footers, for example, unless they contained your address or Social Security number. But if you are sharing data with others, the Document Inspector gives you a quick and easy way to find personal data you might not otherwise have found.

Chapter 4

Using Digital Signatures

Digital signatures are similar to handwritten signatures in that both are intended to provide authenticity to documents. However, although the digital version might include a graphic representation of an actual signature, it also uses cryptography to establish not only a document's authenticity but also the integrity of the file and the identity of the signer. You can add signatures to your own documents and to others' as well. One way to use signatures is to verify that others have read a document (or at least opened it) by adding their signatures.

One important fact about digital signatures is that when you digitally sign a workbook, Excel saves it as a read-only document, preventing you from making further changes. A handwritten signature, being typically the last element you add before sending a letter, in this case ensures that it actually is the last step you perform in a workbook. But don't worry—you can remove and reapply a signature if you need to make changes. The point is you can be sure that a document won't change after you apply a signature.

To accomplish all this, you'll need a valid digital signature, which you must create or obtain separately. Fortunately, Excel provides ways to accomplish this. To begin, click the Microsoft Office Button, click Prepare, and then click Add A Digital Signature to display the message shown in Figure 4-7.

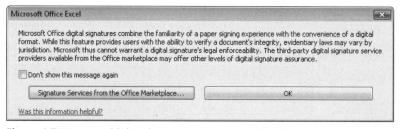

Figure 4-7 You can add digital signatures to your workbooks.

If you don't yet have your own digital signature, you can click Signature Services From The Office Marketplace to open a Web page where you can select and order one from a number of third-party vendors. Clicking OK before you have a signature displays a dialog box where you can select a third-party vendor signature or where you can choose to create your own digital signature. Microsoft is careful to point out that creating your own digital signature lets you verify only the authenticity of your own documents, and even then on only your own computer. The upshot is that you might consider purchasing a verifiable signature, if you think you need one. If, despite these drawbacks, you still want to create your own digital signature, select Create Your Own Digital ID, and then click OK. After you create or purchase a digital ID, the dialog box at the top of Figure 4-8 appears when you click Add A Digital Signature. After you click OK, Excel saves the current workbook as read-only and the second dialog box in Figure 4-9 appears, letting you know that your signature will become invalid if you further modify the workbook.

If after dismissing this last dialog box you try to edit the workbook, you'll see that you can't—the workbook is locked and can't be edited, and a Signatures task pane appears on the right side of the screen, as shown in Figure 4-9.

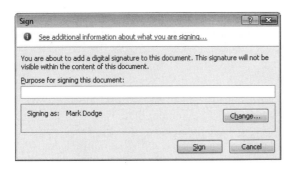

Figure 4-8 For what it's worth, you can create your own digital signature.

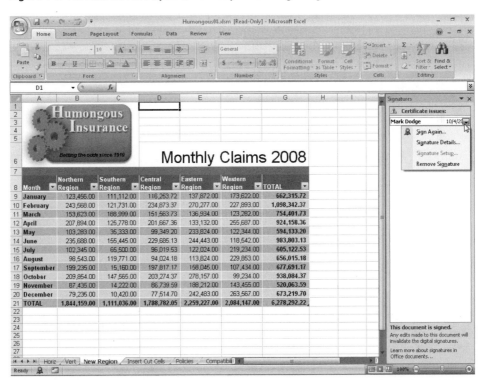

Figure 4-9 The Signatures task pane appears when you attempt to edit a workbook after adding a signature.

Also note in Figure 4-9 that *[Read-Only]* appears in the title bar next to the file name, and a small icon that looks like a certificate ribbon appears next to the word *Ready* in the status bar. You can click this icon to open and close the Signatures task pane, which you can also open and close by clicking the Microsoft Office Button, clicking Prepare, and clicking View Signatures.

To remove a digital signature, click the small downward-pointing arrow next to the signature you want to remove, and click Remove Signature, which again saves the current workbook, this time without the [Read-Only] designation. You can also view more information about the selected signature by clicking Signature Details.

Other Security Features

Several security features in Excel are apropos to topics covered in depth elsewhere in this book:

- For more about worksheet security, see "Protecting Worksheets" on page 156.

- For more about workbook security, see "Hiding and Protecting Workbooks" on page 175.

- To learn about Information Rights Management, see "Controlling Document Access with Information Rights Management" on page 803.

PART 2
Building Worksheets

CHAPTER 5

Planning Your Worksheet Design

In this chapter, we'll pose seven simple questions that might help you greatly when planning a worksheet. Granted, it's not necessary to spend time planning every worksheet you create for personal use, but a little consideration can be helpful when planning worksheets you need to pass on or share with others.

Which Data Should Be in Rows, and Which in Columns?

Sometimes this is rather obvious, but generally speaking, you'll want the data that will be most abundant to fill rows rather than columns. Consider the readability of your data when you make this decision. For example, a month-oriented worksheet like the one in Figure 5-1 can work well with the month labels either across the top or down the left side of the worksheet. But in this case, having the month labels down the side makes it easier to view the worksheet on the screen and makes it easier to fit it on a printed page. The worksheet in Figure 5-1 contains only four columns of detail data, but if your worksheet has more categories of detail data than the number of months, you may want to run the months in columns instead.

Usually the detail you accumulate in a worksheet best fits into rows from top to bottom—relatively speaking, a deep and narrow worksheet. It is not unheard of to build a spreadsheet that is shallow and wide (only a few rows deep, with lots of columns), but you might regret it later. A shallow, wide worksheet can be annoying if you must continually pan to the right to find information or if you have to deal with odd column breaks when printing. If you have a wheel mouse, scrolling up and down is extremely easy to do using the wheel, but panning right and left requires clicking and dragging. And once you have the worksheet filled with data, it's time-consuming to change it—especially when you could have designed it differently from the start.

You might also prefer the worksheet to be long rather than wide so you can use the Page Up and Page Down keys to navigate around the screen. When oriented horizontally, the worksheet shown in Figure 5-1 would still work, as shown in Figure 5-2, but you would have to scroll to the right to view all the data.

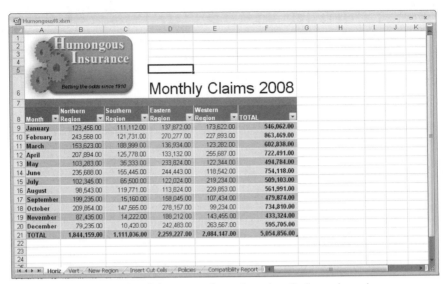

Figure 5-1 Monthly total worksheets are often oriented vertically, as shown here.

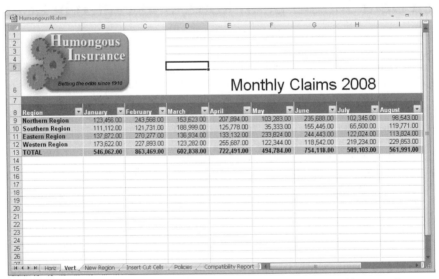

Figure 5-2 Worksheets are often harder to view and print when oriented horizontally.

  You'll find the Humongous08.xlsm, Pacific Sales.xlsm, and Alpacas.xlsm files in the Sample Files section of the companion CD.

Will You Need to Print the Worksheet?

Before you start work on a worksheet, you also need to ask yourself whether you will need to print the worksheet. You might realize that you don't need to worry about printing at all, if, for example, you are going to use the worksheet for information storage or reference purposes only.

If you will want to print the worksheet, consider how your data will look and how the worksheet will work on paper. This will make a huge difference to your overall worksheet design. For example, the worksheet in Figure 5-2 will require two pages to print, even if you orient it horizontally (using Landscape Orientation on the Page Layout tab on the Ribbon). The second page of the printout will contain some of the monthly totals, but you won't see the names of the regions unless you use the Print Titles feature (also on the Page Layout tab) to repeat the headings on each page. For large worksheets in either horizontal or vertical orientation, using Print Titles is an absolute necessity for intelligible printouts.

For more about page setup and print titles, see Chapter 11, "Printing and Presenting."

You also need to consider how you will use the printout. If you're going to use it in a management report, you'll want to try getting the salient information to fit on one page. If it's for a presentation, you might need to distill it further, or create smaller, more digestible chunks of data that can be summarized in a small grid of a dozen or so cells, so it will fit onto a transparency or a slide. If you have massive amounts of data to start with, you can create summary pages for various purposes, as shown in Figure 5-3, or use outlining to collapse the detail in large worksheets, displaying only the totals, as shown in Figure 5-4.

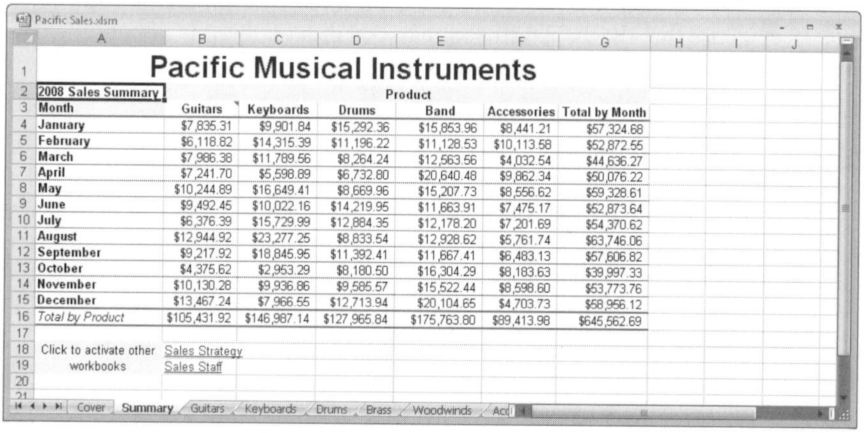

Figure 5-3 If showing all the detail data is too cumbersome, you can create summary sheets for reporting purposes.

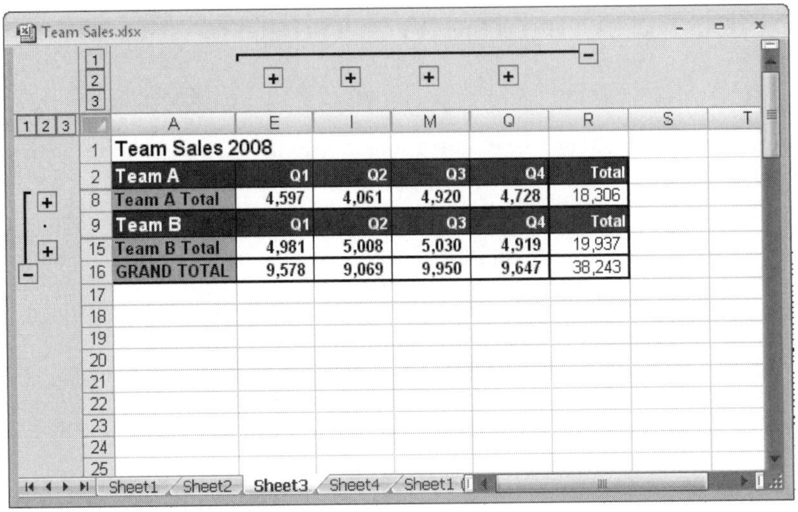

Figure 5-4 You can use outlining to hide the detail for summary purposes.

> **For information about outlining, see "Outlining Worksheets" on page 253.**

If the worksheet is for auditing or reference purposes, you'll probably want to see everything. Orientation is a big issue here. You can print in either landscape (horizontal) or portrait (vertical) format, so design your worksheet accordingly. Sometimes using a landscape orientation helps if you have lots of columns. If you have an inordinate number of columns, you might want to try segmenting your data into an overall system of worksheets—chunks that can be realistically printed without losing context or readability. For example, the sheet tabs at the bottom of the workbook shown in Figure 5-3 give evidence that the displayed summary sheet actually consolidates the data from several other sheets in the same workbook.

Who Is the Audience?

Are you building a worksheet for your own use, or will you be sharing it with others online or in printed form? In other words, does the worksheet need to look marvelous, or is fancy formatting optional? Do you need to create a big-picture summary or overview for others? It's definitely important to consider your audience when deciding how your worksheet is going to look.

If you're close to the data in your worksheet—that is, this is your job—you probably think the details are a lot more interesting than others might. You need to think like the people you will be presenting this information to and tell them what they need to know—no more, and certainly no less. If your worksheet contains a lot of data that your audience doesn't really need to see, *which is almost always the case*, you can create a summary sheet (like the one shown in Figure 5-3) specifically for the purpose of mass consumption. If your worksheet will have more than one type of audience, create different summary sheets for each group, all using the same underlying data.

Would Your Worksheet Survive Without You?

If you are creating worksheets that might at some point be used by others, make sure they are understandable and well documented. Most of us don't think about documentation, but every spreadsheet you create for business or personal use should be created with the possibility in mind that others will need to figure it out someday—possibly without your help. If you change jobs, you will be leaving a good legacy behind for the next person, which reflects well on you. A little documentation goes a long way, as shown in Figure 5-5. You can use the Microsoft Office Excel 2007 Comment command to add notes anywhere a little explanation is in order.

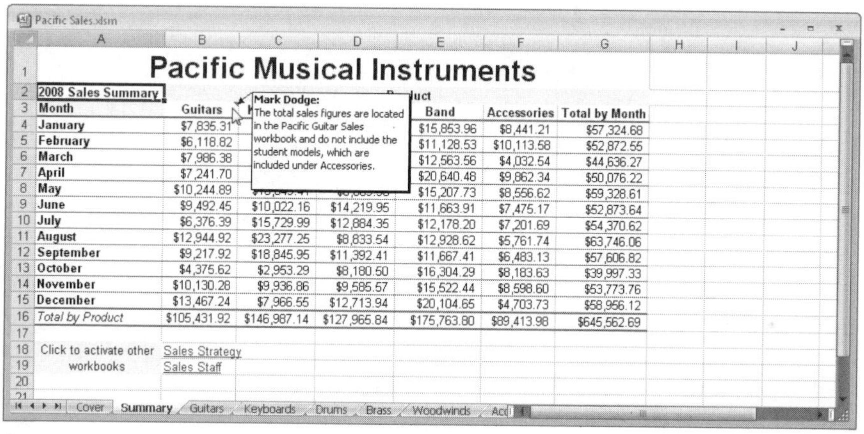

Figure 5-5 Make sure critical worksheets are understandable and well documented.

For information about documenting your worksheets, see "Adding Comments to Cells" on page 251.

You also need to prepare worksheets containing important personal records with survivability in mind. If you were to pass away unexpectedly, you'd want to leave your family with clear financial worksheets.

Does the Worksheet Rely on Imported Data?

Many people work with data that is compiled elsewhere as the basis for their worksheet analyses. For example, a database located either on your computer or somewhere on a network is often the repository for specific information that you extract and analyze. If this is the case, try to make it easy on yourself. Often, people use the "ad hoc" approach to working—that is, they do it quickly, when it's needed, with no particular attention paid to repeatability. If you gather information from a database, you might be able to construct queries that you can execute again and again, on whatever schedule you need, rather than starting from scratch each time. This way, you can ensure that the imported data will be structured in the same way each time. Then you might use the structure of the imported data as the basis for your worksheet design. Or it might make sense to keep the imported data on a separate worksheet no one will see and then construct nicely formatted worksheets you can use to extract only the pertinent information. For example, Figure 5-6 shows just such a worksheet. You can see that the raw data is on a separate worksheet behind the information worksheet.

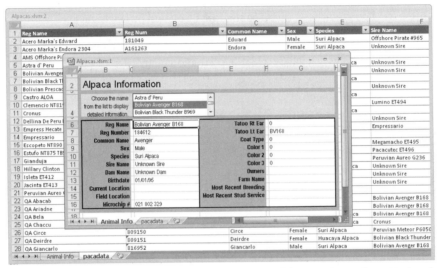

Figure 5-6 You can put raw imported data on its own worksheet and use a formatted worksheet to present the pertinent information.

For information about using information stored elsewhere, see Chapter 23, "Working with External Data," as well as the chapters in Part 8, "Collaborating."

Databases, Fields, and Records

Sometimes when you say the word *database*, you can see people's eyes glaze over in anticipation of a barrage of incomprehensible terminology. Although using a database program can be overwhelmingly complex, consider that many of the worksheets you'll create in Office Excel 2007 (such as the underlying worksheet in Figure 5-6) are actually rudimentary databases. The telephone directory is an example of a database in printed form. In database terminology, each phone listing in the directory is a *record* of the database, and each item of information in a listing (first name, last name, address, and telephone number) is a *field* of the record.

Do You Need More Than One Worksheet?

Spreadsheet programs began as a better way to store, present, and interpret information that previously had been kept on paper and calculated by hand, probably using a 10-key calculator. Often the first worksheets we created when we were climbing the old Excel learning curve were little more than clean, two-dimensional reproductions of what we used to do on paper. One way to step up from the old paper paradigm is to use modular design. *Modular design* is a sort of "structured programming" or "object-oriented" approach, where you carve your data into logical chunks that make sense as stand-alone elements. (The other design approach is called *hierarchical*, where you organize your data for error identification and maximum readability.) Because there's usually no need to keep detail data in any kind of presentable format, why bother? Concentrate your worksheet beautification program on the summary sheets and charts you will share with others. Design a system of worksheets rather than trying to get everything on a single worksheet. Figure 5-6 shows a rudimentary example of modular design—that is, one worksheet contains data, and another worksheet contains a specific type of analysis. In a complex modular system, you might have dozens of worksheets, each dedicated to a specific task.

Have You Allowed Room for New Data?

It's critical to allow for expansion and editing after you have assembled your worksheet. It's generally a good idea to add a few extra rows and columns to the detail area and to keep totals separate from the detail data by a row or column or two, if possible. One of the most common editing actions you'll perform is inserting new rows and columns. Excel has gotten a lot smarter about this over the years, making obsolete some of the rules of thumb that we old-timers have collected. But it's still possible to mess up.

A rather famous folkloric tale tells the story of an accounting person who inserted a row at the bottom of a range of cells but forgot to adjust the totals formulas and was fired because his numbers were off by $200,000. The moral: Edit worksheets carefully, and always guard against introducing new errors along the way.

Chapter 5

In this chapter, we'll cover the basics, including moving around within the massive worksheet grid, entering and selecting data, and working with multiple worksheets and protecting their contents. You probably already know many of these techniques, but here we'll also present alternative methods. You might find a better, or faster, way to do something you do frequently. You'll find that Microsoft Office Excel 2007 offers a lot of alternatives.

Moving Around Regions

You already know how to use scroll bars and the Page Up and Page Down keys. Office Excel 2007 offers many other ways to get around, including some unique tricks you'll find only in Excel 2007.

A *region* is a range of cell entries bounded by blank cells or column and row headings. In Figure 6-1, the range A3:E7 is a region, as are the ranges G3:H7, A9:E10, and G9:H10. (Strictly speaking, cell A1 is also a one-cell region because no adjoining cells contain entries.) For example, cell H10 is within a region, even though it's empty. The *active area* of the worksheet is the selection rectangle that encompasses all regions—that is, all the filled cells in the active worksheet—which in Figure 6-1 is A1:H10.

The techniques used to navigate regions are especially helpful if you typically work with large tables of data. Getting to the bottom row of a 500-row table is easier when you don't have to use the scroll bars. Read on to find out how.

Microsoft Office
Button

Note

The small square in the lower-right corner of the active cell is the *fill handle*. If the fill handle isn't visible on your screen, it means it isn't turned on. To turn it on, click the Microsoft Office Button, click Excel Options, click the Advanced category, and select the Enable Fill Handle And Cell Drag-And-Drop check box.

	A	B	C	D	E	F	G	H	I	J
	Regional Sales.xlsx									
1	Regional Sales									
2										
3	2008	Qtr 1	Qtr 2	Qtr 3	Qtr 4		Total	Average		
4	Region 1	1000	1050	1100	1150		4300	1075		
5	Region 2	1100	1150	1200	1250		4700	1175		
6	Region 3	1200	1250	1300	1350		5100	1275		
7	Region 4	1300	1350	1400	1450		5500	1375		
8										
9	Total	4600	4800	5000	5200		19600	4900		
10	Average	1150	1200	1250	1300		4900			
11										
12										
13										
14										
15										
16										

Figure 6-1 The four blocks of cells on this worksheet are separate regions.

Navigating Regions with the Keyboard

To move between the edges of regions, hold down the Ctrl key, and then press any of the arrow keys. For example, in Figure 6-1, cell A3 is the active cell; press Ctrl+Right Arrow to activate cell E3.

If a blank cell is active when you press Ctrl and an arrow key, Excel moves to the first filled cell in that direction or to the last available cell on the worksheet if it doesn't find any filled cells in that direction. In Figure 6-1, for example, if cell F3 is active when you press Ctrl+Right Arrow, the selection moves to cell G3; if Cell H3 is active, pressing Ctrl+Right Arrow activates cell XFD3—the last available cell in row A3. Just press Ctrl+Left Arrow to return to cell H3.

Navigating Regions with the Mouse

When you move the pointer over the edge of the active cell's border, the pointer changes from a plus sign to an arrow. With the arrow pointer visible, you can double-click any edge of the border to change the active cell to the cell on the edge of the current region in that direction—it is the same as pressing Ctrl and an arrow key in that direction. For example, if you double-click the bottom edge of the active cell in Figure 6-1, Excel selects cell A7.

The left side of the status bar displays the mode indicators in Table 6-1 when the corresponding keyboard mode is active.

Table 6-1 **Keyboard Modes**

Mode	Description
Extend Selection	Press F8 to turn on this mode, which you use to extend the current selection using the keyboard. (Make sure Scroll Lock is off.) This is the keyboard equivalent of selecting cells by dragging the mouse. Furthermore, unlike holding down the Shift key and pressing an arrow key, you can extend the range by pressing only one key at a time. Press F8 again to turn off Extend Selection mode.
Add To Selection	Press Shift+F8 to add more cells to the current selection using the keyboard. The cells need not be adjacent; after pressing Shift+F8, click any cell or drag through any range to add it to the selection. This is the keyboard equivalent of holding down Ctrl and selecting additional cells with the mouse.
Num Lock	Keeps your keypad in numeric entry mode. This is turned on by default, but its status is not usually displayed in the status bar. However, you can make it so by right-clicking the status bar anywhere and clicking Num Lock.
Fixed Decimal	To add a decimal point to the numeric entries in the current selection, click the Microsoft Office Button, click Excel Options, select the Advanced category, and select the Automatically Insert A Decimal Point check box in the Editing Options group. Excel places the decimal point in the location you specify in the Places box. For example, when you turn on Fixed Decimal mode, specify two decimal places, and type the number **12345** in a cell, the value 123.45 appears in the cell after you press Enter. Existing cell entries are not affected unless you edit them. To turn off Fixed Decimal mode, return to the Advanced category in the Excel Options dialog box, and clear the Automatically Insert A Decimal Point check box.
Caps Lock	Press the Caps Lock key to type text in capital letters. (This does not affect number and symbol keys.) To turn off Caps Lock mode, press the Caps Lock key again. The status of this mode does not usually display in the status bar, but you can make it so. Right-click the status bar anywhere, and click Caps Lock.
Scroll Lock	Press Scroll Lock to use the Page Up, Page Down, and arrow keys to move the viewed portion of the window without moving the active cell. When Scroll Lock mode is off, the active cell moves one page at a time when you press Page Up or Page Down and moves one cell at a time when you press one of the arrow keys. To turn off Scroll Lock mode, press the Scroll Lock key again.
End Mode	Press the End key, and then press an arrow key to move the selection to the edge of the region in that direction or to the last worksheet cell in that direction. This mode functions like holding down Ctrl and pressing an arrow key, except you need to press only one key at a time. To turn off End mode, press the End key again. End mode is also turned off after you press one of the arrow keys.
Overtype Mode	Click the formula bar or double-click a cell and press the Insert key to turn on Overtype mode (formerly known as Overwrite mode). Usually, new characters you type in the formula bar are inserted between existing characters. With Overtype mode turned on, the characters you type replace any existing characters to the right of the insertion point. Overtype mode turns off when you press Insert again or when you press Enter or one of the arrow keys to lock in the cell entry.

Chapter 6

Navigating with Special Keys

Table 6-2 shows how you can use the Home and End keys alone and in conjunction with other keys to make selections and to move around a worksheet.

Table 6-2 Keyboard Shortcuts for Navigation

Press	To
Home	Move to the first cell in the current row.
Ctrl+Home	Move to cell A1.
Ctrl+End	Move to the last cell in the last column in the active area. For example, in Figure 6-1, pressing Ctrl+End selects cell H10.
End	Start End mode. Then press an arrow key to move around by cell region.
Scroll Lock+Home	Move to the first cell within the current window.
Scroll Lock+End	Move to the last cell within the current window.

Understanding Selection

Knowing how to select cells, rows, and columns in Excel is fundamental to using the program to its fullest potential. As you will see, there are many more ways to use selection techniques to isolate particular types of data, formats, objects, and even blank cells. Even though some of this information may seem basic, you'll probably encounter a few tips that will make your spreadsheet life a little easier:

- Before you can work with a cell or range, you must select it, and when you do, it becomes *active*.

- The reference of the active cell appears in the Name box at the left end of the formula bar.

- Only one cell can be active at a time, but you can select ranges of cells, and when you do, the active cell is in the upper-left corner of the selected range.

- Select all cells on a worksheet by clicking the Select All box located in the upper-left corner of your worksheet, where the column and row headings intersect.

For more about selection, read on.

Selecting with the Mouse

To select a range of cells, drag the mouse over the range. Alternatively, you can extend using two diagonal corners of the range you want to select. Click a cell at one corner of the range, and then press and hold the Shift key while clicking the cell diagonal to the first cell. For example, to extend the selection A1:B5 so it becomes A1:C10, hold down the Shift key, and click cell C10. When you need to select a large range, this technique is more efficient than dragging the mouse across the entire selection.

Zooming to Select Large Worksheet Areas

It's impossible to see an entire workbook on the screen. Knowing that, what do you do if you need to select a gigantic range of cells? You can drag the pointer past the window border and wait for the automatic scrolling to get you where you need to go, but this method can be frustrating if you have trouble managing the scrolling speed and keep overshooting the target.

A better method is to use the Zoom slider to get a bird's-eye view of the worksheet, as shown in Figure 6-2. Drag the Zoom slider at the bottom of the screen to the percentage you want. You can also click the Zoom percentage indicator adjacent to the slider to open the Zoom dialog box for more zooming options. The Zoom feature is limited to a range from 10 through 400 percent.

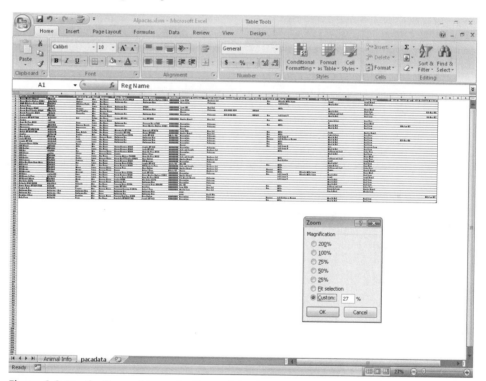

Figure 6-2 Use the Zoom slider or the Zoom dialog box to view large areas of a worksheet for easier selection.

Selecting Columns, Rows, and Multiple Areas

Multiple-area selections (also known as *nonadjacent* or *noncontiguous* selections) are selected cell ranges that do not encompass a single rectangular area, as shown in Figure 6-3. To select multiple-area ranges with the mouse, press the Ctrl key, and drag through each range you want to select. The first cell you click in the last range you select becomes the active cell. As you can see in Figure 6-3, cell G6 is the active cell.

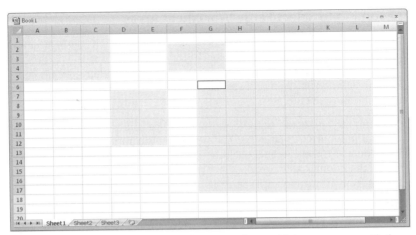

Figure 6-3 Hold down the Ctrl key and drag to select multiple-area ranges with the mouse.

To select an entire column or row, click the column or row heading. In other words, to select cells B1 through B1048576, click the heading for column B. The first visible cell in the column becomes the active cell, so if the first row visible on your screen is row 1048557, then cell B1048557 becomes active when you click the heading for column B, even though all the other cells in the column are selected. To select more than one adjacent column or row at a time, drag through the column or row headings, or click the heading at one end of the range, press Shift, and then click the heading at the other end. To select nonadjacent columns or rows, as shown in Figure 6-4, hold down Ctrl, and click each heading or drag through adjacent headings you want to select.

	A	B	C	D	E	F	G	H	I
1	Regional Sales								
2									
3	2008	Qtr 1	Qtr 2	Qtr 3	Qtr 4	Total	Average		
4	Region 1	1000	1050	1100	1150	4300	1075		
5	Region 2	1100	1150	1200	1250	4700	1175		
6	Region 3	1200	1250	1300	1350	5100	1275		
7	Region 4	1300	1350	1400	1450	5500	1375		
8	Total	4600	4800	5000	5200	19600	4900		
9	Average	1150	1200	1250	1300	4900			
10									
11									
12									
13									
14									
15									

Figure 6-4 Select entire columns and rows by clicking their headings, or hold down the Ctrl key while clicking to select nonadjacent rows and columns.

Use the following methods to select with the keyboard:

- To select an entire column with the keyboard, select any cell in the column, and press Ctrl+Spacebar.

- To select an entire row with the keyboard, select any cell in the row, and press Shift+Spacebar.

- To select several entire adjacent columns or rows with the keyboard, select any cell range that includes cells in each of the columns or rows, and then press Ctrl+Spacebar or Shift+Spacebar, respectively. For example, to select columns B, C, and D, select B4:D4 (or any range that includes cells in these three columns), and then press Ctrl+Spacebar.

- To select the entire worksheet with the keyboard, press Ctrl+Shift+Spacebar.

Selecting Regions

If you hold down the Shift key as you double-click the edge of an active cell's border, Excel selects all the cells from the current selection to the next edge of the region in that direction. The cell from which you start the selection process remains the active cell.

Using the Find & Select Commands

At the right end of the Home tab on the Ribbon, the Find & Select menu displays several helpful selection commands, as shown in Figure 6-5. In the middle of the menu are five commands that used to be buried in dialog boxes and have been promoted in Excel because of their widespread use: Formulas, Comments, Conditional Formatting, Constants, and Data Validation.

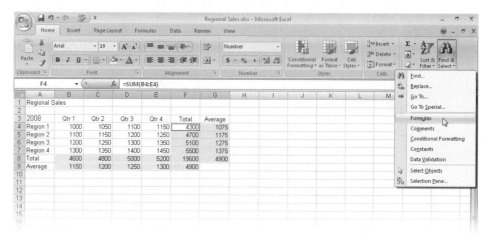

Figure 6-5 Use the Find & Select commands to zero in on specific items.

In Figure 6-5, we used the Formulas command to select all the formulas on the work-sheet, which are highlighted by multiple selection rectangles. You can use these special-ized selection commands for various purposes such as applying specific formatting to formulas and constants or auditing worksheets for errant conditional formatting or data validation cells.

The two Go To commands are also helpful for finding and selecting a variety of work-sheet elements. To quickly move to and select a cell or a range of cells, click Go To (or press F5) to open the Go To dialog box; then type a cell reference, range reference, or defined range name in the Reference box, and press Enter. You can also use Go To to extend a selection. For example, to select A1:Z100, you can click A1, open the Go To dialog box, type **Z100**, and then press Shift+Enter.

> For more about selecting, see "Finding and Replacing Stuff" on page 221 and "Selecting and Grouping Objects" on page 386. For more information about defined range names and references, see "Naming Cells and Cell Ranges" on page 441 and "Using Cell References in Formulas" on page 428.

To move to another worksheet in the same workbook, open the Go To dialog box, and type the name of the worksheet, followed by an exclamation point and a cell name or reference. For example, to go to cell D5 on a worksheet called Sheet2, type **Sheet2!D5**. To move to another worksheet in another open workbook, open the Go To dialog box, and type the name of the workbook in brackets, followed by the name of the worksheet, an exclamation point, and a cell name or reference. For example, to go to cell D5 on a worksheet called Sheet2 in an open workbook called Sales.xlsx, type **[Sales.xlsx]Sheet2!D5**.

Excel keeps track of the last four locations from which you used the Go To command and lists them in the Go To dialog box. You can use this list to move among these loca-tions in your worksheet. This is handy when you're working on a large worksheet or jumping around among multiple locations and worksheets in a workbook. Figure 6-6 shows the Go To dialog box displaying four previous locations.

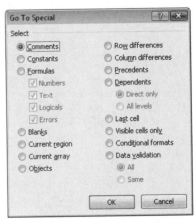

Figure 6-6 The Go To and Go To Special dialog boxes are your selection transporters.

> **Note**
>
> In the Go To dialog box, Excel displays in the Reference box the cell or range from which you just moved. This way, you can easily move back and forth between two locations by pressing F5 and then Enter repeatedly.

Selecting with Go To Special

Find & Select ▾

When you click the Special button in the Go To dialog box (or the Go To Special command on the Find & Select menu), the dialog box shown on the right of Figure 6-6 opens, presenting additional selection options. You can think of the Go To Special dialog box as "Select Special," because you can use it to quickly find and select cells that meet certain specifications.

After you specify one of the Go To Special options and click OK, Excel highlights the cell or cells that match the criteria. With a few exceptions, if you select a range of cells before you open the Go To Special dialog box, Excel searches only the selected range; if the current selection is a single cell or one or more graphic objects, Excel searches the entire active worksheet. The following are guidelines for using the Go To Special options:

- *Constants* refers to any cell containing static data such as numbers or text, but not formulas.

- *Current Region* is handy when you're working in a large, complex worksheet and need to select blocks of cells. (Recall that a *region* is defined as a rectangular block of cells bounded by blank rows, blank columns, or worksheet borders.)

- *Current Array* selects all the cells in an array if the selected cell is part of an array range.

- *Last Cell* selects the cell in the lower-right corner of the range that encompasses all the cells that contain data, comments, or formats. When you select Last Cell, Excel finds the last cell in the active area of the worksheet, not the lower-right corner of the current selection.

- *Visible Cells Only* excludes from the current selection any cells in hidden rows or columns.

- *Objects* selects all graphic objects in your worksheet, regardless of the current selection.

- *Conditional Formats* selects only those cells that have conditional formatting applied. Or you can click the Home tab, and click the Conditional Formatting command on the Find & Select menu.

- *Data Validation* using the All option selects all cells to which data validation has been applied; Data Validation using the Same option selects only cells with the same validation settings as the currently selected cell. You can also click the

Chapter 6

Home tab, and click the Data Validation command on the Find & Select menu, which uses the All option.

For more information about graphic objects, see Chapter 10, "Creating Spiffy Graphics." For more information about conditional formatting, see "Formatting Conditionally" on page 284.

Navigating Multiple Selections

Some of the Go To Special options—such as Formulas, Comments, Precedents, and Dependents—might cause Excel to select multiple nonadjacent cell ranges. After you make the selection, you might want to change the active cell without losing the multi-selection. Or you might want to type entries into multiple ranges you select so you don't have to reach for the mouse. Either way, you can move between selected cells. For example, the worksheet shown here has multiple ranges selected:

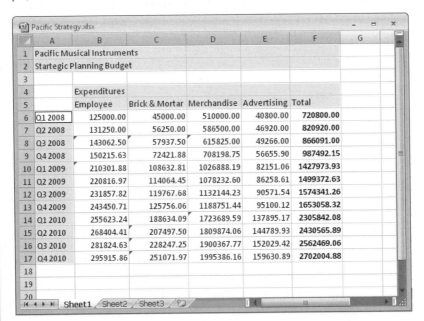

To move the active cell through these ranges without losing the selection, press Enter to move down or to the right one cell at a time; press Shift+Enter to move up or to the left one cell at a time. Or press Tab to move to the right or down; press Shift+Tab to move to the left or up. Pretty cool, eh? You might not think so until you have a lot of noncontiguous, noncolumnar data entry to do, but trust us. So, in the previous worksheet, if you press Enter until cell A17 is selected, the next time you press Enter the selection jumps to the beginning of the next selected region, in this case cell A1. Subsequently pressing Enter selects A2, then B1, then B2, and so on, until the end of the region—cell F2. Then the selection jumps to the next region, cell B4.

Selecting Precedents and Dependents

The Precedents and Dependents options in the Go To Special dialog box let you find cells that are used by a formula or to find cells on which a formula depends. To use the Precedents and Dependents options, first select the cell whose precedents or dependents you want to select. When searching for precedents or dependents, Excel always searches the entire worksheet. When you select the Precedents or Dependents option, Excel activates the Direct Only and All Levels options:

- Direct Only finds only those cells that directly refer to or that directly depend on the active cell.

- All Levels locates direct precedents and dependents plus those cells indirectly related to the active cell.

Depending on the task, you might find the built-in auditing features of Excel to be just the trick. On the Formulas tab on the Ribbon, the Formula Auditing group offers the Track Precedents and Track Dependents buttons. Rather than selecting all such cells like the Go To Special command, clicking these buttons draws arrows showing path and direction in relation to the selected cell. For more information, see "Auditing and Documenting Worksheets" on page 241.

Go To Special Keyboard Shortcuts

If you do a lot of "going to," you'll want to learn a few of these keyboard shortcuts, which will speed things up considerably:

- Press Ctrl+Shift+* to select the current region.
- Press Ctrl+/ to select the current array.
- Press Alt+; to select the visible cells only.
- Press Ctrl+[to select the direct precedents.
- Press Ctrl+Shift+{ to select all the precedents.
- Press Ctrl+] to select the direct dependents.
- Press Ctrl+Shift+} to select all the dependents.
- Press Ctrl+\ to select row differences.
- Press Ctrl+Shift+| to select column differences.

Selecting Row or Column Differences

The Row Differences and Column Differences options in the Go To Special dialog box compare the entries in a range of cells to spot potential inconsistencies. To use these debugging options, select the range before displaying the Go To Special dialog box. The position of the active cell in your selection determines which cells Excel uses to make its comparisons. When searching for row differences, Excel compares the cells in the selection with the cells in the same column as the active cell. When searching for column differences, Excel compares the cells in the selection with the cells in the same row as the active cell.

In addition to other variations, the Row Differences and Column Differences options look for differences in references and select those cells that don't conform to the comparison cell. They also verify that all the cells in the selected range contain the same type of entries. For example, if the comparison cell contains a SUM function, Excel flags any cells that contain a function, formula, or value other than SUM. If the comparison cell contains a constant text or numeric value, Excel flags any cells in the selected range that don't match the comparison value. The options, however, are not case-sensitive.

Techniques for Entering Data

Excel accepts two types of cell entries: constants and formulas. Constants fall into three main categories: numeric values, text values (also called *labels* or *strings*), and date/time values. Excel also recognizes two special types of constants called *logical values* and *error values*.

For more about date/time values, see Chapter 15, "Formatting and Calculating Date and Time."

Making Entries in Cells and in the Formula Bar

To make an entry in a cell, just select the cell, and start typing. As you type, the entry appears both in the formula bar and in the active cell. The flashing vertical bar in the active cell is called the *insertion point*.

After you finish typing, you must "lock in" the entry to store it permanently in the cell by pressing Enter. Pressing Enter normally causes the active cell to move down one row. You can change this so that when you press Enter, either the active cell doesn't change or it moves to an adjacent cell in another direction. Click the Microsoft Office Button, click Excel Options, select the Advanced category, and either clear the After Pressing Enter, Move Selection check box or change the selection in the Direction drop-down list. You also lock in an entry when you move the selection to a different cell by pressing Tab, Shift+Tab, Shift+Enter, or an arrow key, among other methods, after you type the entry, as shown in Table 6-3.

Table 6-3 **Keyboard Shortcuts for Data Entry**

Press	To
Enter	Activate the cell below the active cell, or whatever direction you have selected for the After Pressing Enter, Move Selection check box in the Advanced category in the Excel Options dialog box.
Shift+Enter	Activate the cell above the active cell, or the opposite of the direction set for the After Pressing Enter, Move Selection check box in the Advanced category in the Excel Options dialog box.
Tab	Activate the cell one column to the right of the active cell.
Shift+Tab	Activate the cell one column to the left of the active cell.
Arrow Key	Activate the adjacent cell in the direction of the arrow key you press.

When you begin typing an entry, three buttons appear on the formula bar: Cancel, Enter, and Insert Function. When typing a formula where the entry begins with an equal sign (=), a plus sign (+), or a minus sign (–), a drop-down list of frequently used functions becomes available, as shown in Figure 6-7.

For more about editing formulas, see Chapter 12, "Building Formulas."

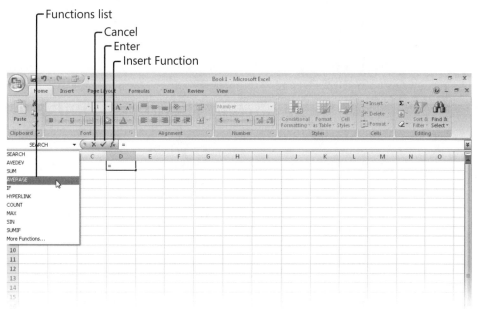

Figure 6-7 When you start entering a formula by typing an equal sign, the formula bar offers ways to help you finish it.

Entering Simple Numeric and Text Values

An entry that includes only numerals 0 through 9 and certain special characters, such as + – E e ( ) . , $ % and /, is a numeric value. An entry that includes almost any other character is a text value. Table 6-4 lists some examples of numeric and text values.

Table 6-4 **Examples of Numeric and Text Values**

Numeric Values	Text Values
123	Sales
123.456	B-1
$1.98	Eleven
1%	123 Main Street
1.23E+12	No. 324

Using Special Characters

A number of characters have special effects in Excel. Here are some guidelines for using special characters:

- If you begin a numeric entry with a plus sign, Excel drops the plus sign.

- If you begin a numeric entry with a minus sign, Excel interprets the entry as a negative number and retains the sign.

- In a numeric entry, the characters *E* and *e* specify an exponent used in scientific notation. For example, Excel interprets 1E6 as 1,000,000 (1 times 10 to the sixth power), which is displayed in Excel as 1.00E+06. To enter a negative exponential number, type a minus sign before the exponent. For example, –1E6 (1 times 10 to the negative sixth power) equals –1,000,000 and is displayed in Excel as –1.00E+06.

- Excel interprets numeric constants enclosed in parentheses as negative numbers, which is a common accounting practice. For example, Excel interprets (100) as –100.

- You can use decimal points and commas as you normally would. When you type numbers that include commas as separators, however, the commas appear in the cell but not in the formula bar; this is the same as if you had applied one of the built-in Excel Number formats. For example, if you type **1,234.56**, the value 1234.56 appears in the formula bar.

- If you begin a numeric entry with a dollar sign ($), Excel assigns a Currency format to the cell. For example, if you type **$123456**, Excel displays $123,456 in the cell and 123456 in the formula bar. In this case, Excel adds the comma to the worksheet display because it's part of the Currency format.

- If you end a numeric entry with a percent sign (%), Excel assigns a Percentage format to the cell. For example, if you type **23%**, Excel displays 23% in the formula bar and assigns a Percentage format to the cell, which also displays 23%.

- If you use a slash (/) in a numeric entry and the string cannot be interpreted as a date, Excel interprets the number as a fraction. For example, if you type **11 5/8** (with a space between the number and the fraction), Excel assigns a Fraction format to the entry, meaning the formula bar displays 11.625 and the cell displays 11 5/8.

> **Note**
> To make sure Excel does not interpret a fraction as a date, precede the fraction with a zero and a space. For example, to prevent Excel from interpreting the fraction 1/2 as January 2, type **0 1/2**.

For more about the built-in Excel Number formats, see "Formatting in Depth" on page 295. For more information about date and time formats, see "How AutoFill Handles Dates and Times" on page 214.

Understanding the Difference Between Displayed Values and Underlying Values

Although you can type 32,767 characters in a cell, a numeric cell entry can maintain precision to a maximum of only 15 digits. This means you can type numbers longer than 15 digits in a cell, but Excel converts any digits after the 15th to zeros. If you are working with figures greater than 999 trillion or decimals smaller than trillionths, perhaps you need to look into alternative solutions, such as a Cray supercomputer.

If you type a number that is too long to appear in a cell, Excel converts it to scientific notation in the cell, if you haven't applied any other formatting. Excel adjusts the precision of the scientific notation depending on the cell width. If you type a very large or very small number that is longer than the formula bar, Excel displays it in the formula bar using scientific notation. In Figure 6-8, we typed the same number in both cell A1 and cell B1; however, because cell B1 is wider, Excel displays more of the number but still displays it using scientific notation.

For more information about increasing the width of a cell, see "Changing Column Widths" on page 335.

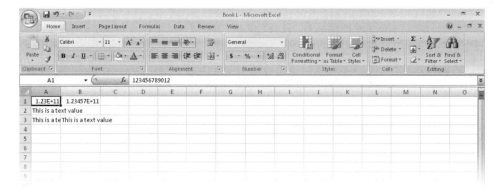

Figure 6-8 Because the number 123,456,789,012 is too long to fit in either cell A1 or cell B1, Excel displays it in scientific notation.

The values that appear in formatted cells are called *displayed values*; the values that are stored in cells and appear in the formula bar are called *underlying values*. The number of digits that appear in a cell—its displayed value—depends on the width of the column and any formatting you have applied to the cell. If you reduce the width of a column that contains a long entry, Excel might display a rounded-off version of the number, a string of number signs (#), or scientific notation, depending on the display format you're using.

> **Note**
>
> If you see a series of number signs (######) in a cell where you expect to see a number, increase the width of the cell to see the numbers again.

TROUBLESHOOTING

My formulas don't add numbers correctly.

Suppose, for example, you write a formula and Excel tells you that $2.23 plus $5.55 equals $7.79, when it should be $7.78. Investigate your underlying values. If you use currency formatting, numbers with more than three digits to the right of the decimal point are rounded to two decimal places. In this example, if the underlying vales are 2.234 and 5.552, the result is 7.786, which rounds to 7.79. You can either change the decimal places or select the Set Precision As Displayed check box (click the Microsoft Office Button, click Excel Options, click the Advanced category, and look in the When Calculating This Workbook area) to eliminate the problem. Be careful if you select Set Precision As Displayed, however, because it permanently changes all the underlying values in your worksheet to their displayed values.

Creating Long Text Values

If you type text that is too long for Excel to display in a single cell, Excel overlaps the adjacent cells, but the text remains stored in the original cell. If you then type text in a cell that is overlapped by another cell, the overlapping text appears truncated, as shown in cell B3 in Figure 6-8. But don't worry—it's still all there.

> **Note**
>
> The easiest way to eliminate overlapping text is to widen the column by double-clicking the column border in the heading. For example, in Figure 6-8, when you double-click the line between the A and the B in the column heading, the width of column A adjusts to accommodate the longest entry in the column.

Using Text Wrapping

If you have long text entries, text wrapping can make them easier to read. Text wrapping lets you type long strings of text that wrap onto two or more lines within the same cell rather than overlapping adjacent cells. Select the cells where you want to use wrapping, then click the Home tab on the Ribbon, and finally click the Wrap Text button, as shown in Figure 6-9. To accommodate the extra lines, Excel increases the height of the row.

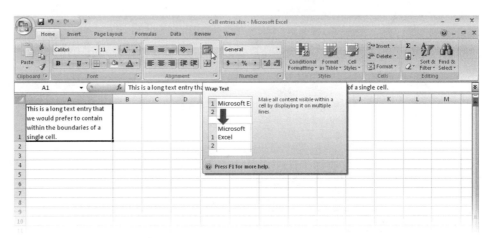

Figure 6-9 Click the Wrap Text button to force long text entries to wrap within a single cell.

For more about wrapping text, see "Wrapping Text in Cells" on page 319.

Chapter 6

Understanding Numeric Text Entries

Sometimes you might want to type special characters that Excel does not normally treat as plain text. For example, you might want +1 to appear in a cell. If you type **+1**, Excel interprets this as a numeric entry and drops the plus sign (as stated earlier). In addition, Excel normally ignores leading zeros in numbers, such as 01234. You can force Excel to accept special characters as text by using numeric text entries.

To enter a combination of text and numbers, such as G234, just type it. Because this entry includes a nonnumeric character, Excel interprets it as a text value. To create a text entry that consists entirely of numbers, you can precede the entry with a text-alignment prefix character, such as an apostrophe. You can also enter it as a formula by typing an equal sign and enclosing the entry with quotation marks. For example, to enter the number 01234 as text so the leading zero is displayed, type either **'01234** or **="01234"** in a cell. Whereas numeric entries are normally right-aligned, a numeric text entry is left-aligned in the cell just like regular text, as shown in Figure 6-10.

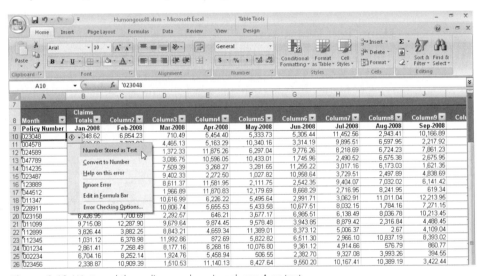

Figure 6-10 We typed the policy numbers in column A as text.

Text-alignment prefix characters, like formula components, appear in the formula bar but not in the cell. Table 6-5 lists all the text-alignment prefix characters.

Table 6-5 Text-Alignment Prefix Characters

Character	Action
' (apostrophe)	Left-aligns data in the cell
" (quotation mark)	Right-aligns data in the cell (see note)
^ (caret)	Centers data in the cell (see note)
\ (backslash)	Repeats characters across the cell (see note)

Only the apostrophe text-alignment prefix character always works with numeric or text entries. The caret, backslash, and quotation mark characters work only if, before typing them, you click the Microsoft Office Button, click Excel Options, select the Advanced category, and then scroll down to the Lotus Compatibility area and select the Transition Navigation Keys check box.

You'll find the Humongous08.xlsx file in the Sample Files section of the companion CD.

When you create a numeric entry that starts with an alignment prefix character, a small flag appears in the upper-left corner of the cell, indicating that the cell has a problem you might need to address. When you select the cell, an error-type smart tag appears to the right. Clicking this smart tag displays a menu of specific commands (refer to Figure 6-10). Because the apostrophe was intentional, you can click Ignore Error.

> **Note**
>
> If a range of cells shares the same problem, as in column A in Figure 6-10, you can select the entire cell range and use the smart tag action menu to resolve the problem in all the cells at the same time. For more information, see "Using Custom AutoCorrect Smart Tags" on page 229.

Entering Symbols

If you ever want to use characters in Excel that are not on your standard computer keyboard, you're in luck. Clicking the Insert tab on the Ribbon and then clicking the Symbol button gives you access to the complete character set for every installed font on your computer. Figure 6-11 shows the Symbol dialog box.

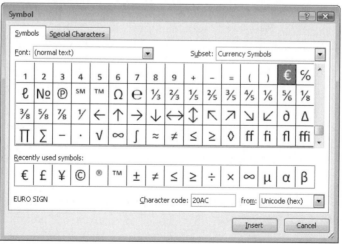

Figure 6-11 You can insert characters from the extended character sets of any installed font.

On the Symbols tab, select the font from the Font drop-down list; the entire character set appears. You can jump to specific areas in the character set using the Subset drop-down list, which also indicates the area of the character set you are viewing if you are using the scroll bar to browse through the available characters. The Character Code box displays the code of the selected character. You can also highlight a character in the display area by typing a character code number. You can select decimal or hexadecimal ASCII character encoding or Unicode using the From drop-down list. If you choose Unicode, you can select from a number of additional character subsets in the Subset drop-down list. The Special Characters tab in the Symbol dialog box gives you quick access to a number of commonly used characters, such as the em dash, the ellipsis, and the trademark and copyright symbols.

Making Entries in Ranges

To make a number of entries in a range of adjacent cells, first select those cells. Then press Enter, Shift+Enter, Tab, or Shift+Tab to move the active cell within the range. For example, to fill in a range of selected cells, select the range, and begin typing entries, as shown in Figure 6-12. Each time you press Enter, the active cell moves to the next cell in the range. The active cell never leaves the selected range until you specifically select another cell or range; in other words, when you reach the edge of the range and press Enter, the active cell jumps to the beginning of the next column or row. You can continue making entries this way until you fill the entire range. The advantage of this trick is that you don't need to take your hands off the keyboard to select cells with the mouse when making many entries at once.

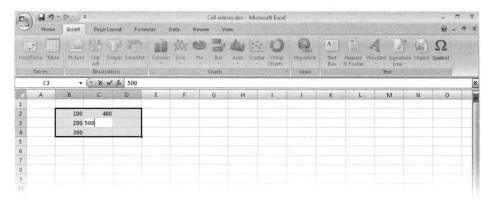

Figure 6-12 You can easily make entries in a range of cells by first selecting the entire range.

> **Note**
> To enter the same value in all selected cells at once, type your entry, and then press Ctrl+Enter.

Editing and Undoing Entries

You can correct simple errors as you type by pressing Backspace before you press Enter to lock in the cell entry, which erases the character to the left of the insertion point. However, to make changes to entries you have already locked in, you first need to enter Edit mode. (The mode indicator at the lower-left corner of the status bar has to change from Ready to Edit.) Use one of the following techniques to enter Edit mode:

- To edit a cell using the mouse, double-click the cell, and position the insertion point at the location of the error.

- To edit a cell using the keyboard, select the cell, and press F2. Use the arrow keys to position the insertion point in the cell.

By selecting several characters before you begin typing, you can replace several characters at once. To select several characters within a cell using the keyboard, enter Edit mode, place the insertion point just before or just after the characters you want to replace, and press Shift+Left Arrow or Shift+Right Arrow to extend your selection.

> **Note**
>
> If you don't want to take your hands off the keyboard to move from one end of a cell entry to the other, press Home or End while in Edit mode. To move through an entry one "word" at a time, press Ctrl+Left Arrow or Ctrl+Right Arrow.

If you need to erase the entire contents of the active cell, press Delete, or press Backspace and then Enter. Pressing Enter acts as a confirmation of the deletion. If you press Backspace accidentally, click the Cancel button or press Esc to restore the contents of the cell before pressing Enter. You can also erase the entire contents of a cell by selecting the cell and typing the new contents to replace the old. Excel erases the previous entry as soon as you begin typing. To revert to the original entry, press Esc before you press Enter.

Undo

Redo

To restore an entry after you press Delete or after you have locked in a new entry, click Edit, Undo; alternatively, press Ctrl+Z. The Undo command remembers the last 16 actions you performed. If you press Ctrl+Z repeatedly, each of the last 16 actions is undone, one after the other, in reverse order. You can also click the small arrow next to the Undo button to display a list of remembered actions. Drag the mouse to select one or more actions, as shown in Figure 6-13. After you release the mouse, all the selected actions are undone. The Redo button works the same way; you can quickly redo what you have just undone, if necessary.

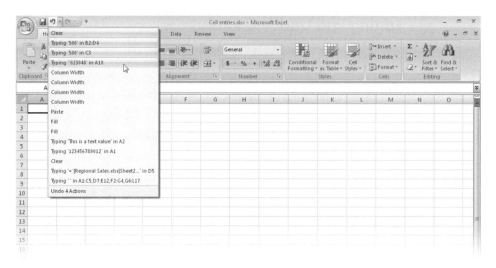

Figure 6-13 Click the small arrow next to the Undo button to select any number of the last 16 actions to undo at once.

Smart Tags

Smart tags give you instant access to commands and actions that are relevant to the current task. Many editing actions, such as copying and pasting cells, invoke a smart tag that appears adjacent to the last cell edited. If you click the tag, a smart tag action menu offers retroactive editing options:

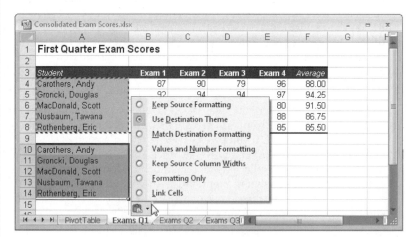

Smart tags appear in many situations, so you will hear about them in other places in this book. For examples of smart tag use, see "Tracing Errors" on page 249, "Pasting Selectively Using Paste Special" on page 186, and "Entering a Series of Dates" on page 523.

> **Note**
> It is important to remember that you can't undo individual actions in the middle of the list. If you select an action, all actions up to and including that action are undone.

Managing Worksheets

You can have as many worksheets in a workbook as your computer's memory will allow (probably hundreds of worksheets, depending on how much data each contains); consequently, you don't need to try to fit everything onto one worksheet. The following sections present the features you can use to organize your worksheet world.

Inserting and Deleting Worksheets

To insert a new worksheet into an existing workbook, click the Insert Worksheet tab, which you can see in Figure 6-14 on the left. The new sheet tab appears to the right of the last worksheet in the workbook. You can also quickly insert worksheets by right-clicking any sheet tab to display the shortcut menu shown in Figure 6-14 on the right. Clicking Insert on this menu opens the Insert dialog box containing other items you can insert besides blank worksheets, including templates and Excel 4.0 macro sheets.

Figure 6-14 To insert a blank worksheet, click the Insert Worksheet tab, or right-click any sheet tab to display a worksheet-focused shortcut menu.

In addition to providing a convenient method for inserting, deleting, renaming, moving, and copying worksheets, this shortcut menu contains the Select All Sheets command. As its name indicates, you use this command to select all the worksheets in a workbook, which you will need to do to perform certain functions, such as copying or formatting, on all the worksheets at once. The View Code command on this shortcut menu launches the Visual Basic Editor, showing the Code window for the current worksheet.

For more information about the Visual Basic Editor, see Chapter 26, "Recording Macros."

> **Note**
>
> As you can see in the shortcut menu shown in Figure 6-14, the sheet tab shortcut menu also contains a Tab Color command. If you are a visually oriented person, you might find color-coding your worksheets to be as useful as changing the worksheet names.

You can also add multiple worksheets to a workbook at the same time. To do so, click a sheet tab, press Shift, and then click other sheet tabs to select a range of worksheets—the same number you want to insert—before clicking Insert Worksheet on the sheet tab shortcut menu. (Notice that Excel adds *[Group]* to the workbook title in the window title bar, indicating you have selected a group of worksheets for editing.) Excel inserts the same number of new worksheets as you selected and places them in front of the first worksheet in the selected range. Note that this does not copy the selected worksheets; it is just a way of telling Excel how many fresh, blank worksheets you want to insert at once.

For more information about group editing, see "Editing Multiple Worksheets" on page 236.

You cannot undo the insertion of a new worksheet. If you do need to delete a worksheet, right-click its sheet tab, and click Delete. If you want to delete more than one worksheet, you can hold down Shift to select a range of worksheets, or you can hold down Ctrl and select nonadjacent worksheets, before you click Delete. Be careful! You cannot retrieve a worksheet after you have deleted it.

Naming and Renaming Worksheets

Notice that Excel numbers the new worksheets based on the number of worksheets in the workbook. If your workbook contains three worksheets, the first worksheet you insert is Sheet4, the next is Sheet5, and so on. If you grow weary of seeing Sheet1, Sheet2, and so on, in your workbooks, you can give your worksheets more imaginative and helpful names by double-clicking the tab and typing a new name.

You can use up to 31 characters in your worksheet names. Nevertheless, you should remember that the name you use determines the width of the corresponding sheet tab, as shown in Figure 6-15. Therefore, you might want to keep your worksheet names concise so you can see more than a couple of sheet tabs at a time.

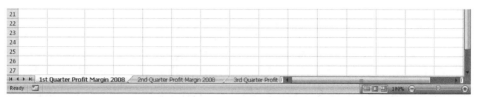

Figure 6-15 Double-click the sheet tab to type a new name. You might want to keep it short.

Moving and Copying Worksheets

As you might expect, Excel provides an easy way to move a worksheet from one place to another in the same workbook. In fact, all you have to do is click a sheet tab to select it and then drag it to its new location. Figure 6-16 shows this process. When you drag a worksheet, a small worksheet icon appears, and a tiny arrow indicates where the worksheet will be inserted in the tab order.

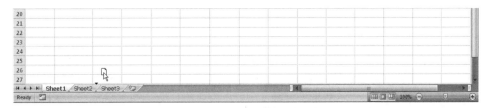

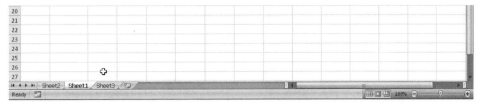

Figure 6-16 Click and drag sheet tabs to rearrange worksheets.

When you move worksheets, remember the following tips:

- If you want to move a worksheet to a location that isn't currently visible on your screen, drag past the visible tabs in either direction. The sheet tabs scroll in the direction you drag.

- You can move several worksheets at the same time. When you select several worksheets and drag, the pointer changes to look like a small stack of pages.

- You can copy worksheets using similar mouse techniques. First, select the worksheets you want to copy, and then hold down Ctrl while you drag the worksheets to the new location. When you copy a worksheet, an identical worksheet appears in the new location. Excel appends a number in parentheses to the copy's name to distinguish it from the original worksheet. For example, making a copy of Sheet1 results in a new worksheet named Sheet1 (2).

- You can move or copy nonadjacent worksheets at the same time by pressing Ctrl while you click to select the sheet tabs. Before dragging, release the Ctrl key to move the selected worksheets, or keep holding it down to create copies.

- You can click Move Or Copy on the sheet tab shortcut menu to handle similar worksheet management functions, including moving and copying worksheets between workbooks.

Chapter 6

Dragging Worksheets Between Workbooks

You can move and copy worksheets between workbooks by dragging. You use the same methods to move and copy that you use for worksheets in the same workbook. For example, with two workbooks arranged horizontally in the workspace, you can move a worksheet from one to the other by dragging it to the new location in the other workbook:

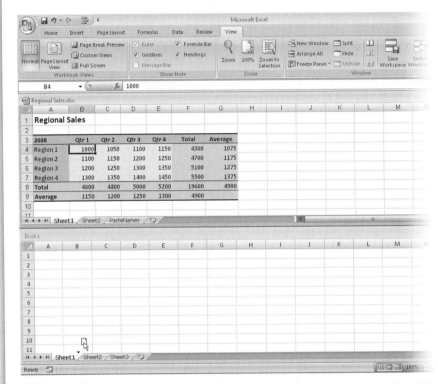

Note that you must arrange the two workbooks together on your screen to allow this to work. To do so, click the View tab on the Ribbon, then click the Arrange All button in the Window group, and finally select an arrangement option.

Viewing Worksheets

Excel provides a few helpful features you can use to change the way worksheets display. You can set up your workspace for specific tasks and then save the same view settings for the next time you need to perform the same task.

Splitting Worksheets into Panes

Worksheet panes let you view different areas of your worksheet simultaneously. You can split any worksheet in a workbook vertically, horizontally, or both vertically and horizontally, with synchronized scrolling capabilities. On the worksheet shown in Figure 6-17, columns B through M and rows 4 through 37 contain data. Column N and row 38 contain the totals. In Normal view, it's impossible to see the totals and the headings at the same time.

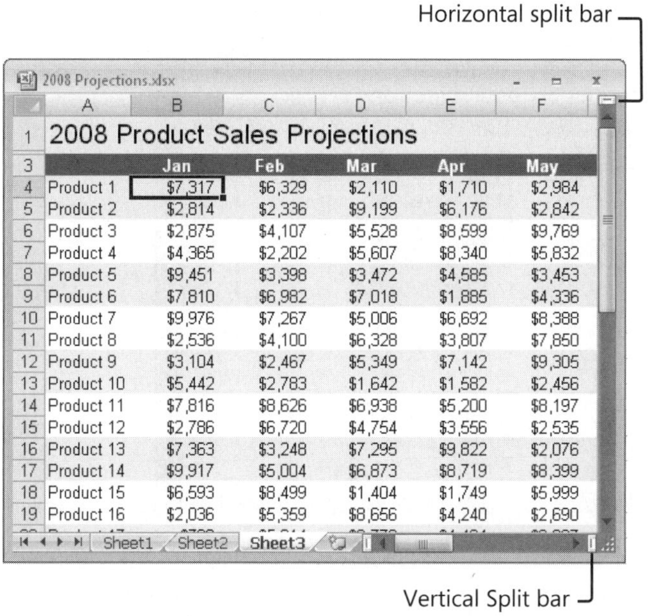

Horizontal split bar ⌐

	A	B	C	D	E	F	
1	**2008 Product Sales Projections**						
3		**Jan**	**Feb**	**Mar**	**Apr**	**May**	
4	Product 1	$7,317	$6,329	$2,110	$1,710	$2,984	
5	Product 2	$2,814	$2,336	$9,199	$6,176	$2,842	
6	Product 3	$2,875	$4,107	$5,528	$8,599	$9,769	
7	Product 4	$4,365	$2,202	$5,607	$8,340	$5,832	
8	Product 5	$9,451	$3,398	$3,472	$4,585	$3,453	
9	Product 6	$7,810	$6,982	$7,018	$1,885	$4,336	
10	Product 7	$9,976	$7,267	$5,006	$6,692	$8,388	
11	Product 8	$2,536	$4,100	$6,328	$3,807	$7,850	
12	Product 9	$3,104	$2,467	$5,349	$7,142	$9,305	
13	Product 10	$5,442	$2,783	$1,642	$1,582	$2,456	
14	Product 11	$7,816	$8,626	$6,938	$5,200	$8,197	
15	Product 12	$2,786	$6,720	$4,754	$3,556	$2,535	
16	Product 13	$7,363	$3,248	$7,295	$9,822	$2,076	
17	Product 14	$9,917	$5,004	$6,873	$8,719	$8,399	
18	Product 15	$6,593	$8,499	$1,404	$1,749	$5,999	
19	Product 16	$2,036	$5,359	$8,656	$4,240	$2,690	

Sheet1 / Sheet2 / **Sheet3**

Vertical Split bar ⌐

Figure 6-17 You can scroll to display the totals in column N or row 38, but you won't be able to see the headings.

You'll find the 2008 Projections.xlsx file in the Sample Files section of the companion CD.

It would be easier to navigate the worksheet in Figure 6-17 if it were split into panes. To do so, click the View tab on the Ribbon, and click Split; the window divides into both vertical and horizontal panes simultaneously, as shown in Figure 6-18. You can use the mouse to drag either split bar to where you need it. If you double-click either split bar icon (located in the scroll bars, as shown in Figure 6-17), you divide the window approximately in half. When you rest your pointer on a split bar, it changes to a double-headed arrow.

> **Note**
>
> Before clicking Window, Split or double-clicking one of the split bar icons, select a cell in the worksheet where you want the split to occur. This splits the worksheet immediately to the left or above the selected cell. If cell A1 is active, the split occurs in the center of the worksheet. In Figure 6-17, we selected cell B4 before choosing the Split command, which resulted in the split panes shown in Figure 6-18.

	A	B	C	D	E	F
1	2008 P roduct Sales Projections					
3		Jan	Feb	Mar	Apr	May
4	Product 1	$7,317	$6,329	$2,110	$1,710	$2,984
5	Product 2	$2,814	$2,336	$9,199	$6,176	$2,842
6	Product 3	$2,875	$4,107	$5,528	$8,599	$9,769
7	Product 4	$4,365	$2,202	$5,607	$8,340	$5,832
8	Product 5	$9,451	$3,398	$3,472	$4,585	$3,453
9	Product 6	$7,810	$6,982	$7,018	$1,885	$4,336
10	Product 7	$9,976	$7,267	$5,006	$6,692	$8,388
11	Product 8	$2,536	$4,100	$6,328	$3,807	$7,850
12	Product 9	$3,104	$2,467	$5,349	$7,142	$9,305
13	Product 10	$5,442	$2,783	$1,642	$1,582	$2,456
14	Product 11	$7,816	$8,626	$6,938	$5,200	$8,197
15	Product 12	$2,786	$6,720	$4,754	$3,556	$2,535
16	Product 13	$7,363	$3,248	$7,295	$9,822	$2,076
17	Product 14	$9,917	$5,004	$6,873	$8,719	$8,399
18	Product 15	$6,593	$8,499	$1,404	$1,749	$5,999
19	Product 16	$2,036	$5,359	$8,656	$4,240	$2,690

Figure 6-18 With the window split, you can scroll each pane independently.

With the window split into four panes, as shown in Figure 6-18, four scroll bars are available (if not visible)—two for each direction. Now you can use the scroll bars to view columns A through N without losing sight of the product headings in column A. In addition, when you scroll vertically between rows 1 and 38, you'll always see the corresponding headings in row 3.

After a window is split, you can reposition the split bars by dragging. If you are ready to return your screen to its normal appearance, click the Split button again to remove all the split bars. You can also remove an individual split by double-clicking the split bar or by dragging the split bar to the top or right side of the window.

Freezing Panes

After you've split a window into panes, you can freeze the left panes, the top panes, or both panes by clicking the View tab on the Ribbon, clicking Freeze Panes, and selecting the corresponding option, as shown in Figure 6-19. When you do so, you lock the data in the frozen panes into place. As you can see in Figure 6-19, the pane divider lines have changed from thick, three-dimensional lines to thin lines.

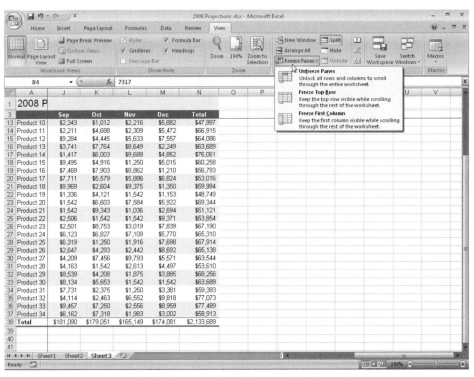

Figure 6-19 Freezing panes locks the top and/or left panes of a split window.

> **Note**
>
> You can split and freeze panes simultaneously at the selected cell by clicking Freeze Panes without first splitting the worksheet into panes. If you use this method, you will simultaneously unfreeze and remove the panes when you click Unfreeze Panes. (The command name changes when panes are frozen.)

Notice also that in Figure 6-18, the sheet tabs are invisible because the horizontal scroll bar for the lower-left pane is so small. After freezing the panes, as shown in Figure 6-19, the scroll bar returns to normal, and the sheet tabs reappear.

> **Note**
>
> To open another worksheet in the workbook if the sheet tabs are not visible, press Ctrl+Page Up to open the previous worksheet or Ctrl+Page Down to open the next worksheet.

After you freeze panes, scrolling within each pane works differently. You cannot scroll the upper-left panes in any direction. You can only scroll the columns (right and left) in the upper-right pane and only the rows (up and down) in the lower-left pane. You can scroll the lower-right pane in either direction.

INSIDE OUT   Make Frozen Panes Easier to See

Generally speaking, all the tasks you perform with panes work better when the windows are frozen. Unfortunately, it's harder to tell that the window is split when the panes are frozen because the thin frozen pane lines look just like cell borders. To make frozen panes easier to see, you can use a formatting clue you will always recognize. For example, select all the heading rows and columns, and fill them with a particular color.

Zooming Worksheets

As mentioned previously, you can use the Zoom control in the bottom-right corner of the screen or click the View tab on the Ribbon and use the two Zoom buttons to change the size of your worksheet display. Clicking a Zoom button displays a dialog box containing one enlargement option, three reduction options, and a Fit Selection option that determines the necessary reduction or enlargement needed to display the currently selected cells. Use the Custom box to specify any zoom percentage from 10 through 400 percent. The Zoom To Selection button enlarges or reduces the size of the worksheet to make all the selected cells visible on the screen. For example, clicking Zoom To Selection with a single cell selected zooms to the maximum 400 percent, centered on the selected cell (as much as possible) in an attempt to fill the screen with the selection.

Note

The Zoom command affects all the selected worksheets; therefore, if you group several worksheets, Excel will display all of them at the selected Zoom percentage. For more about grouping worksheets, see "Editing Multiple Worksheets" on page 236.

For example, to view the entire worksheet shown in Figure 6-17, you can try different Zoom percentages until you get the results you want. Better still, select the entire active area of the worksheet, and click the Zoom To Selection button. Now the entire worksheet appears on the screen, as shown in Figure 6-20. Note that the Zoom percentage resulting from clicking Zoom To Selection is 85 percent, displayed next to the Zoom control at the bottom of the screen.

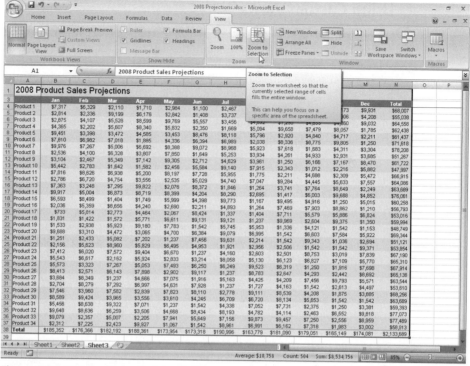

Figure 6-20 Click the Zoom To Selection button with the active area selected to view it all on the screen.

Of course, reading the numbers might be a problem at this size, but you can select other reduction or enlargement sizes for that purpose. While your worksheet is zoomed, you can still select cells, format them, and type formulas as you normally would. The Zoom option in effect when you save the worksheet is the displayed setting when you reopen the worksheet.

> **Note**
>
> The wheel on a mouse ordinarily scrolls the worksheet. You can also use the wheel to zoom. Simply hold down the Ctrl key, and rotate the wheel. If you want, you can make zooming the default behavior of the wheel. To do so, click the Microsoft Office Button, click Excel Options, select the Advanced category, and select the Zoom On Roll With IntelliMouse check box in the Editing Options area.

Using Custom Views

 Suppose you want your worksheet to have particular display and print settings for one purpose, such as editing, but different display and print settings for another purpose, such as an on-screen presentation. By clicking the Custom Views button on the View tab, you can assign names to specific view settings, which include column widths, row heights, display options, window size, position on the screen, pane settings, the cells that are selected at the time the view is created, and, optionally, the print and filter settings. You can then select your saved view settings whenever you need them, rather than manually changing the settings each time.

> **Note**
>
> Before you modify your view settings for a particular purpose, you should save the current view as a custom view, named Normal. This provides you with an easy way to return to the regular, unmodified view. Otherwise, you would have to retrace all your steps to return all the view settings to normal.

In the Custom Views dialog box, the Views list is empty until you click Add to save a custom view. Figure 6-21 shows the Custom Views dialog box with two views added, as well as the Add View dialog box you used to add them.

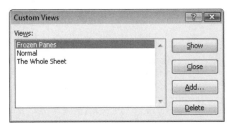

Figure 6-21 Click Add to name the current view and print settings in the Custom Views dialog box.

Protecting Worksheets

In addition to password protection for your files, Excel offers several features that you can use to protect your work—workbooks, workbook structures, individual cells, graphic objects, charts, scenarios, windows, and more—from access or modification by others. You can also choose to allow specific editing actions on protected worksheets.

For information about additional security issues in Excel, see Chapter 4, "Security and Privacy."

Protect Sheet

By default, Excel *locks* (protects) all cells and charts, but the protection is unavailable until you click the Review tab on the Ribbon and click Protect Sheet to access the Protect Sheet dialog box, as shown in Figure 6-22. (You can also click the Format button on the Home tab and then click Protect Sheet.) The protection status you specify applies to the current worksheet only.

Figure 6-22 The Protect Sheet dialog box gives you pinpoint control over many common editing actions.

After protection is turned on, you cannot change a locked item. If you try to change a locked item, Excel displays an error message. As you can see in Figure 6-22, the Allow All Users Of This Worksheet To list contains a number of specific editorial actions you can allow on protected worksheets. In addition to the options visible in Figure 6-22, you can also allow users to sort, use Filter and PivotTable reports, and edit objects or scenarios.

Unlocking Individual Cells

If you click Protect Sheet without specifically unlocking individual cells, you'll lock every cell on the worksheet by default. Most of the time, however, you will not want to lock every cell. For example, you might want to protect the formulas and formatting but leave particular cells unlocked so you can type necessary data without unlocking the entire worksheet. Before you protect a worksheet, select the cells you want to keep unlocked, click Format on the Home tab, and click Lock Cell, as shown in Figure 6-23. Lock Cell is selected by default for all cells, so clicking it deselects it, unlocking the selected cells.

You can easily move between unprotected cells on a locked worksheet by pressing the Tab key.

One way to verify the locked status of a cell is to select it and look at the little padlock icon next to the Lock command. If the icon appears to be clicked already, it means that the selected cell is locked, which is the default state for all cells.

Chapter 6

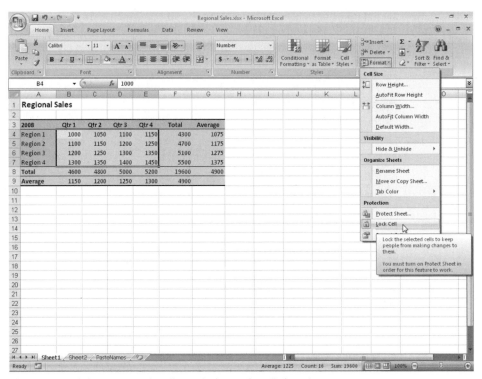

Figure 6-23 Click Format, Lock Cell to unlock specific cells for editing.

> **Note**
>
> Keep in mind that Excel does not provide any on-screen indication of the protection status for individual cells. To distinguish unlocked cells from the protected cells, you might consider applying a specific format, such as cell color or borders.

Protecting the Workbook

You can prevent the alteration of a workbook's structure and lock the position of the workbook window. To do so, click the Review tab on the Ribbon, and click Protect Workbook, Protect Structure And Windows to display the dialog box shown in Figure 6-24.

> **For more information, see "Protecting Workbooks" on page 176.**

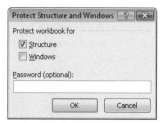

Figure 6-24 Use the Protect Structure And Windows dialog box to set the protection status for the entire workbook.

Allowing Password Access to Specific Cell Ranges

If you need to do more than protect workbooks or individual worksheets, use the Ribbon. Specifically, on the Review tab, in the Changes group, click Allow Users To Edit Ranges. Use the Allow Users To Edit Ranges dialog box, as shown in Figure 6-25, to provide editorial access to specific areas of a protected worksheet. You can even specify exactly who is allowed to do the editing.

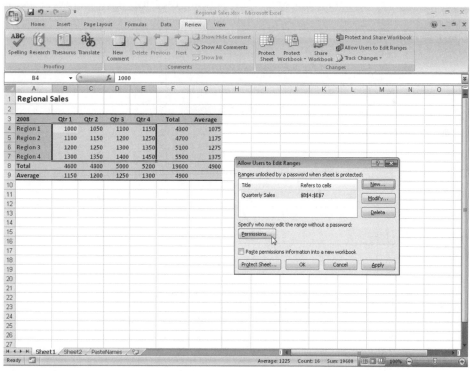

Figure 6-25 You can specify cells that can be edited, as well as the individuals who are allowed to edit them, by using the Allow Users To Edit Ranges dialog box.

When you click New in the Allow Users To Edit Ranges dialog box to add a cell range to the list, the New Range dialog box appears, as shown in Figure 6-26. Type a title for the range of cells you want to allow users to edit. Type a cell range or range name in the Refers To Cells box, or click in the box and drag through the range you want to specify.

Figure 6-26 Specify ranges you want to allow users to edit using the New Range dialog box.

Selecting the Paste Permissions Information Into A New Workbook check box is a handy way to keep track of who and what you've specified in the Permissions list. Note that you can click the Protect Sheet button for quick access to the Protect Sheet dialog box shown in Figure 6-22. You can click the Permissions button to specify individuals who are allowed to edit each range. When you do so, a dialog box like the one in Figure 6-27 appears.

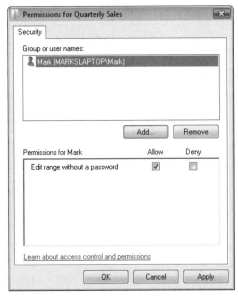

Figure 6-27 Set permissions for individual users by clicking Permissions in the Allow Users To Edit Ranges dialog box.

The Permissions dialog box lists all the users who are authorized to edit the worksheet, as well as whether they will need to use a password to do so. For each item in the Group Or User Names list, you can specify password permissions in the box; click Allow or Deny to restrict editing without a password. This lets you, in effect, employ two levels of restriction, since you are restricting editing access to specified users anyway, and you can force even those users to type a password if you want to do so.

> **Note**
>
> You must specify a password in the New Range dialog box (shown in Figure 6-26) or in the identical Modify Range dialog box to turn on the permissions options that you set. If you don't specify a range password, anyone can edit the range.

You can add users and groups to the list in the Permissions dialog box by clicking Add and then clicking Advanced to display the full dialog box shown in Figure 6-28. Click Find Now to locate all the users and groups available to your system. However, if you are connected to a large network, this might take a long time, so you can use the Common Queries box to restrict your search. You can also use Object Types and Locations to restrict your search further. After you click Find Now, you can select items in the list at the bottom of the dialog box that you want to add. Press the Ctrl key to select multiple items. When you have located the users and groups you want to add, click OK.

> **Note**
>
> To add or change users on your computer, open User Accounts in Control Panel.

Remember, after all this, you still have to activate worksheet protection by clicking Protect Sheet on the Home tab or by clicking Protect Sheet in the Allow Users To Edit Ranges dialog box.

For information about setting file-level permissions, see "Controlling Document Access with Information Rights Management" on page 803. For information about Excel and networks, see "Sharing Workbooks on a Network" on page 790.

Figure 6-28 Click Add in the Permissions dialog box to add to your list of authorized users.

Hiding Cells and Worksheets

In a protected worksheet, if you applied the Hidden protection format to a cell that contains a formula, the formula remains hidden from view in the formula bar, even when you select that cell. To hide a selected cell or cells, click the Format button on the Home tab, and click Cells to display the Format Cells dialog box. Then click the Protection tab, and select the Hidden option. Formulas in hidden cells are still functional, of course; they are just hidden from view. In any case, the displayed result of the formula on the worksheet is still visible.

For information about hiding numbers, see "The Hidden Number Format" on page 315.

You can also hide rows and columns within a worksheet and even hide entire worksheets within a workbook. Any data or calculations in hidden rows, columns, or worksheets are still available through references; the cells or worksheets are hidden from view. To hide a worksheet, click the sheet tab of the worksheet you want to hide, and on the Home tab, click Format, Hide & Unhide, Hide Sheet, as shown in Figure 6-29. Unlike hiding cells, hiding rows, columns, or worksheets happens immediately. Afterward, you can click the corresponding Unhide command to restore the hidden item.

However, if you hide a worksheet and then click Protect Workbook on the Review tab, the Unhide command is no longer available, which helps keep the hidden worksheet even better protected.

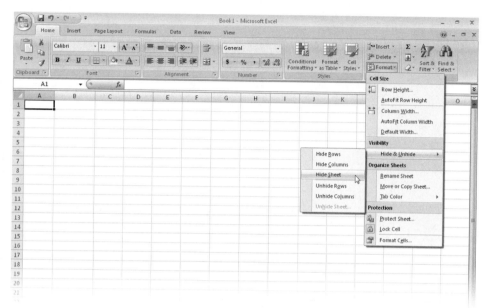

Figure 6-29 Use the Hide & Unhide commands to protect parts of your workbooks.

For more information about workbook protection, see "Hiding and Protecting Workbooks" on page 175.

Using Passwords

When you click Protect Sheet, Protect Workbook, or Protect And Share Workbook on the Review tab, you can assign a password that must be used to disable the protection. You can use unique passwords for each worksheet or workbook you protect.

Protect And Share Workbook

CAUTION

Password protection in Excel is serious business. After you assign a password, you can't unprotect the worksheet or workbook without it. Don't forget your passwords! Remember, capitalization matters.

Chapter 6

How to Work a Workbook

In early versions of Microsoft Excel, worksheets, charts, and macro sheets were stored as separate documents. Since Microsoft Excel 5, however, all these types of data, and more, peacefully coexist in workbooks. You can keep as many worksheets containing as many different types of data as you want in a workbook, you can have more than one workbook open at the same time, and you can have more than one window open for the same workbook. The only limitations to these capabilities are those imposed by your computer's memory and system resources.

Managing Multiple Workbooks

This chapter describes how to protect workbooks, how to use more than one workbook at a time, and how and why to split your view of a workbook into multiple windows. Generally when you start Microsoft Office Excel 2007, a blank workbook appears with the provisional title Book1. The only exceptions occur when you start Office Excel 2007 by opening an existing workbook or when you have one or more Excel files stored in the XLStart folder so that they open automatically.

If you start Excel with Book1 visible and then open an existing Excel file, Book1 disappears unless you have edited it. You can open as many workbooks as you like until your computer runs out of memory.

For more about working with multiple windows, see "Opening Multiple Windows for the Same Workbook" on page 171. For more information about the XLStart folder, see "Opening Files When You Start Excel" on page 65.

Navigating Between Open Workbooks

If you have more than one workbook open, you can activate a particular workbook in any of the following three ways:

- Click its window, if you can see it.

- If you have all your workbook windows maximized, you can shuffle through the open workbooks by pressing Ctrl+Tab to activate each workbook in the order you opened them. Press Shift+Ctrl+Tab to activate them in reverse order.

- On the View tab on the Ribbon, click a window name on the Switch Windows menu, which lists as many as nine open workbooks or, if you have more than nine, displays a More Workbooks command that presents a dialog box that lists all the open workbooks.

INSIDE OUT   Closing the Last Open Excel Window

Over the past few releases of Office, there has been some debate about the relative merits of the multiple document interface (MDI) and the single document interface (SDI). What are we talking about here? It's a difference in how documents are handled in the user interface. Users of previous versions of Excel have grown used to the MDI—where you can have multiple workbooks open but only one icon appears in the Windows system tray. Excel 2007 has switched to the SDI paradigm: Each open workbook creates a new icon in the system tray. A new workbook that appears when you first start Excel (or when you click the Microsoft Office Button and then click New) disappears when you open another workbook unless you have actually edited it. Then, when you click the Close button in the Excel title bar, Excel exits even though you may have thought you had another workbook open to prevent Excel from exiting.

The way to change this default SDI behavior is to click the Microsoft Office Button, click Excel Options, select the Advanced category, and in the Display group clear the Show All Windows In The Taskbar check box. If you still prefer the SDI approach, you can work around this issue by avoiding clicking the Close button and instead clicking the Microsoft Office Button, Close, which closes the active workbook but keeps the program open; by making sure you click the Close button in the workbook window instead of the Close button in the Excel window; or by developing the habit of typing a space character (or any character) in cell A1 as soon as you start Excel just to keep Book1 alive.

Arranging Workbook Windows

To make all open workbooks visible at the same time, click the View tab, and click Arrange All. Excel displays the Arrange Windows dialog box, shown in Figure 7-1, which also shows the workbooks arranged in the Tiled configuration with the screen divided into a patchwork of open documents. Figure 7-2 shows the same workbooks in the Horizontal configuration.

 You'll find the 2008 Projections.xlsx, Humongous08.xlsm, and Pacific Sales.xlsm files in the Sample Files section of the companion CD.

If you select the Windows Of Active Workbook check box in the Arrange Windows dialog box, only the active workbook is affected by the configuration setting, and then only if more than one window is open for the active workbook. Excel arranges those windows according to the option you select under Arrange in the Arrange Windows dialog box. This is handy if you have several workbooks open but you have multiple windows open for one of them and you want only to arrange these windows without closing the other workbooks.

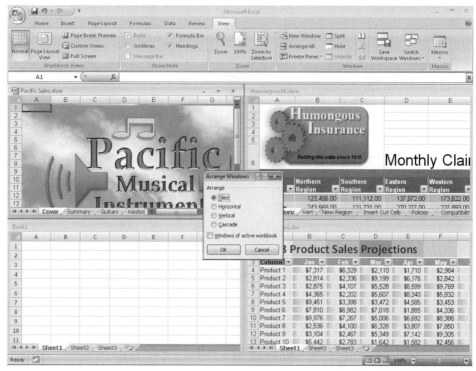

Figure 7-1 Clicking View, Arrange All opens the Arrange Windows dialog box, which gives you a choice of configurations.

For more information about working with multiple worksheets from one workbook, see "Opening Multiple Windows for the Same Workbook" on page 171.

> **Note**
>
> If you're working with several workbooks in a particular arrangement that is often useful, click the View tab, and click Save Workspace in the Window group. This preserves the current settings so you can re-create the window arrangement by opening one file. For more information, see "Saving the Entire Workspace" on page 60.

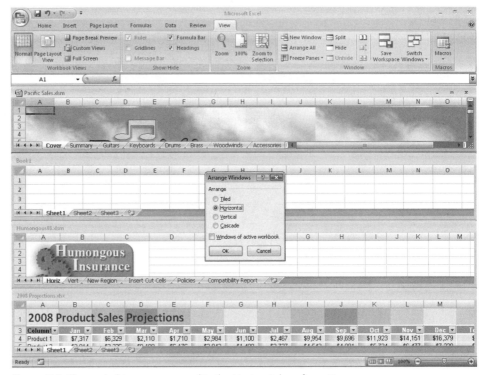

Figure 7-2 These windows are arranged in the Horizontal configuration.

Getting the Most Out of Your Screen

You can maximize the workbook window if you need to see more of the active worksheet, but if that still isn't enough, you can click the Full Screen button on the View tab. When you do so, Excel removes the formula bar, status bar, Quick Access Toolbar, and Ribbon from your screen—everything except the maximized workbook—as shown in Figure 7-3.

To return the screen to its former configuration, press Esc.

For more about maximizing and minimizing windows, see "Resizing the Window" on page 29.

The Full Screen button provides a convenient way to display the most information on the screen without changing the magnification of the data using the Zoom controls. For more information, see "Zooming Worksheets" on page 154.

Column1	Jan	Feb	Mar	Apr	May	Jun	Jul	Aug	Sep	Oct	Nov	Dec
2008 Product Sales Projections												
Product 1	$7,317	$6,329	$2,110	$1,710	$2,984	$1,100	$2,467	$9,954	$9,696	$11,923	$14,151	$16,379
Product 2	$2,814	$2,336	$9,199	$6,176	$2,842	$1,408	$3,737	$4,543	$4,991	$5,734	$6,477	$7,220
Product 3	$2,875	$4,107	$5,528	$8,599	$9,769	$5,557	$3,456	$5,467	$2,311	$4,322	$3,245	$3,267
Product 4	$4,365	$2,202	$5,607	$8,340	$5,832	$2,350	$1,669	$5,094	$3,013	$2,723	$2,434	$2,144
Product 5	$9,451	$3,398	$3,472	$4,585	$3,453	$8,476	$8,118	$5,796	$8,129	$8,796	$9,463	$10,130
Product 6	$7,810	$6,982	$7,018	$1,885	$4,336	$6,394	$6,989	$3,333	$4,660	$4,418	$4,177	$3,935
Product 7	$9,976	$7,267	$5,006	$6,692	$8,388	$9,072	$8,968	$5,923	$6,213	$5,463	$4,713	$3,963
Product 8	$2,536	$4,100	$6,328	$3,807	$7,850	$1,649	$5,253	$6,754	$5,456	$5,487	$5,519	$5,550
Product 9	$3,104	$2,467	$5,349	$7,142	$9,305	$2,712	$4,629	$4,453	$2,115	$2,876	$3,556	$3,428
Product 10	$5,442	$2,783	$1,642	$1,582	$2,456	$5,584	$9,140	$7,915	$11,257	$13,250	$15,244	$17,237
Product 11	$7,816	$8,626	$6,938	$5,200	$8,197	$7,728	$5,955	$5,678	$4,557	$3,624	$2,691	$1,758
Product 12	$2,786	$6,720	$4,754	$3,556	$2,535	$5,029	$4,740	$7,047	$8,150	$9,474	$10,799	$12,124
Product 13	$7,363	$3,248	$7,295	$9,822	$2,076	$8,372	$1,846	$4,462	$4,347	$4,410	$4,473	$4,537
Product 14	$9,917	$5,004	$6,873	$8,719	$8,399	$4,204	$8,290	$3,456	$3,402	$2,327	$1,253	$179
Product 15	$6,593	$8,499	$1,404	$1,749	$5,999	$4,398	$9,773	$5,622	$7,509	$7,933	$8,358	$8,782
Product 16	$2,036	$5,359	$8,656	$4,240	$2,690	$2,211	$4,893	$2,345	$3,447	$3,611	$3,776	$3,941
Product 17	$733	$5,814	$2,773	$4,464	$2,067	$8,424	$1,337	$3,254	$2,889	$2,536	$2,184	$1,831
Product 18	$1,831	$1,422	$1,572	$5,771	$6,611	$9,131	$9,121	$6,654	$7,909	$7,921	$7,933	$7,945
Product 19	$1,533	$2,938	$5,923	$9,180	$7,783	$1,542	$5,745	$5,953	$4,934	$4,805	$4,677	$4,548
Product 20	$9,688	$3,310	$4,472	$3,065	$4,700	$6,384	$9,079	$6,995	$9,185	$10,143	$11,101	$12,059
Product 21	$1,251	$2,433	$5,082	$7,202	$1,237	$7,456	$9,631	$3,456	$7,653	$8,536	$9,419	$10,303
Product 22	$2,156	$5,623	$8,960	$5,829	$6,495	$4,953	$1,921	$6,754	$4,467	$4,242	$4,016	$3,791
Product 23	$7,412	$6,020	$7,572	$9,404	$6,670	$1,237	$4,160	$4,457	$3,202	$2,830	$2,459	$2,087
Product 24	$5,543	$6,617	$2,162	$5,924	$2,833	$3,214	$8,058	$6,755	$9,368	$11,029	$12,690	$14,351
Product 25	$5,573	$3,323	$7,267	$5,053	$7,493	$6,250	$6,249	$9,523	$8,901	$9,510	$10,119	$10,728
Product 26	$8,413	$2,571	$6,143	$7,898	$2,902	$9,117	$1,237	$8,783	$7,951	$8,927	$9,903	$10,879
Product 27	$3,684	$8,349	$1,237	$4,666	$7,075	$1,916	$5,163	$6,789	$5,833	$6,072	$6,311	$6,550
Product 28	$2,704	$8,279	$7,292	$6,997	$4,631	$7,928	$1,237	$3,456	$2,324	$1,980	$2,134	$3,456
Product 29	$7,546	$3,960	$7,582	$2,839	$7,823	$8,110	$2,778	$9,111	$6,589	$6,442	$6,295	$6,148
Product 30	$8,589	$9,424	$3,965	$3,556	$3,610	$4,245	$6,709	$6,720	$8,270	$9,449	$10,628	$11,808
Product 31	$5,456	$8,638	$9,322	$7,071	$1,237	$1,542	$4,338	$7,052	$8,603	$10,627	$12,651	$14,675
Product 32	$9,648	$8,636	$6,259	$3,506	$4,668	$8,434	$8,193	$6,653	$8,416	$8,987	$9,558	$10,130
Product 33	$9,079	$2,357	$5,007	$2,205	$7,941	$5,649	$7,156	$11,232	$10,840	$11,978	$13,116	$14,254
Product 34	$2,312	$7,225	$2,423	$9,927	$1,067	$1,542	$8,961	$8,999	$12,946	$16,068	$19,189	$22,311
Total	$185,352	$176,366	$182,192	$188,361	$173,954	$173,318	$190,996	$210,438	$219,524	$238,452	$254,708	$272,423

Figure 7-3 Clicking View, Full Screen hides the formula bar, status bar, Quick Access Toolbar, and Ribbon to maximize the screen space available for viewing your data.

> **Note**
>
> When you save a workbook, Excel also saves its characteristics, such as the window's size, position on the screen, and display settings. The next time you open the workbook, the window looks the same as it did the last time you saved it. When you open it, Excel even selects the same cells you selected when you saved the file.

Comparing Worksheets Side by Side

View Side By Side

The Arrange All button on the View tab is extremely helpful if you need to compare the contents of two similar workbooks, but another feature makes this task even easier. The View Side By Side button essentially packages the Horizontal window arrangement option with a couple of useful features to make comparison chores a lot easier. The View Side By Side button lives in the Window group on the View tab; it is the top button located to the left of the Save Workspace command, as shown in Figure 7-4.

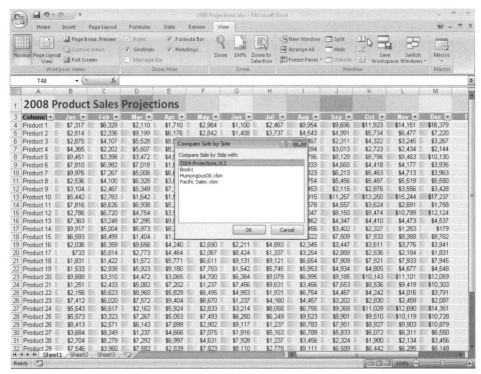

Figure 7-4 If more than two windows are open, select one in the Compare Side By Side dialog box.

Note

The Ribbon on your screen may look different from what you see in this book. The Ribbon display adjusts to the size of your screen, its resolution, and the size of the Excel window. For example, the six buttons in the middle of the Window group on the View tab may not display adjacent text labels if you have a smaller display or if Excel is not maximized.

You can click the View Side By Side button to arrange any two open windows, even if they are windows for the same workbook (as described in the next section). But unlike the Arrange button, View Side By Side performs its trick on no more or less than two windows. After you click the button, you will see a Compare Side By Side dialog box like the one shown in Figure 7-5 if you have more than two windows open. If so, select the window you want to compare, and click OK; this opens and arranges it along with the window that was active when you clicked View Side By Side. (The button name is a little bit misleading, because the windows are actually arranged horizontally—not really "side by side" but one above the other.)

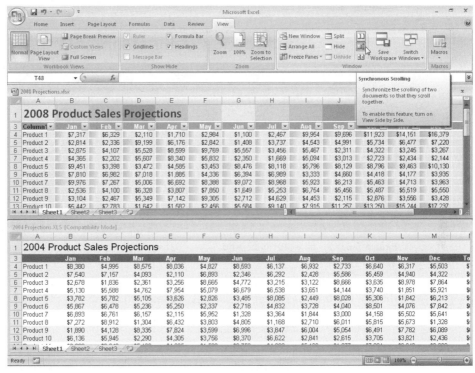

Figure 7-5 The Synchronous Scrolling button locks side-by-side window scrolling.

Synchronous
Scrolling

Reset Window
Position

After you activate "side-by-side mode," the two buttons below the View Side By Side button become active, as shown in Figure 7-5. The Synchronous Scrolling button locks the two windows together wherever they happen to be so when you scroll in any direction, the inactive window scrolls in an identical fashion. The Reset Window Position button puts the active window on top, which is handy. The window that is active when you click the View Side By Side button is the one that appears on top. If you want the other window on top, click the other window, and then click the Reset Window Position button to place it in the top position.

The View Side By Side button is a toggle—to turn off side-by-side mode and return to Normal view, click the View Side By Side button again.

Opening Multiple Windows for the Same Workbook

Suppose you've created a workbook like the one shown in Figure 7-6. You might want to monitor the cells on the summary worksheet while working on one of the other worksheets in the workbook. On the other hand, if you have a large worksheet, you might want to keep an eye on more than one area of the same worksheet at the same time. To perform either of these tasks, you can open a second window for the workbook by clicking New Window on the View tab.

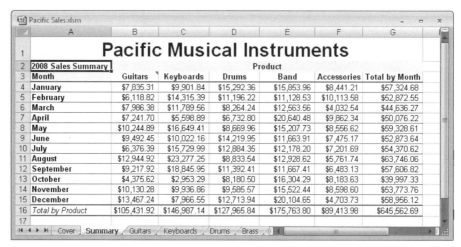

Figure 7-6 You can work on the summary worksheet while viewing supporting worksheets in the same workbook.

To view both windows on your screen, click View, Arrange All, and then select any of the Arrange options except Cascade. If you select the Cascade option, you'll be able to view only the top worksheet in the stack. If you select the Horizontal option, your screen looks similar to the one shown in Figure 7-7.

You might notice that Office Excel 2007 assigned the name Pacific Sales.xlsm:2 to the new workbook window. In addition, it changed the name of the original workbook window to Pacific Sales xlsm:1. Pacific Sales.xlsm:2 now becomes the active window, and as such, it's positioned on top, as indicated by the presence of scroll bars.

> **Note**
>
> Again, if other workbooks are open but you want to view only the windows on the active workbook, select the Windows Of Active Workbook check box in the Arrange Windows dialog box.

You can view any part of the workbook in any window associated with that workbook. In Figure 7-7, Pacific Sales.xlsm:2 originally displayed the summary worksheet when we first created it, because that was the active worksheet when we clicked the New Window button. Then we clicked the Brass tab in the new window, leaving the summary worksheet visible in Pacific Sales.xlsm:1.

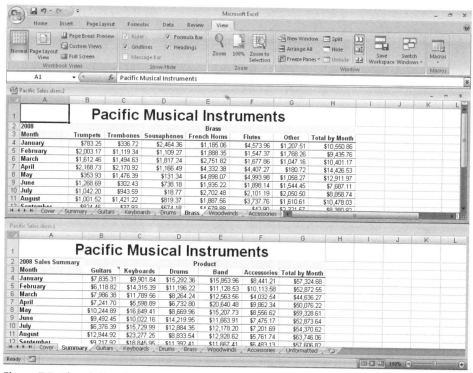

Figure 7-7 After clicking the New Window button to open a second window for the same workbook, select an Arrange option to fit both windows on the screen simultaneously.

Useful Inconsistencies of New Windows

When you create multiple windows of the same workbook, anything you do in one window happens in all windows—almost. New entries; formatting changes; inserted or deleted rows, columns, or worksheets; and just about any other editing changes are reflected in all windows. Display characteristics—or *views*—are not. This means you can zoom in or out and change anything in the Workbook Views and Zoom groups on the View tab as well as the Split and Freeze Panes commands. View adjustments affect only the active window. You can also click the Microsoft Office Button, click Excel Options, select the Advanced category, and then change the settings in the two Display Options sections: Display Options For This Workbook and Display Options For This Worksheet. You can apply these options differently to windows of the same workbook. Just select the name of window you want to change in the drop-down list, as shown in Figure 7-8.

Figure 7-9 shows a somewhat exaggerated example of worksheet auditing. In Pacific Sales.xlsm:1, formulas are displayed; the worksheet is zoomed in; and scroll bars, row and column headings, and gridlines are removed—all in an effort to review the formulas in the summary worksheet to make sure they refer to the proper cells. You can also use this technique to audit your worksheets.

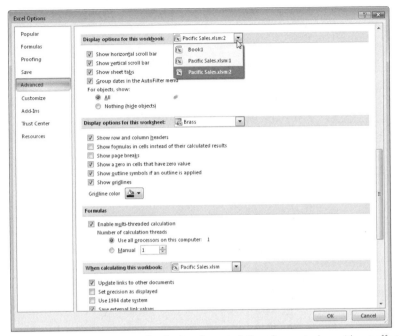

Figure 7-8 You can change the display characteristics of one window without affecting the other.

If you create a view like Pacific Sales.xlsm:1 in Figure 7-9 and want to be able to re-create it in the future, click the Custom Views button in the Workbook Views group on the View tab to save it. If you want to be able to re-create the entire workspace, including additional windows and their view settings, click the Save Workspace button in the Window group on the View tab.

For more information about custom views, see "Using Custom Views" on page 156. For more information about saving workspaces, see "Saving the Entire Workspace" on page 60. For more information about the auditing features in Excel, see "Auditing and Documenting Worksheets" on page 241. For more information about formulas, see Chapter 12, "Building Formulas."

INSIDE OUT   Close the Default Settings Window Last

When you have two windows open in the same workbook and then close one of them, the "number" of the open window isn't important, but the view settings are. In the example shown in Figure 7-9, if we finish our work and close Pacific Sales.xlsm:2, the modified view settings in Pacific Sales.xlsm:1 become the active view for the workbook. If we then save the workbook, we also save the modified view settings. Make sure you close the windows with view settings you don't want to keep before you close the one with the settings you want to use as the default—don't worry about the window number.

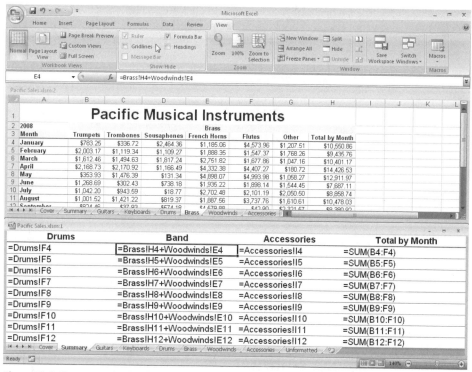

Figure 7-9 You can radically change view options in one window while maintaining a regular view of the same worksheet in another window.

Hiding and Protecting Workbooks

Sometimes you might want to keep certain information out of sight or protect it from inadvertent modification. You can conceal and protect your data by hiding windows, workbooks, or individual worksheets from view.

> For information about protecting individual cells, see "Protecting Worksheets" on page 156.

Hiding Workbooks

At times, you might need to keep a workbook open so you can access the information it contains but not want it to be visible. When several open workbooks clutter your workspace, you can click the Hide button on the View tab to conceal some of them. Office Excel 2007 can still work with the information in the hidden workbooks, but they don't take up space on your screen, and their file names don't appear in the Switch Windows menu on the View tab.

To hide a workbook, activate it, and click View, Hide. Excel removes the workbook from view, but the workbook remains open and available in the workspace. To bring the hidden workbook into view, click View, Unhide, and then select the name of the hidden workbook you want to redisplay. The Unhide command is available only when you have a workbook hidden. The Unhide dialog box, as shown in Figure 7-10, lists all the hidden workbooks.

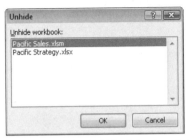

Figure 7-10 The Unhide dialog box lists all the workbooks you currently have hidden.

Clicking the Hide button conceals any open window. However, if you have multiple windows open for the same workbook, clicking the Hide button hides only the active window. The entire workbook isn't hidden. For more information, see "Opening Multiple Windows for the Same Workbook" on page 171.

TROUBLESHOOTING

Nothing happens when you try to open a workbook.

If, when you try to open a workbook, you don't see any error messages or dialog boxes but the workbook doesn't appear to open, the window was probably hidden when it was last saved. The workbook is actually open; you just can't see it.

If, in a previous Excel session, you clicked the Hide button on the View tab and then forgot about the hidden window when you exited Excel, you probably saw a message like "Do you want to save changes you made to Book1?" This would have been the hidden file—the change you made was the act of hiding it. The next time you open the file, it appears that nothing has happened, but if you look at the View tab, the Unhide button is active, which happens only when a hidden window is open in the workspace. Click the Unhide button, select the file name to make it visible once again, and then save it before exiting Excel.

Protecting Workbooks

Protecting a workbook not only prevents changes to the complement of worksheets contained in the workbook but can also prevent modifications to the way the workbook windows are displayed. To protect a workbook, click the Review tab, and click Protect

Workbook, Protect Structure And Windows to display the dialog box shown in Figure 7-11.

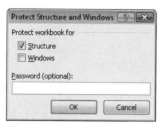

Figure 7-11 Clicking Review, Protect Workbook helps insulate your workbooks from inadvertent modification.

Selecting the Structure check box prevents any changes to the position, the name, and the hidden or unhidden status of the worksheets in the active workbook. When you select the Windows option, the workbook's windows cannot be closed, hidden, unhidden, resized, or moved—in fact, the Minimize, Maximize, and Close buttons disappear. This does not mean you cannot close the workbook; you can still click the Microsoft Office Button and then click Close. However, if you have more than one window open for the workbook, you cannot close any of them individually.

These settings take effect immediately. This command is a toggle—you can turn protection off by clicking Protect Workbook, Protect Structure And Windows again. If protection has been activated, a check mark appears next to the command on the Protect Workbook menu. If you specified a password in the Protect Structure And Windows dialog box, Excel prompts you to supply that password before it turns off the worksheet protection.

The Restrict Permission commands on the Protect Workbook menu control features provided by an Information Rights Management service, which you can use to further protect your critical communications.

For more information, see "Controlling Document Access with Information Rights Management" on page 803.

Encrypting Workbooks

Encrypt Document

You can provide another level of security for your workbooks by adding encryption. Encryption goes beyond simple password protection by digitally obscuring information to make it unreadable without the proper key to "decode" it. (Therefore, encrypted workbooks can be opened only by Excel 2007.) You apply encryption by clicking the Microsoft Office Button, Prepare, Encrypt Document. This displays a dialog box that prompts you for a password and then redisplays itself to confirm the password, as shown in Figure 7-12.

Figure 7-12 Applying a password to encrypt a workbook also turns on protection of the workbook structure.

After you click the Encrypt Document command, you'll need the password you provided to open the workbook again; the Protect Structure And Windows dialog box (refer to Figure 7-11) also uses this password to protect the workbook structure. Even if you turn off workbook protection, encryption is still active until you turn it off it by clicking the Encrypt Document command again and removing the password from the Encrypt Document dialog box.

Saving Workbooks or Windows as Hidden

Sometimes you might want to hide a particular workbook, perhaps even to prevent others from opening and viewing its sensitive contents in your absence. If so, you can save the workbook as hidden. A hidden workbook is not visible when it's opened. You can save a workbook as hidden by following these steps:

1. Close all open workbooks other than the one you want to hide, and then click View, Hide.

2. Exit Excel.

3. When a message appears asking whether you want to save changes to the workbook, click Yes.

The next time the workbook opens, its contents are hidden. To ensure that it cannot be unhidden by others, you might want to assign a password by clicking Review, Protect Workbook before hiding and saving the workbook.

Hiding Worksheets

If you want to hide a particular worksheet in a workbook, click the Home tab, and in the Cells group, click Format. In the menu that appears, click Hide & Unhide, and then click Hide Sheet. When you do so, the active worksheet no longer appears in the workbook. To unhide a hidden worksheet, click Unhide Sheet in the same menu, which becomes active after you have hidden a worksheet. The Unhide dialog box for worksheets is almost identical to the Unhide dialog box for workbooks shown in Figure 7-10. Select the worksheet you want to unhide, and then click OK.

PART 3
Formatting and Editing Worksheets

Worksheet Editing Techniques

Cut and paste. Insert and delete. Undo and redo. It all seems elementary, but as always in Microsoft Office Excel 2007, many other features are hiding beneath the obvious approaches to the simplest tasks; in fact, after reading this chapter, you'll find solutions to problems you probably never even considered. We'll cover all the essential editing techniques, including editing multiple worksheets, checking spelling, selectively pasting entries, creating data series, and outlining and auditing worksheets.

Copying, Cutting, and Pasting

When you copy an item, Office Excel 2007 saves it in memory, using a temporary storage area called the Clipboard. You capture the contents as well as the formatting and any attached comments or objects.

For more information about comments, see "Auditing and Documenting Worksheets" on page 241. For more information about objects, see Chapter 10, "Creating Spiffy Graphics."

When you copy or cut cells, a *marquee* appears around the cell. (We used to refer to this scrolling dotted line as *marching ants*.) This marquee indicates the area copied or cut. You can even paste copied or cut cells onto other worksheets or workbooks without losing the marquee.

Cut

Copy

The Cut and Copy buttons on the Home tab are useful, but you should know the keyboard shortcuts for the quintessential editing commands listed in Table 8-1. You can click the equivalent buttons on the Ribbon, but really, if you never learn another keyboard shortcut, learn these.

Table 8-1 **Essential Keyboard Shortcuts**

Press	To
Ctrl+C	Copy
Ctrl+X	Cut
Ctrl+V	Paste
Ctrl+Z	Undo
Ctrl+Y	Redo

Paste

Copying and Pasting

After you copy, you can paste more than once. As long as the marquee is visible, you can continue to paste the information from the copied cells. You can copy this information to other worksheets or workbooks without losing your copy area marquee. The marquee persists until you press Esc or perform any other editing action. The area you select for copying must be a single rectangular block of cells. If you try to copy nonadjacent ranges, you'll get an error message.

Collecting Multiple Items on the Clipboard

Using the Collect And Copy feature, you can copy (or cut) up to 24 separate items and then paste them where you want them—one at a time or all at once. You do this by displaying the Clipboard task pane shown in Figure 8-1 by clicking the Dialog Box Launcher next to the word *Clipboard* on the Home tab on the Ribbon.

Ordinarily when copying, you can work with only one item at a time. If you copy several items in a row, only the last item you copied is stored in the Clipboard. However, if you first display the Clipboard task pane and then copy or cut several items in succession, each item is stored in the task pane, as shown in Figure 8-1.

You can change the regular collect-and-copy behavior so Excel collects items every time you copy or cut, regardless of whether the Clipboard task pane is present. To do so, click the Options button at the bottom of the Clipboard task pane, as shown in Figure 8-1, and click Collect Without Showing Office Clipboard or Show Office Clipboard Automatically, depending on whether you want the task pane to appear. The latter option activates an additional option, Show Office Clipboard When Ctrl+C Pressed Twice, which is one of the "automatic" methods.

Each time you copy or cut an item, a short representation of the item appears in the Clipboard task pane. Figure 8-1 shows five items in the Clipboard task pane. You can paste any or all of the items wherever you choose. To paste an item from the Clipboard task pane, select the location where you want the item to go, and then click the item in the task pane. To empty the Clipboard task pane for a new collection, click the Clear All button.

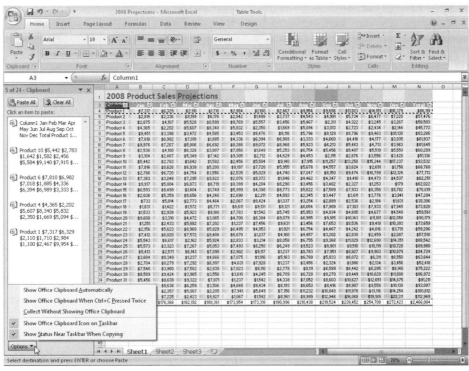

Figure 8-1 The Clipboard task pane stores multiple items that you copy or cut.

Hunting and Gathering

You can use the Clipboard task pane to quickly assemble a list. Although the Collect And Copy feature is useful for editing, it can also be a great tool for gathering information. Copy items such as names or addresses from various locations in the order you want them to appear. Then click the Paste All button in the Clipboard task pane to paste all the items you have collected, in the order collected, into a single column.

Pasting Multiples

After you copy, press Ctrl+V to paste whatever you copied. It's a no-brainer. However, did you know that if you select a range of cells before pasting, Excel fills every cell in that range when you paste? Figure 8-2 illustrates this.

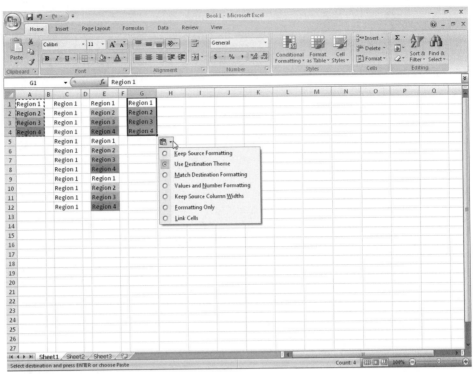

Figure 8-2 Before you paste, select more cells than you copied to create multiple copies of your information.

In Figure 8-2, we did the following:

- Copied cell A1 and then selected the range C1:C12 and pasted, resulting in Excel repeating the copied cell in each cell in the selected range

- Copied Cells A1:A4 and then selected the range E1:E12 and pasted, resulting in Excel repeating the copied range within the range

- Copied cells A1:A4 and then selected cell G1 and pasted, resulting in an exact duplicate of the copied range

> **Note**
>
> If you select a paste range that contains more cells than the copied range, Excel repeats the copied cells until it fills the destination. However, if you select a paste range that is smaller than the copied range, Excel pastes the entire copied range anyway.

Using the Paste Options Smart Tag

Notice in Figure 8-2 that we clicked the Paste Options smart tag action menu that appears near the lower-left corner of the pasted range. This smart tag appears whenever and wherever you paste, offering action options applicable *after* pasting—a sort of "Smart Paste Special." The best part is that you can try each action in turn. Keep selecting paste options until you like what you see, and then press Enter. The following describes each item on the Paste Options smart tag action menu:

- **Use Destination Theme** Changes the formatting of the pasted data to match the theme of the destination. (Themes control the overall look of your documents and include specifications for colors, fonts, and objects.) This is the default action.

- **Match Destination Formatting** Copies formatted data into a differently formatted table without having to redo the formatting.

- **Keep Source Formatting** Retains the copied formatting.

- **Values And Number Formatting** Pastes values without losing number formats.

- **Keep Source Column Widths** Retains column widths. This option is like clicking Keep Source Formatting with the added action of "pasting" the column width.

- **Formatting Only** Leaves the contents of the cells alone and transfers the formatting. This works in the same way as the Format Painter button, located in the Clipboard group on the Home tab.

- **Link Cells** Instead of pasting the contents of the cut or copied cells, pastes a reference to the source cells, ignoring the source formatting.

For more about themes, see "Using Themes and Cell Styles" on page 275.

Cutting and Pasting

When you cut rather than copy cells, subsequent pasting places one copy in the selected destination, removes the copied cells from the Clipboard, removes the copied data from its original location, and removes the marquee. When you perform a cut-and-paste operation, the following rules apply:

- Excel clears both the contents and the formats of the cut range and transfers them to the cells in the paste range. Excel adjusts any formulas outside the cut area that refer to that cell.

- The area you select for cutting must be a single rectangular block of cells. If you try to select nonadjacent ranges, you'll get an error message.

- Regardless of the size of the range you select before pasting, Excel pastes only the exact size and shape of the cut area. The upper-left corner of the selected paste area becomes the upper-left corner of the moved cells.

- Excel overwrites the contents and formats of any existing cells in the range where you paste. If you don't want to lose existing cell entries, be sure your worksheet has enough blank cells below and to the right of the cell you select as the upper-left corner of the paste area to hold the entire cut area.

- You cannot use Paste Special after cutting. Furthermore, no smart tag menu appears when you paste after cutting.

Pasting Selectively Using Paste Special

Paste Special is quite possibly the most useful (and most used) power-editing feature. You can use this feature in many ways, but probably the most popular is copying the value in a cell without copying the formatting or the underlying formula. After you copy a cell or cells, click Paste on the Home tab, and click Paste Special to display the Paste Special dialog box shown in Figure 8-3. (You must copy to use Paste Special. When you cut, Paste Special is unavailable.) The most popular Paste Special actions are directly accessible as commands on the Paste menu on the Home tab, as shown on the left in Figure 8-3.

> **Note**
>
> The Paste menu is actually a button with a downward-pointing arrow below it; clicking the button is equivalent to clicking the Paste command. To display the menu shown on the left in Figure 8-3, click the arrow.

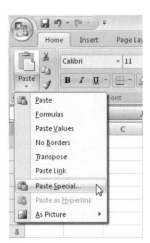

Figure 8-3 Paste Special is probably the most popular power-editing feature, and its most often used options are available as commands on the Paste menu.

> **Note**
>
> You can also open the Paste Special dialog box by right-clicking the cell where you want to paste and then clicking Paste Special.

Here's what the Paste Special options do:

- **All** Predictably, pastes all aspects of the selected cell, which is the same as clicking the Paste command.

- **Formulas** Transfers only the formulas from the cells in the copy range to the cells in the paste range, adjusting relative references. This option is also available as a command on the Paste menu.

- **Values** Pastes static text, numeric values, or only the displayed values resulting from formulas. This option is also available as the Paste Values command on the Paste menu.

- **Formats** Transfers only the formats in the copy range to the paste range.

Format Painter

> **Note**
>
> You can quickly copy and paste formats from a single cell or from a range of cells using the Format Painter button, next to the Paste menu on the Home tab.

- **Comments** Transfers only comments attached to selected cells.

- **Validation** Pastes only the data validation settings you have applied to the selected cells.

- **All Using Source Theme** Transfers only the copied data and applies the theme that has been applied to the destination cells.

For more information about themes, see "Using Themes and Cell Styles" on page 275.

- **All Except Borders** Transfers data without disturbing the border formats you spent so much time applying. This option is also available as the No Borders command on the Paste menu.

- **Column Widths** Transfers only column widths, which is handy when trying to make a worksheet look consistent for presentation.

- **Formulas And Number Formats** Transfers only formulas and number formats, which is helpful when copying formulas to previously formatted areas. Usually,

Chapter 8

you'll want the same number formats applied to formulas you copy, wherever they happen to go.

- **Values And Number Formats** Transfers only the resulting values (but not the formulas) and number formats.

Because the All option pastes the formulas, values, formats, and cell comments from the copy range into the paste range, it has the same effect as clicking Paste, probably making you wonder why Excel offers this option in the Paste Special dialog box. That brings us to our next topic—the Operation options.

Pasting Using Math Operators

You use the options in the Operation area of the Paste Special dialog box to mathematically combine the contents of the copied cells with the contents of the cells in the paste area. When you select any option other than None, Excel does not overwrite the destination cell or range with the copied data. Instead, it uses the specified operator to combine the copy and paste ranges.

For example, say you want to get a quick total of the Northern and Eastern regions in Figure 8-4. First you copy the Northern Region figures to column G, and then you copy the Eastern Region numbers in column D, select cell H9, and click Paste Special. You then select the Values and Add options in the Paste Special dialog box, and after clicking OK, you get the result shown at the bottom of Figure 8-4.

You'll find the Humongous08.xlsm file in the Sample Files section of the companion CD.

The other options in the Operation area of the Paste Special dialog box combine the contents of the copy and paste ranges using the appropriate operators. Just remember that the Subtract option subtracts the copy range from the paste range, and the Divide option divides the contents of the paste range by the contents of the copy range. Also note that if the copy range contains text entries and you use Paste Special with an Operation option (other than None), nothing happens.

Select the Values option when you use any Operation option. As long as the entries in the copy range are numbers, you can use All, but if the copy range contains formulas, you'll get "interesting" results. As a rule, avoid using the Operation options if the paste range contains formulas.

> **Note**
> Excel assigns the value 0 to blank spaces in the copy and paste ranges, regardless of which Operation option you select.

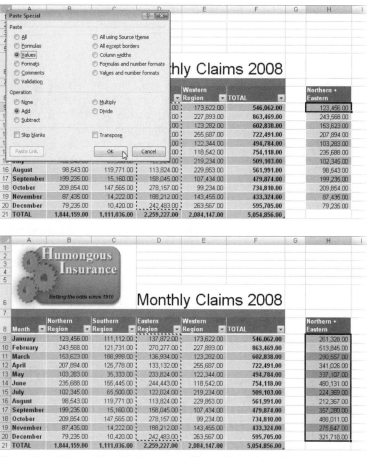

Figure 8-4 We used the Values option of Paste Special to add the totals from column D to those in column G.

Pasting Links

The Paste Link button in the Paste Special dialog box, shown in Figure 8-4, is a handy way to create references to cells or ranges. Although the Paste Special dialog box offers more options, it is more convenient to use the Paste Link command on the Paste menu on the Home tab. When you click Paste Link, Excel enters an *absolute* reference to the copied cell in the new location. For example, if you copy cell A3, then select cell B5, click the Paste menu, then click Paste Link, Excel enters the formula =$A$3 in cell B5.

If you copy a range of cells, Paste Link enters a similar formula for each cell in the copied range to the same-sized range in the new location.

For more information about absolute references, see "Understanding Relative, Absolute, and Mixed References" on page 429.

Skipping Blank Cells

The Paste Special dialog box contains a Skip Blanks check box that you select when you want Excel to ignore any blank cells in the copy range. Generally, if your copy range contains blank cells, Excel pastes those blank cells over the corresponding cells in the paste area. As a result, empty cells in the copy range overwrite the contents, formats, and comments in corresponding cells of the paste area. When you select Skip Blanks, however, the corresponding cells in the paste area are unaffected.

Transposing Entries

One of the often-overlooked but extremely useful Paste Special features is the Transpose check box, which helps you reorient the contents of the copied range when you paste—that is, data in rows is pasted in columns, and data in columns is pasted in rows. (This option is also available as a command on the Paste menu.) For example, in Figure 8-5, we copied the two columns of data shown in cells D2:E6, and then we selected cell G2 and clicked Transpose on the Paste menu on the Home tab. This works both ways. If we subsequently select the range just pasted and click Transpose again, the data is pasted in its original orientation.

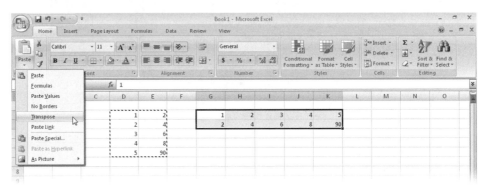

Figure 8-5 We copied cells D2:E6, selected cell G2, and then clicked Home, Paste, Transpose to redistribute the rows of data into columns.

> **Note**
>
> If you transpose cells containing formulas, Excel transposes the formulas and adjusts cell references. If you want the transposed formulas to continue to correctly refer to non-transposed cells, make sure the references in the formulas are absolute before you copy them. For more information about absolute cell references, see "Using Cell References in Formulas" on page 428.

INSIDE OUT   Using Paste Values with Arrays

As with any other formula, you can convert the results of an array formula to a series of constant values by copying the entire array range and—without changing your selection—clicking Home, Paste, Paste Values. When you do so, Excel overwrites the array formulas with their resulting constant values. Because the range now contains constant values rather than formulas, Excel no longer treats the selection as an array. For more information about arrays, see "Using Arrays" on page 468.

Pasting Hyperlinks

The Paste As Hyperlink command on the Paste menu on the Home tab has a specific purpose: to paste a hyperlink that refers to the copied data in the location you specify. When you create a hyperlink, it's as if Excel draws an invisible box, which acts like a button when you click it, and places it over the selected cell.

Hyperlinks in Excel are similar to Web links that, when clicked, launch a Web page. You can add hyperlinks to locations on the Web in your workbooks—a handy way to make related information readily available. You can use hyperlinks to perform similar tasks among your Excel worksheets, such as to provide an easy way to access other worksheets or workbooks that contain additional information. You can even create hyperlinks to other Microsoft Office documents, such as a report created in Microsoft Office Word or a Microsoft Office PowerPoint presentation.

Within Excel, you create a hyperlink by copying a named cell or range, navigating to the location where you want the hyperlink (on the same worksheet, on a different worksheet, or in a different workbook), and then clicking Home, Paste, Paste As Hyperlink. To create a hyperlink in and among Excel worksheets and workbooks, you must first assign a name to the range to which you want to hyperlink. (The easiest method is to select the cell or range and type a name in the name box at the left end of the formula bar.) Note that hyperlinks differ from Excel links, which are actually formulas.

For more information, see "Pasting Links" on page 189. For information about defining names, see "Naming Cells and Ranges" on page 441. For more information about hyperlinks, see Chapter 25, "Collaborating Using the Internet."

When you rest your pointer on a hyperlink, a tip appears showing you the name and location of the document to which the hyperlink is connected, as shown in Figure 8-6. To use a hyperlink, click it and hold the mouse button down until the pointer changes to a hand, and then release the mouse button to open the linked document. (This is an improvement in functionality for Excel 2007; in previous versions, it was the opposite—you clicked to activate the link and held the mouse to select the cell, which made it difficult to select or edit hyperlinked cells.)

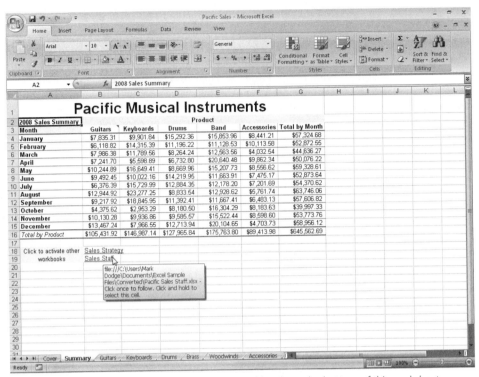

Figure 8-6 We created hyperlinks to supporting workbooks at the bottom of this worksheet.

To edit or delete a hyperlink, right-click it, and then click Edit Hyperlink or Remove Hyperlink.

You'll find the Pacific Sales.xlsm, Pacific Sales Staff.xlsx, and Pacific Strategy.xlsx files in the Sample Files section of the companion CD.

Moving and Copying with the Mouse

Sometimes referred to as *direct cell manipulation*, this feature lets you quickly move a cell or range to a new location. It's that simple. When you select a cell or range, move the pointer over the edge of the selection until the arrow appears, and then click the border and drag the selection to wherever you like. As you drag, an outline of the selected range appears, which you can use to help position the range correctly.

To copy a selection rather than move it, hold down the Ctrl key while dragging. The pointer then appears with a small plus sign next to it, as shown in Figure 8-7, which indicates you are copying rather than moving the selection.

> **Note**
>
> If direct cell manipulation doesn't seem to be working, click the Microsoft Office Button, click the Excel Options button, and in the Advanced category, make sure the Enable Fill Handle And Cell Drag-And-Drop check box is selected.

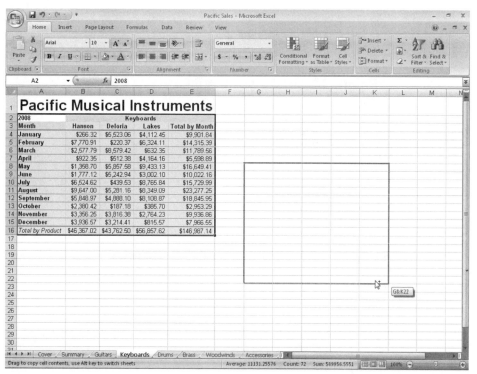

Figure 8-7 Before you finish dragging, press Ctrl to copy the selection. A plus sign and destination reference appear next to the pointer.

You can also use direct cell manipulation to insert copied or cut cells in a new location, moving existing cells out of the way in the process. For example, on the left in Figure 8-8, we selected cells A6:E6 and then dragged the selection while holding down the Shift key. A gray I-beam indicates where Excel will insert the selected cells when you release the mouse button. The I-beam appears whenever the pointer rests on a horizontal or vertical cell border. In this case, the I-beam indicates the horizontal border between rows 8 and 9, but we could just as easily insert the cells vertically (which would produce unwanted results). You'll see the I-beam insertion point flip between horizontal and vertical as you move the pointer around the worksheet. To insert the cells, release the mouse button while still pressing the Shift key. When you release the mouse button, the selected cells move to the new location, as shown on the right in Figure 8-8.

	A	B	C	D	E	F
1	**Pacific Musical Instruments**					
2	2008		Keyboards			
3	Month	Hanson	Deloria	Lakes	Total by Month	
4	January	$266.32	$5,523.06	$4,112.45	$9,901.84	
5	February	$7,770.91	$220.37	$6,324.11	$14,315.39	
6	March	$2,577.79	$8,579.42	$632.35	$11,789.56	
7	April	$922.35	$512.38	$4,164.16	$5,598.89	
8	May	$1,358.70	$5,857.58	$9,433.13	$16,649.41	
9	June	$1,777.12	$5,242.94	$3,002.10	$10,022.16	
10	July	$6,524.62	$439.53	$8,765.84	$ A9:E9	
11	August	$9,647.00	$5,281.16	$8,349.09	$23,277.25	
12	September	$5,848.97	$4,888.10	$8,108.87	$18,845.95	
13	October	$2,380.42	$187.18	$385.70	$2,953.29	
14	November	$3,356.25	$3,816.38	$2,764.23	$9,936.86	
15	December	$3,936.57	$3,214.41	$815.57	$7,966.55	
16	*Total by Product*	$46,367.02	$43,762.50	$56,857.62	$146,987.14	

	A	B	C	D	E	F
1	**Pacific Musical Instruments**					
2	2008		Keyboards			
3	Month	Hanson	Deloria	Lakes	Total by Month	
4	January	$266.32	$5,523.06	$4,112.45	$9,901.84	
5	February	$7,770.91	$220.37	$6,324.11	$14,315.39	
6	April	$922.35	$512.38	$4,164.16	$5,598.89	
7	May	$1,358.70	$5,857.58	$9,433.13	$16,649.41	
8	March	$2,577.79	$8,579.42	$632.35	$11,789.56	
9	June	$1,777.12	$5,242.94	$3,002.10	$10,022.16	
10	July	$6,524.62	$439.53	$8,765.84	$15,729.99	
11	August	$9,647.00	$5,281.16	$8,349.09	$23,277.25	
12	September	$5,848.97	$4,888.10	$8,108.87	$18,845.95	
13	October	$2,380.42	$187.18	$385.70	$2,953.29	
14	November	$3,356.25	$3,816.38	$2,764.23	$9,936.86	
15	December	$3,936.57	$3,214.41	$815.57	$7,966.55	
16	*Total by Product*	$46,367.02	$43,762.50	$56,857.62	$146,987.14	

Figure 8-8 The gray I-beam indicates where Excel will insert selected cells.

For information about using the keyboard for this task, see "Inserting Copied or Cut Cells" on page 197.

If you press Ctrl+Shift while dragging, the selected cells are both copied and inserted instead of moved. Again, a small plus sign appears next to the pointer, and Excel inserts a copy of the selected cells in the new location, leaving the original selected cells intact. You can also use these techniques to select entire columns or rows and then move or copy them to new locations.

Inserting and Deleting

In the realm of spreadsheets, the complementary actions of inserting and deleting are collectively the second most used editing techniques. Inserting and deleting rows and columns of information have some nuances that don't exist in the world of word processing, for example, but that you must consider.

Inserting Columns and Rows

On the Home tab, you can click commands on the Insert menu in the Cells group to add cells, columns, and rows to a worksheet. However, when you need to insert entire rows or columns, it's easiest to right-click the column or row heading, which simultaneously selects the row or column and displays the shortcut menu shown in Figure 8-9.

(You can also drag through several rows or columns and then right-click the selection to insert the same number of columns or rows you selected.) Then just click Insert.

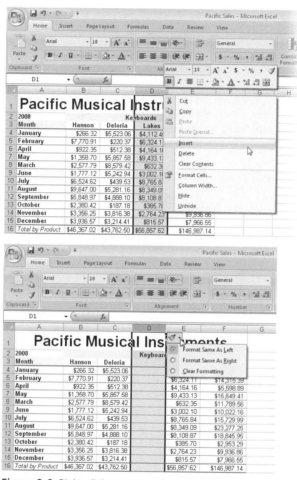

Figure 8-9 Right-click a row or column heading, and click Insert. Click the smart tag after you insert for some post-insertion options.

After inserting the column in Figure 8-9, the contents of column D move to column E, leaving the freshly inserted column D blank and ready for new information. The newly inserted cells take on the same formats as the cells in the column to the left, and Excel adjusts the formulas in cells F4:F15 to account for the expanded range.

A smart tag appears after you insert, which you can use to change the formatting of the inserted cells. Click the smart tag to display the menu shown on the right in Figure 8-9. If you want to extend a table by inserting a column on its right, for example, you might want to use the Format Same As Right or Clear Formatting option. The default Format Same As Left option works for our example.

Note

When you insert a row instead of a column, the smart tag options are Format Same As Above (the default), Format Same As Below, and Clear Formatting.

Handy Keyboard Shortcuts

Some of us are mouse fans; others are keyboard jockeys. If you're a good typist, you might prefer keeping your hands on the keys as much as possible. If so, this table of keyboard shortcuts for typical insertion actions is for you.

Press	To
Alt, I, R	Insert rows
Alt, I, C	Insert columns
Alt, E, D	Delete selected rows or columns
Ctrl+Spacebar	Select columns
Shift+Spacebar	Select rows

Inserting Cells

You can insert cells or cell ranges rather than entire rows or columns by using the shortcut menu technique described earlier or by clicking Home, Insert, Insert Cells, which displays the Insert dialog box shown in Figure 8-10.

Note

The Insert menu is actually a button with an arrow to its right; if you click the button, it is the equivalent of clicking the Insert Cells command, which moves cells either down or to the right, depending on the shape of the selected cell range. To display the menu shown on the left in Figure 8-10, click the arrow.

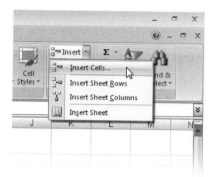 

Figure 8-10 Click the Insert Cells command to choose the direction to move existing cells in your worksheet.

> **Note**
>
> You can insert multiple nonadjacent cells when you use the Insert command, except when inserting cut or copied cells.

Inserting Copied or Cut Cells

Often you need to copy or move existing data to the middle of another area of existing data, moving other data out of the way in the process. You can do this the hard way, by inserting just the right amount of space in the destination area and then copying or cutting cells and pasting them to the new location. However, it's much easier to click Home, Insert, Insert Copied Cells or Insert Cut Cells because this handles all these actions for you. These commands appear on the Insert menu (or on the shortcut menu) only when you have first copied or cut some cells. Sometimes it's obvious what needs to happen. For example, if you cut an entire row, you'll surely want to insert the entire row somewhere else. In these cases, Office Excel 2007 employs some commonsense rules and executes the action without hesitation. If Excel needs more information about how to adjust the worksheet, it will open the Insert Paste dialog box shown in Figure 8-11.

For example, you can use cutting and inserting to add rows for 2007 data in Figure 8-11 by copying the rows containing 2008 data and editing the contents, thereby saving yourself some unnecessary typing. To do so, select cells A6:F9, and press Ctrl+C to copy the range. Then click Home, Insert, Insert Copied Cells to display the Insert Paste dialog box. Then select the Shift Cells Down option, and click OK. Excel inserts the copied data and moves the rest of the table down to accommodate the insertion, as shown in Figure 8-12.

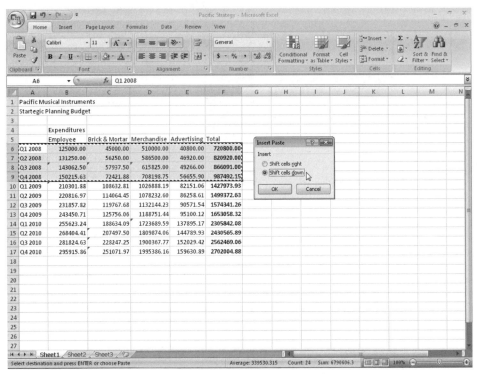

Figure 8-11 When you insert after copying or cutting cells, the Insert Paste dialog box appears.

Deleting Cells, Columns, and Rows

You can use the Delete menu on the Home tab (located in the Cells group) to remove cells, rows, or columns from your worksheet. Delete removes the selected cell or range from the worksheet, shifting cells to fill the empty space you create.

> **Note**
>
> The Delete menu is actually a button with an arrow to its right; if you click the button, it is the equivalent of clicking the Delete Cells command, which moves remaining cells either up or to the left, depending on the shape of the selected cell range. To display the menu, click the arrow.

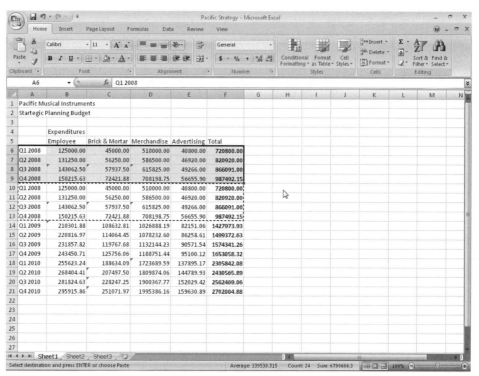

Figure 8-12 Inserting previously copied or cut cells is faster than inserting cells and then copying or cutting data to fill the inserted range.

Here are some guidelines for using Delete:

- You can delete multiple nonadjacent rows by selecting the row heading before clicking Delete. Excel shifts everything below the deleted rows upward and adjusts any formulas accordingly.

- You can delete entire columns by selecting the column heading before clicking Home, Delete. Excel moves everything to the right of the deleted columns left and adjusts any formulas accordingly.

- You can delete multiple nonadjacent selections in one operation as long as you delete either entire rows or entire columns. You cannot delete entire rows and columns at the same time, however, because they overlap.

- You can delete partial rows and columns by selecting a cell or cells and clicking Delete. Excel displays the Delete dialog box shown in Figure 8-13. You can choose the direction you want to shift remaining cells to fill the gap, or you can choose to eliminate the entire rows or columns inhabited by the selected cells.

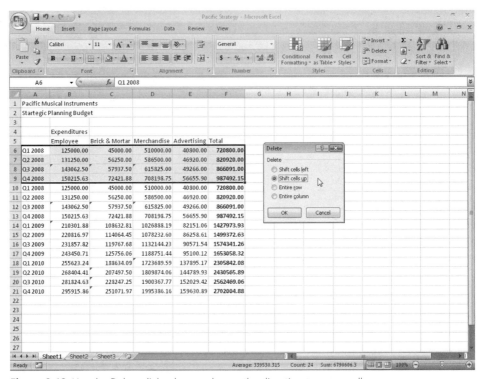

Figure 8-13 Use the Delete dialog box to choose the direction to move cells.

For more information about formulas and cell references, see Chapter 12, "Building Formulas."

When you delete (or insert) partial rows or columns, it's easy to misalign data. For example, in Figure 8-14, we deleted cells B6:E9, with the default Shift Cells Up option selected. This eliminated the cells referred to by the formulas in column F, producing #REF errors. In addition, the column F totals in rows 13 through 20 now refer to the data in rows 9 through 16. This is a case where we might have wanted to clear the cell contents rather than delete the cells.

CAUTION

Although you can generally use Undo to cancel a deletion, you should take heed of these important points. Before you delete an entire column or row, scroll through your worksheet to be sure you're not erasing important information that is not currently visible. Deleting cells that are referred to by formulas can be disastrous, as Figure 8-14 illustrates. Finally, when you delete a column or row referred to by an argument of a function, Excel modifies the argument, if possible, to account for the deletion. This adaptability is a compelling reason to use functions wherever possible. For more about using functions, see Chapter 13, "Using Functions."

Fixing Formula Problems

In the following worksheet, notice that the formulas in row 21 have small triangular indicators in the upper-left corner of each cell (they are green on your screen):

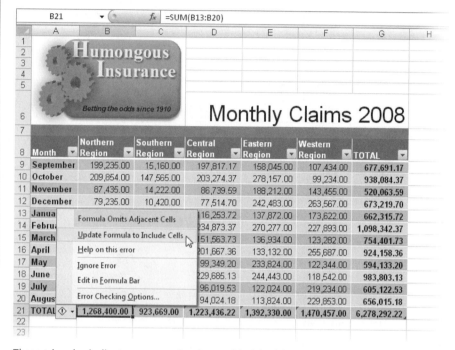

These triangles indicate an anomaly of some kind; in this case, we moved cells around within the table, so the formulas no longer include the cells we moved. Notice in the graphic that the formula bar displays the formula =SUM(B13:B20), omitting cells B9:B12. We used the Insert Cut Cells technique described in this chapter to move the rows containing September through December data from the bottom of the table to the top, which created the problem. When you insert or move rows or columns at the edge of cell ranges referred to by formulas, the formulas might not be able to adjust properly, as is the case here. In the "old days" (a couple of releases ago), you had to figure this out on your own, but Excel 2007 now offers help. As shown here, not only do the little flags appear, but when you select one of the formula cells, a smart tag appears offering a Formula Omits Adjacent Cells menu containing pertinent options.

The Update Formula To Include Cells option works correctly in our example. This is a much easier solution than editing each formula manually.

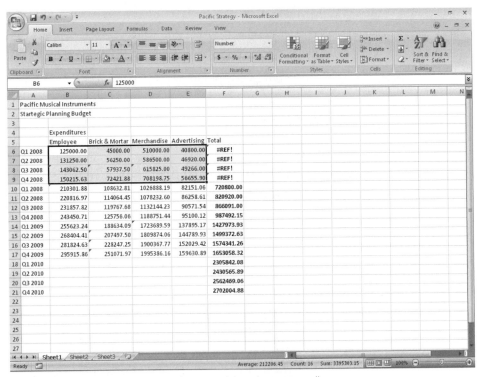

Figure 8-14 You can create errors when you delete the wrong cells.

Clearing Cells

Clear

The difference between deleting and clearing isn't subtle. Although deleting completely removes selected cells, shifting adjacent cells to fill the void, *clearing* leaves selected cells in place and removes contents, formats, and any comments that might be attached. The Home tab includes a Clear menu, which is one of the buttons in the Editing group without a label—the one that is meant to look like an eraser (but really doesn't). Figure 8-15 shows the Clear menu.

Figure 8-15 The commands on the Clear menu remove the corresponding attributes of selected cells without removing the cells.

The commands on the Clear menu perform the following tasks on selected cells:

- **Clear All** removes all text, numbers, formulas, formats, borders, and any attached comments.

- **Clear Formats** removes only formatting and borders.

- **Clear Contents** removes only text, numbers, and formulas.

- **Clear Comments** removes only the attached comments.

CAUTION

The Clear Series command, which was available in previous versions, is no longer available in Excel 2007.

Inserting, Deleting, and Clearing Cells with the Mouse

To perform the next group of operations, you use the fill handle, which appears in the lower-right corner of the *selection rectangle*, the bold border that appears around the selected cell or range. If you select entire rows or columns, the fill handle appears next to the row or column heading.

When you select a single cell and drag the fill handle in any direction, Excel copies the contents of that cell to all the cells through which you drag (with exceptions, which you'll learn later). When you select more than one cell, Excel either copies the range or extends a data series in the direction you drag, depending on the cell contents, the shape of the selection, and whether you are holding down Ctrl. Pressing the Shift key while dragging the fill handle lets you insert blank cells into a worksheet.

In the worksheet on the top in Figure 8-16, we selected A7:H7 and dragged the fill handle one row down while pressing the Shift key. The pointer became a double-headed arrow. The worksheet on the bottom in Figure 8-16 shows the newly inserted blank cells.

You use the same technique to insert entire blank rows or columns—just select the row or column headings, or press Shift and drag the fill handle, which appears adjacent to the row or column headings. You can just as easily delete cells, columns, or rows using a similar technique. To delete the cells we inserted in Figure 8-16, select A8:H8, hold down Shift, and then drag the fill handle up one row. The area turns gray, and the pointer changes to a similar double-headed arrow, with the arrows pointing inward this time. When you release the mouse button, Excel deletes the selection.

	A	B	C	D	E	F	G	H	I	J
1	Regional Sales									
2										
3	2008	Qtr 1	Qtr 2	Qtr 3	Qtr 4		Total	Average		
4	Region 1	1000	1050	1100	1150		4300	1075		
5	Region 2	1100	1150	1200	1250		4700	1175		
6	Region 3	1200	1250	1300	1350		5100	1275		
7	Region 4	1300	1350	1400	1450		5500	1375		
8										
9	Total	4600	4800	5000	5200		19600	4900		
10	Average	1150	1200	1250	1300		4900			

	A	B	C	D	E	F	G	H	I	J
1	Regional Sales									
2										
3	2008	Qtr 1	Qtr 2	Qtr 3	Qtr 4		Total	Average		
4	Region 1	1000	1050	1100	1150		4300	1075		
5	Region 2	1100	1150	1200	1250		4700	1175		
6	Region 3	1200	1250	1300	1350		5100	1275		
7	Region 4	1300	1350	1400	1450		5500	1375		
8										
9										
10	Total	4600	4800	5000	5200		19600	4900		
11	Average	1150	1200	1250	1300		4900			

Figure 8-16 Drag the fill handle while pressing Shift to insert cells.

If you drag the fill handle back over selected cells without pressing Shift, you clear the cell contents instead of deleting the cells. This clears formulas, text, and numbers only. If you hold down the Ctrl key while dragging over a selection, you clear all the cell contents as well as the formatting, borders, and comments.

Fill Handles and Cell Selection Rectangles

The *cell selection rectangle* is the heavy black-bordered box that surrounds the currently selected cells. By default, the *fill handle* is visible in every cell selection rectangle:

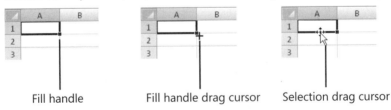

Fill handle   Fill handle drag cursor   Selection drag cursor

Dragging the fill handle extends the selection and performs other feats of prowess, as described in this chapter. Dragging the selection rectangle moves or copies the selection, also as described in this chapter. If the fill handle is not visible, click the Microsoft Office Button, click Excel Options, and then click the Advanced category. In the Editing Options area, select the Enable Fill Handle And Cell Drag-And-Drop check box. The Alert Before Overwriting Cells check box is automatically selected (and recommended).

Dragging with the Right Mouse Button

If you select cells and then drag the selection rectangle using the right mouse button, a shortcut menu appears when you release the button, as shown in Figure 8-17. You can use the options on the shortcut menu to consummate your edit in a variety of ways.

	A	B	C	D	E	F	G	H	I	J	K
1	Team Sales 2008										
2	Team A	Jan	Feb	Mar							
3	Carothers, Andy	321	64	414							
4	DeVoe, Michael	274	467	249							
5	Groncki, Douglas	518	196	279							
6	Hay, Jeff	359	266	497							
7	Ito, Shu	96	117	479							
8	Team A Total	1,568	1,110	1,919							
9	Team B	Jan	Feb	Mar							
10	MacDonald, Scott	389	120	530							
11	Owen, Laura	412	506	445							
12	Parkinson, Eric	425	231	280							
13	Rothenberg, Eric	541	307	89							
14	Steele, Laura C.	164	136	406							
15	Team B Total	1,932	1,299	1,750							
16	GRAND TOTAL	3,500	2,409	3,668							
17											
18											
19											

F2:G16

Move Here
Copy Here
Copy Here as Values Only
Copy Here as Formats Only
Link Here
Create Hyperlink Here
Shift Down and Copy
Shift Right and Copy
Shift Down and Move
Shift Right and Move
Cancel

Figure 8-17 Drag the selection with the right mouse button to display a shortcut menu.

The options on the shortcut menu are as follows:

- **Move Here** Moves the source cells to the selected destination

- **Copy Here** Copies the source cells to the selected destination

- **Copy Here As Values Only** Copies the visible values from the source cells to the selected destination cells but does not copy formulas

- **Copy Here As Formats Only** Copies the formats of the source cells to the destination cells, without affecting the contents

- **Link Here** Creates linking formulas at the destination that refer to the source cells

- **Create Hyperlink Here** Creates a Web-style link to the source cells in the selected destination

- **The Shift options** Lets you copy or move the source cells to a location that contains existing data, shifting it out of the way in the selected direction

Undoing Previous Actions

The word *undo* was never widely used until people started using computers; now it's a verb that we all wish we could apply to more things in life. In Office Excel 2007, you can click the Undo button, located on the Quick Access Toolbar, or press Ctrl+Z to recover from mistakes.

Undo

The Undo button includes a drop-down list of up to the last 100 actions you performed. You can then select and simultaneously undo any number of these actions at once. You display the drop-down list by clicking the small downward-pointing arrow next to the Undo button, as shown in Figure 8-18.

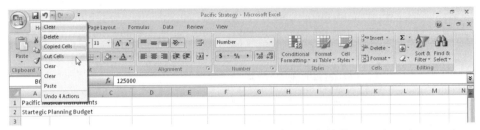

Figure 8-18 Click the arrow next to the Undo button to select and simultaneously undo up to the last 100 actions.

With the drop-down list visible, move your pointer down the list, and select the number of actions you want to undo. When you click, your worksheet reverts to the condition it was in before the selected actions.

Undo reverses the effect of most editing actions and restores any entry in the formula bar. For example, if you accidentally delete a range of data, use Undo to replace the entries. If you edit the contents of a cell and subsequently discover that your changes are incorrect, use Undo to restore the original cell entry. In addition, you can use Undo to reverse formatting and many other types of actions.

Unfortunately, Excel has many actions that Undo can't reverse, such as saving workbooks and deleting worksheets. Closing a workbook erases all the undoable actions displayed in the Undo list. Predictably, actions you cannot undo do not appear in the Undo drop-down list.

Redoing What You've Undone

Redo

After you use Undo, you can then use Redo, which unsurprisingly reverses Undo. You can press Ctrl+Y to redo the last action or click the Redo button on the Quick Access Toolbar, which operates similarly to Undo. Redo also offers a drop-down list with all the undone editing actions. When you redo an action, Excel transfers it to the Undo drop-down list.

You can take advantage of Undo and Redo to see the effects of an editing change in your worksheet. If you edit a cell that is referred to in several formulas, you can use Undo and Redo to get a "before and after" look at the results displayed by the formulas.

Repeating Your Last Action

Repeat

To repeat the last editing action, press Ctrl+Y. (The Repeat button does not ordinarily appear on the Quick Access Toolbar, but you can add it. See "Customizing the Quick Access Toolbar" on page 83.) Redo and Repeat share the same keyboard shortcut, because you can do only one or the other at any given moment. Being able to repeat the last action is a great timesaver and is particularly handy with repetitive chores. The phrase "last action" is the key to understanding the difference between the two faces of this command. Repeat is valid only if Undo was your last action. After you have redone all the "undos" (up to 100), you're back to the "true" last action—that is, the last action you performed before you used Undo.

Unlike Undo, Repeat works with most actions. The only exceptions are those actions you can't logically repeat. For example, if you save a file by clicking the Microsoft Office Button and then Save, you can't repeat the action. Whatever the case, Repeat reflects the last repeatable action.

Editing Cell Contents

You can use the formula bar to edit the contents of a selected cell, or you can perform your editing "on location" in the cell. Office Excel 2007 also includes a few special features you can apply to tasks such as entering date sequences, which once used to involve editing each cell but are now semiautomatic, if you know where to find the "trigger."

Editing in Cells or in the Formula Bar

While typing or editing the contents of a cell, you can use Cut, Copy, Paste, and Clear to manipulate cell entries. Often, retyping a value or formula is easier, but using commands is convenient when you're working with long, complex formulas or with labels. These commands work just as they do in a word-processing program such as Word when you're working in a cell or in the formula bar. For example, you can copy all or part of a formula from one cell to another. For example, suppose cell A10 contains the formula =IF(NPV(.15,A1:A9)>0,A11,A12) and you want to type **=NPV(.15,A1:A9)** in cell B10.

> **Note**
> You can edit the contents of cells without using the formula bar. By double-clicking a cell, you can perform any formula bar editing procedure directly in the cell.

Copy

To do so, select cell A10, and in the formula bar, select the characters you want to copy—in this case, NPV(.15,A1:A9). Then press Ctrl+C, or click the Copy button (located in the Clipboard group on the Home tab). Finally, select cell B10, type **=** to begin a formula, and press Ctrl+V (or click the Paste button).

> **Note**
> Excel does not adjust cell references when you cut, copy, and paste within a cell or in the formula bar. For information about adjustable references, see "How Copying Affects Cell References" on page 432.

When you type or edit formulas containing references, Excel gives you visual aids called *range finders* to help you audit, as shown in Figure 8-19, where we obviously have a problem with our SUM formula.

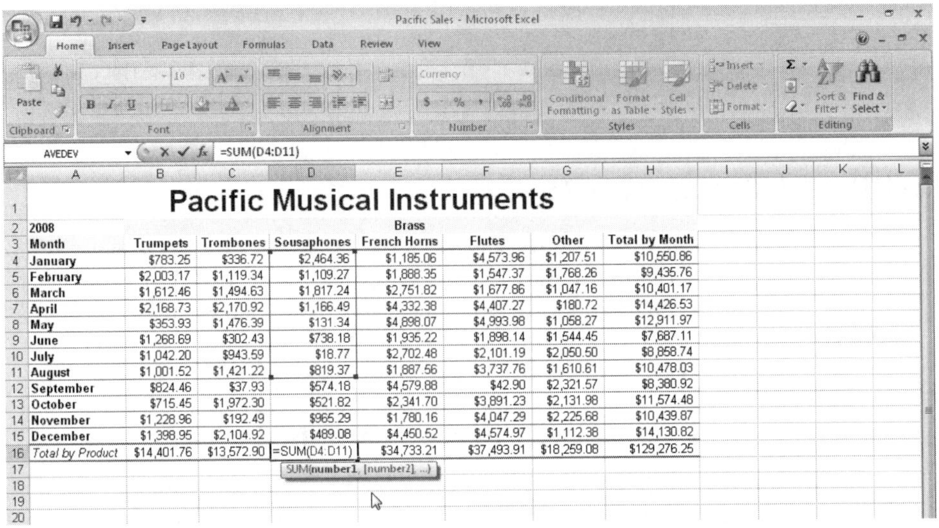

	A	B	C	D	E	F	G	H
1	Pacific Musical Instruments							
2	2008				Brass			
3	Month	Trumpets	Trombones	Sousaphones	French Horns	Flutes	Other	Total by Month
4	January	$783.25	$336.72	$2,464.36	$1,185.06	$4,573.96	$1,207.51	$10,550.86
5	February	$2,003.17	$1,119.34	$1,109.27	$1,888.35	$1,547.37	$1,768.26	$9,435.76
6	March	$1,612.46	$1,494.63	$1,817.24	$2,751.82	$1,677.86	$1,047.16	$10,401.17
7	April	$2,168.73	$2,170.92	$1,166.49	$4,332.38	$4,407.27	$180.72	$14,426.53
8	May	$353.93	$1,476.39	$131.34	$4,898.07	$4,993.98	$1,058.27	$12,911.97
9	June	$1,268.69	$302.43	$738.18	$1,935.22	$1,898.14	$1,544.45	$7,687.11
10	July	$1,042.20	$943.59	$18.77	$2,702.48	$2,101.19	$2,050.50	$8,858.74
11	August	$1,001.52	$1,421.22	$819.37	$1,887.56	$3,737.76	$1,610.61	$10,478.03
12	September	$824.46	$37.93	$574.18	$4,579.88	$42.90	$2,321.57	$8,380.92
13	October	$715.45	$1,972.30	$521.82	$2,341.70	$3,891.23	$2,131.98	$11,574.48
14	November	$1,228.96	$192.49	$965.29	$1,780.16	$4,047.29	$2,225.68	$10,439.87
15	December	$1,398.95	$2,104.92	$489.08	$4,450.52	$4,574.97	$1,112.38	$14,130.82
16	*Total by Product*	$14,401.76	$13,572.90	=SUM(D4:D11)	$34,733.21	$37,493.91	$18,259.08	$129,276.25

Figure 8-19 Double-click a cell containing a formula to edit it and to display range finders.

For more information about auditing, see "Auditing and Documenting Worksheets" on page 241.

> **Note**
>
> You can disable in-cell editing, if you want. To do so, click the Microsoft Office Button, click Excel Options, and in the Advanced category, clear the Allow Editing Directly In Cells check box in the Editing Options area.

Editing Options

The Advanced category in the Excel Options dialog box (click the Microsoft Office Button, Excel Options) contains an assortment of options that control editing-related workspace settings, as shown in Figure 8-20. These options include the following:

- **After Pressing Enter, Move Selection** This locks in the entry and makes the cell below active. To change the direction of the selection after you press Enter, use the Direction drop-down list. When you clear this check box, pressing Enter locks in the entry and leaves the same cell active.

- **Automatically Insert A Decimal Point** Ordinarily you type numbers and decimal points manually. To have Excel enter decimal points for you, select this option, and then select the number of decimal places you want. For example, when you type **12345** with two decimal places specified, Excel enters 123.45 in the cell. When you apply this option, Fixed Decimal appears in the status bar. This option applies only to entries you make after you select it, without altering existing data. It also applies only when you do not type a decimal point. If you type a number including a decimal point, the option has no effect.

- **Enable Fill Handle And Cell Drag-And-Drop** This is required for the direct manipulation of cells using the mouse. See "Moving and Copying with the Mouse" on page 192. Leaving the Alert Before Overwriting Cells option selected is always a good idea.

- **Allow Editing Directly In Cells** This is required for in-cell editing. See "Editing in Cells or in the Formula Bar" on page 207.

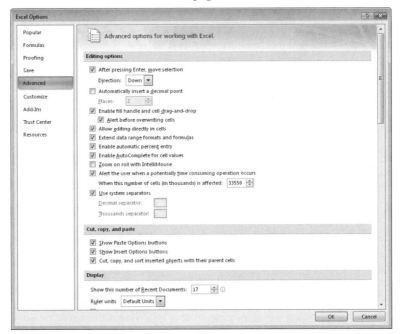

Figure 8-20 Click the Microsoft Office Button, Excel Options, Advanced to display editing-related workspace settings.

- **Extend Data Range Formats And Formulas** This lets Excel apply formatting to new cells entered in a list or table, based on the formats of existing cells. See "Extending Existing Formatting" on page 219.

- **Enable Automatic Percent Entry** This helps you type values in cells with the Percentage format. When you select this check box, all entries less than 1 are multiplied by 100. When you clear this check box, all entries—including those greater than 1—are multiplied by 100. For example, in a cell to which you have already applied the Percentage format, typing either **.9** or **90** produces the same result—90%—in the cell. If you clear the Enable Automatic Percent Entry check box, typing **90** results in the displayed value 9000% (as long as you have applied the Percentage format to the cell).

> **Note**
>
> A quick way to apply the Percentage format to a clean cell is to type a number as a percentage. For example, type **1%** in a cell, and the cell then displays subsequent numbers in the same Percentage format.

- **Enable AutoComplete For Cell Values** This lets Excel suggest cell entries by comparing existing values it finds in the same column as you type. See "Letting Excel Help with Typing Chores" on page 230.

- **Zoom On Roll With IntelliMouse** Ordinarily, if your mouse has a wheel, rotating it causes the worksheet to scroll (or zoom while pressing Ctrl). Select this check box to switch the behavior of the wheel so that the worksheet zooms when you rotate the wheel (or scrolls while you press Ctrl).

- **Alert The User When A Potentially Time-Consuming Operation Occurs** If an editing operation will affect a large number of cells, this option controls whether you will be notified and lets you specify the number of cells it takes to trigger the notification.

- **Use System Separators** Ordinarily, Excel defaults to the designated numeric separators for decimals and thousands (periods and commas, respectively) specified by your Windows system settings. If you want to specify alternative separators, you can do so here.

- **Show Paste Options Buttons/Show Insert Options Buttons** This shows the smart tag menu after pasting or inserting. Ordinarily when you perform a paste or insert operation, a smart tag action menu appears, offering various context-specific actions you can then perform. Clear these options to turn off these features.

- **Cut, Copy, And Sort Inserted Objects With Their Parent Cells** This is required to "attach" graphic objects to cells. See "Tools to Help You Position Objects on the Worksheet" on page 391.

Understanding Fixed and Floating Decimals

The Automatically Insert A Decimal Point option in the Advanced category of the Excel Options dialog box is handy when you need to type long lists of numeric values. (It's equivalent to the floating-decimal feature available on most ten-key calculators.) For example, if you're performing a lengthy data-entry task such as typing multiple dollar values on a worksheet, select the Automatically Insert a Decimal Point option, and click 2 in the Places list. Then just type numbers, and press Enter, saving you an extra keystroke for the decimal point in each entry. If you're entering 1,000 values, typing **295** instead of 2.95 eliminates 25 percent of the keystrokes you would otherwise have to perform. However, you need to be careful to either type trailing zeros or add decimal points to some numbers. For example, you would usually type **5** to enter a 5.00 value, but with two fixed decimal places turned on, the same entry becomes 0.05, making it necessary for you to type either **500** or **5.** to correctly place the decimal point.

Filling and Creating Data Series

As described earlier in this chapter, the fill handle has many talents to make it simple to enter data in worksheets. Uses of the fill handle include quickly and easily filling cells and creating data series using the incredibly useful AutoFill feature.

Take a look at Figure 8-21. If you select cell B2 in this worksheet and drag the fill handle down to cell B5, Excel copies the contents of cell B2 to cells B3 through B5. However, if you click the smart tag action menu that appears after you drag, you can select a different AutoFill action, as shown in Figure 8-22.

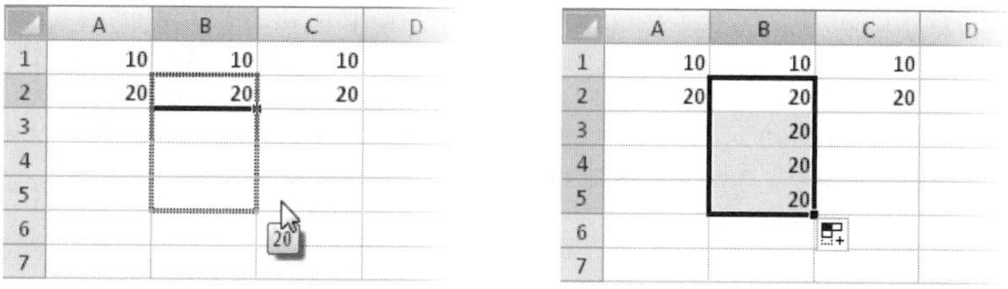

Figure 8-21 Copy the contents of a cell to adjacent cells by dragging the fill handle.

INSIDE OUT   **Create Decreasing Series**

Generally, when you create a series, you drag the fill handle down or to the right, and the values increase accordingly. You can also create a series of decreasing values, however, by dragging the fill handle either up or to the left. Select the starting values in cells at the bottom or to the right of the range you want to fill, and then drag the fill handle back toward the beginning of the range.

AutoFill Options
Smart Tag

Notice that the AutoFill Options smart tag looks a little different from the standard smart tag, a visual clue that you can perform special tasks with the selected cells.

If you click Fill Series on the smart tag action menu, Excel creates the simple series 21, 22, and 23 instead of copying the contents of cell C2. If, instead of selecting a single cell, you select the range C1:C2 in Figure 8-22 and drag the fill handle down to cell C5, you create a series that is based on the interval between the two selected values, resulting in the series 30, 40, and 50 in cells C3:C5. If you click Copy Cells on the AutoFill Options menu, instead of extending the series, Excel copies the cells, repeating the pattern of selected cells as necessary to fill the range. Instead of filling C3:C5 with the values 30, 40, and 50, choosing Copy Cells will enter the values 10, 20, and 10 in C3:C5.

	A	B	C	D	E	F
1	10	10	10			
2	20	20	20			
3		20	20			
4		20	20			
5		20	20			
6						
7				⊙ Copy Cells		
8				○ Fill Series		
9				○ Fill Formatting Only		
10				○ Fill Without Formatting		
11						
12						

	A	B	C	D
1	10	10	10	
2	20	20	20	
3		20	21	
4		20	22	
5		20	23	
6				
7				
8				
9				
10				
11				
12				

Figure 8-22 Create a simple series by dragging the fill handle and then clicking Fill Series on the smart tag action menu.

If you select a text value and drag the fill handle, Excel copies the text to the cells where you drag. If, however, the selection contains both text and numeric values, the AutoFill feature takes over and extends the numeric component while copying the text component. You can also extend dates in this way, using a number of date formats, including Qtr 1, Qtr 2, and so on. If you type text that describes dates, even without numbers (such as months or days of the week), Excel treats the text as a series.

INSIDE OUT   Fill Series Limited to 255 Characters

Excel lets you type up to 32,767 characters in a cell. However, if you want to extend a series using AutoFill, the selected source cells cannot contain more than 255 characters. If you try to extend a series from an entry of 256 characters or more, Excel copies the cells rather than extending the series. This is not really a bug but is a side effect of the Excel column-width limitation of 255 characters. Besides, a 256-character entry is not going to be readable on the screen anyway. If you really need to create series out of humongous cell entries like this, perhaps a little worksheet redesign is in order. Otherwise, you'll have to do it manually.

Figure 8-23 shows some examples of simple data series created by selecting single cells containing values and dragging the fill handle. We typed the values in column A, and we extended the values to the right of column A using the fill handle. Figure 8-24 shows examples of creating data series using two selected values that, in effect, specify the interval to be used in creating the data series. We typed the values in columns A and B and extended the values to the right of column B using the fill handle. These two figures also show how AutoFill can create a series even when you mix text and numeric values in cells. Also note that we extended the values and series in Figure 8-24 by selecting the entire range of starting values in cells A3:B12 before dragging the fill handle to extend them, showing how Excel can extend multiple series at once. (We applied the bold formatting after filling, to make it easier to differentiate the starting values.)

> **Note**
>
> If you select more than one cell and you hold down Ctrl while dragging the fill handle, you suppress AutoFill and copy the selected values to the adjacent cells. Conversely, with a single value selected, holding down Ctrl and dragging the fill handle extends a series, contrary to the regular behavior of copying the cell.

	A	B	C	D	E	F	G	H
1	**Selected Value**	**Resulting Series**						
2								
3	**9:00**	10:00	11:00	12:00	13:00	14:00	15:00	
4	**1/1/2008**	1/2/2008	1/3/2008	1/4/2008	1/5/2008	1/6/2008	1/7/2008	
5	**Qtr 1**	Qtr 2	Qtr 3	Qtr 4	Qtr 1	Qtr 2	Qtr 3	
6	**Jan**	Feb	Mar	Apr	May	Jun	Jul	
7	**January**	February	March	April	May	June	July	
8	**Day 1**	Day 2	Day 3	Day 4	Day 5	Day 6	Day 7	
9	**Mon**	Tue	Wed	Thu	Fri	Sat	Sun	
10	**Product 1**	Product 2	Product 3	Product 4	Product 5	Product 6	Product 7	
11								
12								

Figure 8-23 Create simple data series by selecting a single value and dragging the fill handle.

	A	B	C	D	E	F	G	H
1	**Selected Values**		**Resulting Series**					
2								
3	**9:00**	**10:00**	11:00	12:00	13:00	14:00	15:00	
4	**2007**	**2008**	2009	2010	2011	2012	2013	
5	**1/1/2008**	**2/1/2008**	3/1/2008	4/1/2008	5/1/2008	6/1/2008	7/1/2008	
6	**1/1/2008**	**3/1/2008**	5/1/2008	7/1/2008	9/1/2008	11/1/2008	1/1/2009	
7	**1-Jan**	**2-Jan**	3-Jan	4-Jan	5-Jan	6-Jan	7-Jan	
8	**Dec-07**	**Dec-08**	Dec-09	Dec-10	Dec-11	Dec-12	Dec-13	
9	**Dec-07**	**Dec-09**	Dec-11	Dec-13	Dec-15	Dec-17	Dec-19	
10	**Product 1**	**Product 2**	Product 3	Product 4	Product 5	Product 6	Product 7	
11	**Sat**	**Mon**	Wed	Fri	Sun	Tue	Thu	
12	**1 1/2**	**2 3/4**	4	5 1/4	6 1/2	7 3/4	9	
13								
14								

Figure 8-24 Specify data series intervals by selecting a range of values and dragging the fill handle.

INSIDE OUT

How AutoFill Handles Dates and Times

AutoFill ordinarily increments recognizable date and time values when you drag the fill handle, even if you initially select only one cell. For example, if you select a cell that contains Qtr 1 or 1/1/2008 and drag the fill handle, AutoFill extends the series as Qtr 2, Qtr 3, or 1/2/2008, 1/3/2008, and so on. If you click the smart tag action menu after you drag, you'll see that special options become available if the original selection contains dates or the names of days or months:

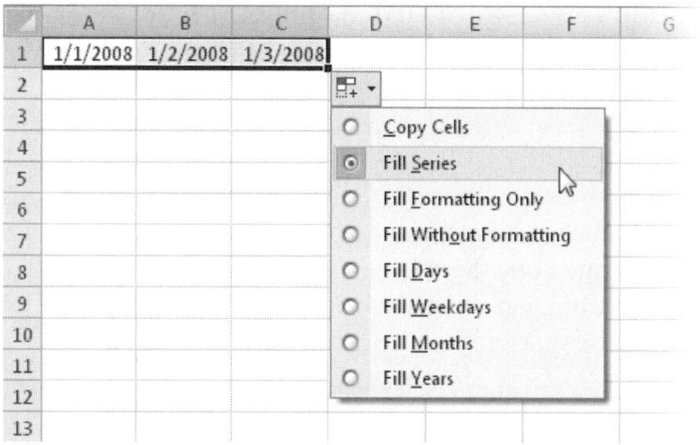

An interesting feature of this menu is Fill Weekdays, which not only increments a day or date series but also skips weekend days. Depending on the original selection, different options might be available on the smart tag action menu.

Extending with AutoFill

Sometimes you can double-click the fill handle to extend a series from a selected range. AutoFill determines the size of the range by matching an adjacent range. For example, in Figure 8-25, we filled column A with a series of values. Then we filled column B by selecting the range B1:B2 and double-clicking the fill handle. The newly created series stops at cell B5 to match the adjacent cells in column A. When the selected cells contain something other than a series, such as simple text entries, double-clicking the fill handle copies the selected cells down to match the length of the adjacent range.

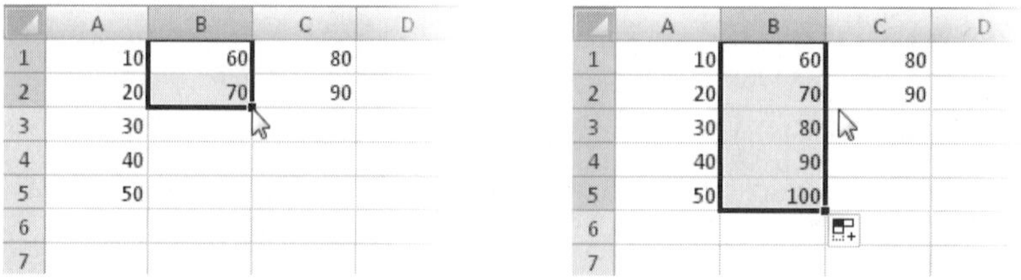

Figure 8-25 We extended a series into B3:B5 by selecting B1:B2 and double-clicking the fill handle.

Dragging the Fill Handle with the Right Mouse Button

When you use the right mouse button to fill a range or extend a series, a shortcut menu appears when you release the button, as shown in Figure 8-26. This menu differs somewhat from the AutoFill Options smart tag menu and lets you specify what you want to happen in advance, as opposed to the smart tag menu's ability to change the action after the fact.

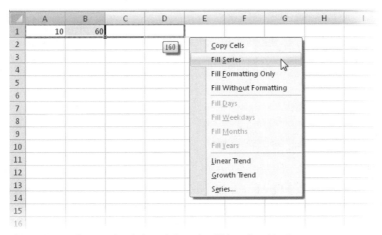

Figure 8-26 If you right-click and drag the fill handle, this shortcut menu appears when you release the mouse button.

The box that appears on the screen adjacent to the pointer indicates what the last number of this sequence would be if we dragged the fill handle like usual (with the left mouse button)—in this case, 160. The Linear Trend command creates a simple linear series similar to that which you can create by dragging the fill handle with the left mouse button. Growth Trend creates a simple nonlinear growth series, using the selected cells to extrapolate points along an exponential growth curve. In Figure 8-27, rows 4 through 6 in column A contain a series created using Linear Trend, and the same rows in column C contain a series created using Growth Trend, using the same starting values.

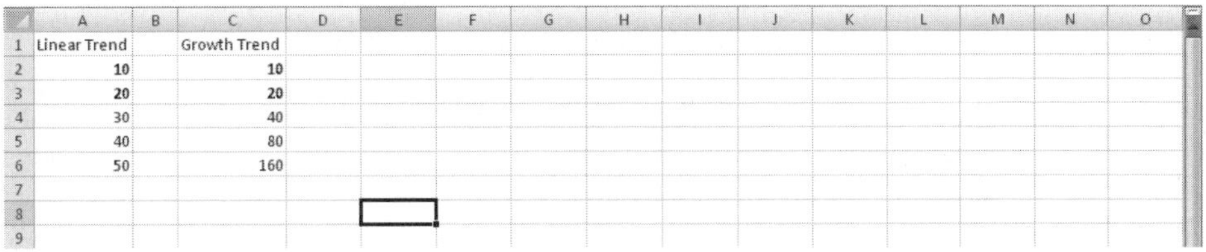

Figure 8-27 We created a linear trend series in column A and a growth trend series in column C.

Using the Series Command

Fill

When you click Series on the shortcut menu that appears when you press the right mouse button and drag the fill handle, the Series dialog box appears, letting you create custom incremental series. Alternatively, you can click the Series command on the Fill menu (located in the Editing group on the Home tab) to display the Series dialog box shown in Figure 8-28.

Figure 8-28   Use the Series dialog box for more control when creating a series.

Use the Series dialog box to specify an interval with which to increment the series (step value) and a maximum value for the series (stop value). Using this method has a couple of advantages over direct mouse manipulation techniques. First, you do not need to select a range to fill, and second, you can specify increments (step values) without first selecting cells containing example incremented values. You can select example values if you want, but it is not necessary.

The Rows option tells Excel to use the first value in each row to fill the cells to the right. The Columns option tells Excel to use the first value in each column to fill the cells below. For example, if you select a range of cells in advance that is taller than it is wide, Excel automatically selects the Columns option when you open the Series dialog box. Excel uses the Type options in conjunction with the start values in selected cells and the value in the Step Value box to create your series. If you select example cells first, Step Value reflects the increment between the selected cells.

The Linear option adds the value specified in the Step Value box to the selected values in your worksheet to extend the series. The Growth option multiplies the last value in the selection by the step value and extrapolates the rest of the values to create the series. If you select the Date option, you can specify the type of date series from the options in the Date Unit area. The AutoFill option works like using the fill handle to drag a series, extending the series using the interval between the selected values; it determines the type of data and attempts to "divine" your intention. Selecting the Trend check box extrapolates an exponential series, but it works only if you select more than one value before displaying the Series dialog box.

For more about typing dates, see "Entering a Series of Dates" on page 523.

Using the Fill Menu Commands

Use the Down, Right, Up, and Left commands on the Fill menu shown in Figure 8-29 to copy selected cells to an adjacent range of cells. Before clicking these commands, select the range you want to fill, including the cell or cells containing the formulas, values, and formats you want to use to fill the selected range. (Comments are not included when you use these Fill commands.)

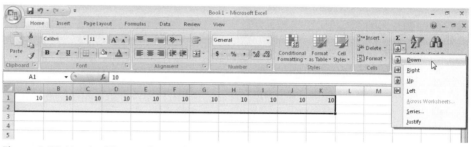

Figure 8-29 Use the Fill menu for quick access to common fill actions.

Suppose cell A1 contains the value 10. In Figure 8-29, we selected the range A1:K2 and then clicked Fill, Right to copy the value 10 across row 1. With the range still selected, we can click Fill, Down to finish filling the selected range with the original value.

> **Note**
> You can also use keyboard shortcuts to duplicate Home, Fill, Down (press Ctrl+D) and Home, Fill, Right (press Ctrl+R).

The Across Worksheets command on the Fill menu copies cells from one worksheet to other worksheets in the same workbook. For more information about using the Across Worksheets command, see "Filling a Group" on page 241.

Distributing Long Entries Using the Justify Command   Clicking Fill, Justify doesn't do what you might think it does. It splits a cell entry and distributes it into two or more adjacent rows. Unlike other Fill commands, Justify modifies the contents of the original cell.

For information about the *other* justify feature—that is, justifying text in a single cell—see "Justifying Text in Cells" on page 319.

For example, in the worksheet on the left in Figure 8-30, cell A1 contains a long text entry. To divide this text into cell-sized parts, select cell A1, and click Home, Fill, Justify. The result appears on the right in Figure 8-30.

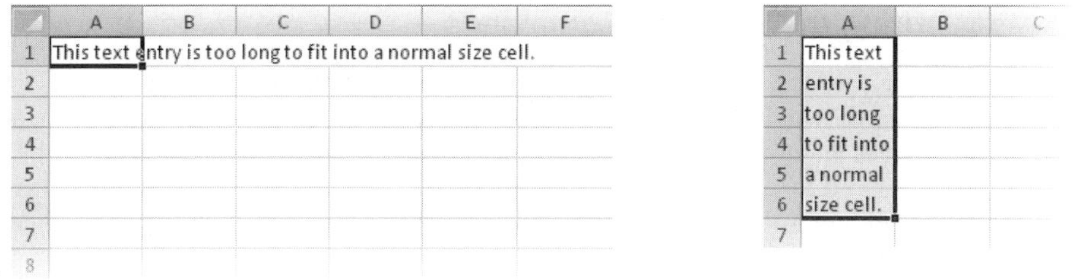

Figure 8-30 Clicking Justify distributes the long label in cell A1 to cells A1:A5.

When you click Justify, Excel displays a message warning you that this command uses as many cells below the selection as necessary to distribute the contents. Excel overwrites any cells that are in the way in the following manner:

- If you select a multirow range, Justify redistributes the text in all selected cells. For example, you can widen column A in Figure 8-30, select the filled range A1:A5, and click Justify again to redistribute the contents using the new column width.

- If you select a multicolumn range, Justify redistributes only the entries in the leftmost column of the range but uses the total width of the range you select as its guideline for determining the length of the justified text. The cells in adjacent columns are not affected, although the justified text will appear truncated if the adjacent column's cells are not empty.

Creating Custom Lists

If you find yourself repeatedly entering a particular sequence in your worksheets, such as a list of names or products, you can use the Excel Custom Lists feature to make entering that sequence as easy as dragging the mouse. After you've created the sequence, you can enter it in any range of cells by typing any item from the sequence in a cell and then dragging the fill handle. For example, Figure 8-31 shows the single name we entered in cell A1 and the custom list we entered in cells A2:A9 by dragging the fill handle.

To create a custom list, follow these steps:

1. Click the Microsoft Office Button, and then click Excel Options.

2. Select the Personalize category. In the Top Options For Working With Excel area, click the Edit Custom Lists button.

3. With NEW LIST selected in the Custom Lists box, type the items you want to include in your list in the List Entries box. Be sure to type the items in the order you want them to appear.

4. Click Add to add the list to the Custom Lists box.

5. Click OK to return to the worksheet.

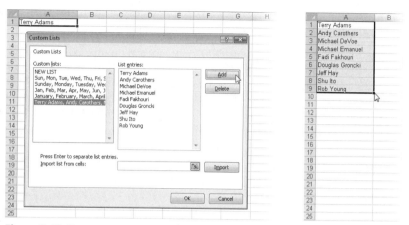

Figure 8-31 You can create custom lists that you can type by dragging the fill handle.

Importing Custom Lists

You can also create a custom list by importing the entries in an existing cell range. To import the entries shown in Figure 8-31, we first selected the range containing the list we wanted before opening the Excel Options dialog box. We then selected the Personalize category and clicked Edit Custom Lists. The address of the selected range appears in the Import List From Cells text box at the bottom of the dialog box. Then we clicked the Import button to add the selected entries as a new list. (You can also select the list after opening the dialog box when the cursor is in the Import List From Cells box.)

Extending Existing Formatting

The automatic-formatting feature lets you add new columns of data to a previously constructed table without having to apply formatting to the new cells. For example, if you want to add another column to the existing table in Figure 8-32, select cell E2, type the column heading, and then continue entering numbers in cells E3–E6.

	A	B	C	D	E	F
1	Regional Sales					
2						
3	2008	Qtr 1	Qtr 2	Qtr 3		
4	Region 1	1000	1050	1100		
5	Region 2	1100	1150	1200		
6	Region 3	1200	1250	1300		
7	Region 4	1300	1350	1400		
8						
9	Total	4600	4800	5000		
10	Average	1150	1200	1250		
11						
12						

	A	B	C	D	E	F
1	Regional Sales					
2						
3	2008	Qtr 1	Qtr 2	Qtr 3	Qtr 4	
4	Region 1	1000	1050	1100	1154	
5	Region 2	1100	1150	1200	1254	
6	Region 3	1200	1250	1300	1353	
7	Region 4	1300	1350	1400		
8						
9	Total	4600	4800	5000		
10	Average	1150	1200	1250		
11						
12						

Figure 8-32 The automatic format extension adds data to an existing table without reformatting.

Excel correctly surmises that you want the new entries to use the same formatting as the adjacent cells in column D. You can turn this feature off by clicking the Microsoft

Office Button, clicking Excel Options, and then in the Advanced category, clearing the Extend Data Range Formats And Formulas check box.

Tables are a new feature in Excel 2007 with special qualities (or, if you prefer, a "reimagining" of the old Lists feature). If you are working in a table, additional options control the extension of formatting and formulas. Click the Microsoft Office Button, click Excel Options, and then select the Proofing category. Click the AutoCorrect Options button to display the AutoCorrect dialog box shown in Figure 8-33. The tab labeled AutoFormat As You Type contains the pertinent options.

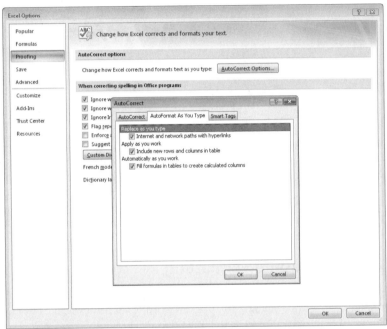

Figure 8-33 The AutoCorrect dialog box controls automatic format and formula extension when working in tables.

As you can see in Figure 8-33, the options on the AutoFormat As You Type tab control whether Excel automatically creates hyperlinks whenever you type recognizable Internet and network paths; the automatic-formatting behavior shown in Figure 8-32; and whether formulas are automatically extended in tables, in a similar fashion as the automatic-formatting feature.

For more about AutoCorrect, see "Fixing Errors As You Type" on page 227. For more about tables, see Chapter 21, "Managing Information in Tables."

Finding and Replacing Stuff

Suppose you've built a large worksheet and you now need to find every occurrence of a specific string of text or values in that worksheet. (In computerese, a *string* is defined as any continuous series of characters—text, numbers, math operators, or punctuation symbols.) You can use the Find & Select menu in the Editing group on the Home tab to locate any string, cell reference, or range name in cells or formulas on a worksheet. In addition to finding strings, you can now also find formatting, with or without strings attached. You can then click Replace to overwrite the strings or formatting you locate with new strings or new formatting.

When you click the Find command on the Find & Select menu (or press Ctrl+F), the Find And Replace dialog box appears, as shown in Figure 8-34. (If yours looks different, click Options to expand the dialog box.)

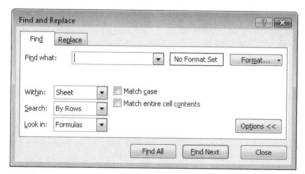

Figure 8-34 Use the Find tab to locate a character string.

Use the options on the Find tab in the following ways:

- **Find What** Type the string of characters you want to find. Be exact. Excel will find exactly what you type, including spaces—nothing more, nothing less.

- **Match Case** Distinguish capital letters from lowercase letters, finding only those occurrences that exactly match the uppercase and lowercase characters of the Find What string. If you leave this check box unselected, Excel disregards the differences between uppercase and lowercase letters.

- **Match Entire Cell Contents** Find only complete and individual occurrences of the string. Ordinarily, Find searches for any occurrence of a string, even if it is part of another string.

- **Within** Search only the active worksheet or the entire workbook.

- **Search** Search by rows or by columns. Ordinarily, your search will take place in the blink of an eye either way, but use this option if you have a large spreadsheet and have some clue where to look. When you select the By Rows option, Excel looks through the worksheet horizontally, row by row, starting with the currently selected cell. Select this option if you think the string is located to the right of the selected cell. The By Columns option searches through the worksheet column by column, beginning with the selected cell. Select this option if you think the string is below the selected cell.

- **Look In**   Choose formulas, values, or comments. When you click Formulas, Excel searches only in formulas. When you select Values, Excel searches any constant values as well as the displayed results of formulas. When you select Comments, Excel examines only text attached as a comment to a cell.

> **Note**
>
> If you want to search the entire workbook or worksheet to locate a string of characters (depending on the selection you make in the Within drop-down list), select a single cell before clicking the Find command. Office Excel 2007 begins its search from that cell and travels through the entire worksheet or workbook. To search only a portion of a worksheet, select the appropriate range before choosing Find.

The nuances of the Look In options, Formulas and Values, can be confusing. Remember that the underlying contents of a cell and the displayed value of that cell are often not the same. When using these options, you should keep in mind the following:

- If a cell contains a formula, the displayed value of the cell is usually the result of that formula.

- If a cell contains a numeric value, the displayed value of the formatted cell may or may not be the same as the cell's underlying value.

- If a cell displays a text value, it is probably the same as the underlying value, unless the cell contains a formula that uses text functions.

- If a cell has the General format, the displayed and underlying values of the cell are usually the same.

For example, if you type **1000** in the Find What text box and select Values as the Look In option, Excel looks at what is displayed in each cell. If you have an unformatted cell with the value 1000 in it, Excel finds it. If another cell has the same value formatted as currency ($1,000), Excel does not find it because the displayed value does not precisely match the Find What string. Because you're searching through values and not formulas, Excel ignores that the underlying content of the cell is 1000. If you select the Formulas option, Excel finds both instances, ignoring the formatting of the displayed values.

> **Note**
>
> If you close the Find And Replace dialog box and want to search for the next occurrence of the same string in your worksheet, you can press F4, the keyboard shortcut for repeating the last search action. You can also repeat your last search (even if you have performed other tasks since that search) by pressing Shift+F4.

Finding Formatting

Excel provides a way to find cells based on formatting in conjunction with other criteria, and even to find and replace specifically formatted cells, regardless of their content. If you click Format in the Find And Replace dialog box shown in Figure 8-35, the Find Format dialog box shown in Figure 8-36 appears. This dialog box has two names—Find Format and Replace Format—depending on whether you clicked the Format button that is adjacent to the Find What text box or the one adjacent to the Replace With text box on the Replace tab. Otherwise, the two dialog boxes are identical. You can select any number of options in this dialog box and, when you are finished, click OK to add them to your criteria.

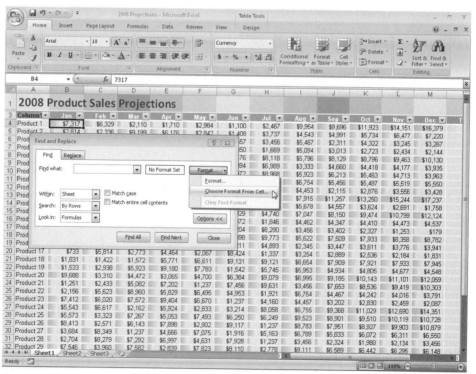

Figure 8-35 Click Choose Format From Cell to use the formatting of a selected cell as search criteria.

Figure 8-36 Click Format in the Find And Replace dialog box to display the Find Format dialog box.

If you click the arrow button next to the Format button to display the Format menu, you can click Choose Format From Cell, as shown in Figure 8-35. Choose Format From Cell is also available as a button at the bottom of the Find Format (or Replace Format) dialog box shown in Figure 8-36.

You'll find the 2008 New Projections.xlsx file in the Sample Files section of the companion CD.

When you click Choose Format From Cell, the Find Format (or Replace Format) dialog box disappears, and a small eyedropper appears next to the cursor. Click a cell that is formatted the way you want, and the Find And Replace dialog box reappears with the word *Preview** in the box that otherwise displays the message *No Format Set*. After you set your formatting criteria, Excel will not find the character strings you search for unless the formatting criteria also match. For example, if you search for the word *Sales* and specify bold type as a formatting criterion, Excel finds any cells containing the word *Sales* in bold type. Excel will find a cell containing the words *Sales Staff* with bold, italic, and underlined formatting because it contains both the word *Sales* and bold formatting, among other things. The more formatting options you set, the narrower the search. Select Clear Find Format in the Format drop-down list shown in Figure 8-35 to remove the formatting criteria.

Specifying Variables Using Wildcard Characters

You can use the wildcard characters ? and * to widen the scope of your searches. Wildcard characters are helpful when you're searching for a group of similar but not identical entries or when you're searching for an entry you don't quite remember. Use them as follows:

- The ? character takes the place of any single character in a Find What string. For example, the Find What string 100? matches the values 1000, 1001, 100A, 100B, and so on.

- The * character takes the place of zero or more characters in a Find What string. For example, the string 12* matches the entries 12, 120, 125, 1200000, and even 123 Maple Street.

You can use the wildcard characters anywhere within a Find What string. For example, you can use the string *s to find all entries that end with s. Alternatively, you can use the string *es* to find each cell that contains the string sequence *es* anywhere in its formula or value.

To search for a string that actually contains a wildcard character (? or *), type a tilde (~) preceding the character. For example, to find the string Who? (including the question mark), type **Who~?** as your Find What text.

Replacing What You Find

Replace works much like Find—in fact, they open the same dialog box. When you click Replace on the Find & Select menu on the Home tab (or press Ctrl+H), you see a dialog box like the one in Figure 8-37 (if yours looks different, click Options to expand the dialog box).

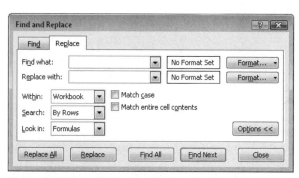

Figure 8-37 You can find and replace character strings and formats by clicking the Replace command on the Find & Select menu.

For example, to replace each occurrence of the name Joan Smith with John Smith, type **Joan Smith** in the Find What text box and **John Smith** in the Replace With text box. You can also find and replace formats using the dual Format buttons. For example, you could search for every occurrence of 14-point, bold, italic Times Roman and replace it with 12-point, double-underlined Arial.

To replace every occurrence of a string or formatting, click Replace All. Instead of pausing at each occurrence to let you change or skip the current cell, Excel locates all the cells containing the Find What string and replaces them.

Note

Although you can use wildcards in the Find What box to aid in your search, if you type wildcard characters in the Replace With box, Excel uses a literal ? or * symbol when it replaces each occurrence of your Find What text.

The Expanding Dialog Box

The Find And Replace dialog box does a neat trick. After you execute a search, the dialog box expands to list all the cells with contents that match your criteria:

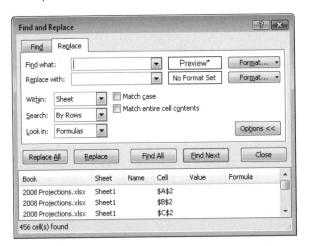

When you select an entry in the list, Excel jumps to that location and selects the cell. You can drag the bottom border of the dialog box to see more of the list. This feature makes it much easier to do extensive find-and-replace tasks because you can see the list at all times; because items remain in the list even after you execute a replacement operation; and because you can keep the dialog box open, change worksheets or workbooks, and utilize the Undo button while you work.

Getting the Words Right

Worksheets are not all numbers, of course, so Office Excel 2007 includes several features to help make typing and editing text easier. AutoCorrect helps you fix common typing errors even before they become spelling problems. For the rest of the words in your worksheets, the spelling checker helps make sure you've entered your text according to Webster. You might even be able to get AutoComplete to do some of the typing for you. And finally, the Research, Thesaurus, and Translate features lend some real clout in your quest for perfect prose.

Fixing Errors As You Type

Perhaps you have to stop and think "*i* before *e* except after *c*" every time you type *receive*. Perhaps you're a blazing typist who constantly hits the second letter of a capitalized word before the Shift key snaps back. The Excel AutoCorrect feature helps fix many common typing and spelling errors on the fly. Click the Microsoft Office Button, Excel Options, and in the Proofing category, click the AutoCorrect Options button to display the AutoCorrect dialog box shown in Figure 8-38.

> **Note**
>
> AutoCorrect works when entering text in cells, formulas, text boxes, on-worksheet controls, and chart labels. AutoCorrect does not work when entering text in dialog boxes.

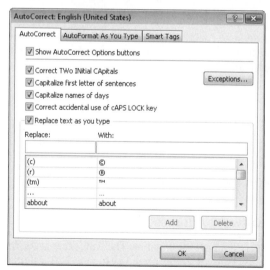

Figure 8-38 You can add your most common typing errors to the AutoCorrect dialog box.

Chapter 8

The AutoCorrect tab in the AutoCorrect dialog box contains the following options:

- **Show Auto Correct Options Buttons** Controls the display of the smart tag action menu when Excel detects an error, listing actions you can perform on the affected cell.

- **Correct TWo INitial CApitals** If a word contains both uppercase and lowercase characters, checks that only one capital letter appears at the beginning of the word. If not, Excel changes subsequent uppercase characters to lowercase. If a word is all caps, Excel leaves it alone (assuming that this was intentional). Auto-Correct does not attempt to modify "mid-cap" words like AutoCorrect, probably because of their increasing usage.

- **Capitalize First Letter Of Sentences** Makes sure you use "sentence case" (even if your sentences aren't grammatically correct), based on the position of periods.

- **Capitalize Names Of Days** Recognizes days and applies initial caps. This does not work on abbreviations like Sat.

- **Correct Accidental Use Of cAPS LOCK Key** Scans for this kind of random Shift-key mistake.

- **Replace Text As You Type** Controls the application of the replacement list at the bottom of the dialog box, which lists a number of common replacement items. You can add your own grammatical faux pas to this list using the Replace and With text boxes and the Add button.

In addition to correcting common typing errors such as replacing *adn* with *and*, Auto-Correct also provides a few useful shortcuts in its replacement list. For example, instead of searching for the right font and symbol to add a copyright mark, you can type **(c)**, and AutoCorrect replaces it with ©.

All these AutoCorrect options use specific rules of order. They use similar, logical methods to determine your real meaning. But don't assume that AutoCorrect (or the spelling checker) knows what you mean. Always proofread important work.

> **Note**
> If you have other Microsoft Office programs installed, anything you add to the AutoCorrect list in Excel will also appear in other Office programs' AutoCorrect lists.

Typing Internet and Network Addresses

We like to refer to this feature as AutoAutoFormat. The AutoFormat As You Type tab in the AutoCorrect dialog box (shown in Figure 8-33 on page 220) offers the Internet And Network Paths With Hyperlinks option under Replace As You Type. This converts a string recognized as a valid uniform resource locator (URL) or network path into an active hyperlink. As you finish typing it, you can click it immediately to go there.

For more about formatting as you type, see "Extending Existing Formatting" on page 219.

Using Custom AutoCorrect Smart Tags

The Smart Tags tab in the AutoCorrect dialog box shown in Figure 8-39 is the repository for customized smart tags. Excel comes with several of them, and you can download additional smart tags as they become available on the Microsoft Office Online Web site (*http://office.microsoft.com/*).

Figure 8-39 The Smart Tags tab in the AutoCorrect dialog box is the control center for all your smart tag needs.

The following smart tag options are available in the AutoCorrect dialog box:

- **Recognizers** Describes the currently installed smart tags in terms of what they look for as you type and includes items such as Date, Financial Symbol, Person Name (e-mail recipient), Telephone Number, and Time. Figure 8-40 shows the smart tag action menus for Financial Symbols and Person Name.

- **Check Workbook** Applies the selected recognizers to existing data in your workbook, letting you add smart tags to existing workbooks. If you do, you need to select the Embed Smart Tags In This Workbook check box.

- **More Smart Tags** Adds custom recognizers found on the Office Update Web site to the Recognizers list. You'll need to be connected to the Internet.

- **Show Smart Tags As** Displays smart tags. Select Indicator And Button (the default), Button Only, or None. Smart tags ordinarily appear as a small triangle in the lower-right corner of the cell (the indicator); in addition, an icon appears when you rest your pointer on the cell (the button).

- **Embed Smart Tags In This Workbook** Permanently attaches smart tags to previously recognized data.

- **Properties** Tells you more about the smart tag you selected in the Recognizers list. You'll need to be connected to the Internet for this one.

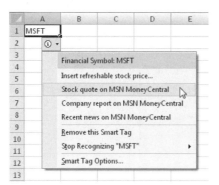
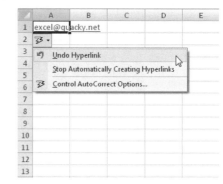

Figure 8-40 Excel includes built-in custom smart tag action menus for stock-ticker symbols and e-mail addresses, among other types of data.

Letting Excel Help with Typing Chores

Often when entering a large amount data in one sitting, you end up typing the same entries repeatedly. The AutoComplete feature cuts down the amount of typing you need to do. It also increases the accuracy of your entries by partially automating them. AutoComplete is on by default, but you can turn it off by clicking the Microsoft Office Button, Excel Options, and the Advanced category and then clearing the Enable Auto-Complete For Cell Values check box in the Editing Options area.

When you begin typing a cell entry, AutoComplete scans all the entries in the same column and, as each character is typed, determines whether the column contains a possible match. (This works only when you are typing in a cell adjacent to other entries.) For example, in Figure 8-41, as soon as we typed **Y** in cell A14, AutoComplete finished the entry with the unique match found in the same column: Young, Rob. The text added by AutoComplete is highlighted, so you can either continue typing, if that wasn't your intended entry, or press Enter or an arrow key to accept the completion and move to another cell.

AutoComplete matches only exact cell entries, not individual words in a cell. For example, if you begin typing **Tony** in column A of the worksheet, AutoCorrect doesn't intervene, because it is not an exact match for any existing entry. Wisely, AutoComplete does not work when you're editing formulas.

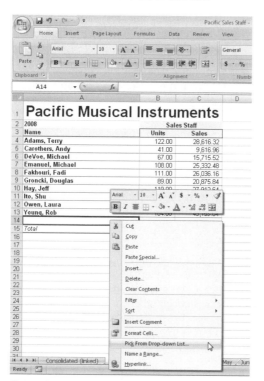

Figure 8-41 Type enough letters to match an existing entry, and AutoComplete finishes it for you. As shown on the right, keep typing to override AutoComplete.

Instead of typing, you can click Pick From Drop-Down List on the shortcut menu to select an existing entry from the same column. To do so, right-click a cell, and click Pick From Drop-Down List in the shortcut menu, as shown in Figure 8-42. After Excel displays the list, click the entry you want, and Excel enters it in the cell. Of course, you can't add new entries this way, as we did in Figure 8-41; only existing entries in the same column are available in the list.

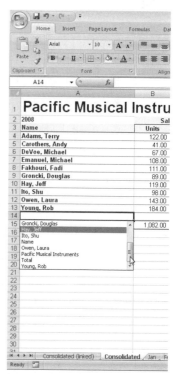

Figure 8-42 Right-click the cell directly below a list, and click Pick From Drop-Down List to display a list of unique entries in the column.

INSIDE OUT   Create Your Own Typing Shorthand

You can use AutoCorrect to monitor your own common typing errors and create your own typing shortcuts. Click the Microsoft Office Button, Excel Options, and then click the AutoCorrect Options button in the Proofing category. Add your shorthand entries in the Replace Text As You Type area on the AutoCorrect tab. (Figure 8-38 on page 227 shows the AutoCorrect dialog box.) Type the characters you want to use as the shorthand "code" in the Replace box, then type the characters with which you want to replace them in the With box, and finally click Add. For example, you can type **MS** in the Replace box and then type **Microsoft Corporation** in the With box. Thereafter, each time you type **MS**, Excel replaces it with the words *Microsoft Corporation*. Make sure you choose unique codes; otherwise, Excel might apply AutoCorrect to entries you don't want changed.

Cheking Yer Speling

Click the Review tab on the Ribbon, and then click Spelling to check the spelling of an entire worksheet or any part of it. If Excel finds any suspect words, the Spelling dialog box shown in Figure 8-43 appears. Keep the following tips in mind when using the spelling checker:

- If you select a single cell, Excel checks the entire worksheet, including all cells, comments, Excel graphic objects, and page headers and footers.

- If you select more than one cell, Excel checks the selected cells only.

- If the formula bar is active, Excel checks only its contents.

- If you select words that are within the formula bar, Excel checks the selected words only.

- If the range you select for checking the spelling contains hidden or outlined cells that are not visible, Excel checks these as well.

- Cells that contain formulas are not checked.

Click Options in the Spelling dialog box to display the Excel Options dialog box. Click the Proofing category, shown in Figure 8-44. Here you can access the AutoCorrect dialog box, choose dictionaries in different languages, and select special options such as the Ignore Internet And File Addresses check box.

> **Note**
> You can press F7 to instantly begin checking the spelling.

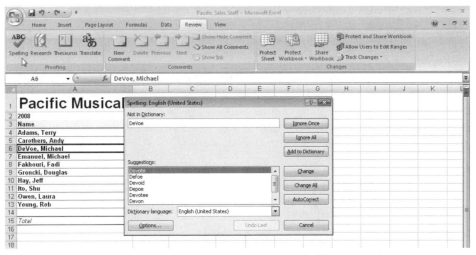

Figure 8-43 Use the Spelling dialog box to review your text and add often-used words to your dictionary.

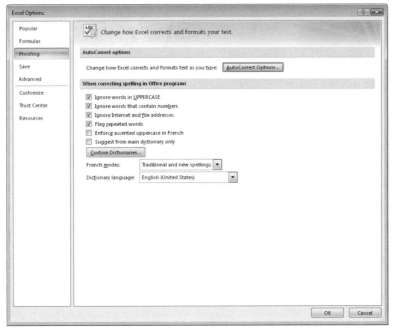

Figure 8-44 Gain more control over spelling with the Proofing tab in the Excel Options dialog box.

Chapter 8

Research Resources

Besides Spelling, the other three buttons in the Proofing group on the Review tab—Research, Thesaurus, and Translate—provide some real horsepower when you are ready to invest time in the word play accompanying your numeric adventures. Perhaps Excel is not the most efficient way to *learn* a foreign language, but the Translate feature is certainly intriguing, especially if you work with international customers or co-workers. Clicking any of these three buttons displays a task pane docked to the right side of the screen, as shown in Figure 8-45. Note that only the Research button is a toggle—clicking it a second time closes the task pane. The other two buttons change what appears within the task pane.

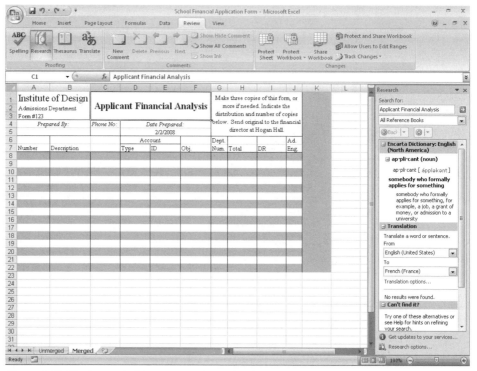

Figure 8-45 The Research, Thesaurus, and Translate buttons on the Review tab open a task pane.

The cell or range selected when you open the task pane automatically appears in the Search For box when you click one of the buttons, and any search results appear in the main area of the task pane. If you already have the task pane open and you want to change the search text, you can either type it or press Alt while clicking a cell containing the text you want, which then appears in the Search For box.

The second box under Search For is a drop-down list that lets you narrow your search to particular resources, as shown in Figure 8-46. Note, however, that when you click the Research button on the Ribbon, the default search is All Reference Books, which also includes the results that would be returned by clicking Thesaurus or Translate. If you scroll to the bottom of the search results, you'll find these categories, plus a Can't Find It? category, offering additional options. As you try different searches in the task pane, click the Back and Next buttons (a.k.a. Previous Search and Next Search) to peruse the various search results.

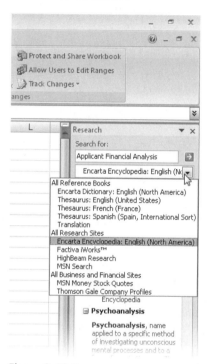

Figure 8-46 You can narrow your search to use specific resources.

You can alter the contents of the drop-down list shown in Figure 8-46 by clicking Research Options, located at the bottom of the task pane, which displays the Research Options dialog box shown in Figure 8-47. Here you can add or remove places to look from the list, update the available options, and specify parental controls, if you are logged on as an administrator. For details on a particular service, select it, and click the Properties button.

At the bottom of the task pane is a Get Updates To Your Services link, which connects you to the Microsoft Office Online Web site where Excel then checks to see whether there are any updates to existing services or any new services available that you can add to your research options.

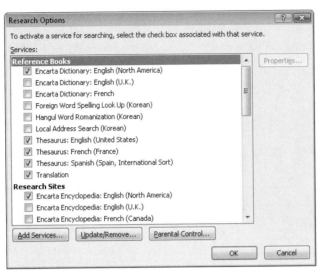

Figure 8-47 Specify the research resources available using the Research Options dialog box.

INSIDE OUT   Task Pane Tricks

You can reposition or resize the task pane by clicking the small arrow next to the Close button and choosing the appropriate command. Clicking the Move command changes the cursor to a four-headed arrow, letting you drag the task pane away from its "docked" position on the right side of the screen. You can let it float above the workspace or dock it on the left side if you prefer. After clicking the Size command, drag the mouse (you don't even need to click) to reposition the border of the task pane to make it wider, up to half the screen width when docked. Click when the size of the task pane is to your liking.

In actuality, you don't need these commands at all. You can drag a task pane away from the dock by its title bar at any time without using the Move command, just as you can drag the inside border of a docked task pane without using the Size command. You can drag the borders of the undocked task pane with impunity, making it as large as you like. To restore a floating task pane to its previous docked configuration, double-click its title bar. To remove a task pane from view, click the Close button in the upper-right corner of the task pane.

Editing Multiple Worksheets

If you need to create a bunch of similar worksheets, Office Excel 2007 helps you save some clicks and keystrokes. For example, if the workbook you're creating calls for a separate worksheet for each month, division, product, or whatever, you can save a lot of time by creating them all at once using the techniques described in this section and then tweak each worksheet as needed.

For information about moving and copying worksheets to other workbooks, see "Dragging Worksheets Between Workbooks" on page 150. For more information about formatting, see Chapter 9, "Worksheet Formatting Techniques."

Grouping Worksheets for Editing

You can group any number of worksheets in a workbook and then add, edit, or format data in all the worksheets in the group at the same time. Use this feature when you're creating or modifying a set of worksheets that are similar in purpose and structure—a set of monthly reports or departmental budgets, for example.

You can select and group worksheets using one of these methods:

- Click the sheet tab of the first worksheet in a range of adjacent worksheets you want to work on, hold down Shift, and click the tab of the last worksheet in the range.

- Click the tab of any of the worksheets you want to work on, hold down Ctrl, and click the tabs of each worksheet you want to include in the group, whether or not the worksheets are adjacent.

- Right-click a sheet tab, and click Select All Sheets on the shortcut menu.

Let's go through the procedure of creating a workbook containing a separate worksheet for each month, starting with a blank workbook:

1. Click the Sheet1 tab, hold down Shift, and then click the Sheet3 tab. The worksheets are now grouped, as shown in Figure 8-48. Notice that the title bar of the workbook displays [Group] after the worksheet name, and all three sheet tabs are white.

2. Right-click any of the selected tabs, and click Move Or Copy on the shortcut menu. In the Before Sheet list in the dialog box that appears, select Move To End. Select the Create A Copy check box, and then click OK. Excel creates three new worksheets, as shown in Figure 8-49.

3. Right-click any tab, and click Select All Sheets on the shortcut menu; then repeat step 2 to create 12 worksheets.

> **Note**
>
> The easiest way to create new, blank worksheets is to click the Insert Worksheet tab, the last sheet tab on the right, which creates a new numbered worksheet. The technique described here is especially useful when you want to create copies of existing worksheets containing data.

Chapter 8

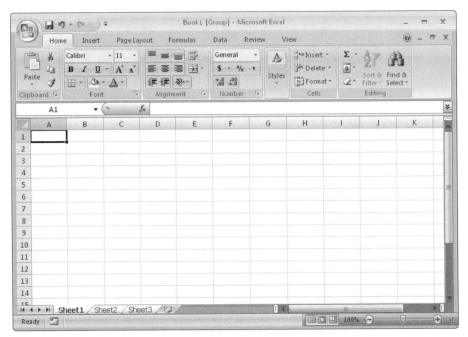

Figure 8-48 The three worksheets are grouped.

4. Rename the worksheets by double-clicking each tab and typing a new name. We used the month abbreviations Jan through Dec.

5. Group all 12 worksheets by selecting their tabs, as shown in step 1. Now, any entries or formatting changes you make in any one of the worksheets is duplicated in all the worksheets in the group.

6. Enter and apply formats as shown in Figure 8-50.

7. When you finish all the entries, common formulas, and formatting, click any worksheet to ungroup, and then make edits to individual worksheets, such as adding each month name and entering units and sales data.

 You'll find the Pacific Brass Sales.xlsx file in the Sample Files section of the companion CD.

You can add formatting, formulas, or any other data to the active worksheet in a group, and Excel modifies all member worksheets simultaneously. Excel transfers any changes you make to column width, row height, view options such as gridlines and scroll bars, and even the location of the active cell to the group.

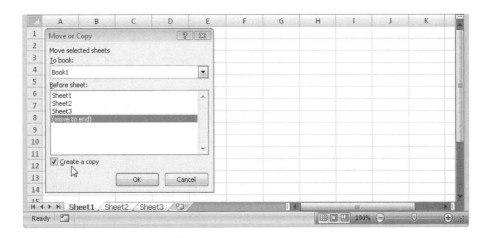

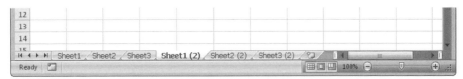

Figure 8-49 Copying a group of worksheets creates the same number of new worksheets.

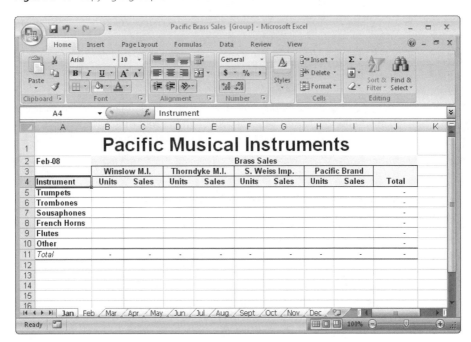

Figure 8-50 With group editing, Excel applies all edits and formats to all the worksheets.

Chapter 8

INSIDE OUT   Group-Editing Tricks

When you group several worksheets and then click one of the worksheets in the group with the intention of editing it individually, you're still in group-editing mode, possibly making inadvertent changes to all your grouped worksheets. Keep your eye on the tabs—when they are white, they are all editable. Getting out of group-editing mode works differently, depending on how many worksheets you have grouped.

If you have grouped all the worksheets in a workbook, clicking any tab except that of the active worksheet exits group-editing mode and removes the [Group] indicator from the title bar of the workbook. However, if you have selected some but not all of the worksheets in a workbook, clicking any other grouped sheet tab makes that worksheet active but does not exit group-editing mode. In this case, click any tab *outside* the group to exit group-editing mode.

Besides using the Move Or Copy command to rearrange and duplicate worksheets in a workbook, you can also use the mouse to perform the same actions directly. Select a group and drag to move it to a different location. The cursor changes to include a little pad of paper, as shown here (top):

To copy a group of worksheets, drag the group, and then press Ctrl before releasing the mouse button. The little pad of paper appears with a plus sign inside it, as shown here (bottom). You can also drag grouped worksheets from one open workbook to another.

What You Can Do in Group-Editing Mode

Use the Excel group-editing feature to perform the following actions on all member worksheets simultaneously:

- **Entering Text** This duplicates what you type in one worksheet in all grouped worksheets.

- **Printing** Using the Print, Print Preview, and Page Setup commands on the Microsoft Office Button affects every worksheet in your group.

- **Viewing** On the View tab, the Zoom, Workbook Views, Show/Hide, and Window options apply to all the selected worksheets.

- **Formatting** This applies any changes to all group members at the same time. Changing row height and column width and applying font formats, Conditional Formatting, and Style options affect all worksheets. You can even click View, Hide to hide all grouped worksheets.

- **Editing** This applies all editing actions including entering formulas, inserting rows and columns, and using Find and Replace to all worksheets in the group.

- **Page Layout** On the Page Layout tab, changes made to Themes, Page Setup options, Scale To Fit, and most Sheet Options apply to the group.

- **Inserting Headers and Footers** Using the Header & Footer command on the Insert tab applies to every worksheet in the group.

Filling a Group

If you aren't starting from scratch but want to duplicate existing data in one worksheet to a number of other worksheets in a workbook, you can click the Across Worksheets command, located on the Fill menu in the Editing group on the Home tab. This option is available only if you first establish a group. When you click this option, Excel displays the Fill Across Worksheets dialog box shown in Figure 8-51.

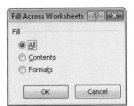

Figure 8-51 Use the Fill Across Worksheets dialog box to copy selected data to all the worksheets in a group.

For example, to copy all the text and formatting of the worksheet shown in Figure 8-50 to all the other grouped worksheets in the workbook (if we hadn't already done that using group-editing mode), we could select the range A1:J110 and then click Fill, Across Worksheets. With the All option selected, Excel transfers all text, formulas, and formatting to every other worksheet in the group. If you select the Contents option, Excel duplicates only text and values; the Formatting option predictably duplicates only the formats. Filling across worksheets does not apply row height, column width, or view options.

Auditing and Documenting Worksheets

Office Excel 2007 has a number of powerful and flexible features that help you audit and debug your worksheets and document your work. Most of the Excel auditing features appear on the Formulas tab in the Formula Auditing group, which is shown in Figure 8-52.

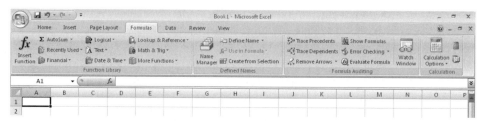

Figure 8-52 The Formula Auditing group on the Formulas tab provides access to most of the Excel 2007 auditing features.

Checking for Errors

Error Checking

Click the Error Checking button to quickly find any error values displayed on the current worksheet and display the Error Checking dialog box, as shown in Figure 8-53. The first erroneous cell in the worksheet is selected, and its contents are displayed in the dialog box, along with a suggestion about the nature of the problem.

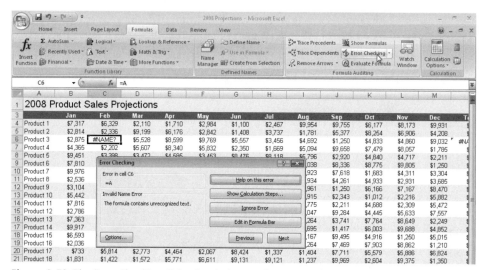

Figure 8-53 The Error Checking dialog box helps you figure out what's wrong with formulas that display error values.

When your problem appears in the dialog box, the following selections are available:

- **Help On This Error** displays a Help topic relating to the problem cell.

- **Show Calculation Steps** displays the Evaluate Formula dialog box. See "Evaluating and Auditing Formulas" on the next page.

- **Ignore Error** skips the selected cell. To "unignore" errors, click Options, and then click Reset Ignored Errors.

- **Edit In Formula Bar** opens the selected cell in the formula bar for editing. When you're finished, click Resume (the Help On This Error button changes to Resume).

Click the Previous and Next buttons to locate additional errors on the current worksheet. Click the Options button to display the Formulas category in the Excel Options dialog box, shown in Figure 8-54. Select or clear the check boxes in the two Error Checking areas to determine the type of errors to look for and the way they are processed. Click the Reset Ignored Errors button if you want to recheck or if you clicked the Ignore Error button in the Error Checking dialog box by mistake.

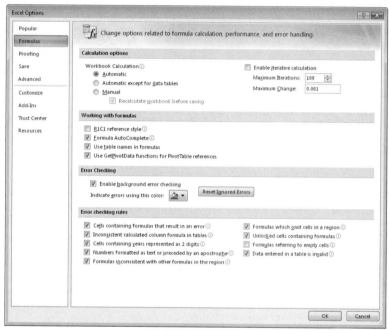

Figure 8-54 Click Options in the Error Checking dialog box to specify error-checking rules.

Evaluating and Auditing Formulas

Evaluate Formula

Sometimes it's difficult to tell what's going on in a complex nested formula. A formula is *nested* when parts of it (called *arguments*) can be calculated separately. For example, in the formula =IF(Pay_Num<>"",Scheduled_Monthly_Payment,""), the named reference Pay_Num indicates a cell that must contain a value in order for the rest of the formula to function. To make this formula easier to read, you can substitute this expression with its result—in this case, 1 (indicating that the expression is TRUE). The formula would then be =IF(1<>"",Scheduled_Monthly_Payment,"").

When you click the Evaluate Formula button on the Formulas tab, you can resolve each nested expression one at a time in complex formulas. Figure 8-55 shows the Evaluate Formula dialog box in action.

For more information about formulas and arguments, see Chapter 12, "Building Formulas."

Click Evaluate to replace each calculable argument with its resulting value. You can click Evaluate as many times as necessary, depending on how many nested levels exist in the selected formula. For example, if you click Evaluate in Figure 8-55, Excel replaces the aforementioned Pay_Num reference with its value. Clicking Evaluate again calculates the next level, and so on, until you reach the end result, which in this case is $188.71, as shown in Figure 8-56.

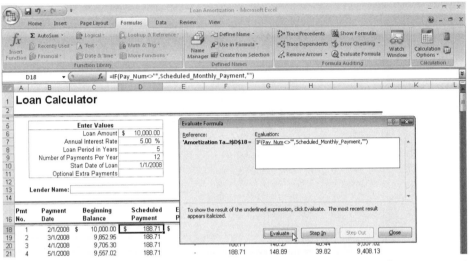

Figure 8-55 Click the Evaluate Formula button on the Formulas tab to systematically inspect nested formulas.

You'll find the Loan Amortization.xlsm file in the Sample Files section of the companion CD.

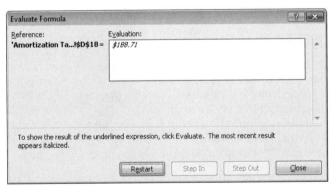

Figure 8-56 Each time you click the Evaluate button, Excel calculates another nested level in the selected formula.

Eventually, clicking Evaluate results in the formula's displayed value, and the Evaluate button changes to Restart, letting you repeat the steps. Click Step In to separate each calculable reference into separate boxes, making the hierarchy more apparent. In our example, the first evaluated reference is to a cell range, which cannot be further evaluated. If the reference is to a cell containing another formula, its address appears in the Evaluate Formula dialog box, as shown in Figure 8-57. Where there are no more steps to be displayed, click Step Out to close the Step In box and replace the reference with the resulting value.

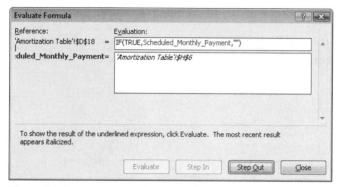

Figure 8-57 Use Step In and Step Out to display calculable arguments separately.

Watching Formulas

Sometimes you might want to keep an eye on a formula as you make changes to other parts of a worksheet, or even when working on other workbooks that supply information to a worksheet. Instead of constantly having to return to the formula's location to see the results of your ministrations, you can use the Watch Window, which provides remote viewing for any cell on any open worksheet.

Select a cell you want to keep an eye on, and click Watch Window on the Formulas tab. Then click Add Watch in the Watch Window, as shown in Figure 8-58.

You can click a cell you want to watch either before or after you display the Add Watch dialog box. Click Add to insert the cell information in the Watch Window. You can dock the Watch Window, as shown in Figure 8-59. You can change its size by dragging its borders or dragging it away from its docked position.

While your workbook is still open, you can select any item in the Watch Window list and delete it by clicking Delete Watch. The Watch Window button is a toggle—click it again to close the window; or click the Close button at the top of the Watch Window. When you close a workbook, Excel removes any watched cells the workbook contains from the Watch Window list.

Tracing Cell References

If you've ever looked at a large worksheet and wondered how you could get an idea of the data flow—that is, how the formulas and values relate to one another—you'll appreciate *cell tracers*. You can also use cell tracers to help find the source of those pesky errors that occasionally appear in your worksheets. The Formula Auditing group on the Formulas tab contains three buttons that control the cell tracers: Trace Precedents, Trace Dependents, and Remove Arrows.

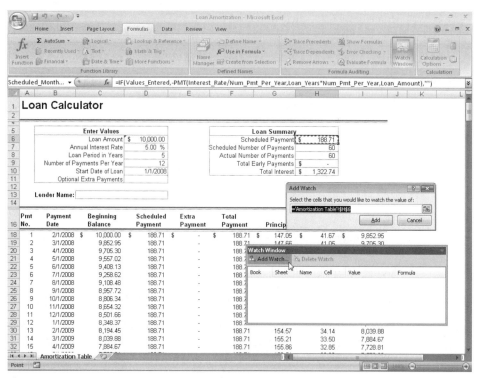

Figure 8-58 Select a cell, and click Watch Window to keep an eye on it, no matter where you are currently working.

INSIDE OUT   Understanding Precedents and Dependents

The terms *precedent* and *dependent* crop up quite often in this section. They refer to the relationships that cells containing formulas create with other cells. A lot of what a spreadsheet is all about is wrapped up in these concepts, so here's a brief description of each term:

- *Precedents* are cells whose values are used by the formula in the selected cell. A cell that has precedents always contains a formula.

- *Dependents* are cells that use the value in the selected cell. A cell that has dependents can contain either a formula or a constant value.

For example, if the formula =SUM(A1:A5) is in cell A6, cell A6 has precedents (A1:A5) but no apparent dependents. Cell A1 has a dependent (A6) but no apparent precedents. A cell can be both a precedent and a dependent if the cell contains a formula and is also referenced by another formula.

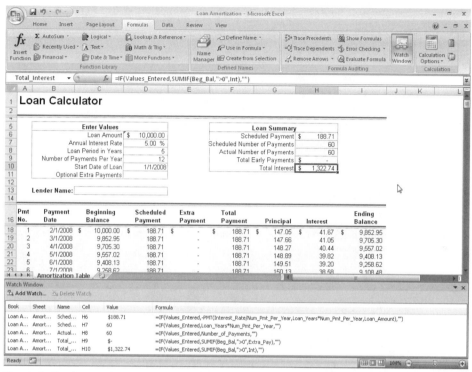

Figure 8-59 The Watch Window displays all the current information for the watched formula.

Tracing Dependent Cells

 In the worksheet in Figure 8-60, we selected cell B2, which contains the hourly rate value. To find out which cells contain formulas that use this value, click the Trace Dependents button. Although this worksheet is elementary to make it easier to illustrate the cell tracers, consider the ramifications of using the cell tracers in a large and complex worksheet.

 You'll find the Audit.xlsx file in the Sample Files section of the companion CD.

The tracer arrows indicate that cell B2 is directly referred to by the formulas in cells C5, C6, C7, and C8. If you click Trace Dependents again, another set of arrows appears, indicating the next level of dependencies—or *indirect* dependents. Figure 8-61 shows the results.

One handy feature of the tracer arrows is that you can use them to navigate, which can be advantageous in a large worksheet. For example, in Figure 8-61 with cell B2 still selected, double-click the arrow pointing from cell B2 to cell C8. The selection jumps to the other end of the arrow, and cell C8 becomes the active cell. Now if you double-click the arrow pointing from cell C8 to cell E8, the selection jumps to cell E8. If you double-click the same again, the selection jumps back to cell C8. If you double-click an arrow that extends beyond the screen, the window shifts to display the cell at the other end. You can use this feature to jump from cell to cell along a path of precedents and dependents.

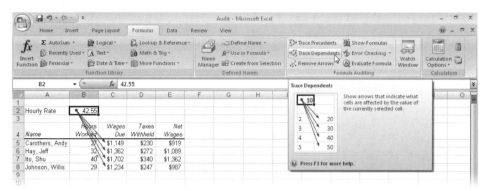

Figure 8-60 When you trace dependents, arrows point to formulas that directly refer to the selected cell.

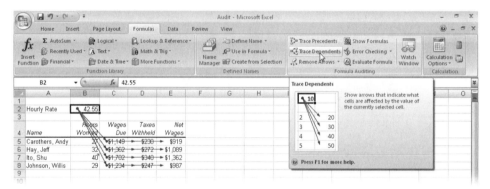

Figure 8-61 When you click Trace Dependents again, arrows point to the next level of formulas, ones that indirectly refer to the selected cell.

Clearing Tracer Arrows

 As you trace precedents or dependents, your screen quickly becomes cluttered, making it difficult to discern the data flow for particular cells. To remove all the tracer arrows from the screen, click the Remove Arrows button in the Formula Auditing group. Alternatively, you can click the small downward-pointing arrow next to the Remove Arrows button to display the Remove Arrows menu, where you can be more selective, using Remove Precedent Arrows or Remove Dependent Arrows.

Tracing Precedent Cells

 You can also trace in the opposite direction by starting from a cell that contains a formula and tracing the cells that are referred to in the formula. In Figure 8-62, we selected cell E5, which contains one of the net wages formulas, and then clicked Trace Precedents twice to show the complete precedent path.

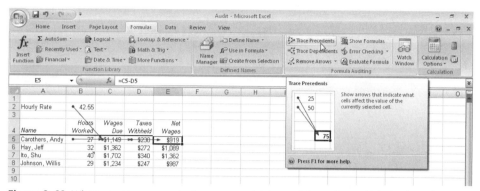

Figure 8-62 When you trace precedents, arrows point from all the cells to which the formula in the selected cell directly refers.

This time, arrows appears with dots in cells B2, B5, C5, and D5, indicating that all these cells are precedents to the selected cell. Notice that the arrows still point in the same direction—toward the formula and in the direction of the data flow—even though we started from the opposite end of the path.

Tracing Errors

Suppose your worksheet displays error values like the ones shown in Figure 8-63. To trace one of these errors to its source, select a cell that contains an error, and click Trace Error, located on the Error Checking menu in the Formula Auditing group on the Formulas tab, as shown in Figure 8-53 on page 242.

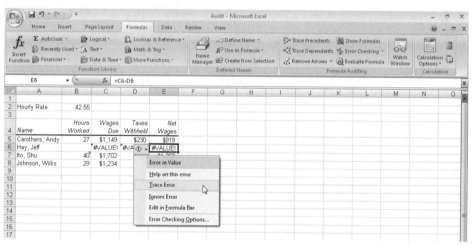

Figure 8-63 Cells with error values display smart tag action menus.

Notice that the cells containing errors display smart tag indicators in their upper-left corners, as shown in Figure 8-63, and when you select one of them, the smart tag action menu appears. The smart tag action menu displays applicable options, including Trace Error, as shown in Figure 8-64.

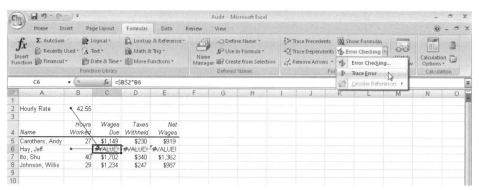

Figure 8-64 Select a cell that contains an error value, and click Trace Error to display arrows that trace the error to its source.

Excel selects the cell that contains the first formula in the error chain and draws red arrows from that cell to the cell you selected. Excel draws blue arrows to the cell that contains the first erroneous formula from the values the formula uses. It's up to you to determine the reason for the error; Excel takes you to the source formula and shows you the precedents. In our example, the error is caused by a space character inadvertently entered in cell B6, replacing the hours-worked figure. This is a common, vexing problem, because cells containing space characters appear to be empty, but a truly empty cell would not have produced an error in this case.

Tracing References to Other Worksheets

If a cell contains a reference to a different worksheet or to a worksheet in another workbook, a dashed tracer arrow appears with a small icon attached, as shown in Figure 8-65. You cannot continue to trace precedents using the same procedure from the active cell when a dashed tracer arrow appears.

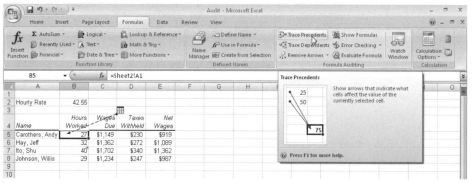

Figure 8-65 If you trace the precedents of a cell that contains a reference to another worksheet or workbook, a special tracer arrow appears.

If you double-click a dashed tracer arrow, the Go To dialog box appears, with the reference displayed in the Go To list. You can select the reference in the list and click OK to activate the worksheet or workbook. However, if the reference is to another workbook that is not currently open, an error message appears.

Adding Comments to Cells

Someday, someone else might need to use your workbooks, so it's good to be clear and to explain everything thoroughly. You can attach comments to cells to document your work, explain calculations and assumptions, or provide reminders. Select the cell you want to annotate, and click the New Comment button in the Comments group on the Review tab (the button changes to Edit Comment after you click it). Then type your message in the box that appears, as shown in Figure 8-66.

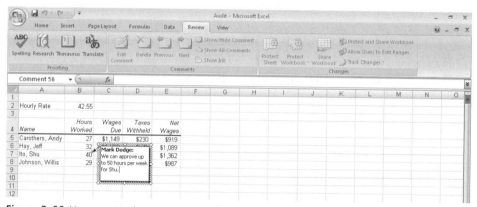

Figure 8-66 You can attach comments to cells to help document your worksheet.

When you add a comment to a cell, your name appears in bold type at the top of the comment box. You can specify what appears here by clicking the Microsoft Office Button, Excel Options and in the Personalize category typing your name (or any other text) in the User Name box. Whatever you type here appears at the top of the comment box, followed by a colon. Although you can attach only one comment to a cell, you can make your comment as long as you like. If you want to begin a new paragraph in the comment box, press Enter. When you're finished, you can drag the handles to resize the comment box.

> **Note**
>
> Ordinarily, a small red triangle appears in the upper-right corner of a cell, indicating the presence of a comment. When you rest the pointer on a cell displaying this comment indicator, the comment appears. To control the display of comments, click the Microsoft Office Button, Excel Options and then the Advanced category. In the Display area, select one of the options under For Cells With Comments, Show.

Tweaking Your Comments

After you've added text to your comments, nothing is set in stone. You can work with comments using the buttons in the Comments group on the Review tab:

- **New Comment/Edit Comment** Click this button to add a comment to the selected cell. If the selected cell already contains a comment, this button changes to Edit Comment, which opens the comment for editing.

- **Previous and Next** Click these buttons to open each comment in the workbook for editing, one at a time. Even if your comments appear on several worksheets in the same workbook, these buttons let you jump directly to each one in succession without using the sheet tabs.

- **Show/Hide Comment** Click this button to display (rather than open for editing) the comment in the selected cell. This button changes to Hide Comment if the comment is currently displayed.

- **Show All Comments** Click this button to display all the comments on the worksheet at once.

- **Delete** Click this button to remove comments from all selected cells.

- **Show Ink** Click this button to show or hide any ink annotations (Tablet PC only).

Printing Comments

To print comments, follow these steps:

1. Click the Page Layout tab on the Ribbon, and click the Dialog Box Launcher in the Page Setup group (the little icon to the right of the group name).

2. Click the sheet tab, and select one of the options in the Comments drop-down list.

   The At End Of Sheet option prints all the comments in text form after the worksheet is printed. The As Displayed On Sheet option prints comments as they appear on the screen (as text boxes) if you display all the comments at once on the worksheet. Be careful, however, because comments printed this way can obscure some contents of the worksheet; and if your comments are clustered together, they might overlap.

3. Click the Print button in the Page Setup dialog box to display the Print dialog box, where you can select additional options before sending your worksheet to the printer.

For more information about printing, see Chapter 11, "Printing and Presenting."

Outlining Worksheets

Many typical spreadsheet models are built in a hierarchical fashion. For example, in a monthly sales worksheet, you might have a column for each month of the year, followed by a totals column, which depends on the numbers in the month columns. You can set up the rows of data hierarchically, with groups of expense categories contributing to category totals. Office Excel 2007 can turn worksheets of this kind into outlines.

Figure 8-67 shows a table of sales figures before outlining, and Figure 8-68 shows the same worksheet after outlining. To accomplish this, we selected cell B3 in the table (any cell would do), clicked the Group menu on the Data tab, and clicked Auto Outline, as shown in Figure 8-67. (To outline a specific range, select the area before choosing Auto Outline.) Figure 8-68 shows how you can change the level of detail displayed after you outline a worksheet.

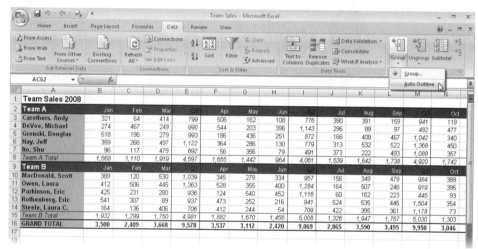

Figure 8-67 Start with a hierarchical worksheet like this one.

You'll find the Team Sales.xlsx file in the Sample Files section of the companion CD.

The difference between the outlined worksheets in Figure 8-68 and Figure 8-69 is that the columns and rows listing the months and individual team members are hidden in Figure 8-69. Without outlining, you would have to hide each group of columns and rows manually; with outlining, you can collapse the outline to change the level of detail instantly. To restore the worksheet to its original state, click Clear Outline, located on the Ungroup menu on the Data tab, as shown in Figure 8-68.

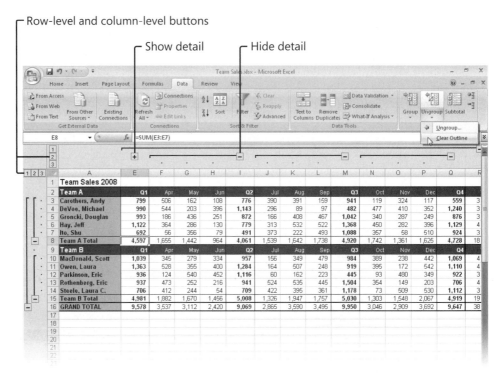

Figure 8-68 Make the worksheet hierarchies collapsible using the Excel outlining features.

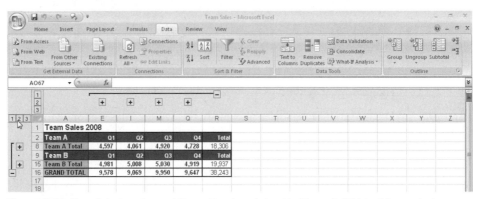

Figure 8-69 Two clicks transformed the outlined worksheet in Figure 8-68 into this quarterly overview.

Outlining a Worksheet with Nonstandard Layout

The standard outline settings reflect the most common worksheet layout. To change these settings, click the Dialog Box Launcher (the little icon to the right of the group name) in the Outline group on the Data tab to display the Settings dialog box shown in Figure 8-70. If your worksheet layout is not typical, such as a worksheet constructed with rows of SUM formulas (or other types of summarization formulas) in rows above the detail rows or with columns of formulas to the left of detail columns, clear the appropriate Direction check box—Summary Rows Below Detail or Summary Columns To Right Of Detail—before outlining.

Figure 8-70 Use the Settings dialog box to adjust for a nonstandard layout.

When you use nonstandard worksheet layouts, be sure the area you want to outline is consistent to avoid unpredictable and possibly incorrect results; that is, be sure all summary formulas appear in the same direction relative to the detail data. After you select or clear one or both Direction options, click the Create button to create the outline.

Extending the Outline to New Worksheet Areas

At times, you might create an outline and then add more data to your worksheet. You might also want to re-create an outline if you change the organization of a specific worksheet area. To include new columns and rows in your outline, repeat the procedure you followed to create the outline in the first place: Select a cell in the new area, and click Auto Outline.

INSIDE OUT   **Just Say No to Automatic Styles**

In the Settings dialog box, the Automatic Styles check box and the Apply Styles button apply rudimentary font formats to your outline that help distinguish totals from detail data. Unfortunately, this isn't very effective. To ensure that the outline is formatted the way you want, you should plan to apply formats manually.

Hiding an Outline

When you outline a worksheet, Excel displays symbols above and to the left of the row and column headings (refer to Figure 8-68). These symbols take up screen space, so if you want to suppress them, you can click the Microsoft Office Button, Excel Options; then click the Advanced category, and clear the Show Outline Symbols If An Outline Is Applied check box in the Display Options For This Worksheet area.

Chapter 8

Collapsing and Expanding Outline Levels

Show Detail

Hide Detail

When you create an outline, the areas above and to the left of your worksheet are marked by one or more brackets that terminate in hide detail symbols, which have minus signs on them. The brackets are called *level bars*. Each level bar indicates a range of cells that share a common outline level. The hide detail symbols appear above or to the left of each level's summary column or row. If you have hidden the outline symbols or if you prefer to use the Ribbon, you can also use the Show Detail and Hide Detail buttons in the Outline group on the Data tab to collapse and expand your outline.

To collapse an outline level so only the summary cells show, click that level's hide detail symbol. For example, if you no longer need to see the sales numbers for January through November in the outlined worksheet (refer to Figure 8-68), click the hide detail symbols above columns E, I, and M. The worksheet then looks like Figure 8-71.

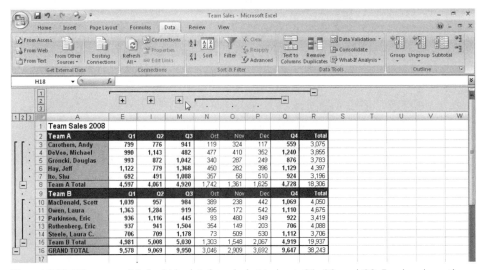

Figure 8-71 When you click the hide detail symbols (–) above Q1, Q2, and Q3, Excel replaces them with show detail symbols (+).

Show detail symbols with a plus sign on them now replace the hide detail symbols above the Q1, Q2, and Q3 columns (columns E, I, and M). To redisplay the hidden details, click the show detail symbols.

Displaying a Specific Outline Level

To collapse each quarter so that only the quarterly totals and annual totals appear, you can click the hide detail symbols above Q1, Q2, Q3, and Q4. The *level symbols*—the squares with numerals at the upper-left corner of the worksheet—provide an easier way, however. An outline usually has two sets of level symbols, one for columns and one for rows. The column level symbols appear above the worksheet, and the row level symbols appear to the left of the worksheet.

INSIDE OUT Collapsing and Expanding with an IntelliMouse Pointing Device

You can use the wheel button on your IntelliMouse pointing device to manipulate an outline without using the detail symbols or level symbols. This is helpful if you prefer to suppress the display of outline symbols to see more of the worksheet on the screen yet you still want to be able to use the outlining feature.

Rest the pointer on the summary row or column you want to expand or collapse; then hold down the Shift key, and rotate the wheel backward (toward your hand) to collapse the outline or forward (away from your hand) to expand it. If you rest the pointer on a cell where a summary row and summary column intersect, the outline collapses or expands in both directions at once.

You can use the level symbols to set an entire worksheet to a specific level of detail. The outlined worksheet shown in Figure 8-68 has three levels each for columns and for rows. By clicking both of the level symbols labeled 2 in the upper-left corner of the worksheet, you can transform the outline shown in Figure 8-68 to the one shown in Figure 8-69.

INSIDE OUT Selecting Only the Visible Cells

When you collapse part of an outline, Excel hides the columns or rows you don't want to see. In Figure 8-71, for example, the detail columns are hidden for the first three quarters of the year. Ordinarily, if you select a range that includes hidden cells, those hidden cells are implicitly selected. Whatever you do with these cells also happens to the hidden cells, so if you want to copy only the displayed totals, using copy and paste won't work. Here's the solution: On the Home tab, click Find & Select, Go To Special, and select the Visible Cells Only option. This is ideal for copying, charting, or performing calculations on only those cells that occupy a particular level of your outline. This feature works the same way in worksheets that have not been outlined; it excludes any cells in hidden columns or rows from the current selection.

Ungrouping and Grouping Columns and Rows

If the default automatic outline doesn't give you the structure you expect, you can adjust it by ungrouping or grouping particular columns or rows. You can easily change the hierarchy of outlined columns and rows by clicking the Group and Ungroup buttons on the Data tab.

For example, you could select row 8 in the outlined worksheet shown in Figure 8-68 and click Ungroup to change row 8 from level 2 to level 1. The outlining symbol to the left of the row moves to the left under the row level symbol labeled 1. To restore the row to its proper level, click Group.

> **Note**
>
> You cannot ungroup or group a nonadjacent selection, and you cannot ungroup a selection that's already at the highest hierarchical level. If you want to ungroup a top-level column or row to a higher level so it appears to be separate from the remainder of the outline, you have to group all the other levels of the outline instead.

Consolidating Worksheets

 You can use the Consolidate button on the Data tab to combine the values from a set of worksheets in the same workbook or from different workbooks. The Consolidate command lets you assemble information from as many as 255 supporting worksheets in a single master worksheet and displays the Consolidate dialog box shown in Figure 8-72.

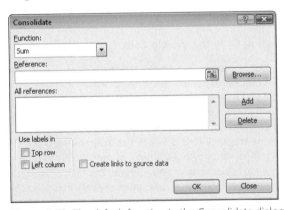

Figure 8-72 The default function in the Consolidate dialog box is Sum.

For example, if you have data for each month in separate worksheets or financial data for several divisions in separate workbooks, you can use the Consolidate command to create a master worksheet that comprises the totals for the corresponding items in each location. You can use the Consolidate command in a number of ways:

- Link the consolidated data to the supporting data so subsequent changes in the supporting worksheets are reflected in the consolidation worksheet.

- Consolidate the source data on an ad hoc basis, without creating a link.

- Consolidate by position, where Office Excel 2007 gathers information from the same cell location in each supporting worksheet.

- Consolidate by category, where Excel uses column or row labels as the basis for associating worksheets. Consolidating by category gives you more flexibility in the way you set up your supporting worksheets. For example, if your January column is column B in one worksheet and column D in another, you can still gather the correct January numbers when you consolidate by category.

- Use any of the functions listed in the Function list in the Consolidate dialog box, including Count (which corresponds to the COUNTA function), Average, Max, Min, Product, Count Nums (which corresponds to the COUNT function), StdDev, StdDevp, Var, and Varp. As shown in Figure 8-72, the default function is Sum.

For more information about functions, see Chapter 13, "Using Functions," and Chapter 14, "Everyday Functions."

- Consolidate worksheets in workbooks that are currently open or in workbooks that are stored on disk. The workbook containing the worksheet that receives the consolidated data must be open, but supporting workbooks can be closed—provided Excel has the correct locations so it can find each workbook file. (This should not be a problem unless you moved them since you last opened them in Excel.) You must save all supporting workbooks before you begin consolidation.

You can also use PivotTable reports to consolidate worksheets. For information, see Chapter 22, "Analyzing Data with PivotTable Reports."

Consolidating by Position

When you consolidate by position, Excel applies the consolidation function (Sum, Average, or whatever else you select) to the same cell references in each supporting worksheet. By Position is the simplest way to consolidate, but your supporting worksheets must have exactly the same layout.

Figure 8-73 shows a simple example of a workbook containing a master worksheet—Consolidated—that matches the layout of 12 supporting monthly worksheets. These worksheets can be consolidated by position because each contains identically structured data.

You'll find the Pacific Brass Sales.xlsx file in the Sample Files section of the companion CD.

To consolidate the monthly worksheets in Figure 8-73 into the worksheet named Consolidated, follow these steps:

1. Open the consolidation worksheet, and select the block of cells that will receive the consolidated data. In Figure 8-73, the destination area is the range B5:I10.

2. Click Data, Consolidate.

3. Select the source range in the first worksheet using the mouse. In this example, we selected B5:I10 in the Jan worksheet.

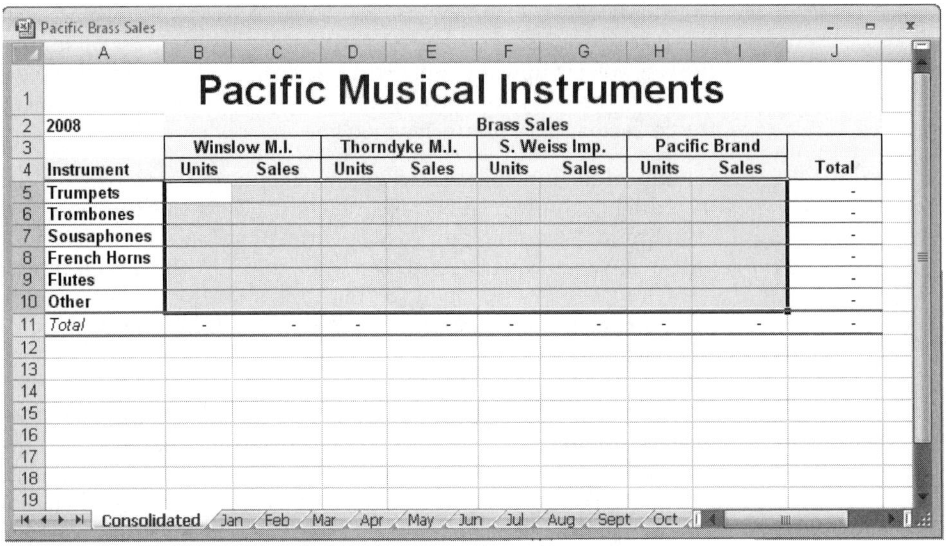

Figure 8-73 All the worksheets in this workbook are identical, which is necessary when consolidating by position.

Note

Make sure all supporting workbooks are open while you are building your consolidation worksheet to make it easier to type references. (If a workbook is closed, you must manually type references to it, and you really don't want that.) After you have the consolidation set up and save the workbook, supporting workbooks can stay closed during future consolidations. If you do have to type a reference, you must use the form [File Name]Sheetname!Reference. If the reference is in the same workbook, the file name (and its surrounding brackets) is unnecessary. If you have assigned the source range a name, you can use this name in place of Reference (highly recommended). For more information, see "Naming Cells and Cell Ranges" on page 441.

---

4. Click Add in the Consolidate dialog box. Excel transfers the reference from the Reference text box to the All References list. Repeat for each worksheet you want to consolidate. Figure 8-74 shows the completed dialog box.

After you add the first range—$B$5:$I$10 in the Jan worksheet—Excel selects the same range in each worksheet when you click its tab. Just click a worksheet tab, and then click Add to add references. Figure 8-75 shows the resulting consolidation.

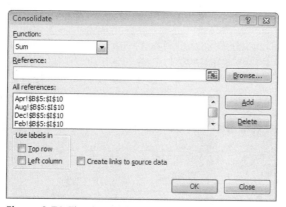

Figure 8-74 The Consolidate command uses the references in the All References list to create the consolidated totals.

Note

After you perform a consolidation, the references you type in the Consolidate dialog box are retained when you save the workbook. The next time you open the workbook and want to refresh the consolidated values, rather than entering the references again, click Consolidate, and click OK.

Chapter 8

Pacific Brass Sales

Pacific Musical Instruments

2008   Brass Sales

Instrument	Winslow M.I.		Thorndyke M.I.		S. Weiss Imp.		Pacific Brand		Total
	Units	Sales	Units	Sales	Units	Sales	Units	Sales	
Trumpets	14.00	3,283.84	1.00	234.56	11.00	2,580.16	2.00	469.12	6,567.68
Trombones	8.00	2,399.84	8.00	2,399.84	3.00	899.94	12.00	3,599.76	9,299.38
Sousaphones	10.00	4,567.80	6.00	2,740.68	8.00	3,654.24	2.00	913.56	11,876.28
French Horns	10.00	3,456.70	6.00	2,074.02	5.00	1,728.35	10.00	3,456.70	10,715.77
Flutes	5.00	943.90	17.00	3,209.26	6.00	1,132.68	8.00	1,510.24	6,796.08
Other	5.00	499.90	7.00	699.86	3.00	299.94	19.00	1,899.62	3,399.32
Total	52.00	15,151.98	45.00	11,358.22	36.00	10,295.31	53.00	11,849.00	48,654.51

Consolidated / Jan / Feb / Mar / Apr / May / Jun / Jul / Aug / Sept / Oct

Figure 8-75 Range B5:I10 in the Consolidated worksheet now contains totals of the corresponding cells in the 12 supporting worksheets.

Consolidating by Category

Now let's look at a more complex example. The Pacific Sales Staff workbook contains monthly sales totals for each salesperson, but each monthly worksheet has different salespeople and a different number of salespeople, as shown in Figure 8-76.

Figure 8-76 Use the categories in the left column of each source worksheet as the basis for this consolidation.

You'll find the Pacific Sales Staff.xlsx file in the Sample Files section of the companion CD.

The consolidation worksheet we'll use for our example has columns for Units and Sales—each worksheet is the same in this respect. When performing a consolidation by category, your consolidation worksheet cannot include row categories, which in our example are the salespeople's names; Excel collects these and adds them as part of the consolidation process. The names are not consistently arranged in the source worksheets, which is why we must use consolidation by category rather than consolidation by position in this example.

To consolidate by category, follow these steps:

1. Select the destination area. This time the destination area must include the row headings—but how many rows? To answer that, you can look at each source worksheet and determine how many unique line items you have. An easier way, however, is to select a single cell—in this case, cell A4—as the destination area. When you specify a single cell as your destination area, the Consolidate command fills in the area below and to the right of that cell as needed. In the example, to preserve the formatting, we inserted more than enough rows to accommodate the data.

2. Click Data, Consolidate.

3. To consolidate by row categories in this example, select the Left Column check box in the Use Labels In area. Click the default Sum function in the Function drop-down list.

4. The consolidation worksheet already has column labels, so you can omit them from the source worksheet references. Each source reference must include row headings, Units and Sales. Select these ranges on each monthly worksheet. For example, on the Jan worksheet, we selected $A$4:$C$8. Unlike when consolidating by position, you have to manually select the ranges in each supporting worksheet, because Excel selects the last range you added, which will not necessarily be what you need in each worksheet.

5. Click OK, and Excel fills out the Consolidated worksheet, as shown in Figure 8-77.

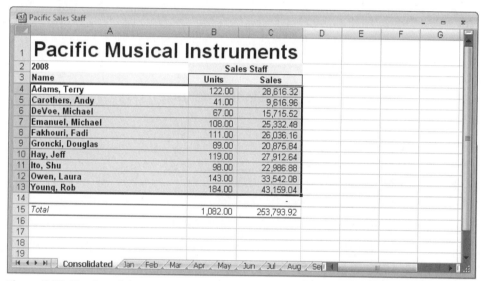

Figure 8-77 The Consolidate command created a separate line item in the consolidation worksheet for each unique item in the source worksheets.

> **Note**
>
> It's important that your categories—in our example, the names of salespeople—are spelled identically on each supporting worksheet. Otherwise, Excel creates a separate line and consolidation for each spelling variation.

Creating Links to the Source Worksheets

The previous examples consolidated numbers with the Sum function, resulting in a range of consolidated constants. Subsequent changes to the source worksheets do not affect the consolidation worksheet until you repeat the consolidation.

You can also use the Consolidate command to create links between the consolidation and source worksheets. To do so, select the Create Links To Source Data check box in the Consolidate dialog box and then consolidate using the same techniques. When you consolidate with links, Excel actually creates an outline in the consolidation worksheet, as shown in Figure 8-78. Each source item is linked separately to the consolidation worksheet, and Excel creates the appropriate summary items. Excel creates additional columns and rows as necessary for each category—one for each unique entry in each worksheet, as shown in rows 35 to 41. Figure 8-78 also shows, in the formula bar, the linking formula for the December units figure in cell C36.

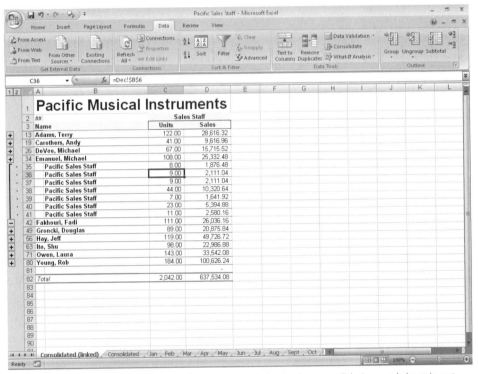

Figure 8-78 When you create links to the source worksheets, the consolidation worksheet is outlined and linking formulas are created in subordinate outline levels.

Note that when you create links, any rows or columns you subsequently add to the source worksheets are not included in the consolidation. However, it is easy to modify the consolidation references. Open the Consolidate dialog box, select the reference you want to change, and click Delete. Then select the modified range, and click Add.

For more information about outlining worksheets, see "Outlining Worksheets" on page 253.

CHAPTER 9

Worksheet Formatting Techniques

When creating a worksheet in Microsoft Office Excel 2007, you probably don't ask yourself the question, why use formats? But we'll answer it anyway. Compare Figure 9-1 to Figure 9-2, and we need say no more. Although the data is the same in both worksheets, the worksheet in Figure 9-2 takes advantage of the formatting features available in Office Excel 2007 and as you can see, it's much easier to read and interpret. In this chapter, you'll learn how to apply basic formatting to help turn your data into information, and we'll discuss advanced formatting features such as themes, cell styles, and conditional formatting.

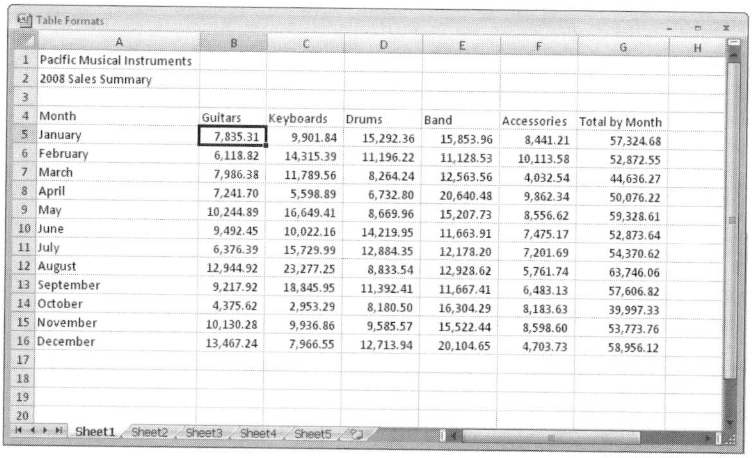

	A	B	C	D	E	F	G	H
1	Pacific Musical Instruments							
2	2008 Sales Summary							
3								
4	Month	Guitars	Keyboards	Drums	Band	Accessories	Total by Month	
5	January	7,835.31	9,901.84	15,292.36	15,853.96	8,441.21	57,324.68	
6	February	6,118.82	14,315.39	11,196.22	11,128.53	10,113.58	52,872.55	
7	March	7,986.38	11,789.56	8,264.24	12,563.56	4,032.54	44,636.27	
8	April	7,241.70	5,598.89	6,732.80	20,640.48	9,862.34	50,076.22	
9	May	10,244.89	16,649.41	8,669.96	15,207.73	8,556.62	59,328.61	
10	June	9,492.45	10,022.16	14,219.95	11,663.91	7,475.17	52,873.64	
11	July	6,376.39	15,729.99	12,884.35	12,178.20	7,201.69	54,370.62	
12	August	12,944.92	23,277.25	8,833.54	12,928.62	5,761.74	63,746.06	
13	September	9,217.92	18,845.95	11,392.41	11,667.41	6,483.13	57,606.82	
14	October	4,375.62	2,953.29	8,180.50	16,304.29	8,183.63	39,997.33	
15	November	10,130.28	9,936.86	9,585.57	15,522.44	8,598.60	53,773.76	
16	December	13,467.24	7,966.55	12,713.94	20,104.65	4,703.73	58,956.12	
17								
18								
19								
20								

Figure 9-1 All entries in this worksheet are displayed in their default formats.

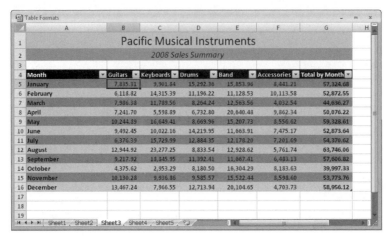

Figure 9-2 The formatted worksheet is easier to read.

Formatting Fundamentals

Worksheet *editing* involves creating and modifying the content, layout, and organization of data, while worksheet *formatting* deals with the appearance and readability of that data. With formatting, you can take mind-numbing detail and turn it into information by highlighting important data, adding visual clues, and enhancing overall readability and organization.

Formatting in Excel is easy: Select the cell or range, and use the appropriate buttons and commands on the Ribbon to apply formatting. Many of the most often used formatting features appear on the Home tab on the Ribbon for quick access, as shown in Figure 9-3. In fact, formatting commands dominate the Home tab; all seven of its Ribbon groups include formatting commands (even the Editing group). Figure 9-3 also shows the Format Cells dialog box, which you access by clicking the Dialog Box Launcher in the Font, Alignment, or Number group on the Home tab on the Ribbon. (The Dialog Box Launcher is the small arrow icon to the right of the title in many Ribbon groups.)

> **Note**
> To quickly access the Format Cells dialog box, press Ctrl+1.

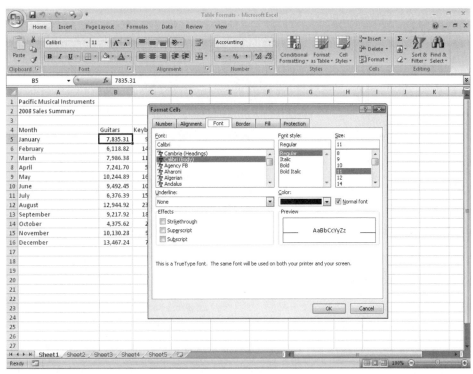

Figure 9-3 The Home tab on the Ribbon and the Format Cells dialog box are your formatting toolboxes.

Here are some fundamental rules of formatting in Excel:

- A formatted cell remains formatted until you remove the format or apply a new format.

- When you overwrite or edit a cell entry, you need not reformat the cell.

- When you copy or cut a cell, the formats applied to that cell travel with it.

> **Note**
>
> Build and edit the worksheet first; apply formatting later. Sometimes, the *least* efficient step you can take is to apply your formatting too soon. Applying, removing, and then reapplying formatting is at least three times the work. Trust us, you'll be doing some reformatting no matter what, so give yourself the freedom to rearrange until the layout becomes clear for your purposes.

Chapter 9

Formatting Tables

In Excel 2007, the concept of a table takes on fresh meaning. Tables are now special objects in Excel that include many features beyond formatting, but you can use the Format As Table button on the Home tab to apply specific font, border, and fill attributes to all the elements of a table at once. The Format As Table palette, shown in Figure 9-4, applies predefined combinations of these formatting criteria.

> **Note**
>
> When you use Format As Table, you apply more than just formatting—you are actually transforming a region of your worksheet into kind of a self-contained entity that not only adds Filters to all column headings but also has special properties that offer extreme editing while preserving the integrity and format of the table structure. Chapter 21, "Managing Information in Tables," covers tables in more detail. You'll want to check out that chapter.

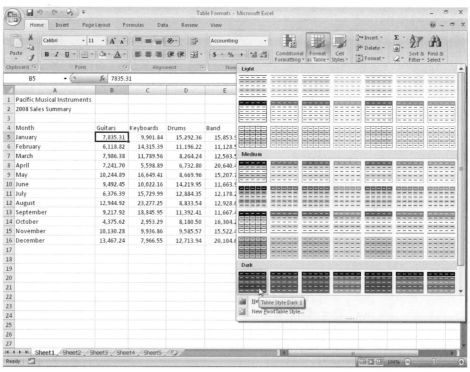

Figure 9-4 The Format As Table palette offers a selection of predefined formats you can apply with one click.

You can apply the Format As Table command to any *region* of cells (that is, a contiguous block of cells on a worksheet). You select a cell anywhere within the region, click Format As Table, and then select one of the sample table formats in the palette. When you do so, Excel displays the Format As Table dialog box, which lets you adjust the selection, as shown in Figure 9-5.

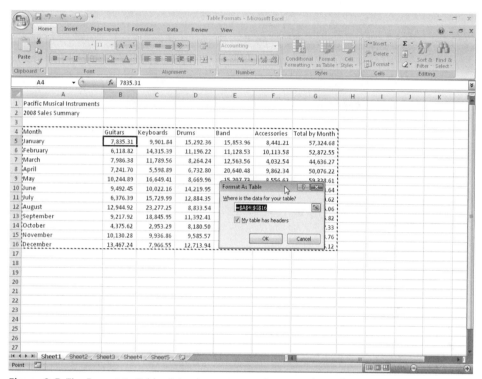

Figure 9-5 The Format As Table dialog box appears after you select a format in the Format As Table palette.

If your table includes headers (as most do), select the My Table Has Headers check box in the Format As Table dialog box. Excel then selects the entire table automatically and applies the selected table format to it.

Here are a few tips to keep in mind when using Format As Table:

Undo

- If you don't like the way something looks, click the Undo button on the Quick Access Toolbar (or press Ctrl+Z).

- The boundaries of a table are defined by blank rows and columns or the edges of the worksheet. Try adding blank columns or rows around your table to effectively fence off areas you don't want Format As Table to touch.

- Select more than one cell before issuing the command so Format As Table affects only the selected cells.

Although Format As Table does a pretty good job with simple tables, you usually need to make a few adjustments afterward. For example, starting with the raw data shown in Figure 9-1, we applied the Dark 8 table format. Figure 9-6 shows the result.

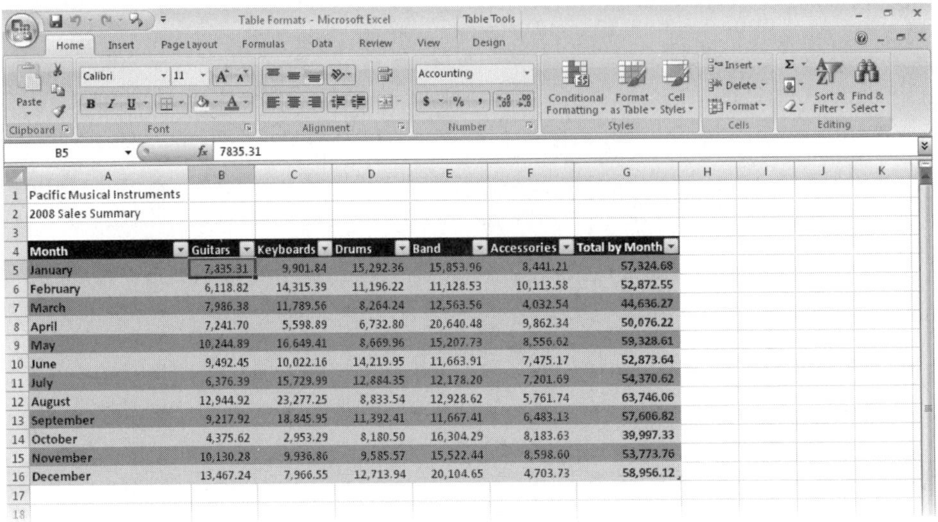

Figure 9-6 In seconds, you can transform a raw worksheet into something more presentable.

As you can see in Figure 9-6, the title and subtitle in cells A1 and A2 were not part of the table, and therefore were not formatted, so we applied additional formatting manually to arrive at the result shown in Figure 9-2. In addition, we applied number formatting to the cells containing data. Nonetheless, using Format As Table speeds up the formatting process and provides at least one formatting feature that is otherwise unavailable: automatic row and column banding, which was one attribute of the automatic format we applied in Figure 9-6. Another cool part of using Format As Table is the automatic preview feature. After you have defined a table using the Format As Table command, you can then use the Format As Table palette to preview other predefined formats. Rest the pointer on any format in the palette, and the associated formatting is temporarily reflected in the table you have already created but is not actually applied unless you click.

After you create a table, a context-triggered tab appears on the Ribbon only when you select a cell or cells within the table. Figure 9-7 shows the Table Tools Design tab.

The Design tab contains formatting commands in the Table Style Options and Table Styles groups. The latter group contains the same palette from the Format As Table command on the Home tab. In Figure 9-7, we selected both the First Column and Last Column check boxes in the Table Style Options group, which, in this particular predefined format, applied bold formatting to the fonts in those columns. You can select and clear check boxes in this group and view the changes immediately. The Header Row check box actually adds or removes the header row from the table. The Totals Row check box adds a double border at the bottom of the table and adds another row containing summary formulas. If you do so, you can select which summary function you want to use by clicking the summary formula in the totals row and then clicking the menu arrow that appears. The menu offers a selection of functions including Sum (the default), Average, Max, and Min, or you can select More Functions to display the Insert Function dialog box.

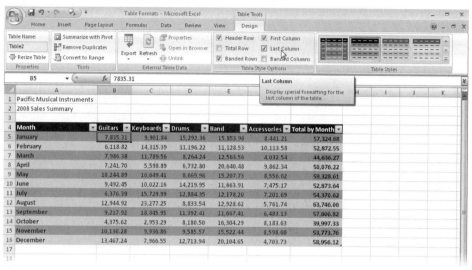

Figure 9-7 The Table Tools Design tab appears on the Ribbon whenever you select a cell in a table.

TROUBLESHOOTING

Did your Design tab disappear?

The Table Tools Design tab appears only when you select a cell that is part of a table. When you select any cell outside the table, this context-triggered tab disappears, and the Home tab is activated.

The two "Banded" check boxes on the Table Tools Design tab—Banded Rows and Banded Columns—are useful. In large worksheets, row banding often makes it easier to track long rows of data across a screen or printed page. In previous versions of Excel, banding required you to construct an esoteric conditional formatting formula using the MOD function. Banding is now easier than ever to apply in Excel thanks to these two options, and unlike the old MOD function approach, these table banding options are smart enough to survive just about any kind of editing, including inserting and deleting rows and columns.

For more information, see "Formatting Conditionally" on page 284 and "Creating Conditional Formatting Formulas" on page 294.

You can insert and delete rows in a table, even at the edges, and the table will automatically do the right thing with formats and formulas. Another great feature of tables is that you can make them bigger just by dragging. As Figure 9-8 shows, the lower-rightmost cell in the lower-rightmost corner of the table contains a small triangular indicator (similar to a cell comment indicator) that you can drag horizontally or vertically to increase (or decrease) the size of the table.

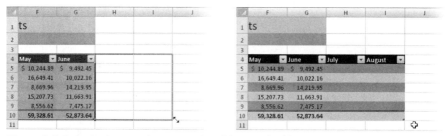

Figure 9-8 Drag the lower-right corner of a table to make it bigger.

Options for Applying Table Formats

When you right-click an item in the Format As Table palette, you'll find a few more tools you can employ when you are working with table formats. Figure 9-9 shows the shortcut menu that appears when you right-click a palette item.

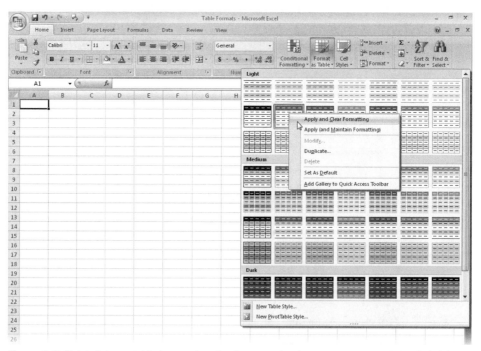

Figure 9-9 Right-click any table format thumbnail to reveal a shortcut menu containing helpful options.

The following are the options:

- Apply And Clear Formatting sounds backward, because what really happens is that Excel removes the existing formatting first before applying the selected table format.

- Apply (And Maintain Formatting) gives you the option of using the selected table format without disturbing any existing format attributes previously applied to the selected cells.

- Duplicate copies the selected table format; opens the Modify Table Quick Style dialog box (which is identical to the New Table Quick Style dialog box shown in Figure 9-10), letting you make modifications; and places the resulting format in the Custom category at the top of the Format As Table palette.

Creating Custom Table Formats

If the built-in palette of table styles doesn't do it for you, you can create your own. To do so, click the Format As Table button on the Home tab, scroll to the bottom of the palette, and click New Table Style to display the New Table Quick Style dialog box shown in Figure 9-10.

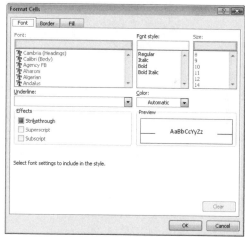

Figure 9-10 Click the New Table Style button on the Format As Table palette to create your own table styles.

In the New Table Quick Style dialog box, you can assign font, border, and fill formats to each item listed in the Table Element box. Select the element you want to format, and click the Format button to display the Format Cells dialog box shown on the right in Figure 9-10. You can click the Clear button to remove the formatting from a selected element; select the Set As Default Table Quick Style For This Document check box to make yours the go-to style whenever you create tables in the current workbook. After you finish specifying formats and click OK, your custom style appears at the top of the Format As Table palette in the Custom category.

Removing the Automatic Table Features

You can use the Convert To Range button in the Tools group on the Table Tools Design tab to remove all the special features applied to a selected table without removing the formatting. (Remember, you need to click a cell in the table to display the Table Tools Design tab.) Figure 9-11 shows the message that appears when you click Convert To Range.

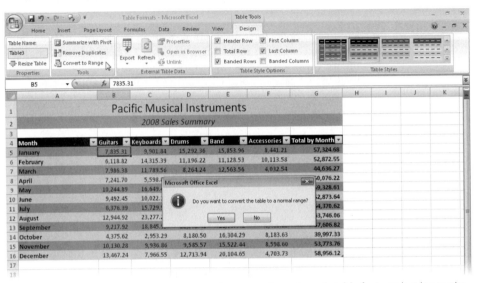

Figure 9-11 The Convert To Range command removes the automatic table features but leaves the formatting.

Convert To Range removes the Filter menus from the selected table, discontinues displaying the Table Tools Design tab, turns off any additional table features such as automatic cell banding and totals, and relegates the range formerly known as Table to simple "formatted cells" status. Any visible table formatting you have already applied remains (including the totals row), but the automatic table functionality disappears. Converting your table in this way makes sense if you don't want to deal with the automatic accoutrements such as Filter menus. It's a great way to take advantage of the automatic table creation features just to apply formatting.

Painting Formats

Format Painter

One of the most useful tools on your formatting tool belt is the Format Painter button. The Clipboard group on the Home tab on the Ribbon is home to the Format Painter button, which looks like a little paintbrush. Select the cell or range from which you want to copy formatting, and click the Format Painter button. (A small paintbrush icon appears next to the pointer.) Then select the cell or drag through the range of cells to which you want to copy the formatting. It's that simple.

If you copy formats from a range of cells and then select a single cell when you paste, the Format Painter selects and formats the same size range, from the selected cell down and to the right. However, if you select a range of cells when you paste formats, the Format Painter limits the pasted formats to the shape of the destination range you select. If the range you want to format is a different shape from the copied range, the pattern is repeated or truncated as necessary.

Clear

> **Note**
>
> To remove all formatting, select a cell or range, click the Clear menu (located in the Editing group on the Ribbon), and click Clear Formats. To remove the values as well as the formatting in selected cells, click Clear All on the menu. For more information, see "Clearing Cells" on page 202.

Using Themes and Cell Styles

Office Excel 2007 now offers a couple of ways to format globally—meaning you can perform certain tasks to help standardize the look of your worksheets and make it easier to create a consistent appearance for all your documents.

Formatting with Themes

Themes are a new concept in Excel 2007. A *theme* is a set of formatting attributes that apply specifically to the line and fill effects, the color palette, and the fonts that are available when formatting documents. The three buttons that control these attributes—Colors, Fonts, and Effects—appear in the Themes group on the Page Layout tab, shown in Figure 9-12. Themes give individuals or workgroups using the Microsoft Office 2007 system programs the ability to use the same sets of basic design attributes for all the documents they create. You'll find corresponding themes in Microsoft Office PowerPoint and Microsoft Office Word as well. You can use themes to standardize all your internal documents, for example, or to maintain a consistent look between pages in a package of presentation handouts.

Themes

When you apply a theme using the Themes button, all applicable formats in the active workbook change instantly, including the colors of text, background, accents and hyperlinks, heading and body text fonts, line and fill effects, and graphic styles, as shown in Figure 9-13.

Just as when you choose a theme, changes you make using the Colors, Fonts, or Effects palettes are reflected immediately throughout the workbook. The Colors palette contains a selection of coordinated color schemes that, when selected, change the available colors in all other palettes where colors are used. The Fonts palette offers a selection of font sets, including two fonts each—one for headings and one for body text. The Effects palette gives you a choice of graphic "looks," accomplished using various applications of line and fill effects using the current color scheme.

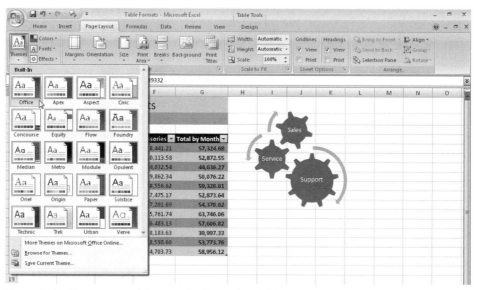

Figure 9-12 Themes control the overall palette of available colors, fonts, and effects.

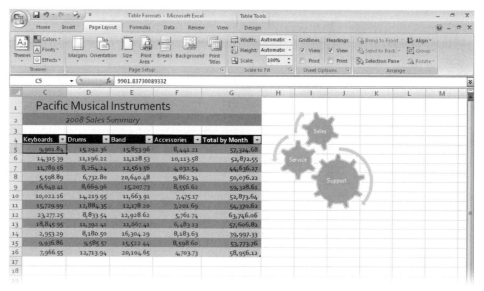

Figure 9-13 Changing the theme instantly changes the look of all the worksheets in the active workbook.

INSIDE OUT   Mousing Around

Microsoft has gone to great lengths in Office 2007 to try to make features more discoverable and self-explanatory. It crafted a new approach for many of the commands that used to live on menus, transforming them into drop-down palettes containing thumbnail representations of the options they offer. In many cases, these palettes exhibit "live preview" functionality, where you can rest the pointer on items in the palette to get a live preview in the worksheet of what would happen if you actually clicked. This is a great feature, but it can be finicky. For example, if you convert an older Excel file and try to use the Themes palette in this way, you might find that not much seems to happen. This can occur when formatting in the old file overrides the default font, color, line, or fill styles controlled by themes. For example, the default font in Excel 2003 is Arial, and the default font in Excel 2007 is Calibri. When you convert an old Excel file, the original fonts carry over as well. Resting the pointer on the Themes palette might not show any changes in the font, and indeed, applying a theme might not have any effect either.

Paste

To get around this problem, you can start with a fresh workbook and type everything again (but who wants to do that?), or you can copy the contents of each worksheet in the old workbook and click Paste, Paste Values (on the Home tab) to add the data to the new workbook. This requires you to redo all the formatting, but that should be a lot easier with the tools in Excel 2007 anyway. Another approach is to reformat all the text in the converted workbook using one of the fonts from the current theme. Use the same approach to convert any colors, lines, or fill styles to use current theme styles.

CAUTION

Themes will have no effect on cells to which you have directly applied font, color, line, or fill formatting using settings that are not part of a theme.

Creating Custom Themes

You can save your own themes using the Save Current Theme command at the bottom of the Themes palette, as you can see in Figure 9-12. Doing so creates a .thmx file and saves it in a special folder on your computer. The name you give the file when you save it becomes the name of the theme, which subsequently appears in the Custom category at the top of the Themes palette, as shown in Figure 9-14. The Custom category appears only if a custom theme exists.

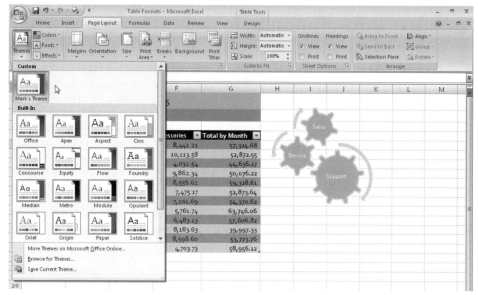

Figure 9-14 The Custom category is created in the Themes palette when you save a custom theme.

The Browse For Themes button at the bottom of the Themes palette lets you load .thmx files from other locations, such as a company theme file on your network, for example. The Search Office Online command opens a browser window and looks for additional predefined themes available on Microsoft Office Online.

Formatting with Cell Styles

The Excel "reimagined" Cell Styles feature bears little resemblance to the old Styles feature, although the basic idea is the same: applying combinations of formatting attributes all at once, eliminating a lot of time clicking buttons, opening dialog boxes, and choosing individual options. Cell styles help you achieve consistency in formatting, both within a worksheet and across worksheets and workbooks. Using cell styles, you can easily modify the formatting characteristics of many cells at once.

> **Note**
>
> Cell styles are based on the formatting attributes of the current theme. Changing the theme will cause the displayed cell styles to update accordingly.

The Cell Styles button appears in the Styles group on the Home tab on the Ribbon. Cell styles wield the following formatting attributes: number and fill formatting, cell alignment, fonts, borders, and even cell-level protection settings. Several built-in cell styles have specific purposes, as you can see in Figure 9-15, and you can create your own custom styles (designed in concert with your company theme, perhaps).

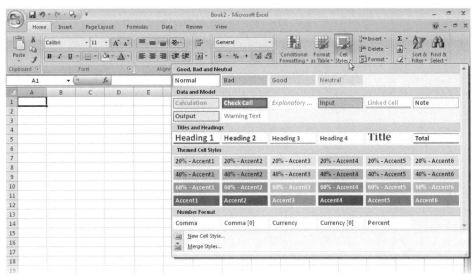

Figure 9-15 The Cell Styles palette offers categories of styles based on the current theme.

You'll find the following six cell style categories, with individual styles that have uses suggested by their titles and the categories in which they live:

- **Good, Bad And Neutral** If you want, you can use these styles when highlighting good news, bad news, and . . . just plain old news. The Normal style also lives here, which you can use to "reset" selected cells to default formatting.

- **Data And Model** These styles are intended for specific purposes, such as Input and Output styles for cells that are meant to accept user input or reveal the results of calculations.

- **Titles And Headings** The intended use is self-explanatory, but it's interesting to note that the top three Heading styles include bottom borders of different weights, making them useful for creating color-coordinated column headers in tables.

- **Themed Cell Styles** These Accent and Emphasis styles are heavily dependent on the current theme colors, offering four graduated percentages of each Accent color for quartile comparisons.

- **Number Format** Included for continuity, these styles are actually more accessible using the Number buttons on the Home tab on the Ribbon.

- **Custom** This category does not appear in the palette until you create a custom style. After you do, the Custom category appears at the top of the palette.

The Cell Styles palette exhibits "mouse hover" functionality, letting you see a live pre-view in selected cells on the worksheet when you rest the pointer on an item in the pal-ette. To apply a style, select the cells you want to format, and click your chosen style in the palette.

Creating Custom Cell Styles

You can create your own styles using one of two different methods: by modifying an existing style or by clicking the New Cell Style command at the bottom of the Cell Styles palette, which displays the Style dialog box shown in Figure 9-16.

Figure 9-16 Use the Style dialog box to create your own cell styles.

The Style dialog box opens with the attributes of the default Normal style displayed. Styles can have a minimum of one and a maximum of six sets of attributes: Number, Alignment, Font, Border, Fill, and Protection, each with a corresponding check box in the Style dialog box. Use the check boxes to specify particular attributes for your cell style. For example, you could clear all but the Protection check box to define a style that does nothing more than change selected cells to "unlocked" status, allowing user entries on a protected worksheet. Using such a style would have no effect on any of the other five style attributes in cells to which it is applied.

To specify style attributes, click the Format button to display the Format Cells dialog box, where you can specify your formatting choices in detail. The Format Cells dialog box contains a separate tab corresponding to the six categories of Style attributes; you can make as many choices as you want on each tab. When you are done with the For-mat Cells dialog box, click OK to close it and return to the Styles dialog box. Then type a name in the Style Name box, and click OK. Your custom style appears in the Custom category at the top of the Cell Styles palette, as shown in Figure 9-17, where we created an Unlocked style.

For more information about the Format Cells dialog box, see "Formatting Numbers" on page 298.

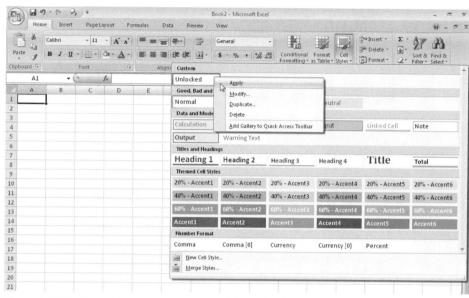

Figure 9-17 Custom styles appear at the top of the Cell Styles palette.

As you can see in Figure 9-17, you can right-click a cell style to display a shortcut menu you can use to delete, modify, or duplicate the style. Duplication is handy if, for example, you want to create a number of related styles such as the predefined Accent styles with different fill percentages. Clicking the Duplication command would make it easier because it would copy all the other attributes for you, so all you have to do is change the fill percentage.

Creating Cell Styles by Example   If you have already formatted a cell using attributes you would like to use often, you can use the style-by-example procedure to encapsulate those attributes in a new style. For example, suppose you format a cell with right alignment and 18-point Arial Black. To make this combination of attributes a new style, follow these steps:

1. Select the cell that contains the formatting you want.

2. On the Ribbon, click Home, Cell Styles, New Cell Style.

3. Type a name such as **HeadRight** in the Style Name box.

4. Clear the Number, Border, Fill, and Protection check boxes in the Style Includes area, and click OK. The new style then appears in the Cell Styles palette.

CAUTION

The safest way to create a style by example is to select only one cell—one you know has all the attributes you want to assign to the new style. If you select two or more cells that are not formatted identically, the new style assumes only those attributes that all cells in the selection have in common.

Modifying and Duplicating Cell Styles The principal advantage of using styles is that if you change your mind about the appearance of a particular element in your workbook, you can revise every instance of that element at once by changing the style. For example, if you'd like the font in the custom HeadRight style—which is now 18-point Arial Black—to also be italic, you can redefine HeadRight.

To modify a style definition, follow these steps:

1. Click Home, Cell Styles.

2. Right-click the thumbnail for the style (in this case, HeadRight) from the palette, and click Modify to display the Style dialog box.

3. Click the Format button to display the Format Cells dialog box, and select the appropriate format options, as shown in Figure 9-18. (For this example, click the Font tab, and select the Italic option in the Font Style list.)

4. Click OK to return to the Style dialog box, then click OK to confirm your changes.

You can also right-click an existing style and click the Duplicate command, which opens a Style dialog box similar to the one shown in Figure 9-18 and appends a number to the end of the style name. You can then change the name if you like and click the Format button to make the desired adjustments to the formatting attributes. Using Duplicate is helpful when you want to create a number of similar styles or when you want to base a custom style on one of the built-in styles. When you finish defining the style, click OK; your new style appears in the Custom category of the Cell Styles palette.

Note

The predefined Normal style is applied to every cell in every new workbook. Thus, if you want to use the standard set of formatting attributes, you don't need to do anything. If, however, you want to change the default attributes for all cells in a worksheet, you can redefine any or all attributes of the Normal style.

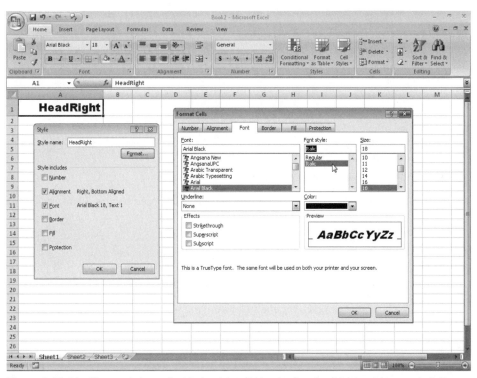

Figure 9-18 Modify an existing cell style by right-clicking its thumbnail in the palette and clicking Modify.

Merging Cell Styles from Different Workbooks   To maintain formatting consistency across a group of worksheets, you can keep the worksheets in the same workbook. If this is impractical but you still want to maintain stylistic consistency, you can copy style definitions between workbooks. (Of course, themes are also helpful in this regard and are covered in "Formatting with Themes" on page 275.)

To copy a style from one workbook to another, take the following steps:

1. Open both the source workbook (the one you're copying from) and the destination workbook (the one you're copying to).

2. Click the destination workbook to make it the active window.

3. On the Ribbon, click Home, Cell Styles, Merge Styles. Excel displays a dialog box listing all the other open workbooks, as shown in Figure 9-19.

4. Select the name of the workbook you want to copy styles from, and click OK.

Figure 9-19 Copy cell styles from any open workbook using the Merge Styles command.

CAUTION!

> If a style in the source workbook has the same name as one already in your destination workbook, a message asks whether you want to merge styles that have the same names. You receive this warning only once, however, no matter how many duplicate style names exist. If you click Yes, the styles from the source workbook override those with the same names in the destination workbook.

Deleting a Cell Style To delete a style, click Home, Cell Styles, and right-click the Custom style you want to delete (you cannot delete a built-in cell style). Then click Delete. Any cells that were formatted using the deleted style revert to the Normal style.

Formatting Conditionally

Conditional formats respond to the contents of cells. They are almost always applied to groups of cells, often rows or columns of totals, if not entire tables. Click Home, Conditional Formatting to display the menu shown in Figure 9-20.

Office Excel 2007 offers five flavors of formatting features you can use for your conditional creations:

- **Highlight Cells Rules** Formatting you apply to cells that stays "asleep" until the values (numeric or text) they contain achieve the specified state. Click Greater Than, Less Than, Between, Equal To, Text That Contains, A Date Occurring, or Duplicate Values to display a dialog box where you can specify the appropriate criteria.

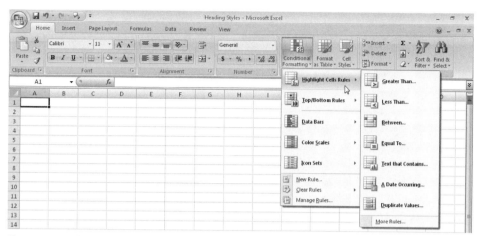

Figure 9-20 The revamped conditional formatting features in Excel 2007 are more powerful and easier to use than previous versions.

- **Top/Bottom Rules** Selected formatting applied to all cells in a range that are greater than or less than a given threshold. Click Top N Items, Top N %, Bottom N Items, Bottom N %, Above Average, or Below Average to display a dialog box where you can specify the appropriate criteria.

- **Data Bars** Gradient fills of color within cells whose lengths indicate the values in the cells relative to all other adjacent cells formatted using the same conditions. Choose from a number of different colors, based on the current theme.

- **Color Scales** Two-color or three-color formats whose color indicates the values in the cells relative to all other adjacent cells formatted using the same conditions. Choose from a number of different color combinations, based on the current theme.

- **Icon Sets** Sets of three, four, or five tiny graphic images placed inside cells whose shape or color indicates the values in the cells relative to all other adjacent cells formatted using the same conditions. Choose from a number of different types of icons.

For example, you could apply conditional formatting to a range of cells that contain sales totals, specifying that if any of the totals drops to less than $1,000, the format of the cell changes to stand out from the other cells. To do so, follow these steps:

1. Select the cells you want to format.

2. Click Conditional Formatting, Highlight Cells Rules, Less Than to display the dialog box shown in Figure 9-21.

3. Type the number you want to use as the threshold for this condition, in this case **1000**.

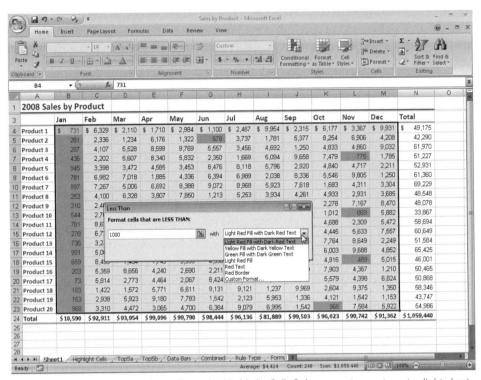

Figure 9-21 Select the Less Than rule on the Highlight Cells Rules menu to create a stoplight chart using conditional formatting.

4. Select one of the options from the drop-down list of available formats.

Notice that when you select a format option in the dialog box, Excel previews it for you in the worksheet. The palette preview functionality does not work from the Conditional Formatting menu with any of the highlight cells rules or top/bottom rules, because they all require additional input first. The Custom Format option at the bottom of the With list (the drop-down list at the right side of the dialog box) does not generate a preview, because clicking it displays a version of the Format Cells dialog box with the Number, Font, Border, and Fill tabs available.

5. Click OK.

Figure 9-22 shows a table after applying conditional formatting. This example was formatted using two highlight cells conditions: one format for numbers greater than 9,000 and a different format for numbers less than 1,000.

You'll find the Sales by Product.xlsx file in the Sample Files section of the companion CD.

	Jan	Feb	Mar	Apr	May	Jun	Jul	Aug	Sep	Oct	Nov	Dec	Total
2008 Sales by Product													
Product 1	$ 731	$ 6,329	$ 2,110	$ 1,710	$ 2,984	$ 1,100	$ 2,467	$ 9,954	$ 2,315	$ 6,177	$ 3,367	$ 9,931	$ 49,175
Product 2	281	2,336	1,234	6,176	1,322	678	3,737	1,781	5,377	8,254	6,906	4,208	42,290
Product 3	287	4,107	5,528	8,599	9,769	5,557	3,456	4,692	1,250	4,833	4,860	9,032	61,970
Product 4	436	2,202	5,607	8,340	5,832	2,350	1,669	5,094	9,658	7,479	775	1,785	51,227
Product 5	945	3,398	3,472	4,585	3,453	8,476	8,118	5,796	2,920	4,840	4,717	2,211	52,931
Product 6	781	6,982	7,018	1,885	4,336	6,394	6,989	2,038	8,336	5,546	9,805	1,250	61,360
Product 7	997	7,267	5,006	6,692	8,388	9,072	8,968	5,923	7,618	1,683	4,311	3,304	69,229
Product 8	253	4,100	6,328	3,807	7,850	1,213	5,253	3,934	4,261	4,933	2,931	3,685	48,548
Product 9	310	2,467	5,349	7,142	2,343	2,712	4,629	3,961	1,250	2,278	7,167	8,470	48,078
Product 10	544	2,783	1,642	1,582	2,456	5,584	1,255	7,915	2,343	1,012	869	5,882	33,867
Product 11	781	8,626	6,938	5,200	8,197	6,542	5,955	1,775	2,211	4,688	2,309	5,472	58,694
Product 12	278	6,720	4,754	3,556	2,535	4,100	4,740	7,047	9,284	4,445	5,633	7,557	60,649
Product 13	736	3,248	7,295	4,344	2,076	8,372	1,846	1,264	3,741	7,764	8,649	2,249	51,584
Product 14	991	5,004	6,873	7,009	8,399	4,204	8,290	2,695	1,417	6,003	9,688	4,852	65,425
Product 15	659	8,499	1,404	1,749	5,999	4,398	2,211	1,167	9,495	4,916	489	5,015	46,001
Product 16	203	5,359	8,656	4,240	2,690	2,211	4,893	1,264	7,469	7,903	4,367	1,210	50,465
Product 17	73	5,814	2,773	4,464	2,067	8,424	1,337	1,404	7,711	5,579	4,398	6,824	50,868
Product 18	183	1,422	1,572	5,771	6,611	9,131	9,121	1,237	9,969	2,604	9,375	1,350	58,346
Product 19	153	2,938	5,923	9,180	7,783	1,542	2,123	5,953	1,336	4,121	1,542	1,153	43,747
Product 20	968	3,310	4,472	3,065	4,700	6,384	9,079	6,995	1,542	965	7,584	5,922	54,986
Total	$ 10,590	$ 92,911	$ 93,954	$ 99,096	$ 99,790	$ 98,444	$ 96,136	$ 81,889	$ 99,503	$ 96,023	$ 99,742	$ 91,362	$ 1,059,440

Figure 9-22 We created two conditions—one to flag high values and one to flag low values. These guys had a rough January.

This procedure is essentially the same for all the highlight cells and top/bottom rules, but several of these rules deserve additional comment:

- **Between** This is obvious perhaps, but although the Greater Than, Less Than, and Equal To rules require you to type a single number criterion, the Between rule requires two criteria.

- **Text That Contains** When you choose this rule, cells containing any form of the text string you type as a criterion are highlighted (entering **and** highlights cells containing *sand*, *Andrew*, and so on).

- **A Date Occurring** This rule always uses the current date as the point of reference. The "occurring" options are all relative to this: Yesterday, Last Week, Next Month, and so on.

- **Duplicate Values** This rule actually has two options, highlighting either Duplicate or Unique values.

The highlight cells rules are the only ones that operate independently of other cells. That is, each cell is evaluated against criteria individually and formatted accordingly. All other conditional formats depend entirely upon the rest of the cell values formatted using the same condition. For example, Figure 9-23 shows the same top/bottom rule applied to two different selected regions (in this case, we specified the top five).

Chapter 9

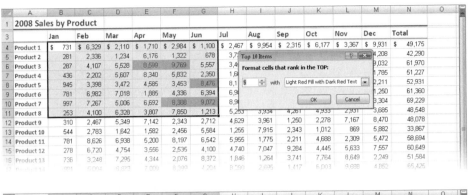

Figure 9-23 We used the same top/bottom rule on two different selections, with different results.

As you can see in Figure 9-23, cell F10 drops out of the top five, and cell C14 is added to the top five when we select a different range of cells. Excel uses all the values in the selected cell range to determine which cells to format. For data bars, color scales, and icon sets, Excel actually applies formatting to every cell in the selected range but adjusts the color, size, or icon based on each cell's value relative to the whole.

Data bars are a unique type of conditional format, because each cell actually contains the same color (actually, a gradation of color) but varies the size of the colored area in each cell to reflect its value relative to the other selected cells. Figure 9-24 shows a live preview of the Orange Databar.

All these conditional formats are pretty flashy, and they definitely help identify relative values in a range, but you can begin to see that too much conditional formatting can become counterproductive. As with any flashy feature, it's easy to love it a little too much, so make sure you're serving the purpose of your worksheet. Figure 9-25 shows what might be considered a more judicious application of conditional formatting, using highlight cells and data bars.

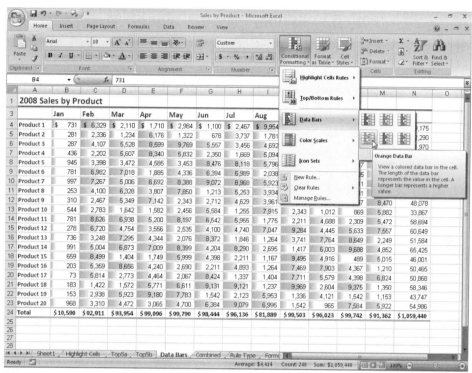

Figure 9-24 You can rest the pointer on items on the Data Bars menu to see a live preview on your worksheet.

	Jan	Feb	Mar	Apr	May	Jun	Jul	Aug	Sep	Oct	Nov	Dec	Total
2008 Sales by Product													
Product 1	$ 731	$ 6,329	$ 2,110	$ 1,710	$ 2,984	$ 1,100	$ 2,467	$ 9,954	$ 2,315	$ 6,177	$ 3,367	$ 9,931	$ 49,175
Product 2	281	2,336	1,234	6,176	1,322	678	3,737	1,781	5,377	8,254	6,906	4,208	42,290
Product 3	287	4,107	5,528	8,599	9,769	5,557	3,456	4,692	1,250	4,833	4,860	9,032	61,970
Product 4	436	2,202	5,607	8,340	5,832	2,350	1,669	5,094	9,658	7,479	775	1,785	51,227
Product 5	945	3,398	3,472	4,585	3,453	8,476	8,118	5,796	2,920	4,840	4,717	2,211	52,931
Product 6	781	6,982	7,018	1,885	4,336	6,394	6,989	2,038	8,336	5,546	9,805	1,250	61,360
Product 7	997	7,267	5,006	6,692	8,388	9,072	8,968	5,923	7,618	1,683	4,311	3,304	69,229
Product 8	253	4,100	6,328	3,807	7,850	1,213	5,253	3,934	4,261	4,933	2,931	3,685	48,548
Product 9	310	2,467	5,349	7,142	2,343	2,712	4,629	3,961	1,250	2,278	7,167	8,470	48,078
Product 10	544	2,783	1,642	1,582	2,456	5,584	1,255	7,915	2,343	1,012	869	5,882	33,867
Product 11	781	8,626	6,938	5,200	8,197	6,542	5,955	1,775	2,211	4,688	2,309	5,472	58,694
Product 12	278	6,720	4,754	3,556	2,535	4,100	4,740	7,047	9,284	4,445	5,633	7,557	60,649
Product 13	736	3,248	7,295	4,344	2,076	8,372	1,846	1,264	3,741	7,764	8,649	2,249	51,584
Product 14	991	5,004	6,873	7,009	8,399	4,204	8,290	2,695	1,417	6,003	9,688	4,852	65,425
Product 15	659	8,499	1,404	1,749	5,999	4,398	2,211	1,167	9,495	4,916	489	5,015	46,001
Product 16	203	5,359	8,656	4,240	2,690	2,211	4,893	1,264	7,469	7,903	4,367	1,210	50,465
Product 17	73	5,814	2,773	4,464	2,067	8,424	1,337	1,404	7,711	5,579	4,398	6,824	50,868
Product 18	183	1,422	1,572	5,771	6,611	9,131	9,121	1,237	9,969	2,604	9,375	1,350	58,346
Product 19	153	2,938	5,923	9,180	7,783	1,542	2,123	5,953	1,336	4,121	1,542	1,153	43,747
Product 20	968	3,310	4,472	3,065	4,700	6,384	9,079	6,995	1,542	965	7,584	5,922	54,986
Total	$ 10,590	$ 92,911	$ 93,954	$ 99,096	$ 99,790	$ 98,444	$ 96,136	$ 81,889	$ 99,503	$ 96,023	$ 99,742	$ 91,362	$ 1,059,440

Figure 9-25 We used highlight cells in the body of this table and data bars in the Totals column.

Creating Conditional Formatting Rules

Excel provides quite a nice variety of conditional formatting options, but you can always create your own as well. You may have noticed the New Rule command at the bottom of the Conditional Formatting menu and the ubiquitous More Rules command on each submenu. These all do essentially the same task—display the New Formatting Rule dialog box shown in Figure 9-26.

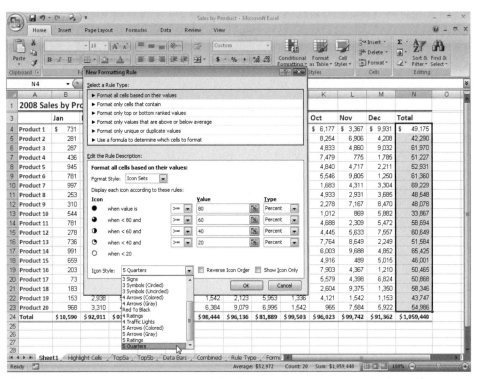

Figure 9-26 Use the New Formatting Rule dialog box to construct your own conditional formats.

All these commands open the same dialog box, but based on the menu or submenu where you clicked the command, a different rule type is selected when it opens. Each rule type displays a different set of rule description criteria below it. In Figure 9-26, we used the Format Style drop-down list to click Icon Sets and then selected 5 Quarters as the icon style. Each format style has a different set of controls for creating conditional formatting rules.

The first rule type—Format All Cells Based On Their Values—contains all the controls for creating data bars, color scales, and icon sets. The coolness factor is admittedly huge using these three format styles, but you have relatively limited control over the actual formatting. You can specify colors (except for icons), but that's about it. All the other rule types give you far greater formatting flexibility. The rule description controls for the second rule type—Format Only Cells That Contain, shown in Figure 9-27—is what you use to create highlight cells rules.

We discuss the last rule type, Use A Formula To Determine Which Cells To Format, in "Creating Conditional Formatting Formulas" on page 294.

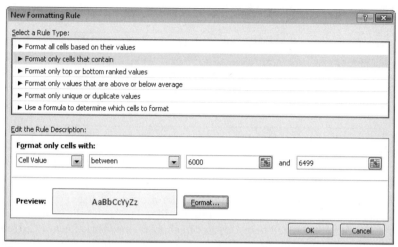

Figure 9-27 Use the second rule type in the New Formatting Rule dialog box to create your own highlight cells rules.

Use the first drop-down list in the Edit The Rule Description area to apply a condition based on the contents of the selected cell. Besides the Cell Value option, you can choose to create a rule for highlighting Specific Text, Dates Occurring (relative to now), Blanks, No Blanks, Errors, or No Errors. The second drop-down list contains the operators Between, Not Between, Equal To, Not Equal To, Greater Than, Less Than, Greater Than Or Equal To, and Less Than Or Equal To. Then you type the comparison values in the next two text boxes. If you select Between or Not Between in the second condition drop-down list, two text boxes appear in which you provide an upper and a lower limit, as shown in Figure 9-27. Otherwise, only one text box appears.

After you establish the Rule Description criteria, click the Format button. An abbreviated version of the Format Cells dialog box appears, containing only Number, Font, Border, and Fill tabs. Specify any combination of formats you want to apply when your rule is triggered. When you are finished, click OK to return to the New Formatting Rule dialog box, and click OK again to save your new rule. You can create as many rules as you want; next, we'll discuss how to work with them.

Managing Conditional Formatting Rules

You can apply as many conditional formats as you think are necessary—using three or more per table is not uncommon. But it is also not uncommon for you to tweak some of the numbers or adjust some of the formatting. To do so, click Home, Conditional Formatting, Manage Rules to display a Conditional Formatting Rules Manager dialog box similar to the one shown in Figure 9-28.

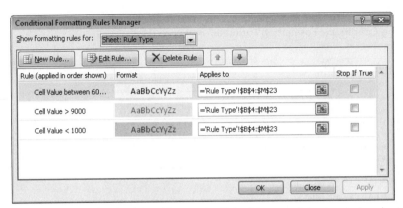

Figure 9-28 Use the Conditional Formatting Rules Manager dialog box to tweak any rules that have been applied in a workbook.

You can use the Show Formatting Rules For drop-down list at the top of the dialog box to choose where to look in the current workbook for rules: Each worksheet in the current workbook is listed here, or you can choose This Worksheet or Current Selection (the default). As you can see in Figure 9-28, you can create, edit, and delete rules using corresponding buttons. When you click New Rule, the now-familiar New Formatting Rule dialog box appears. When you click Edit Rule, a similar dialog box appears (Edit Formatting Rule), with the criteria for the selected rule displayed.

Excel applies the rules listed in the Conditional Formatting Rules Manager dialog box in the order in which they appear in the Rule list—new rules are added to the top of the list and are processed first. Use the two arrow buttons next to Delete Rule to move a selected rule up or down in the precedence list. The Applies To box contains the address of the cell range to which the rule has been applied. If you want to change the cell range, click the Collapse button on the right end of the Applies To text box to collapse the dialog box, letting you see the worksheet, as shown in Figure 9-29. When you do so, you can drag to select the cell range you want and insert the range address in the text box. To restore the dialog box to its original size, click the Collapse (now Expand) button again.

The Stop If True check box is present in this dialog box only for backward compatibility. Previous versions of Excel cannot recognize multiple conditional formatting rules, and instead they apply the rule that occurs last in precedence. If you need to share files with older versions, you'll need to choose which conditional formatting rule you prefer. Select the Stop If True check box for the last rule in the list if you want Excel to use the previous rule; select the Stop If True check box for the last two rules to use the third-to-last rule, and so on.

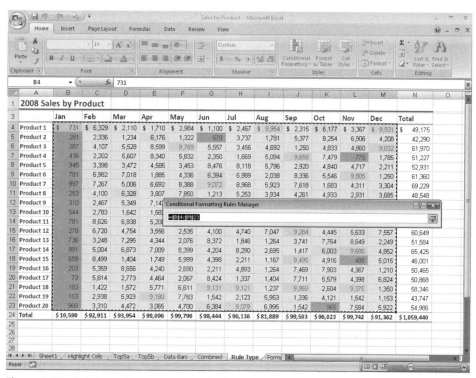

Figure 9-29 Click the Collapse icon in the Applies To text box to minimize the dialog box and allow direct selection of the cell range you want.

> **Note**
>
> When two (or more) conditional rules are true for a particular cell but they are both set to apply a similar format such as font color, the rule that is higher in the Conditional Formatting Rules Manager dialog box's list of precedence wins. Try to make multiple conditions compatible by having each rule apply a different type of format, such as the first rule applying cell color, the second applying font color, and the third applying bold formatting. In addition, conditional formats override manual formats when the condition in the cell is true.

Copying, Clearing, and Finding Conditional Formats

You can copy and paste conditionally formatted cells and use the Fill features or the Format Painter button to copy cells that you have conditionally formatted. When you do so, the conditional rules travel with the copied cells, and a new rule is created that references the new location in the workbook.

To remove conditional formatting rules, click Home, Conditional Formatting, Clear Rules, and then click Selected Cells or Entire Sheet to clear all the corresponding rules. If your conditions have been applied to a table or a PivotTable, additional corresponding commands are available.

You can use two commands on the Find & Select menu on the Home tab to locate cells on the current worksheet that have conditional formats applied to them. The Conditional Formatting command locates and selects all the cells on the current worksheet to which conditional formats have been applied. If conditional formatting exists in more than one cell region on the worksheet, using this command selects all the regions. This makes it easy to edit all the rules using the Conditional Formatting Rules Manager dialog box (refer to Figure 9-28). You can also use the Go To Special command on the Find & Select menu to get a little more specific. Clicking this command displays the Go To Special dialog box, shown in Figure 9-30.

Figure 9-30 Use the Go To Special dialog box to locate all conditional formats or just matching ones.

When you select the Conditional Formats option, two additional options—All and Same—become available. Selecting All is the same as using the Conditional Formatting command on the Find & Select menu, selecting all conditionally formatted cells and regions. If you use the Same option, however, Go To Special finds only those cells that have been formatted using the same condition that exists in the selected cell. Before clicking the Go To Special command, select an example cell containing the conditional format you want to locate.

Creating Conditional Formatting Formulas

The last rule type in the New Formatting Rule dialog box shown in Figure 9-26 offers the ability to create your own conditional formatting formulas. When you select the rule type labeled Use A Formula To Determine Which Cells To Format, the dialog box looks similar to the one shown in Figure 9-31.

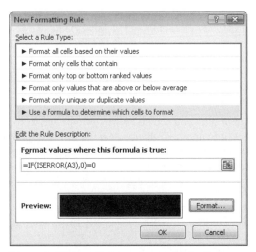

Figure 9-31 Use the last rule type in the list to create your own conditional formatting formulas.

You can create formulas to perform tasks such as identifying dates that fall on specific days of the week, specifying particular values, or doing anything you can't quite accomplish using the built-in conditional formatting tools. For example, using our example worksheet, we typed the following formula in the Format Values Where This Formula Is True text box in the New Formatting Rule dialog box:

=IF(ISERROR(A3),0)=0

Then we clicked the Format button and selected the color black on the Fill tab. The formula applies the selected fill color to any cell that generates an error value. (The cell reference A3 is the relative reference of the top-left cell of the range to which the format is applied.) When you use this technique, you can type any formula that results in the logical values TRUE (1) or FALSE (0). For example, you could use a logical formula such as =N4>AVERAGE($N$4:$N$37), which combines relative and absolute references to apply formatting to a cell when the value it contains is less than the average of the specified range. When you use relative references in this situation, the formatting formulas adjust in each cell where you apply or copy them, as regular cell formulas do.

> For more information, see "Using Cell References in Formulas" on page 428 and "Understanding Logical Functions" on page 507; also see Chapter 14, "Everyday Functions;" and Chapter 15, "Formatting and Calculating Date and Time."

Formatting in Depth

The formatting features in Office Excel 2007 control the display characteristics of numbers and text. It is important to keep in mind the difference between underlying and displayed worksheet values. Formats do not affect the underlying numeric or text values in cells. For example, if you type a number with six decimal places in a cell that is formatted with two decimal places, Excel displays the number with only two decimal places. However, the underlying value isn't changed, and Excel uses the underlying value in calculations.

> **Note**
>
> When you copy a cell or range of cells, you copy both its contents and its formatting. If you then paste this information into another cell or range, the formatting of the source cells replaces any existing formatting. For more information about copying and pasting, see Chapter 8, "Worksheet Editing Techniques."

Most of your formatting needs should be quickly and easily fulfilled using buttons and controls located on the Home tab on the Ribbon, but for more options, you can employ the Format Cells dialog box. To display the Format Cells dialog box, press Ctrl+1. Alternatively, click one of the Dialog Box Launchers adjacent to the titles of the Font, Alignment, and Number groups on the Home tab on the Ribbon. Clicking a Dialog Box Launcher opens the Format Cells dialog box and also activates the corresponding tab. Figure 9-32 shows the Format Cells dialog box.

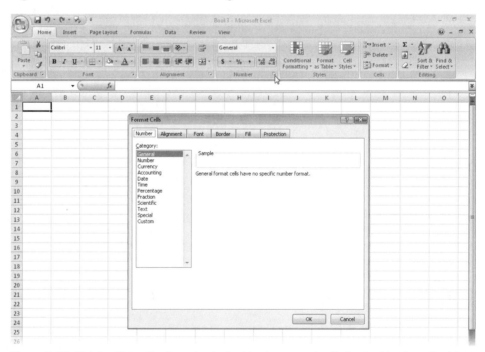

Figure 9-32 Click the Dialog Box Launcher in the Number group to display the Number tab of the Format Cells dialog box.

Throughout the following sections we'll discuss formatting options available directly on the Ribbon, but we'll go into more depth by employing the Format Cells dialog box.

Formatting Individual Characters

If you select a cell and apply formats, the entire contents of the cell receive the formats. However, you can also apply formatting to individual text characters within cells (but not numeric values or formulas). Select individual characters or words inside a cell, and apply the attributes you want. When you are finished, press Enter to see the results, an example of which is shown in Figure 9-33.

For more examples of formatting individual characters, see "Using Fonts" on page 323.

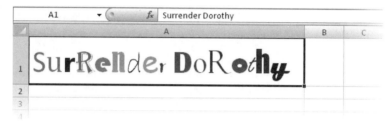

Figure 9-33 You can format individual characters within a cell.

Formatting As You Type

You can include special formatting characters—such as dollar signs, percent signs, commas, or fractions—to format numbers as you type them. When you type numeric-entry characters that represent a format Excel recognizes, Excel applies that format to the cell, on the fly. The following list describes some of the more common special formatting characters:

- If you type **$45.00** in a cell, Excel interprets your entry as the value 45 formatted as currency with two decimal places. Only the value 45 appears in the formula bar after you press Enter, but the formatted value, $45.00, appears in the cell.

- If you type **1 3/8** (with a single space between 1 and 3), 1 3/8 appears in the cell and 1.375 appears in the formula bar. However, if you type **3/8**, then 8-Mar appears in the cell, because date formats take precedence over fraction formats. Assuming you make the entry in the year 2008, then 3/8/2008 appears in the formula bar. To display 3/8 in the cell as a fraction so that 0.375 appears in the formula bar, you must type **0 3/8** (with a space between 0 and 3). For information about typing dates and a complete listing of date and time formats, see "Entering Dates and Times" on page 522.

- If you type **23%** in a cell, Excel applies the no-decimal percentage format to the cell, and 23% appears in the formula bar. Nevertheless, Excel uses the 0.23 decimal value for calculations.

- If you type **123,456** in a cell, Excel applies the comma format without decimal places. If you type **123,456.00**, Excel formats the cell with the comma format including two decimal places.

Understanding the General Format

The General format is the default format for all cells. Although it is not just a number format, it is nonetheless the first category in the drop-down list located in the Number group on the Home tab, as well as on the Number tab in the Format Cells dialog box (refer to Figure 9-32). Unless you specifically change the format of a cell, Excel displays any text or numbers you type in the General format. Except in the cases listed next, the General format displays exactly what you type. For example, if you type **123.45**, the cell displays 123.45. Here are the four exceptions:

- The General format abbreviates numbers too long to display in a cell. For example, if you type **12345678901234** (an integer) into a standard-width cell, Excel displays 1.23457E+13.

- Long decimal values are also rounded or displayed in scientific notation. Thus, if you type **123456.7812345** in a standard-width cell, the General format displays 123456.8. The actual typed values are preserved and used in all calculations, regardless of the display format.

- The General format does not display trailing zeros. For example, if you type **123.0**, Excel displays 123.

- A decimal fraction typed without a number to the left of the decimal point is displayed with a zero. For example, if you type **.123**, Excel displays 0.123.

Formatting Numbers

The Number format is the second option in the drop-down list in the Number group on the Home tab, as well as the second category on the Number tab in the Format Cells dialog box. When you use the drop-down list, selecting Number applies a default number format, with two decimal places and comma separators. For example, if you select the Number format with a cell selected containing 1234.556, the cell displays the number as 1,234.56. Excel rounds the decimal value to two places in the process, which does not change the actual value in the cell, just the displayed value.

Comma Style

> **Note**
> The Comma Style button in the Number group on the Home tab applies the same format as does the Number format in the drop-down list.

In the Format Cells dialog box, the Number category contains additional options, letting you display numbers in integer, fixed-decimal, and punctuated formats, as shown in Figure 9-34. It is essentially the General format with additional control over displayed decimal places, thousand separators, and negative numbers. You can use this category to format any numbers that do not fall into any of the other categories.

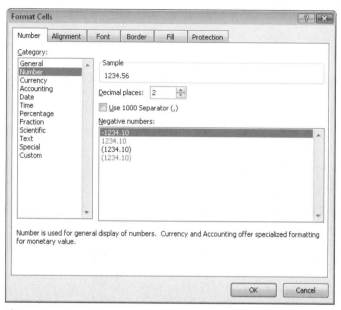

Figure 9-34 Use the Number category for general-purpose, noncurrency numeric formatting.

Follow these guidelines when using the Number category:

- Select the number of decimal places to display (0 to 30) by typing or scrolling to the value in the Decimal Places box.

- Select the Use 1000 Separator (,) check box to add commas between hundreds and thousands, and so on.

- Select an example in the Negative Numbers list to display negative numbers preceded by a minus sign, in red, in parentheses, or in both red and parentheses.

> **Note**
>
> When formatting numbers, always select a cell containing a number before opening the Format Cells dialog box so you can see the results in the Sample area.

Using Currency Formats

The quickest way to apply currency formatting is by clicking Currency in the Number drop-down list in the Number group on the Home tab, as shown in Figure 9-35. This

Currency format is similar to the Number format that precedes it in the drop-down list, except it also includes the default currency symbol for your locale. Notice that most of the commands listed here display little previews showing you what the contents of the active cell will look like if you click that command.

> **Note**
>
> Despite the button's appearance, clicking the $ button on the Home tab actually applies a two-decimal Accounting format, which is similar to, but a little different from, the Currency format. We'll discuss Accounting formats in the next section.

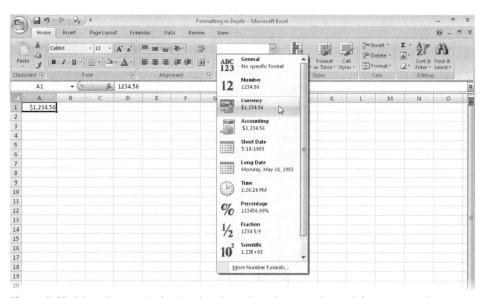

Figure 9-35 Select Currency in the Number drop-down list to apply the default currency format.

For additional currency formatting options, select the Currency category in the Format Cells dialog box, which offers a similar set of options as the Number category (refer to Figure 9-34) but adds a drop-down list of worldwide currency symbols. Besides clicking the Dialog Box Launcher in the Number group on the Home tab to display the Format Cells dialog box, you can also select the More command at the bottom of the Number drop-down list shown in Figure 9-35.

Note

You might notice that the list of currency symbols in the Format Cells dialog box conspicuously lacks an option for the Euro symbol. There is a Euro format you can choose from the menu adjacent to the Accounting Number Format ($) button on the Home tab, which we'll discuss in the next section. Also, some currency conversion tools are available via an add-in that you can install. For more information, see "Using the Euro Currency Tools Add-In" on page 549.

Using the Decimal Buttons

You can change the number of displayed decimal places in any selected cell or range at any time, using two buttons—Increase Decimal and Decrease Decimal—in the Number group on the Home tab:

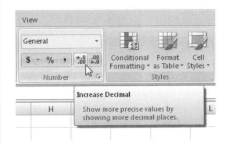

The Increase Decimal button displays an arrow pointing to the left, and the Decrease Decimal button displays an arrow pointing to the right, which might seem backward to those of us in the left-to-right/smaller-to-larger world of Western culture, but of course these buttons address what happens only on the right side of the decimal point. Each click adds or subtracts one decimal place from the displayed value. Interestingly, although you can specify up to 30 decimal places using the Format Cells dialog box, you can increase the number of decimal places to a maximum of 127, one click at a time, using the Increase Decimal button.

Using Accounting Formats

Accounting
Number Format

The most often-used Accounting format is directly available on the Home tab on the Ribbon, using the Accounting Number Format button in the Number group. Clicking this button applies a standard two-decimal-place format with comma separators and currency symbols to the selected cells. Clicking the arrow button adjacent to the Accounting Number Format button displays a menu providing access to a few additional currency symbols, as shown in Figure 9-36.

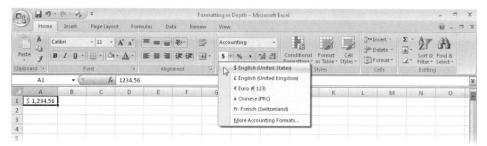

Figure 9-36 The $ button applies a standard Accounting format and offers a few optional currency symbols.

The Accounting formats address the needs of accounting professionals, but they benefit the rest of us as well. When you use one of these formats with the Single Accounting or Double Accounting font formats (to add underlines to your numbers), you can easily create profit and loss (P&L) statements, balance sheets, and other schedules that conform to generally accepted accounting principles (GAAP). The Accounting formats correspond roughly to the Currency format in appearance—you can display numbers with or without your choice of currency symbols and specify the number of decimal places. However, the two formats have some distinct differences. The rules governing the Accounting formats are as follows:

- The Accounting format displays every currency symbol flush with the left side of the cell and displays numbers flush with the right side, as shown in Figure 9-36. The result is that all the currency symbols in the same column are vertically aligned, which looks much cleaner than Currency formats.

- In the Accounting format, negative values are always displayed in parentheses and always in black—displaying numbers in red is not an option.

- The Accounting format includes a space equivalent to the width of a parenthesis on the right side of the cell so that numbers line up evenly in columns of mixed positive and negative values.

- The Accounting format displays zero values as dashes. The spacing of the dashes depends on whether you select decimal places. If you include two decimal places, the dashes line up under the decimal point.

- Finally, the Accounting format is the only built-in format that includes formatting criteria for text. It includes spaces equivalent to the width of a parenthesis on each side of text so that it, too, lines up evenly with the numbers in a column.

Typically, when creating a GAAP-friendly worksheet of currency values, you would use currency symbols only in the top row and in the totals row at the bottom of each column of numbers. This makes good sense, because all those dollar signs would make for a much busier table if every number in the table displayed them. The middle of the table is then formatted using a compatible format without currency symbols, as shown in Figure 9-37.

	A	B	C	D	E	F	G	H	I	J	K	L	M	N	O
1	2008 Sales by Product														
3		Jan	Feb	Mar	Apr	May	Jun	Jul	Aug	Sep	Oct	Nov	Dec	Total	
4	Product 1	$ 731	$ 6,329	$ 2,110	$ 1,710	$ 2,984	$ 1,100	$ 2,467	$ 9,954	$ 2,315	$ 6,177	$ 3,367	$ 9,931	$ 49,175	
5	Product 2	281	2,336	1,234	6,176	1,322	678	3,737	1,781	5,377	8,254	6,906	4,208	42,290	
6	Product 3	287	4,107	5,528	8,599	9,769	5,557	3,456	4,692	1,250	4,833	4,860	9,032	61,970	
7	Product 4	436	2,202	5,607	8,340	5,832	2,350	1,669	5,094	9,658	7,479	775	1,785	51,227	
8	Product 5	945	3,398	3,472	4,585	3,453	8,476	8,118	5,796	2,920	4,840	4,717	2,211	52,931	
9	Product 6	781	6,982	7,018	1,885	4,336	6,394	6,989	2,038	8,336	5,546	9,805	1,250	61,360	
10	Product 7	997	7,267	5,006	6,692	8,388	9,072	8,968	5,923	7,618	1,683	4,311	3,304	69,229	
11	Product 8	253	4,100	6,328	3,807	7,850	1,213	5,253	3,934	4,261	4,933	2,931	3,685	48,548	
12	Product 9	310	2,467	5,349	7,142	2,343	2,712	4,629	3,961	1,250	2,278	7,167	8,470	48,078	
13	Product 10	544	2,783	1,642	1,582	2,456	5,584	1,255	7,915	2,343	1,012	869	5,882	33,867	
14	Product 11	781	8,626	6,938	5,200	8,197	6,542	5,955	1,775	2,211	4,688	2,309	5,472	58,694	
15	Product 12	278	6,720	4,754	3,556	2,535	4,100	4,740	7,047	9,284	4,445	5,633	7,557	60,649	
16	Product 13	736	3,248	7,295	4,344	2,076	8,372	1,846	1,264	3,741	7,764	8,649	2,249	51,584	
17	Product 14	991	5,004	6,873	7,009	8,399	4,204	8,290	2,695	1,417	6,003	9,688	4,852	65,425	
18	Product 15	659	8,499	1,404	1,749	5,999	4,398	2,211	1,167	9,495	4,916	489	5,015	46,001	
19	Product 16	203	5,359	8,656	4,240	2,690	2,211	4,893	1,264	7,469	7,903	4,367	1,210	50,465	
20	Product 17	73	5,814	2,773	4,464	2,067	8,424	1,337	1,404	7,711	5,579	4,398	6,824	50,868	
21	Product 18	183	1,422	1,572	5,771	6,611	9,131	9,121	1,237	9,969	2,604	9,375	1,350	58,346	
22	Product 19	153	2,938	5,923	9,180	7,783	1,542	2,123	5,953	1,336	4,121	1,542	1,153	43,747	
23	Product 20	968	3,310	4,472	3,065	4,700	6,384	9,079	6,995	1,542	965	7,584	5,922	54,986	
24	Total	$10,590	$92,911	$93,954	$99,096	$99,790	$98,444	$96,136	$81,889	$99,503	$96,023	$99,742	$91,362	$1,059,440	
25															
26															

Figure 9-37 It is standard practice to use currency symbols only in the top and bottom rows of a table.

Luckily, Excel makes it easy to format this way, using buttons in the Number group on the Home tab on the Ribbon. Despite seemingly incompatible button names, both the Accounting Number Format button and the Comma Style button apply accounting formats, adhering to the rules described earlier. So, to format the numeric entries in the table shown in Figure 9-37, select the first and last rows, click the Accounting Number Format button, then select all the cells in between, and finally click the Comma Style button. (We then selected all the numeric cells in the table and clicked the Decrease Decimal button twice to hide all the decimal values.)

Using Accounting Underlines

Generally accepted accounting principles specify the proper usage of single and double underlines in tables. The Underline button on the Home tab includes a menu letting you select Single or Double underlines, but unfortunately these do not rise to the accepted standard. But fear not—Office Excel 2007 provides two Underline formats in a drop-down list of the same name on the Font tab in the Format Cells dialog box. These differ from their regular counterparts in two ways. First, accounting underlines are applied to the entire width of the cell (minus a parenthesis-sized space on each side), whereas regular underlines are applied only under the actual characters in a cell. If the cell contains a text entry that extends beyond the cell border, the accounting underlines stop at the cell border. Second, the accounting underline formats appear near the bottom of cells, unlike regular underlines, which are applied much closer to the numbers or text in the cell, drawing annoying lines through commas and the descenders of letters like g and p. Of course, you can also apply single-line and double-line cell borders instead of underline formats, which is the approach used when you add a totals row to a table using the Totals Row option on the Table Tools Design tab.

For information about font formats, see "Using Fonts" on page 323. For information about tables, see "Formatting Tables" on page 268, and see Chapter 21.

Formatting Percentages

Percent Style

Not surprisingly, using the Percentage format displays numbers as percentages. The decimal point of the formatted number, in effect, moves two places to the right, and a percent sign appears at the end of the number. For example, if you choose a percentage format without decimal places, the entry **0.1234** will be displayed as 12%; if you select two decimal places, the entry **0.1234** will be displayed as 12.34%. Remember that you can always adjust the number of displayed decimal places using the Increase Decimal and Decrease Decimal buttons.

An interesting (and helpful) quirk about percentage formats is that they behave differently depending on whether you type a number and then apply the format or type a number in a previously formatted cell. For example, Figure 9-38 shows two cells formatted as percentages. We typed the same number—**22.33**—in each cell, but only cell A1 was previously formatted with the Percentage format; we clicked the Percent Style button *after* typing the value in cell A2.

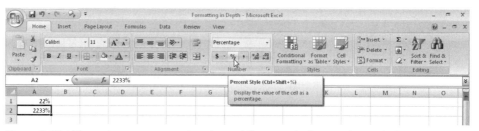

Figure 9-38 When using percentages, it makes a difference whether you format before or after typing values.

As you can see, it makes a world of difference which way you do this. So, why is this behavior helpful? For example, if a worksheet contains a displayed value of 12% and you need to change it to 13%, it is not particularly intuitive to type **.13** in the cell (including the leading decimal point). Usability studies show that most people would type **13** in this situation, which would result in a displayed value of 1300% (if not for the quirky behavior). If you really did intend to type **1300%** and saw 13% displayed, you'd catch it and fix it right away, no harm done. But if you apply the Percentage format to a range of cells that already contain values (or formulas that result in values), check all the cells afterward to make sure you get the intended results.

Formatting Fractions

The formats in the Fraction category in the Format Cells dialog box, shown in Figure 9-39, display fractional numbers as actual fractions rather than as decimal values. As with all number formats, the underlying value does not change despite the displayed value of the fraction.

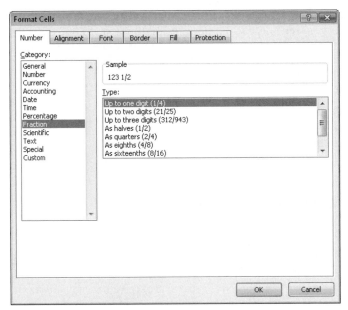

Figure 9-39 Excel provides many fraction-formatting options.

You can generate some wild, nonstandard fractions unless you apply constraints using options in the Format Cells dialog box. Here is how Office Excel 2007 applies different fraction formats:

● The Up To One Digit (single-digit) fraction format displays 123.456 as 123 1/2, rounding the display to the nearest value that can be represented as a single-digit fraction.

● The Up To Two Digits (double-digit) fraction format uses the additional precision allowed by the format and displays 123.456 as 123 26/57.

● The Up To Three Digits (triple-digit) fraction format displays 123.456 as the even more precise 123 57/125.

● The remaining six fraction formats specify the exact denominator you want by rounding to the nearest equivalent, displaying 123.456 using the As Sixteenths format, or 123 7/16.

You can also apply fraction formatting on the fly by typing fractional values in a specific way. Type a number (or a zero), type a space, and then type the fraction, as in 123 1/2. For more details, see "Formatting As You Type" on page 297.

Formatting Scientific (Exponential) Values

The Scientific format displays numbers in exponential notation. For example, a two-decimal Scientific format (the default) displays the number 98765432198 as 9.88E+10 in a standard-width cell. The number 9.88E+10 is 9.88 times 10 to the 10th power. The symbol E stands for *exponent*, a synonym here for 10 to the *n*th power. The expression "10 to the 10th power" means 10 times itself 10 times, or 10,000,000,000. Multiplying this value by 9.88 gives you 98,800,000,000, an approximation of 98,765,432,198. Increasing the number of decimal places (the only option available for this format) increases the precision and will likely require a wider cell to accommodate the displayed value.

You can also use the Scientific format to display very small numbers. For example, this format displays 0.000000009 as 9.00E−09 in a standard-width cell, which equates to 9 times 10 to the negative 9th power. The expression "10 to the negative 9th power" means 1 divided by 10 to the 9th power, 1 divided by 10 nine times, or 0.000000001. Multiplying this number by nine results in our original number, 0.000000009.

Understanding the Text Format

Applying the Text format to a cell indicates that the entry in the cell is to be treated as text, even if it's a number. For example, a numeric value is ordinarily right-aligned in its cell. If you apply the Text format to the cell, however, the value is left-aligned as if it were a text entry. For all practical purposes, a numeric constant formatted as text is still considered a number because Excel is capable of recognizing its numeric value anyway.

Using the Special Formats

The four Special formats shown in Figure 9-40 are a result of many requests from users. These generally noncalculated numbers include two ZIP code formats, a phone number format (complete with the area code in parentheses), and a Social Security number format. Using each of these Special formats, you can quickly type numbers without having to type the punctuation characters.

The following are guidelines for using the Special formats:

- **Zip Code** Leading zeros are retained to correctly display the code, as in 04321. In Normal format, if you type **04321**, Excel drops the zero and displays 4321.

- **Phone Number** Excel applies parentheses around the area code and dashes between the digits, making it much easier to type many numbers at the same time, because you don't have to move your hand from the keypad. Furthermore, the numbers you type remain numbers instead of becoming text entries, which they would become if you typed parentheses or dashes in the cell.

- **Social Security Number** Excel places dashes after the third and fifth numbers. For example, if you type **123456789**, Excel will display 123-45-6789.

- **Locale** This drop-down list lets you select from more than 120 locations with unique formats. For example, if you select Vietnamese, only two Special formats are available: Metro Phone Number and Suburb Phone Number.

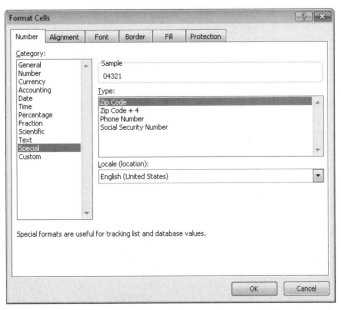

Figure 9-40 Excel provides several frequently requested formats in the Special category.

Creating Custom Number Formats

Most number formats you need are available using commands and buttons on the Ribbon, but you can use the Format Cells dialog box to accomplish minor feats of formatting that might surprise you. We'll use the Custom category on the Number tab in the Format Cells dialog box, shown in Figure 9-41, to create custom number formats using special formatting codes. (To quickly display the Format Cells dialog box, press Ctrl+1.) Excel adds new formats to the bottom of the list of formatting codes in the Type list, which also includes built-in formats. To delete a custom format, select the format in the Format Cells dialog box, and click Delete. You cannot delete built-in formats.

Creating New Number Formats   The quickest way to start creating a custom format is to use one of the existing custom formats as a starting point. Here's an easy way to build on an existing format, as well as to see what the codes in the Type list mean:

1. Type a number (or, in the case of our example, a date), and apply the built-in format that most closely resembles the custom format you want to create. Leave this cell selected.

2. On the Number tab in the Format Cells dialog box, select the Custom category. The format you selected is highlighted in the Type list, representing the code equivalent of the format you want to modify, as shown in Figure 9-41.

3. Edit the contents of the Type text box, using the codes listed in Table 9-1. The original format isn't affected, and the new format is added to the bottom of the Type list.

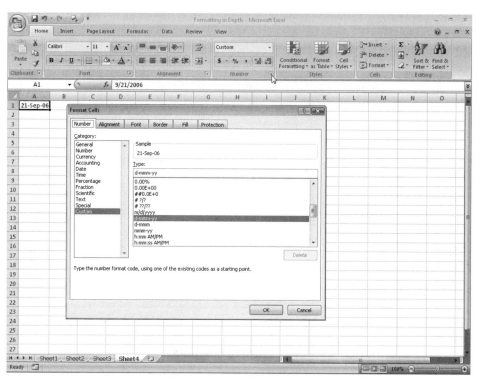

Figure 9-41 Use the Custom category to create new formats using special codes.

For example, to create a format that displays the date and time with the longest available format for day, month, year, start by typing a date in a cell, and then select it. In the Custom category in the Format Cells dialog box, edit the format in the Type text box to read *dddd, mmmm dd, yyyy – hh:mm AM/PM* (including spaces and commas), and then click OK. Figure 9-42 shows the result.

> **Note**
>
> Saving the workbook saves your new formats, but to carry special formats from one workbook to another, you must copy and paste a cell with the Custom format. For easy access to special formats, consider saving them in one workbook.

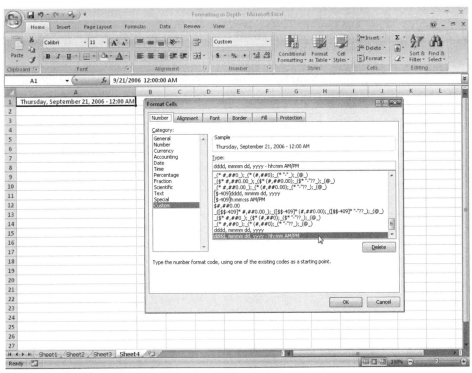

Figure 9-42 We created a custom format by typing codes in the Type text box.

You can create any number format using the codes in Table 9-1.

Table 9-1 Custom Format Symbols

Symbol	Meaning
0	**Digit placeholder.** This symbol ensures that a specified number of digits appear on each side of the decimal point. For example, if the format is *0.000*, the value .987 is displayed as 0.987. If the format is *0.0000*, the value .987 is displayed as 0.9870. If a number has more digits to the right of the decimal point than the number of zeros specified in the format, the number in the cell is rounded. For example, if the format is *0.00*, the value .987 is displayed as 0.99; if the format is *0.0*, .987 is rounded to 1.0.
?	**Digit placeholder.** This symbol follows the same rules as the 0 placeholder, except that space is left for insignificant zeros on either side of the decimal point. This placeholder aligns numbers on the decimal points. For example, 1.4 and 1.45 would line up on the decimal point if both were formatted as *0.??*.

Symbol	Meaning
#	**Digit placeholder.** This symbol works like 0, except that extra zeros do not appear if the number has fewer digits on either side of the decimal point than # placeholders specified in the format. This symbol shows Excel where to display commas or other separating symbols. The format #,###, for example, tells Excel to display a comma after every third digit to the left of the decimal point.
.	**Decimal point.** This symbol determines how many digits (0 or #) appear to the right and left of the decimal point. If the format contains only # placeholders to the left of this symbol, Excel begins numbers less than 1 with a decimal point. To avoid this, use 0 as the first digit placeholder to the left of the decimal point instead of #. If you want Excel to include commas and display at least one digit to the left of the decimal point in all cases, specify the format #,##0.
%	**Percentage indicator.** This symbol multiplies the entry by 100 and inserts the % character.
/	**Fraction format character.** This symbol displays the fractional part of a number in a nondecimal format. The number of digit placeholders that surround this character determines the accuracy of the display. For example, the decimal fraction 0.269 when formatted with # ?/? is displayed as 1/4, but when formatted with # ???/??? is displayed as 46/171.
,	**Thousands separator.** If the format contains a comma surrounded by #, 0, or ? placeholders, Excel uses commas to separate hundreds from thousands, thousands from millions, and so on. In addition, the comma acts as a rounding and scaling agent. Use one comma at the end of a format to tell Excel to round a number and display it in thousands; use two commas to tell Excel to round to the nearest million. For example, the format code #,###,###, would round 4567890 to 4,568, whereas the format code #,###,###,, would round it to 5.
E– E+ e– e+	**Scientific format characters.** If a format contains one 0 or # to the right of an E–, E+, e–, or e+, Excel displays the number in scientific notation and inserts E or e in the displayed value. The number of 0 or # placeholders to the right of the E or e determines the minimum number of digits in the exponent. Use E– or e– to place a negative sign by negative exponents; use E+ or e+ to place a negative sign by negative exponents and a positive sign by positive exponents.
$ – + / ( ) space	**Standard formatting characters.** Typing any of these symbols adds the actual corresponding character directly into your format.
\	**Literal demarcation character.** Precede each character you want to display in the cell—except for : $ – + / ( ) and space—with a backslash. (Excel does not display the backslash.) For example, the format code #,##0 \D;-#,##0 \C displays positive numbers followed by a space and a D and displays negative numbers followed by a space and a C. To insert several characters, use the quotation-mark technique described in the "Text" table entry.
_	**Underscore.** This code leaves space equal to the width of the next character. For example, _) leaves a space equal to the width of the close parenthesis. Use this formatting character for alignment purposes.

Symbol	Meaning
"Text"	**Literal character string.** This formatting code works like the backslash technique except that all text can be included within one set of double quotation marks without using a separate demarcation character for each literal character.
*	**Repetition initiator.** This code repeats the next character in the format enough times to fill the column width. Use only one asterisk in the format.
@	**Text placeholder.** If the cell contains text, this placeholder inserts that text in the format where the @ appears. For example, the format code *"This is a"* @ displays "This is a debit" in a cell containing the word *debit*.

Table 9-2 lists the built-in formats and indicates how these codes relate to the other categories on the Number tab. (This table does not list Date and Time codes, which are covered in Chapter 15.)

Table 9-2 Built-In Custom Format Codes

Category	Custom Format Codes
0	Digit
General	No specific format
Number	0
	0.00
	#,##0
	#,##0.00
	#,##0_);(#,##0)
	#,##0_);[Red](#,##0)
	#,##0.00_);(#,##0.00)
	#,##0.00_);[Red](#,##0.00)
Currency	$#,##0_);($#,##0)
	$#,##0_);[Red]($#,##0)
	$#,##0.00_);($#,##0.00)
	$#,##0.00_);[Red]($#,##0.00)
Percentage	0%
	0.00%
Scientific	0.00E+00
	##0.0E+0
Fraction	# ?/?
	# ??/??
Date	(See Chapter 15)

Category	Custom Format Codes
Time	(See Chapter 15)
Text	@
Accounting	_($* #,##0_);_($* (#,##0);_($* "-"_);_(@_)
	_(* #,##0_);_(* (#,##0);_(* "-"_);_(@_)
	_($* #,##0.00_);_($* (#,##0.00);_($* "-"??_);_(@_)
	_(* #,##0.00_);_(* (#,##0.00);_(* "-"??_);_(@_)

Creating Four-Part Formats Within each custom format definition, you can specify completely different formats for positive, negative, zero, and text values. You can create custom formats with as many as four parts, separating the portions by semicolons—Positive Number; Negative Number; Zero; Text. Figure 9-43 shows how three different formats are constructed using codes.

	B	C	D	E	F	G
2	**Syntax:**	**Positive Number code**	**Negative Number code**	**Zero code**	**Text code**	
3	**Accounting #3**	_($* #,##0.00_);	_($* (#,##0.00);	_($* "-"??_);	_(@_)	
4	**Value in cell**	123.45	-123.45	0	see note	
5	**Displayed Value**	$ 123.45	$ (123.45)	$ -	see note	
6	**Custom Billing**	"Amount due: "$#,##0.00_);	"Credit: "($#,##0.00);	"Let's call it even.";	"Please note: "@	
7	**Value in cell**	123.45	-123.45	0	due 3/15	
8	**Displayed Value**	Amount due: $123.45	Credit: ($123.45)	Let's call it even.	Please note: due 3/15	
9	**Custom Part #**	"Part # "### ####				
10	**Value in cell**	1234567				
11	**Displayed Value**	Part # 123-4567				
12						

Figure 9-43 You can create your own four-part formats.

You'll find the Formatting Numbers.xlsx file in the Sample Files section of the companion CD. It contains many of the custom formatting code examples described in this section.

Among the built-in formats, only the Accounting formats use all four parts, as shown in Figure 9-43, which breaks down each part of the third Accounting format in Table 9-2. The following are some guidelines for creating multipart formats:

- If your custom format includes only one part, Excel applies that format to positive, negative, and zero values.

- If your custom format includes two parts, the first part applies to positive and zero values; the second part applies to only negative values.

- If your custom format has three parts, the third part controls the display of zero values.

- The fourth and last element in a four-way format controls text-value formatting. Any formats with three or fewer elements have no effect on text entries.

> **Note**
>
> If you prefer, you can suppress the display of all zero values in a worksheet, including the displayed values of formulas with a zero result. Click the Microsoft Office Button, Excel Options, and then click the Advanced category. In the Display Options For This Worksheet area, clear the Show A Zero In Cells That Have Zero Value check box.

Adding Color to Formats   You can also use the Number formats to change the color of selected cell entries. For example, you might use color to distinguish categories of information or to make totals stand out. You can even create formats that assign different colors to specific numeric ranges so that, for example, all values greater than or less than a specified value appear in a different color.

Create Custom Billing and Part Number Formats

Suppose you create a billing statement and you want to format the totals in the Amount Due column so they display differently depending on the value in each cell. You might create the Custom Billing format shown in Figure 9-43, which was created using the following code:

```
"Amount due: "$#,##0.00_);"Credit: "($#,##0.00);"Let's call it even. ";"Please note: "@
```

Suppose you're creating an inventory worksheet and you want all the entries in a particular column to appear in the format *Part # XXX-XXXX*, shown as the *Custom Part #* format in Figure 9-43, which was created using the following code:

```
"Part # "###-####
```

Using this code lets you type your part numbers as actual numbers rather than as text entries, which happens if you include any non-numeric characters, including dashes. This way, you can sort your part numbers properly and otherwise manipulate them as numeric data.

> **Note**
>
> You can create codes that assign different colors based on the value in the cell, but an easier way is built into Excel: You can use the Conditional Formatting menu on the Home tab on the Ribbon. For more information, see "Formatting Conditionally" on page 284.

To change the color of an entry, type the name of the new color, in brackets, in front of each segment of code. For example, if you want to apply a blue Currency format with two decimal places, edit the *$#,##0.00_);($#,##0.00)* format as follows:

```
[Blue]$#,##0.00_);( $#,##0.00)
```

When you apply this format to a worksheet, positive and zero values appear in blue, and text and negative values appear as usual, in black. The following simple four-part format code displays positive values in blue, negative values in red, zero values in yellow, and text in green (with no additional number formatting specified).

```
[Blue];[Red];[Yellow];[Green]
```

You can specify the following color names in your formats: Black, Blue, Cyan, Green, Magenta, Red, White, and Yellow. You can also specify a color as COLOR*n*, where *n* is a number in the range 1 through 16. Excel selects the corresponding color from your worksheet's current 16-color palette.

> **Note**
>
> If you define colors that are not among your system's repertoire of solids, Excel produces them by mixing dots from solid colors. Such blended colors, which are said to be *dithered*, work well for shading. But for text and lines, Excel always uses the nearest solid color in preference to a dithered color.

TROUBLESHOOTING

Decimal points in my Currency formats don't line up.

Sometimes when you use Currency formats with trailing characters, such as the French Canadian dollar (23.45 $), you want to use the GAAP practice of using currency symbols only at the top and bottom of a column of numbers. The numbers between should not display any currency symbols, so how do you make all the decimal points line up properly?

You can create a custom format code to apply to the noncurrency format numbers in the middle of the column. An underscore character (_) in the format code tells Excel to leave a space that is equal in width to the character that follows it. For example, the code _$ leaves a space equal to the width of the dollar sign. Thus, the following code does the trick for you:

```
#,##0.00 _$;[Red]#,##0.00 _$
```

Make sure you add a space between the zeros and the underscores to properly line the numbers up with the built-in French Canadian dollar format.

Using Custom Format Conditional Operators   You can create custom formats that are variable. To do so, you can add a conditional operator to the first two parts of the standard four-part custom format. This, in effect, replaces the positive/negative formats with either/or formats. The third format becomes the default format for values that don't match the other two conditions, or the "else" format. You can use the conditional operators <, >, =, <=, >=, and <> with any number to define a format.

For example, suppose you are tracking accounts-receivable balances. To display accounts with balances of more than $50,000 in blue, negative values in parentheses and in red, and all other values in the default color, create this format:

```
[Blue][>50000]$#,## 0.00_);[Red][<0]($# ,##0.00);$#,##0.00_)
```

Using these conditional operators can also be a powerful aid if you need to scale numbers. For example, if your company produces a product that requires a few milliliters of a compound for each unit and you make thousands of units every day, you need to convert from milliliters to liters and kiloliters when you budget the use of this compound. Excel can make this conversion with the following numeric format:

```
[>999999]#,##0,," kl";[>999]##," L";#" ml"
```

The following table shows the effects of this format on various worksheet entries:

Entry	Display
72	72 ml
7286957	7 kl
7632	8 L

As you can see, using a combination of conditional formats, the thousands separator, and text with spaces within quotation marks can improve both the readability and the effectiveness of your worksheet, without increasing the number of formulas.

The Hidden Number Format

To hide values in a worksheet, assign a null format to them. To create a null format, type only the semicolon separator for that portion of the format. For example, to hide negative and zero values only, use this format:

```
$#,##0.00;;
```

To hide all entries in a cell, use this format:

```
;;;
```

The null format hides the cell contents in the worksheet, but the entry is still visible in the formula bar and accessible via reference in formulas. To hide the cell contents so they don't appear in the worksheet or the formula bar, use the worksheet and cell protection features. For more information, see "Protecting Worksheets" on page 156.

Aligning Data in Cells

The Alignment group on the Home tab on the Ribbon, shown in Figure 9-44, contains the most useful tools for positioning data within cells. For more precise control and additional options, click the Dialog Box Launcher adjacent to the title of the Alignment group to display the Format Cells dialog box shown in Figure 9-45.

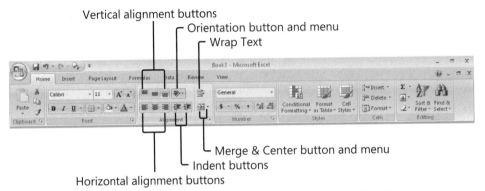

Figure 9-44 Excel can address most of your alignment needs via tools on the Ribbon.

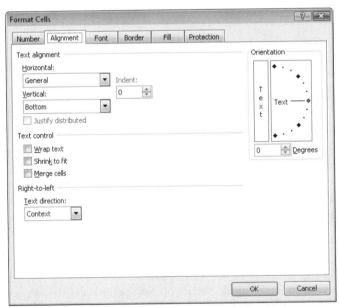

Figure 9-45 Alignment means a lot more than just right, left, or justified.

The Alignment tab in the Format Cells dialog box includes the following options:

- **Horizontal** These options control the right or left alignment within the cell. The General option, the default for Horizontal alignment, right-aligns numeric values and left-aligns text values.

- **Vertical** These options control the top-to-bottom position of cell contents within cells.

- **Text Control** These three check boxes wrap text in cells, reduce cell contents until they fit in the current cell width, and merge selected cells into one.

- **Text Direction** The options on this drop-down list format individual cells for right-to-left languages. The default option is Context, which responds to the regional settings on your computer. (This feature is applicable only if support is available for right-to-left languages.)

- **Orientation** These controls let you precisely specify the angle of text within a cell, from vertical to horizontal, and anywhere in between.

Aligning Text Horizontally

Align Left

Center

Align Right

The Align Left, Center, and Align Right buttons on the Ribbon correspond to three of the options on the Horizontal drop-down list on the Alignment tab in the Format Cells dialog box: Left (Indent), Center, and Right (Indent). These options align the contents of the selected cells, overriding the default cell alignment. Figure 9-46 shows the Horizontal alignment options in action, all of which we'll discuss in detail in the following sections.

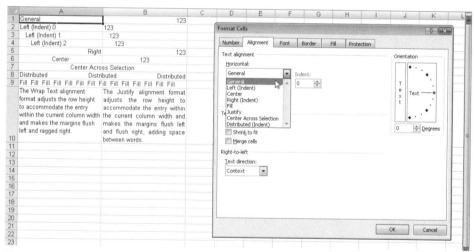

Figure 9-46 Use the Horizontal alignment options to control the placement of text from left to right.

Decrease Indent

Increase Indent

Indenting Cell Contents The Increase Indent button in the Alignment group on the Home tab simultaneously applies left alignment to the selected cells and indents the contents by the width of one character. (One character width is approximately the width of the capital X in the Normal cell style.) Each click increments the amount of indentation by one. The adjacent Decrease Indent button does just the opposite, decreasing the indentation by one character width with each click.

Chapter 9

In the Format Cells dialog box, the corresponding options are Left (Indent) and Right (Indent). These are linked to the Indent control, located next to the Horizontal drop-down list shown in Figure 9-46. Ordinarily, the value in the box is zero—the standard left-alignment setting. Each time you increase this value by one, the entry in the cell begins one character width to the right. For example, in Figure 9-46, row 2 is formatted with no left indent, row 3 with a left indent of 1, and row 4 with a left indent of 2. The maximum indent value you can use is 250.

Distributing Cell Contents   Using the Distributed (Indent) option in the Horizontal drop-down list, you can position text fragments contained in a cell with equal spacing within the cell. For example, in Figure 9-46, we first merged cells A8:B8 into one cell, then typed the word **Distributed** three times in the merged cell, and then applied the Distributed (Indent) horizontal alignment. The result shows that Excel expanded the spaces between words in equal amounts to justify the contents within the cell.

To learn about merging, see "Merging and Unmerging Cells" on page 337.

Centering Text Across Columns   The Center Across Selection option in the Horizontal text alignment drop-down list centers text from one cell across all selected blank cells to the right or to the next cell in the selection that contains text. For example, in Figure 9-46, we applied the Center Across Selection format to cells A7:B7. The centered text is in cell A7.

> Note
>
> Although the results might look similar, the Center Across Selection alignment option does not merge cells. When you use Center Across Selection, the text from the leftmost cell remains in its cell but is displayed centered across the entire selected range.

Filling Cells with Characters   The Fill option in the Horizontal alignment drop-down list repeats your cell entry to fill the width of the column. For example, in Figure 9-46, cells A9:B9 contain the single word *Fill* and a space character, with the Fill alignment format applied. Only the first cell in the selected range needs to contain text. Excel repeats the text to fill the range. Like the other Format commands, the Fill option affects only the appearance, not the underlying contents, of the cell.

CAUTION

> Because the Fill option affects numeric values, as well as text, it can cause a number to look like something it isn't. For example, if you apply the Fill option to a ten-character-wide cell that displays 3, the cell appears to contain the number 3333333333.

Wrap Text

Wrapping Text in Cells   If you type a label that's too wide for the active cell, Excel extends the label past the cell border and into adjacent cells—provided those cells are empty. If you click the Wrap Text button on the Home tab (or the Wrap Text option on the Alignment tab in the Format Cells dialog box), Excel displays your label entirely within the active cell. To accommodate it, Excel increases the height of the row in which the cell is located and then wraps the text onto additional lines within the same cell. As shown in Figure 9-46, cell A10 contains a multiline label formatted with the Wrap Text option.

Justifying Text in Cells   The Alignment tab in the Format Cells dialog box provides two justify options—one in the Horizontal drop-down list and one in the Vertical drop-down list. The Horizontal Justify option not only forces text in the active cell to align flush with the right margin, as shown in cell B10 in Figure 9-46, but also wraps text within the cell and adjusts the row height accordingly.

> **Note**
>
> Do not confuse the Horizontal Justify option with the Justify command (on the Fill menu in the Editing group on the Home tab), which redistributes a text entry into as many cells as necessary below the selected cell, dividing the text into separate chunks. For more information about the Justify command on the Fill menu, see "Distributing Long Entries Using the Justify Command" on page 217.

The Vertical Justify option performs essentially the same task as its Horizontal counterpart, except it adjusts cell entries relative to the top and bottom of the cell rather than the sides, as shown in cell E3 of Figure 9-47.

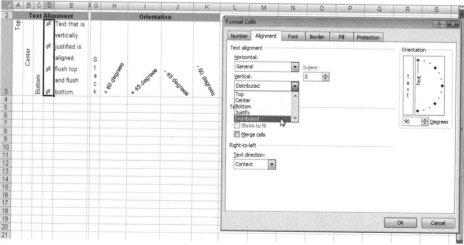

Figure 9-47 Use the Vertical options to control placement of text from top to bottom.

Chapter 9

The Justify Distributed option becomes available only when you select one of the Distributed options in either the Horizontal drop-down list or the Vertical drop-down list. It combines the effect of the Justify option with that of the Distributed option by not only wrapping text in the cell and forcing it to align flush right but by also spacing the contents of the cell as evenly as possible within each wrapped line of text.

Aligning Text Vertically

Top Align

Middle Align

Bottom Align

The Top Align, Middle Align, and Bottom Align buttons on the Home tab control the vertical placement of cell contents and fulfill most of your needs in this regard. The Vertical drop-down list, on the Alignment tab in the Format Cells dialog box, includes two additional alignment options—Justify and Distributed—which are similar to the corresponding Horizontal alignment options. Cells A3:C3 in Figure 9-47 show examples of the first three alignment options. As noted earlier, cell E3 shows the Justify option in action. We formatted cell D3, containing the percent signs, using the Distributed option.

The options in the Vertical drop-down list create the following effects:

- **Top, Center, and Bottom** These options force cell contents to align to each respective location within a cell. The default vertical cell orientation in new worksheets is Bottom.

- **Justify** This option expands the space between words so that text entries align flush with the top and bottom of the cell.

- **Distributed** This option spreads the contents of the cell evenly from top to bottom, making the spaces between words as close to equal as possible.

Controlling Text Orientation

Orientation

The default action of the Orientation button in the Alignment group on the Home tab is to angle the contents of the selected cell to a 45-degree angle. Clicking the arrow next to the Orientation button displays the menu shown in Figure 9-48, offering additional Orientation commands.

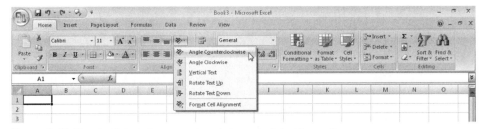

Figure 9-48 Use the Orientation menu to rotate or stack text in a cell.

The Orientation area on the Alignment tab in the Format Cells dialog box contains additional controls, letting you change the angle of cell contents to read at any angle from 90 degrees counterclockwise to 90 degrees clockwise.

Chapter 9

A Cool Application of Angled Text

Many times the label at the top of a column is much wider than the data stored in it. You can use the Wrap Text option to make a multiple-word label narrower, but sometimes that's not enough. Vertical text is an option, but it can be difficult to read and takes a lot of vertical space. Try using rotated text and cell borders:

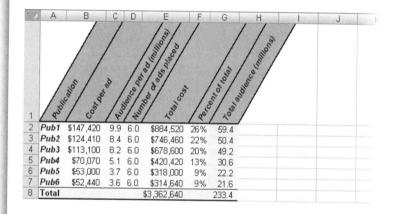

Here's how to do it:

1. Select the cells you want to format, and click the Dialog Box Launcher in the Font group on the Home tab to display the Format Cells dialog box.

2. Click the Border tab, and apply vertical borders to the left, right, and middle of the range.

3. Click the Alignment tab, and use the Orientation controls to select the angle you want. (It's usually best to select a positive angle from 30 to 60 degrees.)

4. In the Horizontal Text Alignment drop-down list, select Center, and then click OK. Excel rotates the left and right borders along with the text.

5. Drag down the bottom border of the row 1 header (the line between 1 and 2) to make it deep enough to accommodate the labels without wrapping.

6. Select all the active columns, and double-click any one of the lines between the selected column headers (for example, the line between the column letters C and D) to shrink all the columns to their smallest possible width.

Using the Angle Counterclockwise command on the Orientation button's menu (in the Alignment group on the Home tab) will rotate the text to +45 degrees for you, but because we wanted to apply borders and alignment options as well, using the Format Cells dialog box was a more efficient method.

> **Note**
>
> Interestingly, as you experiment with orientation, you won't see a Horizontal option on the Orientation button's menu, requiring you to use either the Format Cells dialog box or the Undo command (Ctrl+Z) to restore cells to their default orientation.

Excel automatically adjusts the height of the row to accommodate vertical orientation unless you manually set the row height, either before or after changing text orientation. Cell G3 in Figure 9-47 shows what happens when you click the tall, skinny Text button on the left side of the Orientation area. Although the button is labeled Text, you can also apply this "stacked letters" effect to numbers and formulas.

The angle controls let you rotate text to any point in a 180-degree arc. You can use either the Degrees box at the bottom or the large dial above it to adjust text rotation. To use the dial, click and drag the Text pointer to the angle you want, and the number of degrees appears in the spinner below. You also can click the small up and down arrows in the Degrees box to increment the angle one degree at a time from horizontal (zero), or you can highlight the number displayed in the Degrees box and type a number from −90 through 90. Cells H3:K3 in Figure 9-47 show some examples of rotated text.

You'll find the Angled Text.xlsx file in the Sample Files section of the companion CD.

For more about cell borders, see "Customizing Borders" on page 325. For more about row heights, see "Changing Row Heights" on page 336.

Shrinking Text to Fit in Cells

The Shrink To Fit check box on the Alignment tab in the Format Cells dialog box reduces the size of the font in the selected cell until the contents can be completely displayed in the cell. This is useful when you have a worksheet in which adjusting the column width to allow a particular cell entry to be visible has undesirable effects on the rest of the worksheet or where angled text, vertical text, and wrapped text aren't feasible solutions. In Figure 9-49, we typed the same text in cells A1 and A2 but applied the Shrink To Fit option to cell A2.

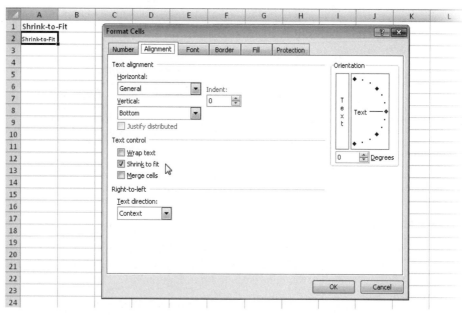

Figure 9-49 The Shrink To Fit alignment option reduces the font size until the cell contents fit within the cell.

The Shrink To Fit format is dynamic and readjusts if you change the column width, either increasing or decreasing the font size as needed. The assigned size of the font does not change; therefore, no matter how wide you make the column, the font expands only to the assigned size.

The Shrink To Fit option can be a good way to solve a problem, but keep in mind that this option reduces the font to as small a size as necessary. If the cell is narrow enough and the cell contents long enough, the result might be too small to read.

Using Fonts

The term *font* refers to a typeface (such as Arial), along with its attributes (such as point size and color). The Font group on the Home tab on the Ribbon, shown in Figure 9-50, is the easiest way to apply general font formatting to selected cells. Here are a few facts about the controls in the Font group:

- The Font, Font Size, Underline, Borders, Fill Color, and Font Color buttons all include arrows to their right, which you can click to display a menu or palette with additional options.

- The appearance of the Font Color, Fill Color, and Borders buttons changes to reflect the last-used option. This lets you apply the same option again by clicking the button, without using the menu or palette.

- The Bold and Italic buttons are toggles; click once to apply the format, and click again to remove it.

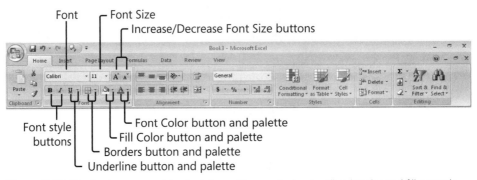

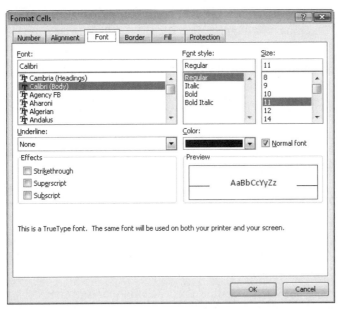

Figure 9-50 The Font group contains font-formatting controls, as well as border and fill controls.

For more extensive control over fonts, use the Font tab in the Format Cells dialog box. To specify a font, select the cell or range; then click the Dialog Box Launcher in the Font group, and click the Font tab, shown in Figure 9-51.

Figure 9-51 On the Font tab you can assign fonts, character styles, sizes, colors, and effects to your cell entries.

> **Note**
> You can also press Ctrl+1 to display the Format Cells dialog box.

The numbers in the Size list show the point sizes at which Excel can optimally print the selected font, but you can type any number in the text box at the top of the list—even fractional point sizes up to two decimal places. Unless you preset it, Excel adjusts the row height as needed to accommodate the largest point size in the row. The available font styles vary, depending on the font you select in the Font list. Most fonts offer italic, bold, and bold italic styles. To reset the selected cells to the font and size defined as the Normal cell style, select the Normal Font check box.

For more information about using the cell styles, see "Formatting with Cell Styles" on page 278.

INSIDE OUT   Automatic Font Color Isn't Really Automatic

If you select Automatic (the default font color option) in the Color drop-down list (or use its equivalent in the Font group on the Home tab on the Ribbon), Excel displays the contents of your cell in black. You might think that Automatic should select an appropriate color for text, based on the color you apply to the cell, but this isn't the case. If, for example, you apply a black background to a cell, you might think the automatic font color would logically be white. This isn't so; Automatic is always black unless you have selected another Window Font color in the Display Properties dialog box (accessed from Windows Control Panel). For more information about applying colors to cells, see "Applying Colors and Patterns" on page 329.

Customizing Borders

Borders

Borders and shading can be effective devices for defining areas in your worksheet or for drawing attention to important cells, and the Borders button in the Font group on the Home tab is the easiest way to apply them. Clicking this button applies the last-used border format and displays a thumbnail representation of it on the button. Click the arrow to the right of the button to display the menu shown in Figure 9-52.

Note

Like the image displayed on the button, when you rest the pointer on the button to display a tip, the button name also reflects the last-used border format.

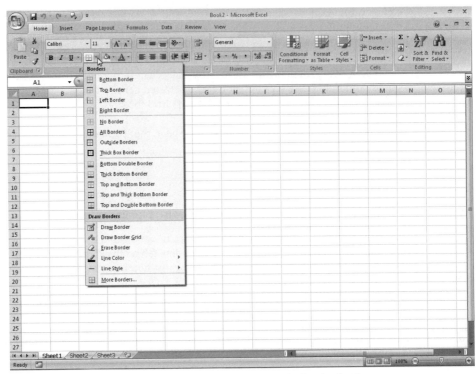

Figure 9-52 Click the arrow next to the Borders button to display the Borders menu.

The most often-used border options are represented on the Borders menu, but for more precise control, click the More Borders command on the menu to display the Border tab in the Format Cells dialog box shown in Figure 9-53. (As always, the Dialog Box Launcher next to the Font group opens the dialog box as well.) If you have more than one cell selected when you open the dialog box, the Border preview area includes tick marks in the middle and at the corners, as shown in Figure 9-53.

> **Note**
> A solid gray line in the preview area means that the format applies to some, but not all, of the selected cells.

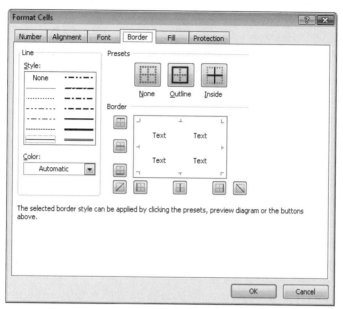

Figure 9-53 Using the Border tab, you can assign 13 styles of borders in 70 colors.

To apply borders, either you can click the preview area where you want the border to appear or you can click the buttons located around the preview area. An additional preset button, Inside, becomes active only when you have more than one cell selected. If you click the Outline button, borders are applied to only the outside edge of the entire selection. The None preset removes all border formats from the selection.

> **Note**
>
> Borders often make a greater visual impact on your screen when you remove worksheet gridlines. Click the View tab on the Ribbon, and clear the Gridlines check box in the Show/Hide group to remove gridlines from your worksheet. For more information about gridlines, see "Controlling Other Elements of the Excel Interface" on page 96.

The default, or Automatic, color for borders is black. To select a line style, click the type of line you want to use in the Line area, and then click any of the buttons in the Border area or click the preview box directly to apply that style in the selected location. (The first finely dotted line in the Style area is a solid hairline when printed.) To remove a border, click the corresponding button, or the line in the preview window, without selecting another style.

An Angled Border Trick

Sometimes you might want to use that pesky cell that generally remains empty in the upper-left corner of a table. You can use an angled border to create dual-label corner cells:

	A	B	C	D	E	F	G
1	First Quarter Exam Scores						
2							
3	Exam # / Student	1	2	3	4	Average	
4	Adams	87	90	79	96	88.00	
5	Carothers	92	94	94	97	94.25	
6	Devoe	96	95	95	80	91.50	
7	Gronicki	85	87	87	88	86.75	
8	Ito	81	88	88	85	85.50	
9							
10							

Here's how to do it:

1. Select the cell you want to format, and type about 10 space characters. You can adjust this later (there are 20 spaces before the Exam # label in the example).

2. Type the label you want to correspond to the column labels across the top of the table.

3. Hold down the Alt key, and press Enter twice to create two line breaks in the cell.

4. Type the second label, which corresponds to the row labels down the left side of the table, and press Enter.

5. With the cell selected, click the More Borders command on the Borders menu.

6. Select a line style, and click the upper-left to lower-right angled border button.

7. Click the Alignment tab, select the Wrap Text check box, and then click OK.

You will probably need to fine-tune a bit by adjusting the column width and row height and by adding or removing space characters before the first label. In the example, we also selected cells B3:F3 and then clicked the Top Align button in the Alignment group on the Home tab on the Ribbon so that all the labels line up across the top of the table.

For more information about alignment, see "Aligning Data in Cells" on page 316. For more about entering line breaks and tabs in cells, see "Formula-Bar Formatting" on page 454.

You'll find the Angled Borders.xlsx file in the Sample Files section of the companion CD.

By using the group of Draw Borders commands at the bottom of the Borders menu shown in Figure 9-52, you can create complex borders quickly and easily. When you click Draw Border, you enter "border-drawing mode," which persists until you click Draw Border again or press Esc. After you activate this mode, you can drag to create lines and boxes along cell gridlines, as shown in Figure 9-54. If you click Draw Border

Grid, not only are borders drawn along the boundaries of the selected cells but also they're drawn along all the gridlines in the selection rectangle, as shown at the bottom of Figure 9-54.

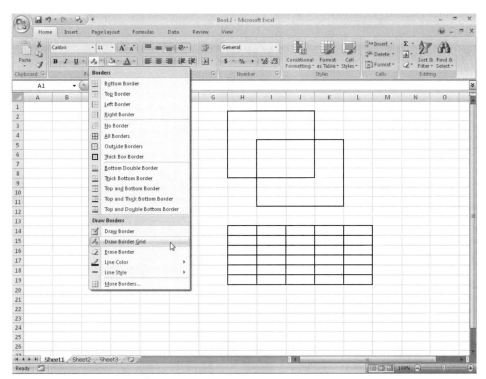

Figure 9-54 We created two boxes using the Draw Border command and another using the Draw Border Grid command.

If you make selections in the Line Color and Line Style palettes at the bottom of the Borders menu prior to using either Draw Border command, the borders you draw reflect your color and style selections. Clicking Erase Border predictably activates the opposite of border-drawing mode: "border-erasing mode." Dragging while in erase mode removes all borders within the selection rectangle.

Applying Colors and Patterns

Fill Color

The Fill Color button in the Font group on the Home tab offers colors you can apply to selected cells. Click the button's arrow to display the palette shown in Figure 9-55.

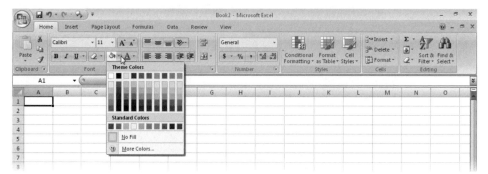

Figure 9-55 Use the Fill Color palette to add color to cells.

If you want to do more than just fill cells with color, the Fill tab in the Format Cells dialog box provides additional control. (Click the Dialog Box Launcher in the Font group on the Ribbon to display the Format Cells dialog box.) The main feature of the Fill tab is a palette of colors, mimicking the palette available on the Ribbon. A feature not available on the Ribbon is the Pattern Style drop-down palette, as shown in Figure 9-56. You use this palette to select a pattern for selected cells and the Pattern Color drop-down palette above it to choose its color.

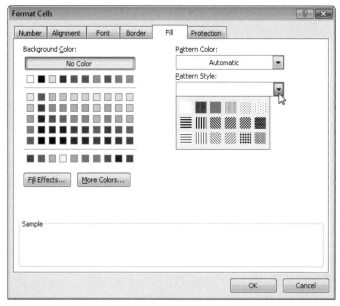

Figure 9-56 Using the Fill tab, you can select colors and patterns for cell backgrounds.

Follow these guidelines when using the Fill tab:

- The Color area controls the background of selected cells. When you choose a color and do not select any pattern, Excel applies a solid colored background.

- To return the background color to its default state, click No Color.

- If you pick a background color and then select a pattern style, the pattern is overlaid on the solid background. For example, if you select red from the Color area and then click one of the dot patterns, the result is a cell that has a red background and black dots.

- The Pattern Color palette controls the color of the pattern, not the cell. For example, if you leave Background Color set to No Color and select a red for Pattern Color and any dot pattern in the Pattern Style palette, the cell will have a white background with red dots.

> **Note**
> When selecting colors for cell backgrounds, select one on which you can easily read the text and numbers that are formatted using the default color, black. For example, yellow is the most visible background color you can choose to complement black text, which is why you see this combination on road signs. A dark blue background with black text—that's not so good.

The More Colors button on the Fill tab displays the dialog box shown in Figure 9-57, where you can select colors that are not otherwise represented on the color palettes. The Standard tab in the Colors dialog box displays a stylized color wheel using the current theme colors, most of which are already available on the palettes. The Custom tab shown in Figure 9-57 lets you pinpoint colors, use specific color values, and switch between the default RGB (red, green, blue) color model or HSL, a color model defined by hue, saturation, and luminosity values instead of RGB color values.

The Fill Effects button on the Fill tab in the Format Cells dialog box opens up another world of possibility, offering gradient fills you can apply to cells. Clicking this button displays the Fill Effects dialog box shown in Figure 9-58. You can select different colors and shading styles, but this version of the Fill Effects dialog box offers only two-color effects. The One Color, Preset, and Transparency options are not available. Note that Fill Effects gradient fills are static, unlike data bars, which are conditional gradient fills that respond to cell values and interact with adjacent cells by applying proportional amounts of fill to each cell.

For more about gradients, see "Filling an Area with a Color Gradient" on page 638. For more about Data Bars, see "Formatting Conditionally" on page 284.

Chapter 9

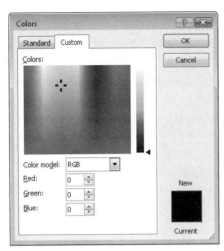

Figure 9-57 Click the More Colors button on the Fill tab in the Format Cells dialog box to select the colors you need.

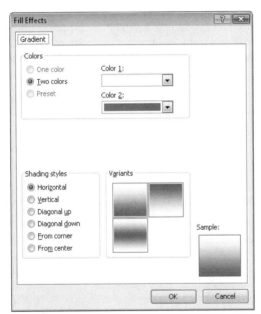

Figure 9-58 Click the Fill Effects button on the Fill tab in the Format Cells dialog box to use gradient fills in cells.

Adding Graphic Backgrounds to Worksheets

Adding background images to worksheets is easy. Click the Page Layout tab on the Ribbon, and click the Background button. A standard Windows file-management dialog box appears, from which you can open most types of image files, located anywhere on your computer or network. Excel then applies the graphic image to the background of the active worksheet, as shown in Figure 9-59.

Figure 9-59 Add a background graphic to any worksheet.

Here are some tips for working with background images:

- The example in Figure 9-59 is a cover sheet for a large workbook; be careful when using backgrounds behind data. It could be difficult to read cell entries with the wrong background applied.

- You might want to turn off the display of gridlines, as shown in Figure 9-59. To do so, clear the Gridlines View check box, which is also located on the Page Layout tab.

- If you don't like the way the background looks with your data, click the Background button again, whose name changes to Delete Background when a background is present.

- The graphic image is tiled in the background of your worksheet, which means the image is repeated as necessary to fill the worksheet.

- Cells to which you have assigned a color or pattern override the graphic background. For example, the large box under the Pacific Musical Instruments logo in

Figure 9-59 is a single merged cell with a diagonal gradient fill applied, designed as a place to put titles or instructions for the opening page of the workbook.

- Backgrounds are preserved when you save the workbook as a Web page.

For more information about saving workbooks as Web pages, see Chapter 25, "Collaborating Using the Internet."

Controlling the Size of Cells

The primary methods you use to control the size of cells are adjusting the row height and changing the column width. In addition, you can adjust the size of cells by merging several cells into one or by unmerging previously merged cells. The Format menu, located in the Cells group on the Home tab, is the central command location for cell sizing, as shown in Figure 9-60.

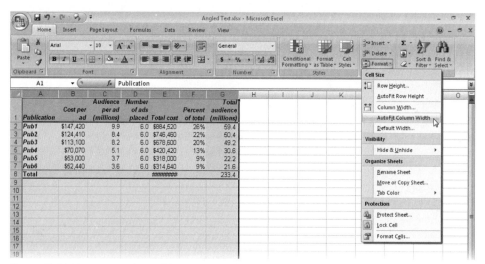

Figure 9-60 You can use the Cell Size commands on the Format menu to manage row height and column width.

Here are the options you can use:

- **Column Width and Row Height** These two commands display a dialog box where you can type a different value to be applied to selected cells. Column width is limited to 255, and row height can be up to 409. The default column width for Excel is 8.43 characters; however, this does not mean each cell in your worksheet can display 8.43 characters. Because Excel uses proportionally spaced fonts (such as Arial) as well as fixed-pitch fonts (such as Courier), different characters can take up different amounts of space. A default-width column, for example, can display about eight numerals in most 10-point fixed-pitch fonts.

- **AutoFit Row Height** This command adjusts the row height in selected cells by adjusting them to accommodate the tallest item in the row. (Row height is usually self-adjusting based on font size.)

- **AutoFit Column Width** This command adjusts column widths in selected cells by adjusting them to accommodate the widest entry in the column.

- **Default Width** This command displays a dialog box where you can change the starting column width for all selected worksheets in the current workbook. This has no effect on columns whose width you have previously specified.

Changing Column Widths

If the standard column width isn't enough to display the complete contents of a cell, one of the following will occur:

- Text that is too long runs over into adjacent cells.

- Long text entries are truncated at the border if the adjacent cell isn't empty.

- Long numbers appear in scientific notation (for example, 1.23E+12).

- A series of number signs (#) appears if you assign a numeric format.

To change column widths using the mouse, drag the lines between column headings. As you drag, the width of the column and the number of pixels appear in a tip, as shown in Figure 9-61. This figure also illustrates how to change the width of multiple columns at the same time: Drag to select column headings; alternatively, hold down Ctrl, and click headings to select nonadjacent columns. Then, when you drag the line to the right of any selected column, all the selected column widths change simultaneously.

Figure 9-61 The cursor looks like a double-headed arrow when adjusting column width or row height with the mouse.

Note

Depending on the font you are using, characters that appear to fit within a column on your screen might not fit when you print the worksheet. You can preview your output before printing by pressing Ctrl+P to display the Print dialog box and by clicking the Preview button to display the worksheet as it will look when printed. For information about Print Preview, see Chapter 11, "Printing and Presenting."

Chapter 9

Tricks for Tailoring Cells

Here are a few methods you can use to speed up your cell-sizing chores:

- When you select a number of rows or columns, you can tailor all of them to fit their contents—essentially the same as using one of the AutoFit commands—by double-clicking any line to the right of a selected column header or any line below a selected row header. Doing so automatically snaps all the selected cells to accommodate the widest or tallest displayed values.

- To tailor all the cells in the worksheet at once, first click the gray square at the intersection of the row and column headers to select the entire worksheet (or press Ctrl+A). Then double-click any line in the row header to autofit all rows, and double-click any line in the column header to autofit all columns.

- To change the widths of all the columns in the current worksheet, select any entire row by clicking a row heading (or pressing Shift+Spacebar), and then click the Width command on the Format menu on the Home tab.

- To change the height of all of the rows in the current worksheet, select any entire column by clicking a column heading (or pressing Ctrl+Spacebar), and then click the Height command on the Format menu on the Home tab.

Changing Row Heights

The height of a row always changes dynamically to accommodate the largest font used in that row. Thus, you don't usually need to worry about characters being too tall to fit in a row. Adjusting row height is the same as adjusting column width–just drag one of the lines between row headings.

To restore the default height of one or more rows, select any cells in those rows, and click AutoFit on the Format menu on the Home tab. Unlike column width, you cannot define a standard row height. The AutoFit command serves the same function, returning empty rows to the standard height needed to accommodate the default font and fitting row heights to accommodate the tallest entry. When you create or edit a multiline text entry using the Wrap Text button or the Justify option on the Alignment tab in the Format Cells dialog box, Excel automatically adjusts the row height to accommodate it.

For more information, see "Wrapping Text in Cells" on page 319 and "Justifying Text in Cells" on page 319.

Hiding a Column or Row

If you want to hide information within a worksheet, you can hide entire columns or rows. To do so, select any cell in the row or column you want to hide. Then on the Format menu on the Home tab, click Hide & Unhide, and then click Hide Rows or Hide Columns. This sets the width of the column to zero. You can also hide rows and columns by dragging the line between headings up or to the left until the height or width is zero. When a row or column's width is set to 0, Excel skips over it when you move the active cell, and the column letter or row number disappears. For example, if you hide column C, the column heading line reads A, B, D, and so on.

To redisplay a hidden row or column, drag to select the headings on both sides, and click Unhide Rows or Unhide Columns on the Hide & Unhide menu. The Hidden check box on the Protection tab of the Format Cells dialog box hides only formulas in the formula bar.

Merging and Unmerging Cells

Merge & Center

The spreadsheet grid is arguably the most versatile type of document, and the ability to merge cells makes it all the more versatile. Select the cells you want to merge, and click the arrow to the right of the Merge & Center button in the Alignment group on the Home tab to display the menu shown in Figure 9-62.

CAUTION

When you merge several cells that contain data, only the data in the uppermost, leftmost cell is preserved. Excel overwrites data in subsidiary cells. Copy any data you need to another location before merging.

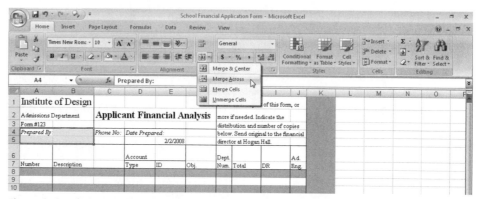

Figure 9-62 The Merge & Center button offers a variety of merge commands.

Chapter 9

When you merge cells, you end up with a single cell that comprises the original cells. If, in the worksheet shown in Figure 9-63, we were to select cells A4:B5 and click the Merge Across command, the result would be two merged cells, A4 and A5, each spanning two columns. Here are the differences between the Merge & Center commands:

- **Merge & Center** This command consolidates all selected cells into one big cell and centers the contents across the newly merged cell.

- **Merge Across** This command consolidates each row of selected cells into one wide cell per row.

- **Merge Cells** This command consolidates all selected cells into one big cell.

- **Unmerge Cells** This command returns a merged cell to its original component cells and places its contents in the upper-leftmost cell. Clicking the Merge & Center button (not the Merge & Center command) when a merged cell is selected has the same effect, like a toggle "turning off" the merge.

Figure 9-63 shows the same worksheet shown in Figure 9-62, after merging cells A1:B3, C1:F3, G1:J5, A4:B4, A5:B5, D4:F4, D5:F5, and D6:E6. We had to shuffle some of the text, premerge, so that we wouldn't lose it to the merging process. For example, the text in the original range G1:J5 was unevenly spaced because of the different row heights needed to accommodate the text in cells A1 and C2. To eliminate this problem, we used the Merge Cells command on the range A1:B3, we used the Merge & Center command on the ranges C1:F3 and G1:J5, and then we reentered the text.

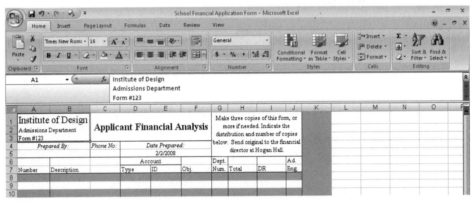

Figure 9-63 Most of the cells in the top five rows of this worksheet, and a couple in the sixth row, were merged in various combinations.

You'll find the School Financial Application.xlsx file in the Sample Files section of the companion CD.

When you merge cells, the new *big cell* uses the address of the cell in the upper-left corner, as shown in Figure 9-63. Cell A1 is selected, as you can see in the name box. (In the figure, we also expanded the formula bar to show the three rows of text in the merged cell.) The headings for rows 1, 2, and 3 and columns A and B are highlighted, which would ordinarily indicate that the range A1:B3 is selected. For all practical purposes, however, cells A2:A3 and B1:B3 no longer exist. The other merged cells, or the subsidiary cells, act like blank cells when referred to in formulas and return zero (or an error value, depending on the type of formula).

> **Note**
>
> In Figure 9-63, the information in the formula bar is on three lines. To enter line breaks within a cell, press Alt+Enter. For more information, see "Formula-Bar Formatting" on page 454.

Merging cells obviously has interesting implications, considering that it seems to violate the grid—one of the defining attributes of spreadsheet design. That's not as bad as it sounds, but keep in mind these tips:

- If you select a range to merge and any single cell contains text, a value, or a formula, the contents are relocated to the new big cell.

- If you select a range of cells to merge and more than one cell contains text or values, only the contents of the uppermost, leftmost cell are relocated to the new big cell. Contents of subsidiary cells are deleted; therefore, if you want to preserve data in subsidiary cells, make sure you add it to the upper-left cell or relocate it.

- Formulas adjust automatically. A formula that refers to a subsidiary cell in a merged range changes to refer to the address of the new big cell. If a merged range of cells contains a formula, relative references adjust. For more about references, see "Using Cell References in Formulas" on page 428.

- You can copy, delete, cut and paste, or click and drag big cells as you would any other cell. When you copy or move a big cell, it replaces the same number of cells at the destination. The original location of a cut or deleted big cell returns to individual cells.

- You can drag the fill handle of a big cell as you can drag the fill handle of regular cells. When you do so, the big cell is replicated, in both size and content, replacing all regular cells in its path. For more about using the fill handle, see "Filling and Creating Data Series" on page 211.

- If you merge cells containing border formatting other than along any outer edge of the selected range, border formats are erased.

Using Template Files to Store Formatting

A *template* is a model that can serve as the basis for new worksheets. A template can include both data and formatting information. Template files are great timesavers. They're also an ideal way to ensure a consistent look among reports, invoices, and other documents you tend to create repeatedly. Figure 9-64 shows an example of a template for an expense report. This worksheet would make a good template because expense reports are used repeatedly, but each time you'll want to start with a fresh, clean copy.

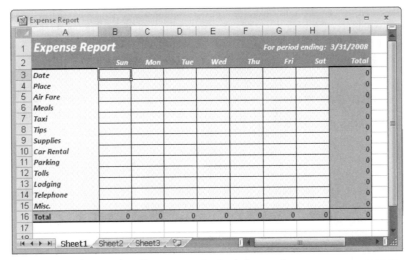

Figure 9-64 This template file serves as the basis for creating new expense reports.

You'll find the Expense Report.xltx file in the Sample Files section of the companion CD.

The advantages to using templates are standardization and protection. It is difficult to overwrite the original accidentally, because when you save a new template-based workbook for the first time, you must supply a new name for it. This way you can repeatedly create new workbooks with the same appearance without worrying about overwriting the original.

To create a template file, follow these steps:

1. Open the workbook you want to use as a template.

2. Click the Microsoft Office Button, Save As, and supply a file name.

3. Choose Excel Template (*.xltx) from the Save As Type drop-down list, and click Save.

When you choose the Excel Template format in the Save As dialog box, Excel switches to the Template folder and saves your new template there. This is the location that ensures your template is always available when you click the New command on the Microsoft Office Button and double-click My Templates.

You can use any Excel workbook as a template, even if you did not save it in template format. When you installed Excel, a folder named Templates was installed on your hard disk in the following location:

- **Windows Vista:** C:\Users\<your name>\AppData\Roaming\Microsoft\Templates

- **Windows XP:** C:\Documents and Settings\<your name>\Application Data\ Microsoft\Templates

When you open a template, a fresh copy of the workbook is created, and the copy is given a temporary name consisting of the original file name plus a number. If the template file is named Expenses, for example, the working copy is named Expenses1.

INSIDE OUT   Full Disclosure

Microsoft Windows tries to keep secrets from you—for your own good, of course. But fearless readers of this book need no such accommodation, so here are a couple of actions you can take to make life a little easier. First, let's show hidden files and folders. If you go looking, the Template folders described in this chapter can be hard to find, because they are in locations Windows likes to keep hidden from view. To make them more findable, click the Windows Start menu, Control Panel, Appearance And Personalization, Folder Options, and on the View tab, select Show Hidden Files And Folders. Second, let's display all the file extensions. The old-style MS-DOS extensions used to be three characters in length and now can be four, such as .xltx for template and .xlsx for regular workbook. These may be "retro," but they also still helpful, letting you tell at a glance in which format a file was saved. To make extensions visible, clear the Hide File Extensions For Known File Types check box, which is also on the View tab in the Folder Options dialog box.

Chapter 9

Adding Graphics and Printing

Creating Spiffy Graphics

Microsoft Office Excel 2007 gives you the tools to create a variety of graphic objects—boxes, lines, circles, ovals, arcs, freeform polygons, text boxes, buttons, and a wide assortment of complex predefined shapes, clip art, and the new SmartArt graphics. If you already have graphics created in other programs, Office Excel 2007 imports those graphics as well. Throughout this chapter, you'll learn how to add graphics to worksheets, but you can also use many of the same kinds of effects when creating charts. First we'll discuss creating and inserting various kinds of graphic objects, and then we'll cover formatting and working with them.

Most of your graphic adventures will begin using the buttons and menus found on the Insert tab on the Ribbon, shown in Figure 10-1.

> **For more information about charts, see Part 6, "Creating Charts."**

Figure 10-1 The Insert tab contains most of the drawing tools.

Using the Shapes Tools

The Excel graphics tool chest contains many of the powerful capabilities of dedicated illustration programs. Using only the tools in the Shapes palette on the Ribbon, you can create lines, rectangles, and ovals; smooth and freeform curves; linked objects using connectors; basic and not-so-basic shapes, such as pentagons and lightning bolts; a variety of straight, curved, three-dimensional (3-D), and multiheaded arrows; stars, emblems, and banners; and even a variety of callouts. Click the Shapes button to display the palette shown in Figure 10-2.

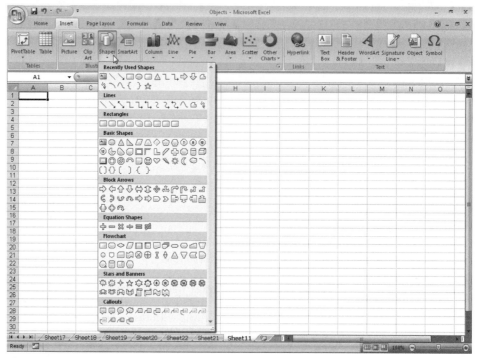

Figure 10-2 The Shapes palette provides a wealth of graphic options.

If you have ever used a drawing program, such as Microsoft Paint or CorelDRAW, you already know how to create lines, arrows, ovals, and rectangles. In Excel, as in graphics programs, click the tool you want, and then drag the pointer to create the object. When you drag a simple box shape using the Rectangle tool, for example, Excel displays *Rectangle 1* in the Name box at the left end of the formula bar. Excel refers to new graphic objects by category and numbers them in the order in which you create them.

Objects you create appear to float over the worksheet or chart in a separate layer. Objects are separate from the worksheet or chart, and you can group and format them as discrete items. Here are a few more important facts you should know about using the drawing tools:

- Excel enters *drawing mode* when you click a Shapes tool and exits drawing mode when you finish drawing an object. You can cancel drawing mode by clicking the same tool again.

- Formatting you apply to underlying worksheet cells has no effect on objects.

- When you move the pointer over an object, the pointer changes to a four-headed move arrow. You can then select the object or move it elsewhere by dragging.

- After you select an object, you can stretch and resize it by dragging the handles that appear on its perimeter.

- If you drag a center handle, you change the object's height or width.

- When you select a graphic object in Excel, one or more new tabs appear on the Ribbon, depending on the type of object you select. Figure 10-3 shows the Format tab under Drawing Tools. These tabs offer additional formatting and effects you can apply to selected objects.

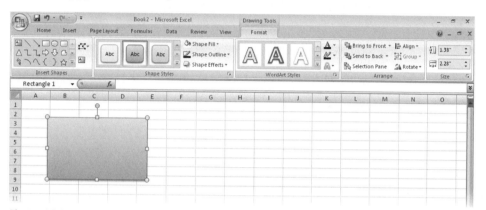

Figure 10-3 New tabs appear, under Drawing Tools, when you select a graphic object.

Drawing Constrained Objects

The word *constrain* has a somewhat negative connotation, but in computer lingo, a constraint is usually a good thing. If you apply a constraint to an object you draw, for example, you force the object to adhere to a specific angle or proportion. Using constraints is the easiest way to create perfect circles and squares. For example, you can hold down Shift (and sometimes Ctrl) while creating objects to constrain them, as Figure 10-4 illustrates.

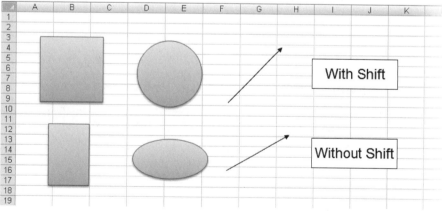

Figure 10-4 When you create or size objects, hold down Shift to constrain them.

The key you use to constrain your object depends on the type of constraint you want to cause. The following lists describe the types of constraints created using each method.

Holding down the Shift key causes the following constraints:

- The Line and Arrow tools draw perfectly horizontal or vertical lines or diagonal lines constrained to exact 15-degree increments (0°, 15°, 30°, 45°, 90°, and so on).

- The Rectangle tool draws perfect squares.

- The Oval tool draws perfect circles.

- Other shapes are drawn to predefined, roughly symmetrical constraints. Shapes come in many different forms, so the effect of the Shift key varies considerably, depending on the shape.

Holding down the Ctrl key causes the following constraints:

- While dragging to create rectangles, ovals, text boxes, and AutoShapes, the object is centered on the point at which you click. Objects grow out from the center point as you drag.

- When dragging a handle to resize a previously drawn object, the object remains centered on its original center point and resizes equally in all directions.

- When dragging an object to move it, holding down Ctrl creates a copy of the object, leaving the original in place.

- You can use Ctrl+Shift to create symmetrical objects such as squares, circles, and stars that are centered on the point you click.

Holding down the Alt key causes the following constraint:

- You can hold down Alt while creating objects to use the gridlines on a worksheet as a drawing grid. The edges of your objects are then forced to follow the gridlines. Note, however, that if you use Shift and Alt together to draw a square or a circle aligned to the grid, Excel does its best, but the result might not be perfect. This is because the default height and width of the cells on a worksheet might not provide an ideal grid for perfect squares or circles.

Drawing Freehand Lines and Polygons

The tools on the Shapes palette are extremely easy to use. Just click a tool, and then click and drag to create the object on the worksheet. A few tools would benefit from a little additional information, however, and we'll discuss them in the following list:

Curve

- **Curve** Draws smoothly curved lines between clicked points.

Freeform

- **Freeform** Draws combined freehand lines and straight lines.

Scribble

- **Scribble** Draws unconstrained lines. (However, when you release the mouse button, the resulting line is smoothed somewhat.)

INSIDE OUT   Selecting Objects

When you work with objects, it's almost as if another program with a transparent desktop is floating over the worksheet—as if the objects you draw are in another dimension. In a sense, they are. What goes on in the grid of Excel has little to do with what goes on in the drawing layer, although you do have opportunities to create interaction between objects and worksheets using macros and formulas.

When you are working in cells, you can click any graphic object to select it and then click the worksheet to select cells. You can hop back and forth between the object and worksheet, no problem. But they are still parallel universes, which becomes apparent when you try to select multiple items. For example, you can drag to select a range of cells, but you cannot drag a selection rectangle around a group of objects to select them; instead, you end up selecting a cell in that "other dimension" as soon as you click. You can press Ctrl and click to add nonadjacent cells to a selection on the worksheet, and this method works similarly with objects. In fact, you can select an object, then hold down either Shift or Ctrl, and click additional objects to add them to the selection—either method accomplishes the same result. You can also press Ctrl+A to "select all" in either the worksheet or the object layer. If you do so with a cell selected, all cells are selected; if you do so with an object selected, all objects are selected. But you can't select cells and objects together. You might want this when you're copying a portion of a worksheet to another location and you want to copy adjacent objects as well. You can actually accomplish this by selecting the underlying cells and pasting them in the new location. The objects may not be selected, but they are usually linked to a cell location. Unless you specify otherwise, objects will travel with their underlying cells if you move or copy them. For more information, see "Positioning Objects" on page 387.

The Freeform and Curve buttons are different from the others in that when you release the mouse button, you're not done drawing. To finish drawing using either of these buttons, you must click the starting point to close the loop and create a solid object; or to create a line, double-click where you want the line to end. Figure 10-5 shows a few objects created using these buttons.

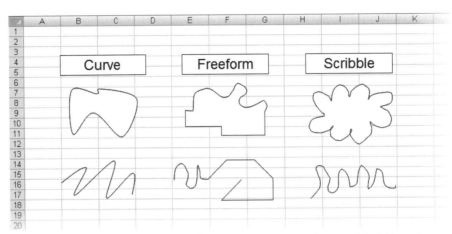

Figure 10-5 A sampling of objects created using the Curve, Freeform, and Scribble tools.

For example, if you click the Freeform tool and then click anywhere on the worksheet or chart to begin drawing, the line remains anchored to the point you clicked. If you release the mouse button, the line remains "attached," stretching from the anchor point to the crosshairs pointer like a rubber band. If you stretch the line and click again, you create a segment that is anchored between the first and second point. You can continue this as long as you want, creating additional segments with each new anchor point. If you drag, you create a curved freehand line. By combining these methods, you can create a hybrid object with both straight and curved lines. If you click the beginning of the line, you create a solid object, or you can double-click at any time to finish drawing.

Adjusting Freehand Shapes with the Edit Points Command

Edit Shape

Drawing an attractive freehand line or polygon shape with a mouse can be challenging. If you have difficulty dragging the shape you want, use the Edit Points command, which changes a line or polygon created with the Scribble, Curve, or Freeform tool into a series of points you can drag to reshape the object.

To adjust a Scribble, Curve, or Freeform shape, right-click the object, and then click Edit Points. (The Edit Points command also appears on the Edit Shape menu on the Format tab under Drawing Tools, which appears only when you select an object.) After you click Edit Points, a new set of handles appears on the object, following its curves and corners. You can then drag as many of the handles as necessary to new positions. For example, we used the Freeform button to create the shape on the left in Figure 10-6, and then we selected the shape. The shape on the right is the same freeform polygon after we clicked Edit Points.

After you click Edit Points, you can add or delete any of the handles on an object. If you want to clean up your drawing by eliminating some of the points, press the Ctrl key, and click each handle you want to delete. If you want to add points, press Ctrl, and click anywhere on a line where you want a handle to appear.

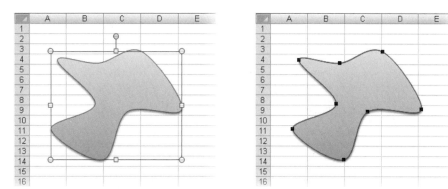

Figure 10-6 When you click Edit Points, handles appear at each vertex, as in the polygon on the right.

Working with Curves

When you edit the points in an object you created using the Scribble, Curve, or Free-form tool, you can fine-tune the curves even further by using commands on the short-cut menu that appears when you right-click any edit point, as shown in Figure 10-7.

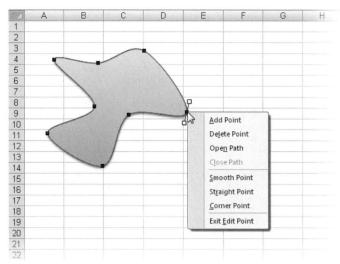

Figure 10-7 Change the type of a selected edit point by right-clicking it and then clicking commands on the shortcut menu.

If you click any edit point, *vertex handles* become visible that you can drag to modify the curve or angle at that vertex, as shown in Figure 10-8. These handles give you total control over the shape of a curve. The longer the vertex handle, the flatter the curve in the direction you drag.

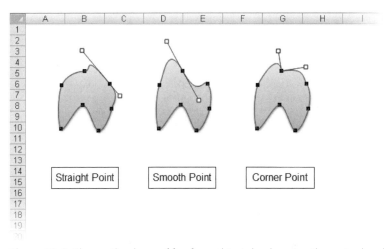

Figure 10-8 Change the shape of freeform objects by dragging the vertex handles that appear when you click a point.

Excel 2007 offers three types of points. You can right-click any existing point and change it to a different type of point using the corresponding command on the shortcut menu:

- **Straight Point** Creates a gradual transition between the lines flowing out from either side, which can be unequal, and displays vertex handles when selected. You can drag each vertex handle separately. The longer the vertex handle, the more gradual the curve on that side of the point.

- **Smooth Point** Lines flowing out from either side of a smooth point are equally curved and display vertex handles of equal length when you select them. Drag a vertex handle, and the opposite handle moves equally in the opposite direction, creating an equal curve on either side of the point.

- **Corner Point** Creates an abrupt transition between the lines flowing out from either side and displays vertex handles when selected, which can be dragged separately. The Scribble button always creates corner points.

Working with Text Boxes

Use the Text Box button in the Text group on the Insert tab to add notes, headings, legends, and other text to your worksheets and charts to give more impact or to clarify the data you're presenting.

Click the Text Box button, point to a location on your worksheet, and drag to create a box. A blinking cursor appears in the box, indicating you can begin typing. After you are finished, you can select and format text using the same commands you use for text in cells. When you select a text box, drag any of its eight perimeter handles to resize it.

> **Note**
>
> If you click the Spelling command with a single cell selected, all the text on the current worksheet is checked, including text in text boxes. If you click Spelling while a text box (or any object) is selected, only the text contained in that text box (or object) is checked.

Adding Text to Other Shapes

The Text Box button is quick and easy to use, but if you want to add graphic assistance to your message, you can add text to two-dimensional shapes created by using the Shapes palette on the Insert tab, including arrows, as shown in Figure 10-9, as well as banners, boxes, and just about any shape except lines and connectors.

Figure 10-9 Text boxes are only one of the many graphic objects that can display text.

To create one of these custom text boxes, just draw the shape you want, and then start typing. Resize the object as needed, and give the shape and its text the look you want using the Format tab under Drawing Tools, which appears on the Ribbon when you select a shape.

> **Create Linked Objects**
>
> You can create a link from a text box—or any other shape containing text—to a cell so you can display that cell's contents in the text box. First draw a text box. With the text box selected, type an equal sign in the formula bar, and then type a cell reference or defined name. For example, suppose cell D3 contains a formula that returns the value $123.45. When you type **=$D$3** into the formula bar while you have a text box selected, the value $123.45 appears in the text box. When you link a text box in this way, you cannot type additional text into it. To remove the link, select the text box, and delete the reference formula in the formula bar. For more about formulas and the formula bar, see Chapter 12, "Building Formulas."

Working with Shapes

The Shapes palette on the Insert tab offers dozens of predrawn shapes you can use to add effective visual communication to your worksheets. Most shapes display a yellow, diamond-shaped handle somewhere on the perimeter. If you drag this handle, you can control a specific dimension of the shape, as Figure 10-10 illustrates.

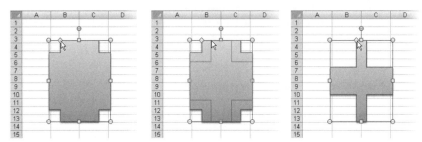

Figure 10-10 Many shapes have special diamond-shaped handles that you can drag to control a specific feature of the shape.

In addition to the diamond handle, all two-dimensional objects in Excel display a panhandle that you drag to rotate the object, as shown in Figure 10-11.

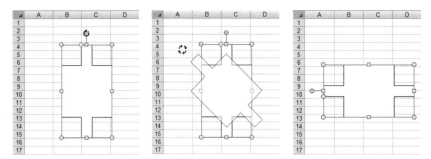

Figure 10-11 Drag the panhandle of any two-dimensional object to rotate it.

Using Connectors and Callouts

Most shapes are easy to use and somewhat self-explanatory. Connectors and callouts, however, have some special qualities that bear mentioning. If you've ever spent time creating drawings using simple lines and boxes, you know what a problem it can be when you need to reposition any of the objects. You usually end up spending as much time fine-tuning the drawing as you spent drawing it in the first place. *Connectors*, which are special kinds of lines that are "sticky" on both ends, can help. You use them when you want to connect shapes using lines that remain attached and stretch, making it easier to reposition objects later with a minimum of tweaking.

The connector tools are the six tools located in the middle of the Lines group on the Shapes palette, as shown in Figure 10-12. After you click one of these tools, special points appear when you rest the pointer on any existing shape. These are *connection points*, and if you click one of them, the connector line attaches to that point. The second click attaches the other end of the connector line to a point on another object and finishes the connector line.

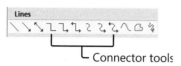

Figure 10-12 The connector tools appear in the Lines group on the Shapes palette.

As Figure 10-13 shows, the resulting connector line stays attached to the two points even when you move the shapes. You don't have to attach connectors to anything. For example, you can connect one end to a shape and leave the other end free to create your own custom callout.

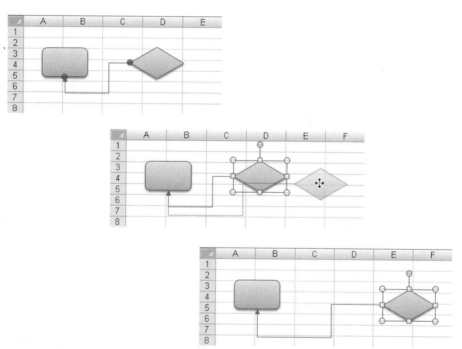

Figure 10-13 Connector lines remain attached to the points where you place them, even when you drag the shape to a new location.

Connectors are particularly useful for creating flow charts. First, sketch your ideas using connectors with the Flowchart tools on the Shapes palette. You can move flow chart symbols as you work, and the connector lines reroute themselves as necessary.

> You can also use SmartArt graphics to create flow charts and other types of diagrams. For more information, see "Creating SmartArt" on page 358.

Callouts are special text boxes with connector lines already attached. You can use them to add labels to important information or to describe important items. The most familiar type of callout is the kind you see in comics. Excel includes several of these balloon callouts, shown in Figure 10-14 with additional text formatting applied. Note that in this type of callout, the tip of the balloon pointer is the sticky point.

Figure 10-14 Callouts help you describe important items or call attention to important messages.

After drawing a callout, you can immediately begin typing the text you want in the callout. Then drag the diamond-shaped handle to move the tip of the callout indicator to the location you want.

Creating WordArt

The WordArt button on the Insert tab opens a palette containing a number of fancy text styles you can employ to create impressive logos and headings. After you click the effect you want in the palette, a new WordArt graphic object appears on the worksheet. You can then type your text and modify the WordArt object using controls on the Format tab under Drawing Tools; this tab appears on the Ribbon when you select the WordArt object, as shown in Figure 10-15.

Notice that in Figure 10-15, selected WordArt objects display the same handles as shapes, including the free rotate panhandle. After you create your WordArt or anytime you select a WordArt object, the Format tab under Drawing Tools appears on the Ribbon, as shown in Figure 10-15. The Shape Styles group and the WordArt Styles group contain controls you use to change the look of the WordArt object.

The WordArt Styles palette on the Format tab displays a selection of WordArt effects. This palette is similar to the one displayed by clicking the WordArt button on the Insert tab, except that instead of creating a new WordArt object, the WordArt Styles palette lets you modify an existing WordArt object. You can select styles that apply only to selected text in the object (or only to the word containing the active cursor), or you can select styles that apply to all the text in the object. The Clear WordArt command at the bottom of the palette does not remove the object or the text, just the fancy formatting, resulting in a WordArt object of the same dimensions but formatted as plain text.

Text Effects

The Text Effects button displays a menu containing six palettes of special effects you can apply to your WordArt object, as shown in Figure 10-16.

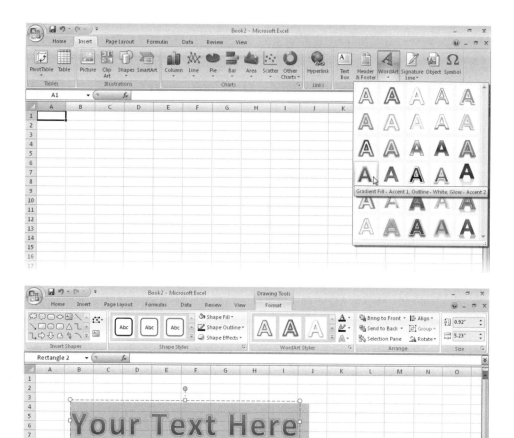

Figure 10-15 Use the WordArt button to create stunning logos and headings.

As with most palettes in Office Excel 2007, the palettes on the Text Effects menu allow you to rest the pointer on an icon in the palette to see a live preview of how the effect will look if you apply it to the selected WordArt object. The same behavior is exhibited by the palette in the Shape Styles group, although the results may not be what you expect. Applying Shape Styles does not change the look of the text but instead adds lines, colors, and fills to the area behind the text.

The rest of the controls on the Format tab under Drawing Tools apply to other objects as well as WordArt and are described in "Formatting Objects That Contain Text" on page 382 and in "Positioning Objects" on page 387.

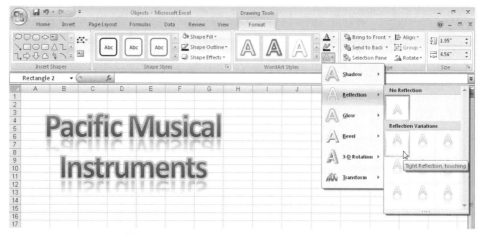

Figure 10-16 The Text Effects menu offers advanced formatting effects.

Creating SmartArt

The SmartArt button on the Insert tab represents a significant new set of features in the 2007 Microsoft Office system. SmartArt replaces the Organization Chart feature with all that and more—a comparative cornucopia of new functionality and graphic complexity. SmartArt graphics are prepackaged sets of graphic objects designed to address a variety of presentation tasks, such as creating timelines and decision trees, illustrating procedural steps and relationships, and, yes, even creating organizational charts.

Help

> **Note**
>
> The feature formerly known as Microsoft Organization Chart 2.0 is still available as an add-in, which you can add to your Microsoft Office System installation by exiting all programs and using Windows installation tools. For details, click the Help button, and under "Working With Graphics," read "Where Can I Find Microsoft Office Organization Chart?"

When you click the SmartArt button, the Choose A SmartArt Graphic dialog box shown in Figure 10-17 appears.

The categories on the left represent conceptual approaches you can select to narrow the SmartArt graphics available in the main area of the dialog box:

- **List** Creates a list of information that does not need to be in any particular order

- **Process** Illustrates sequential steps to achieve a goal

- **Cycle** Describes processes that are cyclical rather than goal oriented

- **Hierarchy** Creates organizational charts or decision trees
- **Relationship** Shows connections
- **Matrix** Illustrates relationships that are interdependent
- **Pyramid** Shows relationships that are proportional in size or importance

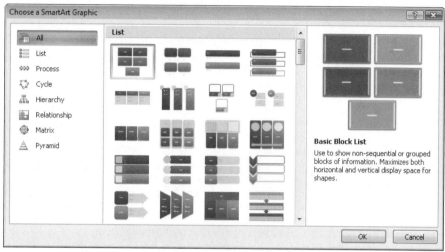

Figure 10-17 SmartArt graphics help you illustrate conceptual information.

After you select a SmartArt graphic in the dialog box, click OK to add it to your worksheet, as shown in Figure 10-18.

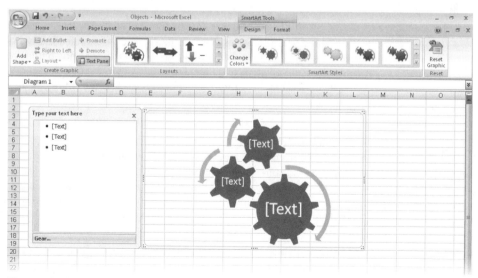

Figure 10-18 You can type your text into the box on the left, and it appears in the graphic to the right.

The SmartArt graphic comprises several components: the text pane with its Name box at the bottom displaying the currently active item; the SmartArt graphic; and the border surrounding the SmartArt like a picture frame. The text pane and the border appear only when you select the graphic. Similarly, two tabs appear on the Ribbon, under SmartArt Tools, only when you select a SmartArt graphic: Design and Format. The text pane makes organizing large charts and diagrams a lot easier and lets you easily perform editing tasks such as indenting bullet lists and rearranging hierarchical items. Here's more information about the text pane and the border:

- Resize the graphic by dragging any of the eight dotted handles on the border.

- Move the graphic by dragging the border; the text pane will follow.

- Enter text directly into graphic items by clicking and typing.

- Redisplay a closed text pane by clicking the tab that appears in its place on the border or by clicking the Text Pane button on the Design tab under SmartArt Tools.

If you change your mind about your original SmartArt selection, the Layouts palette on the Design tab under SmartArt Tools lets you switch to a different graphic arrangement within the same SmartArt category, without having to start from scratch. Or click the More Layouts command at the bottom of the Layouts palette to switch to a different SmartArt category.

The SmartArt Styles palette offers different graphic treatments and gives you thumbnail previews using your selected graphic, as shown in Figure 10-19. Both of these palettes exhibit live preview functionality, allowing you to rest the pointer on each thumbnail in the palette to quickly view your graphic in each style.

> **Note**
>
> The Layouts and SmartArt Styles palettes share a clever design feature with a number of other palettes on the Ribbon. The top two arrows on the right side of the palette allow you to scroll up and down through the available styles in the palette without obscuring the worksheet; clicking the bottom arrow button displays the entire palette.

The buttons in the Create Graphic group on the Design tab under SmartArt Tools offer ways to modify your graphic, and how they work depends on the particular graphic you're using. For example, the Add Bullet button works perfectly in most List graphics but not so well in the gear graphic shown in Figure 10-19. Experimentation is inevitable and rewarding. You can always press Ctrl+Z to undo any changes or click the Reset Graphic button on the Design tab under SmartArt Tools. Here is some more information about buttons in the Create Graphic group:

- **Add Shape** Inserts another shape similar to those already in the selected graphic. Clicking the arrow displays a menu of commands that allow you to choose where to put the new shape: above, below, after, or before the active shape. The Add

Assistant command applies only to Hierarchical Organization Chart graphics; it adds a box outside the hierarchy that is typically used for administrative assistants or other positions outside the normal chain of command.

- **Add Bullet** Creates a new bullet item, subordinate to the active bullet.

- **Right To Left** Flips the horizontal orientation of applicable graphics.

- **Layout** Controls the horizontal orientation of an organization chart. Menu commands include Standard, Left Hanging, Right Hanging, and Both (left *and* right hanging). This is available only when an Organization Chart graphic is selected.

- **Promote and Demote** Change the hierarchical position of a selected bullet. Promoting to the highest level creates a new shape in the SmartArt graphic. Similarly, demoting a top-level bullet removes the corresponding shape in the graphic and adds its text as subordinate to the previous bullet. Only in Organization Chart graphics, these buttons move the selected shape up or down the hierarchy and do not add or remove shapes from the graphic.

We discuss the controls available on the Format tab under SmartArt Tools in "Formatting Graphics" on page 368.

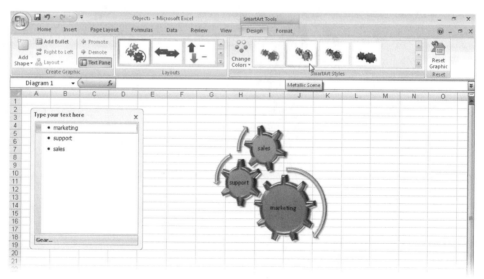

Figure 10-19 Use the SmartArt Styles palette on the Design tab under SmartArt Tools to add graphic interest to your SmartArt.

Chapter 10

Inserting Graphics

Although the Excel graphic toolbox is overflowing with ways to create impressive graphic objects from scratch, you can also employ several methods to insert ready-made graphics from other programs, to insert pictures, and to insert other types of graphic content onto your worksheets.

Inserting Clip Art and Media Files

If you don't have the time or inclination to create your own artwork, you can instantly call on the talents of numerous professional illustrators using the Clip Art button on the Insert tab. You can resize and reposition artwork, add borders, and sometimes even add fills and patterns to clip art objects. Click the Clip Art button to display the Clip Art task pane, shown in Figure 10-20.

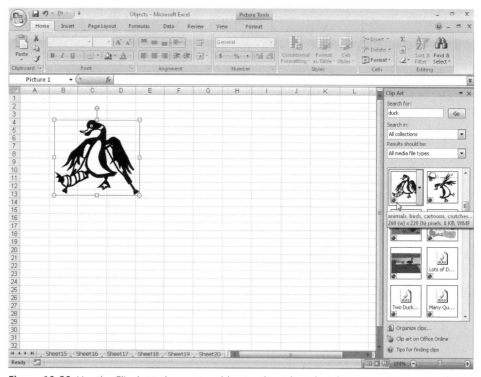

Figure 10-20 Use the Clip Art task pane to add not only art but also photos, movies, or sounds to your worksheets.

To find appropriate pieces of clip art, you must first provide some criteria in the Search For text box in the Clip Art task pane. The first time you click the Go button to initiate a search, you'll see a message box asking whether you want to include images found on Microsoft Office Online. A wealth of graphic content is available online—far more than ships with the program—so it's a good idea to click the Yes button if you'd like to see the maximum number of available graphic options. If you click No, you can always click the Search In drop-down list in the task pane and select the Web Collections check box. The other options in this list are My Collections, comprising your own media files, and Office Collections, installed with your Microsoft Office system programs.

Figure 10-20 shows a piece of clip art inserted on the worksheet, which was accomplished by simply clicking the thumbnail image in the task pane. When you rest the pointer on a thumbnail image, a ScreenTip reveals information about the item, including its size, three-character file type designation, and some of the keywords associated with it. Notice also in Figure 10-20 the three items at the bottom of the thumbnail window in the Clip Art task pane, which are displayed as generic icons. These are .wav files—sound clips you can insert just like pieces of clip art. The Clip Art task pane lets you search for and insert not only clip art but also photos, movies, and sound files. You can specify the type of media you want using the Results Should Be drop-down list in the task pane, which ordinarily displays the words *All media file types*.

When you rest the pointer on a clip in the task pane, a bar with an arrow appears to the right. Click the bar to display a menu with additional options you can apply to the selected clip. Several commands on this menu will benefit from some additional explanation:

- **Copy/Move To Collection** Adds or relocates the selected clip to one of your own collections by displaying the Copy To Collection dialog box. You can create a new collection or add to an existing personal collection.

- **Edit Keywords** Displays a dialog box where you can add or modify any keywords associated with the selected clip.

- **Find Similar Style** Searches for any clips that were created using a similar illustration style. Unfortunately, this depends on a style code embedded in each preinstalled clip, rather than a subjective artistic evaluation of the artwork (although this would probably involve a lot more computing power than most of us have on the desktop). Don't expect this command to work on clips you add from your own archives.

- **Make Available Offline** Displays a dialog box that lets you add clips found on the Web to one of the collections installed on your computer or to a new collection you create.

- **Preview/Properties** Displays the Preview/Properties dialog box shown in Figure 10-21, which lists all the pertinent information about the clip. This is a handy way to find out the format of the clip, the keywords associated with it, and more.

Managing Clips

You can go straight to the source of the content displayed in the Clip Art task pane by clicking Organize Clips at the bottom of the Clip Art task pane, which displays a dialog box similar to the one shown in Figure 10-22. The contents of the Collection List depend on the clips cataloged on your system.

Chapter 10

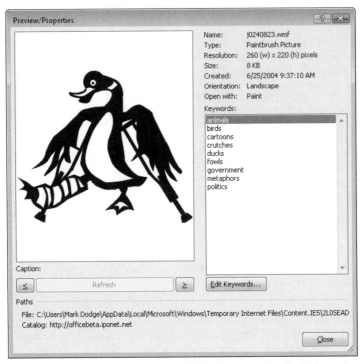

Figure 10-21 The Preview/Properties dialog box gives detailed information about the selected clip.

The Microsoft Clip Organizer isn't just a dialog box but a separate program with its own interface and Help system. Although most of the functionality you need is available from the task pane, more options are available using the menus and buttons of the Microsoft Clip Organizer. Here are a few highlights:

- Click the Search button to display a Search pane similar to the one in the Clip Art task pane. Click the Collection List button to return to the list.

- Click the Clips Online button to open your Web browser and display the Microsoft Office Online Clip Art page.

- Click File, New Collection to create a new category in the Collection List task pane. This command is available only when you select My Collections or one of its subfolders in the Collection List task pane.

- Click File, Add Clips To Organizer, and click one of the commands on the menu to catalog and add clips located on your computer or on a connected camera or scanner. Clicking Automatically scans your computer and collects all eligible clips; clicking On My Own lets you specify folders.

- Click Tools, Compact to remove unused space. Clips that come with Microsoft Office are already compacted, but you can click this command if you add your own clips.

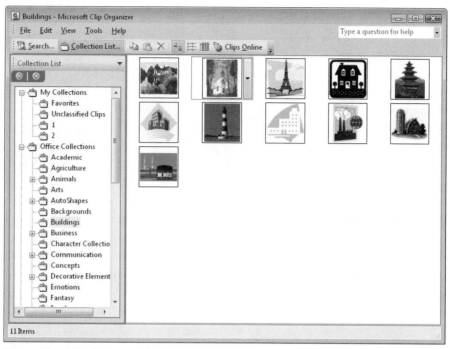

Figure 10-22 The Microsoft Clip Organizer is the wizard behind the curtain of the Clip Art task pane.

Inserting Pictures

The Picture button on the Insert tab lets you insert graphics in your workbooks that have been saved in a variety of file formats. Clicking Picture displays a dialog box that is functionally identical to the Open dialog box, which you can use to find image files in any location to which your computer has access. The File Type drop-down list to the right of the File Name text box lets you zero in on a particular file type but is set to All Pictures by default. You can choose different ways to look at files by clicking the Views button; Thumbnail view is the default.

For more information about the Open dialog box, see "Opening Files" on page 63.

Importing Pictures

You can import pictures into Excel from other programs that produce files compatible with the Clipboard. Simply copy the image in the source program; then on the Home tab in Excel, click the Paste menu, and then click Paste Special, which allows you to select from several options, as shown in Figure 10-23. The options available in this dialog box depend on the type of picture with which you are working.

 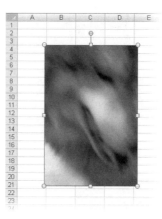

Figure 10-23 Images copied from other programs can usually be pasted in more than one format using Paste Special.

The image used in Figure 10-23 was copied from Adobe ImageReady and pasted in the Bitmap format. If the program used to create the graphic you want to import into Excel supports linking, you might also be able to establish a link between the source file and the graphic, allowing the graphic to be automatically updated in your workbook whenever you make changes to the original using the source program. The Paste Link option becomes available in the Paste Special dialog box, if and when linking is possible.

For more information about linking, see Chapter 30, "Linking and Embedding."

Inserting Other Objects

The Object button on the Insert tab gives you direct access to other programs you can use to create objects. The difference between inserting a picture and inserting an object is that a picture is always static and cannot be directly edited, whereas an inserted object retains a connection to its source program and is said to be *embedded* on a worksheet. You can open an embedded object for editing by double-clicking it.

When you click the Object button, a dialog box appears with two tabs—Create New and Create From File. The Create New tab, shown in Figure 10-24, starts the program selected in the Object Type list, allowing you to create the object directly in the program. The contents of this list vary depending on the configuration of your system and the programs you have installed.

When you select an item in the Object Type list, a small frame is inserted on the current worksheet at the location of the active cell, and the program needed to create or edit that object type is started. For example, if you select Bitmap Image in the Object Type list, Microsoft Paint starts, and you can begin creating a new image within the frame. Elements of the program's interface appear without completely displacing the Excel interface, as shown in Figure 10-25. The degree to which this blending of interfaces occurs depends on the chosen program.

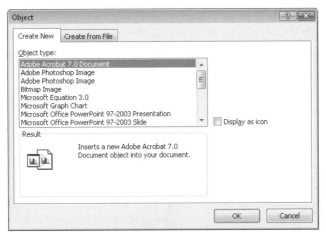

Figure 10-24 You can use the Create New tab of the Object dialog box to simultaneously insert an object and start the program used to create it.

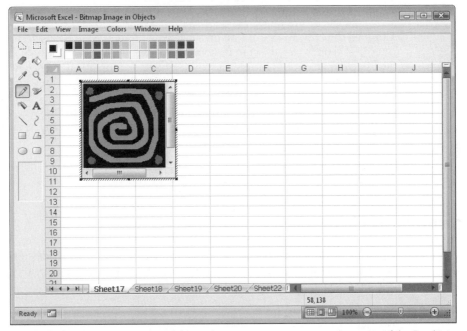

Figure 10-25 When you insert an object, the source program opens, but parts of the Excel interface are still visible.

When you are finished editing the inserted object, click anywhere outside the frame to return to the Excel interface. Figure 10-26 shows the Create From File tab in the Object dialog box. You can use this tab to insert an existing file as an embedded object rather than create a new object with the Create New tab. Again, the object types you can embed depend on the programs installed on your computer.

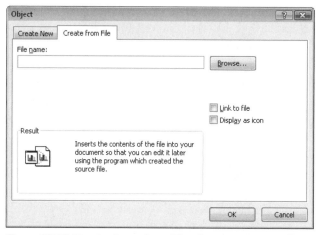

Figure 10-26 Use the Create From File tab to insert existing files into your workbooks.

Although the Link To File option on the Create From File tab isn't selected by default, you can still open the object in its source program by double-clicking it. If you do select the Link To File option, the object will be updated automatically whenever the source file changes. The Display As Icon option embeds the selected file in your workbook as an icon. This option is particularly convenient if an embedded object is long, large, or more easily viewed in its source program. However, if you distribute the workbook to other users, be sure the same program is available on their computers, or they will not be able to open the embedded icon for viewing.

To make changes to any embedded object, double-click the object. The source program starts, and the object file opens, allowing you to make modifications.

Formatting Graphics

After you create or insert a graphic object, Office Excel 2007 provides tools you can use to modify it. Most of these tools are on hidden Ribbon tabs that appear only when an object is selected.

> **Note**
>
> This is the exception that proves the rule: No additional tabs appear on the Ribbon when an embedded object is selected. For more about embedded objects, see "Inserting Other Objects" on page 366.

Three types of hidden tabs exist, depending on the object you select: SmartArt Tools, Drawing Tools, or Picture Tools appear on a menu bar above the new tabs. All three types include a Format tab; SmartArt Tools includes an additional tab, Design, which is discussed in "Creating SmartArt" on page 358. The controls available on the Format tab change depending on the type of object selected.

When you select a picture or a piece of clip art, for example, you can use the Format tab under Picture Tools to make some rather extreme adjustments to the image. Although the source program that created an imported picture probably offers more control, you can do a fair amount of formatting from within Excel as well, such as changing its shape, adding a border, and adjusting brightness and contrast. Figure 10-27 shows the picture we imported in Figure 10-23.

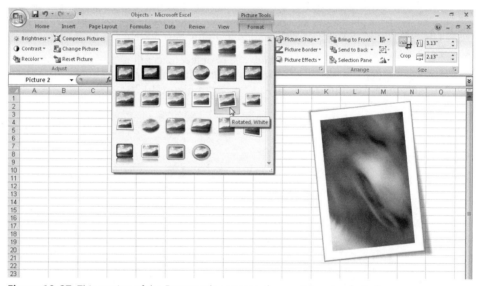

Figure 10-27 This version of the Format tab appears when a picture is selected.

- **Brightness and Contrast** Offer control over the exposure of the selected picture.

- **Recolor** Offers color tinting options based on the current theme colors, plus Sepia, Grayscale, Washout, and more.

- **Change Picture** Lets you switch to a different image without changing the size or formatting of the selected picture.

- **Reset Picture** Discards any applied formatting and returns the selected picture to its original form.

- **Picture Shape** Offers a palette similar to the Shapes palette on the Insert menu. Select the shape you want to apply to the selected picture. This palette does not support live preview.

Chapter 10

• **Picture Border** Applies a border to the picture and lets you select its color, size, and type.

 • **Picture Effects** Displays a menu of special effects you can apply to the selected picture, including Shadow, Reflection, Glow, Soft Edges, and 3-D Rotation.

 • **Crop** Displays handles on the picture that you can drag to change its displayed area. The Height and Width controls are linked so that changing one dimension causes the other to change proportionally.

As Figure 10-27 shows, simply resting the pointer on a thumbnail in the Picture Styles palette temporarily displays the selected picture using that style. The same functionality applies to most other palettes available on the Format tab. Here are some details about selected controls available on the Format tab:

Height

When you select any other type of object (except for embedded objects), the Format tab under Drawing Tools appears, containing many of the same controls as the Format tab under Picture Tools, as you can see in Figure 10-28.

Width

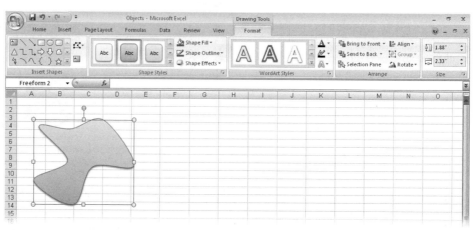

Figure 10-28 This version of the Format tab appears when any Shape, Text Box, or WordArt object is selected.

Here are details about the formatting controls available on the Format tab under Drawing Tools that are different from those on the Format tab under Picture Tools:

• **Shape Fill** This palette lets you select colors, textures, gradients, and even pictures you can use to fill the selected shape.

 • **Shape Outline** This palette offers options you can apply to the outline of the selected shape, including color, line weight, and line style. Other than the name on the button, this palette is otherwise identical to the Picture Border palette, described earlier.

 • **Shape Effects** Displays a menu of special effects you can apply to the selected picture, including Shadow, Reflection, Glow, Soft Edges, and 3-D Rotation. Other than the name on the button, this palette is otherwise identical to the Picture Effects palette, described earlier.

The Format tab under Drawing Tools and the Format tab under Picture Tools contain groups covered elsewhere in this book. For more about the Insert Shapes group, see "Using the Shapes Tools" on page 345. To read about the WordArt group, see "Creating WordArt" on page 356. For information about the Arrange group, see "Positioning Objects" on page 387.

Formatting Text in Graphics

Most of what you can do with text in cells applies to text in graphics as well. You can use the tools in the Font group on the Home tab to accomplish most of what you need to do in either cells or text-capable objects. However, you can employ a few additional text-formatting options when working with text in objects.

To see what we're talking about, click Shapes on the Insert menu, draw any kind of two-dimensional object such as a rectangle, and then type some text. Drag through the text you just typed to select it, then right-click the selected text, and finally click Font to display the Font dialog box like the one shown in Figure 10-29.

> Note
>
> You can also display the Font dialog box by selecting any text-capable object and clicking the Dialog Box Launcher in the Font group on the Home tab.

Chapter 10

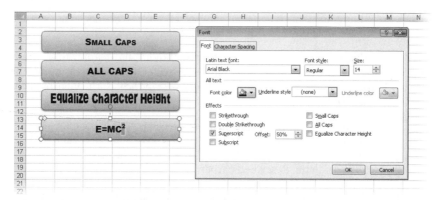

Figure 10-29 The Font dialog box offers a few formatting options not found elsewhere.

The Font dialog box shares many of the same controls found in the Format Cells dialog box that you use to format text in cells. The Font dialog box additionally offers the following options:

- **Double Strikethrough** This effect draws two lines through the middle of the selected text.

- **Offset** When the Superscript or Subscript effect is turned on, Offset offers precise control over the distance of selected text from the baseline, as shown in Figure 10-29.

- **Small Caps** This effect changes lowercase characters in selected text to small capital letters, as shown in Figure 10-29. Text typed as capital letters is unaffected.

- **All Caps** This effect changes all the selected lowercase characters into capital letters, as shown in Figure 10-29.

- **Equalize Character Height** This effect changes the size of each selected character so they all occupy the same amount of vertical space, as shown in Figure 10-29. Characters with descenders are moved above the baseline.

- **Character Spacing** On the Character Spacing tab in the Font dialog box, this effect lets you expand or condense the space between characters of selected text by a specified number of points, as shown in Figure 10-30.

- **Kerning** This effect applies special spacing rules to correct problematic character pairs and lets you specify a font size above which kerning is applied.

In Figure 10-30, the first text box is formatted as usual; kerning was applied to the second text box. The effect is subtle, but you can see that the spacing between each letter pair in the second box is a little tighter. Kerning is particularly noticeable when applied to large display fonts and logos.

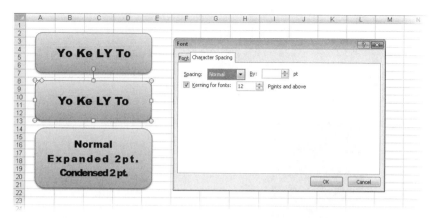

Figure 10-30 Adjust the space between letters in graphic objects using the Character Spacing tab.

Note

Chapter 9, "Worksheet Formatting Techniques," discusses the overall formatting features of Excel 2007; we discuss text formatting in depth in "Using Fonts" on page 323.

Applying Compression to Pictures

When you import pictures using the Picture button on the Insert tab, you can choose to optimize the storage of these bitmap images, along with your worksheet, to decrease the amount of disk space they consume. Clicking the Compress Pictures button on the Format tab under Picture Tools displays a dialog box of the same name; clicking its Options button displays the Compression Settings dialog box. Figure 10-31 shows both.

Here are details about the options in the Compress Pictures and Compression Settings dialog boxes:

- **Apply To Selected Pictures Only** Ordinarily, all the images in your workbook are compressed at once. Select this check box to compress only the currently selected images.

- **Automatically Perform Basic Compression On Save** Excel applies compression whenever you save your workbook. To prevent this, clear this check box.

- **Delete Cropped Areas Of Pictures** This discards any nonvisible portions of pictures you have cropped using the options in the Size group on the Format tab under Picture Tools. This is the default setting and is nonreversible.

- **Target Output options** These options allow you to specify the number of dots per inch (dpi) to suit your output requirements: Print, Screen, or E-Mail.

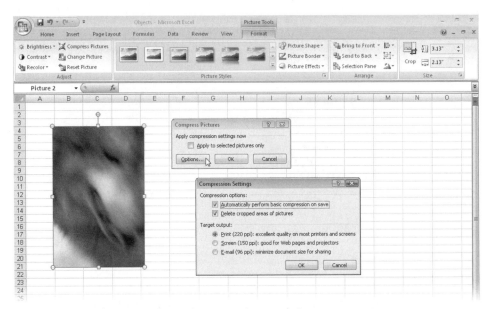

Figure 10-31 Apply compression settings to any imported picture.

Using the Format Shape Dialog Box

Most of the graphic formatting controls you need are right up front on the Ribbon—the "dashboard" of Excel. The Ribbon offers easy access to buttons and palettes as well as live preview functionality. However, a few additional options are not available on the Ribbon. To access them, right-click any graphic object (except an embedded object), and click either Format Shape or Format Picture to display the dialog box shown in Figure 10-32. (The command is Format Picture when you select clip art or an inserted picture, but the dialog box is the same either way.)

Not only does the Format Shape dialog box offer a few additional controls, but you might also find it convenient, because you can leave it open and move it out of the way while you work. For more information, see the sidebar "A Dialog Apart" on the next page.

The categories on the left side of the Format Shape dialog box are always the same, no matter what type of object you select. However, the options available in each category change based on the object type. For example, the settings in the Text Box category are unavailable when you select a picture.

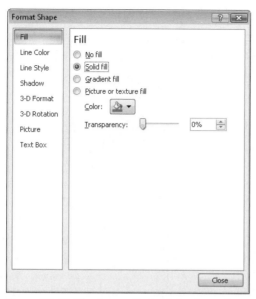

Figure 10-32 The Format Shape dialog box offers central control of graphic-object formatting.

Undo

A Dialog Apart

Although you don't get the full "mouse hover" live preview functionality you get using the Ribbon, you do see results on the worksheet after you make a change in the Format Shape dialog box. You can change settings in each category listed on the left, and you'll see your progress reflected in the selected graphic object in real time, not after you dismiss the dialog box. This is a departure from "old" dialog box functionality, in which you can make all the changes you want but clicking the Cancel button discards anything you did while the dialog box was open. But you'll notice there is no Cancel button, or even an OK button, in the Format Shape dialog box. Your changes apply instantly, but you can also undo instantly by clicking the Undo button on the Quick Access Toolbar. It gets better: With the Format Shape dialog box open, you can select different objects on the worksheet; click Ribbon tabs and buttons; use the Quick Access Toolbar; display other dialog boxes; and even change worksheets. The Format Shape dialog box functions like a toolbar or a task bar that you can drag anywhere on your screen (or off your screen and onto a second monitor's screen, if you have one).

Much of what you'll find in the Format Shape dialog box is self-explanatory, but we'll hit the high points for you in the following sections, which will also serve to describe some of the inner workings of equivalent Ribbon-based controls.

Formatting Fills and Lines

The first two categories in the Format Shape dialog box, Fill and Line Color, contain options that change the controls displayed in the dialog box, as shown in Figure 10-33. For example, in Figure 10-33 you can see the differences between the controls available when the Gradient Fill and Picture Or Texture Fill options are selected. As always, any changes you make in the dialog box are reflected immediately in the selected object.

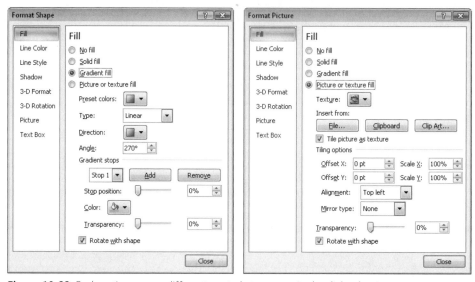

Figure 10-33 Each option causes different controls to appear in the dialog box.

Note

The most often used controls in the Fill, Line Color, and Line Style categories in the Format Shape dialog box are available directly on the Ribbon. On the Format tab under Drawing Tools, which appears when you select a graphic object, click the Shape Fill or Shape Outline button.

Gradient Fills   Gradient Fill is the third option in the Fill category in the Format Shape dialog box; a *gradient fill* consists of two or more colors, cross-fading from light to dark. You can choose from a number of presets in the Preset Colors drop-down list, or you can customize your own. In the Type drop-down list, select from Linear, Rectangular, Radial, or Path, which follows the contours of the selected object. You can select a fill direction for any gradient type except Path. You can specify an angle from 0 to 359.9 degrees, which is the point from which a gradient emanates. The Direction settings are presets of the Angle setting; both settings are applicable only to linear gradients.

Gradient Stops   You can create complex, nonlinear gradients using the Gradient Stops option, which lets you specify up to 10 intervals of gradation using varying amounts of color and transparency. To get an idea how they work, select any of the more colorful samples in the Preset Colors list, and then look at the Gradient Stops drop-down list. For example, the preset named Rainbow has seven gradient stops, each set to a different color. The Stop Position control determines where along the gradient path the selected stop comes into play. For example, if you wanted to create a three-color gradient, you could add stops at 50 percent and 100 percent for a fairly even gradient or at 10 percent and 80 percent to emphasize the middle color. You can also use the Transparency slider to add varying amounts of transparency to each gradient stop. For example, you could set a shape to be 0 percent transparent on one end of the scale and 80 percent on the other end, revealing varying amounts of the worksheet below the shape.

> **Note**
>
> If you find that you keep applying the same formatting options to objects you create, you can easily make these hard-earned formats the default for all new objects you create. Right-click any object formatted the way you like, and click Set As Default Shape. The command name may change, depending on the object you select. Note that you must right-click the *border* of a text box, not the text area, to display the Set As Default Shape command.

Picture or Texture Fill   Selecting the Picture Or Texture Fill option in the Fill category in the Format Shape dialog box reveals the controls shown on the right in Figure 10-33. You can select one of the preset textures in the Texture drop-down list, or you can import an image from a file on disk, a piece of clip art, or even the current contents of the Clipboard by clicking the appropriate Insert From button. The Tile Picture As Texture option repeats an image as needed to fill the selected shape, or if not selected, it places a single instance of an image in the center of the selected shape. The Tiling Options let you offset the image from the edges of the shape, giving you control over the percentage of offset from the left, right, top, or bottom of the shape.

Line Colors and Styles   The Line Color and Line Style categories in the Format Shape dialog box don't contain any surprises; these categories are where you control the formatting of lines and arrows. You can create gradient lines and compound lines; you can specify different styles of dashed lines and arrowheads; you can add square, round, or flat caps to the end of lines; you can specify a percentage of transparency to solid lines; and you can specify round, bevel, or miter intersections where lines meet.

Applying Shadows

You can use the Shadow category in the Format Shape dialog box to add depth to any graphic object. In Figure 10-34, we created a shape and right-clicked it, then clicked Format Shape and clicked the Shadow category, and then applied shadow effects. When you click the Presets button, a palette appears with a number of built-in shadow configurations. After you apply a shadow effect, you can modify it using the sliders in the dialog box.

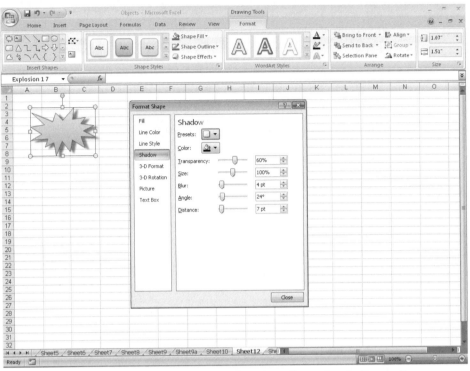

Figure 10-34 You can create an infinite number of shadow effects using the Format Shape dialog box.

> **Note**
> The same shadow presets in the Format Shape dialog box are available on the Ribbon; on the Format tab under Drawing Tools, which appears when a graphic object is selected, you can find the shadow presets by clicking the Shape Effects button and then clicking Shadow.

Applying 3-D Effects

Click the 3-D Format category in the Format Shape dialog box to apply three-dimensional effects to the selected shape. If you apply one of the Bevel presets, several formats are applied to the selected object: color and amount of depth and contour, surface type, and lighting type. In Figure 10-35, we created a shape and applied the Convex preset from the Top drop-down list.

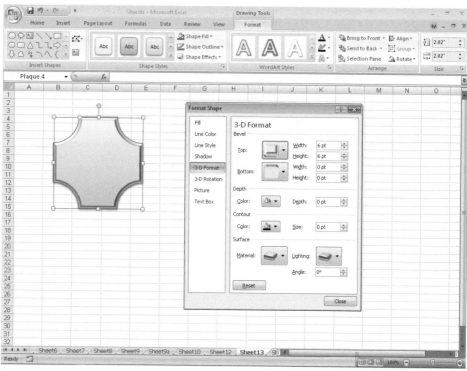

Figure 10-35 Start with a basic shape, and give it depth.

> **Note**
> The most often used controls in the 3-D Format and 3-D Rotation categories in the Format Shape dialog box are available directly on the Ribbon. On the Format tab under Drawing Tools, which appears when you select a graphic object, click the Shape Effects button, and then click the commands on the Bevel menu and the 3-D Rotation menu.

With the controls in the 3-D Rotation category, you can control the attitude of the selected shape in all three dimensions. We'll describe the controls in the two 3-D categories in the Format Shape dialog box in detail.

- **Bevel (in the 3-D Format category)**   Controls the amount of "extrusion" applied to the selected shape, giving it the appearance of having a beveled edge. You can create extrusions on both sides; the Top drop-down list controls the front of the shape, and the Bottom drop-down list controls the back, as shown in Figure 10-36. (To see the results of the Bottom settings, you must rotate the shape using controls in the 3-D Rotation category.) The Width settings control the width of the beveled edge, and the Height settings control the distance the bevel is extruded from the surface of the shape.

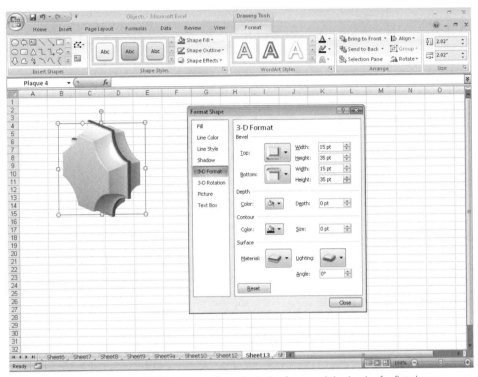

Figure 10-36 You can "extrude" 3-D bevels from both the front and the back of a flat shape.

- **Depth (in the 3-D Format category)** Controls the thickness and color of the shape. (To see the results of the Depth settings, you must rotate the shape using controls in the 3-D Rotation category.)

- **Contour (in the 3-D Format category)** Controls the size and color of a raised border applied to the perimeter of the selected shape.

- **Surface (in the 3-D Format category)** Includes two palettes you can use to select types of surface treatment and lighting effects. Materials include surfaces such as plastic and metal, translucent, and special effects such as soft edge and wireframe. Choose from lighting effects such as Three-Point, Sunset, and Chilly, and choose the angle from which the light originates.

- **Rotation (in the 3-D Rotation category)** Contains controls to adjust the position of the selected object in three-dimensional space. The x-axis is horizontal, the y-axis is vertical, and the z-axis is front to back.

- **Perspective (in the 3-D Rotation category)** Controls the amount of foreshortening applied to a shape, if applicable. *Foreshortening* makes shapes that are closer look larger. You use this control to make shapes appear to tilt forward or backward. It is easiest to start by clicking one of the Perspective options in the Presets drop-down list; then you can change the angle of foreshortening using the Perspective controls.

- **Keep Text Flat (in the 3-D Rotation category)**   Prevents any text typed in a shape from rotating along with the shape, effectively separating the text from the shape.

Formatting Pictures

The Picture category in the Format Picture (or Format Shape) dialog box contains Brightness and Contrast sliders, which give you control over exposure characteristics of bitmap images. Also, a Recolor drop-down list offers a number of special effects, as shown in Figure 10-37.

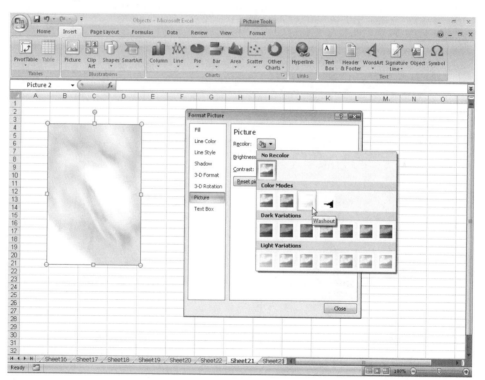

Figure 10-37 The Recolor drop-down list offers special effects you can apply to bitmap images.

> **Note**
>
> The most often used controls in the Picture category of the Format Shape dialog box are available directly on the Ribbon. On the Format tab under Picture Tools, which appears when you select a picture, use the buttons in the Adjust group. For more information, see "Formatting Graphics" on page 368.

Formatting Objects That Contain Text

Besides objects you actually create with the Text Box button on the Insert tab, many of the objects you can create in Excel are de facto text boxes. Figure 10-38 shows two objects, one created with the Text Box tool and another created with one of the Star tools in the Shapes palette. Both objects are subject to the influence of the Text Box controls in the Format Shape dialog box, as are most two-dimensional shapes and even WordArt and SmartArt objects.

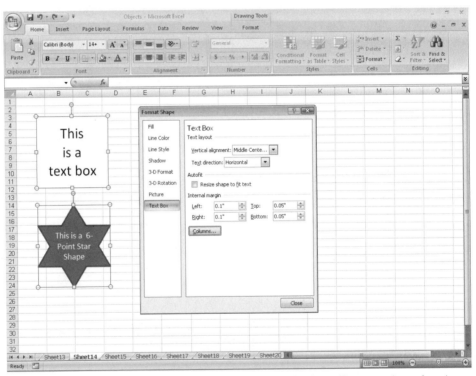

Figure 10-38 The Text Box category of the Format Shape dialog box offers controls not found on the Ribbon.

> **Note**
>
> The most often used controls in the Text Box category of the Format Shape dialog box are available directly on the Ribbon. On the Home tab, use the buttons in the Font and Alignment groups. For more information, see the following topics: "Using Fonts" on page 323 and "Aligning Data in Cells" on page 316. For more about text boxes, see "Working with Text Boxes" on page 352.

Middle Align

The Text Layout controls perform some of the same tasks as the buttons in the Alignment group on the Home tab of the Ribbon. You can see in Figure 10-38 that both the Middle Align and Center buttons on the Ribbon are highlighted, indicating that the selected objects have those attributes applied. The corresponding setting in the Vertical Alignment category in the dialog box is also selected.

Center

If you select the Resize Shape To Fit Text check box, the object shrinks (or expands) to fit the text it contains, as typed and formatted. The Internal Margin settings add or decrease the amount of space between the edge of a shape and the text it contains. The Columns button displays a dialog box you can use to create columns of text within any text-capable object, as shown in Figure 10-39.

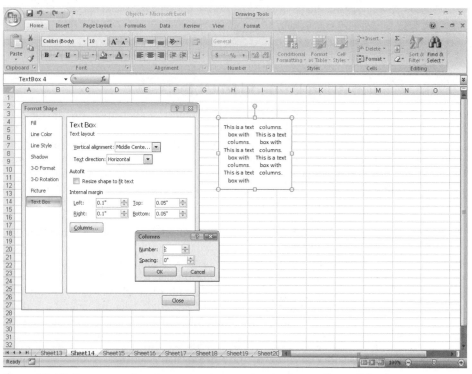

Figure 10-39 You can create columnar text boxes using the Format Shape dialog box.

Chapter 10

Selecting Text or Shapes

You have two ways to select objects containing text: Either you select the text area or you select the entire object. When you select the text area, you can edit it; when you select the object, you can move it. You tell the difference by looking at the object's border. When you click a shape created using the Text Box tool on the Insert tab, the border is a dashed line at first, indicating the text area is ready for editing. Click the border of the box, and the border changes to a solid line, indicating the object is now selected:

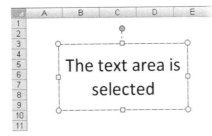 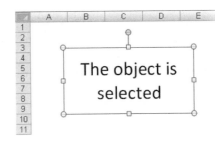

For shapes other than text boxes, it depends on whether the shape contains text: Click near the text, and the text area is selected; otherwise, the shape is selected. If a non-text-box shape doesn't contain text, you can't activate the text area, but you don't need to do so—just start typing after you select the object to create a text area.

Formatting Embedded Objects

As mentioned earlier in this chapter, objects you create using the Object button on the Insert tab cannot be formatted using the Format Shape dialog box, and they do not display additional formatting tabs on the Ribbon. So to apply formatting to embedded objects, right-click an embedded object, and click the Format Object command (or Format Picture, depending on the object). When you do so, a dialog box like the one shown in Figure 10-40 appears. Note that, depending on the type of object selected, some of the options available in this dialog box will have no effect.

For more information about embedded objects, see "Inserting Other Objects" on page 366.

The Colors And Lines tab in the Format Object dialog box gives you control over the style, color, and weight of the object's border, as well its fill color and pattern. In Figure 10-40, we applied a gradient fill to an embedded Microsoft Equation Editor object and added 75 percent transparency and a 3-point border. In general, the options available in this dialog box are self-explanatory, but here are a few facts that might be less obvious:

- The Color options on the Colors And Lines tab include 56 standard colors that are not controlled by the current theme settings.

- On the Colors And Lines tab, the Fill Effects option in the Color drop-down list displays the Fill Effects dialog box, which you can use to add patterns, gradient fills, pictures, or textures, such as wood, marble, canvas, and even a paper bag effect, to your objects.

- If you apply a pattern using the Pattern tab in the Fill Effects dialog box, the color you select for the foreground is assigned to the pattern itself and is reflected in the sample pattern thumbnails displayed in the dialog box. The color you select for the background is assigned to the white areas of the pattern.

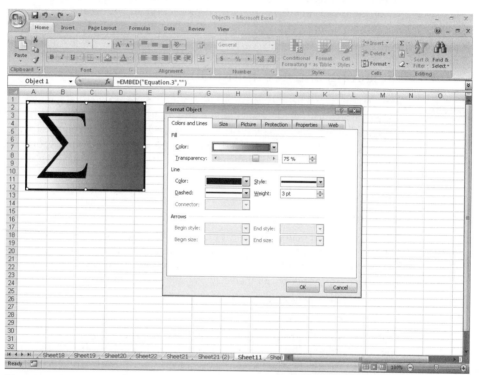

Figure 10-40 Your formatting options are more limited with embedded objects.

- On the Picture tab, the Color drop-down list in the Image Control area includes the same options you can find using the Recolor button on the Format tab under Picture Tools, described in "Formatting Graphics" on page 368.

- Click the Reset button on the Picture tab to return all settings to their original values.

- Click the Compress button on the Picture tab to display the Compress Pictures dialog box, which includes the same options as in the Compression Settings dialog box, described in "Applying Compression to Pictures" on page 373.

- The settings on the Properties tab allow you to specify how Excel handles objects when editing the underlying cells on a worksheet. For details about the equivalent options in the Size And Properties dialog box, see "Positioning Objects" on the next page.

Working with Graphic Objects

After you create graphic objects on your worksheet, you'll need to move them and format them. You can also control their protection attributes and specify the way objects respond to changes in the position of underlying cells. The following sections discuss the many ways you can use Office Excel 2007 to help you accomplish these tasks.

Selecting and Grouping Objects

Sometimes you'll find it convenient to move, resize, or even reformat more than one object at a time. If you create a logo using multiple objects, for example, you will want to move all objects as a single unit, preserving their positions relative to one another. For these purposes, Excel includes the Group button in the Arrange group on the Page Layout tab, which is a menu containing the Group, Ungroup, and Regroup commands.

> **Note**
> You can select multiple objects by clicking individual objects while holding down Shift. You can select all the objects on the current worksheet by clicking one to select it and then pressing Ctrl+A (Select All). You can also select all objects by clicking Home, Find & Select, Go To Special and then selecting the Objects option.

After you select a group of objects, you can lock them together either by using the Group button on the Page Layout tab or by right-clicking any of the selected objects, clicking Group, and then clicking one of the Group commands, as shown in Figure 10-41.

When you group objects, the sets of handles around each selected object are then replaced by a single set of handles for the entire group, as shown in Figure 10-41. After you group the objects, you can manipulate the set of objects as a single object. You can resize, move, and apply formatting to them as a group. When you apply formatting, however, the separate objects might behave differently, especially if you have grouped different kinds of objects with different formats. It's best to apply formatting before you group objects, unless the objects are similar.

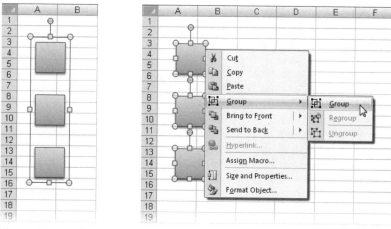

Figure 10-41 Select a group of objects, and then right-click any one of them to display a shortcut menu of applicable commands.

To ungroup a set of objects, select the group, right-click, and then click Group, Ungroup. You can use the Regroup command to reconstitute the group of objects you most recently ungrouped. For example, this is handy if you ungrouped a set of objects to make changes to one or more of them. Rather than selecting them again and clicking Group, just click Regroup.

> **Note**
>
> Unlike with other objects, when you click an object containing text and a dotted border appears around it, the text area—not the object—is selected. To select the object, click the border; when the border appears as a solid line, the object is selected. If you want to move an object containing text while its text area is active, you can drag it by its border.

Positioning Objects

Think of the objects on a worksheet as stacked on top of each other. Each new object you draw is placed on top of the stack. You can adjust the position of objects in the stack using the Bring To Front and Send To Back buttons in the Arrange group on the Page Layout tab. You can also right-click an object and then use the equivalent commands on the shortcut menu.

Figure 10-42 shows two identical sets of ungrouped objects. In the set on the right, we positioned the banner in front of the other objects in the stack using the Bring To Front button, and we positioned the star behind the other objects using the Send To Back button.

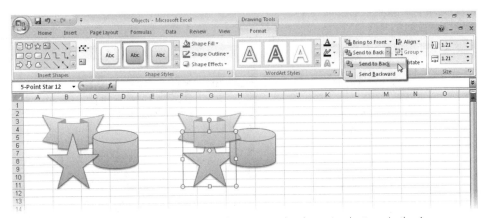

Figure 10-42 You can reposition objects in relation to each other using buttons in the Arrange group on the Page Layout tab.

As you can see in Figure 10-42, the Send To Back button is both a menu and a button—clicking the main part of the button issues the Send To Back command, while clicking its arrow displays a short menu. The same is true for the Bring To Front button. These mini-menus offer the additional Bring Forward and Send Backward commands, which move the object higher or lower in the stack, one layer at a time.

If you need to work with multiple objects on a worksheet, you can gain a little more control using the Selection Pane button. Click the Selection Pane button in the Arrange group on the Page Layout tab to display a task pane like the one shown in Figure 10-43.

You can use the buttons at the bottom of the Selection And Visibility task pane to show and hide all objects on the worksheet and to move selected objects up and down in the object stack. You can click the little eyeball icon to the right of an object name to hide that object; click again to unhide it. You can also edit the names of the objects by simply clicking the name once to select it and then clicking it again to edit its text.

> **Note**
>
> The Selection Pane button is also available on the Format tabs under both Drawing Tools and Picture Tools; these tabs appear when you select a picture, a shape, WordArt, a text box, or clip art.

You can change the relationship of objects to the underlying worksheet using the options on the Properties tab in the Size And Properties dialog box. Right-click an object, and click the Size And Properties command to display the dialog box shown in Figure 10-44. For SmartArt objects, you'll find the command when you right-click the graphic frame; the command is not available for embedded objects.

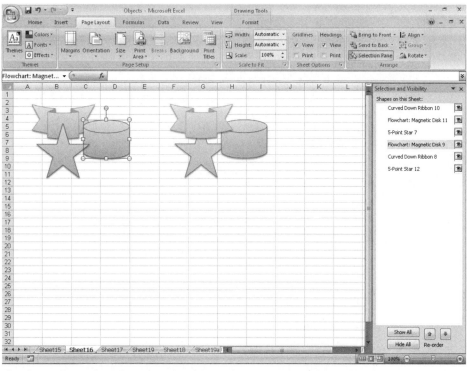

Figure 10-43 Use the Selection And Visibility task pane to control the display of multiple objects.

Figure 10-44 You can control how objects respond to changes on the worksheet.

> **Note**
>
> The Size And Properties dialog box is also available by clicking the Dialog Box Launcher in the Size group on the Format tabs under both Drawing Tools and Picture Tools; these tabs appear when you select a picture, a shape, WordArt, a text box, or clip art.

The default Object Positioning option is Move And Size With Cells, meaning that if you do anything to change the size or shape of the underlying cells, the object adjusts accordingly. An underlying cell is any cell whose right or bottom border is between the upper-left corner and the lower-right corner of the object. Here are some facts you need to know about the Object Positioning options:

- If you insert columns or rows to the left of an object formatted with the Move And Size With Cells option, the object moves accordingly.

- If you insert columns or rows between the first and last cells underlying an object formatted with the Move And Size With Cells option, the object stretches to accommodate the insertion.

- If you select the Move But Don't Size With Cells option and then insert or delete columns or rows, the object moves but retains its shape and proportion.

- If you select the Don't Move Or Size With Cells option, the object floats above the worksheet and isn't affected by any changes you make to the underlying cells.

- The Print Object check box is ordinarily selected. If you turn it off, the selected object isn't printed when you print the worksheet.

> **Note**
>
> In addition to moving and sizing objects with cells, Excel lets you control what happens when you cut, copy, or sort cells to which objects are attached. Click the Microsoft Office Button, click Excel Options, select the Advanced category, and in the Cut, Copy, And Paste group, select or clear the Cut, Copy, And Sort Inserted Objects With Their Parent Cells check box.

The Size tab in the Size And Properties dialog box offers precise control over the height, width, angle of rotation, scale, and cropping of the selected object. You can perform these tasks directly by dragging, but you might find it helpful to display the dialog box if you want to resize objects proportionally using the Lock Aspect Ratio option.

What Is Alt Text?

In Figure 10-44, notice that the dialog box contains an Alt Text tab. If you click it, you'll see that the only option is to add alternative text—known in Web parlance as *alt text*:

(Also notice in Figure 10-40 on page 385, the Format Object dialog box has a Web tab that does the same job for embedded objects.) When you save an Excel document as a Web page, graphics are converted to their Web-based equivalents. In HTML, the language of the Web, alternative text is added to images for four reasons. First, alt text appears in the browser while an image is loading, which is particularly helpful for large images over slow connections. Second, when you rest the pointer on an image containing alt text, the text appears in a pop-up window in your browser. Third, alt text is used by text-reading software commonly used by the blind, allowing them to hear a description of the image. And fourth, Web search engines index alt text along with the other "visible" text on your Web site, so descriptions added to images adds to the text indexed by Web search engines. If you're planning to save your workbook in HTML format, you should consider adding alternative text to all your graphics. For more information about Excel and the Web, see Chapter 25, "Collaborating Using the Internet."

Tools to Help You Position Objects on the Worksheet

Align

It's great to be able to create cool graphics with Excel, but the free-floating nature of graphic objects sometimes makes it hard to maintain a semblance of order on your worksheet. The Align button, in the Arrange group on the Page Layout tab, contains commands you can use to straighten up your worksheet, as shown in Figure 10-45.

Chapter 10

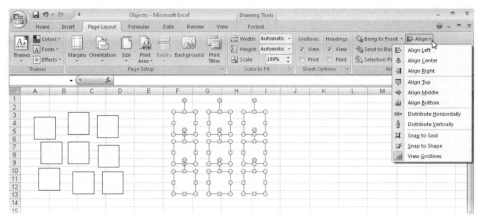

Figure 10-45 Use the Align commands to straighten up objects.

> **Note**
>
> You can also find the Align button on the Format tab under Drawing Tools; this tab appears when you select most types of objects (except embedded objects). The Align button also appears in its button-only form (without the word *Align* displayed) on the Format tab under Picture Tools, which appears when you select a bitmap image or clip art.

Suppose you have a number of objects that you want to be evenly spaced, like the ones shown in Figure 10-45. You can start by selecting the top row of objects, using the Align Top command to line them up, and then selecting Distribute Horizontally to space them evenly. Then you can use the other alignment and distribution commands to position the rest of the objects to your liking. Here are some key points to remember about using these object-positioning commands:

- **Snap To Grid**   Uses the columns and rows of the worksheet to align objects. Preexisting objects don't line up with the grid when you choose this command, but as soon as you create or drag an object, it snaps to the nearest column and row borders. The Snap To Grid command is a toggle—that is, you click once to turn it on and click again to turn it off.

- **Snap To Shape**   Turns on the Snap To Grid command when you choose it, activating its functionality. It adds to the spreadsheet grid virtual gridlines tangent to the edges of any existing objects, making it easy to align objects to one another. If you turn off the To Grid command, the To Shape command is turned off as well. The Snap To Shape command is also a toggle.

- **The Align and Distribute commands**   Arrange the selected objects relative to each other. These buttons are available only when you select two or more objects.

- **Align Left/Right/Top/Bottom** Lines up the edges of all selected objects with the corresponding edge of the leftmost, rightmost, top, or bottom object selected.

- **Align Center** Lines up the centers of objects along a vertical axis and finds the average common centerline of all selected objects.

- **Align Middle** Lines up the centers of objects along a horizontal axis and finds the average common centerline of all selected objects.

- **Distribute Horizontally/Vertically** Calculates the total amount of space between the selected objects and divides the space as equally as possible among them. The first and last objects (leftmost and rightmost or top and bottom) do not move—all the objects in between are adjusted as necessary.

> **Note**
> You can use the arrow keys on your keyboard to nudge selected objects 1 pixel at a time. If the Snap To Grid command is turned on, pressing an arrow key moves the selected object to the next gridline in that direction.

Protecting Objects

Objects are ordinarily prevented from being selected, moved, formatted, or sized. You can change this by right-clicking the object, clicking the Size And Properties command, and on the Properties tab, selecting or clearing the Locked check box. You can also select the Lock Text check box, which is available only when you select a text-capable object, to protect an object's text contents. Figure 10-46 shows the Properties tab. Newly drawn objects are assigned Locked status. However, to activate worksheet security and protection, you must also click Protect Sheet on the Review tab. For more information about protection, see "Protecting Worksheets" on page 156.

Chapter 10

> **Controlling the Display of Objects**
>
> You might want to suppress the display of objects in a workbook for security reasons or to simply speed up scrolling on an older computer. To do so, click the Microsoft Office Button, click Excel Options, and select the Advanced category. In the Display Options For This Workbook area, the For Objects, Show All option is ordinarily selected. Selecting the Nothing (Hide Objects) option prevents both their display and printing.
>
> Although you cannot directly modify objects when they are hidden, some actions still change them. If you select anything other than Don't Move Or Size With Cells on the Properties tab in the Size And Properties dialog box, hidden objects still respond to adjustments made to the column width or row height of underlying cells.

Figure 10-46 You can lock objects and the text they contain to prevent changes when the workbook is protected.

More Tricks with Graphic Objects

But wait, there's more! We'll now describe a few features that are hard to classify with the other graphics features. You can essentially turn any graphic object into a button by assigning a macro to it. In addition, you can take pictures of your worksheets and use those pictures in Excel workbooks (or even in other programs); they can appear as static bitmaps or dynamic windows to display what's happening in other areas of the workbook or in other workbooks.

Assigning Macros to Objects

You can attach a macro to any object, allowing you to activate the macro by simply clicking the object. To attach a macro to an object, do the following:

1. Right-click the object, and click the Assign Macro command.

2. When the Assign Macro dialog box appears (shown in Figure 10-47), assign a macro to the object by clicking New to create a new macro using the Visual Basic Editor, by clicking Record to create a new macro by example, or by selecting an existing macro from the list.

For more information about macros, see Chapter 26, "Recording Macros."

Figure 10-47 Assigning macros to objects turns them into buttons.

INSIDE OUT   Grouped Objects and Macros

Assigning macros to objects is a cool way to create some crazy-looking "buttons." You can also assign macros to grouped objects, or to individual objects that you subsequently group, but you can't do both. For example, say you assign macros to two objects and then group the objects. You can click each object to run each macro, just as if they were ungrouped. But if you assign another macro to the grouped object, the new macro overrides the existing macros.

Taking Pictures of Your Worksheets

Excel provides techniques for taking pictures of your worksheets: You can use the Copy As Picture, Paste As Picture, and Paste Picture Link commands on the Paste menu on the Home tab, and you can use the Camera button, which you can add to the Quick Access Toolbar.

Using the Camera Button

Camera

With the Camera button, you can copy an image of a range of cells and paste the image anywhere on the same worksheet, on another worksheet in the same workbook, or in another workbook. Copying an image isn't the same as copying the cells using the Copy button. When you use the Camera button, you copy a *linked image* of selected cells, not their contents. As a result, the image changes dynamically if the contents of the original cells change.

Chapter 10

> **Note**
> To add the Camera button to a toolbar, click the Microsoft Office Button, Excel Options, Customize. In the Choose Commands From drop-down list, select All Commands, select Camera in the list, and then click the Add button.

Figure 10-48 shows two worksheets side by side. If you select the range G3:G16 in the Pacific Sales Summary worksheet on the left and click the Camera button, the pointer changes from a plus sign to a crosshairs. Click anywhere in Book2 to select it, and then use the crosshairs pointer to click where you want the upper-left corner of the picture to appear. Excel embeds the picture as shown on the right in Figure 10-48.

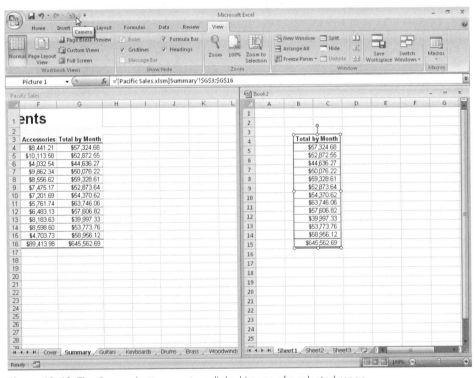

Figure 10-48 The Camera button creates a linked image of a selected range.

> **Note**
> Any graphic objects that happen to be within or overlapping the selected range also display in the linked picture.

After you paste the picture, you can change its size and proportions by dragging its selection handles and treating it just like any other graphic object. Changes in shape, size, and formatting do not affect the dynamic updating of the data displayed in the picture.

If you select the embedded picture, the formula bar displays a formula much like any other cell-linking formula, as shown in Figure 10-48. After you create the picture, you can edit the formula in the formula bar, and the picture changes accordingly. You can even change the reference formula to link a completely different worksheet or workbook. The link between the source and destination documents has another distinctive and useful characteristic. Suppose you close the Pacific Sales worksheet in Figure 10-48. If you then double-click the embedded image in Book2, Pacific Sales opens automatically, with the pictured range selected.

For more information about linking formulas, see "Formula Fundamentals" on page 427.

Using the Copy As Picture and Paste As Picture Commands

The Copy As Picture command rather unintuitively lives on the As Picture menu that you can find by clicking the Paste menu on the Home tab. It creates an image of a selected area of the worksheet just as the Camera button does, but with an important difference. The copied picture is static, with no links to any worksheet. Static pictures are useful when you don't need to update data or when the speed with which Excel recalculates the worksheet is more important. You can use the Copy As Picture command to add images of worksheets and charts to reports or other documents via the Clipboard. After you take the picture, you can paste it in another Excel document or in a document from any program that accepts Clipboard images.

Before clicking the Copy As Picture command, select the cells, object, or chart you want to copy. When you click the command, the dialog box in Figure 10-49 appears.

Figure 10-49 Use the Copy As Picture command to create "screen shots" of selected areas of your worksheets.

The options in the Copy Picture dialog box are as follows:

- **As Shown On Screen** Reproduces the selection at the moment you take the picture.

- **As Shown When Printed** Reproduces the selection according to the settings in the Page Setup dialog box that control the printing of gridlines and row and column headings.

- **Picture** Copies the picture in a format that can be displayed on monitors with different resolutions. This is useful if the picture will be viewed on different computers.

- **Bitmap** Copies the picture in a format that is correct only when the display resolution is the same as the screen from which it was copied.

After you copy an image to the Clipboard, you can paste the image anywhere you want—in another location on the worksheet, on another worksheet, or even in a document from another program. The Paste As Picture command is similar to Copy As Picture, except you don't see the Copy Picture dialog box. Instead, the image is pasted using the default As Shown When Printed option as the default format.

The Paste Picture Link command creates a linked image just like the Camera button does, except that the resulting image also uses the As Shown When Printed format instead of the As Shown On Screen option, as the Camera button does.

Gallery of Spiffy Examples

This section includes a few samples of what you can do in Office Excel 2007. With the exception of a couple of scanned personal photos, we created all the effects represented here with the tools and clip art that come with Excel.

Figure 10-50 shows a logo for a fictitious company called Fabrikam, Inc. We created the logo using the following tools:

- Insert tab, SmartArt, Stacked Venn diagram

- Insert tab, WordArt button

- Home tab, Font controls

You'll find the Graphics Gallery.xlsx file in the Sample Files section of the companion CD.

We created the Pacific Musical Instruments logo shown in Figure 10-51 on a page with a picture applied to the background by clicking the Background button on the Page Layout tab. We imported the speaker and musical note graphics from another program. Otherwise, we used the following tools to create the logo:

- Insert tab, Text Box button

- Format tab under Drawing Tools, Rotate, Flip Horizontal

- Home tab, Merge & Center button (the block of cells below the logo that is formatted with a gradient fill)

Figure 10-50 This logo shows a different use for a diagram.

Figure 10-51 You can do a lot with text boxes.

Figure 10-52 shows a picture applied to the background using the Background button on the Page Layout tab and the following tools:

- Insert tab, Shapes, Callouts, Rounded Rectangular Callout
- Format tab under Drawing Tools, Shape Styles, Subtle Effect, Accent 4

Chapter 10

Figure 10-52 This shows how you can use a background picture and some cartoon callouts.

The Adventure Works worksheet in Figure 10-53 has an interesting argyle background created by first selecting A1:E4 and then enlarging the cells by changing the row heights and column widths. With the cell range still selected, we then clicked the Dialog Box Launcher in the Font group on the Home tab and then, on the Border tab, clicked both diagonal border preset buttons. Then we clicked the Fill tab and selected a fill color. We did the rest of the work with the following tools:

- Insert tab, Clip Art button

- Insert tab, Shapes, Rectangle

- Insert tab, WordArt button

- Format tab under Drawing Tools, Text Effects button, Shadow, Outer Shadow

- Format tab under Drawing Tools, Shape Fill button, Gradient

Figure 10-54 shows a logo for a fictitious company called Lucerne Publishing that includes a personal photo inserted using the Picture button on the Insert tab. Otherwise, we created the logo using the following tools:

- Insert tab, Text Box button

- Insert tab, Shapes, Rectangle

- Format tab under Drawing Tools, Dialog Box Launcher in the Shape Styles group, Line Style tab

- Format tab under Drawing Tools, Text Effects button, Shadow

- Insert tab, WordArt

- Format tab under Drawing Tools, Text Fill button, Picture

- Home tab, Dialog Box Launcher in the Font group, Font tab, Equalize Character Height option

Figure 10-53 You can use cell borders to create patterned backgrounds.

Figure 10-54 You can apply a picture to WordArt as a fill color.

You can use any of the graphics shown in this section in workbooks, or you can use Copy As Picture to copy and paste them into other documents created in other programs. For more information about the Copy As Picture command, see "Using the Copy As Picture and Paste As Picture Commands" on page 397.

Printing and Presenting

M icrosoft Office Excel 2007 makes it easy for you to produce polished, professional-looking reports. In this chapter, we explain how to define the layout of your printed pages, control page breaks, and preview your pages for printing.

Controlling the Appearance of Your Pages

The most often used options affecting the appearance of your printed pages are available on the Page Layout tab on the Ribbon, shown in Figure 11-1. This is the central control panel for setting up paper sizes, margins, and page orientation, as well as for working with page breaks, print areas, and other printing options. For even more control over your printouts, click the Dialog Box Launcher in the Page Setup group on the Page Layout tab to display the Page Setup dialog box, also shown in Figure 11-1.

Setting Page Options

The Page tab in the Page Setup dialog box, shown in Figure 11-1, is the tab you'll use most often; it contains settings that control page orientation, scaling, paper size, print quality, and page numbering.

Printing Wide or Tall

Orientation

The Orientation button on the Page Layout tab offers two options: Portrait and Landscape. These options determine whether Office Excel 2007 prints your worksheet vertically (Portrait) or horizontally (Landscape). Portrait, the default setting, offers more room for rows but less room for columns. Select Landscape if you have more columns but fewer rows on each page. You can also find these options on the Page tab in the Page Setup dialog box.

Specifying Paper Size

The Size button on the Page Layout tab includes options for nearly every size of paper available (not just the sizes supported by your printer). You can additionally control the quality of your printout by clicking the Size button and then clicking More Paper Sizes (or clicking the Dialog Box Launcher in the Page Setup group) to display the Page tab in the Page Setup dialog box. The Print Quality drop-down list shows the print quality settings available for your printer. A laser printer, for example, might offer print-quality settings of 600 dots per inch (dpi), 300 dpi, and 150 dpi. Higher dpi settings look better but take longer to print. If the Print Quality drop-down list is not available, you might also be able to adjust these settings, and more, using your printer driver's dialog box, which you can access by clicking the Options button on the Page tab in the Page Setup dialog box.

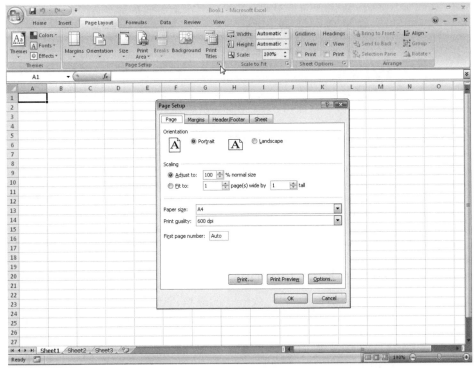

Figure 11-1 The Page Layout tab on the Ribbon and the Page Setup dialog box control most printing options.

For more information about printer drivers, see "Setting Printer Driver Options" on page 422.

> ### AutoLetter/A4 Paper Resizing
>
> Excel includes help for folks who routinely share work across international borders. In much of the world, the standard paper size is Letter (8.5 by 11 inches), but A4 paper (210 by 297 millimeters) is also widely used. Now you can print worksheets set for A4 paper on printers loaded with standard Letter paper (and vice versa), and Excel adjusts the page setup accordingly. Excel does this on the fly, without changing the page size setting in the Page Setup dialog box. If you want to turn this feature off, click the Microsoft Office Button, click Excel Options, select the Advanced category, and in the General group clear the Scale Content For A4 Or 8.5 × 11" Paper Sizes check box.

Setting a Reduction Ratio

Using the Scaling settings on the Page tab in the Page Setup dialog box, you can override the default size of your printouts in one of two ways: by specifying a scaling factor (from 10 percent through 400 percent) or by fitting the report to a specified number of pages. Excel always scales in both the horizontal and vertical dimensions. For example, if the full size of your print area is two pages deep but only one page wide and you tell Excel to scale it to a single page, the resulting printout will be both narrower and shallower. The Fit To options are a great way to print a worksheet that is ordinarily just a bit too large to fit on a single printed page. If you want to return to a full-size printout after selecting a scaling option, you can select the Adjust To option and type **100** in the % Normal Size box.

Setting the First Page Number

If you want to control the numbering of pages in your printout's header or footer—an essential tool when printing multipage worksheets—use the First Page Number box on the Page tab in the Page Setup dialog box. You can type any starting number, including 0 or negative numbers. By default, this option is set to Auto, but you can change it to any number you want.

Working in Page Layout View

The new Page Layout view in Excel 2007 represents a major upgrade to the worksheet-printing workflow, in comparison with the "old" ways of doing things. In previous versions of Excel, the last task you performed, after creating and formatting a worksheet, was to view the worksheet in Print Preview to see how it was going to fit on a page. This is partly because Print Preview is minimally interactive—you can drag to change margins and column widths, but that's all. In Page Layout view, however, Excel is fully functional. To see for yourself, click the Page Layout View button on the View tab. Page Layout view, shown on the next page, could become your preferred working environment, if you don't mind the considerable slowdown in performance that comes with a more graphically intensive interface.

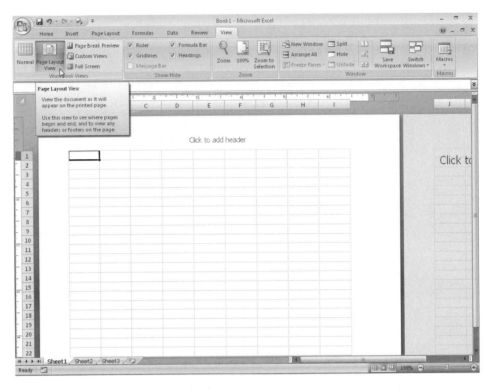

In Page Layout view, you can do the following:

- Drag lines between row and column headers to adjust row height and column width.

- Refer to the rulers to see the actual dimensions of your data relative to the printed page.

- Drag the edge between the shaded and white areas on the rulers to adjust margins.

- Click the Page Layout tab and change settings in the Page Setup group to see the changes immediately reflected in graphical pages that appear as separate sheets of paper on your screen.

- Click and type directly in headers and footers.

- Click other tabs on the Ribbon to zoom, apply formatting, and add formulas, graphics, charts, and so on.

In fact, we couldn't find anything you couldn't do in Page Layout view. Page Layout view is applied per worksheet; you can specify a different view for each open worksheet, and the settings are saved with the workbook.

Setting Margins

You can adjust the margins of your printouts to allow the maximum amount of data to fit on a page, to customize the amount of space available for headers and footers, or to accommodate special requirements such as three-hole-punched paper. The Margins button on the Page Layout tab, shown in Figure 11-2, provides three settings that may meet most of your needs: Normal, Wide, and Narrow. These settings refer to the size of the margins, not the size of the printed area. For example, to fit more data on a page, use the Narrow setting. Note that when you apply your own margin settings, the Last Custom Setting command appears as the first item in the Margins menu, as Figure 11-2 shows. This command does not appear unless you have specified your own margin settings.

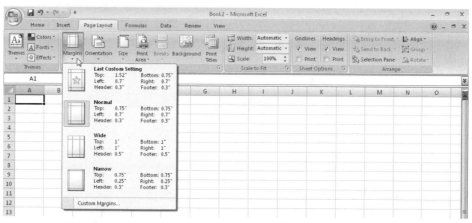

Figure 11-2 Click the Margins button on the Page Layout tab to choose a basic margin setting.

The Margins tab in the Page Setup dialog box offers precise control over the top, bottom, left, and right margins of your printed worksheets. You can display the Margins tab by clicking the Margins button and then clicking Custom Margins. As shown in Figure 11-3, the default settings are .75 inch for the top and bottom margins and 0.7 inch for the left and right margins.

When you click in any of the text boxes on the Margins tab, a line appears in the sample page in the middle of the dialog box, showing you where the selected margin will appear.

If you want a header or footer to appear on each page, the top and bottom margins need to be large enough to accommodate them. For more information about setting up a header and footer, see "Creating a Header and Footer" on the next page.

Chapter 11

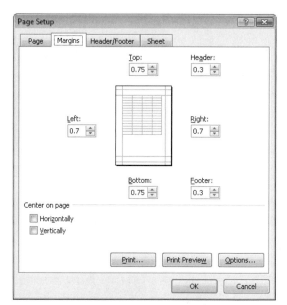

Figure 11-3 You can specify precise margin settings on the Margins tab in the Page Setup dialog box.

> **Centering Your Work on the Page**
>
> Excel aligns worksheets to the upper-left corner of the printed page by default. If you want Excel to center your printout on the page vertically, horizontally, or both, select the Center On Page check boxes at the bottom of the Margins tab in the Page Setup dialog box (refer to Figure 11-3).

Creating a Header and Footer

On the Header/Footer tab in the Page Setup dialog box, you can provide essential information about your printout—such as file name, creation date, page number, and author's name—by including a header (printed at the top of each page) or footer (printed at the bottom of each page). By default, Excel prints footers .3 inch from the bottom edge and headers .3 inch from the top edge, but you can change this on the Margins tab in the Page Setup dialog box.

The drop-down lists that appear immediately under the words *Header* and *Footer* in the dialog box shown in Figure 11-4 offer predefined options you can use to customize your headers and footers. When you select an option in the drop-down list, the preview area adjacent to the list displays a sample of the selected option. In Figure 11-4, we selected predefined options for both Header and Footer, which are reflected in the previews.

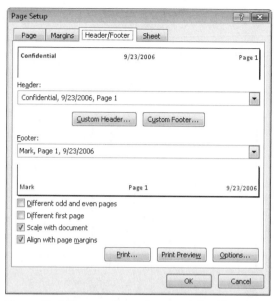

Figure 11-4 You can choose from predefined headers and footers or create your own using the Header/Footer tab in the Page Setup dialog box.

Creating Custom Headers and Footers

If you don't find what you need in the list of predefined headers and footers, you can create your own or modify one that Excel offers. If you create custom headers or footers for the current workbook, Excel adds them to these drop-down lists. Click the Custom Header button to open the Header dialog box shown in Figure 11-5, or click the Custom Footer button to open a similar dialog box.

Create a Default Header and Footer

If you want your header and footer to be the same in every workbook you create, you can create a default header and footer. Open a new, blank workbook, and set the header and footer the way you want them to be every time. Next, save the workbook using the name Book.xls. Store this file in the XLStart folder:

- **Windows Vista** C:\Users\<your name>\AppData\Roaming\Microsoft\Excel\ XLStart

- **Windows XP** C:\Documents and Settings\<your name>\Application Data\ Microsoft\Excel\XLStart

Whenever you open a new workbook, it will have your header and footer already in place.

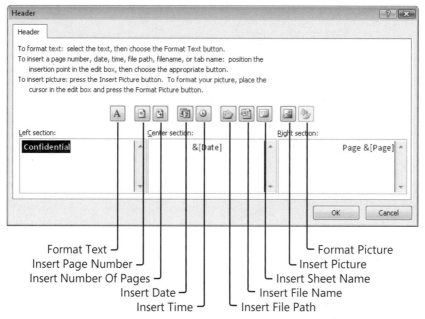

Figure 11-5 The Header dialog box contains tools to make creating a header a snap.

Excel uses various codes to represent information you might want to put in your headers and footers—such as the current time, current date, and current page number. Fortunately, you don't have to learn these codes to create headers and footers. Click the appropriate box (Left Section, Center Section, or Right Section) to indicate where you want the information to appear, and then click the appropriate buttons to add the information to your header or footer. Here's what each button does:

- **Format Text** Displays the Font dialog box, letting you specify the font and font style for the selected text

- **Insert Page Number** Inserts the page number in the selected section

- **Insert Number Of Pages** Inserts the total number of pages in the selected section; typically used in conjunction with the page number in a "Page x of y" construction

- **Insert Date** Inserts the date of printing in the selected section

- **Insert Time** Inserts the time of printing in the selected section

- **Insert File Path** Inserts the folder path and file name of the workbook in the selected section

- **Insert File Name** Inserts only the file name of the current workbook in the selected section

- **Insert Sheet Name** Inserts the name of the current worksheet in the selected section

- **Insert Picture** Displays the Insert Picture dialog box, letting you add a picture to the selected section

- **Format Picture** Displays the Format Picture dialog box, letting you adjust the settings of an inserted picture

To specify text in your header or footer, click the appropriate text box, and type your text. To divide the text between two or more lines, press Enter at the end of each line. To include an ampersand in your text, type two ampersands.

Adding Pictures to Headers and Footers

You can add pictures to custom headers and footers using the Insert Picture and Format Picture buttons (refer to Figure 11-5). For example, you can insert pictures to add company logos or banners to your documents. Click the Insert Picture button to access the Insert Picture dialog box, which you use to locate the picture you want to use. When you insert the picture, Excel displays *&[Picture]* in the section box of the Header (or Footer) dialog box. (Unlike other header and footer codes, you can't just type this code—you have to use the Insert Picture button.)

After you insert the picture, click the Format Picture button to specify the size, brightness, and contrast of the picture and to rotate, scale, or crop the picture. (You can't directly manipulate Header or Footer pictures—you must use the Format Picture button.) It might take some trial and error to obtain the result you want, adjusting the size of the picture as well as the top or bottom margins to accommodate it. Figure 11-6 shows a sample of a picture used in a header, displayed in Page Layout view.

 You'll find the Fabrikam.xlsx file in the Sample Files section of the companion CD.

To arrive at the example shown in Figure 11-6, we did the following:

- In the left section, we added the date and changed the font to 10-point, italic Arial Black.

- In the center section, we inserted a picture; then we clicked Format Picture and reduced its size.

- In the right section, we added the time and changed the font to 10-point, italic Arial Black.

- We dismissed the Header dialog box and selected both the Vertically and Horizontally check boxes below Center On Page on the Margins tab in the Page Setup dialog box.

- We dismissed the Page Setup dialog box and dragged the top margin to accommodate the graphic in Page Layout view.

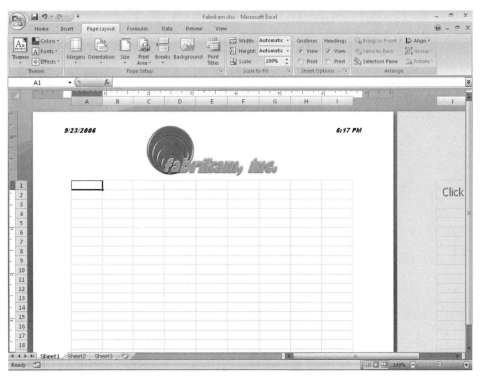

Figure 11-6 You can manipulate the fonts and even add pictures to headers and footers.

Changing Fonts in Headers and Footers

The Excel default font for headers and footers is 10-point Arial. To select a different font, point size, or font style, select the code or text in the section you want to change, and click the Format Text button to access the Font dialog box. Note that the font options you select apply only to the highlighted text or code in the section box. You can assign different font options to each section, even to individual elements within each section.

Setting Worksheet Options

Clicking the Dialog Box Launcher in the Page Setup group on the Page Layout tab displays the Page Setup dialog box. Click the Sheet tab, shown in Figure 11-7, to access settings specific to the active worksheet. You can specify different worksheet options for each worksheet in a workbook. (You can also display the Sheet tab by clicking the Print Titles button.)

  You'll find the 2008 Projections.xlsx file in the Sample Files section of the companion CD.

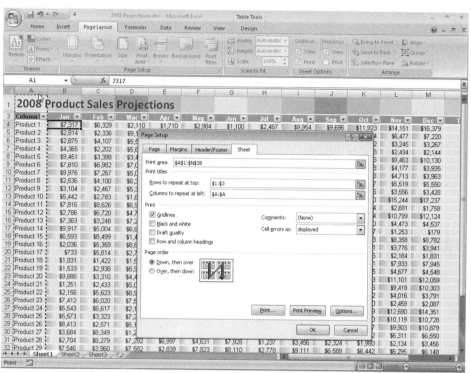

Figure 11-7 Use the Sheet tab in the Page Setup dialog box to set the area to print and the row and column titles to print on each page of your worksheet.

Specifying the Area to Be Printed

The first item on the Sheet tab in the Page Setup dialog box is the Print Area text box, which you use to specify the exact cell range (or ranges) you want to print. If you do not specify an area to print, Excel prints the entire active area of the selected worksheet(s). If you expect to print the same area of a given worksheet repeatedly, you can save yourself some steps by defining the print area. To do so, click in the Print Area text box, and then drag to select the cells on the worksheet you want to include. When you do this, the dialog box collapses so you can see more of the worksheet, and Excel inserts the cell range reference of the area you selected in the Print Area text box, as shown in Figure 11-7. You can select multiple nonadjacent cell ranges by selecting a range, typing a comma, and then selecting the next range. Each range you select prints on a separate page.

You can also use the Print Area button on the Page Layout tab to specify the area or areas you want to print. To use this method, first select the range or ranges you want to print, click Print Area, and then click Set Print Area, which adds the range references to the Page Setup dialog box. The other option on the Print Area menu is Clear Print Area, which removes all the range references from the Print Area text box in the Page Setup dialog box.

> **Note**
>
> To remove your print area definition, you can return to the Page Setup dialog box and delete the cell references. You can also use the Define Name dialog box by pressing Ctrl+F3 and deleting the name *Print_Area*. For more information, see "Naming Cells and Cell Ranges" on page 441.

Specifying Rows and Columns to Print on Every Page

On most worksheets, the column and row labels that identify information categories appear in only the first couple of columns and top few rows. When Excel breaks up a large report into pages, those important column and row labels might appear only on the first page of the printout. You can use the Sheet tab in the Page Setup dialog box to force Excel to print the contents of one or more columns, one or more rows, or a combination of columns and rows on every page of a report. You can display the Sheet tab by clicking the Print Titles button on the Page Layout tab on the Ribbon.

Suppose you want to print the contents of column A and rows 1, 2, and 3 on all the pages of a lengthy report. First, click in the Rows To Repeat At Top text box, and then select the headings for rows 1 through 3. (To select multiple contiguous row headings, drag through them.) Click in the Columns To Repeat At Left text box, and then select the column A heading (or any cell in column A). Figure 11-8 shows the result in Page Layout view. (Note that to apply print titles, you need to click OK in the Page Setup dialog box. In Figure 11-8, we did this, and then we redisplayed the dialog box and dragged it out of the way for illustration purposes.)

Notice in Figure 11-8 that the column containing the product numbers appears on both pages displayed in Page Layout view. Without using print titles, the first column on the second page of the printout would have displayed the August totals instead of the product numbers. You can specify separate print titles for each worksheet in your workbook. Excel remembers the titles for each worksheet.

> **Note**
>
> To remove your print title definitions, you can return to the Page Setup dialog box and delete the cell references. You can also use the Define Name dialog box by pressing Ctrl+F3 and deleting the name *Print_Titles*. For more information, see "Naming Cells and Cell Ranges" on page 441.

Printing Gridlines and Headings

By default, Excel does not print gridlines or row and column headings, regardless of whether you have them displayed on your worksheet. If you want to print gridlines or headings, select the corresponding Print check box in the Sheet Options group on the

Page Layout tab. You can also select the Gridlines or Row And Column Headings check box on the Sheet tab in the Page Setup dialog box.

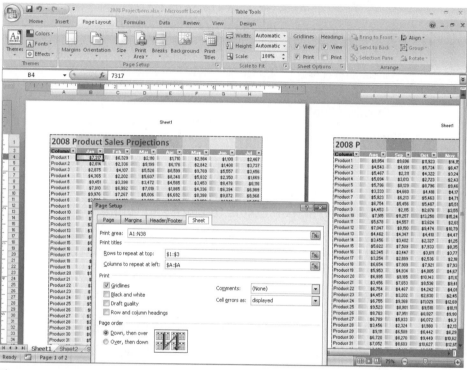

Figure 11-8 We defined the print titles and used Page Layout view to see the results.

Printing Comments and Errors

Comments are annotations you create by clicking New Comment on the Review tab on the Ribbon. To make sure the comments in your worksheet are included with your printout, select one of the Comments options on the Sheet tab in the Page Setup dialog box. If you select At End Of Sheet from the drop-down list, Excel adds a page to the end of the printout and prints all your notes together, starting on that new page. If you select As Displayed On Sheet, Excel prints the comments as pop-up windows wherever they are located on a worksheet. Note that the latter option may cause the comments to obscure worksheet data.

> **Note**
>
> You can display all comments on the worksheet by clicking the Show All Comments button on the Page Layout tab. This gives you an idea of how the worksheet will look when printed if you select the As Displayed On Sheet option in the Page Setup dialog box.

Chapter 11

The Cell Errors As drop-down list on the Sheet tab in the Page Setup dialog box gives you options for how error codes that are displayed on the worksheet should be printed. Ordinarily, error codes such as #NAME? are printed just as they appear on your screen, but you can change this so cells containing error codes print as blank cells or with a double hyphen (--) or #NA displayed instead of the error code.

For more about creating comments, see "Adding Comments to Cells" on page 251. For more about error codes, see "Understanding Error Values" on page 437.

Printing Drafts

If your printer offers a draft-quality mode, you can obtain a quicker, though less attractive, printout by selecting the Draft Quality check box on the Sheet tab in the Page Setup dialog box. This option has no effect if your printer has no draft-quality mode and is most useful for dot matrix or other slow printers.

Translating Screen Colors to Black and White

If you've assigned colors and patterns to your worksheet but you want to see what it will look like when printed on a black-and-white printer, select the Black And White check box on the Sheet tab in the Page Setup dialog box, which tells Excel to use only black and white when printing. If you are using a black-and-white printer, you probably won't need to worry about this option, but if you seem to be having trouble, try selecting it.

Setting the Printing Order of Large Print Ranges

When you print a large report, Excel breaks the report into page-sized sections based on the current margin and page-size settings. If the print range is both too wide and too deep to fit on a single page, Excel ordinarily works in "down and then over" order. For example, suppose your print range measures 120 rows by 20 columns and Excel can fit 40 rows and 10 columns on a page. Excel prints the first 40 rows and first 10 columns on page 1, the second 40 rows and first 10 columns on page 2, and the third 40 rows and first 10 columns on page 3. On page 4, Excel prints the first 40 rows and second 10 columns, and so on. If you prefer to have Excel print each horizontal chunk before moving to the next vertical chunk, select the Over, Then Down option on the Sheet tab in the Page Setup dialog box.

Specifying What and Where to Print

Click the Microsoft Office Button, click Print, and then click OK to send the entire active area of the current worksheet immediately to the printer. For all but the most basic of worksheets, you'll probably need to provide a bit more information, beginning with specifying exactly what you want to print. To do so, click the Print button on the Sheet tab in the Page Setup dialog box to display the Print dialog box. (Or you can click the Microsoft Office Button, Print.)

You can print only a particular range of pages by typing the starting and ending page numbers in the From and To text boxes in the Print Range area in the Print dialog box, shown in Figure 11-9.

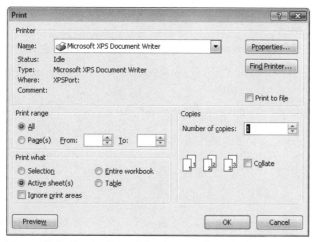

Figure 11-9 Use the Print dialog box to tell Excel what you want to print and how many copies you want.

The Print dialog box contains these options for specifying what, where, and how you want Office Excel 2007 to print:

- **Name** Displays the name of your default printer. To use a different printer, click the small arrow to display a list of available printers, and then select the printer you want to use.

> **Note**
>
> The Find Printer button shown in Figure 11-9 is useful when you are connected to a network. Click this button to search for all the printers that are available anywhere on your network.

- **Selection** Prints only the currently selected area of a worksheet.

- **Active Sheet(s)** Prints a worksheet or a group of worksheets but not the entire workbook. Select the worksheets you want to print as a group before clicking File, Print. If you have defined a print area on any or all of the specified worksheets, Excel prints only those ranges. For more information about selecting a group of worksheets, see "Editing Multiple Worksheets" on page 236.

- **Entire Workbook** Prints the entire workbook, not just the current worksheet. If you have defined a print area on any or all of the specified worksheets, Excel prints only those ranges.

- **Table** Prints only the currently selected table.

- **Ignore Print Areas** If you have defined print areas on the worksheet or worksheets specified for printing, select this check box to disregard them.

- **Copies** Specifies the number of copies you want. You can instruct Excel to print up to 32,767 copies at a time.

- **Collate** If your worksheet is more than one page long and you plan to print multiple copies, have Excel collate the copies for you. For example, instead of printing five copies of page 1 followed by five copies of page 2, Excel prints page 1 and page 2 together, prints the next set, and so on. Collated copies are more convenient but might take longer to print.

- **Print To File** Sends the selected data to a file on disk, instead of to the printer.

For more information about defining range names, see "Naming Cells and Cell Ranges" on page 441.

Printing Immediately

Quick Print

To bypass the Print dialog box, you can click the Quick Print button on the Quick Access Toolbar to start printing immediately using the default Active Sheet(s) option in the Page Setup dialog box. If the Quick Print button is not visible, click the arrow to the right of the Quick Access Toolbar to display the Customize Quick Access Toolbar menu, and click Quick Print to add the button to the toolbar.

For more information, see "Using the Quick Access Toolbar" on page 38.

Printing to a File

The Print To File check box is in many ways an anachronism—a remnant of computing days of yore. It was often used to facilitate *batch printing*—that is, unattended printing of multiple files—back before print spooling was the norm. You can still use Print To File if you want to print a document from a different computer on which Excel isn't installed.

When you print to a file, Excel sends the same stream of data that would ordinarily go straight to your printer to a file on your hard disk. This isn't an Excel document file but a printer document file. Excel saves all the necessary information from your document so that line and page breaks, spacing, and fonts (if you're lucky) remain the same. Unfortunately, your results can vary depending on the type of printer, the fonts you use, and the complexity of your document. For this reason, it's advisable to test printer files before relying on them for critical work.

Here's the key to making this process work: You have to use MS-DOS to send the file to your printer. In Windows (either Vista or XP), click Start, All Programs, Accessories, Command Prompt. At the command prompt, type the following:

copy <file name> lpt1: /b

This assumes the printer file is located in the same folder where you are issuing the command and that the printer is directly attached to the computer. You can, of course, get around this assumption by specifying a full path name instead of just a file name.

Adjusting Page Breaks

Breaking pages across printed sheets of paper is often challenging using word-processing programs, but it can be even more challenging when planning the printing strategy for large spreadsheet models. Office Excel 2007 makes it easy to adjust the positions of page breaks by offering a couple of approaches: the Breaks button on the Page Layout tab on the Ribbon and the Page Break Preview button on the View tab.

Using Page Break Preview

`Page Break Preview`   Clicking the Page Break Preview button results in a view of your worksheet like the one shown in Figure 11-10. You can move page breaks by dragging them. You can even edit your worksheet while in Page Break Preview mode. Page Break Preview mode zooms out to give you a bird's-eye view of the entire worksheet, but you can use the Zoom controls in the lower-right corner of the screen to adjust the zoom percentage.

Using Page Break Preview lets you see both the positions of your page breaks and the page numbers Excel will use when you print. Default page breaks—the ones Excel proposes to use if you don't intervene—appear as heavy dashed lines. If you're not happy with the position of a default break, drag the line where you want it. Your page break then becomes a manual page break and appears as a solid line. To exit Page Break Preview, click either the Normal button or the Page Layout View button on the View tab.

> **Note**
>
> After you apply any Page Setup options, Excel displays dashed lines in Normal view wherever a page break will occur. If you'd rather not see these lines, click the Microsoft Office Button, click Excel Options, select the Advanced category, and in the Display Options For This Worksheet section, clear the Show Page Breaks check box.

If you attempt to extend the dimensions of a page beyond the maximum width or depth according to the current page setup, Excel scales the worksheet to make it fit and displays an adjusted percentage value in the Scaling options shown on the Page tab in the Page Setup dialog box.

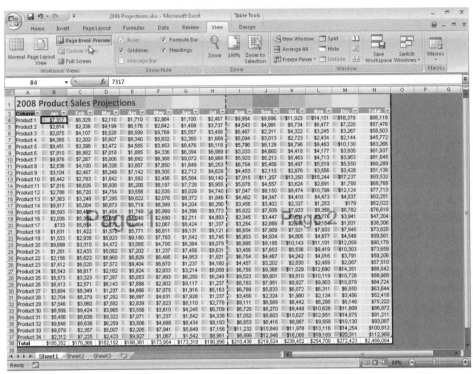

Figure 11-10 Page Break Preview shows default page breaks with heavy dashed lines, which you can reposition by dragging.

If, after trying different page breaks, you want to revert to the automatic page breaks (heavy dashed lines), drag the manual page breaks (solid lines) to the left past the row headers or up past the column headers. After you have removed all manual page breaks, the automatic breaks reappear in their default locations.

Inserting and Removing Manual Page Breaks

Spreadsheet pagination can be problematic, given that rows and columns of numbers often don't fit into the 8.5-by-11-inch world of printing. This is why Excel provides yet another method you can use to manually adjust page breaks. To add a page break in Normal view, select any cell of the row directly beneath or in the column directly to the right of where you want the break to occur, click the Breaks button on the Page Layout tab, and then click Insert Page Break. If you select a cell where data appears both below and to the right, Excel applies page breaks both horizontally and vertically. To remove a break, select a cell in the row below a horizontal break, or in the column to the right of a vertical break, click the Breaks button, and then click either Remove Page Break or Reset All Page Breaks.

TROUBLESHOOTING

My manual page breaks don't work.

In the Page Setup dialog box, selecting the Fit To option on the Page tab can cause Excel to override manual page breaks. Fit To applies reduction sufficient to fit the entire print area into a specific number of pages. To derail this override, switch to the Adjust To option. This sets the worksheet to print according to your manual page breaks.

If you prefer the compressed Fit To "look" but still want to control page breaks, you can define the print area using multiple nonadjacent ranges—one range per page. Excel automatically prints each nonadjacent range as a separate page. Select the first range you want to print, hold down Ctrl, and select the next range. Select as many ranges (pages) as you want. Then click the Print Area button on the Page Layout tab, and click Set Print Area.

Using Print Preview

The Print Preview feature gives you a glimpse of your worksheets the way they will look on paper. Although Page Layout view is generally better at helping you visualize your printed pages, it still displays your entire worksheet. Even if you specify smaller areas to print using the Print Area button or the equivalent settings in the Page Setup dialog box, Page Layout view displays everything and indicates your defined print areas using dotted lines. Using Print Preview displays only what will be printed and nothing more, including the effects of page breaks, margins, and formatting, before you needlessly waste paper with multiple test printouts. To access Print Preview, use one of the following methods:

- Click the Microsoft Office Button, Print, Print Preview.

- Click the Preview button in the Print dialog box.

- Click the Print Preview button in the Page Setup dialog box.

If you're not satisfied with the appearance of your worksheet, you can access most page layout settings from within Print Preview. Click the Page Setup button to display the Page Setup dialog box, and change any page setting. You can also change the margins and column widths without leaving Print Preview by clicking the Show Margins check box, as shown in Figure 11-11. To adjust a margin, drag a dotted line; to adjust a column's width, drag the column handle. As you drag, the page-number indicator in the lower-left corner of the screen changes to display the name and setting for the margin or the width of the selected column. To turn off the display of margin lines and column handles, clear the Show Margins check box.

The following buttons help you move around within Print Preview mode:

- You can move forward or backward a page at a time by clicking the Next Page and Previous Page buttons.

Chapter 11

- Click the Zoom button to display the page at the same size you see in Normal view. Click Zoom again to return to the normal Print Preview whole-page view. Alternatively, you don't need to use Zoom at all. Click anywhere (except on a displayed margin line), and the preview zooms in; click anywhere in zoomed mode, and the preview returns to whole-page view.

After you're satisfied with the appearance of your document, you can click the Print button to print the document or click the Close Print Preview button to return to the previous view.

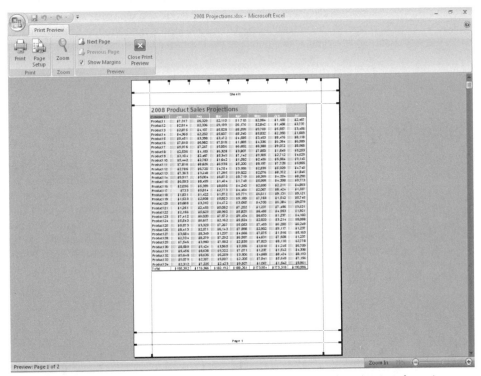

Figure 11-11 You can display lines and handles that you can use to adjust the size of margins, headers, footers, and columns in Print Preview by clicking the Show Margins check box.

Setting Printer Driver Options

Occasionally while working in Office Excel 2007, you might need to set options that only your printer driver provides. For example, you might need to switch from automatic to manual paper feed or from one paper tray to another. You can do this by clicking either the Properties button in the Print dialog box (refer to Figure 11-9) or the Options button in the Page Setup dialog box (refer to Figure 11-7) to open the Properties dialog box for the selected printer.

Creating Portable Documents

The new Microsoft XML Paper Specification (XPS) document format lets you create a representation of "electronic paper" that displays your data on the screen as it would look when printed, similar to the ubiquitous Portable Document Format (PDF). One of the benefits of portable document formats is the ability to share documents you do not want others to modify. Both formats require freely downloadable software for viewing and promise cross-platform consistency and format compatibility, regardless of the software and fonts available on your computer.

You can search the contents of XPS documents, and you can preview them in applications that support them such as Microsoft Office Outlook 2007. Worksheets you save in XPS format are also viewable using an XPS-enabled Web browser or a stand-alone XPS viewer.

> **Note**
>
> If you are just one XPS viewer short of being able to see your XPS documents, click the Microsoft Office Button, Excel Options, Resources, and then click the Go Online button to launch your Web browser and connect to Microsoft Office Online. Click Downloads, and type **XPS** in the Search box to find and download the available XPS add-ins.

Microsoft XPS Document Writer is listed as one of the "printers" available in the Name drop-down list in the Print dialog box. If you select this option and click OK to start printing, Excel displays a version of the Save As dialog box where you specify a file name, reminiscent of the Print To File option (discussed in "Printing to a File" on page 418). "Printing" an XPS document is like using your hard disk as the paper tray, generating pages of electronic output instead of wood pulp–based output. When you select Microsoft XPS Document Writer in the Print dialog box and then click Properties, the Microsoft XPS Document Writer Properties dialog box appears. Click the XPS Documents tab to display the dialog box, as shown in Figure 11-12.

The Layout tab in the Microsoft XPS Document Writer Properties dialog box offers a choice between portrait and landscape modes, but the Page Setup dialog box (or Ribbon group) sets the orientation, so you don't need to worry about this setting. The XPS Documents tab offers an Automatically Open XPS Documents Using The XPS Viewer check box. When you select this check box, the XPS file opens in your Web browser as soon as Excel is finished saving it, as shown in Figure 11-13.

If you want to be able to save your workbooks in PDF, you can install an add-in that makes this possible. To install it, click the Microsoft Office Button, Excel Options, Resources, and then click the Go Online button to launch your Web browser and connect to Microsoft Office Online. Click Downloads, and type **PDF** in the Search box to find and download the Microsoft Save As PDF add-in.

Chapter 11

Figure 11-12 Learn more about XPS documents by clicking the link at the bottom of the Microsoft XPS Document Writer Properties dialog box.

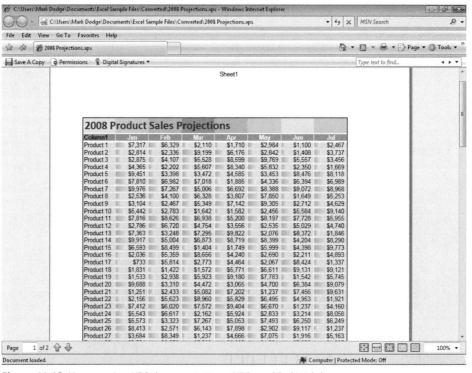

Figure 11-13 You can view XPS documents in an XPS-enabled Web browser.

PART 5

Creating Formulas and Performing Data Analysis

Building Formulas

Formulas are the heart and soul of a spreadsheet, and Microsoft Office Excel 2007 offers a rich environment in which to build complex formulas. Armed with a few mathematical operators and rules for cell entry, you can turn a worksheet into a powerful calculator. In this chapter, we'll cover the basics, and then we'll look closer at using functions, defining names, building structured references, working with arrays, creating linking formulas, and constructing conditional tests.

Formula Fundamentals

All formulas in Excel begin with an equal sign. The equal sign tells Excel that the succeeding characters constitute a formula. If you omit the equal sign, Excel might interpret the entry as text.

To show how formulas work, we'll walk you through some rudimentary ones. Begin by selecting blank cell A10. Then type **=10+5**, and press Enter. The value 15 appears in cell A10. Now select cell A10, and the formula bar displays the formula you just typed. What appears in the cell is the displayed value; what appears in the formula bar is the underlying value, which in this case is a formula.

Understanding the Precedence of Operators

Operators are symbols that represent specific mathematical operations, including the plus sign (+), minus sign (–), division sign (/), and multiplication sign (*). When performing these operations in a formula, Excel follows certain rules of precedence:

- Excel processes expressions within parentheses first.

- Excel performs multiplication and division before addition and subtraction.

- Excel calculates consecutive operators with the same level of precedence from left to right.

Type some formulas to see how these rules apply. Select an empty cell, and type **=4+12/6**. Press Enter, and you see the value 6. Excel first divides 12 by 6 and then adds the result (2) to 4. If Excel used different precedence rules, the result would be different. For example, select another empty cell, and type **=(4+12)/6**. Press Enter, and you see the value 2.666667. This demonstrates how you can change the order of precedence using parentheses. The formulas in Table 12-1 contain the same values and operators, but note the different results because of the placement of parentheses.

Table 12-1 Placement of Parentheses

Formula	Result
=3*6+12/4–2	19
=(3*6)+12/(4–2)	24
=3*(6+12)/4–2	11.5
=(3*6+12)/4–2	5.5
=3*(6+12/(4–2))	36

If you do not include a closing parenthesis for each opening parenthesis in a formula, Excel displays the message "Microsoft Excel found an error in this formula" and provides a suggested solution. If the suggestion matches what you had in mind, simply press Enter, and Excel completes the formula for you.

When you type a closing parenthesis, Excel briefly displays the pair of parentheses in bold. This feature is handy when you are typing a long formula and are not sure which pairs of parentheses go together.

> **Note**
>
> If you are unsure of the order in which Excel will process a sequence of operators, use parentheses—even if the parentheses aren't necessary. Parentheses also make your formulas easier to read and interpret, which is helpful if you or someone else needs to change them later.

Using Cell References in Formulas

A cell reference identifies a cell or group of cells in a workbook. When you include cell references in a formula, the formula is said to be *linked* to the referenced cells. The resulting value of the formula depends on the values in the referenced cells and changes automatically when the values in the referenced cells change.

To see cell referencing at work, select cell A1, and type the formula **=10*2**. Now select cell A2, and type the formula **=A1**. The value in both cells is 20. If at any time you change the value in cell A1, the value in cell A2 changes also. Now select cell A3, and type **=A1+A2**. Excel returns the value 40. Cell references are especially helpful when you create complex formulas.

Entering Cell References by Clicking

You can save time and increase accuracy when you enter cell references in a formula by selecting them with your pointer. For example, to enter references to cells A9 and A10 in a formula in cell B10, do the following:

1. Select cell B10, and type an equal sign.

2. Click cell A9, and type a plus sign.

3. Click cell A10, and press Enter.

When you click each cell, a marquee surrounds the cell, and Excel inserts a reference to the cell in cell B10. After you finish entering a formula, be sure to press Enter. If you do not press Enter and then select another cell, Excel assumes you want to include the cell reference in the formula.

The active cell does not have to be visible in the current window for you to enter a value in that cell. You can scroll through the worksheet without changing the active cell and click cells in remote areas of your worksheet, in other worksheets, or in other workbooks, as you build a formula. The formula bar displays the contents of the active cell, no matter which area of the worksheet is currently visible.

> **Note**
>
> If you scroll through your worksheet and the active cell is no longer visible, you can redisplay it by pressing Ctrl+Backspace. You can return to the upper-left corner of the worksheet by pressing Ctrl+Home.

Understanding Relative, Absolute, and Mixed References

Relative references—the type we've used so far in the sample formulas—refer to cells by their position in relation to the cell that contains the formula, such as "the cell two rows above this cell." *Absolute references* refer to cells by their fixed position in the worksheet, such as "the cell located at the intersection of column A and row 2." A *mixed reference* contains a relative reference and an absolute reference, such as "the cell located in column A and two rows above this cell." Absolute and mixed references are important when you begin copying formulas from one location to another in your worksheet. When you copy and paste, relative references adjust automatically, while absolute references do not. For information about copying cell references, see "How Copying Affects Cell References" on page 432.

A relative reference to cell A1, for example, looks like this: =A1. An absolute reference to cell A1 looks like this: =$A$1. You can combine relative and absolute references to cell A1 to create these mixed references: =$A1 or =A$1.

If the dollar sign precedes only the letter (A, for example), the column coordinate is absolute, and the row is relative. If the dollar sign precedes only the number (1, for example), the column coordinate is relative, and the row is absolute.

While entering or editing a formula, press F4 to change reference types quickly. The following steps show how:

1. Select cell A1, and type **=B1+B2** (but do not press Enter).

2. Press F4 to change the reference nearest to the flashing cursor to absolute. The formula becomes =B1+$B$2.

3. Press F4 again to change the reference to mixed (relative column coordinate and absolute row coordinate). The formula becomes =B1+B$2.

4. Press F4 again to reverse the mixed reference (absolute column coordinate and relative row coordinate). The formula becomes =B1+$B2.

5. Press F4 again to return to the original relative reference.

When you use this technique to change reference types, activate the formula bar by clicking it, and then you can either click in the cell reference you want to change before pressing F4 or drag to select one or more cell references in the formula and change all the selected references at the same time.

Creating References to Other Worksheets in the Same Workbook

You can refer to cells in other worksheets within the same workbook just as easily as you refer to cells in the same worksheet. For example, to enter a reference to cell A9 in Sheet2 into cell B10 in Sheet1, do this:

1. Select cell B10 in Sheet1, and type an equal sign.

2. Click the Sheet2 tab.

3. Click cell A9, and then press Enter.

After you press Enter, Sheet1 becomes active. Select cell B10, and you will see that it contains the formula =Sheet2!A9.

The worksheet portion of the reference is separated from the cell portion by an exclamation point. Note also that the cell reference is relative, which is the default when you select cells to create references to other worksheets.

Creating References to Worksheets in Other Workbooks

You can refer to cells in worksheets in separate workbooks in the same way you refer to cells in other worksheets within the same workbook. These references are called *external references*. For example, to enter a reference to Book2 in Book1, follow these steps:

Microsoft Office
Button

1. Create a new workbook—Book2—by clicking the Microsoft Office Button, clicking New, selecting Blank Workbook, and clicking OK.

2. Click the View tab, click Arrange All, select the Vertical option, and click OK.

3. Select cell A1 in Sheet1 of Book1, and type an equal sign.

4. Click anywhere in the Book2 window to make the workbook active.

5. Click the Sheet2 tab at the bottom of the Book2 window.

6. Click cell A2. Before pressing Enter to lock in the formula, your screen should look similar to Figure 12-1.

7. Press Enter to lock in the reference.

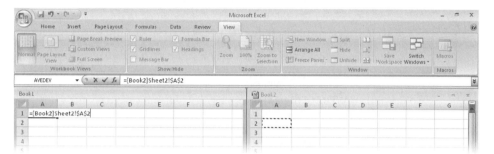

Figure 12-1 Enter external references easily by clicking the cell to which you want to refer.

Understanding Row-Column Reference Style

In the regular A1 reference style, rows are numbered, and columns are designated by letters. In R1C1 reference style, both rows and columns are numbered. The cell reference R1C1 means row 1, column 1; therefore, R1C1 and A1 refer to the same cell. Although R1C1 reference style isn't widely used anymore, it was the standard in some "classic" spreadsheet programs, such as Microsoft Multiplan.

To turn on the R1C1 reference style, click the Microsoft Office Button, click Excel Options, select the Formulas category, select the R1C1 Reference Style check box, and then click OK. The column headers change from letters to numbers, and the cell references in all your formulas automatically change to R1C1 format. For example, cell M10 becomes R10C13, and cell XFD1048576, the last cell in your worksheet, becomes R1048576C16384.

In R1C1 notation, a relative cell reference displays in terms of its relationship to the cell that contains the formula rather than by its actual coordinates. This can be helpful when you are more interested in the relative position of a cell than in its absolute position. For example, suppose you want to enter in cell R10C2 (B10) a formula that adds cells R1C1 (A1) and R1C2 (B1). After selecting cell R10C2, type an equal sign, select cell R1C1, type a plus sign, select cell R1C2, and then press Enter. When you select cell R10C2, the formula =R[−9]C[−1]+R[−9]C appears in the formula bar. Negative row and column numbers indicate that the referenced cell is above or to the left of the formula cell; positive numbers indicate that the referenced cell is below or to the right of the formula cell. The brackets indicate relative references. This formula reads, "Add the cell nine rows up and one column to the left to the cell nine rows up in the same column."

A relative reference to another cell must include brackets. Otherwise, Excel assumes you're using absolute references. For example, if we select the entire formula we created in the previous paragraph in the formula bar and press F4, the formula changes to =R1C1+R1C2 using absolute references.

How Copying Affects Cell References

One of the handiest benefits of using references is the capability to copy and paste formulas. But you need to understand what happens to your references after you paste so you can create formulas with references that operate the way you want them to operate.

Copying Relative References   When you copy a cell containing a formula with relative cell references, Excel changes the references automatically, relative to the position of the cell where you paste the formula. Referring to Figure 12-2, suppose you type the formula **=AVERAGE(B4:E4)** in cell F4. This formula averages the values in the four-cell range that begins four columns to the left of cell F4.

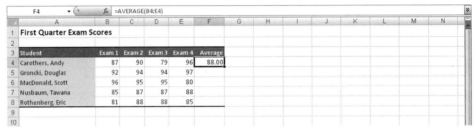

Figure 12-2 Cell F4 contains relative references to the cells to its left.

 You'll find the Exams.xlsx file in the Sample Files section of the companion CD.

You want to repeat this calculation for the remaining rows as well. Instead of typing a new formula in each cell in column F, you select cell F4 and press Ctrl+C to copy it (or click the Copy button in the Clipboard group on the Home tab). Then you select cells F5:F8, click the arrow next to the Paste button on the Home tab, click Paste Special, and then select the Formulas And Number Formats option (to preserve the cell and border formatting). Figure 12-3 shows the results. Because the formula in cell F4 contains a relative reference, Excel adjusts the references in each copy of the formula. As a result, each copy of the formula calculates the average of the cells in the corresponding row. For example, cell F5 contains the formula =AVERAGE(B5:E5).

Copying Absolute References   If you want cell references to remain the same when you copy them, use absolute references. For example, in the worksheet on the left in Figure 12-4, cell B2 contains the hourly rate at which employees are to be paid, and cell C5 contains the relative reference formula =B2*B5. Suppose you want to copy the formula in C5 to the range C6:C8. The worksheet on the right in Figure 12-4 shows what happens if you copy the existing formula to this range: You get erroneous results. Although the formulas in cells C6:C8 should refer to cell B2, they don't. For example, cell C8 contains the incorrect formula =B5*B8.

| F5 | | ▾ | f_x =AVERAGE(B5:E5) | | | | | | | | | | | | |

	A	B	C	D	E	F	G	H	I	J	K	L	M	N
1	First Quarter Exam Scores													
2														
3	Student	Exam 1	Exam 2	Exam 3	Exam 4	Average								
4	Carothers, Andy	87	90	79	96	88.00								
5	Groncki, Douglas	92	94	94	97	94.25								
6	MacDonald, Scott	96	95	95	80	91.50								
7	Nusbaum, Tawana	85	87	87	88	86.75								
8	Rothenberg, Eric	81	88	88	85	85.50								
9														
10														

Figure 12-3 We copied the relative references from cell F4 to cells F5:F8.

C5		▾		f_x =B2*B5

	A	B	C	D
2	Hourly Rate	22.25		
		Hours	Wages	
4	Name	Worked	Due	
5	DeVoe, Michael	27	600.75	
6	Fakhouri, Fadi	32		
7	Ito, Shu	40		
8	Ortiz, David J.	29		
9				
10				

C8		▾		f_x =B5*B8

	A	B	C	D
2	Hourly Rate	22.25		
		Hours	Wages	
4	Name	Worked	Due	
5	DeVoe, Michael	27	600.75	
6	Fakhouri, Fadi	32	0.00	
7	Ito, Shu	40	#VALUE!	
8	Ortiz, David J.	29	783.00	
9				
10				

Figure 12-4 The formula in cell C5 contains relative references. We copied the relative formula in cell C5 to cells C6:C8, producing incorrect results.

You'll find the Wages.xlsx file in the Sample Files section of the companion CD.

Because the reference to cell B2 in the original formula is relative, it changes as you copy the formula to the other cells. To correctly apply the wage rate in cell B2 to all the calculations, you must change the reference to cell B2 to an absolute reference before you copy the formula.

To change the reference style, click the formula bar, click the reference to cell B2, and then press F4. The result is the following formula: =$B$2*B5.

When you copy this modified formula to cells C6:C8, Excel adjusts the second cell reference, but not the first, within each formula. In Figure 12-5, cell C8 now contains the correct formula: =$B$2*B8.

Copying Mixed References   You can use mixed references in your formulas to anchor a portion of a cell reference. (In a mixed reference, one portion is absolute, and the other is relative.) When you copy a mixed reference, Excel anchors the absolute portion and adjusts the relative portion to reflect the location of the cell to which you copied the formula.

To create a mixed reference, you can press the F4 key to cycle through the four combinations of absolute and relative references—for example, from B2 to $B$2 to B$2 to $B2.

C8		f_x	=$B$2*B8	
	A	B	C	D
2	**Hourly Rate**	22.25		
4	*Name*	*Hours Worked*	*Wages Due*	
5	DeVoe, Michael	27	600.75	
6	Fakhouri, Fadi	32	712.00	
7	Ito, Shu	40	890.00	
8	Ortiz, David J.	29	645.25	
9				
10				

Figure 12-5 We created an absolute reference to cell B2 before copying the formula.

The loan payment table in Figure 12-6 uses mixed references (and an absolute reference). You need to enter only one formula in cell C6 and then copy it down and across to fill the table. Cell C6 contains the formula = –PMT($B6,$C$3,C$5) to calculate the annual payments on a $10,000 loan over a period of 15 years at an interest rate of 6 percent. We copied this formula to cells C6:F10 to calculate payments on three additional loan amounts using four additional interest rates.

C6			f_x	=-PMT($B6,$C$3,C$5)		
A B	C	D	E	F	G	
1						
2	**Loan Payment Calculator**					
3	*Years:* 15					
4			**Loan Amount**			
5	*Rate:*	$ 10,000	$ 20,000	$ 30,000	$ 40,000	
6	6.00%	1,030	2,059	3,089	4,119	
7	6.50%	1,064	2,127	3,191	4,254	
8	7.00%	1,098	2,196	3,294	4,392	
9	7.50%	1,133	2,266	3,399	4,531	
10	8.00%	1,168	2,337	3,505	4,673	
11						
12						

Figure 12-6 This loan payment table uses formulas that contain mixed references.

You'll find the Loan.xlsx file in the Sample Files section of the companion CD.

The first cell reference, $B6, indicates we always want to refer to the values in column B but the row reference (Rate) can change. Similarly, the mixed reference, C$5, indicates we always want to refer to the values in row 5 but the column reference (Loan Amount) can change. For example, cell E8 contains the formula = –PMT($B8,$C$3,E$5). Without mixed references, we would have to edit the formulas manually in each of the cells in the range C6:F10.

TROUBLESHOOTING

Inserted cells are not included in formulas.

If you have a SUM formula at the bottom of a row of numbers and then insert new rows between the numbers and the formula, the range reference in the SUM function doesn't include the new cells. Unfortunately, you can't do much about this. This is an age-old worksheet problem, but Excel attempts to correct it for you automatically. Although the range reference in the SUM formula will not change when you insert the new rows, it will adjust as you type new values in the inserted cells. The only caveat is that you must enter the new values one at a time, starting with the cell directly below the column of numbers. If you begin entering values in the middle of a group of newly inserted rows or columns, the range reference remains unaffected. For more information about the SUM function, see "Using the SUM Function" on page 497.

Editing Formulas

You edit formulas the same way you edit text entries. To delete characters in a formula, drag through the characters in the cell or the formula bar, and press Backspace or Delete. To replace a character, highlight it, and type its replacement. To replace a reference, highlight it, and click the new cell you want the formula to use; Excel enters a relative reference automatically. You can also insert additional cell references in a formula. For example, to insert a reference to cell B1 in the formula =A1+A3, simply move the insertion point between A1 and the plus sign, and either type **+B1** or type a plus sign and click cell B1. The formula becomes =A1+B1+A3.

Understanding Reference Syntax

So far, we have used the default worksheet and workbook names for the examples in this book. When you save a workbook, you must give it a permanent name. If you create a formula first and then save the workbook with a new name, Excel adjusts the formula accordingly. For example, if you save Book2 as Sales.xlsx, Excel changes the remote reference formula =[Book2]Sheet2!$A$2 to =[Sales.xlsx]Sheet2!$A$2. And if you rename Sheet2 of Sales.xlsx to February, Excel changes the reference to =[Sales.xlsx]February!$A$2. If the referenced workbook is closed, Excel displays the full path to the folder where the workbook is stored in the reference, as shown in the example ='C:\Work\[Sales.xlsx]February'!$A$2.

In the preceding example, note that apostrophes surround the workbook and worksheet portion of the reference. Excel adds the apostrophes around the path when you close the workbook. If you type a new reference to a closed workbook, however, you must add the apostrophes yourself. To avoid typing errors, open the closed workbook, and click cells with your cursor to enter references so that Excel inserts them in the correct syntax for you.

Chapter 12

Using Numeric Text in Formulas

The seemingly oxymoronic term *numeric text* refers to an entry that is not strictly numbers but includes both numbers and a few specific text characters. You can perform mathematical operations on numeric text values as long as the numeric string contains only the following characters:

```
0 1 2 3 4 5 6 7 8 9 . + – E e
```

In addition, you can use the / character in fractions. You can also use the following five number-formatting characters:

```
$ , % ( )
```

You must enclose numeric text strings in quotation marks. For example, if you type the formula **=$1234+$123**, Excel displays an error message stating that Excel found an error in the formula you typed. (The error message also offers to correct the error for you by removing the dollar signs.) But the formula ="$1234"+"$123" produces the result 1357 (ignoring the dollar signs). When Excel performs the addition, it automatically translates numeric text entries into numeric values.

For more information about number-formatting characters, see "Formatting As You Type" on page 297.

About Text Values

The term *text values* refers to any entry that is neither a number nor a numeric text value (see the previous section); Excel treats the entry as text only. You can refer to and manipulate text values using formulas. For example, if cell A1 contains the text *First* and you type the formula **=A1** in cell A10, cell A10 displays First.

For more information about manipulating text with formulas, see "Understanding Text Functions" on page 502.

You can use the & (ampersand) operator to *concatenate*, or join, several text values. Extending the preceding example, if cell A2 contains the text *Quarter* and you type the formula **=A1&A2** in cell A3, then cell A3 displays *FirstQuarter*. To include a space between the two strings, change the formula to =A1&" "&A2. This formula uses two concatenation operators and a *literal string*, or *string constant* (a space enclosed in quotation marks).

You can use the & operator to concatenate strings of numeric values as well. For example, if cell A3 contains the numeric value 867 and cell A4 contains the numeric value 5309, the formula =A3&A4 produces the string 8675309. This string is left-aligned in the cell because it's considered a text value. (Remember, you can use numeric text values to perform any mathematical operation as long as the numeric string contains only the numeric characters listed at the top of this page.)

Finally, you can use the & operator to concatenate a text value and a numeric value. For example, if cell A1 contains the text *January* and cell A3 contains the numeric value 2009, the formula =A1&A3 produces the string January2009.

Practical Concatenation

Depending on the kind of work you do, the text manipulation prowess of Excel may turn out to be the most important skill you learn in this book. If you deal with a lot of mailing lists, for example, you probably use a word-processing application such as Microsoft Office Word 2007. But read on—you might find that Excel has the tools you've been wishing for, and it just might become your text manipulation application of choice.

Suppose you have a database of names in which the first and last names are stored in separate columns. This example shows you how to generate a list of full names:

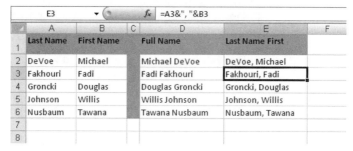

We created the full names listed in columns D and E using formulas like the one visible in the formula bar. For example, the formula in cell D2 is =A2&" "&B2, which concatenates the contents of the cells in columns A and B and adds a space character in between. The formula in cell E2 (shown in the illustration) reverses the position of the first and last names and adds a comma before the space character.

Pretty soon, you'll be using the term *concatenate* in everyday conversation. Instead of the old "ducks in a row" metaphor, you'll be saying, "We must concatenate our ducks." Caution is advised.

 You'll find the Concatenation.xlsx file in the Sample Files section of the companion CD.

Understanding Error Values

An *error value* is the result of a formula that Excel can't resolve. Table 12-2 describes the seven error values.

Table 12-2 Error Values

Error Value	Cause
#DIV/0!	You attempted to divide a number by zero. This error usually occurs when you create a formula with a divisor that refers to a blank cell.
#NAME?	You typed a name that doesn't exist in a formula. You might have mistyped the name or typed a deleted name. Excel also displays this error value if you do not enclose a text string in quotation marks.
#VALUE	You entered a mathematical formula that refers to a text entry.
#REF!	You deleted a range of cells whose references are included in a formula.
#N/A	No information is available for the calculation you want to perform. When building a model, you can type **#N/A** in a cell to show you are awaiting data. Any formulas that reference cells containing the #N/A value return #N/A.
#NUM!	You provided an invalid argument to a worksheet function. #NUM! can indicate also that the result of a formula is too large or too small to be represented in the worksheet.
#NULL!	You included a space between two ranges in a formula to indicate an intersection, but the ranges have no common cells.

Using Functions: A Preview

In simplest terms, a *function* is a predefined formula. Many Excel functions are shorthand versions of frequently used formulas. For example, compare the formula =A1+A2+A3+A4+A5+A6+A7+A8+A9+A10 with the formula =SUM(A1:A10). The SUM function makes the formula a lot shorter, easier to read, and easier to create. Some Excel functions perform complex calculations. For example, using the PMT function, you can calculate the payment on a loan at a given interest rate and principal amount.

All functions consist of a function name followed by a set of *arguments* enclosed in parentheses. (In the preceding example, A1:A10 is the argument in the SUM function.) If you omit a closing parenthesis when you enter a function, Excel adds the parenthesis after you press Enter, as long as it's obvious where the parenthesis is supposed to go. (Relying on this feature can produce unpredictable results; for accuracy, always verify your parentheses.)

For more information about functions, see Chapter 13, "Using Functions." For more about the SUM function, see Chapter 14, "Everyday Functions."

Using the Sum Button

Sum

No surprise—the SUM function is used more often than any other function. To make this function more accessible, Excel includes the Sum button on the Home tab on the Ribbon, which inserts the SUM function into a cell. (This button has an alter ego with identical functionality on the Formulas tab on the Ribbon, where it is called the Auto-Sum button.)

> **Note**
>
> You can quickly enter a SUM function in the selected cell by pressing Alt+=.

To see how this works, do the following:

1. Enter a column of numbers, like we did in Figure 12-7.

2. Select the cell below the column of numbers, and click the Sum button in the Editing group on the Home tab. The button inserts the entire formula for you and suggests a range to sum.

3. If the suggested range is incorrect, simply drag through the correct range, and press Enter.

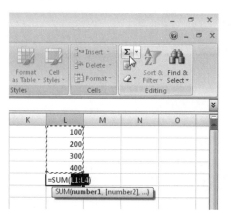 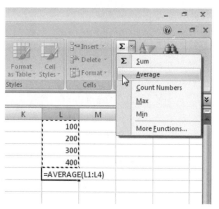

Figure 12-7 Use the Sum button to add a summary formula in a cell adjacent to columns or rows of numbers.

The Sum button includes a menu that appears when you click the arrow next to the button, as shown in Figure 12-7. You can enter the AVERAGE, COUNT, MAX, or MIN function almost as easily as you can enter the SUM function—all it takes is an extra click to select the function you want from the Sum menu. The More Functions command opens the Insert Function dialog box, where you can access any Excel function. If you select a contiguous cell range that is adjacent to rows or columns of numbers before clicking the Sum button, Excel enters SUM functions in each cell.

> **Note**
>
> Get a quick sum by selecting the cells you want to sum and then looking at the status bar, where Excel automatically displays the sum, the average, and the count (the total number of cells containing entries) of the selected range. Right-click the status bar to add more readouts for minimum, maximum, and numerical count. For more information, see "Quick Totals on the Status Bar" on page 45.

For more information, see "Using the SUM Function" on page 497.

Inserting a Function

When you want to use a built-in function, click the Insert Function button on the Formulas tab on the Ribbon (or the little *fx* icon located on the formula bar). When you do so, the Insert Function dialog box shown in Figure 12-8 appears. For details about using the Insert Function dialog box, see "Inserting Functions" on page 492.

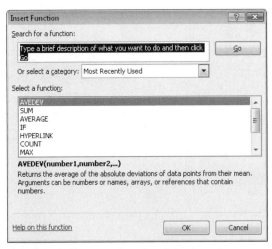

Figure 12-8 The Insert Function dialog box gives you access to all the built-in functions in Excel.

Using Formula AutoComplete

Excel 2007 makes it a little easier to create formulas with a new feature called *Formula AutoComplete*. Figure 12-9 illustrates what happens when you type an equal sign followed by the letter *S*—Excel lists all functions that begin with that letter. Formula AutoComplete also provides lists of defined names and function arguments, as well as special codes and names used in structured references and Cube functions.

For more about defined names, see "Using Names in Formulas" on page 442; for more about structured references, see "Using Structured References" on page 454.

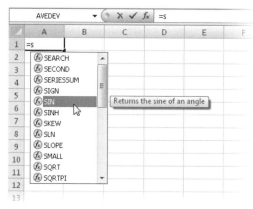

Figure 12-9 When you start to type a function, Excel lists all the functions that begin with that letter or letters.

You can just keep typing your formula, or you can click any of the items in the Auto-Complete list to see a pop-up description of what that function does. Scroll down the list to see more functions; to insert one of the functions into your formula, double-click it. You can type additional characters to narrow the list further. For example, typing **=si** in the example shown in Figure 12-9 would narrow the AutoComplete list to three functions: SIGN, SIN, and SINH. Formula AutoComplete also works within nested formulas. For example, if you started typing a formula such as **=SUM(SIN(A4),S** into a cell, the AutoComplete list would appear and readjust its contents for each letter you type in the formula.

Working with Formulas

We've covered most of the basics you need to know about how formulas and references work. In the following sections, we'll dig deeper, covering how to use defined names, intersections, structured references, and three-dimensional (3-D) formulas.

Naming Cells and Cell Ranges

If you find yourself repeatedly typing cryptic cell addresses, such as **Sheet3!A1:AJ51**, into formulas, we'll show you a better approach. You can assign a short, memorable name to any cell or range and then use that name instead of the cryptogram in formulas. Naming cells has no effect on either their displayed values or their underlying values—you are just assigning "nicknames" you can use when creating formulas.

Chapter 12

After you define names in a worksheet, those names become available to any other worksheets in the workbook. A name defining a cell range in Sheet6, for example, is available for use in formulas in Sheet1, Sheet2, and so on, in the workbook. As a result, each workbook contains its own set of names. You can also define worksheet-level names that are available only on the worksheet in which they are defined.

For more information about worksheet-level names, see "Workbook-Wide vs. Worksheet-Only Names" on page 445.

Using Names in Formulas

When you use the name of a cell or a range in a formula, the result is the same as if you typed the cell or range address. For example, suppose you typed the formula **=A1+A2** in cell A3. If you assigned the name Mark to cell A1 and the name Vicki to cell A2, the formula =Mark+Vicki has the same result and is easier to read.

The easiest way to define a name follows:

1. Select a cell.

2. Click the Name box on the left end of the formula bar, as shown in Figure 12-10.

3. Type **TestName**, and then press Enter.

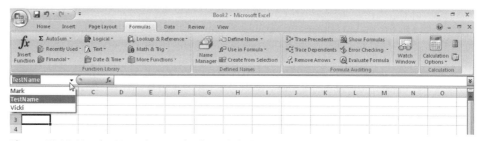

Figure 12-10 Use the Name box on the formula bar to quickly assign names to cells and ranges.

Keep the following basics in mind when using names in formulas:

- The Name box usually displays the address of the selected cell. If you have named the selected cell or range, the name takes precedence over the address, and Excel displays it in the Name box.

- When you define a name for a range of cells, the range name does not appear in the Name box unless you select the same range.

- When you click the Name box and select a name, the cell selection switches to the named cells.

- If you type a name in the Name box that you have already defined, Excel switches the selection instead of redefining the name.

- When you define a name, the stored definition is an absolute cell reference that includes the worksheet name. For example, when you define the name TestName for cell A3 in Sheet1, the actual name definition is recorded as Sheet1!$A$3.

For more information about absolute references, see "Understanding Relative, Absolute, and Mixed References" on page 429.

Defining and Managing Names

Instead of coming up with new names for cells and ranges, you can simply use existing text labels to create names. Click the Define Name button on the Formulas tab on the Ribbon to display the New Name dialog box shown in Figure 12-11. In this example, we selected cells B4:E4 before clicking the Define Name button, and Excel correctly surmised that the label *Region 1* was the most likely name candidate for that range. If you are happy using the adjacent label as a name, just press Enter to define the name, or you can first add a note in the Comment box if you want to provide some helpful documentation.

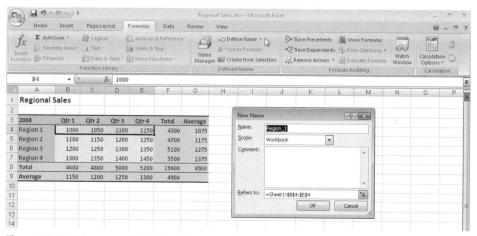

Figure 12-11 When you click Define Name on the Formulas tab, Excel suggests any label in an adjacent cell in the same row or column as a name.

You can, of course, define a name without first selecting a cell or range on the worksheet. For example, in the New Name dialog box, type **Test2** in the Name text box, and then type **=D20** in the Refers To text box. Click OK to add the name, which also closes the New Name dialog box. To see a list of the names you have defined, click the Name Manager button on the Formulas tab. The Name Manager dialog box appears, as shown in Figure 12-12.

The Name Manager dialog box lists all the names along with their values and locations. You'll see that the Refers To text box shows the definition of the name we just added, =Sheet1!D20. Excel adds the worksheet reference for you, but note that the cell reference stays relative, just as you typed it, while the Region_1 definition created by Excel uses absolute references (indicated by the dollar signs in the Refers To definition). Also note that if you do not enter an equal sign preceding the reference, Excel interprets the definition as text. For example, if you typed **D20** instead of **=D20**, the Refers To text box would display the text constant ="D20" as the definition of the name Test2.

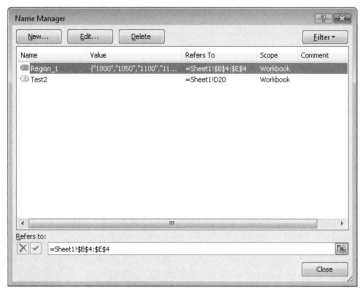

Figure 12-12 The Name Manager dialog box provides central control over all the names in a workbook.

When working with tables created using the new table features in Excel, some names are created automatically, and others are implied. If this sounds intriguing, see "Using Structured References" on page 454.

Editing Names

Although it is possible to edit name references directly using the Refers To text box in the Name Manager dialog box, it is preferable to click the Edit button at the top of the dialog box. Doing so opens the Edit Name dialog box, which is otherwise the same as the New Name dialog box shown in Figure 12-11. Although you can edit name references directly in the Name Manager dialog box, the Edit Name dialog box offers additional opportunities to change the name and to add a comment.

In the Edit Name dialog box, you can change cell references in the Refers To text box by typing or by directly selecting cells on the worksheet. When you click OK in the Edit Name dialog box, the Name Manager dialog box reappears, displaying the updated name definition. Clicking the New button in the Name Manager dialog box predictably displays the New Name dialog box; clicking the Delete button removes all selected names from the list in the Name Manager dialog box. Keep in mind that when you delete a name, any formula in the worksheet referring to that name returns the error value #NAME?.

Rules for Naming

The following rules apply when you name cells and ranges in Excel:

- You must begin all names with a letter, a backslash (\), or an underscore (_). You cannot use any other symbol.

- You cannot use spaces; Excel translates blank spaces in labels to underscores in defined names.

- You can't use names that resemble cell references (for example, AB$5 or R1C7).

- You can use single letters, with the exception of the letters *R* and *C* (uppercase and lowercase), as names.

- You can also use numbers, periods, and underscore characters.

A name can contain 255 characters. Excel does not distinguish between uppercase and lowercase characters in names. For example, if you create the name Tax and then create the name TAX in the same workbook, the second name overwrites the first.

Workbook-Wide vs. Worksheet-Only Names

Names in Excel usually function on a workbook-wide basis. That is, a name you define on any worksheet is available for use in formulas on any other worksheet. But you can also create names whose scope is limited to the worksheet level—that is, names that are available only on the worksheet in which you define them. You might want to do this if, for example, you have a number of worksheets doing similar jobs in the same workbook and you want to use the same names to accomplish similar tasks on each worksheet. To define a worksheet-only name, click the Scope drop-down list in the New Name dialog box, and select the name of the worksheet to which you want to limit the scope of the name.

TROUBLESHOOTING

My old worksheet-level names have changed.

In previous versions of Excel, you created worksheet-level names by preceding the name (not the cell reference) with the name of the worksheet, followed by an exclamation point. This no longer works in Excel 2007, and it's easier now anyway, using the Scope options in the New Name dialog box. If you have existing worksheet-level names in workbooks that you created using previous versions of Excel, they will still work after you import the workbooks into Excel 2007, but Excel modifies the name by removing the old designation that was part of the name (the worksheet name and exclamation point) and adds the Scope designation instead.

For example, to define TestSheetName as a worksheet-only name in Sheet1, select the range you want, click the Define Name button on the Formulas tab, type **TestSheet-Name** in the Name text box, and then select Sheet1 from the Scope drop-down list, as shown in Figure 12-13.

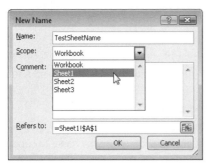

Figure 12-13 Use the Scope drop-down list to specify a worksheet to which you want to restrict a name's usage.

The following are some additional facts to keep in mind when working with worksheet-only and workbook-level names:

- Worksheet-only names do not appear in the Name box on the formula bar in worksheets other than the one in which you define them.

- When you select a cell or range to which you have assigned a worksheet-only name, the name appears in the Name box on the formula bar, but you have no way of knowing its scope. You can consider adding clues for your own benefit, such as including the word *Sheet* as part of all worksheet-only names when you define them.

- If a worksheet contains a duplicate workbook-level and worksheet-only name, the worksheet-level name takes precedence over the book-level name on the worksheet where it lives, rendering the workbook-level version of the name useless on that worksheet.

- You can use a worksheet-only name in formulas on other worksheets by adding the name of the worksheet followed by an exclamation point (no spaces) preceding the name in the formula. For example, you could type the formula **=Sheet1!TestSheetName** in a cell on Sheet3.

- You can't change the scope of an existing name.

Creating Names Semiautomatically

You can click the Create From Selection button on the Formulas tab on the Ribbon to name several adjacent cells or ranges at once, using row labels, column labels, or both. When you choose this command, Excel displays the Create Names From Selection dialog box shown in Figure 12-14.

Selecting Cells While a Dialog Box Is Open

The Refers To text boxes in the New Name and Name Manager dialog boxes (and many other text boxes in other dialog boxes) contain a *collapse dialog button*, which indicates that this is a text box from which you can navigate and select cells on the worksheet. For example, after you click the Refers To text box, you can click outside the dialog box to select any other worksheet tab, drag scroll bars, switch workbooks, or make another workbook active. In addition, if you click the collapse dialog button, sure enough, the dialog box collapses, letting you see more of the worksheet:

	A	B	C	D	E	F	G	H
1	**Regional Sales**							
2								
3	2008	Qtr 1	Qtr 2	Qtr 3	Qtr 4	Total	Average	
4	Region 1	1000	1050	1100	1150	4300	1075	
5	Region 2	1100	1150	1200	1250	4700	1175	
6	Region 3	1200	125					
7	Region 4	1300	135					
8	Total	4600	480					
9	Average	1150	120	1250	1300	4900		
10								

New Name - Refers to:

=Sheet1!$B$4:$E$4

You can drag the collapsed dialog box around the screen using its title bar. When you finish, click the collapse dialog button again, and the dialog box returns to its original size.

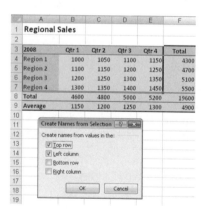

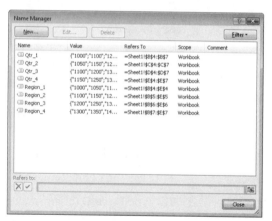

Figure 12-14 Use the Create Names From Selection dialog box to name several cells or ranges at once using labels.

Excel assumes that labels included in the selection are the names for each range. For example, Figure 12-14 shows that with A3:E7 selected, the Top Row and Left Column options in the Create Names dialog box are automatically selected, creating a set of names for each quarter and each product. Note that when using Create From Selection, you need to select the labels as well as the data. When you click the Name Manager button, you'll see the names you just created listed in the dialog box.

Naming Constants and Formulas

You can create names that are defined by constants and formulas instead of by cell references. You can use absolute and relative references, numbers, text, formulas, and functions as name definitions. For example, if you often use the value 8.3% to calculate sales tax, you can click the Define Name button, type the name **Tax** in the Name box, and then type **8.3%** (or **.083**) in the Refers To text box. Then you can use the name Tax in a formula, such as **=Price+(Price*Tax)**, to calculate the cost of items with 8.3 percent sales tax. Note that named constants and formulas do not appear in the Name box on the formula bar, but they do appear in the Name Manager dialog box.

You can also enter a formula in the Refers To text box. For example, you might define the name Price with a formula, such as =Sheet1!A1*190%. If you define this named formula while cell B1 is selected, you can then type **=Price** in cell B1, and the defined formula takes care of the calculation for you. Because the reference in the named formula is relative, you can then type **=Price** in any cell in your workbook to calculate a price using the value in the cell directly to the left. If you type a formula in the Refers To text box that refers to a cell or range in a worksheet, Excel updates the formula whenever the value in the cell changes.

Using Relative References in Named Formulas   When you are creating a named formula that contains relative references, such as =Sheet1!B22+1.2%, Excel interprets the position of the cells referenced in the Refers To text box as relative to the cell that is active when you define the name. Later, when you use such a name in a formula, the named formula uses whatever cell corresponds to the relative reference. For example, if cell B21 was the active cell when you defined the name Fees as =Sheet1!B22+1.2%, the name Fees always refers to the cell one row below the cell in which the formula is currently located.

Creating Three-Dimensional Names

You can create three-dimensional names, which use 3-D references as their definitions. For example, suppose you have a 13-worksheet workbook containing one identical worksheet for each month plus one summary sheet. You can define a 3-D name that you can use to summarize totals from each monthly worksheet. To do so, follow these steps:

1. Select cell B5 in Sheet1 (the summary sheet).

2. Click the Define Name button.

3. Type **Three_D** (or any name you choose) in the Name box, and type **=Sheet2: Sheet13!B5** in the Refers To text box.

4. Press Enter (or click OK).

Now you can use the name Three_D in formulas that contain any of the following functions: SUM, AVERAGE, AVERAGEA, COUNT, COUNTA, MIN, MINA, MAX, MAXA, PRODUCT, STDEV, STDEVA, STDEVP, STDEVPA, VAR, VARA, VARP, and VARPA. For example, the formula =MAX(Three_D) returns the largest value in the three-dimensional range named Three_D. Because you used relative references in step 3, the definition of the range Three_D changes as you select different cells in the worksheet. For example, if you select cell C3 and display the Name Manager dialog box, =Sheet2: Sheet13!C3 appears in the Refers To text box.

For more information on three-dimensional references, see "Creating Three-Dimensional Formulas" on page 453.

Using Names in Formulas

After you define one or more names in your worksheet, you can insert those names in formulas using one of several methods. First, if you know at least the first letter of the name you want to use, you can simply start typing to display the Formula AutoComplete drop-down list containing all the names beginning with that letter (along with any built-in functions that begin with that letter), as shown in Figure 12-15. To enter one of the names in your formula, double-click it.

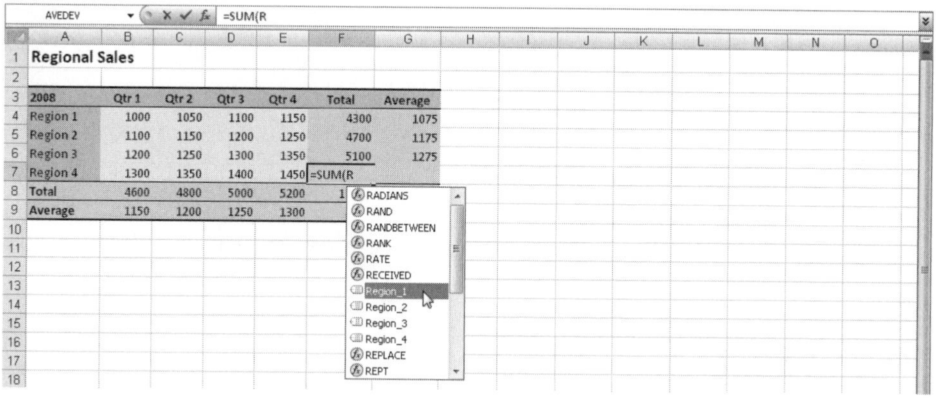

Figure 12-15 Names you define appear in the Formula AutoComplete list when you type a formula.

For more information, see "Using Formula AutoComplete" on page 440.

You can also find a list of all the names relevant to the current worksheet when you click the Use In Formula button on the Formulas tab on the Ribbon, which you can click while in the process of entering a formula, as shown in Figure 12-16.

Clicking the Paste Names command at the bottom of the Use In Formula menu displays the Paste Name dialog box shown on the left in Figure 12-17 when you are editing a formula. If you click the command when you are not in Edit mode, a different version of the dialog box appears, as shown on the right in Figure 12-17. The difference is the Paste List button, which we'll discuss in the next section.

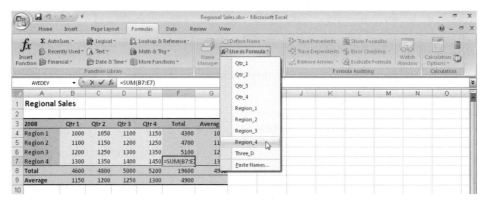

Figure 12-16 Click the Use In Formula button, and select a name to enter it into the selected cell.

Figure 12-17 The Paste Name dialog box changes, depending on whether you are editing within a cell.

Creating a List of Names

In large worksheet models, it's easy to accumulate a long list of defined names. To keep a record of all the names used, you can paste a list of defined names in your worksheet by clicking Paste List in the Paste Name dialog box, as shown in Figure 12-18. Excel pastes the list in your worksheet beginning at the active cell. Worksheet-only names appear in the list only when you click Paste List on the worksheet where they live. Paste List is really the only useful feature in the Paste Name dialog box, given the superior methods of using names described in the previous section.

> **Note**
> When Excel pastes the list of names, it overwrites any existing data without asking for permission first. If you inadvertently overwrite data, press Ctrl+Z to undo it.

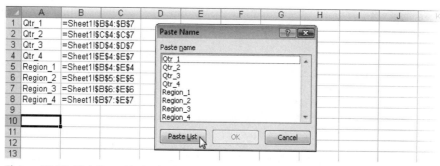

Figure 12-18 Click Paste List in the Paste Name dialog box to create a list of names and references starting at the active cell.

Replacing References with Names

You can replace cell references with their corresponding names all at once using the Apply Names command, which you access by clicking the arrow next to the Define Name button on the Formulas tab on the Ribbon. When you do so, Excel locates all cell and range references for which you have defined names and replaces them with the appropriate name. If you select a single cell before you click the Apply Names command, Excel applies names throughout the active worksheet; if you select a range of cells first, Excel applies names to only the selected cells.

Figure 12-19 shows the Apply Names dialog box, which lists all the cell and range names you have defined. Select each name you want to apply, and then click OK.

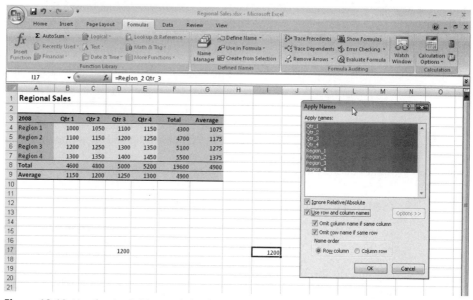

Figure 12-19 Use the Apply Names dialog box to substitute names for cell and range references in your formulas. Click Options to display all the options shown here.

Excel ordinarily does not apply the column or row name if either is superfluous. For example, Figure 12-19 shows a worksheet after we applied names using the default options in the Apply Names dialog box. Cell I17 is selected, and the formula bar shows it contains the formula =Region_2 Qtr_3, which before applying names contained the formula =D5. Because cell I17 isn't in the same row or column as any of the defined ranges, both the row and column names are included in the new formula. Cell D17 contained the same formula, =D5. But because D17 is in the same column as the referenced cell, only the row name is needed thanks to implicit intersection, resulting in the formula =Region_2.

If you prefer to see both the column and row names even when they are not necessary, clear the Omit Column Name If Same Column check box and the Omit Row Name If Same Row check box.

The Name Order options control the order in which row and column components appear. For example, if we applied names using the Column Row option, the formula in cell I17 in Figure 12-19 would become =Qtr_3 Region_2.

For more information about implicit intersection, see "Getting Explicit About Intersections" below.

Select the Ignore Relative/Absolute check box to replace references with names regardless of the reference type. In general, leave this check box selected. Most name definitions use absolute references (the default when you define and create names), and most formulas use relative references (the default when you paste cell and range references in the formula bar). If you clear this check box, absolute, relative, and mixed references are replaced with name definitions only if the definitions use the same reference style.

The Use Row And Column Names check box is necessary if you want to apply names in intersection cases, as we have shown in the examples. If you define names for individual cells, however, you can clear the Use Row And Column Names check box to apply names to only specific cell references in formulas.

Using Go To with Names

When you click the Find & Select button on the Home tab and click Go To (or press F5), any names you have defined appear in the Go To list, as shown in Figure 12-20. Select a name, and click OK to jump to the range to which the name refers. Note that names defined with constants or formulas do not appear in the Go To dialog box.

Getting Explicit About Intersections

In the worksheet in Figure 12-19, if you type the formula **=Qtr_l*4** in cell I4, Excel assumes you want to use only one value in the Qtr_1 range B4:B7—the one in the same row as the formula that contains the reference. This is called *implicit intersection*. Because the formula is in row 4, Excel uses the value in cell B4. If you type the same formula in cells I5, I6, and I7, each cell in that range contains the formula =Qtr_1*4, but at I5 the formula refers to cell B5, at I6 it refers to cell B6, and so on.

Figure 12-20 Use the Go To dialog box to select a cell or range name so you can move to that cell or range quickly.

Explicit intersection refers to a specific cell with the help of the intersection operator. The *intersection operator* is the space character that appears when you press the Spacebar. If you type the formula **=Qtr_1 Region_1** at any location on the same worksheet, Excel knows you want to refer to the value at the intersection of the range labeled Qtr 1 and the range labeled Region 1, which is cell B4.

Creating Three-Dimensional Formulas

You can use references to perform calculations on cells that span a range of worksheets in a workbook. These are called *3-D references*. Suppose you set up 12 worksheets in the same workbook—one for each month—with a year-to-date summary sheet on top. If all the monthly worksheets are laid out identically, you could use 3-D reference formulas to summarize the monthly data on the summary sheet. For example, the formula =SUM(Sheet2:Sheet13!B5) adds all the values in cell B5 on all the worksheets between and including Sheet2 and Sheet13.

> You can also use 3-D names in formulas. For more information, see "Creating Three-Dimensional Names" on page 448.

To construct this three-dimensional formula, follow these steps:

1. In cell B5 of Sheet1, type **=SUM(**.

2. Click the Sheet2 tab, and select cell B5.

3. Click the right tab-scrolling button (located to the left of the worksheet tabs) until the Sheet13 tab is visible.

4. Hold down the Shift key, and click the Sheet13 tab. All the tabs from Sheet2 through Sheet13 change to white, indicating they are selected for inclusion in the reference you are constructing.

5. Select cell B5 in Sheet13.

6. Type a closing parenthesis, and then press Enter.

Chapter 12

For more information about group editing, see "Editing Multiple Worksheets" on page 236.

You can use the following functions with 3-D references: SUM, AVERAGE, AVERAGEA, COUNT, COUNTA, MIN, MINA, MAX, MAXA, PRODUCT, STDEV, STDEVA, STDEVP, STDEVPA, VAR, VARA, VARP, and VARPA.

Formula-Bar Formatting

You can enter spaces and line breaks in a formula to make it easier to read in the formula bar without affecting the calculation of the formula. To enter a line break, press Alt+Enter. Figure 12-21 shows a formula that contains line breaks. To see all of the formula in the formula bar, click the Expand Formula Bar button (the one with the chevron) at the right end of the formula bar.

A1			f_x	=(((C1*C2)+(D1*D2)+(E1*E2))*I1)											
				+(((F1*F2)+(G1*G2)+(H1*H2))*I2)											
	A	B	C	D	E	F	G	H	I	J	K	L	M	N	O
1	24.44			1	3	5	7	9	11	0.05					
2				2	4	6	8	10	12	0.08					
3															
4															
5															
6															
7															
8															

Figure 12-21 You can enter line breaks in a formula to make it more readable.

Using Structured References

Creating names to define cells and ranges makes complex formulas easier to create and easier to read, and *structured references* offer similar advantages, and much more, whenever you create formulas in tables or formulas that refer to data in tables. Structured references are dynamic; formulas that use them automatically adjust to any changes you make to the table.

Table

Structured references rely on the structure imposed when you create a table using the Table button on the Insert tab on the Ribbon. Excel recognizes distinct areas of a table as separate components you can refer to using *specifiers* that are either predefined or derived from the table. Figure 12-22 shows a modified version of the Regional Sales worksheet that we converted to a table. We'll refer to this table as we discuss structured references.

For more information about creating tables, see Chapter 21, "Managing information in Tables."

When you refer to data in tables using formulas created by direct manipulation—that is, when you click or drag to insert cell or range references in formulas—Excel creates structured references automatically in most cases. (If a structured reference is not applicable, Excel inserts cell references instead.) Excel builds structured references using the table name and the column labels. (Excel automatically assigns a name to the table when you create one.) You can also type structured references using strict syntax guidelines that we'll explain later in this section.

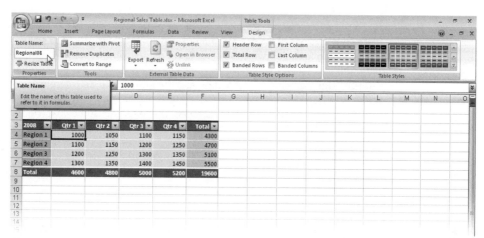

Figure 12-22 We created this table to illustrate the power of structured references.

> **Note**
>
> The capability to create structured references automatically using direct manipulation with the mouse is an option that is ordinarily turned on. To disable this feature, click the Microsoft Office Button, Excel Options, and then in the Formulas category, clear the cryptically titled Use Table Names In Formulas check box.

All Excel tables contain the following areas of interest, as far as structured references are concerned:

- **The table** Excel automatically applies a table name when you create a table, which appears in the Table Name text box in the Properties group on the Table Tools Design tab that appears when you select a table. Excel named our table Table3 in this example, but we changed it to Regional08 by typing in the Table Name text box, as shown in Figure 12-22. The table name actually refers to all the data in the table, excluding the header and total rows.

- **Individual columns of data** Excel uses your column headers in *column specifiers*, which refer to the data in each column, excluding the header and the total row. A *calculated column* is a column of formulas inside the table structure, such as F4:F7 in our example, which, again, does not include the header or total rows.

- **Special items** These are specific areas of a table, including the total row, the header row, and other areas specified by using *special item specifiers*—fixed codes that are used in structured references to zero in on specific cells or ranges in a table. We'll explain these later in this section.

For details about calculated columns in tables, see Chapter 21, "Managing Information in Tables."

No More Natural-Language Formulas

In previous versions of Excel, you could use adjacent labels instead of cell references when creating formulas, which was like using names without actually having to define them. This was called the *natural-language formulas* feature, but it was riddled with problems and has been replaced in Excel 2007 with structured references, which work much better. However, when you open a workbook created with a previous version of Excel containing natural-language formulas, the following, somewhat frightening, error message appears:

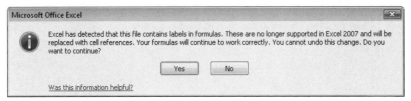

Despite the admonition that "Excel cannot undo this change," this mandatory conversion has little effect on your worksheets other than changing some of the underlying formulas. Excel correctly identifies the offending labels and replaces them for you with the correct cell references. If you still want your formulas to be more readable, you can then rebuild them using names or structured references.

Let's look at an example of a structured reference formula. Figure 12-23 shows a SUM formula that we created by first typing **=SUM(**, then clicking cell B4, then typing another comma, and finally clicking cell C4. Because the data we want to use resides within a table and our formula is positioned in one of the same rows, Excel automatically uses structured references when we use the cursor to select cells while building formulas.

| H4 | | | f_x | =SUM(Regional08[[#This Row],[Qtr 1]],Regional08[[#This Row],[Qtr 2]]) | | | | | | | | | |

	A	B	C	D	E	F	G	H	I	J	K	L	M	N
1	Regional Sales Table													
2														
3	2008	Qtr 1	Qtr 2	Qtr 3	Qtr 4	Total		1st Half	2nd Half					
4	Region 1	1000	1050	1100	1150	4300		2050						
5	Region 2	1100	1150	1200	1250	4700								
6	Region 3	1200	1250	1300	1350	5100								
7	Region 4	1300	1350	1400	1450	5500								
8	Total	4600	4800	5000	5200	19600								
9														
10														
11														
12														
13														

Figure 12-23 We created the formula in cell H4 by dragging to select cells in the table.

The result shown in the formula bar appears to be much more complex than necessary because we could just type **=SUM(B4:C4)** to produce the same result in this worksheet. But the structured formula is still quite easy to create using the mouse, and it has the distinct advantage of being able to automatically accommodate even the most radical changes to the table, which ordinary formulas are not nearly as good at accommodating.

Let's examine a little more closely the structured reference contained within the parentheses of the SUM function shown in Figure 12-23. The entire reference string shown here is equivalent to the expression (B4,C4), which combines the cells on both sides of the comma. The portion of the reference string in bold represents a single, complete structured reference.

`Regional08[[#This Row],[Qtr 1]],Regional08[[#This Row],[Qtr 2]])`

Here's how the reference string breaks down:

- The first item, Regional08, is the table specifier, which is followed by an opening bracket. Just like parentheses in functions, brackets in structured references always come in pairs. The table name is a little bit like a function, in that it always includes a pair of brackets that enclose the rest of the reference components. This tells Excel that everything within the brackets applies to the Regional08 table.

- The second item, [#This Row], is one of the five special item specifiers and tells Excel that the following reference components apply only to those portions of the table that fall in the current row. (Obviously, this wouldn't work if the formula were located above or below the table.) This represents an application of implicit intersection (see "Getting Explicit About Intersections" on page 452).

- The third item, [Qtr 1], is a column specifier. In our example, this corresponds to the range B4:B7. However, because it follows the [#This Row] specifier, only those cells in the range that happen to be in the same row as the formula are included, or cell B4 in the example.

- The second reference follows the second comma in the string and is essentially the same as the first, specifying the other end of the range, or cell C4 in the example.

Understanding Structured Reference Syntax

Here are some of the general rules governing the creation of structured references:

- Table naming rules are the same as those of defined names. See "Naming Cells and Cell Ranges" on page 441.

- You must enclose all specifiers in matching brackets.

- To make structured references easier to read, you can add a single space character in any or all of the following locations:

  - After the first opening (left) bracket (but not in subsequent opening brackets)

  - Before the last closing (right) bracket (but not in subsequent closing brackets)

  - After a comma

Chapter 12

- Column headers are always treated as text strings in structured references, even if the column header is a number.

- You cannot use formulas in brackets.

- You need to use double brackets in column header specifiers that contain one of the following special characters: tab, line feed, carriage return, comma, colon, period, opening bracket, closing bracket, pound sign, single quotation mark, double quotation mark, left brace, right brace, dollar sign, caret, ampersand, asterisk, plus sign, equal sign, minus sign, greater than symbol, less than symbol, and division sign; for example, Sales[[$Canadian]]. Space characters are permitted.

Using Operators with Column Specifiers

You can use three *reference operators* with column specifiers in structured references—a colon (:), which is the range operator; a comma (,), which is the union operator; and a space character ( ), which is the intersection operator.

For example, the following formula calculates the average combined sales for quarters 1 and 4 using a comma (the union operator) between the two structured references:

```
=AVERAGE(Regional08[Qtr 1],Regional08[Qtr 4])
```

The following formula calculates the average sales for quarters 2 and 3 by using colons (the range operator) to specify contiguous ranges of cells in each of the two structured references within the parentheses and by using a space character (the intersection operator) between the two structured references, which combines only the cells that overlap (Qtr 2 and Qtr 3):

```
=AVERAGE(Regional08[[Qtr 1]:[Qtr 3]] Regional08[[Qtr 2]:[Qtr 4]])
```

About the Special Item Specifiers

Excel provides five special codes you can use with your structured references that refer to specific parts of a table. You've already seen the special item specifier [#This Row] being used in previous examples. Here are all five special item specifiers:

- **[#This Row]** This specifier identifies cells at the intersection created in conjunction with column specifiers; you cannot use it with any of the other special item specifiers in this list.

- **[#Totals]** This refers to cells in the total row (if one exists) and otherwise returns a null value.

- **[#Headers]** This refers only to cells in the header row.

- **[#Data]** This refers only to cells in the data area between the header row and the total row.

- **[#All]** This refers to the entire table, including the header row and the total row.

Are Your References Qualified?

Two kinds of structured references exist: *qualified* and *unqualified*. Generally, you can use unqualified references in formulas that you construct within a table because the formulas are insulated from errors that may be introduced by inserting, deleting, or moving cells by virtue of the robust infrastructure of the table. When building formulas outside the protective structure of a table, it is advisable to use qualified references to protect against such errors. Here is an example of an unqualified reference that will work only within a table, followed by a qualified reference that produces the same result outside the table:

```
=[Qtr 1]/[Total]
```

```
=Regional08[[#This Row],[Qtr 1]]/Regional08[[#This Row],[Total]]
```

Using Formula AutoComplete with Structured References

As you enter your formulas, the Formula AutoComplete feature is there to help you along by displaying lists of applicable functions, defined names, and structured reference specifiers as you type. For example, Figure 12-24 shows a formula being constructed using a SUM function, along with an AutoComplete drop-down list displaying all the defined items that are available that begin with the opening bracket character (also called a *display trigger* in AutoComplete parlance) that you just typed in the formula. Notice that the list includes all the column specifiers for the example table, as well as all the special item specifiers, all of which begin with a bracket.

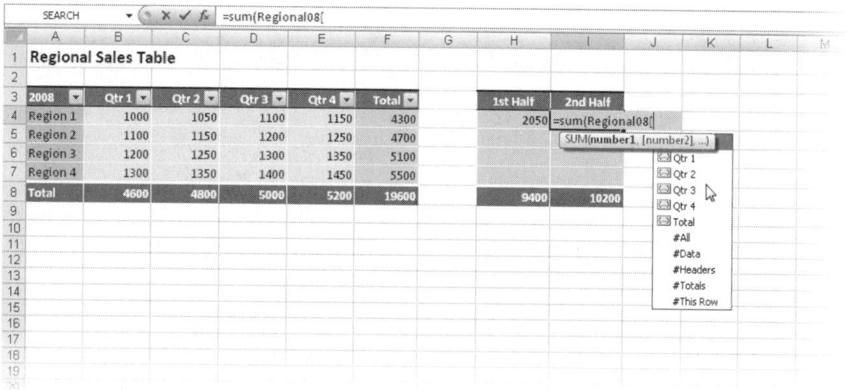

Figure 12-24 Structured reference specifiers automatically appear in the AutoComplete drop-down list if they are applicable when creating a formula.

To enter one of the items in the list in the formula, double-click it. The Formula AutoComplete list will most likely open more than once as you type formulas, offering any and all options that begin with the entered letters or display triggers. For example, the AutoComplete list appeared after we typed **=S** with a list of all the items beginning with that letter and again after typing the **R** in Regional08.

For more information, see "Using Formula AutoComplete" on page 440.

Filling and Copying Structured References

As a rule, structured references do not adjust like relative cell references when you copy or fill them—the reference remains the same. The exceptions to this rule occur with column specifiers when you use the fill handle to copy fully qualified structured references outside the table structure. For example, in the worksheet shown in Figure 12-25, we dragged the fill handle to copy the % of Total formula in cell K4 to the right, and the column specifiers in the formulas adjusted accordingly.

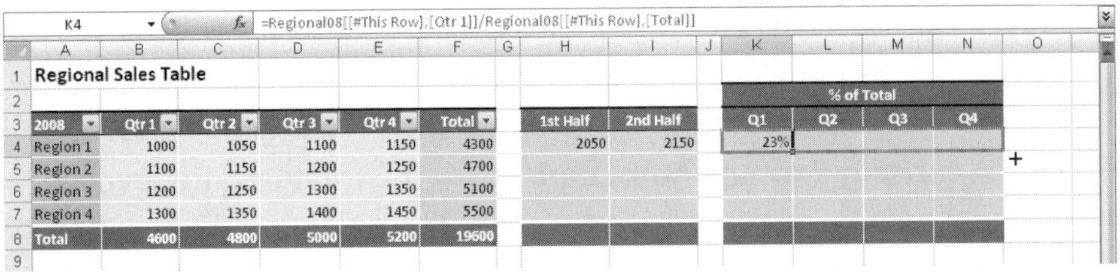

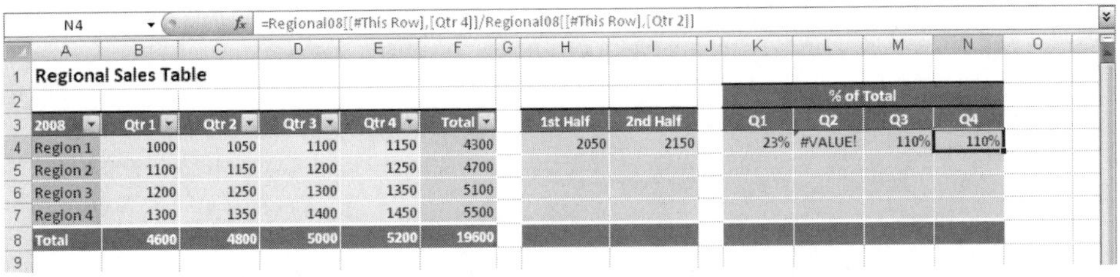

Figure 12-25 You can drag the fill handle to extend structured reference formulas into adjacent cells, but they behave a little bit differently than regular formulas.

The results illustrate some interesting structured reference behavior. Notice that the first formula shown in cell K4 divides the value in the Qtr 1 column by the value in the Total column. After we filled to the right, the resulting formula in cell N4 divides the value in the Qtr 4 column by the value in the Qtr 2 column. How did this happen?

As far as filling cells is concerned, tables act like little traps—you can check in, but you can't check out. The top formula shown in Figure 12-25 has two column specifiers: Qtr 1 and Total. When we filled to the right, the Qtr 1 reference extended the way we wanted, extending to Qtr 2, Qtr 3, and Qtr 4 in each cell to the right. However, the Total reference, instead of extending to the right (G4, H4, I4) like a regular series fill would, "wrapped" around the table (2008, Qtr 1 and Qtr 2), resulting in the formula displayed in cell N4 at the bottom of Figure 12-25. This is interesting behavior, and we're sure people will figure out ways to put it to good use.

For more information about using the fill handle, see "Filling and Creating Data Series" on page 211.

What we need is a way to "lock" the Total column reference, but Excel doesn't offer any way to create "absolute" column specifiers like we can with cell references. We can substitute a cell reference for the entire Total reference, as shown in Figure 12-26. We used a mixed reference in this case, specifying the absolute column $F but letting the row number adjust so we could fill down as well.

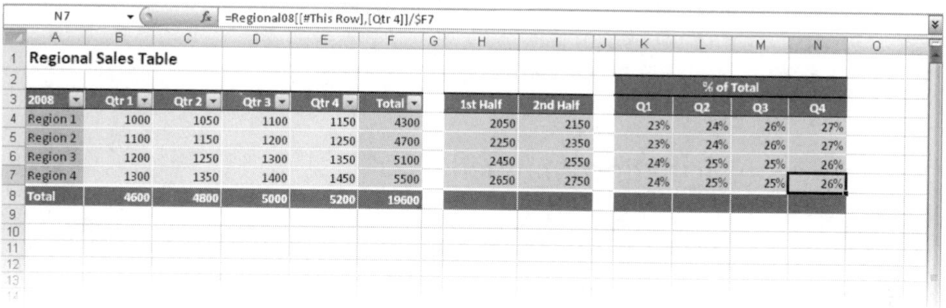

	N7			f_x =Regional08[[#This Row],[Qtr 4]]/$F7												
	A	B	C	D	E	F	G	H	I	J	K	L	M	N	O	
1	Regional Sales Table															
2													% of Total			
3	2008	Qtr 1	Qtr 2	Qtr 3	Qtr 4	Total		1st Half	2nd Half		Q1	Q2	Q3	Q4		
4	Region 1	1000	1050	1100	1150	4300		2050	2150		23%	24%	26%	27%		
5	Region 2	1100	1150	1200	1250	4700		2250	2350		23%	24%	26%	27%		
6	Region 3	1200	1250	1300	1350	5100		2450	2550		24%	25%	25%	26%		
7	Region 4	1300	1350	1400	1450	5500		2650	2750		24%	25%	25%	26%		
8	Total	4600	4800	5000	5200	19600										
9																
10																
11																
12																
13																

Figure 12-26 We replaced the second structured reference with an absolute cell reference to make filling these formulas work properly.

Note that if we were to select cell H4 in Figure 12-26 and drag the fill handle down, the formulas in each cell would not appear to adjust at all, and yet they would work perfectly. (The formula in cell H4 appears in Figure 12-23.) This is because explicit intersection, the built-in behavior of column specifiers, and the functionality of the [#This Row] specifier eliminate the need to adjust row references.

> **Note**
>
> When dragging the fill handle to the right in a cell containing a structured reference formula, pressing Ctrl prevents the column specifiers from adjusting as they usually would and instead copies the formula to the right without adjustment.

Worksheet Calculation

When you change the value in any of the cells to which a formula refers, Excel updates the displayed values of the formula as well. This updating process is called *recalculation*, and it affects only those cells containing references to cells that have changed. By default, Excel recalculates whenever you make changes to a cell. If a large number of cells must be recalculated, the word *Calculating* appears in the status bar, along with a percentage of progress meter if it's going to take a particularly long time. You can interrupt the recalculation process simply by doing something, such as using commands or making cell entries; Excel pauses and then resumes recalculation when you are finished.

Chapter 12

> **Note**
>
> When you open an Excel 2007 workbook, Excel recalculates only those formulas that depend on cell values that have changed. However, because of changes in the way Excel 2007 recalculates, when you open a workbook that was created using a previous version of Excel (or saved in a previous Excel file format), Excel recalculates all the formulas in the workbook each time you open it. To avoid this, save it in the Excel 2007 (.xlsx or .xlsm) file format.

Recalculating Manually

To save time, particularly when you are making entries into a large workbook with many formulas, you can switch from automatic to manual recalculation; that is, Excel will recalculate only when you tell it to do so. To set manual recalculation, click the Calculation Options button on the Formulas tab on the Ribbon, and choose the Manual option. You can also click the Microsoft Office Button, Excel Options, and then select the Formulas category to display the additional options shown in Figure 12-27.

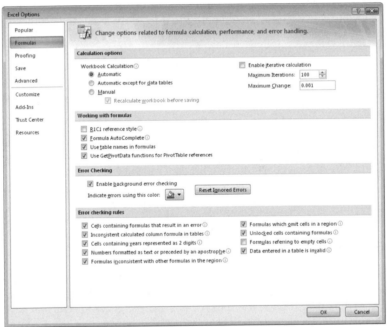

Figure 12-27 The Formulas category in the Excel Options dialog box controls worksheet calculation and iteration.

Here are a few facts to remember about calculation options:

- With worksheet recalculation set to manual, the status bar displays the word *Calculate* if you make a change; click it to initiate recalculation immediately.

- The Recalculate Workbook Before Saving check box helps make sure the most current values are stored on disk.

- To turn off automatic recalculation only for data tables, select the Automatic Except For Data Tables option. For more information, see "Using Data Tables" on page 583.

Calculate Now

- To recalculate all open workbooks, click the Calculate Now button in the Calculation group on the Formulas tab on the Ribbon, or press F9.

Calculate Sheet

- To calculate only the active worksheet in a workbook, click the Calculate Sheet button in the Calculation group on the Formulas tab on the Ribbon, or press Shift+F9.

Multithreaded Calculation

If you have a computer with multiple processors or a hyperthreaded processor, Excel takes full advantage of the additional power by dividing the workload among available processors. Click the Microsoft Office Button, Excel Options, Advanced category, and look in the Formulas area. Excel automatically detects additional processors and displays the total number adjacent to the Use All Processors On This Computer option. The number of processors also appears in the status bar next to the word *Calculating*, if you have enough formulas to slow the calculation process enough for it to appear. If you want, you can turn this option off if you want to reserve some of your computer's processing bandwidth for other programs you need to run simultaneously.

Calculating Part of a Formula

You might want to see the result of just one part of a complex formula if, for example, you are tracking down a discrepancy. To change only part of a formula to a value, select the part you want to change, and press F9. You also can use this technique to change selected cell references in formulas to their values. Figure 12-28 shows an example.

If you're just verifying your figures, press the Esc key to discard the edited formula. Otherwise, if you press Enter, you replace the selected portion of the formula.

Chapter 12

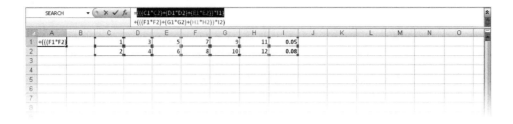

Figure 12-28 Select any part of a formula, and press F9 to convert it to its resulting value.

> **Note**
>
> You can also click the Evaluate Formula button on the Formulas tab to troubleshoot your workbook models. For more information, see "Evaluating and Auditing Formulas" on page 243.

Working with Circular References

A *circular reference* is a formula that depends on its own value. The most obvious type is a formula that contains a reference to the same cell in which it's entered. For example, if you type **=C1-A1** in cell A1, Excel displays the error message shown in Figure 12-29. After you click OK, Excel opens the Help dialog box, which displays a pertinent topic.

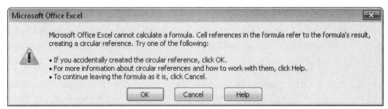

Figure 12-29 This error message appears when you attempt to enter a formula that contains a circular reference.

If a circular reference warning surprises you, this usually means you made an error in a formula. If the error isn't obvious, verify the cells that the formula refers to using the built-in formula-auditing features. For details, see "Auditing and Documenting Worksheets" on page 241.

When a circular reference is present in the current worksheet, the status bar displays the text *Circular References* followed by the cell address, indicating the location of the circular reference on the current worksheet. If *Circular References* appears without a cell address, then the circular reference is located on another worksheet.

As you can see in Figure 12-30, when you click the arrow next to the Error Checking button on the Formulas tab and click Circular Reference, any circular references that exist on the current worksheet are listed on a menu that appears only if a circular reference is present. Click the reference listed on this menu to activate the offending cell.

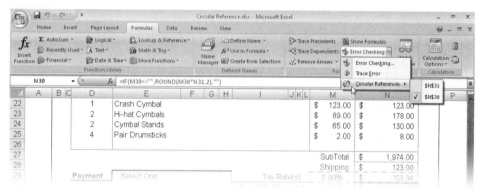

Figure 12-30 The Circular References menu appears if any circular references are present.

You can resolve many circular references. Some circular formulas are useful or even essential, such as the set of circular references shown in Figure 12-31. These formulas are circular because the formula in cell M30 depends on the value in M31, and the formula in M31 depends on the value in M30.

Figure 12-31 illustrates a useful circular reference scenario called *convergence*: The difference between results decreases with each iterative calculation. In the opposite process, called *divergence*, the difference between results increases with each calculation.

When Excel detects a circular reference, tracer arrows appear on the worksheet. To draw additional arrows to track down the source of an unintentional circular reference, select the offending cell, and then click Trace Precedents on the Formulas tab to draw tracer arrows to the next level of precedent cells, as shown in Figure 12-31.

For more information about tracer arrows and other auditing features, see "Auditing and Documenting Worksheets" on page 241.

You'll find the Circular Reference.xlsx file in the Sample Files section of the companion CD.

Chapter 12

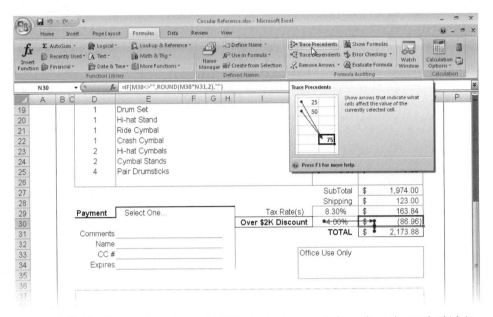

Figure 12-31 The discount formula in cell M29 is circular because it depends on the total, which in turn depends on the discount value in M29.

After you dismiss the error message shown in Figure 12-29, the formula will not resolve until you allow Excel to recalculate in controlled steps. To do so, click the Microsoft Office Button, Excel Options, Formulas category, and in the Calculation Options section, select the Enable Iterative Calculation check box. Excel recalculates all the cells in any open worksheets that contain a circular reference.

If necessary, the recalculation repeats the number of times specified in the Maximum Iterations box (100 is the default). Each time Excel recalculates the formulas, the results in the cells get closer to the correct values. If necessary, Excel continues until the difference between iterations is less than the number typed in the Maximum Change text box (0.001 is the default). Thus, using the default settings, Excel recalculates either a maximum of 100 times or until the values change less than 0.001 between iterations, whichever comes first.

If the word *Calculate* appears in the status bar after the iterations are finished, more iterations are possible. You can accept the current result, increase the number of iterations, or lower the Maximum Change threshold. Excel does not repeat the "Cannot Resolve Circular Reference" error message if it fails to resolve the reference. You must determine when the answer is close enough. Excel can perform iterations in seconds, but in complex circular situations, you might want to set the Calculation option to Manual; otherwise, Excel recalculates the circular references every time you make a cell entry.

The Solver add-in, a "what-if" analysis tool, offers more control and precision when working with complex iterative calculations. For details, see "Using the Solver" on page 601.

Understanding the Precision of Numeric Values

Here are three interesting facts about numeric precision in Excel:

- Excel stores numbers with as much as 15-digit accuracy and converts any digits after the 15th to zeros.

- Excel drops any digits after the 15 in a decimal fraction.

- Excel uses scientific notation to display numbers that are too long for their cells.

TROUBLESHOOTING

Rounded values in my worksheet don't add up.

Your worksheet can appear erroneous if you use rounded values. For example, if you use cell formatting to display numbers in currency format with two decimal places, Excel displays the value 10.006 as the rounded value $10.01. If you add 10.006 and 10.006, the correct result is 20.012. If all of these numbers are formatted as currency, however, the worksheet displays the rounded values $10.01 and $10.01, and the rounded value of the result is $20.01. The result is correct, as far as rounding goes, but its appearance might be unacceptable for a particular purpose, such as a presentation or an audit.

You can correct this problem by changing the currency format, or you can click the Microsoft Office Button, Excel Options, Advanced category and in the section entitled When Calculating This Workbook, select the Set Precision As Displayed check box. However, you should select this check box only with extreme caution because it permanently changes the underlying values in your worksheet to their displayed values. For example, if a cell containing the value 10.006 is formatted as currency, selecting the Set Precision As Displayed check box permanently changes the value to 10.01. For more information, see "Formatting Numbers" on page 298.

Table 12-3 contains examples of how Excel treats integers and decimal fractions longer than 15 digits when they are typed in cells with the default column width of 8.43 characters.

Table 12-3 Examples of Numeric Precision

Typed Entry	Displayed Value	Stored Value
123456789012345678	1.23457E+17	123456789012345000
1.23456789012345678	1.234568	1.23456789012345
1234567890.12345678	1234567890	1234567890.12345
123456789012345.678	1.23457E+14	123456789012345

Excel can calculate positive values as large as 9.99E+307 and approximately as small as 1.00E−307. If a formula results in a value outside this range, Excel stores the number as text and assigns a #NUM! error value to the formula cell.

Using Arrays

Arrays are familiar concepts to computer programmers. Simply defined, an *array* is a collection of items. Excel is one of the few applications that facilitate array operations, in which items that comprise an array can be individually or collectively addressed in simple mathematical terms. Here is some basic array terminology you should know:

- An *array formula* acts on two or more sets of values, called *array arguments*, to return either a single result or multiple results.

- An *array range* is a block of cells that share a common array formula.

- An *array constant* is a specially organized list of constant values that you can use as arguments in array formulas.

Arrays perform calculations in a way unlike anything else. You can use them for worksheet security, alarm monitors, linear regression tables, and much more.

One-Dimensional Arrays

The easiest way to learn about arrays is to look at a few examples. For instance, you can calculate the averages shown in Figure 12-32 by entering a single array formula.

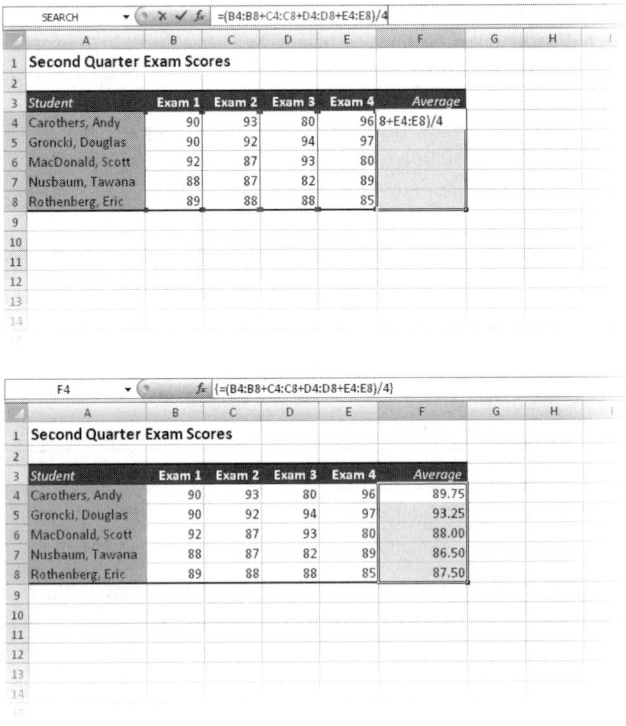

Figure 12-32 We entered a single array formula in the selected range F4:F8.

This particular example might be used to help protect the formulas from tampering because modifying individual formulas in cells that are part of an array is impossible. To enter this formula, do the following:

1. Select the range F4:F8.

2. Type the formula in the formula bar, as shown in Figure 12-32.

3. Press Ctrl+Shift+Enter.

The resulting single array formula exists in five cells at once. Although the array formula seems to be five separate formulas, you can't make changes to any one formula without selecting the entire formula—that is, the entire range F4:F8.

You can identify an array formula by looking at the formula bar. If the active cell contains an array formula, the entire formula, including the equal sign, is enclosed in braces—{ }—in the formula bar, as you can see in Figure 12-32.

Array Formula Rules

To enter an array formula, first select the cell or range that will contain the results. If the formula produces multiple results, you must select a range the same size and shape as the range or ranges on which you perform your calculations.

Follow these guidelines when entering and working with array formulas:

- Press Ctrl+Shift+Enter to lock in an array formula. Excel will then place a set of curly braces around the formula in the formula bar to indicate that it's an array formula. Don't type the braces; if you do, Excel interprets your entry as text.

- You can't edit, clear, or move individual cells in an array range, and you can't insert or delete cells. You must treat the cells in the array range as a single unit and edit them all at once.

- To edit an array, select the entire array, click the formula bar, and edit the formula. Then press Ctrl+Shift+Enter to lock in the formula.

- To clear an array, select the entire array, and press Delete.

- To select an entire array, click any cell in the array, and press Ctrl+/.

- To move an array range, you must select the entire array and either cut and paste the selection or drag the selection to a new location.

- You can't cut, clear, or edit part of an array, but you can assign different formats to individual cells in the array. You can also copy cells from an array range and paste them in another area of your worksheet.

Two-Dimensional Arrays

In the preceding example, the array formula resulted in a vertical, one-dimensional array. You also can create arrays that include two or more columns and rows, otherwise known as *two-dimensional arrays*. Figure 12-33 shows an example.

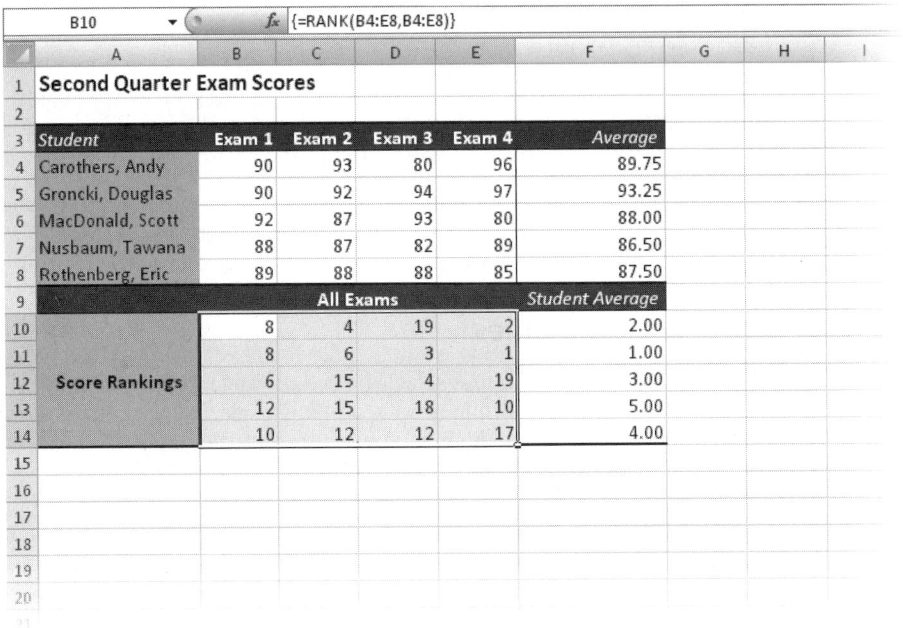

	B10	▼		f_x	{=RANK(B4:E8,B4:E8)}			
	A	B	C	D	E	F	G	H	I
1	**Second Quarter Exam Scores**								
2									
3	*Student*	**Exam 1**	**Exam 2**	**Exam 3**	**Exam 4**	*Average*			
4	Carothers, Andy	90	93	80	96	89.75			
5	Groncki, Douglas	90	92	94	97	93.25			
6	MacDonald, Scott	92	87	93	80	88.00			
7	Nusbaum, Tawana	88	87	82	89	86.50			
8	Rothenberg, Eric	89	88	88	85	87.50			
9			**All Exams**			*Student Average*			
10		8	4	19	2	2.00			
11		8	6	3	1	1.00			
12	**Score Rankings**	6	15	4	19	3.00			
13		12	15	18	10	5.00			
14		10	12	12	17	4.00			
15									
16									
17									
18									
19									
20									
21									

Figure 12-33 We used a two-dimensional array formula in B10:E14 to compute the rank of each exam score. A similar one-dimensional array appears in F10:F14.

To enter a two-dimensional array, do the following:

1. Select a range to contain your array that is the same size and shape as the range you want to use.

2. Type your formula in the formula bar, and press Ctrl+Shift+Enter.

> **Note**
> Unfortunately, you can't create three-dimensional arrays across multiple worksheets in workbooks.

Single-Cell Array Formulas

You can perform calculations on a vast collection of values within a single cell by using an array formula that produces a single value as a result. For example, you can create a simple single-cell array formula to multiply the values in a range of cells by the values in an adjacent range, as shown in Figure 12-34.

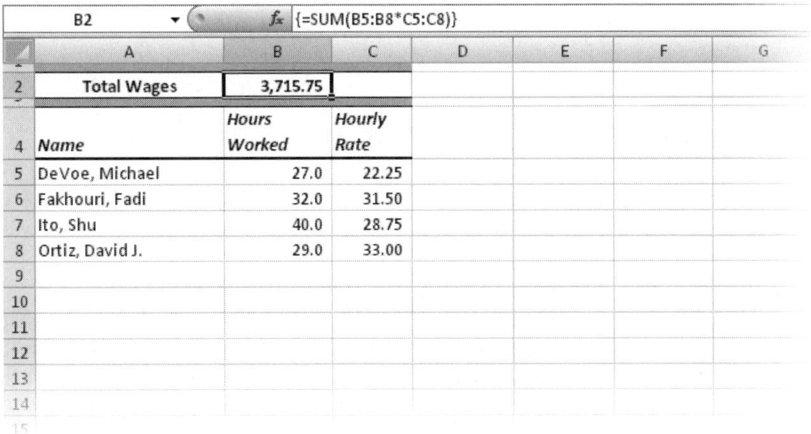

Figure 12-34 To calculate total wages paid, we used a single-cell array formula in B3 to multiply hours worked by wages due for each employee individually.

In the example shown in Figure 12-34, you must enter the formula as an array formula (by pressing Ctrl+Shift+Enter); entering it as a regular formula results in a #VALUE error. Our example shows a tiny worksheet, but an array formula like this can make fast work of giant tables.

Using Array Constants

An array constant is a specially organized list of values that you can use as arguments in your array formulas. Array constants can consist of numbers, text, or logical values. Although Excel adds braces for you when you enter array formulas, you must type braces around array constants and separate their elements with commas and semicolons. Commas indicate values in separate columns, and semicolons indicate values in separate rows. The formula in Figure 12-35, for example, performs nine computations in one cell.

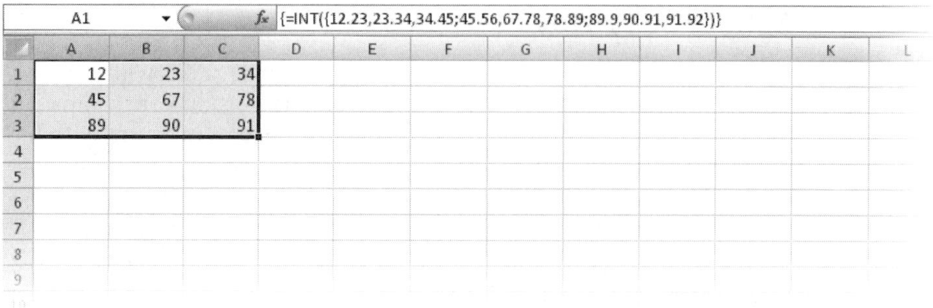

| A1 | | ▼ | fx | {=INT({12.23,23.34,34.45;45.56,67.78,78.89;89.9,90.91,91.92})} |

Figure 12-35 An array constant is the argument for this array formula.

A Single-Cell Array Formula Application

Suppose you want the total number of items in a table that satisfy two criteria. You want to know how many transactions of more than $1,000 occurred after a specified date. You could add a column to the table containing an IF function to find each transaction that satisfies these criteria and then total the results of that column. A simpler way to do this is to use a single array formula like this one: =SUM((A1:A100>39448)*(C1:C100>999)).

The 39448 in the formula is the serial date value for January 1, 2008. Enter the formula by pressing Ctrl+Shift+Enter. Each item in the first parenthetical expression evaluates to either a 1 (TRUE) or a 0 (FALSE), depending on the date; each item in the second parenthetical expression evaluates also to either a 1 or a 0, depending on whether its value is greater than 999. The formula then multiplies the 1s and 0s, and when both evaluate to TRUE, the resulting value is 1. The SUM function adds the 1s and gives you the total. You can add more criteria by adding more parenthetical elements to the formula; any expression that evaluates to FALSE (0) eliminates that transaction because anything multiplied by 0 is 0.

You could enhance this formula in several ways. For example, replace the serial date number with the DATEVALUE function so you can use "*1/1/2008*" as an argument instead of having to find the date value yourself. Even better, use cell references as arguments to each element so you can type variable criteria in cells rather than editing the formula. For information about the DATEVALUE function, see Chapter 15, "Formatting and Calculating Date and Time."

To enter a formula using an array constant, follow these steps:

1. Select a range of cells the size you need to contain the result. In Figure 12-35, the argument to the INT function contains three groups (separated by semicolons) of three values (separated by commas), which produces a three-row, three-column range.

2. Enter an equal sign to begin the formula and, optionally, a function name and opening parenthesis.

3. Type the array argument enclosed in braces to indicate that the enclosed values make up an array constant. If you entered a function, type its closing parenthesis.

4. Press Ctrl+Shift+Enter. The resulting array formula contains two sets of curly braces—one set encloses the array constant, and the other encloses the entire array formula.

When entering array constants, remember that commas between array elements place those elements in separate columns, and semicolons between array elements place those elements in separate rows.

Understanding Array Expansion

When you use arrays as arguments in a formula, all your arrays should have the same dimensions. If the dimensions of your array arguments or array ranges do not match, Excel often expands the arguments for you. For example, to multiply all the values in cells A1:B5 by 10, you can use either of the following array formulas: { =A1:B5*10} or { ={ 1,2;3,4;5,6;7,8;9,10}*10}.

Note that neither of these two formulas are balanced; ten values are on the left side of the multiplication operator but only one is on the right. Excel expands the second argument to match the size and shape of the first. In the preceding example, the first formula is equivalent to { =A1:B5*{ 10,10;10,10;10,10;10,10;10,10} }, and the second is equivalent to { ={ 1,2;3,4;5,6;7,8;9,10}*{ 10,10;10,10;10,10;10,10;10,10} }.

When you work with two or more sets of multivalue arrays, each set must have the same number of rows as the argument with the greatest number of rows, and each must have the same number of columns as the argument with the greatest number of columns.

Linking Workbooks

Creating dynamic links between workbooks using external reference formulas provides a number of advantages. For example, you could break a large, complex company budget model into more manageable departmental models. Then you could link all the departmental workbooks (supporting workbooks) to a master budget workbook (a dependent workbook). In addition to creating more manageable and flexible models, linked workbooks can save recalculation time and memory.

The following sections discuss some special considerations to be aware of when working with workbooks linked by external reference formulas. For more information about external references, see "Creating References to Other Worksheets in the Same Workbook" on page 430 and "Creating References to Worksheets in Other Workbooks" on page 430.

Saving Linked Workbooks

When you create a set of linked workbooks, you should save the supporting workbooks before you save the dependent workbooks. For example, suppose you are modeling your company's 2008 budget in an unsaved workbook called Book1. When you save the workbook, you give it the name Budget.

Now suppose you have another active workbook in which you plan to enter actual (as opposed to budgeted) expenditures; you have already saved the workbook with the name Actual. This workbook contains links to your Budget workbook and, therefore, depends on the Budget workbook for some of its information. When you first created these links, the Budget workbook was identified as Book1.

If you save Book1 as Budget while the Actual workbook is still open, all references to Book1 in the Actual workbook change automatically to Budget. For example, if Actual contains the reference =[Book1]Sheet1!$A$1, the reference changes to ='[Budget.xlsx]Sheet1'!$A$1.

If you try to close the dependent Actual workbook before you save the supporting Book1 (Budget) workbook, however, you see the "Save Actual with references to unsaved documents?" warning. Click OK to save and close it. When you then save Book1 as Budget, Excel doesn't update the references to Book1 in the Actual workbook because it isn't open; the formulas continue to reference Book1. When you reopen Actual, Excel first displays a security warning, alerting you that automatic links are present. Click the Options button to display the dialog box shown in Figure 12-36, where you can select Enable This Content to allow linking formulas to function.

After you enable links, Excel then displays a message box that prompts you to update the linked information. If you click the Edit Links button, the dialog box shown in Figure 12-37 appears.

Excel is, of course, unable to find Book1. You need to click the Change Source button to locate the Actual workbook so Excel can reestablish the links.

Opening a Dependent Workbook

When you save a workbook that contains dependent formulas, Excel stores the most recent results of those formulas. If you open and edit the supporting workbook after closing the dependent workbook, the values of edited cells in the supporting workbook might be different. When you open the dependent workbook again, the workbook contains the old values of the external references in the dependent formulas, and Excel displays a security warning, alerting you that automatic links are present. Click the Options button to display the dialog box shown in Figure 12-36, where you can select Enable This Content to update the linked formulas. Excel then searches for the supporting workbook. If it finds the workbook, Excel reads the supporting values and updates the dependent formulas in the dependent workbook. Excel does not open the supporting workbook; it merely reads the appropriate values from it.

If Excel can't find the supporting workbook, it displays the alert "This workbook contains one or more links that cannot be updated." You can click Continue to open the workbook anyway, or you can click the Edit Links button to display the dialog box shown in Figure 12-37.

Figure 12-36 Excel disables external links by default, requiring your intervention.

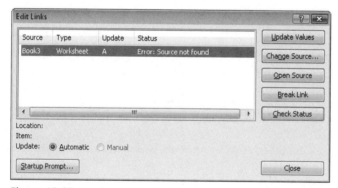

Figure 12-37 Use the Edit Links dialog box to manage all your external links.

Editing Links

 You can open supporting workbooks, as well as specify different supporting workbooks, when you click the Edit Links button, located in the Connections group on the Data tab on the Ribbon. When you do so, a dialog box like the one shown in Figure 12-37. Here is some helpful information about using the Edit Links dialog box:

- An A in the Status column indicates a link that is updated automatically.

- An M in the Status column indicates a manual link that isn't updated until you click Update Values.

- Click Open Source to open the supporting workbook.

Chapter 12

- Click Change Source to select a different supporting workbook.

- Click Break Link to convert all existing external references in formulas to their current values. You can't undo this action, so proceed with caution.

- Click Update Values to fetch the latest figures from the supporting workbook without having to open it.

- You can link objects and documents created in other applications, such as Word, to Excel worksheets and charts. When you do so, the Type column displays the application name and the object type.

Clicking the Startup Prompt button displays the Startup Prompt dialog box shown in Figure 12-38, which you can use to specify how links are handled whenever the workbook is opened.

Figure 12-38 The Startup Prompt dialog box lets you customize the startup behavior of external links.

Ordinarily, Excel displays a security alert when you open a workbook containing linking formulas, which individual Excel users can choose to suppress on their computers. If you would prefer to suppress the security alert for the current workbook, you can do so by selecting either Don't Display The Alert And Don't Update Automatic Links or Don't Display The Alert And Update Links in the Startup Prompt dialog box.

> **Note**
>
> To change the default behavior of disabling automatic links, click the Microsoft Office Button, Excel Options, Advanced category, and then in the General section, clear the Ask To Update Automatic Links option.

Copying, Cutting, and Pasting in Linked Workbooks

You can use relative or absolute references to cells in other workbooks as you do in a single workbook. Relative and absolute references to cells in supporting workbooks respond to the Copy, Cut, and Paste commands and toolbar buttons in much the same way as references to cells in the same workbook do.

For example, suppose you type the formula **=[Form2.xlsx]Sheet1!F1** in cell A1 on Sheet1 of Form1 and then use Copy and Paste to copy this formula to cell B1. The formula in cell B1 becomes =[Form2.xlsx]Sheet1!G1. The original formula changes when you copy it to cell B1 because the reference to cell F1 is relative. However, if the formula in cell A1 of Form1 contained an absolute reference, such as =[Form2.xlsx]Sheet1!$F$1, the reference in the copied formula would not change.

Copying and Pasting Between Workbooks

When you copy a dependent formula from one workbook to another and that formula includes a relative reference to a third workbook, Excel adjusts the reference to reflect the new position of the formula. For example, suppose that cell A1 in Form1 contains the formula =[Form2.xlsx]Sheet1!A1. If you copy and paste that formula into cell B5 in Form3, the result is the formula =[Form2.xlsx]Sheet1!B5. Excel adjusts the formula to reflect its new relative position.

If you copy a formula that contains an absolute reference to another workbook, the formula remains the same. For example, suppose cell A1 in Form1 contains the formula =[Form2.xlsx]Sheet1!$A$1. If you copy and paste that formula into cell B5 in Form3, the resulting formula is the same.

Even if you copy a dependent formula to the workbook to which the formula refers, it's still a dependent formula. For example, if you copy the formula =[Form2.xlsx]Sheet1!$A$1 from cell A1 of Form1 to cell A3 on Sheet1 of Form2, the resulting formula is essentially the same, except that the book reference isn't necessary because the formula is in the same workbook. As a result, the formula becomes =Sheet1!$A$1.

Cutting and Pasting Between Workbooks

Excel does not adjust the relative references in a formula when you cut it from one workbook and paste it in another, as it does when you copy a formula. For example, suppose that cell A1 on Sheet1 of Form1 contains the formula =[Form2.xlsx]Sheet1!A1. If you cut that formula and paste it into cell B5 of Form3, the formula does not change.

When you cut and paste cells, Excel usually adjusts any references to those cells in the formulas of the workbook. Dependent formulas, however, do not follow the same rules. When you cut and paste a cell referred to by a dependent formula in a closed workbook, that formula isn't adjusted to reflect the change.

For example, suppose you create the formula =[Form2.xlsx]Sheet1!A10 in cell A1 in Form1. If you close Form1 and use Cut and Paste to move the entry to cell B10 of Form2, the formula in cell A1 of Form1 remains the same. You might expect the link to be broken because the worksheet containing the formula was closed when you modified the referenced cell. However, Excel manages to keep track of everything.

Creating Conditional Tests

A conditional test formula compares two numbers, functions, formulas, labels, or logical values. You can use conditional tests to flag values that fall outside a given threshold, for example. You can use simple mathematical and logical operators to construct logical formulas, or you can use an assortment of built-in functions. For information about using conditional test functions, see "Understanding Logical Functions" on page 507.

> You might also be able to satisfy some of your conditional curiosities by using the conditional formatting feature in Excel. For details, see "Formatting Conditionally" on page 284.

Conditional Formatting ▾

Each of the following formulas performs a rudimentary conditional test:

```
=A1>A2
=5-3<5*2
=AVERAGE(B1:B6)=SUM(6,7,8)
=C2="Female"
=COUNT(A1:A10)=COUNT(B1:B10)
=LEN(A1)=10
```

Every conditional test must include at least one logical operator, which defines the relationship between elements of the conditional test. For example, in the conditional test A1>A2, the greater than (>) logical operator compares the values in cells A1 and A2. Table 12-4 lists the six logical operators.

Table 12-4 Logical Operators

Operator	Definition
=	Equal to
>	Greater than
<	Less than
> =	Greater than or equal to
< =	Less than or equal to
< >	Not equal to

The result of a conditional test is either the logical value TRUE (1) or the logical value FALSE (0). For example, the conditional test =A1=10 returns TRUE if the value in A1 equals 10 or FALSE if A1 contains any other value.

Using the Conditional Sum and Lookup Wizards

Excel includes two useful tools called *wizards* that help you assemble frequently used yet confusing types of formulas. The Conditional Sum Wizard and the Lookup Wizard are provided as add-ins, which are special types of macros designed to integrate seamlessly into Excel. To see whether you have these wizards installed, look at the Formulas tab. If you see the Conditional Sum or Lookup buttons, as shown in Figure 12-39, then the respective wizards are installed.

Figure 12-39 The Conditional Sum and Lookup buttons live on the Formulas tab when installed.

If you don't see buttons for either add-in, click the Microsoft Office Button, Excel Options, and then click the Add-Ins category. In the Manage drop-down list at the bottom of the dialog box, select Excel Add-Ins, and then click the Go button to display the Add-Ins dialog box shown in Figure 12-40.

Figure 12-40 Use the Add-Ins dialog box to install additional tools.

In the Add-Ins dialog box, select the check boxes for both the Conditional Sum Wizard and the Lookup Wizard (and any others you want), and then click OK to install them. Excel will prompt you for permission to proceed—more than once, if you selected more than one add-in to install.

> **Note**
>
> The buttons you use to launch all but two of the Excel add-ins appear in the Solutions group on the Formulas tab; buttons for the Analysis Toolpak and the Solver add-in both appear in the Analysis group on the Data tab. For more information about the Analysis Toolpak, see Chapter 13, "Using Functions"; for more information about the Solver add-in, see Chapter 18, "Performing What-If Analysis."

Chapter 12

Creating Conditional Sum Formulas

The Conditional Sum Wizard creates formulas using the SUM and IF functions. This wizard not only makes constructing these formulas easier and faster but also shows you how these formulas are constructed so you can build your own conditional formulas without the wizard.

For more information about the IF function, see "Understanding Logical Functions" on page 507.

To build a conditional formula, follow these steps:

1. Select the table or list containing the values you want to use, and click the Conditional Sum button on the Formulas tab to display the wizard page shown in Figure 12-41.

   If you click anywhere in the table before you start the wizard, Excel automatically selects the current region for you. If Excel selects the correct region, click Next. Otherwise, drag to select the range you want to use. Remember to include the row and column labels. After clicking Next, the page shown on the left in Figure 12-42 appears.

2. In the Column To Sum list, select the name of the column from which you want to extract totals.

   This is why you need to select the labels in Step 1 of the wizard. If the column labels do not appear in the list, click Back, and reselect the range.

 You'll find the Pacific Sales Transactions.xlsx file in the Sample Files section of the companion CD.

3. Still in Step 2 of the wizard, specify the condition to use when selecting the values you want to include in the total. In the Column list, select the name of the column containing the labels you want to conditionally check, select an operator in the Is list, and then select a value in the This Value list.

   The contents of the This Value list change depending on the column selected in the Column list. The This Value list displays only the unique values in the selected column, ignoring duplicates.

4. Click Add Condition.

   The criteria you specify are added to the list at the bottom of the page. You can add as many as seven conditions. If you change your mind about any condition, select the condition from the list, and click Remove Condition. When you have finished editing conditions, click Next.

5. In Step 3 of the wizard, either choose Copy Just The Formula To A Single Cell or choose Copy The Formula And Conditional Values.

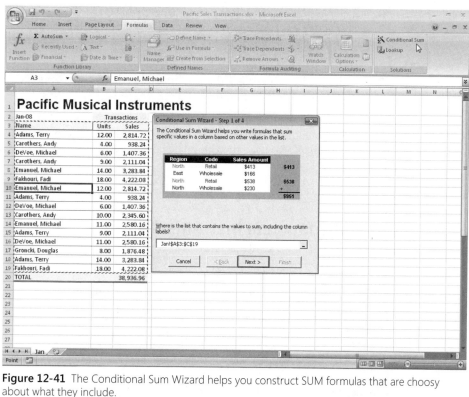

Figure 12-41 The Conditional Sum Wizard helps you construct SUM formulas that are choosy about what they include.

Conditional Sum Wizard - Step 2 of 4

Which column contains the values to sum? Select the column label.

Column to sum: Sales

Next, select a column you want to evaluate, and then type or select a value to compare with data in that column.

Column: Is: This value:

Name   =   Adams, Terry

Add Condition   Remove Condition

Name=Adams, Terry

Cancel   < Back   Next >   Finish

Conditional Sum Wizard - Step 3 of 4

The Conditional Sum Wizard can copy the formula to your worksheet in two different forms.

⦿ Copy just the formula to a single cell.

9,147.84

○ Copy the formula and conditional values.

Adams, Terry   9,147.84

Cancel   < Back   Next >   Finish

Figure 12-42 These wizard pages let you select the cells to include in your calculation.

6. Click Next, and then select the cell where you want to place the resulting formula. Or, if you chose the Copy The Formula And Conditional Values option in Step 3 of the wizard, the wizard adds an intervening step, letting you first select the cell where you want the conditional value to go.

7. Click Finish. Excel pastes the resulting formula (and the optional conditional value) in the worksheet in the locations specified.

You can add more conditional formulas, or if you already have a list of unique values you can use for comparison (such as salesperson names), you can copy the formula as needed (but only if you used the Copy The Formula And Conditional Values option in Step 3 of the wizard), as shown in Figure 12-43.

F4			fx {=SUM(IF($A$4:$A$19=E4,$C$4:$C$19,0))}						
	A	B	C	D	E	F	G	H	I

Pacific Musical Instruments

	Name	Units	Sales		Salesperson	Total Sales
2	Jan-08		Transactions			
4	Adams, Terry	12.00	2,814.72		Adams, Terry	9,147.84
5	Carothers, Andy	4.00	938.24		Carothers, Andy	5,394.88
6	DeVoe, Michael	6.00	1,407.36		DeVoe, Michael	5,394.88
7	Carothers, Andy	9.00	2,111.04		Emanuel, Michael	8,678.72
8	Emanuel, Michael	14.00	3,283.84		Fakhouri, Fadi	8,444.16
9	Fakhouri, Fadi	18.00	4,222.08		Groncki, Douglas	1,876.48
10	Emanuel, Michael	12.00	2,814.72			
11	Adams, Terry	4.00	938.24			
12	DeVoe, Michael	6.00	1,407.36			
13	Carothers, Andy	10.00	2,345.60			
14	Emanuel, Michael	11.00	2,580.16			
15	Adams, Terry	9.00	2,111.04			
16	DeVoe, Michael	11.00	2,580.16			
17	Groncki, Douglas	8.00	1,876.48			
18	Adams, Terry	14.00	3,283.84			
19	Fakhouri, Fadi	18.00	4,222.08			
20	TOTAL		38,936.96			

Figure 12-43 We added a list of unique salesperson names (conditions) in column E and copied the conditional sum formula to cells F5:F9.

The resulting formula shown in the formula bar in Figure 12-43 is enclosed in braces, indicating an array formula. For more information about arrays, see "Using Arrays" on page 468.

INSIDE OUT   **Watch Out for Spaces**

The Conditional Sum Wizard isn't smart about space characters. For example, if a label in the column of criteria includes an invisible space character at the end of the text string, Excel excludes it from the total, even if all the instances are otherwise identical.

Creating Lookup Formulas

The Lookup Wizard creates formulas using the INDEX and MATCH functions. Like the Conditional Sum Wizard, it makes constructing lookup formulas easier and faster, and it also illustrates how these formulas are constructed so you can build them yourself later. For more information about the INDEX and MATCH functions, see "Understanding Lookup and Reference Functions" on page 512. To build a lookup formula, follow these steps:

1. Click the Lookup button on the Formulas tab to display the wizard page shown on the left in Figure 12-44.

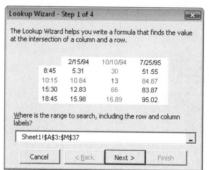
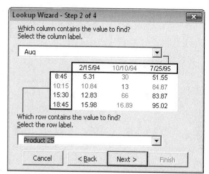

Figure 12-44 Specify the lookup range and the row and column you want to find using the first two steps of the Lookup Wizard.

> **Note**
>
> If the Lookup button does not appear on the Formulas tab, you need to install the add-in. See "Using the Conditional Sum and Lookup Wizards" on page 478.

2. Select the table or list containing the values you want to use. If you click anywhere in the table before you start the wizard, Excel automatically selects the current

region for you. If Excel selects the correct region, click Next; otherwise drag to select the range you want to use. Remember to include the row and column labels.

3. Click Next. The page shown on the right in Figure 12-44 appears.

4. Select the name of the column containing the value you want from the Select The Column Label drop-down list. (This is why you need to select the labels in Step 1 of the wizard.) If the labels don't appear in the list, click the Back button, and reselect the range.

5. Click Next, and then decide whether you want the lookup parameters as well as the result to be inserted in your worksheet, as shown in Figure 12-45. We recommend inserting the parameters (conditions), as we will show later. Select the Copy The Formula And Lookup Parameters option, and then click Next.

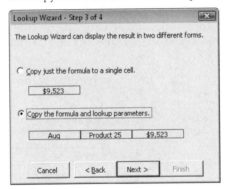

Figure 12-45 If you copy the formula to a single cell, the parameters are fixed; copying both the formula and the parameters lets you create a lookup table.

6. Select the cell where you want the resulting formula to be placed. If you chose the Copy The Formula And Lookup Parameters option in Step 3 of the wizard, the wizard adds two extra steps. If you did this, select the cell where you want the first parameter to go, click Next, and click a cell for the second parameter. Then click Next, and click the cell where you want the conditional formula to go.

7. Click Finish.

Figure 12-46 shows an example of how you can use the Lookup Wizard to build a lookup table.

As mentioned previously, when you select the Copy The Formula And Lookup Parameters option in Step 3 of the Lookup Wizard, Excels inserts the parameters in your worksheet; in our example, we specified cells P5 and Q5. The resulting lookup formula (in cell R5) refers to these inserted values using relative references. As you can see in the formula bar in Figure 12-46, the first arguments for the MATCH functions are relative references to our specified cells. Using relative references in this way, you can perform two tasks. First, you can type other valid parameters (Sept, Product 12, or both, for example) in the parameter cells (P5 and Q5), and the lookup formula finds the corresponding value at the new intersection. Second, because the parameter references are relative, you can copy the formula to additional cells and type additional parameters into cells in the same relative locations.

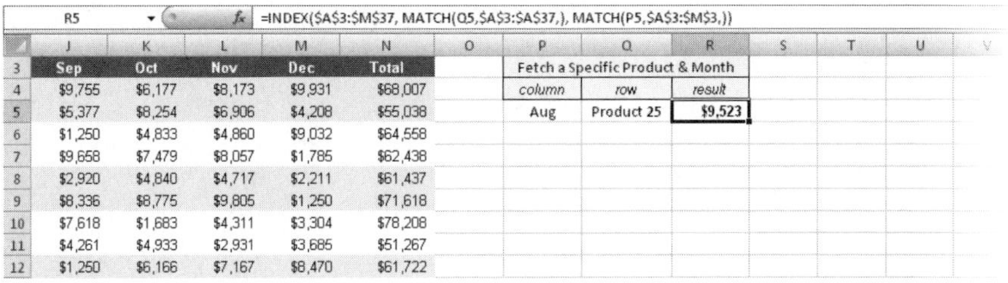

R5			fx	=INDEX($A$3:$M$37, MATCH(Q5,$A$3:$A$37,), MATCH(P5,$A$3:$M$3,))								
	J	K	L	M	N	O	P	Q	R	S	T	U	V
3	**Sep**	**Oct**	**Nov**	**Dec**	**Total**		Fetch a Specific Product & Month						
4	$9,755	$6,177	$8,173	$9,931	$68,007		*column*	*row*	*result*				
5	$5,377	$8,254	$6,906	$4,208	$55,038		Aug	Product 25	$9,523				
6	$1,250	$4,833	$4,860	$9,032	$64,558								
7	$9,658	$7,479	$8,057	$1,785	$62,438								
8	$2,920	$4,840	$4,717	$2,211	$61,437								
9	$8,336	$8,775	$9,805	$1,250	$71,618								
10	$7,618	$1,683	$4,311	$3,304	$78,208								
11	$4,261	$4,933	$2,931	$3,685	$51,267								
12	$1,250	$6,166	$7,167	$8,470	$61,722								

Figure 12-46 You can enter different months and product numbers to change the corresponding value in cell R5.

Using Functions

Worksheet *functions* are special tools that perform complex calculations quickly and easily. They work like the special keys on sophisticated calculators that compute square roots, logarithms, and statistical evaluations—except Microsoft Office Excel 2007 has hundreds of these special functions. Some functions, such as SIN and FACT, are the equivalent of lengthy mathematical formulas you would otherwise have to create by hand. Other functions, such as IF and VLOOKUP, can't be otherwise duplicated by formulas. When none of the built-in functions is quite what you need, you can create custom functions, as explained in Chapter 27, "Creating Custom Functions."

Using the Built-In Function Reference in Excel

While preparing this book, we had to make some tough choices. Fully describing each of the hundreds of worksheet functions would fill an entire book—or two, perhaps. To provide the greatest benefit, we had to decide which functions to focus on and which to mention only briefly. Admittedly, we tend to devote more ink to financial, information, and lookup functions than we do to engineering or trigonometric functions. We think this makes sense for the majority of our readers. If you need more information about functions that we do not cover in great detail, Excel offers several built-in resources:

Help

- **The online Help system** The Excel Help system includes a detailed description of each worksheet function. Just press F1 to display the Excel Help window, and then type a function name in the Search text box to find all the relevant Help topics. You can also click Function Reference in the Table Of Contents, where the functions are grouped into categories to help you find the one you need. For example, clicking the Logical category and then the Logical Functions topic displays the information shown in Figure 13-1.

> **For more information, see "Using the Online Help System" on page 73.**

- **The Insert Function dialog box** You can use this dialog box, shown in Figure 13-2, to browse through the entire list of functions if you're not sure which function you need. To display the Insert Function dialog box, click the Insert Function button on the formula bar.

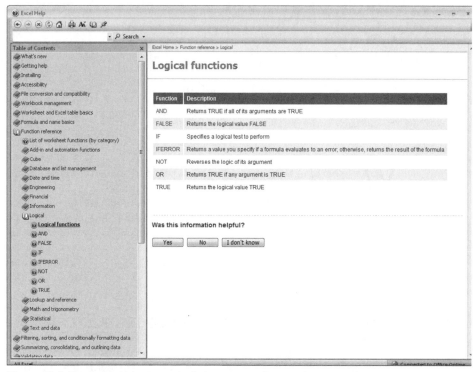

Figure 13-1 The online Help system includes a comprehensive function reference.

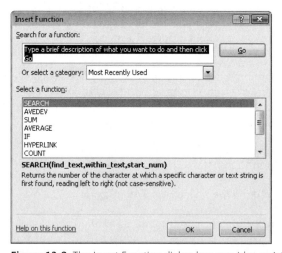

Figure 13-2 The Insert Function dialog box provides assistance with using functions.

● **The Function Arguments dialog box** This dialog box, shown in Figure 13-3, provides details about the function, and the required arguments appear as separate text boxes in the middle of the dialog box. Notice also the link to the relevant Help topic at the bottom of the dialog box. To display the Function Arguments dialog box, click the Insert Function button on the formula bar, select a function, and click OK. You can also click the Insert Function button while you are in the process of entering a formula *after* you type a valid function name and an open parenthesis to display the Function Arguments dialog box.

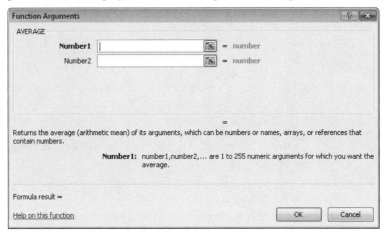

Figure 13-3 The Function Arguments dialog box provides assistance with entering function arguments.

Note

Drag the Function Arguments dialog box around the screen if you need to see the cells behind it. For maximum viewing, make the dialog box smaller by clicking one of the collapse dialog buttons on the right side of the argument boxes.

● **Function ScreenTips** These little pop-up descriptions that appear below selected formulas are useful if you are unsure about the syntax of a function as you type a formula; you can get help without even leaving the cell. After you type the required open parenthesis following any valid function name, the appropriate ScreenTip appears, as shown in Figure 13-4. The ScreenTip shows you the correct function syntax and any available alternate versions of the function (also shown in Figure 13-4). You can also click the function name in the ScreenTip to display the relevant topic from the online Help system. If you click an argument name in the ScreenTip, the corresponding section of the formula is highlighted for you, making it easy to identify each argument, as shown in Figure 13-4.

Figure 13-4 Click an argument name in the Function ScreenTip, which appears when you click an existing function, to highlight the corresponding argument in the cell.

Microsoft Office
Button

> **Note**
>
> To turn off Function ScreenTips, click the Microsoft Office Button, click Excel Options, select the Advanced category, and then in the Display area, clear the Show Function ScreenTips check box.

- **Formula AutoComplete** As you type a formula, Excel provides pop-up lists that offer function names and defined names that match the letters you are typing in the formula. For example, if you type **=S** in a cell, Excel displays a scrolling list of all functions (and defined names, if any) that begin with the letter S that you can then double-click to insert into your formula.

For details, see "Using Formula AutoComplete" on page 440 and "Naming Cells and Ranges" on page 441.

Exploring the Syntax of Functions

Worksheet functions have two parts: the name of the function and the arguments that follow. Function names—such as SUM and AVERAGE—describe the operation the function performs. Arguments specify the values or cells to be used by the function. For example, the function ROUND has the following syntax: =ROUND(*number, num_digits*), as in the formula =ROUND(M30,2). The M30 part is a cell reference entered as the *number* argument—the value to be rounded. The 2 part is the *num_digits* argument. The result of this function is a number (whatever the contents of cell M30 happens to be) rounded to two decimal places.

Parentheses surround function arguments. The opening parenthesis must appear immediately after the name of the function. If you add a space or some other character between the name and the opening parenthesis, the error value #NAME? appears in the cell.

> **Note**
>
> A few functions, such as PI, TRUE, and NOW, have no arguments. (You usually nest these functions in other formulas.) Even though they have no arguments, you must place an empty set of parentheses after them, as in =NOW( ).

When you use more than one argument in a function, you separate the arguments with commas. For example, the formula =PRODUCT(C1,C2,C5) tells Excel to multiply the numbers in cells C1, C2, and C5. Some functions, such as PRODUCT and SUM, take an unspecified number of arguments. You can use as many as 255 arguments in a function, as long as the total length of the formula does not exceed 8,192 characters. However, you can use a single argument, or a range that refers to any number of cells in your worksheet, as a formula. For example, the function =SUM(A1:A5,C2:C10,D3:D17) has only three arguments but actually totals the values in 29 cells. (The first argument, A1:A5, refers to the range of five cells from A1 through A5, and so on.) The referenced cells can, in turn, also contain formulas that refer to more cells or ranges.

Expressions as Arguments

You can use combinations of functions to create an expression that Excel evaluates to a single value and then interprets as an argument. For example, in the formula =SUM(SIN(A1*PI( )),2*COS(A2*PI( ))) the comma separates two complex expressions that Excel evaluates and uses as the arguments of the SUM function.

Types of Arguments

In the examples presented so far, all the arguments have been cell or range references. You can also use numbers, text, logical values, range names, arrays, and error values as arguments.

Numeric Values

The arguments to a function can be numeric. For example, the SUM function in the formula =SUM(327,209,176) adds the numbers 327, 209, and 176. Usually, however, you type the numbers you want to use in cells of a worksheet and then use references to those cells as arguments to your functions.

Text Values

You can also use text as an argument to a function. For example, in the formula =TEXT(NOW( ),"*mmm d, yyyy*") the second argument to the TEXT function, *mmm d, yyyy*, is a text argument specifically recognized by Excel. It specifies a pattern for converting the serial date value returned by NOW into a text string. Text arguments can be text strings enclosed in quotation marks or references to cells that contain text.

For more about text functions, see "Understanding Text Functions" on page 502.

Logical Values

The arguments to a few functions specify only that an option is either set or not set; you can use the logical values TRUE to set an option and FALSE to specify that the option isn't set. A logical expression returns the values TRUE or FALSE (which evaluate to 1 and 0, respectively) to the worksheet or the formula containing the expression. For example, the first argument of the IF function in the formula =IF(A1=TRUE,"Future ", "Past ")&"History" is a logical expression that uses the value in cell A1. If the value in A1 is TRUE (or 1), the expression A1=TRUE evaluates to TRUE, the IF function returns Future, and the formula returns the text Future History to the worksheet.

For more about logical functions, see "Understanding Logical Functions" on page 507.

Named References

You can use a defined name as an argument to a function. For example, if you click the Formulas tab on the Ribbon and use the Define Name button to assign the name Qtrly-Income to the range C3:C6, you can use the formula =SUM(QtrlyIncome) to total the numbers in cells C3, C4, C5, and C6.

For more about names, see "Naming Cells and Cell Ranges" on page 441.

Arrays

You can use an array as an argument in a function. Some functions, such as TREND and TRANSPOSE, require array arguments; other functions don't require array arguments but do accept them. Arrays can consist of numbers, text, or logical values.

For more about arrays, see "Using Arrays" on page 468.

Mixed Argument Types

You can mix argument types within a function. For example, the formula =AVERAGE(Group1,A3,5*3) uses a defined name (Group1), a cell reference (A3), and a numeric expression (5*3) to arrive at a single value. All three are acceptable.

Inserting Functions

Insert Function

The easiest way to locate and insert built-in functions is by clicking the Insert Function button. This button has two versions—one is the little *fx* button that appears on the formula bar, and the other is located in the Function Library group on the Formulas tab on the Ribbon. Either way, when you click Insert Function, the dialog box shown in Figure 13-2 appears. If you're not sure what function you need, type a description of what you are trying to do in the Search text box. For example, if you type **how many cells contain values** and then click the Go button, the Insert Function dialog box returns a list of recommended functions, similar to the list shown in Figure 13-5. As it turns out, the first function in the list of suggestions fills the bill. If you don't find the function you're look-ing for, try rewording your query.

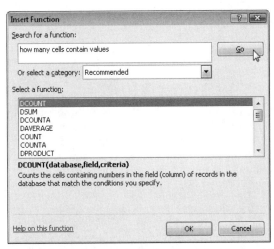

Figure 13-5 Ask a question in the Search text box, and Excel suggests some possible functions you can try.

You can also select a function category from the Or Select A Category drop-down list to display all the applicable functions available. Function categories include Financial, Date & Time, Lookup & Reference, Text, and more. The Recommended category keeps track of any functions returned as a result of using the Search text box.

When you select a function, the syntax and a brief description appear at the bottom of the dialog box. You can obtain help on a function selected in the Select A Function list by clicking the Help On This Function link at the bottom of the dialog box. When you select a function and click OK, Excel enters an equal sign to start a formula in the active cell, inserts the function name and a set of parentheses, and displays the Function Arguments dialog box, shown in Figure 13-3.

The Function Arguments dialog box contains one text box for each argument of the selected function. If the function accepts a variable number of arguments (such as SUM), the dialog box gets bigger as you type additional arguments. A description of the argument text box currently containing the insertion point appears near the bottom of the dialog box. To the right of each argument text box, a display area shows the current value of the argument. This display is handy when you are using references or defined names, because the value of each argument is calculated for you. The current value of the function (Formula Result) appears at the bottom of the dialog box.

Some functions, such as INDEX, have more than one form. When you select a function from the Insert Function dialog box that has more than one form, Excel presents the Select Arguments dialog box, shown in Figure 13-6, in which you select the form you want to use.

Chapter 13

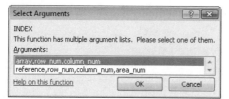

Figure 13-6 If a function has more than one form, the Select Arguments dialog box appears.

You can also use the Function Library group on the Formulas tab on the Ribbon to insert functions. Each of the categories listed in the Insert Function dialog box has a button or menu in the Function Library group. For example, clicking the More Functions button reveals a menu containing additional categories of functions, as shown in Figure 13-7. When you click one of the functions listed on any of these menus, Excel inserts the selected function in the formula bar, and the Function Arguments dialog box appears.

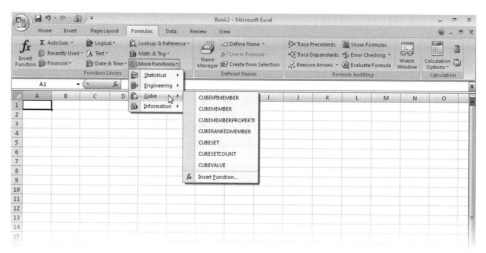

Figure 13-7 The Function Library group on the Formulas tab provides direct access to the built-in functions in Excel.

TROUBLESHOOTING

I get a #NAME? error.

You might get the #NAME? error for a few reasons, but one of the more common is typing the function name incorrectly. Here's a good habit to acquire if you type functions: Use lowercase letters. When you press Enter, Excel converts the name of the function to uppercase letters if you typed it correctly. If the letters don't change to uppercase, you probably typed the name of the function incorrectly. If you're not sure of the exact name or if you continue to get an error, perhaps it's time to consult Help or use the Insert Function dialog box.

Inserting References and Names

As with any other formula, you can insert cell references and defined names into your functions easily using the mouse. For example, to enter a function in cell C11 that averages the cells in the range C2:C10, select cell C11, type **=average(** and then select the range C2:C10. A marquee appears around the selected cells, and a reference to the selected range appears in the formula. Then type the closing parenthesis. If you define named ranges, constants, or formulas in your worksheets, you can insert them in your formulas. To do this, click the Formulas tab, click the Use In Formula button in the Defined Names group, and then select the name you want to use. When you click the name, it appears at the insertion point in the formula.

This chapter describes some of the more useful functions Microsoft Office Excel 2007 has to offer. To keep this book from threatening the structural integrity of your bookshelf, we've had to make some hard choices about which functions to highlight. Therefore, this chapter (along with Chapters 15, 16, and 17) by no means represents a comprehensive reference. For complete information about all the built-in functions that Office Excel 2007 has to offer, you can use a number of on-screen tools, covered in "Using the Built-In Function Reference in Excel" on page 487. And Appendix C, "Function Reference," lists every function available in Excel, along with the basic information you need to put each one to use, and includes cross-references to any information available in this and other chapters.

For more information, see Chapter 15, "Formatting and Calculating Date and Time"; Chapter 16, "Functions for Financial Analysis"; and Chapter 17, "Functions for Analyzing Statistics."

Understanding Mathematical Functions

Most of the work you do in Excel will probably involve at least a few mathematical functions. The most popular among these is the SUM function, but Excel is capable of calculating just about anything. In the next sections, we'll discuss some of the most used (and most useful) mathematical functions in Excel.

Using the SUM Function

The SUM function totals a series of numbers. It takes the form =SUM(number1, number2, . . .). The *number* arguments are a series of as many as 30 entries that can be numbers, formulas, ranges, or cell references that result in numbers. SUM ignores arguments that refer to text values, logical values, or blank cells.

> **Note**
> You can create powerful conditional SUM formulas using add-in tools. See "Using the Conditional Sum and Lookup Wizards" on page 478.

The Sum Button

Sum

Because SUM is such a commonly used function, Excel provides the Sum button on the Home tab on the Ribbon, as well as the AutoSum button on the Formulas tab. These buttons also include a menu of commonly used functions, including SUM. If you select a cell and click the Sum button, Excel creates a SUM formula and guesses which cells you want to total. To enter SUM formulas in a range of cells, select the cells before clicking Sum.

Automatic Range Expansion

Ever since the first spreadsheet program was created, one of the most common problems has been inserting cells at the bottom or to the right of a range that is already referenced in a formula. For example, suppose you type the formula **=SUM(A1:A4)** in cell A5 and then select row 5 and insert a new row. The new row is inserted above the selected row, thus pushing the SUM formula down to cell A6. It used to be that any numbers in the new inserted cell A5 were not included in the SUM formula. A few versions ago, Excel changed all that. Now you can insert cells at the bottom or to the right of a range referenced by a formula, and Excel adjusts the formulas for you—and this is key—*as soon as you type values in the new, inserted cells*. In other words, the SUM formula does not change unless and until you type a value in the inserted cell, now or later. This also works if, rather than inserting cells, you simply place the formula away from a column of numbers—in fact, it doesn't matter how many rows are between the formula and the values, as long as they are blank to start. (This does not work with formulas placed to the right of values that refer to columns.) If you type a value in the cell directly below the column of values that are referenced in the formula, the formula adjusts to accommodate it.

This works only immediately to the right or below a referenced range. Inserting cells at the top or to the left of a referenced range still involves editing the referencing formulas manually.

Using Selected Mathematical Functions

Math & Trig

Excel has 60 built-in math and trigonometry functions; the following sections brush only the surface, covering a few of the more useful or misunderstood functions. You can access them directly by clicking the Math & Trig button on the Formulas tab on the Ribbon.

The PRODUCT and SUMPRODUCT Functions

The PRODUCT function multiplies all its arguments and can take as many as 255 arguments that are text or logical values; the function ignores blank cells.

You can use the SUMPRODUCT function to multiply the value in each cell in one range by the corresponding cell in another range of equal size and then add the results. You can include up to 255 arrays as arguments, but each array must have the same dimensions. (Non-numeric entries are treated as zero.) For example, the following formulas are essentially the same:

```
=SUMPRODUCT(A1:A4, B1:B4)
{=SUM(A1:A4*B1:B4)}
```

The only difference between them is that you must enter the SUM formula as an array by pressing Ctrl+Shift+Enter.

For more information about arrays, see "Using Arrays" on page 468.

The MOD Function

The MOD function returns the remainder of a division operation (modulus). It takes the arguments (*number, divisor*). The result of the MOD function is the remainder produced when *number* is divided by *divisor*. For example, the function =MOD(9, 4) returns 1, the remainder that results from dividing 9 by 4.

A MOD Example

Here's a practical use of the MOD function that you can ponder:

1. Select a range of cells such as A1:G12, click Conditional Formatting on the Home tab on the Ribbon, and then click New Rule.

2. Select the Use A Formula To Determine Which Cells To Format option in the Select A Rule Type list.

3. In the text box, type the formula =**MOD(ROW(), 2)=0**.

4. Click the Format button, and select a color on the Fill tab to create a format that applies the selected color to every other row. Note that if you select a single cell in an odd-numbered row before creating this formatting formula, nothing seems to happen, but if you copy or apply the format to other rows, you'll see the result. Click OK.

This formula identifies the current row number using the ROW function, divides it by 2, and if there is a remainder (indicating an odd-numbered row), returns FALSE because the formula also contains the conditional test =0. If MOD returns anything but 0 as a remainder, the condition tests FALSE. Therefore, Excel applies formatting only when the formula returns TRUE (in even-numbered rows). For more information about conditional formatting, see "Formatting Conditionally" on page 284.

Chapter 14

The COMBIN Function

The COMBIN function determines the number of possible combinations, or groups, that can be taken from a pool of items. It takes the arguments (*number, number_chosen*), where *number* is the total number of items in the pool and *number_chosen* is the number of items you want to group in each combination. For example, to determine how many different 12-player football teams you can create from a pool of 17 players, type the formula **=COMBIN(17, 12)**. The result indicates that you could create 6,188 teams.

> ### Try Your Luck
>
> The COMBIN function can help you figure out just how slim a chance you have of getting the elusive ace-high straight flush in a game of five-card stud. You express the number of card combinations using the formula =COMBIN(52, 5), resulting in 2,598,960. That's not too bad when you consider the odds of winning the lottery. To figure that out, you need to know the number of possible combinations when choosing 6 numbers out of a total of 49. Type the formula **=COMBIN(49, 6)**, and the result is 13,983,816 possibilities. You'd better keep your day job either way.

The RAND and RANDBETWEEN Functions

The RAND function generates a random number between 0 and 1. It's one of the few Excel functions that doesn't take an argument, but you must still type a pair of parentheses after the function name. The result of a RAND function changes each time you recalculate your worksheet. This is called a *volatile* function. If you use automatic recalculation, the value of the RAND function changes each time you make a worksheet entry.

The RANDBETWEEN function provides more control than RAND. With RAND-BETWEEN, you can specify a range of numbers within which to generate random integer values. The arguments (*bottom, top*) represent the smallest and largest integers that the function should use. The values for these arguments are inclusive. For example, the formula =RANDBETWEEN(123, 456) can return any integer from 123 up to and including 456.

Using the Rounding Functions

Excel includes several functions devoted to the seemingly narrow task of rounding numbers by a specified amount.

The ROUND, ROUNDDOWN, and ROUNDUP Functions

The ROUND function rounds a value to a specified number of decimal places, rounding digits less than 5 down and digits greater than or equal to 5 up. It takes the arguments (*number, num_digits*). If *num_digits* is a positive number, then *number* is rounded to the specified number of decimal points; if *num_digits* is negative, the function rounds to the left of the decimal point; if *num_digits* is 0, the function rounds to the nearest integer. For example, the formula =ROUND(123.4567, −2) returns 100, and the formula =ROUND(123.4567, 3) returns 123.457. The ROUNDDOWN and ROUNDUP functions take the same form as ROUND. As their names imply, they always round down or up, respectively.

Accounting
Number Format

> **Note**
>
> Don't confuse the rounding functions with rounded number formats, such as the one applied when you click the Accounting Number Format button on the Home tab on the Ribbon. When you format the contents of a cell to a specified number of decimal places, you change only the display of the number in the cell; you don't change the cell's value. When performing calculations, Excel always uses the underlying value, not the displayed value. Conversely, the rounding functions change the actual values of numbers.

The EVEN and ODD Functions

The EVEN function rounds a number up to the nearest even integer. The ODD function rounds a number up to the nearest odd integer. Negative numbers are correspondingly rounded down. For example, the formula =EVEN(22.4) returns 24, and the formula =ODD(−4) returns −5.

The FLOOR and CEILING Functions

The FLOOR function rounds a number down to its nearest given multiple, and the CEILING function rounds a number up to its nearest given multiple. These functions take the arguments (*number, multiple*). For example, the formula =FLOOR(23.4, 0.5) returns 23, and the formula =CEILING(5, 1.5) returns 6, the nearest multiple of 1.5.

> ### Using the Flexible MROUND Function
>
> Suppose you want to round a number to a multiple of something other than 10—for example, rounding numbers to sixteenths so that when formatted as fractions they never appear with a denominator larger than 16. The MROUND function rounds any number to a multiple you specify.
>
> The function takes the form =MROUND(number, multiple). For example, typing the formula =**MROUND(A1, .0625)** rounds the number displayed in cell A1 in increments of one-sixteenth. The function rounds up if the remainder after dividing *number* by *multiple* is at least half the value of *multiple*. If you want to apply this to an existing formula, just wrap the MROUND formula around it by replacing A1 (in the example) with your formula.

Chapter 14

The INT Function

The INT function rounds numbers down to the nearest integer. For example, the formulas

```
=INT(100.01)
=INT(100.99999999)
```

both return the value 100, even though the number 100.99999999 is essentially equal to 101. When a number is negative, INT also rounds that number down to the next integer. If each of the numbers in the examples were negative, the resulting value would be –101.

The TRUNC Function

The TRUNC function truncates everything to the right of the decimal point in a number, regardless of its sign. It takes the arguments (*number, num_digits*). If *num_digits* isn't specified, it's set to 0. Otherwise, TRUNC truncates everything after the specified number of digits to the right of the decimal point. For example, the formula =TRUNC(13.978) returns the value 13; the formula =TRUNC(13.978, 1) returns the value 13.9.

AVERAGE vs. AVG

Some other spreadsheet programs use the AVG statistical function to compute averages. In some previous versions of Excel, typing the formula **=AVG(2, 4, 5, 8)** would result in a #NAME? error. Excel now accepts AVG, although when you type the function, an error dialog box appears, asking whether you want to change the function to AVERAGE. That's still kind of rude, but it works. Presumably, one reason why Excel doesn't just change AVG to AVERAGE for you is so you will learn to start using the correct function name.

When you use this function, Excel ignores cells containing text, logical values, or empty cells but includes cells containing a zero value. You can also choose the AVERAGEA function, which operates in the same way as AVERAGE except it includes text and logical values in the calculation.

Understanding Text Functions

 Text functions in Excel are some of the most useful word-processing and data-management tools you'll find anywhere—they perform tasks word-processing programs can't do. You'll find them conveniently listed for you when you click the Text button on the Formulas tab on the Ribbon.

Paste

You can use the TRIM and CLEAN functions to remove extra spaces and nonprinting characters, which is great for cleaning up imported data—a task that ranges from difficult to impossible using search and replace. The UPPER, LOWER, and PROPER functions change the case of words, sentences, and paragraphs with no retyping. You might find yourself copying text from other documents into Excel just so you can apply these functions. After using text functions, select the cells containing the formulas, press Ctrl+C to copy, click the Paste button on the Home tab, and then click Paste Values to convert the formulas to their resulting (text) values. You can then copy the edited text into the original document.

In the following sections, we'll discuss the most useful Excel text functions.

Using Selected Text Functions

Text functions convert numeric entries, as well as *numeric text* entries, into text strings so you can manipulate the text strings themselves. Numeric text is a type of numeric entry that provides a few specific text characters in addition to numeric characters. For details, see "Using Numeric Text in Formulas" on page 436.

The TEXT Function

The TEXT function converts a number into a text string with a specified format. Its arguments are (*value, format_text*), where *value* represents any number, formula, or cell reference; and *format_text* is the format for displaying the resulting string. For example, the formula =TEXT(98/4, "0.00") returns the text string 24.50. You can use any Excel formatting symbol ($, #, 0, and so on) except the asterisk (*) to specify the format you want, but you can't use the General format.

For information about formatting symbols and codes, see Table 9-1, "Custom Format Symbols," on page 309 and Table 9-2, "Built-In Custom Format Codes," on page 311.

The DOLLAR Function

Like the TEXT function, the DOLLAR function converts a number into a string. DOLLAR, however, formats the resulting string as currency with the number of decimal places you specify. The arguments (*number, decimals*) specify a number or reference and the number of decimal places you want. For example, the formula =DOLLAR(45.899, 2) returns the text string $45.90. Notice that Excel rounds the number when necessary.

If you omit *decimals*, Excel uses two decimal places. If you add a comma after the first argument but omit the second argument, Excel uses zero decimal places. If you use a negative number for *decimals*, Excel rounds to the left of the decimal point.

The LEN Function

The LEN function returns the number of characters in an entry. The single argument can be a number, a string enclosed in double quotation marks, or a reference to a cell. Trailing zeros are ignored. For example, the formula =LEN("Test") returns 4.

The LEN function returns the length of the displayed text or value, not the length of the underlying cell contents. For example, suppose cell A10 contains the formula =A1+A2+A3+A4+A5+A6+A7+A8 and its result is the value 25. The formula =LEN(A10) returns the value 2, which indicates the length of the resulting value 25. The cell referenced as the argument of the LEN function can contain another string function. For example, if cell A1 contains the function =REPT("–*", 75), which enters the two-character hyphen and asterisk string 75 times in a cell, the formula =LEN(A1) returns the value 150.

The ASCII Functions: CHAR and CODE

Every computer uses numeric codes to represent characters. The most prevalent system of numeric codes is ASCII, or American Standard Code for Information Interchange. ASCII uses a number from 0 to 127 (or in some systems, to 255) to represent each number, letter, and symbol.

The CHAR and CODE functions deal with these ASCII codes. The CHAR function returns the character that corresponds to an ASCII code number; the CODE function returns the ASCII code number for the first character of its argument. For example, the formula =CHAR(83) returns the text S. The formula =CODE("S") returns the ASCII code 83. If you type a literal character as the text argument, be sure to enclose the character in quotation marks; otherwise, Excel returns the #NAME? error value.

> **Note**
> If you use certain ASCII symbols often, you can use the ASCII code number with the CHAR function to create a symbol without using the Symbol button on the Insert tab on the Ribbon. For example, to create a registered trademark symbol (®) just type **=CHAR(174)**.

The Cleanup Functions: TRIM and CLEAN

Leading and trailing blank characters often prevent you from correctly sorting entries in a worksheet or a database. If you use string functions to manipulate text in your worksheet, extra spaces can prevent your formulas from working correctly. The TRIM function eliminates leading, trailing, and extra blank characters from a string, leaving only single spaces between words.

The CLEAN function is similar to TRIM, except it operates on only nonprintable characters, such as tabs and program-specific codes. CLEAN is especially useful if you import data from another program or operating system, because the translation process often introduces nonprintable characters that appear as symbols or boxes. You can use CLEAN to remove these characters from the data.

The EXACT Function

The EXACT function is a conditional function that determines whether two strings match exactly. The function ignores formatting, but it is case sensitive, so uppercase letters are considered different from lowercase letters. If both strings are identical, the function returns TRUE. Both arguments must be literal strings enclosed in quotation marks, references to cells that contain text, numeric values, or formulas that evaluate to numeric values. For example, if cell A5 and cell A6 on your worksheet both contain the text Totals, the formula =EXACT(A5, A6) returns TRUE.

For information about comparing strings, see "Creating Conditional Tests" on page 478.

The Case Functions: UPPER, LOWER, and PROPER

Three functions manipulate the case of characters in text strings. The UPPER and LOWER functions convert text strings to all uppercase or all lowercase letters. The PROPER function capitalizes the first letter in each word, capitalizes any other letters in the text string that do not follow another letter, and converts all other letters to lowercase. For example, if cell A1 contains the text *mark Dodge*, you can type the formula **=UPPER(A1)** to return MARK DODGE. Similarly, the formula =LOWER(A1) returns mark dodge, and **=PROPER(A1)** returns Mark Dodge.

Unexpected results can occur when the text contains punctuation, however. For example, if cell A1 contains the text *it wasn't bad*, the PROPER function converts it to It Wasn'T Bad.

Using the Substring Text Functions

The following functions locate and return portions of a text string or assemble larger strings from smaller ones: FIND, SEARCH, RIGHT, LEFT, MID, SUBSTITUTE, REPLACE, and CONCATENATE.

The FIND and SEARCH Functions

You use the FIND and SEARCH functions to locate the position of a substring within a string. Both functions return the position in the string of the character you specify. (Excel counts blank spaces and punctuation marks as characters.) These two functions work the same way, except FIND is case sensitive and SEARCH allows wildcards. Both functions take the same arguments: (*find_text, within_text, start_num*). The optional *start_num* argument is helpful when *within_text* contains more than one occurrence of *find_text*. If you omit *start_num*, Excel reports the first match it locates. For example, to locate the *p* in the string A Night At The Opera, you would type the formula **=FIND("p", "A Night At The Opera")**. The formula returns 17, because *p* is the 17th character in the string.

If you're not sure of the character sequence you're searching for, you can use the SEARCH function and include wildcards in your *find_text* string. Suppose you've used the names Smith and Smyth in your worksheet. To determine whether either name is in cell A1, type the formula **=SEARCH("Sm?th", A1)**. If cell A1 contains the text John Smith or John Smyth, the SEARCH function returns the value 6—the starting point of the string Sm?th.

If you're not sure of the number of characters, use the * wildcard. For example, to find the position of Allan or Alan within the text (if any) stored in cell A1, type the formula **=SEARCH("A*an", A1)**.

The RIGHT and LEFT Functions

The RIGHT function returns the rightmost series of characters from a specified string; the LEFT function returns the leftmost series of characters. These functions take the same arguments: (*text, num_chars*). The *num_chars* argument indicates the number of characters to extract from the *text* argument.

These functions count blank spaces in the *text* argument as characters; if *text* contains leading or trailing blank characters, you might want to use a TRIM function within the RIGHT or LEFT function to ensure the expected result. For example, suppose you type **This is a test** in cell A1 on your worksheet. The formula =RIGHT(A1, 4) returns the word *test*.

The MID Function

You can use the MID function to extract a series of characters from a text string. This function takes the arguments (*text, start_num, num_chars*). For example, if cell A1 contains the text This Is A Long Text Entry, you can type the formula **=MID(A1, 11, 9)** to extract the characters Long Text from the entry in cell A1.

The REPLACE and SUBSTITUTE Functions

The REPLACE and SUBSTITUTE functions substitute new text for old text. The REPLACE function replaces one string of characters with another string of characters and takes the arguments (*old_text, start_num, num_chars, new_text*). Suppose cell A1 contains the text Eric Miller, CEO. To replace the first four characters with the string Geof, type the formula **=REPLACE(A1, 1, 4, "Geof")**. The result is Geof Miller, CEO.

With the SUBSTITUTE function, you specify the text to replace. The function takes the arguments (*text, old_text, new_text, instance_num*). Suppose cell A1 contains the text Mandy and you want to place it in cell A2 but change it to Randy. Type **=SUBSTITUTE(A1, "M", "R")** in cell A2.

The *instance_num* argument optionally replaces only the specified occurrence of *old_text*. For example, if cell A1 contains the text *through the hoop*, the 4 in the formula =SUBSTITUTE(A1, "h", "l", 4) tells Excel to substitute an l for the fourth *h* found in cell A1. If you don't include *instance_num*, Excel changes all occurrences of *old_text* to *new_text*.

> **Note**
>
> You can create an array formula using the SUBSTITUTE function to count the number of occurrences of a text string in a range of cells. Use the formula =SUM(LEN(<range>)–LEN(SUBSTITUTE(<range>, "text", "")))/LEN("text") to count the number of times *text* appears in <range>. Type the formula, and press Ctrl+Shift+Enter.

The CONCATENATE Function

To assemble strings from up to 255 smaller strings or references, the CONCATENATE function is the function equivalent of the & character. For example, if cell B4 contains the text Pacific with a trailing space character, the formula =CONCATENATE(B4, "Musical Instruments") returns Pacific Musical Instruments.

TROUBLESHOOTING

Concatenated dates become serial numbers.

If you try to concatenate the contents of a cell formatted as a date, the result is probably not what you expect. Because a date in Excel is only a serial number, what you usually see is a formatted representation of the date. But when you concatenate the contents of a date-formatted cell, you get the unformatted version of the date. To avoid this problem, use the TEXT function to convert the serial number to a recognizable form. For example, suppose cell A1 contains the text *Today's Date is* and cell A2 contains the function =NOW() and is formatted to display the date in dd/mm/yyyy format. Nonetheless, the formula =CONCATENATE(A1, " ", A2) results in the value Today's Date is 39511 (or whatever the current date serial number happens to be). To remedy this problem, type the TEXT function as follows: **=CONCATENATE(A1, " ", TEXT(A2, "dd/mm/yyyy")).**

This version returns the value Today's Date is 03/04/2008 (or whatever today's date happens to be). Note that the formula includes a space character as a separate argument (" ") between the two cell reference arguments.

Understanding Logical Functions

 You use logical functions to test for specific conditions. These functions are often called *logical operators* in discussions of Boolean logic, which is named after George Boole, the British mathematician. You might have run across logical operators in *set theory*, used when teaching logical concepts in high school. You use logical operators to arrive at one of two conclusions: TRUE or FALSE. We'll discuss the most useful logical functions in the following sections. You can access the logical functions by clicking the Logical button on the Formulas tab on the Ribbon.

Using Selected Logical Functions

Excel has a rich set of logical functions. Most logical functions use conditional tests to determine whether a specified condition is TRUE or FALSE.

For more information about conditional tests, see "Creating Conditional Tests" on page 478.

INSIDE OUT   Streamline Formulas Using the SUMIF Function

If you find yourself frequently using the IF function to perform conditional tests on individual rows or columns and then using the SUM function to total the results, the SUMIF function might make your work a little easier. With SUMIF, you can add specific values in a range, based on a criterion you supply. For example, you can type the formula **=SUMIF(C12:C27, "Yes", A12:A27)** to find the total of all numbers in A12:A27 in which the cell in the same row in column C contains the word Yes. This performs all the calculations you need in one cell and eliminates having to create a column of IF formulas. For more information about SUMIF, see "The SUMIF, SUMIFS, and COUNTIF Functions" on page 555.

The IF Function

The IF function returns values based on supplied conditional tests. It takes the arguments (*logical_test, value_if_true, value_if_false*). For example, the formula =IF(A6<22, 5, 10) returns 5 if the value in cell A6 is less than 22; otherwise, it returns 10. You can nest other functions within an IF function. For example, the formula =IF(SUM(A1:A10)>0, SUM(A1:A10), 0) returns the sum of A1 through A10 if the sum is greater than 0; otherwise, it returns 0.

You can also use text arguments to return nothing instead of zero if the result is false. For example, the formula =IF(SUM(A1:A10)>0, SUM(A1:A10), " ") returns a null string (" ") if the conditional test is false. The *logical_test* argument can also consist of text. For example, the formula =IF(A1="Test", 100, 200) returns the value 100 if cell A1 contains the string Test or returns 200 if it contains any other entry. The match between the two text entries must be exact except for case.

The AND, OR, and NOT Functions

Three additional functions help you develop compound conditional tests: AND, OR, and NOT. These functions work with the logical operators =, >, <, >=, <=, and <>. The AND and OR functions can each have as many as 255 logical arguments. The NOT function takes only one argument. Arguments can be conditional tests, arrays, or references to cells that contain logical values.

Suppose you want Excel to return the text Pass only if a student has an average score greater than 75 and fewer than five unexcused absences. In Figure 14-1, we typed the formula **=IF(OR(G4<5,F4>75), "Pass", "Fail")**. This fails the student in row 5 because of the five absences. If you use AND instead of OR in the formula shown in Figure 14-1, all students would pass.

H4				f_x	=IF(OR(G4<5,F4>75),"Pass","Fail")				

	A	B	C	D	E	F	G	H	I	J	K
1	**Math Exam Scores**										
2	Ms. Nagata										
3	*Student*	**Exam 1**	**Exam 2**	**Exam 3**	**Exam 4**	*Average*	*Absences*	*Pass/Fail*			
4	Carothers, Andy	87	90	79	96	88.00	2	Pass			
5	Groncki, Douglas	92	94	94	97	94.25	5	Fail			
6	MacDonald, Scott	96	95	95	80	91.50	0	Pass			
7	Nusbaum, Tawana	85	87	87	88	86.75	4	Pass			
8	Rothenberg, Eric	81	88	88	85	85.50	1	Pass			
9											
10											
11											
12											
13											
14											
15											

Figure 14-1 You can create complex conditional tests using the OR function.

You'll find the And Or Not.xlsx file in the Sample Files section of the companion CD.

The OR function returns the logical value TRUE if any one of the conditional tests is true; the AND function returns the logical value TRUE only if all the conditional tests are true.

Because the NOT function negates a condition, you usually use it with other functions. NOT instructs Excel to return the logical value TRUE if the argument is false or the logical value FALSE if the argument is true. For example, the formula =IF(NOT(A1=2), "Go", " ") tells Excel to return the text Go if the value of cell A1 is anything but 2.

Nested IF Functions

Sometimes you can't resolve a logical problem using only logical operators and the AND, OR, and NOT functions. In these cases, you can nest IF functions to create a hierarchy of tests. For example, the formula =IF(A1=100, "Always", IF(AND(A1>=80, A1<100), "Usually", IF(AND(A1>=60, A1<80), "Sometimes", "Who cares?"))) states, in plain language, the following: If the value is 100, return Always; if the value is from 80 through 99, return Usually; if the value is from 60 through 79, return Sometimes; or finally, if none of these conditions is true, return Who cares?. You can create formulas containing up to 64 levels of nested functions.

Other Uses for Conditional Functions

You can use all the conditional functions described in this section as stand-alone formulas. Although you usually use functions, such as AND, OR, NOT, ISERROR, ISNA, and ISREF, within an IF function, you can use formulas, such as =AND(A1>A2, A2<A3), also to perform simple conditional tests. This formula returns the logical value TRUE if the value in A1 is greater than the value in A2 and the value in A2 is less than the value in A3. You might use this type of formula to assign TRUE and FALSE values to a range of numeric database cells and then use the TRUE and FALSE conditions as selection criteria for printing a specialized report.

Understanding Information Functions

More Functions

The information functions could be considered the internal monitoring system in Excel. Although they perform no specific calculations, you can use them to find out about elements of the Excel interface and then use that information elsewhere. We'll discuss the most useful of these functions in the following sections. You'll find these functions by clicking the More Functions button on the Formulas tab on the Ribbon and then clicking Information.

Using Selected Information Functions

With information functions, you can gather information about the contents of cells, their formatting, and the computing environment as well as perform conditional tests for the presence of specific types of values.

The TYPE and ERROR.TYPE Functions

The TYPE function determines whether a cell contains text, a number, a logical value, an array, or an error value. The result is a code for the type of entry in the referenced cell: 1 for a number (or a blank cell), 2 for text, 4 for a logical value (TRUE or FALSE), 16 for an error value, and 64 for an array. For example, if cell A1 contains the number 100, the formula =TYPE(A1) returns 1. If A1 contains the text Microsoft Excel, the formula returns 2.

Like the TYPE function, the ERROR.TYPE function detects the contents of a cell, except it detects different types of error values. The result is a code for the type of error value in the referenced cell: 1 for #NULL!, 2 for #DIV/0!, 3 for #VALUE!, 4 for #REF!, 5 for #NAME!, 6 for #NUM!, and 7 for #N/A. Any other value in the referenced cell returns the error value #N/A. For example, if cell A1 contains a formula that displays the error value #NAME!, the formula =ERROR.TYPE(A1) returns 5. If A1 contains the text Microsoft Excel, the formula returns #N/A.

The COUNTBLANK Function

The COUNTBLANK function counts the number of empty cells in the specified range, which is its only argument. This function is tricky because formulas that evaluate to null text strings, such as =" ", or to zero might seem empty, but they aren't and therefore won't be counted.

Using the IS Information Functions

You can use the ISBLANK, ISERR, ISERROR, ISEVEN, ISLOGICAL, ISNA, ISNON-TEXT, ISNUMBER, ISODD, ISREF, and ISTEXT functions to determine whether a referenced cell or range contains the corresponding type of value.

All the IS information functions take a single argument. For example, the ISBLANK function takes the form =ISBLANK(value). The *value* argument is a reference to a cell. If *value* refers to a blank cell, the function returns the logical value TRUE; otherwise, it returns FALSE.

TROUBLESHOOTING

My IS function returns unexpected results.

Although you can use a cell range (rather than a single cell) as the argument to any IS function, the result might not be what you expect. For example, you might think the ISBLANK function would return TRUE if the referenced range is empty or FALSE if the range contains any values. Instead, its behavior depends on where the range is in relation to the cell containing the formula. If the argument refers to a range that intersects the row or column containing the formula, ISBLANK uses implicit intersection to arrive at the result. In other words, the function looks at only one cell in the referenced range and only if it happens to be in the same row or column as the cell containing the function. The function ignores the rest of the range. If the range shares neither a row nor a column with the formula, however, the result is always FALSE. For more about intersection, see "Getting Explicit About Intersections" on page 452.

An ISERR Example

You can use ISERR to avoid getting error values as formula results. For example, suppose you want to call attention to cells containing a particular character string, such as 12A, resulting in the word Yes appearing in the cell containing the formula. If the string isn't found, you want the cell to remain empty. You can use the IF and FIND functions to perform this task, but if the value isn't found, you get a #VALUE! error rather than a blank cell.

To solve this problem, add an ISERR function to the formula. The FIND function returns the position at which a substring is found within a larger string. If the substring isn't there, FIND returns #VALUE!. The solution is to add an ISERR function, such as =IF(ISERR(FIND("12A", A1)), " ", "Yes"). Because you're not interested in the error, which is simply a by-product of the calculation, this traps the error, leaving only the results in which you are interested.

> **Note**
>
> When you type numeric values as text, such as ="**21**", the IS function, unlike other functions, does not recognize them as numbers. Therefore, the formula =ISNUMBER("21") returns FALSE.

Understanding Lookup and Reference Functions

Lookup &
Reference

Lookup and reference functions help you use your own worksheet tables as sources of information to be used elsewhere in formulas. You can use three primary functions to look up information stored in a list or a table or to manipulate references: LOOKUP, VLOOKUP, and HLOOKUP. Some powerful lookup and reference functions in addition to these three are available; we describe many of them in the following sections. You'll find a list of all these functions by clicking the Lookup & Reference button on the Formulas tab on the Ribbon.

Using Selected Lookup and Reference Functions

VLOOKUP and HLOOKUP are nearly identical functions that look up information stored in tables you have constructed. VLOOKUP and HLOOKUP operate in either vertical or horizontal orientation (respectively), but LOOKUP works either way.

When you look up information in a table, you usually use a row index and a column index to locate a particular cell. Excel derives the first index by finding the largest value in the first column or row that is less than or equal to a lookup value you supply and then uses a row number or column number argument as the other index. Make sure the table is sorted by the row or column containing the lookup values.

> **Creating Automated Lookup Formulas**
>
> You can create powerful lookup formulas using add-in tools. (The tools don't actually use any of the lookup functions.) For more information, see "Using the Conditional Sum and Lookup Wizards" on page 478.

These functions take the following forms:

```
=VLOOKUP(lookup_value, table_array, col_index_num, range_lookup)
=HLOOKUP(lookup_value, table_array, row_index_num, range_lookup)
```

Table 14-1 lists LOOKUP function arguments and their descriptions. The LOOKUP function takes two forms; the first is called the *vector form*, and the second is called the *array form*:

```
=LOOKUP(lookup_value, lookup_vector, result_vector)
=LOOKUP(lookup_value, array)
```

Table 14-1 **LOOKUP Function Arguments**

Argument	Description
lookup_value	The value, cell reference, or text (enclosed in quotation marks) that you want to find in a table or a range.
table_array	A cell range or name that defines the table in which to look.
row_index_num *col_index_num*	The row or column number of the table from which to select the result, counted relative to the table (not according to the actual row and column numbers).
range_lookup	A logical value that determines whether the function matches *lookup_value* exactly or approximately. Type **FALSE** to match *lookup_value* exactly. The default is TRUE, which finds the closest match.
lookup_vector	A one-row or one-column range that contains numbers, text, or logical values.
result_vector	A one-row or one-column range that must be the same size as *lookup_vector*.
array	A range containing numbers, text, or logical values to compare with *lookup_value*.

The difference between the lookup functions is the type of table each function uses: VLOOKUP works only with vertical tables (tables arranged in columns); HLOOKUP works only with horizontal tables (tables arranged in rows). You can use the *array form* of LOOKUP with either horizontal tables or vertical tables, and you can use the *vector form* with single rows or columns of data.

The array form of LOOKUP determines whether to search horizontally or vertically based on the shape of the table defined in the *array* argument. If the table has more columns than rows, LOOKUP searches the first row for *lookup_value*; if the table has more rows than columns, LOOKUP searches the first column for *lookup_value*. LOOKUP always returns the last value in the row or column containing the *lookup_value* argument; or you can specify a row or column number using VLOOKUP or HLOOKUP.

The VLOOKUP and HLOOKUP Functions

For the VLOOKUP and HLOOKUP functions, whether Excel considers a lookup table to be vertical or horizontal depends on where the comparison values (the first index) are located. If the values are in the leftmost column of the table, the table is vertical; if they are in the first row of the table, the table is horizontal. (In contrast, LOOKUP uses the shape of the table to determine whether to use the first row or column as the comparison values.) The comparison values can be numbers or text, but it is essential that they be sorted in ascending order. No comparison value should be used more than once in a table.

The *index_num* argument (sometimes called the *offset*) provides the second index and tells the lookup function which column or row of the table to look in for the function's result. The first column or row in the table has an index number of 1; therefore, the *index_num* argument must be greater than or equal to 1 and must never be greater than the number of rows or columns in the table. For example, if a vertical table is three columns wide, the index number can't be greater than 3. If any value does not meet these rules, the function returns an error value.

You can use the VLOOKUP function to retrieve information from the table in Figure 14-2.

	C1		▾		f_x	=VLOOKUP(41,A3:C7,3)			
	A	B	C	D	E	F	G	H	I
1			14						
2									
3	10	17.98	5						
4	20	5.89	8						
5	30	5.59	11						
6	40	23.78	14						
7	50	6.79	17						
8									
9									
10									
11									
12									
13									
14									

Figure 14-2 You can use the VLOOKUP function to retrieve information from a vertical table like this one.

You'll find the Lookup.xlsx file in the Sample Files section of the companion CD.

Remember that these lookup functions usually search for the greatest comparison value that is less than or equal to the lookup value, not for an exact match between the comparison values and the lookup value. If all the comparison values in the first row or column of the table range are greater than the lookup value, the function returns the #N/A error value. If all the comparison values are less than the lookup value, however, the function returns the value that corresponds to the last (largest) comparison value in the table, which might not be what you want. If you require an exact match, type **FALSE** as the *range_lookup* argument.

The worksheet in Figure 14-3 shows an example of a horizontal lookup table using the HLOOKUP function.

A1				f_x	=HLOOKUP(6,B2:E7,3)			
	A	B	C	D	E	F	G	H	I
1	101								
2		3	6	10	16				
3		5	100	99	1				
4		10	101	98	2				
5		25	105	95	3				
6		30	110	94	2				
7		35	125	90	1				
8									
9									
10									
11									
12									
13									

Figure 14-3 You can use the HLOOKUP function to retrieve information from a horizontal table like this one.

The LOOKUP Function

The LOOKUP function is similar to VLOOKUP and HLOOKUP and follows the same rules, but it is available in two forms, *vector* and *array*, whose arguments are described in Table 14-1.

Like HLOOKUP and VLOOKUP, the *vector form* of LOOKUP searches for the largest comparison value that isn't greater than the lookup value. It then selects the result from the corresponding position in the specified result range. The *lookup_vector* and *result_vector* arguments are often adjacent ranges, but they don't have to be when you use LOOKUP. They can be in separate areas of the worksheet, and one range can be horizontal and the other vertical. The only requirement is that they must have the same number of elements.

For example, consider the worksheet in Figure 14-4, where the ranges are not parallel. Both the *lookup_vector* argument, A1:A5, and the *result_vector* argument, D6:H6, have five elements. The *lookup_value* argument, 3, matches the entry in the third cell of the *lookup_vector* argument, making the result of the formula the entry in the third cell of the result range: 300.

The *array form* of LOOKUP is similar to VLOOKUP and HLOOKUP but works with either a horizontal table or a vertical table, using the dimensions of the table to figure out the location of the comparison values. If the table is taller than it is wide or the table is square, the function treats it as a vertical table and assumes that the comparison values are in the leftmost column. If the table is wider than it is tall, the function views the table as horizontal and assumes that the comparison values are in the first row of the table. The result is always in the last row or column of the specified table; you can't specify column or row numbers.

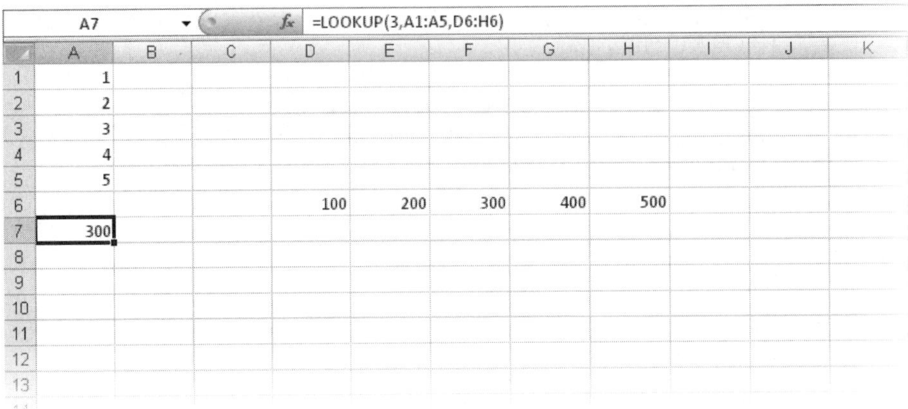

Figure 14-4 The vector form of the LOOKUP function can retrieve information from a nonparallel cell range.

Because HLOOKUP and VLOOKUP are more predictable and controllable, you'll generally find using them preferable to using LOOKUP.

The ADDRESS Function

The ADDRESS function provides a handy way to build a cell reference using numbers typed into the formula or using values in referenced cells. It takes the arguments (*row_num, column_num, abs_num, a1, sheet_text*). For example, the formula =ADDRESS(1, 1, 1, TRUE, "Data Sheet") results in the reference 'Data Sheet'!$A$1.

The CHOOSE Function

You use the CHOOSE function to retrieve an item from a list of values. The function takes the arguments (*index_num, value 1, value 2, . . .*) and can include up to 254 values. The *index_num* argument is the position in the list you want to return; it must be positive and can't exceed the number of elements in the list. The function returns the value of the element in the list that occupies the position indicated by *index_num*. For example, the function =CHOOSE(2, 6, 1, 8, 9, 3) returns the value 1, because 1 is the second item in the list. (The *index_num* value isn't counted as part of the list.) You can use individual cell references for the list, but you can't specify ranges. You might be tempted to create a function, such as =CHOOSE(A10, C1:C5), to take the place of the longer function in the preceding example. If you do, however, the result is a #VALUE! error value.

The MATCH Function

The MATCH function is closely related to the CHOOSE function. However, whereas CHOOSE returns the item that occupies the position in a list specified by the *index_num* argument, MATCH returns the position of the item in the list that most closely matches a lookup value.

> **Note**
>
> You can create powerful lookup formulas using add-in tools that use the MATCH and INDEX functions. See "Using the Conditional Sum and Lookup Wizards" on page 478.

This function takes the arguments (*lookup_value, lookup_array, match_type*), where *lookup_value* and the items in the *lookup_array* can be numeric values or text strings, and *match_type* defines the rules for the search, as shown in Table 14-2.

Table 14-2 MATCH Function Arguments

match_type	Description
1 (or omitted)	Finds the largest value in the specified range (which must be sorted in ascending order) that is less than or equal to *lookup_value*. If no items in the range meet these criteria, the function returns #N/A.
0	Finds the first value in the specified range (no sorting necessary) that is equal to *lookup_value*. If no items in the range match, the function returns #N/A.
–1	Finds the smallest value in the specified range (which must be sorted in descending order) that is greater than or equal to *lookup_value*. If no items in the range meet these criteria, the function returns #N/A.

When you use MATCH to locate text strings, you should specify a *match_type* argument of 0 (an exact match). You can then use the wildcards * and ? in the *lookup_value* argument.

The INDEX Function

The INDEX function has two forms: an array form, which returns a value, and a reference form, which returns a cell reference. The forms of these functions are as follows:

```
=INDEX(array, row_num, column_num)
=INDEX(reference, row_num, column_num, area_num)
```

The *array form* works only with an array argument; it returns the value of the result, not the cell reference. The result is the value at the position in *array* indicated by *row_num* and *column_num*. For example, the formula

```
=INDEX({10,20,30;40,50,60} , 1, 2)
```

returns the value 20, because 20 is the value in the cell in the second column and first row of the array.

> **Note**
>
> Each form of the INDEX function offers an advantageous feature. Using the reference form of the function, you can use multiple, nonadjacent areas of the worksheet as the *reference* lookup range. Using the array form of the function, you can get a range of cells, rather than a single cell, as a result.

The *reference form* returns a cell address instead of a value and is useful when you want to perform operations on a cell (such as changing the cell width), rather than on its value. This function can be confusing, however, because if an INDEX function is nested in another function, that function can use the value in the cell whose address is returned by INDEX. Furthermore, the reference form of INDEX doesn't display its result as an address; it displays the value(s) at that cell address. Remember that the result is an address, even if it doesn't look like one.

Here are a few guidelines to keep in mind when using the INDEX function:

- If you type **0** as the *row_num* or *column_num* argument, INDEX returns a reference for the entire row or column, respectively.

- The *reference* argument can be one or more ranges, which are called *areas*. Each area must be rectangular and can contain numbers, text, or formulas. If the areas are not adjacent, you must enclose the *reference* argument in parentheses.

- You need the *area_num* argument only if you include more than one area in *reference*. The *area_num* argument identifies the area to which the *row_num* and *column_num* arguments will be applied. The first area specified in *reference* is designated area 1, the second area 2, and so on.

Let's consider some examples to see how all this works. Figure 14-5 shows an example of an INDEX function. The formula in cell A1 uses the row coordinate in cell A2 and the column coordinate in cell A3 to return the contents of the cell in the third row and second column of the specified range.

The following example is a bit trickier: Using the same worksheet in Figure 14-5, the formula =INDEX(C3:E6, 0, 2) displays the #VALUE! error value because the *row_num* argument of 0 returns a reference to the entire column specified by the *column_num* argument of 2, or the range D3:D6. Excel can't display a range as the result. However, try nesting this formula in another function, as follows: =SUM(INDEX(C3:E6, 0, 2)). The result is 2600, the sum of the values in D3:D6. This illustrates the utility of obtaining a reference as a result.

Now we'll show how the INDEX function works with multiple ranges in the *reference* argument. (When you're using more than one range, you must enclose the argument in parentheses.) For example, in the formula =INDEX((A1:C5,D6:F10), 1, 1, 2), the *reference* range comprises two areas: A1:C5 and D6:F10. The *area_num* argument (2) tells INDEX to work on the second of these areas. This formula returns the address D6, which is the cell in the first column and first row of the range D6:F10. The displayed result is the value in that cell.

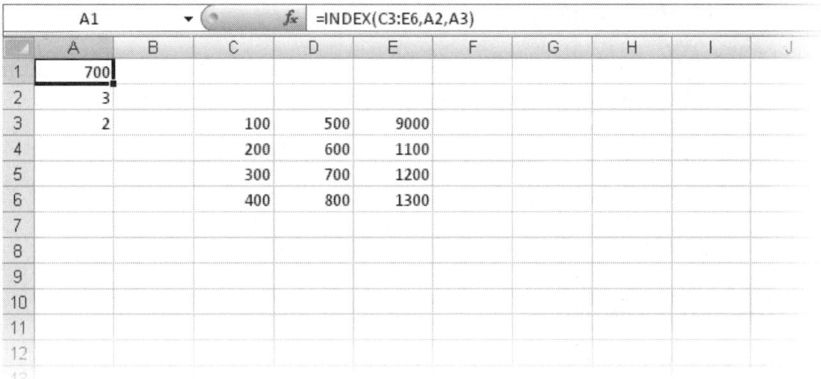

A1				f_x	=INDEX(C3:E6,A2,A3)					
	A	B	C	D	E	F	G	H	I	J
1	700									
2	3									
3	2		100	500	9000					
4			200	600	1100					
5			300	700	1200					
6			400	800	1300					
7										
8										
9										
10										
11										
12										

Figure 14-5 Use the INDEX function to retrieve the address or value in a cell where information is located.

The INDIRECT Function

The INDIRECT function returns the contents of a cell using its reference. It takes the arguments (*ref_text, a1*), where *ref_text* is an A1-style or R1C1-style reference or a cell name. The *a1* argument is a logical value indicating which type of reference you're using. If *a1* is FALSE, Excel interprets *ref_text* as R1C1 format; if *a1* is TRUE or omitted, Excel interprets *ref_text* as A1 format. For example, if cell C6 on your worksheet contains the text value B3 and cell B3 contains the value 2.888, the formula =INDIRECT(C6) returns the value 2.888. If your worksheet is set to display R1C1-style references and cell R6C3 contains the text reference R3C2 and cell R3C2 contains the value 2.888, then the formula =INDIRECT(R6C3, FALSE) also returns the value 2.888.

For information about A1-style and R1C1-style references, see "Understanding Row-Column Reference Style" on page 431.

The ROW and COLUMN Functions

The result of the ROW and COLUMN functions is the row or column number, respectively, of the cell or range referred to by the function's single argument. For example, the formula =ROW(H5) returns the result 5. The formula =COLUMN(C5) returns the result 3 because column C is the third column on the worksheet.

If you omit the argument, the result is the row or column number of the cell that contains the function. If the argument is a range or a range name and you enter the function as an array by pressing Ctrl+Shift+Enter, the result of the function is an array that consists of the row or column numbers of each row or column in the range. For example, suppose you select cells B1:B10, type the formula **=ROW(A1:A10)**, and then press Ctrl+Shift+Enter to enter the formula in all cells in the range B1:B10. That range will contain the array result {1;2;3;4;5;6;7;8;9;10}, the row numbers of each cell in the argument.

Chapter 14

Chapter 14

The ROWS and COLUMNS Functions

The ROWS and COLUMNS functions return the number of rows or columns, respectively, referenced by the function's single argument in a reference or an array. The argument is an array constant, a range reference, or a range name. For example, the result of the formula =ROWS({100,200,300;1000,2000,3000}) is 2, because the array consists of two rows (separated by a semicolon). The formula =ROWS(A1:A10) returns 10, because the range A1:A10 contains ten rows. And the formula =COLUMNS(A1:C10) returns 3, because the range A1:C10 contains three columns.

The AREAS Function

You can use the AREAS function to determine the number of areas in a reference. *Areas* refer to individual cell or range references, not regions. The single argument to this function can be a cell reference, a range reference, or several range references. If you use several range references, you must enclose them in a set of parentheses so Excel doesn't misinterpret the commas that separate the ranges. (Although this function takes only one argument, Excel still interprets unenclosed commas as argument separators.) For example, suppose you assign the name Test to the group of ranges A1:C5,D6,E7:G10. The function =AREAS(Test) returns 3, the number of areas in the group.

The TRANSPOSE Function

The TRANSPOSE function changes the horizontal or vertical orientation of an array. It takes a single argument, *array*. If the argument refers to a vertically oriented range, the resulting array is horizontal. If the range is horizontal, the resulting array is vertical. The first row of a horizontal array becomes the first column of the vertical array result, and vice versa. You must type the TRANSPOSE function as an array formula in a range that has the same number of rows and columns as the *array* argument has columns and rows, respectively.

For quick and easy transposition, select the range you want to transpose, press Ctrl+C to copy the range, click the cell where you want the upper-left corner of the transposed range to begin, click the Paste button on the Home tab, and then click Transpose.

Formatting and Calculating Date and Time

You can use date and time values to stamp documents and to perform date and time arithmetic. Creating a production schedule or a monthly billing system is relatively easy with Microsoft Office Excel 2007. Although Office Excel 2007 uses numeric values to count each nanosecond, starting from the beginning of the 20th century, you can use formatting to display those numbers in whatever form you want.

Understanding How Excel Records Dates and Times

Excel assigns serial values to days, hours, minutes, and seconds, which makes it possible for you to perform sophisticated date and time arithmetic. The basic unit of time in Excel is the day. Each day is represented by a serial date value. The base date, represented by the serial value 1, is Sunday, January 1, 1900. When you enter a date in your worksheet, Excel records the date as a serial value that represents the number of days between the base date and the specified date. For example, Excel represents the date January 1, 2008, by the serial value 39,448, representing the number of days between the base date–January 1, 1900–and January 1, 2008.

The time of day is a decimal value that represents the portion of a day that has passed from its beginning–midnight–to the specified time. Therefore, Excel represents noon by the value 0.5, because the difference between midnight and noon is exactly half a day. Excel represents the time/date combination 12:59:54 PM, October 6, 2006, by the serial value 38996.54159, because October 6, 2006, is day 38,996 (counting January 1, 1900, as day 1), and the interval between midnight and 12:59:54 PM amounts to .54159 of a whole day.

> **Note**
>
> You can see the serial value of a formatted date by selecting the cell containing the date and pressing Ctrl+Shift+tilde (~). To return the cell to its date format, press Ctrl+Z.

Using the 1904 Date System

If you transfer documents between Excel for the Macintosh and Excel for Windows, the proper date system for the worksheet is automatically set for you. When the date system changes, existing serial date values display different dates, but the underlying values do not change. If you change date systems after you have begun entering dates in a worksheet, all your dates will be off by four years.

Microsoft Office
Button

You can change the base date (the date that corresponds to the serial value 1) from January 1, 1900—used by Excel for Windows—to January 2, 1904—used by Excel for the Macintosh. Click the Microsoft Office Button, click Excel Options, select the Advanced category, and select the Use 1904 Date System check box in the When Calculating This Workbook area.

When you select this check box, the serial date values in your worksheet remain the same, but the display of all dates changes so that the serial values of any dates you enter on your Excel for Windows worksheets match corresponding serial values from Excel for the Macintosh worksheets. If you transfer information into Excel for Windows from a worksheet created in Excel for the Macintosh, selecting this option ensures that Excel evaluates the serial date values correctly. In this book, we use the 1900 date system.

Entering Dates and Times

Although Excel records dates and times as serial date values, you don't have to type them that way. You can manipulate dates and times in your worksheet formulas just as you manipulate other types of values. You enter date values in formats that Excel automatically applies. To enter date values in this way, type the date in one of the following formats: m/d/yy, d-mmm-yy, d-mmm, or mmm-yy. (You can also type four-digit years for any of these formats.)

Note

You can change the default date, time, currency, and numbering settings through the Clock, Language, And Region item in Windows Vista Control Panel (Date, Time, Language, And Regional Options in Windows XP). These settings will determine how Excel interprets your date entries. For example, with regional options set to Italian, typing a date in d/m/yy format will result in a properly displayed date, but if you type the same date with regional options set to English, the entry is interpreted as text.

If your entry doesn't match any of the built-in date or time formats, Excel picks the format that's most similar to your entry. For example, if you type **1 dec**, you see the formatted entry 1-Dec in the cell. In the formula bar, the entry appears as 12/1/2008 (if the current year is 2008) so you can edit the date more easily.

You can also type times in a time format. Select a cell, and type the time in one of the following forms: h:mm AM/PM, h:mm:ss AM/PM, h:mm, h:mm:ss, or the combined date and time format, m/d/yy h:mm. Notice that you must separate the hours, minutes, and seconds of the time entries by colons.

> For more information about custom formats, see "Creating Your Own Date and Time Formats" on page 527.

If you don't include AM, PM, A, or P with the time, Excel uses the 24-hour (military) time convention. In other words, Excel always assumes that the entry 3:00 means 3:00 AM, unless you specifically enter **PM**.

You can enter the current date in a cell or formula by holding down Ctrl and pressing the semicolon (;) key. This enters the date stamp in the current short-date format, as set in Control Panel. Enter the current time in a cell or formula by holding down Ctrl+Shift and pressing the colon (:) key. This enters the time stamp in h:mm AM/PM format. (Of course, the colon and semicolon occupy the same key—the Shift key changes the entry to a time stamp.)

INSIDE OUT   The Magic Crossover Date

December 31, 2029, is the default magic crossover date—that is, the last day Microsoft Windows assumes is in the future if you enter the year using only two digits. For example, if you type **12/31/29** in a cell, Windows assumes you mean the year 2029. If, however, you type **1/1/30** in a cell, Windows interprets it to mean January 1, 1930.

You can change this magic crossover date by changing the setting on the Date tab in the Customize Regional Options dialog box. To access this dialog box, open Control Panel, and then click Clock, Language, And Region. Next, click Regional And Language Options, and then click the Customize This Format button. Finally, click the Date tab, and change the last date (2029) to the value of your choice. Of course, you're still limited to a 100-year span; if you change the last date Windows recognizes as being in the future, the corresponding beginning date—January 1, 1900—changes accordingly. Therefore, if you need to enter century-spanning dates, you should get into the habit of typing the full four-digit year to avoid surprises.

Entering a Series of Dates

You can create an evenly spaced series of dates in a row or column in several ways, but the job is especially easy when you use the fill handle. Suppose you want to create a series of dates in row 1. The series begins with March 1, 2008, and the dates must be exactly one month apart.

If you type **3/1/2008** in cell A1 and drag the fill handle to the right, Excel extends the series of dates incrementally by days, as shown in Figure 15-1. After you drag, Excel displays a smart tag adjacent to the selection. Click the smart tag to display the smart tag action menu shown in Figure 15-1, which displays a number of AutoFill options; select Fill Months to convert the already-extended day series into a month series.

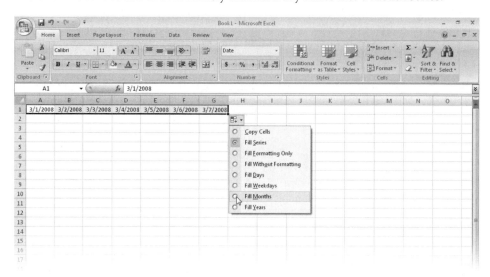

Figure 15-1 After you drag the fill handle to extend a date series, use the smart tag action menu to adjust the series.

If you drag the fill handle by right-clicking it, a shortcut menu that is similar to the smart tag action menu appears. You can use this shortcut menu to select a fill command before performing any fill action. If what you want to do isn't represented on the menu, click the Series command to display the Series dialog box.

Fill

You can use the Series command to tend to a series of dates with a bit more flexibility than using the fill handle. To use this approach, type the starting date, select the range of cells you want to fill (including the starting date), click the Fill button on the Home tab on the Ribbon, and click Series to display the Series dialog box shown in Figure 15-2.

When extending a series of dates, remember the following:

- You can use the Series In options to choose whether to extend the selected date across the current row or down the current column.

- You can use the Step Value option to specify the interval between cells. For example, by typing **2** in the Step Value text box and selecting Month in the Date Unit area, you can create a series of dates occurring every other month. By typing a negative number in the Step Value text box, you can create a series that decreases (goes backward in time).

- You can use the Stop Value text box to set an ending date for the series. Using this method, you can use the Series command without having to figure out how many cells to select in advance. For example, to enter a series of dates that extends from 1/1/08 through 12/31/10, type **1/1/08** in a cell. Then select only that cell, display the Series dialog box, select the Columns option, and type **12/31/10** in the Stop Value text box. Excel extends a series of dates following the original cell.

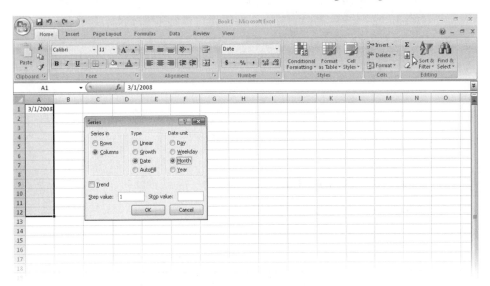

Figure 15-2 Use the Series dialog box to create date series.

For more information about AutoFill and the Series command, see "Filling and Creating Data Series" on page 211.

Extending an Existing Date Series

The AutoFill feature uses the selected cells to determine the type of series you intend to create when you drag the fill handle. AutoFill copies text and nonsequential values and increments sequential numeric values. Because dates are stored as serial values, Auto-Fill extends them sequentially, as illustrated in Figure 15-3.

When you use the fill handle to extend the value in a single selected cell, Excel assumes you want to increment the numeric value in each cell. (If you want to copy the cell instead, hold down Ctrl while dragging the fill handle.) Notice that in Figure 15-3 the entries in rows 7 through 11 contain text values. AutoFill recognizes text entries for days and months and extends them as if they were numeric values. In addition, when a cell contains a mixed text and numeric entry (as in row 11), AutoFill copies the text portion if it's not the name of a month or day and extends the numeric portion if it occurs at either end of the entry.

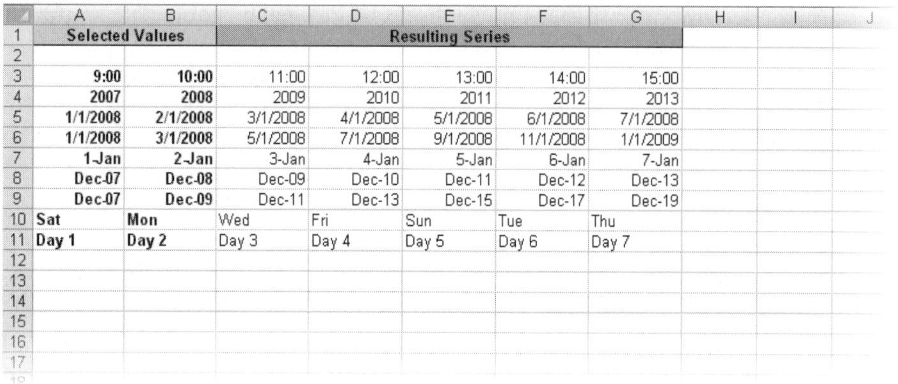

	A	B	C	D	E	F	G	H	I	J
1	Selected Values				Resulting Series					
2										
3	9:00	10:00	11:00	12:00	13:00	14:00	15:00			
4	2007	2008	2009	2010	2011	2012	2013			
5	1/1/2008	2/1/2008	3/1/2008	4/1/2008	5/1/2008	6/1/2008	7/1/2008			
6	1/1/2008	3/1/2008	5/1/2008	7/1/2008	9/1/2008	11/1/2008	1/1/2009			
7	1-Jan	2-Jan	3-Jan	4-Jan	5-Jan	6-Jan	7-Jan			
8	Dec-07	Dec-08	Dec-09	Dec-10	Dec-11	Dec-12	Dec-13			
9	Dec-07	Dec-09	Dec-11	Dec-13	Dec-15	Dec-17	Dec-19			
10	Sat	Mon	Wed	Fri	Sun	Tue	Thu			
11	Day 1	Day 2	Day 3	Day 4	Day 5	Day 6	Day 7			
12										
13										
14										
15										
16										
17										

Figure 15-3 Starting with the values in the Selected Values area, we created the values to the right by dragging the fill handle.

Formatting Dates and Times

After you type a date or time in a cell, you can use the Number Format drop-down list on the Home tab on the Ribbon to change its format using the most popular date and time formats, or you can click More Number Formats at the bottom of the list to select any of the built-in formats. In the Format Cells dialog box, select the Date or Time category to display the list of available formats in the Type box on the right. A preview of the format appears in the Sample box in the upper-right corner, as shown in Figure 15-4.

> **Note**
>
> At the top of the list of Date and Time formats you'll see several types that begin with an asterisk (*). These formats respond to changes in the settings available on the Date and Time tabs in the Customize Regional Options dialog box, which you access by opening Control Panel, clicking Regional And Language Options, and then clicking the Customize button on the Formats tab. All other formats remain unaffected by these Control Panel settings.

Most of the Date and Time formats are easy to understand, but a few special formats exist:

- The 13:30 and 13:30:55 time formats use the 24-hour (military) time convention.
- The 30:55.2 time format displays only minutes and seconds; Excel displays a fraction of a second as a decimal value.
- The 37:30:55 time format displays elapsed time.

> **Note**
> You can press Ctrl+1 to quickly display the Format Cells dialog box.

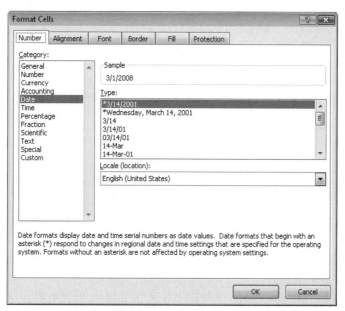

Figure 15-4 Use the Number tab in the Format Cells dialog box to apply Date and Time formats to cells.

Creating Your Own Date and Time Formats

To supplement the standard Date and Time formats, you can create custom formats using the same technique you use for creating custom numeric formats.

For more information about custom formats, see "Creating Custom Number Formats" on page 307.

For example, you can create a format that displays all the available date and time information. The entry 2/24/08 would appear as Tuesday, February 24, 2008 0:00:00.0. To create this format, follow these steps:

1. Select the cell that contains the date.

2. Press Ctrl+1 to display the Format Cells dialog box, and if necessary, click the Number tab.

3. Select the Custom category.

4. Highlight the entry in the text box at the top of the Type list, and type the following custom format code: **dddd mmmm dd, yyyy h:mm:ss.0**.

5. Click OK. Excel stores the new format in the Type list for the Custom category and displays the date using the new format in the selected cell.

You can use the same procedure to display only a portion of the date or the time information available. For example, if you create the format mmmm, Excel displays the date 2/24/2008 as February.

Table 15-1 shows the formatting codes you can use to create custom date and time formats. Be sure to keep two facts in mind. First, Excel assumes that m means months. If, on the other hand, you type the code **m** immediately after an **h**, or the code **mm** immediately after an **hh**, Excel displays minutes instead of months. Second, if you include one of the codes AM/PM, am/pm, A/P, or a/p in a time format, Excel uses the 12-hour time convention; if you omit these codes, Excel uses the 24-hour (military) time convention.

After you add a custom date or time format to the Type list, you can apply it to any date or time entry. Select the Custom category and select the format you entered from the Type list (new custom formats appear at the bottom of the list), and click OK to apply the format.

Measuring Elapsed Time

You can enclose time codes in brackets, as listed at the bottom of Table 15-1, to display more than 24 hours, more than 60 minutes, or more than 60 seconds in a time value. The brackets must always appear around the first code in the format. Excel provides one built-in elapsed time code, [h]:mm:ss, available in the Custom category Type list. Other valid codes for measuring elapsed time include [mm]:ss and [ss].

Bracketed codes have no effect if you use them in any position of the format other than first. For example, if you use the code h:[mm]:ss, Excel ignores the brackets and displays the time using the regular h:mm:ss format.

> **Note**
> One format in the Time category on the Number tab in the Format Cells dialog box represents elapsed time: 37:30:55. This is the same as the [h]:mm:ss format in the Custom category.

Suppose you want to determine the elapsed time between two dates. Type the following formulas in cells A1, A2, and A3, respectively: **11/23/08 13:32**, **11/25/08 23:59**, and **=A2−A1**.

If you apply the built-in format 37:30:55 ([h]:mm:ss) to cell A3, the result of the formula is 58:27:00—the elapsed time between the two dates. If you apply the standard 1:30:55 PM (h:mm:ss) format to cell A3 instead, the result is 10:27:00—the difference between the two times. Without the elapsed time format code, Excel ignores the difference in dates.

Table 15-1 Codes for Creating Custom Date and Time Formats

Code	Display
General	Number in General (serial value) format.
d	Day number without leading zero (1–31).
dd	Day number with leading zero (01–31).
ddd	Day-of-week abbreviation (Sun–Sat).
dddd	Complete day-of-week name (Sunday–Saturday).
m	Month number without leading zero (1–12).
mm	Month number with leading zero (01–12).
mmm	Month name abbreviation (Jan–Dec).
mmmm	Complete month name (January–December).
yy	Last two digits of year number (00–99).
yyyy	Complete four-digit year number (1900–2078).
h	Hour without leading zero (0–23).
hh	Hour with leading zero (00–23).
m	Minute without leading zero (0–59).
mm	Minute with leading zero (00–59).
s	Second without leading zero (0–59).
ss	Second with leading zero (00–59).
s.0	Second and tenths of a second without leading zero.
s.00	Second without leading zero and hundredths of a second without leading zero.
ss.0	Second without leading zero and tenths of a second with leading zero.
ss.00	Second and hundredths of a second with leading zero.
AM/PM	Time in AM/PM notation.
am/pm	Time in am/pm notation.
A/P	Time in A/P notation.
a/p	Time in a/p notation.
[ ]	Brackets display the absolute elapsed time when used to enclose a time code, as in [h]. You can use brackets around only the first component of the code.

Chapter 15

TROUBLESHOOTING

I can't enter a number of hours greater than 9999.

Suppose you have a worksheet in which you keep a running total of flying time for pilots, using the time formats in Excel. Whenever you try to enter a number of hours greater than 9999 (which isn't uncommon), Excel treats the entry as text. What's wrong?

Nothing is wrong—that's just a built-in limitation of Excel. Here are a couple of ways to work with this limitation:

- Use an elapsed time format. In the Cells group on the Home tab, click Format, click Format Cells, click the Number tab if necessary, select the Custom category, and then select [h]:mm:ss in the Type list to apply the one built-in elapsed time format. If you don't need to record seconds, you can delete :ss. Elapsed time formats can store and display an unlimited number of hours.

- If you need to enter more than 9999 hours at a time, you'll have to break it into two smaller chunks and type it in two cells.

You should also know that when you type a time greater than 24 hours (even 24:01), Excel adds a date in the formula bar. Unless the number of hours typed exceeds a year's worth, the added date will be sometime in 1900; you'll just have to live with that. You can select the year in the formula bar and type the correct year, but then the year will be displayed in the cell along with the time. Otherwise, the date doesn't show in the cell unless you format it accordingly.

Calculating with Date and Time

Because Excel records dates as serial date values, you can use dates in formulas and functions as you would any other value. Suppose you want to find the date that falls exactly 200 days after July 4, 2008. If cell A1 contains the entry 7/4/08, you can type the following formula to compute the date 200 days later, which is 1/20/09 (or 39,833): **=A1+200**.

As another example, suppose you want to find the number of weeks between October 31, 2003, and May 13, 2008. Type the formula **=(("5/13/08")−("10/31/03"))/7**, which returns approximately 236.6 weeks.

You can also use times in formulas and functions; however, the results of time arithmetic are not as easy to understand as the results of date arithmetic. For example, you can determine how much time has elapsed between 8:22 AM and 10:45 PM by typing the formula **="22:45"−"8:22"**. The result is .599306, which can be formatted using a 24-hour time format (one that doesn't include AM/PM) to display 14:23. Excel displays the result relative to midnight.

Suppose you want to determine the time that is 2 hours, 23 minutes, and 17 seconds after 12:35:23 PM. The formula **=("12:35:23 PM")+("2:23:17")** returns the correct answer, .624074, which can be formatted as 14:58:40. In this formula, 2:23:17 represents not an absolute time (2:23:17 AM) but an interval of time (2 hours, 23 minutes, and 17 seconds). This format is perfectly acceptable to Excel.

TROUBLESHOOTING

Excel displays my time as #####.

Usually, a cell full of number signs means the cell isn't wide enough to show its displayed contents. But Excel can't display negative numbers as dates or times. If the result of a date or time calculation is negative and you attempt to display this result in a date or time format, you will see a cell full of number signs, no matter how much you widen the cell. This typically happens when you subtract a later time of day from an earlier time of day. You can work around the problem by converting the result to elapsed hours. To do that, multiply the result by 24, and display it in a numeric format, not a date or time format.

Working with Date and Time Functions

Using the Excel date and time functions, you can perform worksheet calculations quickly and accurately. For example, if you use your worksheet to calculate your company's monthly payroll, you might use the HOUR function to determine the number of hours worked each day and the WEEKDAY function to determine whether employees should be paid at the standard rate (for Monday through Friday) or at the overtime rate (for Saturdays and Sundays).

 In the following sections, we'll explore a few of the most useful date and time functions in detail. You can access all 20 of the date and time functions available in Excel by clicking the Date & Time button on the Formulas tab on the Ribbon. For complete information about all the functions Excel has to offer, you can read about a number of tools in "Using the Built-In Function Reference in Excel" on page 487.

Using the TODAY and NOW Functions

You can type **=TODAY( )** in a cell or a formula to insert the serial value of the current date. If you type the function in a cell with the General format (which is the default), Excel displays the resulting value in mm/dd/yyyy format. Although this function takes no arguments, you must remember to include the empty parentheses. (You'll remember that *arguments* are variables that supply the values a function needs to perform its calculations. You place arguments between the parentheses of functions that require them.)

Similarly, you can type **=NOW( )** in a cell or formula to insert the current date and time. This function also takes no arguments. The result of the function is a serial date and time value that includes an integer (the date) and a decimal value (the time). Excel doesn't update the value of NOW continuously. If the value of a cell that contains the

NOW function isn't current, you can update the value by recalculating the worksheet. (You recalculate the worksheet by making a new entry or by pressing F9.) Excel also updates the NOW function whenever you open or print the worksheet.

The NOW function is an example of a *volatile* function—that is, a function whose calculated value is subject to change. Anytime you open a worksheet that contains one or more NOW functions and close the worksheet, Excel prompts you to save your changes regardless of whether you've made any, because the current value of NOW has changed since the last time you used the worksheet. (Another example of a volatile function is RAND.)

For more about the RAND function, see "The RAND and RANDBETWEEN Functions" on page 500.

Using the WEEKDAY Function

The WEEKDAY function returns the day of the week for a specific date and takes the arguments (*serial_number*, *return_type*). The *serial_number* argument can be a serial date value; a reference to a cell that contains either a date function or a serial date value; or text, such as 1/27/08 or January 27, 2008. If you use text, be sure to enclose the text in quotation marks. The function returns a number that represents the day of the week on which the specified date falls. The optional *return_type* argument determines the way the result is displayed. Table 15-2 lists the available return types.

Table 15-2 **Return Type Codes**

If *return_type* Is . . .	WEEKDAY Returns . . .
1 or omitted	A number from 1 through 7 where 1 is Sunday and 7 is Saturday
2	A number from 1 through 7 where 1 is Monday and 7 is Sunday
3	A number from 0 through 6 where 0 is Monday and 6 is Sunday

Note

You might want to format a cell containing the WEEKDAY function with a custom day-of-week format, such as dddd. By applying this custom format, you can use the result of the WEEKDAY function in other functions and still have a meaningful display on the screen.

Using the YEAR, MONTH, and DAY Functions

The YEAR, MONTH, and DAY functions return the value of the year, month, and day portions of a serial date value. All three take a single argument, which can be a serial date value; a reference to a cell that contains either a date function or a serial date value; or a text date enclosed in quotation marks. For example, if cell A1 contains the date

3/25/2008, the formula =YEAR(A1) returns the value 2008, the formula =MONTH(A1) returns the value 3, and the formula =DAY(A1) returns the value 25.

Using the HOUR, MINUTE, and SECOND Functions

Just as the YEAR, MONTH, and DAY functions extract the value of the year, month, and day portions of a serial date value, the HOUR, MINUTE, and SECOND functions extract the value of the hour, minute, and second portions of a serial time value. For example, if cell B1 contains the time 12:15:35 PM, the formula =HOUR(B1) returns the value 12, the formula =MINUTE(B1) returns the value 15, and the formula =SECOND(B1) returns the value 35.

Using the DATEVALUE and TIMEVALUE Functions

The DATEVALUE function translates a date into a serial value. You must type the single argument as text, using any date from 1/1/1900 to 12/31/9999, and you must add quotation marks around the text. You can enter the argument using any of the built-in Date formats; however, if you type the date without a year, Excel uses the current year from your computer's internal clock. For example, the formula =DATEVALUE("December 31, 2010") returns the serial value 40,543.

Similarly, the TIMEVALUE function translates a time into a decimal value. You must type its single argument as text. You can use any of the built-in Time formats, but you must add quotation marks around the text. For example, the formula =TIMEVALUE("4:30 PM") returns the decimal value 0.6875.

Working with Specialized Date Functions

Excel includes a set of specialized date functions that perform operations such as calculations for the maturity dates of securities, for payroll, and for work schedules.

Using the EDATE and EOMONTH Functions

You can use the EDATE function to calculate the exact date that occurs an indicated number of months before or after a given date. It takes the arguments (*start_date, months*), where *start_date* is the date you want to use as a starting point and *months* is an integer value that indicates the number of months before or after the start date. If the *months* argument is positive, the function returns a date after the start date; if the *months* argument is negative, the function returns a date before the start date. For example, to find the date that falls exactly 23 months after June 12, 2008, type the formula **=EDATE("6/12/08", 23)**, which returns the value 40310, or May 12, 2010.

The EOMONTH function returns a date that is an indicated number of months before or after a given date. Although EOMONTH is similar to EDATE and takes the same arguments, the value returned is always rounded up to the last day of the month. For example, to calculate the serial date value that is the last day of the month 23 months after June 12, 2008, type the formula **=EOMONTH("6/12/2003", 23)**, which returns 40329, or May 31, 2010.

Using the YEARFRAC Function

The YEARFRAC function calculates a decimal number that represents the portion of a year that falls between two given dates. This function takes the arguments (*start_date, end_date, basis*), where *start_date* and *end_date* specify the period of time you want to convert to a fractional year. The *basis* argument is the type of day count you want to use, as described in Table 15-3.

Table 15-3 **Basis Codes**

If *basis* Is . . .	YEARFRAC Returns . . .
0 (or omitted)	30/360, or 30 days per month and 360 days per year, as established in the United States by the National Association of Security Dealers (NASD)
1	Actual/actual, or the actual number of days in the month(s)/actual days in the year
2	Actual/360
3	Actual/365
4	European 30/360

For example, to determine what fraction of a year is represented from 4/12/08 to 12/15/08, you can type the formula **=YEARFRAC("4/12/04", "12/15/04")**. This formula returns 0.675, based on the default 30-day month and 360-day year.

Using the WORKDAY and NETWORKDAYS Functions

The WORKDAY and NETWORKDAYS functions are invaluable for anyone who calculates payroll and benefits or determines work schedules. Both functions return values based on working days, excluding weekend days. In addition, you can choose whether to include holidays and specify the exact dates.

The WORKDAY function returns the date that is an indicated number of working days before or after a given date. This function takes the arguments (*start_date, days, holidays*), where *start_date* is the date you want the function to count from and *days* is the number of workdays before or after the start date, excluding weekends and holidays. Use a positive value for days to count forward from the start date; use a negative value to count backward. The optional *holidays* argument can be an array or a reference to a cell range that contains any dates you want to exclude from the calculation. If you leave *holidays* blank, the function counts all weekdays from the start date. For example, to determine the date that is 100 working days, not counting holidays, from the current date, type the formula **=WORKDAY(NOW( ),100)**.

Similarly, the NETWORKDAYS function calculates the number of working days between two given dates. It takes the arguments (*start_date, end_date, holidays*). For example, to determine the number of working days from January 15, 2008 to June 30, 2008, type the formula **=NETWORKDAYS("1/15/08", "6/30/08")**, which results in a value of 120.

Functions for Financial Analysis

With the financial functions provided with Microsoft Office Excel 2007, you can perform common business calculations, such as net present value and future value, without building long and complex formulas. These functions are the heart of spreadsheets—the word *spreadsheet* itself refers to the seemingly antiquated system of using special grid paper to track financial information. Functions have taken the place of the old 10-key calculator sequences (*algorithms*) used by accounting professionals before computers revolutionized the discipline.

Office Excel 2007 offers more than 50 financial functions, and in this chapter, we'll touch on most of them, with special emphasis on those most often used, needed, or misunderstood. For complete information about all the built-in functions that Excel has to offer, you can use some on-screen tools, covered in "Using the Built-In Function Reference in Excel" on page 487.

Calculating Investments

The financial functions built into Excel fall into three major categories: investments, depreciation, and securities. The functions included within each category accept similar arguments. To streamline this chapter, we'll first define the common arguments, and we'll then discuss their implementation in the individual functions.

Table 16-1 lists all the arguments used in functions dedicated to calculating investments.

Table 16-1 Investment Function Arguments

Argument	Description
Future value	The value of an investment at the end of the term (0 if omitted)
value1, value2, . . . value n	Periodic payments (*inflows*) when individual amounts differ
Number of periods	Term of investment
Payment	Periodic payments when individual amounts are the same
Type	When payment is to be made (0 if omitted); 0 = at end of period; 1 = at beginning of period
Period	Number of an individual periodic payment

Argument	Description
Present value	Value of investment today
Rate	Discount rate or interest rate
Guess	A starting interest rate for iterative calculations (10 percent if omitted)
Finance rate	The rate at which you borrow money to purchase an investment
Reinvestment rate	The rate at which you reinvest cash received from an investment

The PV Function

Present value is one of the most common methods for measuring the attractiveness of a long-term investment. *Present value* is today's value of the investment. It's determined by discounting the inflows (payments received) from the investment back to the present time. If the present value of the inflows is greater than the cost of the investment, the investment is a good one.

The PV function computes the present value of a series of equal periodic payments or of a lump-sum payment. (A series of equal payments is often called an *ordinary annuity*.) This function takes the arguments (*rate, number of periods, payment, future value, type*); for definitions of these arguments, see Table 16-1. To compute the present value of a series of payments, type a value for the *payment* argument, or to compute the present value of a lump-sum payment, type a value for the *future value* argument. For an investment with both a series of payments and a lump-sum payment, use both arguments.

Here's a real-world example of how this function works: Suppose you are presented with an investment opportunity that returns $1,000 each year over the next five years. To receive this annuity, you must invest $4,000. Are you willing to pay $4,000 today to earn $5,000 over the next five years? To decide whether this investment is acceptable, you need to determine the present value of the stream of $1,000 payments you will receive.

Because you could invest your money in a five-year CD money-market account at 4.5 percent, we'll use 4.5 percent as the discount rate of the investment. (Because this discount rate is a sort of hurdle over which an investment must leap before it becomes attractive to you, it's often called the *hurdle rate*.) To determine the present value of this investment, use the formula =PV(4.5%, 5,1000), which returns the value −4389.98, meaning you should be willing to spend $4,389.98 now to receive $5,000 over the next five years. (Negative values indicate money going out; positive values indicate money coming in.) Because your investment is only $4,000, you can surmise that this is an acceptable investment.

Suppose you're offered $5,000 at the end of five years instead of $1,000 for each of the next five years. Is the investment still as attractive? To find out, use the formula =PV(4.5%, 5,,5000). (Include a comma as a placeholder for the unused *payment* argument.) This formula returns the present value −4012.26, which means that, at a hurdle rate of 4.5 percent, you should be willing to spend $4,012.26 to receive $5,000 in five years. Although the proposal may not be nearly as attractive under these terms, it's still acceptable because your investment is only $4,000. However, it also makes a guaranteed 4.5 percent CD look much more attractive by comparison.

The NPV Function

The NPV function calculates the net present value, which is another common method for determining the profitability of an investment. In general, any investment that yields a net present value greater than zero is considered profitable. This function takes the arguments (*rate, value1,value2, . . .*); for definitions of these arguments, see Table 16-1. You can use as many as 254 inflow values as arguments, but you can include any number of values by using an array as an argument.

NPV differs from PV in two important respects. Whereas PV assumes constant inflow values, NPV allows variable payments. The other major difference is that PV allows payments and receipts to occur at either the beginning or the end of the period, whereas NPV assumes that all payments and receipts are evenly distributed and that they occur at the end of each period. If the cost of the investment must be paid up front, you should not include the cost as one of the function's inflow arguments but should subtract it from the result of the function. On the other hand, if the cost must be paid at the end of the first period, you should include it as a negative first inflow argument. Let's consider an example to help clarify this distinction.

Suppose you are contemplating an investment on which you expect to incur a loss of $85,000 at the end of the first year, followed by gains of $95,000; $140,000; and $185,000 at the ends of the second, third, and fourth years. You will invest $250,000 up front, and the hurdle rate is 8 percent. To evaluate this investment, use the formula =NPV(8%, –85000, 95000, 140000, 185000) –250000.

The result, –139.48, tells you not to expect a net profit from this investment. Note that the negative values in this formula indicate the money you spend on your investment. (You can use the Goal Seek command to determine what initial cost or interest rate would justify the investment. For more information about this command, see "Using the Goal Seek Command" on page 599.)

This formula does not include the up-front cost of the investment as an argument for the NPV function. However, if you fund the initial $250,000 investment at the end of the first year instead of at the beginning, the formula is =NPV(8%,(–250000–85000), 95000, 140000, 185000). The result, $18,379.04, would suggest that this might be a profitable investment.

The FV Function

The FV function determines the future value of an investment and is essentially the opposite of present value, computing the value at some future date of an investment that makes payments as a lump sum or as a series of equal periodic payments. This function takes the arguments (*rate, number of periods, payment, present value, type*); for definitions of these arguments, see Table 16-1. Use the *payment* argument to compute the future value of a series of payments and the *present value* argument to compute the future value of a lump-sum payment.

Suppose you're thinking about starting an IRA. You plan to deposit $4,000 in the IRA at the beginning of each year, and you expect the average rate of return to be 6 percent per year for the entire term. Assuming you're now 30 years old, how much money will your account accumulate by the time you're 65? Use the formula =FV(6%, 35, –4000,, 1) to learn that your IRA balance will be $472,483.47 at the end of 35 years.

Now assume you started an IRA account three years ago and have already accumulated $7,500 in your account. Use the formula =FV(6%, 35, –4000, –7500, 1) to learn that your IRA will grow to $530,129.12 at the end of 35 years.

In both of these examples, the *type* argument is 1, because payments occur at the beginning of the period. Including this argument is particularly important in financial calculations that span many years. If you omit the *type* argument (1) in the preceding formula, Excel assumes you add money to your account at the end of each year and returns the value $503,384.77—a difference of $26,744.35!

The PMT Function

The PMT function computes the periodic payment required to amortize a loan over a specified number of periods. This function takes the arguments (*rate, number of periods, present value, future value, type*); for definitions of these arguments, see Table 16-1.

Suppose you want to take out a 30-year mortgage for $300,000. Assuming an interest rate of 6 percent, what will your monthly payments be? First, divide the 6 percent interest rate by 12 to arrive at a monthly rate (0.5 percent). Next, convert the number of periods into months by multiplying 30 by 12 (360). You can include these computations as arguments using the formula =PMT((6%/12), (30*12), 300000) to compute the monthly mortgage payment, which turns out to be –$1,798.65. (The result is negative because it's a cost to you.)

The IPMT Function

The IPMT function computes the interest part of an individual payment made to repay an amount over a specified time period, with constant periodic payments and a constant interest rate. This function takes the arguments (*rate, period, number of periods, present value, future value, type*); for definitions of these arguments, see Table 16-1.

Suppose you borrow $200,000 for 30 years at 6 percent interest. The formula =IPMT((6/12)%, 1, 360, 200000) tells you that the interest component of the payment due for the first month is an even –$1,000.00. The formula =IPMT((6/12)%, 360, 360, 200000) tells you that the interest component of the final payment of the same loan is –$5.97.

TROUBLESHOOTING

The PMT function produces unrealistic results.

Sometimes you might find that the PMT function seems to produce unrealistic results—such as payments that are excessively large. As is the case with all functions used for calculating investments, make sure you are using the same units for both the *rate* and *nper* (*number of periods*) arguments. If, for example, you type **6%** for the rate, you must type the *nper* argument in years, because 6 percent is an annual rate. If you type **6%** for the rate and **360** as the term, Excel returns the payment required to amortize a loan at either 6 percent per month for 30 years or 6 percent per year for 360 years! You can resolve your problem by either dividing 6 percent by 12 (which is the standard way of expressing a loan) or typing **30** for *nper*, indicating the term in years. Note, however, that these two options are not equivalent—they yield very different results because of the way interest is calculated. You should use the same units that your lender uses, which is probably annual interest rate divided by 12 and *nper* expressed in months.

The PPMT Function

The PPMT function is similar to the IPMT function, except it computes the principal component of an individual payment when a loan is repaid over a specified time with constant periodic payments and a constant interest rate. If you compute both IPMT and PPMT for the same period, you can add the results to obtain the total payment. The PPMT function takes the arguments (*rate, period, number of periods, present value, future value, type*); for definitions of these arguments, see Table 16-1.

If you borrow $200,000 for 30 years at 6 percent interest, the formula =PPMT((6/12)%, 1, 360, 200000) tells you that the principal component of the payment for the first month of the loan is –$199.10. The formula =PPMT((6/12)%, 360, 360, 200000) tells you that the principal component of the final payment of the same loan is –$1193.14.

The NPER Function

The NPER function computes the number of periods required to amortize a loan, given a specified periodic payment. This function takes the arguments (*rate, payment, present value, future value, type*); for definitions of these arguments, see Table 16-1.

Suppose you can afford mortgage payments of $2,000 per month and you want to know how long it will take to pay off a $300,000 loan at 6 percent interest. The formula =NPER((6/12)%, –2000, 300000) tells you that your mortgage payments will extend over 278 months.

If the payment is too small to amortize the loan at the indicated rate of interest, the function returns an error value. The monthly payment must be at least equal to the period interest rate times the principal amount; otherwise, the loan will never be

Chapter 16

amortized. For example, the formula =NPER((6/12)%, −1000, 300000) returns the #NUM! error value. In this case, the monthly payment must be at least $1,501 to amortize the loan (although it would take more than 120 years worth of payments at that amount).

The RATE Function

The RATE function determines the rate of return of an investment that generates a series of equal periodic payments or a single lump-sum payment. This function takes the arguments (*number of periods, payment, present value, future value, type, guess*); for definitions of these arguments, see Table 16-1. You use either the *payment* argument to compute the rate for a series of equal periodic payments or the *future value* argument to compute the rate of a lump-sum payment.

Suppose you're considering an investment that will pay you four annual $1,000 payments. The investment costs $3,000. To determine the actual annual rate of return on your investment, type the formula =**RATE(4, 1000, −3000)**. This formula returns 13 percent, an excellent rate of return on this investment.

> **Note**
>
> The RATE function uses *iteration* to compute the rate of return. The function begins by computing the net present value of the investment at the *guess* rate. If that first net present value is greater than zero, the function selects a higher rate and repeats the net present value calculation; if the first net present value is less than zero, the function selects a lower rate for the second iteration. RATE continues this process until it arrives at the correct rate of return or until it has gone through 20 iterations. For more information about iteration, see "Working with Circular References" on page 464.

If you receive the #NUM! error value when you enter the RATE function, Excel probably cannot calculate the rate within 20 iterations. Try typing a different *guess* rate to give the function a running start. A rate from 10 percent through 100 percent usually works.

The IRR Function

The IRR function determines the internal rate of return of an investment, which is the rate that causes the net present value of the investment to equal zero. In other words, the internal rate of return is the rate that causes the present value of the inflows from an investment to equal the cost of the investment.

Internal rate of return, like net present value, compares one investment opportunity with another. An attractive investment is one whose net present value, discounted at the appropriate hurdle rate, is greater than zero. Turn that equation around, and you can see that the discount rate required to generate a net present value of zero must be greater than the hurdle rate. Thus, an attractive investment is one for which the discount rate required to yield a net present value of zero—that is, the internal rate of return—is greater than the hurdle rate.

The IRR function takes the arguments (*values, guess*). (For definitions of these arguments, see Table 16-1.) The *values* argument is an array or a reference to a range of cells that contain numbers. Only one *values* argument is allowed, and it must include at least one positive and one negative value. IRR ignores text, logical values, and blank cells. IRR assumes that transactions occur at the end of a period and returns the equivalent interest rate for that period's length. The *guess* argument is optional, but if you receive the #NUM! error value, try including a *guess* to help Excel reach the answer.

Suppose you agree to buy an income property for $350,000 and rent it. Over the next ten years, you expect to receive net rental income starting at $40,000 the first year, increasing by $1,000 per year. You can set up a simple worksheet that contains your investment and income information. Type the 11 values, starting with the initial investment amount, in cells A1:A11 on the worksheet. (Be sure to type the initial $350,000 investment in cell A1 as a negative value.) Then the formula **=IRR(A1:A11)** returns the internal rate of return of 4.46 percent. If the hurdle rate is 3.5 percent, you can consider this property to be a good investment.

The MIRR Function

The MIRR function calculates the modified internal rate of return of an investment. The difference from the IRR function is that MIRR takes into account the cost of the money you borrow to finance the investment. MIRR assumes you'll reinvest the cash it generates and that transactions occur at the end of a period. It then returns the equivalent interest rate for that period's length.

The MIRR function takes the arguments (*values, finance rate, reinvestment rate*). (For definitions of these arguments, see Table 16-1.) The *values* argument must be an array or a reference to a range of cells that contain numbers. This argument represents a series of payments and income occurring at regular periods. You must include at least one positive and one negative value in the *values* argument.

Suppose you borrow $120,000 at 7 percent interest to acquire an investment that will return increasing amounts of income over five years. If cells A1 through A6 contain the values –120000, 22000, 24000, 28000, 31000, and 33000, representing the initial investment (as a negative value) and the subsequent cash inflows from that investment, the formula =MIRR(A1:A6, 7%, 3.5%) returns a modified internal rate of return of 4 percent.

Calculating Depreciation

Depreciation has an enormous effect on the bottom line of any business, and accurately calculating depreciation is crucial if you want to avoid triggering a detailed scrutiny of your records by the IRS. These functions help you precisely determine the depreciation of an asset for a specific period. Table 16-2 lists the common arguments used in these functions.

Table 16-2 Depreciation Function Arguments

Argument	Description
Cost	Initial cost of the asset
Life	Length of time the asset will be depreciated
Period	Individual time period to be computed
Salvage	Asset's remaining value after it has been fully depreciated

The SLN Function

The SLN function determines the straight-line depreciation for an asset for a single period. This depreciation method assumes that the depreciation is uniform throughout the useful life of the asset. The cost or basis of the asset, less its estimated salvage value, is deductible in equal amounts over the life of the asset. This function takes the arguments (*cost, salvage, life*). (For definitions of these arguments, see Table 16-2.)

Suppose you want to determine the depreciation for each year of a machine that costs $8,000 new; has a life of 10 years; and has a salvage value of $500. The formula =SLN(8000, 500, 10) tells you that each year's straight-line depreciation is $750.

The DDB and DB Functions

The DDB (double declining balance) function computes an asset's depreciation at an accelerated rate—more in the early periods and less later. Using this method, depreciation is computed as a percentage of the net book value of the asset (the cost of the asset less any prior years' depreciation).

The function takes the arguments (*cost, salvage, life, period, factor*). All DDB arguments must be positive numbers, and you must use the same time units for life and period; that is, if you express life in months, period must also be in months. The *factor* argument is optional and has a default value of 2, which indicates the normal double declining balance method. Using 3 for the *factor* argument specifies the triple declining balance method. For other argument definitions, see Table 16-2.

Suppose you want to calculate the depreciation of a machine that costs $5,000 new and that has a life of five years (60 months) and a salvage value of $100. The formula =DDB(5000, 100, 60, 1) tells you that the double declining balance depreciation for the first month is $166.67. (Note that *life* is expressed in months.) The formula =DDB(5000, 100, 5, 1) tells you that the double declining balance depreciation for the first year is $2,000.00. (Note that *life* is expressed in years.)

The DB (declining balance) function is similar to the DDB function except it uses the fixed declining balance method of depreciation and can calculate depreciation for a particular period in the asset's life. It takes the arguments (*cost, salvage, life, period, month*).

The *life* and *period* arguments must use the same units. The optional *month* argument is the number of months depreciated in the first year, which, if omitted, is 12–a full year. For example, to calculate the real depreciation for the first period on a $1,000,000 item with a salvage value of $100,000; a life of six years; and seven months in the first year; use the formula =DB(1000000, 100000, 6, 1, 7), which returns $186,083.33.

The VDB Function

The VDB (variable declining balance) function calculates the depreciation of an asset for any complete or partial period, using either the double declining balance or another accelerated-depreciation factor you specify.

This function takes the arguments (*cost, salvage, life, start, end, factor, no switch*). The *start* argument is the period after which depreciation will be calculated, and *end* is the last period for which depreciation will be calculated. These arguments determine the depreciation for any length of time during the life of the asset. The *life*, *start*, and *end* arguments must all use the same units (days, months, or years). The optional *factor* argument is the rate at which the balance declines. If you omit *factor*, Excel assumes that the argument is 2 and uses the double declining balance method. The optional *no switch* argument is a value that specifies whether to switch to straight-line depreciation when the straight-line depreciation is greater than the declining balance. If you omit *no switch* or type **0 (FALSE)**, Excel switches to straight-line depreciation; to prevent the switch, type **1 (TRUE)**. For other argument definitions, see Table 16-2.

Suppose you purchased a $15,000 asset at the end of the first quarter of the current year and that this asset will have a salvage value of $2,000 after five years. To determine the depreciation of this asset next year (the fourth to seventh quarters of its use), use the formula =VDB(15000, 2000, 20, 3, 7). The depreciation for this period is $3,760.55. The units used here are quarters. Notice that the *start* argument is 3, not 4, because we are jumping over the first three periods to start in the fourth.

The SYD Function

The SYD function computes an asset's depreciation for a specific time with the sum-of-the-years'-digits method. The SYD function takes the arguments (*cost, salvage, life, period*). (For definitions of these arguments, see Table 16-2.) You must use the same units for life and period. Using the sum-of-the-years'-digits method, Excel calculates depreciation on the cost of the item less its salvage value. Like the double declining balance method, the sum-of-the-years'-digits method is an accelerated depreciation method.

Suppose you want to determine the depreciation of a machine that costs $15,000; has a life of three years; and a salvage value of $1,250. The formula =SYD(15000, 1250, 3, 3) tells you that the sum-of-the-years'-digits depreciation for the third year is $2,291.67.

Chapter 16

Analyzing Securities

 The Financial button on the Formulas tab offers a group of functions designed for specific tasks related to computing and analyzing various types of securities.

> **Note**
>
> In previous versions of Excel, these functions were part of the Analysis Toolpak add-in, but at long last, Microsoft has fully integrated these functions into Excel 2007. As a result of this change, the functions may produce slightly different results, but Microsoft says they're so insignificantly different that the results are nonetheless "equally correct." Although its worksheet functions have been integrated into Excel, the Analysis Toolpak is still available as an add-in with sophisticated data analysis tools. For more information, see "Installing the Analysis Toolpak" on page 567.

Many of these functions share similar arguments. We'll describe the most common ones in Table 16-3 to avoid revisiting the same information in the function discussions that follow.

Table 16-3 Security-Analysis Function Arguments

Argument	Description
Basis	Day count basis of the security. If omitted, defaults to 0, indicating U.S. (NASD) 30/360 basis. Other basis values include 1 = actual/actual, 2 = actual/360, 3 = actual/365, and 4 = European 30/360.
Coupon	The security's annual coupon rate.
Frequency	Number of coupon payments made per year: 1 = annual, 2 = semiannual, 4 = quarterly.
Investment	Amount of investment in the security.
Issue	Issue date of the security.
Maturity	Maturity date of the security, which must be greater than the settlement date.
Par	Par value (face value) of the security; $1,000 if omitted.
Price	Price of the security.
Rate	Interest rate of the security at the issue date, which must be greater than or equal to zero.
Redemption	Value of the security at redemption.
Settlement	Settlement date of the security (the day you have to pay for it), which must be greater than the issue date.
Yield	Annual yield of the security, which must be greater than or equal to zero.

You can type dates by using any of the following: the date's serial number, the date enclosed in quotation marks, or a reference to a cell that contains a date. For example, you can type the date June 30, 2008 as the serial date value *39629*, as *6/30/08*, or as a reference to a cell containing this date. If the security-analysis function results in a #NUM! error value, be sure the dates are in the correct form and that they meet the criteria described in Table 16-3.

For more information about serial date values, see "Understanding How Excel Records Dates and Times" on page 521.

The DOLLARDE and DOLLARFR Functions

One of this pair of functions converts the familiar fractional pricing of securities to decimals, and the other converts decimals to fractions. The DOLLARDE function takes the arguments (*fractional dollar, fraction*), and the DOLLARFR function takes the arguments (*decimal dollar, fraction*). The *fractional dollar* argument is the value you want to convert expressed as an integer, followed by a decimal point and the numerator of the fraction you want to convert. The *decimal dollar* argument is the value you want to convert expressed as a decimal. The *fraction* argument is an integer indicating the denominator you want to use in the conversion. For the DOLLARFR function, *fraction* is the unit that the function should use when converting the decimal value, effectively rounding the decimal number to the nearest half, quarter, eighth, sixteenth, thirty-second, and so on.

For example, the formula =DOLLARDE(1.03, 32) translates as 1+3/32, which is equivalent to 1.09375. On the other hand, the formula =DOLLARFR(1.09375, 32) returns the result 1.03.

The ACCRINT and ACCRINTM Functions

The ACCRINT function returns the interest accrued by a security that pays interest on a periodic basis. This function takes the arguments (*issue, first interest, settlement, rate, par, frequency, basis, calculation method*), in which *first interest* indicates the date on which interest is first accrued and *calculation method* is a logical value (1 or True; 0 or False). The default value of True for *calculation method* returns the total accrued interest; a value of False returns the interest accrued after the *first interest* date. For other argument definitions, see Table 16-3. For example, suppose a U.S. Treasury bond has an issue date of March 1, 2008; a settlement date of April 1, 2008; a first interest date of September 1, 2008; a 7 percent coupon rate with semiannual frequency; a par value of $1,000; and a basis of 30/360. The accrued interest formula is =ACCRINT("3/1/08", "9/1/08", "4/1/08", 0.07, 1000, 2, 0), which returns 5.833333, indicating that $5.83 accrues from March 1, 2008, to April 1, 2008.

Similarly, the ACCRINTM function returns the interest accrued by a maturity security (a type of security with not only a rhyming name but that also pays interest at maturity). This function takes the arguments (*issue, settlement, rate, par, basis*). Using the preceding example with a maturity date of July 31, 2012, the accrued interest formula is =ACCRINTM("3/1/08", "7/31/12", 0.07, 1000, 0), which returns 309.1667, indicating that the $1,000 bond will pay $309.17 interest on July 31, 2012.

Chapter 16

The INTRATE and RECEIVED Functions

The INTRATE function calculates the rate of interest, or discount rate, for a fully invested security. This function takes the arguments (*settlement, maturity, investment, redemption, basis*); for argument definitions, see Table 16-3. For example, suppose a bond has a settlement date of March 31, 2008, and a maturity date of September 30, 2008. A $1,000,000 investment in this bond will have a redemption value of $1,032,324, using the default 30/360 basis. The bond's discount rate formula is =INTRATE("3/31/08", "9/30/08", 1000000, 1032324, 0), which returns 0.064648, or 6.46 percent.

Similarly, the RECEIVED function calculates the amount received at maturity for a fully invested security and takes the arguments (*settlement, maturity, investment, discount, basis*). Using the preceding example with a 5.5 percent discount rate, the formula =RECEIVED("3/31/08", "9/30/08", 1000000, 0.055, 0) returns the mature value $1,028,277.63.

The PRICE, PRICEDISC, and PRICEMAT Functions

The PRICE function calculates the price per $100 of face value of a security that pays interest on a periodic basis. This function takes the arguments (*settlement, maturity, rate, yield, redemption, frequency, basis*); for argument definitions, see Table 16-3. For example, suppose a bond's settlement date is March 31, 2008; its maturity date is July 31, 2008; and the interest rate is 5.75 percent, with semiannual frequency. The security's annual yield is 6.50 percent, its redemption value is $100, and it's calculated using the standard 30/360 basis. The bond price formula is =PRICE("3/31/08", "7/31/08", 0.0575, 0.065, 100, 2, 0), which returns $99.73498.

Similarly, the PRICEDISC function returns the price per $100 of face value of a security that is discounted, instead of paying periodic interest. This function takes the arguments (*settlement, maturity, discount, redemption, basis*). Using the preceding example with the addition of a discount amount of 7.5 percent, the formula =PRICEDISC("3/31/08", "7/31/08", 0.075, 100, 0) returns a price of $97.50.

Finally, the PRICEMAT function returns the price per $100 of face value of a security that pays its interest at the maturity date. This function takes the arguments (*settlement, maturity, issue, rate, yield, basis*). Using the preceding example with a settlement date of July 31, 2008; an issue date of March 1, 2008; and the maturity date changed to July 31, 2009; the formula =PRICEMAT("7/31/08", "7/31/09", "3/31/08", 0.0575, 0.065, 0) returns $99.18.

The DISC Function

The DISC function calculates the discount rate for a security and takes the arguments (*settlement, maturity, price, redemption, basis*). (For argument definitions, see Table 16-3.) For example, suppose a bond has a settlement date of June 15, 2008; has a maturity date of December 31, 2008; has a price of $96.875; has a $100 redemption value; and uses the standard 30/360 basis. The bond discount rate formula =DISC("6/15/08", "12/31/08", 96.875, 100, 0) returns 0.057398, or 5.74 percent.

The YIELD, YIELDDISC, and YIELDMAT Functions

The YIELD function determines the annual yield for a security that pays interest on a periodic basis and takes the arguments (*settlement, maturity, rate, price, redemption, frequency, basis*); for definitions of these arguments, see Table 16-3. For example, suppose a bond has a settlement date of February 15, 2008; has a maturity date of December 1, 2008; has a coupon rate of 5.75 percent with semiannual frequency; has a price of $99.2345; has a $100 redemption value, and uses the standard 30/360 basis. The annual bond yield formula =YIELD("2/15/08", "12/1/08", 0.0575, 99.2345, 100, 2, 0) returns 0.067406, or 6.74 percent.

The YIELDDISC function, on the other hand, calculates the annual yield for a discounted security. It takes the arguments (*settlement, maturity, price, redemption, basis*). Using the preceding example but changing the price to $96.00, the bond yield formula =YIELDDISC("2/15/08", "12/1/08", 96, 100, 0) returns 0.052448, or 5.25 percent.

The YIELDMAT function calculates the annual yield for a security that pays its interest at maturity. This function takes the arguments (*settlement, maturity, issue, rate, price, basis*). Using the arguments from the YIELD example but adding an issue date of January 1, 2008, and changing the price to $99.2345, the yield-at-maturity formula =YIELDMAT("2/15/08", "12/1/08", "1/1/08", 0.0575, 99.2345, 0) returns 0.067178, or 6.72 percent.

The TBILLEQ, TBILLPRICE, and TBILLYIELD Functions

The TBILLEQ function calculates the bond-equivalent yield for a U.S. Treasury bill. It takes the arguments (*settlement, maturity, discount*). (For argument definitions, see Table 16-3.) For example, suppose a U.S. Treasury bill has a settlement date of February 1, 2008; a maturity date of July 1, 2008; and a discount rate of 8.65 percent. The formula for calculating the bond yield that is equivalent to the yield of a U.S. Treasury bill is =TBILLEQ("2/1/08", "7/1/08", 0.0865), which returns 0.091, or 9.1 percent.

You use the TBILLPRICE function to calculate the price per $100 of face value for a U.S. Treasury bill. This function takes the arguments (*settlement, maturity, discount*). Using the preceding example, the formula to calculate the price per $100 of face value, =TBILLPRICE("2/1/08", "7/1/08", 0.0865), returns 96.3718, or $96.37.

Finally, the TBILLYIELD function calculates a U.S. Treasury bill's yield. It takes the arguments (*settlement, maturity, price*). Using the preceding example with its result, a price of $96.37, the yield formula =TBILLYIELD("2/1/08", "7/1/08", 96.37) returns the yield 0.089803, or 9 percent.

The COUPDAYBS, COUPDAYS, COUPDAYSNC, COUPNCD, COUPNUM, and COUPPCD Functions

This group of functions performs calculations relating to bond coupons. For all the sample formulas in this section, we'll use as our example a bond with a settlement date of March 1, 2008, and a maturity date of December 1, 2008. Its coupons are payable semiannually, using the actual/actual basis (that is, a *basis* argument of 1). All these functions take the same arguments: (*settlement, maturity, frequency, basis*). (For definitions of these arguments, see Table 16-3.)

The COUPDAYBS function calculates the number of days from the beginning of the coupon period to the settlement date. Using our sample data, the formula =COUPDAYBS("3/1/08", "12/1/08", 2, 1) returns 91.

The COUPDAYS function calculates the number of days in the coupon period that contains the settlement date. Using our sample data, the formula =COUPDAYS("3/1/08", "12/1/08", 2, 1) returns 183.

The COUPDAYSNC function calculates the number of days from the settlement date to the next coupon date. Using our sample data, the formula =COUPDAYSNC("3/1/08", "12/1/08", 2, 1) returns 92.

The COUPNCD function calculates the next coupon date after the settlement date. Using our sample data, the formula =COUPNCD("3/1/08", "12/1/08", 2, 1) returns 39600, or June 1, 2008.

The COUPNUM function calculates the number of coupons payable between the settlement date and the maturity date and rounds the result to the nearest whole coupon. Using our sample data, the formula =COUPNUM("3/1/08", "12/1/08", 2, 1) returns 2.

The COUPPCD function calculates the coupon date before the settlement date. Using our sample data, the formula =COUPPCD("3/1/08", "12/1/08", 2, 1) returns 39417, or December 1, 2007.

The DURATION and MDURATION Functions

The DURATION function calculates the annual duration for a security whose interest payments are made on a periodic basis. *Duration* is the weighted average of the present value of the bond's cash flow and measures how a bond's price responds to changes in the yield. This function takes the arguments (*settlement, maturity, coupon, yield, frequency, basis*). (For argument definitions, see Table 16-3.)

For example, suppose a bond has a settlement date of January 1, 2008; has a maturity date of December 31, 2013; has a semiannual coupon rate of 8.5 percent; has a yield of 9.5 percent; and uses the default 30/360 basis. The resulting formula, =DURATION("1/1/08", "12/31/13", 0.085, 0.095, 2, 0), returns a duration of 4.78708.

The MDURATION function calculates the annual modified duration for a security with interest payments made on a periodic basis, adjusted for market yield per number of coupon payments per year. This function takes the arguments (*settlement, maturity, coupon, yield, frequency, basis*). Using the values from the DURATION formula, the modified duration formula looks like =MDURATION("1/1/08", "12/31/13", 0.085, 0.095, 2, 0) and returns a value of 4.57.

Using the Euro Currency Tools Add-In

Now that the euro is a well-established standard currency, you might find that the Euro Currency Tools add-in can make life simpler. To install this add-in, click the Microsoft Office Button, click Excel Options, select the Add-Ins category, and click the Go button to display the dialog box shown in Figure 16-1. Select the Euro Currency Tools check box, and then click OK. Click Yes to confirm you want to install the add-in (which may take a few minutes).

Figure 16-1 The Euro Currency Tools add-in can help when you need to work with euros.

To see what this add-in provides, click the Formulas tab on the Ribbon. The Solutions group appears on the right end of the Formulas tab and includes the Euro Conversion command, the Euro Formatting command, and a list of conversion options, as shown in Figure 16-2.

Select any conversion in the Euro Currency drop-down list, and see what the value in the selected cell would be if converted to the selected currency. The result, which you can also select and copy, appears in the box to the right of the Euro Conversion button in the Solutions group on the Formulas tab, as shown in Figure 16-2.

Chapter 16

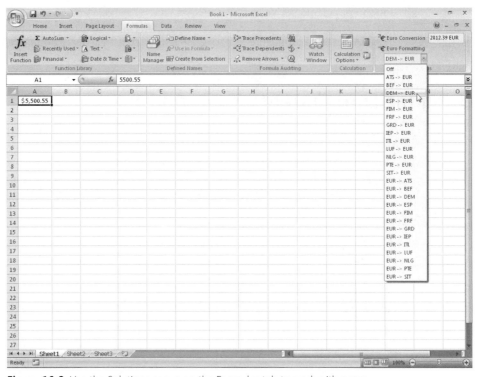

Figure 16-2 Use the Solutions group on the Formulas tab to work with euros.

If you need to convert the values in a worksheet full of cells (or just one cell) from one European Union member currency to another, use the Euro Conversion button, which displays the dialog box shown on the left in Figure 16-3. Options in this dialog box work as follows:

- The Source Range box, when selected, lets you drag to select the range you want to convert. You can select a matching range for the results using the Destination Range box, but you need to select only one cell, which will become the upper-left corner of the resulting range.

- The From and To boxes in the Currency Conversion area select the European Union member currency of the Source Range and Destination Range, respectively.

- You use the Output Format list to select a format for the resulting values: the corresponding currency format; the International Standardization Organization (ISO) format, which uses the appropriate ISO three-letter code instead of currency symbols; or None if you prefer unformatted numbers.

Clicking the Advanced button displays the Advanced Euro Options dialog box, shown on the right in Figure 16-3, which contains the following options:

- **Convert To Values Only** Converts all numbers and formulas in Source Range to raw values, which is the default option.

- **Prompt To Convert Formulas** Displays a dialog box during the conversion process in which you can specify conversion options for each formula, including three that are not available in the Advanced Options dialog box. You can copy the original formula instead of creating a conversion formula in the destination cell, you can choose to leave the cell blank, or you can edit each formula individually.

- **Link New Formulas To Original Data** Pastes formulas instead of values in Destination Range for any corresponding Source Range cells that contain formulas. These new formulas use the EUROCONVERT function with the same references used in the source formulas, creating dynamically updating conversion formulas.

- **Output Full Precision** Controls the rounding of numbers. Usually, based on European Union rules, Excel calculates converted currency values with a rounding factor that uses six significant digits of precision. To suppress this rounding factor, select the Output Full Precision check box.

- **Set Triangulation Precision To** Determines the number of significant digits of precision, from 3 through 15, to be used in the intermediate calculations when converting between two European Union member currencies, which are performed in euros.

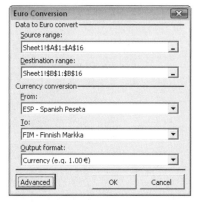
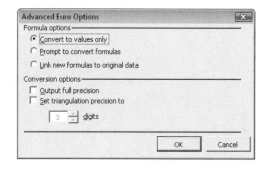

Figure 16-3 Click the Euro Conversion button to convert all the values in a cell range from one euro currency to another.

Chapter 16

Microsoft Office Excel 2007 provides a wide range of features that can help you analyze statistical data. A number of functions that assist in simple analysis tasks, such as AVERAGE, MEDIAN, and MODE, are built into the program. If the built-in statistical functions aren't enough, you can turn to the Analysis Toolpak, an add-in that provides a collection of tools to augment the built-in analytical capabilities of Office Excel 2007. You can use these tools to create histograms, create rank-and-percentile tables, extract samples from a data set, perform regression analysis, generate special random-number sets, apply Fourier and other transformations to your data, and more. In this chapter, we'll explore the most important statistical analysis functions that are built into Excel, as well as those included with the Analysis Toolpak.

Analyzing Distributions of Data

In statistics, a collection of measurements is called a *distribution*. Excel has several methods you can use to analyze distributions: built-in statistical functions, the sample and population statistical functions, or the rank-and-percentile functions together with the Rank And Percentile tool.

> **Note**
> You can also analyze distributions using the Descriptive Statistics and Histogram tools, both of which are included in the Analysis Toolpak add-in. For more information, see "Using the Analysis Toolpak Data Analysis Tools" on page 567.

Using Built-In Statistical Functions

More Functions

You use the built-in statistical functions to analyze a group (or population) of measurements. In the following sections, the discussion is limited to the most commonly used statistical functions. To quickly access these functions, click the More Functions button on the Formulas tab on the Ribbon, and then click Statistical to display a menu of statistical functions.

> **Note**
>
> Excel also offers the advanced statistical functions LINEST, LOGEST, TREND, and GROWTH, which operate on arrays. For more information, see "Understanding Linear and Exponential Regression" on page 559.

The AVERAGE Function

The AVERAGE function computes the arithmetic mean, or average, of the numbers in a range by summing a series of numeric values and then dividing the result by the number of values. This function takes the arguments (*number1, number2, . . .*), can include up to 255 arguments, and ignores blank cells and cells containing logical and text values. For example, to calculate the average of the values in cells B4 through B15, you could use the formula =(B4+B5+B6+B7+B8+B9+B10+B11+B12+B13+B14+B15)/12, but it's obviously more efficient to use =AVERAGE(B4:B15).

For more information about this function, see the sidebar "AVERAGE vs. AVG" on page 502.

The MEDIAN, MODE, MAX, MIN, and COUNT Functions

These functions all take the same arguments, essentially just a cell range or a list of numbers separated by commas, such as (*number1, number2, . . .*). They can accept up to 255 arguments, ignoring text, error values, and logical values. Here's a brief description of each:

- **MEDIAN** Computes the median of a set of numbers. The median is the number in the middle of the set, that is, an equal number of values are higher and lower than the median. If the numbers specified include an even number of values, the value returned is the average of the two that lie in the middle of the set.

- **MODE** Determines which value occurs most frequently in a set of numbers. If no number occurs more than once, MODE returns the #N/A error value.

- **MAX** Returns the largest value in a range.

- **MIN** Returns the smallest value in a range.

- **COUNT** Tells you how many cells in a given range contain numbers, including dates and formulas that evaluate to numbers.

> **Note**
>
> To count all nonblank cells, regardless of what they contain, you can use the COUNTA function. For more information about this function, see "The A Functions" on page 556.

The SUMIF, SUMIFS, and COUNTIF Functions

The SUMIF function is similar to SUM but first tests each cell using a specified conditional test before adding it to the total. This function takes the arguments (*range, criteria, sum_range*). The *range* argument specifies the range you want to test, the *criteria* argument specifies the conditional test to be performed on each cell in the range, and the *sum_range* argument specifies the cells to be totaled. For example, if you have a worksheet with a column of month names defined using the range name Months and an adjacent column of numbers named Sales, use the formula =SUMIF(Months, "June", Sales) to return the value in the Sales cell that is adjacent to the label June. Alternatively, you can use a conditional test formula, such as =SUMIF(Sales, ">=999", Sales), to return the total of all sales figures that are more than $999.

The SUMIFS function does similar work to that of the SUMIF function, except you can specify up to 127 different ranges to sum, each with their own criteria. Note that the *sum_range* argument is in the first position instead of the third position in this function: (*sum_range, criteria_range1, criteria1, criteria_range2, criteria2, . . .*). The sum range and each criteria range must all be the same size and shape. Using a similar example to the one we used for the SUMIF function, suppose we also created defined names for cell ranges Months, Totals, and Product1, Product2, and so on. The formula =SUMIFS(Totals, Product3, "<=124", Months, "Jun") returns the total sales for the month of June when sales of Product2 were less than or equal to $124.

> You can use the Conditional Sum Wizard add-in to help you construct formulas. For more information, see "Using the Conditional Sum and Lookup Wizards" on page 478.

Similarly, COUNTIF counts the cells that match specified criteria and takes the arguments (*range, criteria*). Using the same example, you can find the number of months in which total sales fell to less than $600 using a conditional test, as in the formula =COUNTIF(Totals, "<600").

> For more information about conditional tests, see "Creating Conditional Tests" on page 478. For more about using range names, see "Naming Cells and Cell Ranges" on page 441.

Using Functions That Analyze Rank and Percentile

Excel includes several functions that extract rank and percentile information from a set of input values: PERCENTRANK, PERCENTILE, QUARTILE, SMALL, LARGE, and RANK.

The PERCENTRANK Function

The PERCENTRANK function returns a percentile ranking for any member of a data set. You can use this function to create a percentile table that's linked to the input range so that the percentile figures are updated if the input values change. We used this function to create the percentile ranking in column E of Figure 17-1.

Chapter 17

	A	B	C	D	E	F	G	H	I	J	K	L
	E2		▾	f_x =PERCENTRANK(D2:D1001,D2,4)								
1	Student ID	Verbal	Math	Total	Percentile							
2	722-4499	418	518	936	3%							
3	605-3475	465	557	1022	34%							
4	546-3500	463	549	1012	27%							
5	655-8550	466	587	1053	55%							
6	812-6448	520	544	1064	62%							
7	814-6503	470	537	1007	24%							
8	332-3453	533	549	1082	73%							
9	55-0476	476	570	1046	49%							
10	745-0539	468	548	1016	30%							
11	675-1544	441	562	1003	21%							
12	836-6513	570	560	1130	94%							
13	146-4509	503	554	1057	57%							
14	45-9450	551	556	1107	86%							
15	924-3538	498	562	1060	59%							
16	664-9559	466	525	991	17%							
17	596-5425	414	549	963	8%							
18	914-1483	497	545	1042	46%							
19	266-3469	581	519	1100	82%							
20	116-2492	402	568	970	9%							
21	524-5404	488	539	1027	37%							
22	883-4501	547	536	1083	73%							
23	275-2453	456	567	1023	34%							
24	475-1532	536	559	1095	80%							
25	864-9444	546	551	1097	81%							

Figure 17-1 PERCENTRANK links percentile figures to input values.

You can find the SAT Scores.xlsx file in the Sample Files section of the companion CD.

The PERCENTRANK function takes the arguments (*array, x, significance*). The *array* argument specifies the input range (which is D2:D1001, in our example), and *x* specifies the value whose rank you want to obtain. The *significance* argument, which is optional, indicates the number of digits of precision you want; if omitted, results are rounded to three digits (*0.xxx* or *xx.x%*).

The A Functions

Excel includes a set of functions that give you more flexibility when calculating data sets that include text or logical values. These functions are AVERAGEA, COUNTA, MAXA, MINA, STDEVA, STDEVPA, VARA, and VARPA, all of which accept a series of up to 255 arguments (*value1, value2, . . .*).

Ordinarily, the non-A versions of these functions ignore cells containing text values. For example, if a range of 10 cells contains one text value, AVERAGE ignores that cell and divides by 9 to arrive at the average, whereas AVERAGEA considers the text value part of the range and divides by 10. This is helpful if you always want to include all referenced cells in your calculations, especially if you use formulas that return text flags, such as "none," if a certain condition is met. For more information about STDEVA, STDEVPA, VARA, and VARPA, see "Using Sample and Population Statistical Functions" on page 558.

The PERCENTILE and QUARTILE Functions

You use the PERCENTILE function to determine which member of an input range stands at a specified percentile ranking; it takes the arguments (*array, k*). You must express the percentile k as a decimal fraction from 0 to 1. For example, to find out which score in Figure 17-1 represents the 87th percentile, you can use the formula =PERCENTILE(D2:D1001, 0.87).

The QUARTILE function, which takes the arguments (*array, quart*), works much like the PERCENTILE function, except it returns the value that represents the lowest percentile, or any quarter-percentile in the input set. The *array* argument specifies the input range. The *quart* argument specifies the value to be returned, as shown in Table 17-1.

Table 17-1 **The *Quart* Argument**

Quart	Returns
0	Lowest value
1	25th-percentile value
2	Median (50th-percentile) value
3	75th-percentile value
4	Highest value

INSIDE OUT   Use MIN, MEDIAN, and MAX

QUARTILE is a powerful function, but if you don't need to return 25th or 75th percentile values, you will get faster results using other functions, particularly when working with large data sets. Use the MIN function instead of QUARTILE(*array*, 0), the MEDIAN function instead of QUARTILE(*array*, 2), and the MAX function instead of QUARTILE(*array*, 4).

The SMALL and LARGE Functions

The SMALL and LARGE functions return the kth smallest and kth largest values in an input range; both take the arguments (*array, k*), where k is the position from the largest or smallest value to the value in the array you want to find. For example, to find the 15th highest score in Figure 17-1, you can use the formula =LARGE(D2:D1001, 15).

The RANK Function

The RANK function returns the ranked position of a particular number within a set of numbers and takes the arguments (*number, ref, order*). The *number* argument is the number for which you want to find the rank, *ref* is the range containing the data set, and *order* optionally ranks the number as if it were in a ranking list in an ascending or

Chapter 17

descending (the default) order. For example, to find out which ranking the score 1200 has in the data set in Figure 17-1, you can use the formula =RANK(1200, D2:D1001).

By default, the highest value is ranked 1, the second highest is ranked 2, and so on. If RANK can't find an exact match between its first argument and an input value, it returns the #N/A error value.

Using Sample and Population Statistical Functions

Variance and standard deviation are statistical measurements of the dispersion of a group, or population, of numbers. The standard deviation is the square root of the variance. As a rule, about 68 percent of a normally distributed population falls within one standard deviation of the mean, and about 95 percent falls within two standard deviations. A large standard deviation indicates that the population is widely dispersed from the mean; a small standard deviation indicates that the population is tightly packed around the mean.

Four statistical functions—VAR, VARP, STDEV, and STDEVP—compute the variance and standard deviation of the numbers in a range of cells. Before you calculate the variance and standard deviation of a group of values, you must determine whether those values represent the total population or only a representative sample of that population. The VAR and STDEV functions assume that the values represent only a sample of the total population; the VARP and STDEVP functions assume that the values represent the total population.

Calculating Sample Statistics: VAR and STDEV

The VAR and STDEV functions compute variance and standard deviation, assuming that their arguments represent only a sample of the total population. These functions both take the arguments (*number1, number2, . . .*) and accept up to 255 arguments. The worksheet in Figure 17-2 shows exam scores for five students and assumes that the scores in cells B4:E8 represent only a part of the total population.

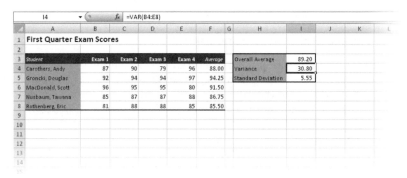

Figure 17-2 The VAR and STDEV functions measure the dispersion of sample exam scores.

You can find the VAR.xlsx file in the Sample Files area of the companion CD.

Cell I4 uses the VAR function =VAR(B4:E8) to calculate the variance for this sample group of test scores. Cell I5 uses the STDEV function =STDEV(B4:E8) to calculate the standard deviation.

Assuming that the test scores in the example are normally distributed, we can deduce that about 68 percent of the students (the general-rule percentage) achieved scores from 83.65 (the average 89.20 minus the standard deviation 5.55) to 94.75 (89.20 plus 5.55).

Calculating Total Population Statistics: VARP and STDEVP

If the numbers you're analyzing represent an entire population rather than a sample, use the VARP and STDEVP functions to calculate variance and standard deviation. These functions both take the arguments (*number1, number2, . . .*) and accept up to 255 arguments.

Assuming that cells B4:E8 in the worksheet shown in Figure 17-2 represent the total population, you can calculate the variance and standard deviation with the formulas =VARP(B4:E8) and =STDEVP(B4:E8). The VARP function returns 29.26, and the STDEVP function returns 5.41.

> **Note**
>
> The STDEV, STDEVP, VAR, and VARP functions do not include text values or blank cells in their calculations. If you want to include blanks or text, use the A versions: STDEVA, STDEVPA, VARA, and VARPA. For more information, see "The A Functions" on page 556.

Understanding Linear and Exponential Regression

Excel includes several array functions for performing linear regression (LINEST, TREND, FORECAST, SLOPE, and STEYX) and for performing exponential regression (LOGEST and GROWTH). You enter these functions as array formulas, and they produce array results. You can use each of these functions with one or several independent variables. The following list defines the different types of regression:

- **Linear regression** Produces the slope of a line that best fits a single set of data. Based on a year's worth of sales figures, for example, linear regression can tell you the projected sales for March of the following year by giving you the slope and y-intercept (that is, the point where the line crosses the y-axis) of the line that best fits the sales data. By following the line forward in time, you can estimate future sales, if you can safely assume that growth will remain linear.

- **Exponential regression** Produces an exponential curve that best fits a set of data that you suspect does not change linearly with time. For example, a series of

Chapter 17

measurements of population growth will nearly always be better represented by an exponential curve than by a line.

- **Multiple regression** Is the analysis of more than one set of data, which often produces a more realistic projection. You can perform both linear and exponential multiple regression analyses. For example, suppose you want to project the appropriate price for a house in your area based on square footage, number of bathrooms, lot size, and age. Using a multiple regression formula, you can estimate a price, based on a database of information gathered from existing houses.

Regressing into the Future?

The concept of regression might sound strange because the term is usually associated with movement backward, whereas in the world of statistics, regression is often used to predict the future. Simply put, *regression* is a statistical technique that finds a mathematical expression that best describes a set of data.

Often businesses try to predict the future using sales and percent-of-sales projections based on history. A simple percent-of-sales technique identifies assets and liabilities that vary along with sales, determines the proportion of each, and assigns them percentages. Although using percent-of-sales forecasting is often sufficient for slow or steady short-term growth, the technique loses accuracy as growth accelerates.

Regression analysis uses more sophisticated equations to analyze larger sets of data and translates them into coordinates on a line or curve. In the not-so-distant past, regression analysis was not widely used because of the large volume of calculations involved. Since spreadsheet applications, such as Excel, began offering built-in regression functions, the use of regression analysis has become more widespread.

Calculating Linear Regression

The equation $y = mx + b$ algebraically describes a straight line for a set of data with one independent variable where x is the independent variable, y is the dependent variable, m represents the slope of the line, and b represents the y-intercept. If a line represents a number of independent variables in a multiple regression analysis to an expected result, the equation of the regression line takes the form

$$y = m_1 x_1 + m_2 x_2 + \ldots + m_n x_n + b$$

in which y is the dependent variable, x_1 through x_n are n independent variables, m_1 through m_n are the coefficients of each independent variable, and b is a constant.

The LINEST Function

The LINEST function uses this more general equation to return the values of m_1 through m_n and the value of b, given a known set of values for y and a known set of values for each independent variable. This function takes the form =LINEST(*known_y's, known_x's, const, stats*).

The *known_y's* argument is the set of *y*-values you already know. This argument can be a single column, a single row, or a rectangular range of cells. If *known_y's* is a single column, each column in the *known_x's* argument is considered an independent variable. Similarly, if *known_y's* is a single row, each row in the *known_x's* argument is considered an independent variable. If *known_y's* is a rectangular range, you can use only one independent variable; *known_x's* in this case should be a range of the same size and shape as *known_y's*. If you omit the *known_x's* argument, Excel uses the sequence 1, 2, 3, 4, and so on.

The *const* and *stats* arguments are optional. If either is included, it must be a logical constant—either TRUE or FALSE. (You can substitute 1 for TRUE and 0 for FALSE.) The default settings for *const* and *stats* are TRUE and FALSE, respectively. If you set *const* to FALSE, Excel forces *b* (the last term in the straight-line equation) to be 0. If you set *stats* to TRUE, the array returned by LINEST includes the following validation statistics:

se_1 through se_n	Standard error values for each coefficient
se_b	Standard error value for the constant *b*
r^2	Coefficient of determination
se_y	Standard error value for *y*
F	*F* statistic
D_f	Degrees of freedom
ss_{reg}	Regression sum of squares
ss_{resid}	Residual sum of squares

Before creating a formula using LINEST, you must select a range large enough to hold the result array returned by the function. If you omit the *stats* argument (or set it explicitly to FALSE), the result array encompasses one cell for each of your independent variables and one cell for *b*. If you include the validation statistics, the result array looks like the following example. After selecting a range to contain the result array, type the function, and then press Ctrl+Shift+Enter to enter the function in each cell of the result array.

m_n	m_{n-1}	. . .	m_2	m_1	b
se_n	se_{n-1}	. . .	se_2	se_1	se_b
r^2	se_y				
F	D_f				
ss_{reg}	ss_{resid}				

Note that, with or without validation statistics, the coefficients and standard error values for your independent variables are returned in the opposite order from your input data. For example, if you have four independent variables organized in four columns, LINEST evaluates the leftmost column as x_1, but it returns m_1 in the fourth column of the result array.

Figure 17-3 shows a simple example of the use of LINEST with one independent variable. The entries in column B of this worksheet represent monthly product demand for a small business. The numbers in column A represent the months in the period. Suppose you want to compute the slope and y-intercept of the regression line that best describes the relationship between the demand and the months. In other words, you want to describe the trend of the data. To do this, select the range F6:G6, type the formula **=LINEST(B2:B19, A2:A19)**, and press Ctrl+Shift+Enter. The resulting number in cell F6 is 20.613, the slope of the regression line; the number in cell G6 is 4002.065, the y-intercept of the line.

	A	B	C	D	E	F	G	H	I	J	K
						F6		f_x {=LINEST(B2:B19,A2:A19)}			
1	Month	Demand, thousands	Trend								
2	1	4039	4022.67836								
3	2	4057	4043.29137								
4	3	4052	4063.90437								
5	4	4094	4084.51737			Linear Estimation					
6	5	4104	4105.13037			20.613003	4002.0654				
7	6	4110	4125.74338								
8	7	4154	4146.35638								
9	8	4161	4166.96938								
10	9	4186	4187.58239								
11	10	4195	4208.19539								
12	11	4229	4228.80839								
13	12	4244	4249.4214								
14	13	4242	4270.0344								
15	14	4283	4290.6474								
16	15	4322	4311.26041								
17	16	4333	4331.87341								
18	17	4368	4352.48641								
19	18	4389	4373.09942								
20											
21											
22											
23											

Figure 17-3 The LINEST function computes the slope and y-intercept of a regression line.

You can find the Analysis.xlsx file in the Sample Files area of the companion CD.

The LINEST and LOGEST functions return only the y-axis coordinates used for calculating lines and curves. The difference between them is that LINEST projects a straight line and LOGEST projects an exponential curve. You must be careful to match the appropriate function to the analysis at hand. The LINEST function might be more appropriate for sales projections, and the LOGEST function might be more appropriate for statistical analyses or population trends. For more information, see "The LOGEST Function" on page 566.

INSIDE OUT   A Real (Estate) Regression Application

One often-used regression model is sometimes known as the Competitive Market Analysis (CMA). Realtors use CMAs to arrive at an estimated selling price for a home, based on historical sales data for comparable homes in the area. Here is a sample Excel-based version of this tool, called the Home Price Estimator:

Home Price Estimator   For sample use only - results not guaranteed.

What You Want	
Square Footage	2400
Number of Bathrooms	3
Number of Bedrooms	2
Age of Home	15
Esimated Price	**$230,209**

To use this worksheet, first enter data for the house you want to find (in the blue cells), then enter data for selected homes in the same neighborhood that have recently been listed or sold.

Input Data	Home 1	Home 2	Home 3	Home 4	Home 5
Square Footage	2500	3200	2200	3450	2675
Number of Bathrooms	2.5	3	2.75	3.75	2.5
Number of Bedrooms	4	3	4	6	4
Age of Home	25	7	40	22	68
Price	$285,000	$325,500	$249,500	$379,500	$305,000

This application uses the LINEST function to analyze the statistics in the Input Data area and generate an array of results based on similar statistics in the What You Want area. The LINEST array is actually located in hidden rows below the visible area of the worksheet, as shown next. The first row of values in the LINEST data array is used by the Estimated Price formula to extrapolate an estimated value.

D26	f_x	{=LINEST(prices,inputs,TRUE,TRUE)}				
A B	C	D	E	F	G	H	I

		D	E	F	G	H
25						
26	Array Outputs	58.05735057	15739.49919	-25459.2084	100.0201939	34188.10582
27		0	0	0	0	0
28		1	0	#N/A	#N/A	#N/A
29		#NUM!	0	#N/A	#N/A	#N/A
30						
31						
32	Transposed Inputs	2500	2.5	4	25	285000
33		3200	3	3	7	325500
34		2200	2.75	4	40	249500
35		3450	3.75	6	22	379500
36		2675	2.5	4	68	305000
37						
38						

Usually in this workbook, row and column headings are hidden, rows 25 through 37 are hidden, worksheet protection is turned on, and cells are locked with entries allowed only in the designated input areas. Real estate tip: As the note on the worksheet implies, you can use listed home prices to arrive at an estimated price, but actual sale prices are more realistic, if you can get them.

You can find the Home Price Estimator.xlsx file in the Sample Files area of the companion CD.

The TREND Function

LINEST returns a mathematical description of the straight line that best fits known data. TREND finds points that lie along that line and that fall into the unknown category. You can use the numbers returned by TREND to plot a trendline—a straight line that helps make sense of actual data. You can also use TREND to *extrapolate*, or make intelligent guesses about, future data based on the tendencies exhibited by known data. (Be careful. Although you can use TREND to plot the straight line that best fits the known data, TREND can't tell you whether that line is a good predictor of the future. Validation statistics returned by LINEST can help you make that assessment.) The TREND function takes the form =TREND(*known_y's, known_x's, new_x's, const*).

The first two arguments represent the known values of your dependent and independent variables. As in LINEST, the *known_y's* argument is a single column, a single row, or a rectangular range. The *known_x's* argument also follows the pattern described for LINEST. The third and fourth arguments are optional. If you omit *new_x's*, the TREND function considers *new_x's* to be identical to *known_x's*. If you include *const*, the value of that argument must be TRUE or FALSE (or 1 or 0). If *const* is TRUE, TREND forces *b* to be 0.

To calculate the trendline data points that best fit your known data, simply omit the third and fourth arguments from this function. The results array will be the same size as the *known_x's* range. In Figure 17-4, we used TREND to find the value of each point on the regression line that describes the data set from the example in Figure 17-3. To create these values, we selected the range C2:C19 and entered =TREND(B2:B19, A2:A19) as an array formula using Ctrl+Shift+Enter.

To extrapolate from existing data, you must supply a range for *new_x's*. You can supply as many or as few cells for *new_x's* as you want. The result array will be the same size as the *new_x's* range. In Figure 17-5 we used TREND to calculate demand for the 19th, 20th, and 21st months. To arrive at these values, we typed **19** through **21** in A21:A23, selected C21:C23, and entered **=TREND(B2:B19, A2:A19, A21:A23)** as an array formula by pressing Ctrl+Shift+Enter.

The FORECAST Function

The FORECAST function is similar to TREND, except it returns a single point along a line rather than returning an array that defines the line. This function takes the form =FORECAST(*x, known_y's, known_x's*).

The *x* argument is the data point for which you want to extrapolate a value. For example, instead of using TREND, we can use the FORECAST function to extrapolate the value in cell C23 in Figure 17-5 by using the formula =FORECAST(21, B2:B19, A2:A19) where the *x* argument refers to the 21st data point on the regression line. You can use this function if you want to calculate any point in the future.

	C2		f_x	{=TREND(B2:B19,A2:A19)}							
	A	B	C	D	E	F	G	H	I	J	K
1	Month	Demand, thousands	Trend								
2	1	4039	4022.67836								
3	2	4057	4043.29137								
4	3	4052	4063.90437								
5	4	4094	4084.51737			Linear Estimation					
6	5	4104	4105.13037			20.613003	4002.0654				
7	6	4110	4125.74338								
8	7	4154	4146.35638								
9	8	4161	4166.96938								
10	9	4186	4187.58239								
11	10	4195	4208.19539								
12	11	4229	4228.80839								
13	12	4244	4249.4214								
14	13	4242	4270.0344								
15	14	4283	4290.6474								
16	15	4322	4311.26041								
17	16	4333	4331.87341								
18	17	4368	4352.48641								
19	18	4389	4373.09942								
20											

Figure 17-4 The TREND function creates a data series that can be plotted as a line on a chart.

	C21		f_x	{=TREND(B2:B19,A2:A19,A21:A23)}							
	A	B	C	D	E	F	G	H	I	J	K
1	Month	Demand, thousand s	Trend								
2	1	4039	4022.6784								
3	2	4057	4043.2914								
4	3	4052	4063.9044								
5	4	4094	4084.5174			Linear Estimation					
18	17	4368	4352.4864								
19	18	4389	4373.0994								
20											
21	19		4393.7124								
22	20		4414.3254								
23	21		4434.9384								
24											
25											

Figure 17-5 TREND can predict the sales figures for months 19, 20, and 21.

The SLOPE Function

The SLOPE function returns the slope of the linear regression line. The slope is defined as the vertical distance divided by the horizontal distance between any two points on the regression line. Its value is the same as the first number in the array returned by the LINEST function. In other words, SLOPE calculates the trajectory of the line used by the FORECAST and TREND functions to calculate the values of data points. The SLOPE function takes the form =SLOPE(*known_y's, known_x's*).

Chapter 17

To find the slope of the regression line that describes the data set from the example shown in Figure 17-5, we can use =SLOPE(B2:B19, A2:A19) as an array. This returns a value of 20.613.

The STEYX Function

The STEYX function calculates the standard error of a regression, a measure of the amount of error accrued in predicting a *y* for each given *x*. This function takes the form =STEYX(*known_y's, known_x's*). If we apply this function to the worksheet shown in Figure 17-5, the formula =STEYX(B2:B19, A2:A19) returns a standard error value of 12.96562.

Calculating Exponential Regression

Unlike linear regression, which plots values along a straight line, exponential regression describes a curve by calculating the array of values needed to plot it. The equation that describes an exponential regression curve is as follows:

$$y = b * m_1^{x1} * m_2^{x2} * \ldots * m_n^{xn}$$

If you have only one independent variable, the equation is as follows:

$$y = b * m^x$$

The LOGEST Function

The LOGEST function works like LINEST, except you use it to analyze data that is nonlinear, and it returns the coordinates of an exponential curve instead of a straight line. LOGEST returns coefficient values for each independent variable plus a value for the constant *b*. This function takes the form =LOGEST(*known_y's, known_x's, const, stats*).

LOGEST accepts the same arguments as the LINEST function and returns a result array in the same fashion. If you set the optional *stats* argument to TRUE, the function also returns validation statistics. For more information about the LOGEST function's underlying equations and its arguments, see "The LINEST Function" on page 560.

> **Note**
>
> The LINEST and LOGEST functions return only the y-axis coordinates used for calculating lines and curves. The difference between them is that LINEST projects a straight line and LOGEST projects an exponential curve. You must be careful to match the appropriate function to the analysis at hand. The LINEST function might be more appropriate for sales projections, and the LOGEST function might be more suited to applications such as statistical analyses or population trends.

The GROWTH Function

Where the LOGEST function returns a mathematical description of the exponential regression curve that best fits a set of known data, the GROWTH function finds points that lie along that curve. The GROWTH function works like its linear counterpart, TREND, and takes the form =GROWTH(*known_y's, known_x's, new_x's, const*). For more information about the GROWTH function's arguments, see "The TREND Function" on page 564.

Using the Analysis Toolpak Data Analysis Tools

The Analysis Toolpak add-in is part of the deal when you purchase Excel 2007, although you might not know it. *Add-ins* are little packages of tools that more or less seamlessly integrate into the user interface of Excel. However, they require you to install them first. The following sections discuss the installation of, and the tools included with, the Analysis Toolpak.

Installing the Analysis Toolpak

To see whether you have the Analysis Toolpak installed, click the Data tab on the Ribbon. If the Data Analysis button is there, then you're good to go. If not, click the Microsoft Office Button, click Excel Options, and select the Add-Ins category. In the Manage list at the bottom of the dialog box, select Excel Add-Ins, and then click the Go button to display the dialog box shown in Figure 17-6. In the Add-Ins dialog box, select the Analysis Toolpak check box, and then click OK to install it. Excel prompts you for permission to proceed. Click Yes.

Figure 17-6 Use the Add-Ins dialog box to install the Analysis Toolpak.

When you click the Data Analysis button on the Data tab, the Data Analysis dialog box appears, as shown in Figure 17-7.

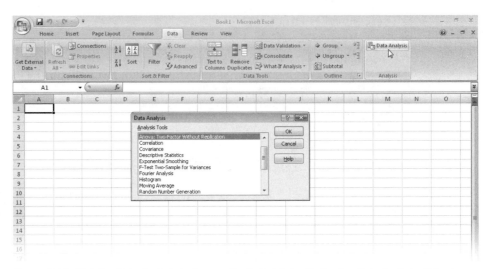

Figure 17-7 Click the Data Analysis button on the Data tab to display the Data Analysis dialog box.

Using the Descriptive Statistics Tool

The Descriptive Statistics tool provides a table of statistics for one or more sets of input values, showing the general tendencies and variability of the data. For each variable in the input range, this tool's output range includes a detailed list of statistics, as shown in Figure 17-8. To use the Descriptive Statistics tool, click the Data Analysis button on the Data tab on the Ribbon, select Descriptive Statistics, and click OK. The Descriptive Statistics dialog box shown in Figure 17-8 appears.

The Descriptive Statistics tool requires an input range that consists of one or more variables and an output range. You must also indicate whether the variables are to be arranged by column or by row. If you include a row of labels, be sure to select the Labels In First Row option. Excel then uses the labels to identify the variables in its output table. Select the Summary Statistics option only if you want a detailed output table as shown in Figure 17-8; otherwise, leave this check box empty.

Like the other tools in the Analysis Toolpak, Descriptive Statistics creates a table of constants. If a table of constants doesn't suit your needs, you can obtain most of the same statistical data from other Analysis Toolpak tools or from formulas that use the Excel worksheet functions. Table 17-2 lists the statistics and formulas.

Table 17-2 Descriptive Statistics Formulas

Statistic	Formula
Mean	=AVERAGE(*number1, number2, . . .*)
Standard error	Similar to =STEYX (*known_y's, known_x's*) but uses the ±-distribution rather than the standard regular distribution.
Median	=MEDIAN(*number1, number2, . . .*)
Mode	=MODE(*number1, number2, . . .*)

Statistic	Formula
Standard deviation	=STDEV(*number1, number2, . . .*)
Variance	=VAR(*number1, number2, . . .*)
Kurtosis	=KURT(*number1, number2, . . .*)
Skewness	=SKEW(*number1, number2, . . .*)
Range	=MAX(*number1, number2*)–MIN (*number1, number2, . . .*)
Minimum	=MIN(*number1, number2, . . .*)
Maximum	=MAX(*number1, number2, . . .*)
Sum	=SUM(*number1, number2, . . .*)
Count	=COUNT(*value1, value2, . . .*)
*k*th largest	=LARGE(*array, k*)
*k*th smallest	=SMALL(*array, k*)
Confidence	Similar to =CONFIDENCE (*alpha, standard_dev, size*) but uses a different algorithm

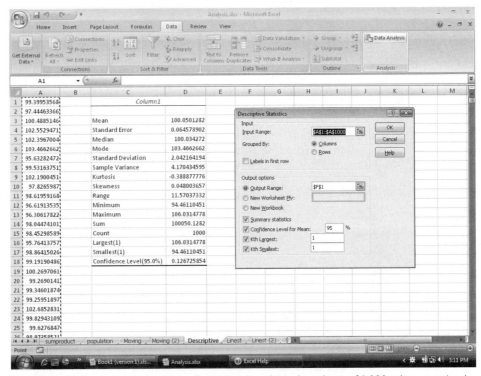

Figure 17-8 We generated this table of statistics describing the column of 1,000 values contained in Column A using the Descriptive Statistics tool.

Chapter 17

Creating Histograms

A *histogram* is a chart (usually a simple column chart) that takes a collection of measurements and plots the number of measurements (called the *frequency*) that fall within each of several intervals (called *bins*).

To see how the Histogram tool works, we'll use a table of 1,000 test scores. (The input range must contain numeric data only.) To see a breakdown of the total scores at 50-point intervals, begin by setting up the distribution bins shown in column F of Figure 17-9.

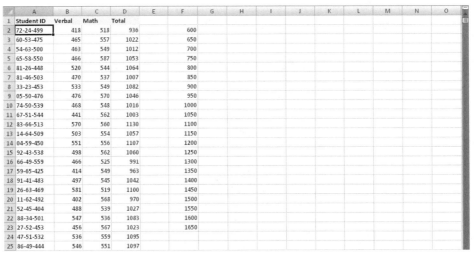

	A	B	C	D	E	F	G	H	I	J	K	L	M	N	O
1	Student ID	Verbal	Math	Total											
2	72-24-499	418	518	936		600									
3	60-53-475	465	557	1022		650									
4	54-63-500	463	549	1012		700									
5	65-58-550	466	587	1053		750									
6	81-26-448	520	544	1064		800									
7	81-46-503	470	537	1007		850									
8	33-23-453	533	549	1082		900									
9	05-50-476	476	570	1046		950									
10	74-50-539	468	548	1016		1000									
11	67-51-544	441	562	1003		1050									
12	83-66-513	570	560	1130		1100									
13	14-64-509	503	554	1057		1150									
14	04-59-450	551	556	1107		1200									
15	92-43-538	498	562	1060		1250									
16	66-49-559	466	525	991		1300									
17	59-65-425	414	549	963		1350									
18	91-41-483	497	545	1042		1400									
19	26-63-469	581	519	1100		1450									
20	11-62-492	402	568	970		1500									
21	52-45-404	488	539	1027		1550									
22	88-34-501	547	536	1083		1600									
23	27-52-453	456	567	1023		1650									
24	47-51-532	536	559	1095											
25	86-49-444	546	551	1097											

Figure 17-9 Column F contains the distribution bins.

The distribution bins don't have to be equally spaced like the ones in Figure 17-9 are, but they must be in ascending order. Click the Data Analysis button on the Data tab, select the Histogram tool, and then click OK. Figure 17-10 shows the Histogram dialog box.

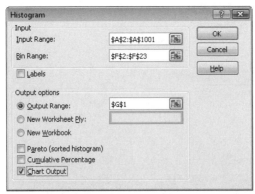

Figure 17-10 This dialog box appears after you select the Histogram tool in the Data Analysis dialog box.

The Histogram tool can take three items of information: the location of the data (in this case, D2:D1001), the location of the bins (F2:F22), and the upper-left cell of the range where you want the analysis to appear (G1). After you click OK, Excel writes its analysis in columns G and H, as shown in Figure 17-11.

	A	B	C	D	E	F	G	H	I	J	K	L
1	Student ID	Verbal	Math	Total			Bin	Frequency	Cumulative %			
2	722-4499	418	518	936		600	600	0	0.00%			
3	605-3475	465	557	1022		650	650	0	0.00%			
4	546-3500	463	549	1012		700	700	0	0.00%			
5	655-8550	466	587	1053		750	750	0	0.00%			
6	812-6448	520	544	1064		800	800	0	0.00%			
7	814-6503	470	537	1007		850	850	0	0.00%			
8	332-3453	533	549	1082		900	900	3	0.30%			
9	55-0476	476	570	1046		950	950	48	5.10%			
10	745-0539	468	548	1016		1000	1000	155	20.60%			
11	675-1544	441	562	1003		1050	1050	329	53.50%			
12	836-6513	570	560	1130		1100	1100	291	82.60%			
13	146-4509	503	554	1057		1150	1150	150	97.60%			
14	45-9450	551	556	1107		1200	1200	23	99.90%			
15	924-3538	498	562	1060		1250	1250	1	100.00%			
16	664-9559	466	525	991		1300	1300	0	100.00%			
17	596-5425	414	549	963		1350	1350	0	100.00%			
18	914-1483	497	545	1042		1400	1400	0	100.00%			
19	266-3469	581	519	1100		1450	1450	0	100.00%			
20	116-2492	402	568	970		1500	1500	0	100.00%			
21	524-5404	488	539	1027		1550	1550	0	100.00%			
22	883-4501	547	536	1083		1600	1600	0	100.00%			
23	275-2453	456	567	1023		1650	1650	0	100.00%			
24	475-1532	536	559	1095			More	0	100.00%			
25	864-9444	546	551	1097								

Figure 17-11 This analysis tells us that three scores were at least 900 but less than 950; 48 are at least 950 but less than 1,000; and so on.

Note

We created our own distribution bins for this model, but you can let the Histogram tool determine the divisions for you. Leave the Bin Range box blank to create evenly distributed bin intervals using the minimum and maximum values in the input range as beginning and ending points. The number of intervals is equal to the square root of the number of input values.

Here are a few facts to keep in mind when using the Histogram tool:

- In the Frequency column, the histogram reports the number of input values that are equal to or greater than the bin value but less than the next bin value.

- The last value in the table reports the number of input values equal to or greater than the last bin value.

- Select the Pareto check box in the Histogram dialog box to sort the output in descending order.

- Select the Cumulative Percentage option to create a table that lists the cumulative percentages of each bin level.

- If you select the Chart Output option in the Histogram dialog box, the Histogram tool simultaneously generates a chart and places it next to the frequency distribution table.

For everything you need to know about charts, see Part 6, "Creating Charts."

INSIDE OUT   Beware of Bin Formulas

Notice that the Histogram tool duplicates your column of bin values in the Bin column, which is convenient if you place the output somewhere else in your workbook. But because the Histogram tool copies the bin values, it's best if the bin range contains numeric constants rather than formulas. If you do use formulas, be sure they don't include relative references; otherwise, when Histogram copies the range, the formulas might produce unwanted results.

Analyzing Distribution with the FREQUENCY Function

It's easy to generate a new frequency distribution table using the Histogram tool whenever you change the input values, but the Histogram tool generates static numbers (numeric constants). If you'd rather create formulas linked to the input values, you can use the built-in FREQUENCY array function, which calculates the number of times specified values occur in a population and takes the arguments (*data_array, bins_array*). Figure 17-12 shows the FREQUENCY function applied to the data shown in Figure 17-9.

	A	B	C	D	E	F	G	H	I	J	K	L
		G2		fx	{=FREQUENCY(D2:D1001,F2:F20)}							
1	Student ID	Verbal	Math	Total								
2	722-4499	418	518	936		600	0					
3	605-3475	465	557	1022		650	0					
4	546-3500	463	549	1012		700	0					
5	655-8550	466	587	1053		750	0					
6	812-6448	520	544	1064		800	0					
7	814-6503	470	537	1007		850	0					
8	332-3453	533	549	1082		900	3					
9	55-0476	476	570	1046		950	48					
10	745-0539	468	548	1016		1000	155					
11	675-1544	441	562	1003		1050	329					
12	836-6513	570	560	1130		1100	291					
13	146-4509	503	554	1057		1150	150					
14	45-9450	551	556	1107		1200	23					
15	924-3538	498	562	1060		1250	1					
16	664-9559	466	525	991		1300	0					
17	596-5425	414	549	963		1350	0					
18	914-1483	497	545	1042		1400	0					
19	266-3469	581	519	1100		1450	0					
20	116-2492	402	568	970		1500	0					
21	524-5404	488	539	1027		1550	0					
22	883-4501	547	536	1083								
23	275-2453	456	567	1023								
24	475-1532	536	559	1095								
25	864-9444	546	551	1097								

Figure 17-12 Use the FREQUENCY function to link the distribution analysis to the input data.

To use the FREQUENCY function, set up a column of bin values, just as you would with the Histogram tool, and then select the entire range where you want the output to appear, which in our example would be G2:G21—the cells in column G that are directly adjacent to the bin values in column F. (This range must be a column, because FREQUENCY can't use a row or multicolumn range as its output range.) Then type the formula, specifying the input range as the first argument and the bin range as the second. Press Ctrl+Shift+Enter to lock in the array formula. For more information about arrays, see "Using Arrays" on page 468.

Using the Rank And Percentile Tool

Suppose you want to rank the scores shown in Figure 17-9. You could rank them by sorting the data in descending order, with the best score at the top and the worst score at the bottom of the column. To find the rank of any score, you might want to create an ascending series of numbers beside the sorted scores, with 1 beside the best score and 1,000 beside the worst.

The Rank And Percentile tool not only performs these tasks for you but also creates percentile figures for each value in your input range. To use this tool, click the Data Analysis button on the Data tab on the Ribbon, select Rank And Percentile, and then click OK. Figure 17-13 shows the Rank And Percentile dialog box.

> **Note**
> If the Data Analysis button does not appear on the Data tab, see "Installing the Analysis Toolpak" on page 567.

Here's how to read the output of the Rank And Percentile tool, shown at the bottom of Figure 17-13. The first row of the output table (F2:I2) tells us that the 285th item in the input range is a total score of 1,206, which ranks first and is better than 100 percent of the other scores. Here are some hints to remember when using the Rank And Percentile tool:

- It's best to use the Labels In First Row option in the Rank And Percentile dialog box and then include the column heading in the input range. This way, the second column in the output table uses the same label. If you do not include the label in the input range, the output column is labeled Column1.

> **Note**
> If you select the Labels In First Row option but do not actually include the cell containing the label in your input range, the first value in the input range becomes the title. For example, if the input range in Figure 17-13 were $D$2:$D$1001, the resulting label in column G would be 936 instead of Total.

- In Figure 17-13, we analyzed a single column of data, but we could analyze the Verbal, Math, and Total columns together. In that case, we would specify the input range B1:D1001, and the tool would generate 12 columns of output, four for each input column.

- You can also have the output table placed on a new worksheet or workbook, which is a good idea if you select multiple columns of input data resulting in a large output table.

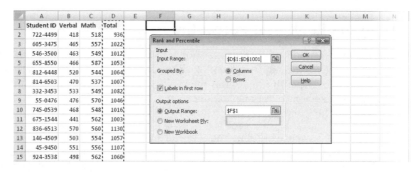

Figure 17-13 Use the Rank And Percentile tool to generate an output table like the one shown in the lower figure.

Generating Random Numbers

The built-in random-number function, RAND, generates a uniform distribution of random real numbers from 0 to 1. In other words, all values from 0 to 1 share the same probability of being returned by a set of formulas based on the RAND function. Because the sample is relatively small, the distribution is by no means perfectly uniform. Nevertheless, repeated tests demonstrate that the RAND function doesn't favor any position within its spectrum of distribution. For more information, see "The RAND and RAND-BETWEEN Functions" on page 500.

Correlating Tables

The input and output tables, shown at the bottom of Figure 17-13, share a common column of data—the Total column—and the same number of rows. But because the two tables are sorted differently, the rows don't match. The easiest solution is to sort the output table by the Point column; in this context, *Point* indicates the position of the corresponding data point in the input range. Therefore, sorting the output table by the Point column puts it in the same order as the input table:

	A	B	C	D	E	F	G	H	I	J	K
1	Student ID	Verbal	Math	Total		Point	Total	Rank	Percent		
2	722-4499	418	518	936		1	936	972	2.70%		
3	605-3475	465	557	1022		2	1022	657	33.90%		
4	546-3500	463	549	1012		3	1012	726	26.60%		
5	655-8550	466	587	1053		4	1053	447	54.60%		
6	812-6448	520	544	1064		5	1064	379	61.70%		
7	814-6503	470	537	1007		6	1007	756	23.80%		
8	332-3453	533	549	1082		7	1082	270	72.60%		
9	55-0476	476	570	1046		8	1046	502	49.50%		
10	745-0539	468	548	1016		9	1016	693	29.90%		
11	675-1544	441	562	1003		10	1003	779	21.30%		
12	836-6513	570	560	1130		11	1130	61	93.70%		
13	146-4509	503	554	1057		12	1057	419	57.60%		
14	45-9450	551	556	1107		13	1107	140	85.50%		
15	924-3538	498	562	1060		14	1060	403	59.20%		

If you want to add information from the output table to the existing input table, you can delete the Point column (because the Point column simply indicates the row number), the Total column (because the input table already has a Total column), and the blank column in the output table, creating a single, correlated table.

TROUBLESHOOTING

Random numbers keep changing.

The RAND function is one of Excel's *volatile* functions—that is, it recalculates every time the worksheet recalculates, which happens every time you make an entry in a cell. If you want to generate a set of random numbers and then "freeze" them, select all the RAND formulas in your worksheet, and press Ctrl+C to copy them. Then click the Paste button on the Home tab on the Ribbon, and click Paste Values to replace the volatile formulas with fixed values. Or, instead of using the RAND function, use the Random Number Generation tool (described next), which produces constants instead of formulas.

The Random Number Generation tool creates sets of random numbers that are not uniformly distributed. You can then use the Histogram tool to sort and plot the results for Monte Carlo decision analysis and other kinds of simulations. Six distribution types are available: Uniform, Normal, Bernoulli, Binomial, Poisson, and Discrete (user-defined). In addition, you can select Patterned in the Distribution list to create nonrandom

Chapter 17

numbers at specified intervals. Click the Data Analysis button on the Data tab on the Ribbon, select Random Number Generation, and then click OK to display a dialog box like the one shown in Figure 17-14.

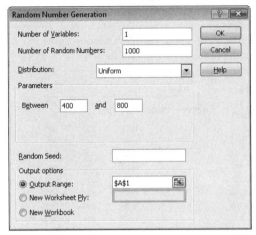

Figure 17-14 The Parameters area in the Random Number Generation dialog box changes to reflect the distribution type you select.

Here are a couple of important points regarding using the Random Number Generation tool:

- In the Number Of Variables and Number Of Random Numbers text boxes, you indicate how many columns of numbers you want and how many numbers you want in each column. For example, if you want 10 columns of 100 numbers each, specify 10 in the Number Of Variables text box and 100 in the Number Of Random Numbers text box.

- You can also specify a seed value. However, each time you generate a random-number set with a particular distribution type using the same seed value, you get the same sequence of numbers; therefore, you should specify a seed value only if you need to be able to reproduce a random-number sequence.

Random Number Distribution Methods

In the Random Number Generation dialog box, the parameters shown directly below the Distribution list change, depending on the type of distribution you select. As Figure 17-14 shows, when you select Uniform in the Distribution list, you can specify the beginning and ending points of the distribution in the Between and And text boxes.

Distributing Random Numbers Uniformly

This option asks you to specify two numbers between (and including) which to generate a set of random numbers, and it works much the same way as the RANDBETWEEN function, generating an evenly distributed set of real numbers. You can use this option as a more convenient alternative to RAND if you want endpoints other than 0 and 1 or if you want sets of numbers to be based on the same seed value.

Distributing Random Numbers Normally

Normal distribution has the following characteristics:

- One particular value, the mean, is more likely to occur than any other value.

- Values greater than the mean are as likely to occur as values less than it.

- Values close to the mean are more likely to occur than values distant from the mean.

To generate normally distributed random numbers, you specify two parameters: the mean and the standard deviation. The standard deviation is the average absolute difference between the random numbers and the mean. (Approximately 68 percent of the values in a normal distribution will fall within one standard deviation of the mean.)

Generating Random Numbers Using Bernoulli Distribution

The Bernoulli Distribution option simulates the probability of success of a number of trials, given that all trials have an equal probability of succeeding and that the success of one trial has no impact on the success of subsequent trials. (Note that success in this context has no value implication. In other words, you can use this distribution to simulate failure as readily as success.) All values in the Bernoulli distribution's output are either 0 or 1.

The probability that each cell will return a 1 is given by the distribution's sole parameter—P Value—for which you supply a number from 0 to 1. For example, if you want a sequence of 100 random Bernoulli values whose most likely sum is 27, you define a 100-cell output range and specify a P Value of 0.27.

Generating Random Numbers Using Binomial Distribution

The Binomial Distribution option simulates the number of successes in a fixed number of trials, given a specified probability rate. As with the Bernoulli Distribution option, the trials are assumed to be independent; that is, the outcome of one has no effect on any other. To generate binomially distributed numbers, you specify Number Of Trials and the P Value (probability) that any trial will succeed. (Again, success in this context has no value implication. In other words, you can use this distribution to simulate failure as readily as success.)

For example, suppose you make 10 sales presentations a week, you close the sale 20 percent of the time, and you would like to know what your success rate might be over the next year. Type **50** (for 50 working weeks in the year) in the Number Of Random Numbers text box, **0.2** in the P Value text box, and **10** in the Number Of Trials text box to learn that you can expect to make no sales four weeks in the coming year.

Chapter 17

Generating Random Numbers Using Poisson Distribution

The Poisson Distribution option simulates the number of times an event occurs within a particular time span, given a certain probability of occurrence. The occurrences are assumed to be independent; that is, each occurrence has no effect on the likelihood of others.

The Poisson Distribution option takes a single parameter, Lambda, which represents the expected outcome of an individual occurrence. For example, suppose you receive an average of 10 service calls a day. You want to know how often you can expect to get 18 or more service calls in a day over a year. To get this information, type **260** (52 weeks times 5 days) in the Number Of Random Numbers box and **10** in the Lambda box (the expected average). You can then use the COUNTIF function to count the number of times 18 shows up in the output range. For more information, see "The SUMIF, SUMIFS, and COUNTIF Functions" on page 555.

Generating Random Numbers Using Discrete Distribution

Use the Discrete Distribution option to create a custom distribution pattern by specifying a table of possible outcomes along with the probability associated with each outcome. The probability values must be from 0 to 1, and the sum of the probabilities in the table must equal 1. To use the Discrete Distribution option, specify the possible outcomes and their probabilities as a two-column range whose reference is the only parameter used by this option.

For example, you could create a custom distribution pattern to generate random snow-shovel sales patterns based on a two-column input range: Month Number and Probability of Snow.

Generating Semi-Random Numbers Using Patterned Distribution

Selecting Patterned in the Distribution list in the Random Number Generation dialog box generates numbers that are both random and part nonrandom. Selecting the Patterned option displays the dialog box shown in Figure 17-15.

You can think of the Patterned option as a fancy Fill Series command. It creates one or more arithmetic series with optional internal repetitions. For example, to create the series shown in Figure 17-15, complete the dialog box as shown, requesting two sequences of the numbers 1 through 10, using a step interval of 3, and repeating each number twice within each cycle.

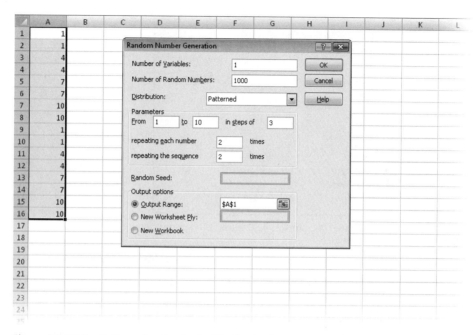

Figure 17-15 The Patterned option in the Distribution list creates an arithmetic series with operational repetitions.

For more information, see "Filling and Creating Data Series" on page 211.

If the step interval takes the series beyond the specified upper value, the output range includes the upper value because the last interval is truncated. For example, if you specify a step interval of 4 and the numbers 1 through 10, Excel creates the series 1, 5, 9, and 10.

Sampling a Population of Numbers

The Sampling tool extracts a subset of numbers from a larger group (or population) of numbers. From an input range, you can sample a specified number of values at random or at every nth value. The Sampling tool copies the extracted numbers to an output range you specify. Click the Data Analysis button on the Data tab on the Ribbon, select Sampling, and then click OK to display the Sampling dialog box, like the one shown in Figure 17-16.

The values in the input range must be numeric. They can include blank values and dates, provided you type the dates as numbers, not text. For example, to simplify a chart of daily commodity prices, you can use the Sampling tool to extract every nth data point and then create a new plot from the extracted data.

Chapter 17

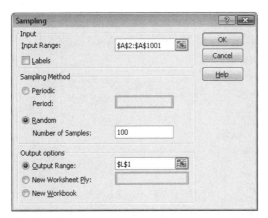

Figure 17-16 The Sampling tool extracts a random or periodic subset of a numeric population.

> **Note**
>
> To perform the equivalent of sampling from a range containing text values, set up a series of ascending integers beginning at 1 in a column alongside the text values, and then use the Sampling tool to extract numbers from this series. Then you can assemble a list of sampled text values by using the resulting numbers as arguments to the INDEX function. For more information, see "The INDEX Function" on page 517.

Calculating Moving Averages

A *moving average* is a forecasting technique that simplifies trend analysis by smoothing fluctuations that occur in measurements taken over time. These fluctuations can be caused by random noise that is often a by-product of the measurement technique. For example, measurements of the height of a growing child will vary with the accuracy of the ruler and whether the child is standing straight or slouching. You can take a series of measurements, however, and smooth them over time, resulting in a curve that reflects the child's actual growth rate. Fluctuations in measurements can result from other temporary conditions that introduce bias. Monthly sales, for example, might vary with the number of working days in the month or the absence of a star salesperson who takes a vacation.

Suppose you have created the 18-month demand curve shown in Figure 17-17. To generate a less noisy trendline from this data, you can plot a six-month moving average. The first point in the moving average line is the average of the first six monthly figures (January through June 2008). The next point averages the second-through-seventh monthly figures (February through July 2008), and so on. You can use the Moving Average tool to perform this analysis for you. Click the Data Analysis button on the Data tab on the

Ribbon, select Moving Average, and then click OK to display the Moving Average dialog box, as shown in Figure 17-18.

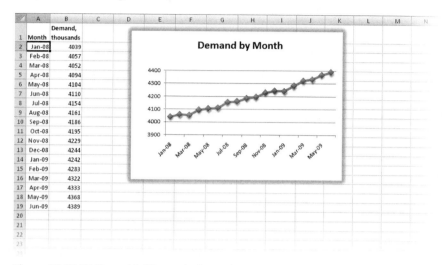

Figure 17-17 We'll use this 18-month demand curve to demonstrate the Moving Average tool.

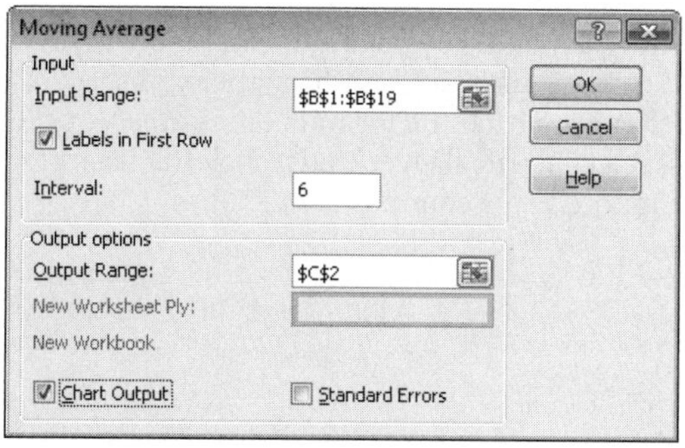

Figure 17-18 The Moving Average tool helps smooth out bumpy curves to reveal the trend.

The Moving Average tool requires three pieces of information: the input range that contains the data you want to analyze, the output range where the averaged data will appear, and the interval over which the data is averaged. To determine a three-month moving average, for example, specify an interval of 3.

Figure 17-19 shows a six-month moving average superimposed over the original demand curve in Figure 17-18. The Moving Average tool produced the data in column C, which was used to create the straighter plot line in the chart. Notice that the first five cells in the tool's output range contain #N/A error values. Where the interval is n, you will always have $n-1$ #N/A error values at the beginning of the output. Including those values in a chart presents no problem, because Excel leaves the first area of the plot line blank.

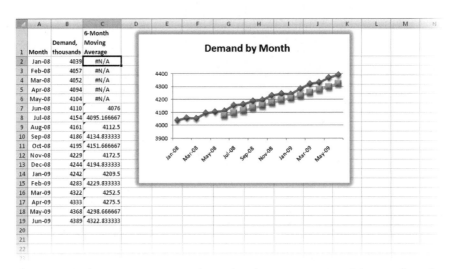

	Month	Demand, thousands	6-Month Moving Average
1	Month	thousands	Average
2	Jan-08	4039	#N/A
3	Feb-08	4057	#N/A
4	Mar-08	4052	#N/A
5	Apr-08	4094	#N/A
6	May-08	4104	#N/A
7	Jun-08	4110	4076
8	Jul-08	4154	4095.166667
9	Aug-08	4161	4112.5
10	Sep-08	4186	4134.833333
11	Oct-08	4195	4151.666667
12	Nov-08	4229	4172.5
13	Dec-08	4244	4194.833333
14	Jan-09	4242	4209.5
15	Feb-09	4283	4229.833333
16	Mar-09	4322	4252.5
17	Apr-09	4333	4275.5
18	May-09	4368	4298.666667
19	Jun-09	4389	4322.833333
20			
21			
22			

Figure 17-19 The Moving Average tool provides a better perspective of the overall trend.

In Figure 17-19 we applied some judicious formatting to the rather plain chart generated by the Moving Average tool. To learn more about charts, see Part 6, "Creating Charts."

Notice that each cell containing a moving average value in Figure 17-19 displays a flag in the upper-left corner of the cell. This is an error flag; after you select the cell, a smart tag action menu appears alerting you that the formula omits adjacent cells. In this case, it's OK. To remove the flags, select all the flagged cells, click the smart tag to display its menu, and then choose the Ignore Error command.

Performing What-If Analysis

One of the most important benefits of spreadsheet software is that it performs a what-if analysis quickly and easily. Change key variables, and instantly see the effect. For example, if you're using Microsoft Office Excel 2007 to decide whether to lease or purchase a car, you can test your financial model with different assumptions about interest rates and down payments, and you can see the effects of varying rates on bottom-line costs you will pay, such as the total interest. Office Excel 2007 offers a number of advanced what-if features, which are discussed in this chapter.

Using Data Tables

 A data table, or sensitivity table, summarizes the impact of one or two variables on formulas that use those variables. You can click the What-If Analysis button in the Data Tools group on the Data tab and then click Data Table to create two kinds of data tables: tables based on a single input variable that test the variable's impact on more than one formula and tables based on two input variables that test their impact on a single formula.

Data Tables Based on One Input Variable

Suppose you're considering buying a house that requires you to take on a 30-year, $200,000 mortgage, and you need to calculate monthly payments on the loan for several interest rates. A one-variable data table, such as the one shown in Figure 18-1, can give you the information you need.

 You can find the Goal Seek.xlsx file in the Sample Files section of the companion CD.

To create this table, type the interest rates you want to test, as shown in cells B3:B9 in Figure 18-1. This is the *input range*, because it contains the input values you want to test. Type the loan amount in a cell outside the data table area. We typed **$200,000** in cell C1. This allows us to easily change the loan amount to test various scenarios. Enter the formula that uses the input variable. In this case, type the formula **=PMT(A2/12, 360, C1)** in cell C2. In this formula, A2/12 is the monthly interest rate, 360 is the term of the loan in months, and C1 refers to the cell containing the loan principal.

C2		▾	f_x	=PMT(A2/12,360,C1)							
	A	B	C	D	E	F	G	H	I	J	K	L
1		Loan Amount:	$200,000.00								
2			(555.56)								
3			4.0%								
4			4.5%								
5			5.0%								
6			5.5%								
7			6.0%								
8			6.5%								
9			7.0%								
10											
11											
12											
13											
14											
15											

Figure 18-1 Begin building the data table by typing the interest rates and the PMT function in the worksheet.

> **Note**
>
> Notice that the formula in cell C2 refers to cell A2, which is blank. Because A2 is blank, the function returns a spurious result: the payment required to amortize the loan at an interest rate of 0 percent. Cell A2 is a placeholder through which Excel will feed the values in the input range to create the data table. Because Excel never changes the underlying value of this cell, this placeholder can be any cell, but it must be located outside the data table.

After you have entered the inputs and the formula, select the data table—the smallest rectangular block that includes the formula and all the values in the input range. In this case, select the range B2:C9, and then click the What-If Analysis button in the Data Tools group on the Data tab, and click Data Table.

In the Data Table dialog box, shown in Figure 18-2, specify the location of the input cell in the Row Input Cell or Column Input Cell box. The *input cell* is the placeholder cell referred to by the table formula—in this example, A2. If the input values are arranged in a row, type the input cell reference in the Row Input Cell box. If the values in the input range are arranged in a column, as in our example, use the Column Input Cell box.

Figure 18-2 Use the Data Table dialog box to specify the input cell.

After you click OK, Excel enters the results of the table formula (one result for each input value) in the available cells of the data table range. In this example, Excel enters six results in the range C3:C9, as shown in Figure 18-3, with a little formatting added for easier reading.

	C9		f_x	{=TABLE(,A2)}									
	A	B	C	D	E	F	G	H	I	J	K	L	
1		Loan Amount:	$200,000.00										
2			(555.56)										
3		4.0%	(954.83)										
4		4.5%	(1,013.37)										
5		5.0%	(1,073.64)										
6		5.5%	(1,135.58)										
7		6.0%	(1,199.10)										
8		6.5%	(1,264.14)										
9		7.0%	(1,330.60)										
10													
11													
12													
13													
14													
15													

Figure 18-3 The monthly loan payments for each interest rate now appear in the data table.

When you create this data table, Excel enters the array formula { =TABLE(,A2)} in each cell in the *results range* C3:C9. In the sample data table, the formula computes the results of the PMT function using each of the interest rates in column B. After you have built the table, you can change the loan amount or any of the interest rate values to see the results immediately.

> **Note**
>
> The TABLE function is an internal function, meaning that you can't select it in the Insert Function dialog box or type it manually.

Single-Variable Tables with More Than One Formula

When you create a single-variable data table, you can include as many output formulas as you want. If your input range is in a column, type the second output formula directly to the right of the first one, the third to the right of the second, and so on. You can use different formulas for different columns, but they must all use the same input cell.

Suppose you're thinking about buying a house that would require you to take out a $180,000 mortgage. You want to know what your monthly payments would be on that mortgage at each of the interest rates in the input range, and you want to be able to compare these payments with those for the $200,000 mortgage calculated in Figure 18-3. You can expand the table in Figure 18-3 to include both formulas.

To add a new formula to the existing data table, type the new formula in cell D2. For this example, we typed **=PMT(A2/12, 360, D1)**. This formula must also refer to cell A2, the same input cell as in the first formula. Then type **$180,000** in cell D1, and select the table range B2:D9. Then click the What-If Analysis button on the Data tab, and click

Data Table. Finally, type the same input cell reference ($A$2) in the Column Input Cell box. Figure 18-4 shows the result.

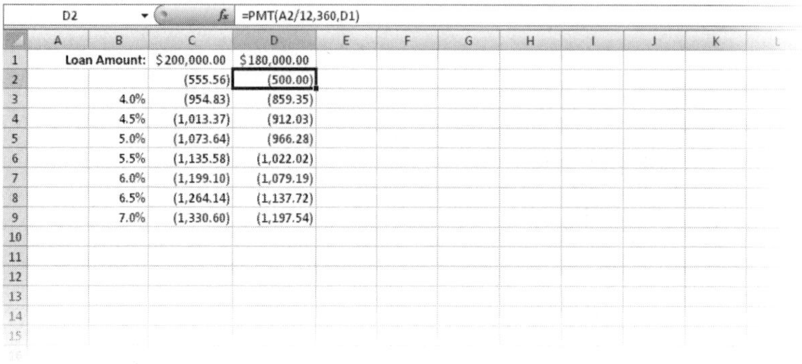

	D2		f_x	=PMT(A2/12,360,D1)								
	A	B	C	D	E	F	G	H	I	J	K	L
1		Loan Amount:	$200,000.00	$180,000.00								
2			(555.56)	(500.00)								
3		4.0%	(954.83)	(859.35)								
4		4.5%	(1,013.37)	(912.03)								
5		5.0%	(1,073.64)	(966.28)								
6		5.5%	(1,135.58)	(1,022.02)								
7		6.0%	(1,199.10)	(1,079.19)								
8		6.5%	(1,264.14)	(1,137.72)								
9		7.0%	(1,330.60)	(1,197.54)								

Figure 18-4 This data table computes the monthly payments on two different loan amounts at various interest rates.

Data Tables Based on Two Input Variables

Suppose you want to build a data table that computes the monthly payment on a $200,000 mortgage, but this time you want to vary not only the interest rate but also the term of the loan. You want to know what effect changing the interest rate and the term will have on your monthly payment.

To create this table, you can again type seven interest rates in cells B3:B9, and then type the second set of input values—the loan terms, in months—in a row above and to the right of the first set, as shown in Figure 18-5.

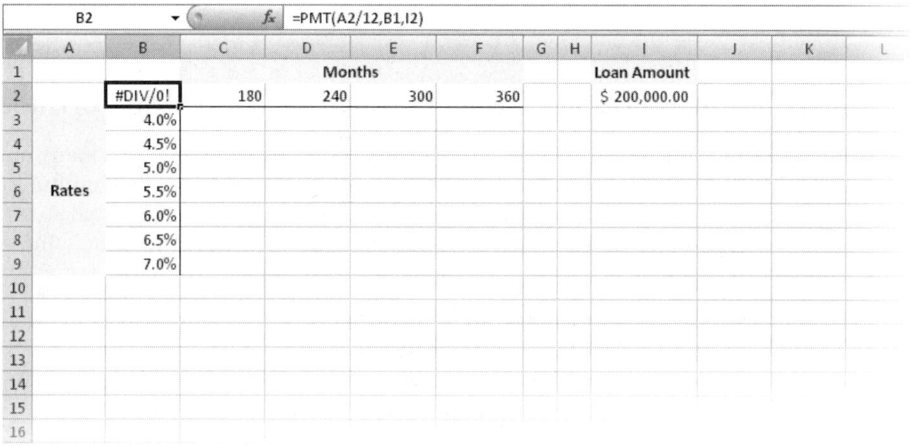

	B2		f_x	=PMT(A2/12,B1,I2)								
	A	B	C	D	E	F	G	H	I	J	K	L
1				Months					Loan Amount			
2		#DIV/0!	180	240	300	360			$ 200,000.00			
3		4.0%										
4		4.5%										
5		5.0%										
6	Rates	5.5%										
7		6.0%										
8		6.5%										
9		7.0%										

Figure 18-5 Cell B2 contains the formula for this two-variable table.

After you type the loan amount in a cell outside the table area (cell I2 in this example), you can create the table formula. Because this is a two-variable table, you must type the formula in the cell at the intersection of the row and column that contain the two sets of input values—cell B2, in this example. Although you can include as many formulas as you want in a single-variable data table, you can include only one output formula in a two-variable table. The formula for the table in this example is =PMT(A2/12, B1, I2).

You'll notice immediately that the formula in cell B2 returns the #DIV/ 0! error value. This is because the two blank cells, A2 and B1, when used as arguments, produce a number that is either too large or too small for Excel to represent. As you'll see, this spurious result does not affect the performance of the table.

Finally, select the data table—the smallest rectangular block that includes all the input values and the table formula. In this example, the table range is B2:F9. Click the What-If Analysis button on the Data tab, then click Data Table, and finally specify the (empty) input cells. Because this is a two-variable table, you must define two input cells. For this example, type the reference for the first input cell, $B$1, in the Row Input Cell box, and then type the reference for the second input cell, $A$2, in the Column Input Cell box. Figure 18-6 shows the result.

	C3			f_x {=TABLE(B1,A2)}								
	A	B	C	D	E	F	G	H	I	J	K	L
1				Months					Loan Amount			
2		#DIV/0!	180	240	300	360			$ 200,000.00			
3		4.0%	(1,479.38)	(1,211.96)	(1,055.67)	(954.83)						
4		4.5%	(1,529.99)	(1,265.30)	(1,111.66)	(1,013.37)						
5		5.0%	(1,581.59)	(1,319.91)	(1,169.18)	(1,073.64)						
6	Rates	5.5%	(1,634.17)	(1,375.77)	(1,228.17)	(1,135.58)						
7		6.0%	(1,687.71)	(1,432.86)	(1,288.60)	(1,199.10)						
8		6.5%	(1,742.21)	(1,491.15)	(1,350.41)	(1,264.14)						
9		7.0%	(1,797.66)	(1,550.60)	(1,413.56)	(1,330.60)						
10												
11												
12												
13												
14												
15												

Figure 18-6 This data table calculates the monthly payments using various interest rates and terms.

TROUBLESHOOTING

The results in my two-input data table are wrong.

Be careful not to reverse the input cells in a two-variable table. If you do, Excel uses the input values in the wrong place in the table formula, which creates a set of meaningless results. For example, if you reverse the input cells in the example shown in Figure 18-6, Excel uses the values in the input range C2:F2 as interest rates and the values in the input range B3:B9 as terms, resulting in monthly payments in the $20 million range!

To make sure you're using the correct input cells, you need to look at the formula. In our example formula =PMT(A2/12, B1, I2), A2 appears in the first argument, which is *rate*. Because the rates are arranged in a column, A2 is the column input cell.

Chapter 18

Editing Tables

Although you can edit the input values or formulas in the left column or top row of a table, you can't edit the contents of any individual cell in the results range because the data table is an array. If you make a mistake when you set up a data table, you must select all the results, press the Delete key, and then recompute the table.

You can copy the table results to a different part of the worksheet. You might want to do this to save the table's current results before you change the table formula or variables. In Figure 18-7, we copied the values from C3:F9 to C10:F16. When you do this, the copied values are constants, not array formulas. Excel automatically changes the results of the table from a set of array formulas to their numeric values if you copy the results out of the table range.

	A	B	C	D	E	F	G	H	I	J	K	L
			C11			f_x -1479.37585121851						
1					Months				Loan Amount			
2		#DIV/0!	180	240	300	360			$ 200,000.00			
3		4.0%	(1,479.38)	(1,211.96)	(1,055.67)	(954.83)						
4		4.5%	(1,529.99)	(1,265.30)	(1,111.66)	(1,013.37)						
5		5.0%	(1,581.59)	(1,319.91)	(1,169.18)	(1,073.64)						
6	Rates	5.5%	(1,634.17)	(1,375.77)	(1,228.17)	(1,135.58)						
7		6.0%	(1,687.71)	(1,432.86)	(1,288.60)	(1,199.10)						
8		6.5%	(1,742.21)	(1,491.15)	(1,350.41)	(1,264.14)						
9		7.0%	(1,797.66)	(1,550.60)	(1,413.56)	(1,330.60)						
10												
11			(1,479.38)	(1,211.96)	(1,055.67)	(954.83)						
12			(1,529.99)	(1,265.30)	(1,111.66)	(1,013.37)						
13			(1,581.59)	(1,319.91)	(1,169.18)	(1,073.64)						
14			(1,634.17)	(1,375.77)	(1,228.17)	(1,135.58)						
15			(1,687.71)	(1,432.86)	(1,288.60)	(1,199.10)						
16			(1,742.21)	(1,491.15)	(1,350.41)	(1,264.14)						
17			(1,797.66)	(1,550.60)	(1,413.56)	(1,330.60)						
18												
19												
20												
21												
22												
23												
24												

Figure 18-7 Copying the results range to another part of the worksheet transfers the numeric values, not the formulas used to compute them.

Using the Scenario Manager

To model more complicated problems than data tables can handle, involving as many as 32 variables, you can call on the services of the Scenario Manager by clicking the What-If Analysis button in the Data Tools group on the Data tab and then clicking Scenario Manager. A *scenario* is a named combination of values assigned to one or more variable cells in a what-if model. The worksheet in Figure 18-8 is a what-if model, set up so you can type variable figures and watch the effect on dependent computed values. The Scenario Manager records, tracks, and applies combinations of variable values.

	B	C	D	E
1	**Revenue**	Name	Total per week	Total per year
2	Revenues per Customer Visit	*Revenue*	34.78	
3	Direct Costs per Customer Visit	*DirCosts*	30.12	
4	Gross Profit per Customer Visit	*GrossProfitVisit*	4.66	
5	Average Customer Visits	*AvgCustVisits*	33,759	
6	*Gross Profit*		157,317	8,180,481
7	**Overhead**			
8		*Payroll*		3,494,046
9		*Facilities*		1,635,511
10		*Depreciation*		453,305
11		*Advertising*		291,647
12		*Supplies*		496,944
13		*Other*		1,295,828
14	*Subtotal*			7,667,281
15				
16	**Operating Profit**			513,200
17				
18				
19				
20				
21				
22				

Figure 18-8 We'll use the Scenario Manager to model the effects of changing values in D2:D3, D5, and E8:E13 of this worksheet.

You can find the Revenue Scenarios.xlsm file in the Sample Files section of the companion CD.

Here are some of the tasks you can do with the Scenario Manager:

- Create multiple scenarios for a single what-if model, each with its own sets of variables. You can create as many scenarios as your model requires.

- Distribute a what-if model to other members of your group so they can add their own scenarios. Then you can collect the multiple versions and merge all the scenarios into a single worksheet.

- Track changes made to scenarios easily with the version-control features of the Scenario Manager by recording the date and the user name each time a scenario is added or modified.

- Print reports detailing all the changing cells and result cells.

- Password-protect scenarios from modification, and even hide them from view.

- Examine relationships between scenarios created by multiple users, using Scenario Summary and PivotTable reports. For more about PivotTables, see Chapter 22, "Analyzing Data with PivotTable Reports."

Imagine that you manage a grocery store whose profit picture is modeled by the worksheet in Figure 18-8. The numbers in D2:D5 and E8:E13 are historic averages; column C contains the range names applied to the relevant cells in columns D and E. You're interested in testing the impact of changes in these cells on the bottom line in cell E16.

Chapter 18

> **Note**
>
> Cell references are OK, but before you begin using the Scenario Manager, it's a good idea to name the cells you plan to use for your variables, as well as any cells containing formulas whose values depend on your variable cells. This step isn't required, but it makes the scenario reports, as well as some of the dialog boxes, more intelligible. For more information, see "Naming Cells and Cell Ranges" on page 441.

Defining Scenarios

To define a scenario, follow these steps:

1. Click the What-If Analysis button on the Data tab, and click Scenario Manager.

2. In the Scenario Manager dialog box, shown in Figure 18-9, click Add.

Figure 18-9 When you click the What-If Analysis button on the Data tab and then click Scenario Manager, Excel displays the Scenario Manager dialog box.

3. In the Add Scenario dialog box, shown in Figure 18-10, type a name for your scenario. (Note that as soon as you type cell references in the Add Scenario dialog box, the title of the dialog box changes to Edit Scenario.)

> **Note**
>
> It's a good idea to define the values you begin with as a scenario before changing any of them. You can name this scenario something like Starting Values or Last Year, as in our example. If you don't name the starting scenario, you'll lose your original what-if assumptions when you display the new changing cell values on your worksheet.

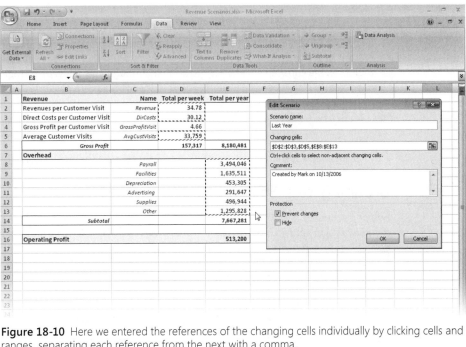

Figure 18-10 Here we entered the references of the changing cells individually by clicking cells and ranges, separating each reference from the next with a comma.

4. In the Changing Cells box, type or select the cells you plan to vary. Select nonadjacent cells and ranges by pressing the Ctrl key before selecting the cells or by separating their references or names with commas, as shown in Figure 18-10.

5. Click OK to create the first scenario. The Scenario Values dialog box appears, displaying a box for each changing cell. If you have named the changing cells, the names appear adjacent to the boxes, as shown in Figure 18-11; otherwise, the references of the changing cells appear.

6. To complete a scenario, edit these values; however, for this example, leave the values as they are, and just click OK.

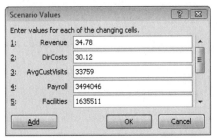

Figure 18-11 Because we previously named each changing cell, the names appear in the Scenario Values dialog box.

> **Note**
>
> In each text box in the Scenario Values dialog box, you can type either a constant or a formula. For example, to increase the value of the first variable in Figure 18-11, click in front of the value in the first variable's box, and type **=1.1*** to create a formula that multiplies the current value by 1.1. (Note that although you can type formulas in the Scenario Values dialog box, Excel alerts you that the formulas are converted to their resulting values after you click OK.)

7. To create another scenario, click Add to return to the Add Scenario dialog box.

Browsing Your Scenarios

Select a scenario name in the Scenario Manager dialog box, and click Show. The Scenario Manager replaces the variable values currently on the worksheet with the values you specified when you created the scenario. In Figure 18-12, the example worksheet has a scenario showing average customer visits increased by 5 percent and revenues per customer visit decreased by 5 percent.

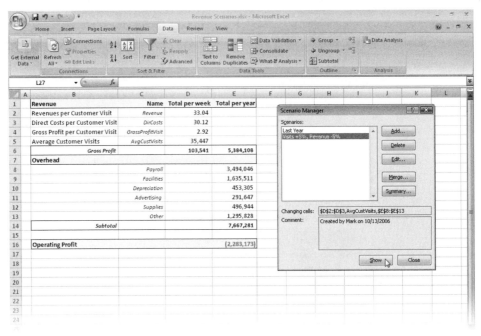

Figure 18-12 Clicking Show replaces your current worksheet values with the values of a specified scenario.

The Scenario Manager dialog box remains on the screen after you click the Show button so you can look at the results of other scenarios without returning to the worksheet. If you click Close or press Esc to close the Scenario Manager dialog box, the values from the last scenario you browsed remain on the worksheet. (This is a good reason to create a starting values scenario, as mentioned earlier.)

Adding, Editing, and Deleting Scenarios

Excel saves scenarios with all other worksheet data when you save them. Each worksheet in a workbook can contain its own set of scenarios. In the Scenario Manager dialog box, you add new scenarios by clicking Add, and you edit existing scenarios by clicking Edit, which displays the Edit Scenario dialog box (which is functionally the same as the Add Scenario dialog box shown in Figure 18-10). You can change the name of the selected scenario, add or remove changing cells, or add comments in the Edit Scenario dialog box.

Tracking Changes

If someone edits a scenario, Excel adds a Modified By entry to the Comment box in the Scenario Manager dialog box, beneath the Created By entry that appears when you first add a scenario. Each time a scenario is modified, Excel adds the name of the user and the date of modification. This information is particularly helpful if you route your what-if models to others and then merge their scenarios into a single what-if model, as discussed in the following section.

INSIDE OUT   Comment Modifications

When you edit scenarios, you can modify the contents of the Comment box; those modifications persist in all dialog boxes, including the creation and modification dates. You might not want this to happen if you really want to track changes or prevent tampering. If you don't want these comments modified, make sure you take advantage of the preventative measures discussed in "Protecting Worksheets" on page 156.

Routing and Merging Scenarios

If part of your job is to develop what-if models or projections for your company, you probably spend a lot of time gathering information about trends and market forces that might affect the company in the future. Often you need input from several people, each of whom knows about a particular aspect of the business, such as payroll costs or sales trends. Excel includes a scenario-merging feature to make this sort of information gathering easier.

For example, suppose you want to distribute a what-if model to your co-workers: Vicki has expertise about customer trends, Max knows the payroll story, and Regina keeps track of advertising. You can distribute individually named copies of the workbook to each person, and after your co-workers add their what-if scenarios and return the workbook or workbooks, you can merge the scenarios into a master worksheet. Simply open all the workbooks containing the scenarios you want, open the worksheet where you want the result to go, and click Merge in the Scenario Manager dialog box. When you do so, a dialog box like the one in Figure 18-13 appears.

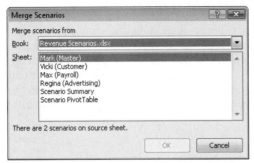

Figure 18-13 Clicking Merge in the Scenario Manager dialog box displays the Merge Scenarios dialog box, with which you can import scenarios from any worksheet in any open workbook.

INSIDE OUT   Request Only the Data You Need

Merging scenarios works best if the basic structure of all the worksheets is identical. Although this uniformity isn't a strict requirement, merging scenarios from worksheets that are laid out differently can cause changing cell values to appear in unexpected locations. For this reason, and because it's generally difficult to ascertain the skill level of everyone contributing data, you might try a different approach. Distribute a questionnaire requesting only the data you need, use external cell references to link the requested data with the appropriate locations on your master worksheet, and create the scenarios yourself.

In the Merge Scenarios dialog box, you select the workbook and worksheet from which you want to merge scenarios. As shown in Figure 18-13, if you select a worksheet in the Sheet list, a message at the bottom of the dialog box tells you how many scenarios exist on that worksheet. When you click OK, the scenarios on that worksheet are copied to the active worksheet. After merging all the scenarios from your co-workers, the Scenario Manager dialog box for this example looks like the one shown in Figure 18-14.

Notice in Figure 18-14 that the Comment box displays the name of the creator and modifier of the selected scenario. If the Scenarios list includes similarly named scenarios, Excel appends a creator name, date, or number to the name. You can use the Edit button to rename the scenarios if you want.

Figure 18-14 The merged scenarios are now available on the same worksheet.

Each group of scenarios provided by the co-workers uses different changing cells. Vicki's scenarios change the values in cells D2, D3, and D5; Max's scenarios change only the value in E8; and Regina's scenarios change only the value in E11. You can display these different scenarios together and watch how the combinations affect the bottom line.

Creating Scenario Reports

The Revenue Scenarios workbook with its merged scenarios has become a somewhat complex what-if model. However, you can create models that are far more complex, which can include as many scenarios as you want (or as many as your computer can handle) with up to 32 variables per scenario. The Scenario Manager summary reports help you keep track of the possibilities, and PivotTable reports give you additional what-if functionality by allowing you to manipulate the elements of the report. However, although you can create as many scenarios as you like, the Scenario Summary report will display only the first 251 of them.

Clicking Summary in the Scenario Manager dialog box displays the dialog box shown in Figure 18-15. Use it to create reports that show the values each scenario assigns to each changing cell.

At the bottom of the dialog box, you identify result cells that you want to appear in the report, separated by commas. You want cells that are dependent on the most changing cells—in this case, the Operating Profit value in cell E16, as well as cell E6, the yearly Gross Profit value.

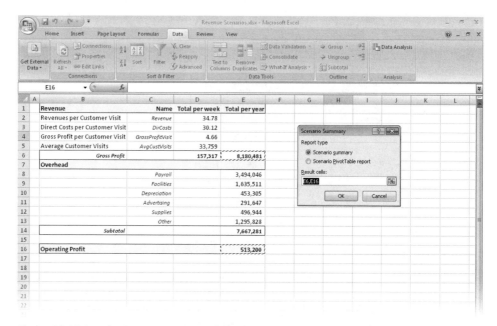

Figure 18-15 Use the Scenario Summary dialog box to specify the type of report and the result cells you want to see.

The Scenario Summary Report

The Scenario Summary is a fully formatted report placed on a new worksheet, as shown in Figure 18-16.

In Figure 18-16, notice that all the changing cell values in column E are shaded in gray. The shading indicates cells that change in the scenario named at the top of the column.

Notice also that outlining symbols appear above and to the left of the summary report, allowing you to show and hide details. As you can see in Figure 18-17, clicking the outline plus sign symbol displays hidden data—the contents of the Comment box in the Scenario Manager dialog box, including the creation and modification dates of each scenario.

For information about working with worksheet outlines, see "Outlining Worksheets" on page 253.

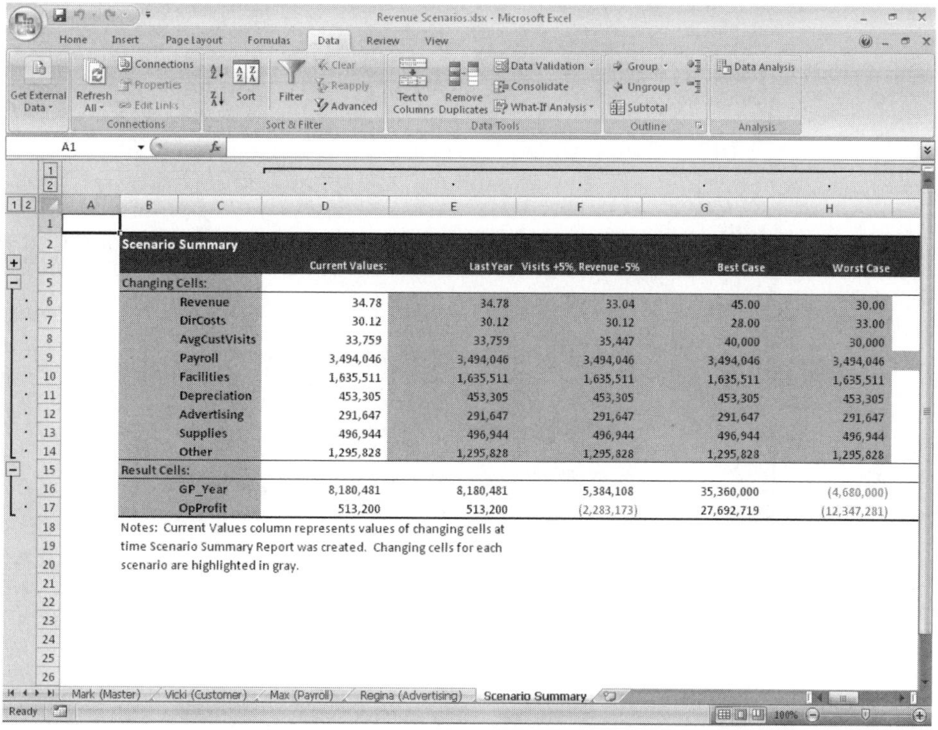

Figure 18-16 The Scenario Summary option creates a report on a new worksheet named Scenario Summary.

The Scenario PivotTable Report

Like the Scenario Summary report, the Scenario PivotTable report is created as a new worksheet in your workbook. However, PivotTables are what-if tools in their own right, allowing you to use direct mouse-manipulation techniques to mix and match different scenarios in the report and watch the effects on result cells. Figure 18-18 shows a Scenario PivotTable report created from a version of the Revenue Scenarios workbook.

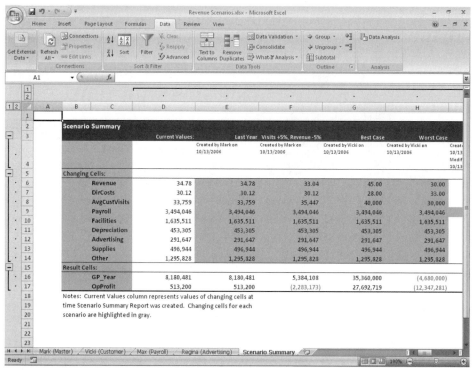

Figure 18-17 The comments entered in the Scenario Manager dialog box are hidden in row 4 of the Scenario Summary report.

For information about how to use PivotTables, see Chapter 22.

Use Scenario Summary Reports

PivotTables are powerful analysis tools best suited to complex what-if models that include scenarios with different sets of changing cells created by different people. The more one-dimensional your what-if model, the less useful a PivotTable becomes. Pivot-Tables take longer to create and consume more memory than summary reports. If you create all the scenarios yourself and use the same set of changing cells in each, you might find it easier to use Scenario Summary reports because you won't be able to make use of the advantages offered by the PivotTable.

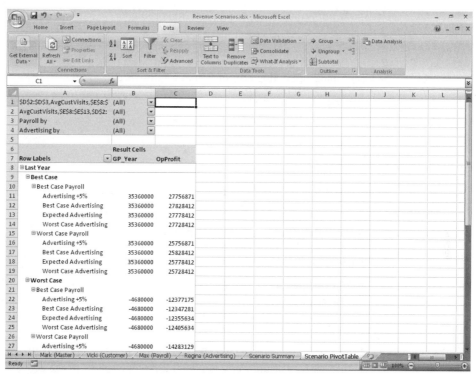

Figure 18-18 The Scenario PivotTable report manipulates the actual data in the report.

Using the Goal Seek Command

By clicking the What-If Analysis button on the Data tab and then clicking Goal Seek, you can compute an unknown value that produces the result you want. For example, suppose you want to know the maximum 30-year mortgage you can afford if the interest rate is 6.5 percent and if you must limit your monthly payments to $2,000. To use the Goal Seek command to answer this question, first set up the problem using trial values. For example, in the mortgage problem shown in Figure 18-19, a $500,000 mortgage would require monthly payments in excess of the $2,000 target.

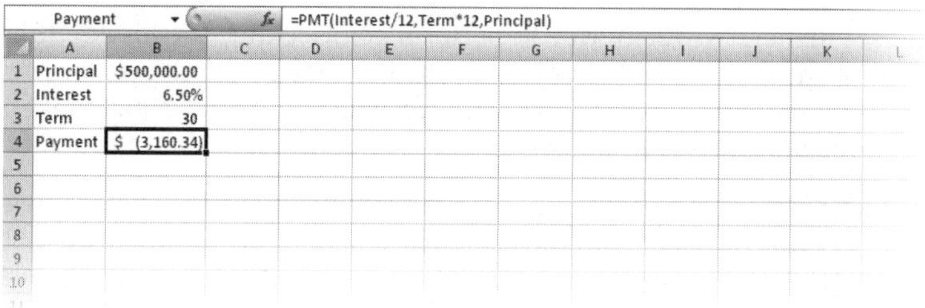

Figure 18-19 Use the Goal Seek command to find the maximum mortgage you can borrow if you want to keep your payments under a certain limit.

Here's how to perform goal seeking on this problem:

1. Select the formula cell—in this case, B4—to make it the active cell.

2. Click the What-If Analysis button on the Data tab, and click Goal Seek to display the Goal Seek dialog box shown in Figure 18-20.

Figure 18-20 To use goal seeking, complete the Goal Seek dialog box.

3. Accept the value in the Set Cell box (make sure it specifies the cell containing the formula). In the To Value box, type the maximum value you want as the result of the formula—in this case, **–2000**. (You type a negative number because the payment represents cash spent rather than received.)

4. In the By Changing Cell box, type the reference or click the cell on the worksheet whose value is unknown—in this case, cell B1 (the Principal value). Alternatively, if you have assigned a name, such as Principal, to cell B1, you can type that name in the By Changing Cell box.

5. Click OK, or press Enter. Excel displays the Goal Seek Status dialog box shown in Figure 18-21. The answer you are looking for appears in the cell specified in the By Changing Cell box.

6. To type this value on the worksheet, click OK in the Goal Seek Status dialog box. To restore the value that was in B1 before you used the Goal Seek command, click Cancel.

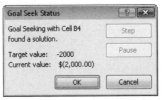

Figure 18-21 The Goal Seek Status dialog box informs you when Excel finds a solution.

Excel uses an iterative technique to perform goal seeking. It tries one value after another for the variable cell specified in the By Changing Cell box until it arrives at the solution you requested. Excel solves the mortgage problem we just looked at quickly. Other problems might take longer, and some might not be solvable at all.

While Excel is working on a complex goal-seeking problem, you can click Pause in the Goal Seek Status dialog box to interrupt the calculation, and then click Step to display the result of each successive iteration. A Continue button appears in the dialog box if you are solving a problem in this stepwise fashion. To resume full-speed goal seeking, click Continue.

Precision and Multiple Solutions

Suppose you enter the formula =A2^2 in cell A1 of a blank worksheet and then use the Goal Seek command to find the value of A2 that will make A1 equal to 4. (In other words, in the Goal Seek dialog box, type **$A$1** in the Set Cell box, **4** in the To Value box, and **$A$2** in the By Changing Cell box.) The result, shown in Figure 18-22, might be surprising. Excel seems to be telling you that the closest value it can find to the square root of 4 is 2.000023.

By default, the Goal Seek command stops when it has either performed 100 iterations (trial solutions) or found an answer that comes to within 0.001 of your specified target value. If you need greater precision than this, you can change the default limits by clicking the Microsoft Office Button, clicking Excel Options, selecting the Formulas category, and then changing the Maximum Iterations value to a number greater than 100 or setting the Maximum Change value to a number less than 0.001, or both.

For more information about worksheet calculation options, see Chapter 12, "Building Formulas."

	A1			f_x	=A2^2							
	A	B	C	D	E	F	G	H	I	J	K	L
1	4.000092											
2	2.000023											
3												
4												
5												
6												
7												
8												

Figure 18-22 The Goal Seek command returns this result when asked to find the square root of 4.

This example illustrates another factor you should be aware of when you use the Goal Seek command. The Goal Seek command finds only one solution, even though your problem might have several. In this case, the value 4 has two square roots: +2 and −2. In situations like this, the Goal Seek command gives you the solution with the same sign as the starting value. For instance, if you start with a value of −1 in cell A2, the Goal Seek command reports the solution as −1.999917, instead of +2.000023.

Using the Solver

The Goal Seek command is handy for problems that involve an exact target value that depends on a single unknown value. For problems that are more complex, you should use the Solver add-in. The Solver can handle problems that involve many variable cells and can help you find combinations of variables that maximize or minimize a target cell. It also specifies one or more constraints—conditions that must be met for the solution to be valid.

> **Note**
>
> The Solver is an add-in. If the Solver button does not appear on the Data tab on the Ribbon, click the Microsoft Office Button, Excel Options, Add-Ins category, and then click the Go button. Then select the Solver Add-In check box, and click OK to install it. Click Yes to confirm that you want to install the Solver add-in.

As an example of the kind of problem that the Solver can tackle, imagine you are planning an advertising campaign for a new product. Your total budget for print advertising is $12,000,000; you want to expose your ads at least 800 million times to potential readers; and you've decided to place ads in six publications—we'll call them Pub1 through Pub6. Each publication reaches a different number of readers and charges a different rate per page. Your job is to reach the readership target at the lowest possible cost with the following additional constraints:

- At least six advertisements should run in each publication.

- No more than a third of your advertising dollars should be spent on any one publication.

- Your total cost for placing advertisements in Pub3 and Pub4 must not exceed $7,500,000.

Figure 18-23 shows one way to lay out the problem.

	A	B	C	D	E	F	G	H	I	J	K
1	Publication	Cost per ad	Audience per ad (millions)	Number of ads placed	Total cost	Percent of total	Total audience (millions)				
2	Pub1	$147,420	9.9	6.0	$884,520	26%	59				
3	Pub2	$124,410	8.4	6.0	$746,460	22%	50				
4	Pub3	$113,100	8.2	6.0	$678,600	20%	49				
5	Pub4	$70,070	5.1	6.0	$420,420	13%	31				
6	Pub5	$53,000	3.7	6.0	$318,000	9%	22				
7	Pub6	$52,440	3.6	6.0	$314,640	9%	22				
8	Total				$3,362,640		233				
9	Total Pub3+Pub4				$1,099,020						
10											
11			Constraints:		Total advertising budget		$12,000,000				
12					Total budget for Pub3+Pub4		$7,500,000				
13					Minmum total audience (millions)		800				
14					Maximum % of budget spent on any publication		33.30%				
15					Maximum number of ads per publication		6				
16											
17											
18											
19											
20											
21											

Figure 18-23 You can use the Solver to determine how many advertisements to place in each publication to meet your objectives at the lowest possible cost.

You can find the Advertising.xlsx file in the Sample Files section of the companion CD.

> **Note**
>
> This section merely introduces the Solver. A complete treatment of this powerful tool is beyond the scope of this book. For more details, including an explanation of the Solver error messages, see the online Help system. For background material about optimization, we recommend *Financial Models Using Simulation and Optimization II: Investment* by Wayne L. Winston (Palisade Corporation, 2001).

You might be able to work out this problem yourself by substituting many alternatives for the values currently in D2:D7, keeping your eye on the constraints, and noting the impact of your changes on the total expenditure figure in E8. In fact, that's what the Solver does for you—but it does it more rapidly, and it uses some analytic techniques to home in on the optimal solution without having to try every conceivable alternative.

Click the Solver button on the Data tab to display the dialog box shown in Figure 18-24. To complete this dialog box, you must give the Solver three sets of information: your objective, or *target* (minimizing total expenditure); your variables, or *changing cells* (the number of advertisements you will place in each publication); and your *constraints* (the conditions summarized at the bottom of the worksheet in Figure 18-23).

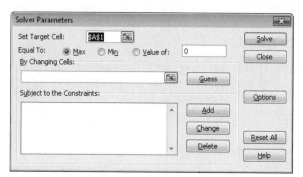

Figure 18-24 Use the Solver Parameters dialog box to set up your problem.

Stating the Objective

In the Set Target Cell box, you indicate the goal, or target, that you want Solver to achieve. In this example, you want to minimize your total cost—the value in cell E8—so you specify your objective by typing **E8** in the Set Target Cell box (or by clicking the cell). In this example, because you want the Solver to set your target cell to its lowest possible value, you select Min as the Equal To option.

> **Note**
> It's a good idea to name all the important cells of your model before you put the Solver to work. If you don't name the cells, the Solver reports construct names based on the nearest column-heading and row-heading text, but these constructed names don't appear in the Solver dialog boxes. For more information, see "Naming Cells and Cell Ranges" on page 441.

You don't have to specify an objective. If you leave the Set Target Cell box blank, then click Options, and finally select the Show Iteration Results check box, you can use the Solver to step through some or all the combinations of variable cells that meet your constraints. You will then receive an answer that solves the constraints but isn't necessarily the optimal solution.

For more information about the Show Iteration Results option, see "Viewing Iteration Results" on page 609.

Specifying Variable Cells

The next step is to tell the Solver which cells to change. In our example, the cells whose values can be adjusted are those that specify the number of advertisements to be placed in each publication, or cells D2:D7. Alternatively, you can click Guess, and the Solver proposes the appropriate changing cells based on the target cell you specified.

Specifying Constraints

The last step, specifying constraints, is optional. To specify a constraint, click Add in the Solver Parameters dialog box, and complete the Add Constraint dialog box. Figure 18-25 shows how you express the constraint that total advertising expenditures (the value in cell E8 in the model) must be less than or equal to the total budget (the value in cell G11).

Figure 18-25 Click Add in the Solver Parameters dialog box to add constraints.

Figure 18-26 shows how the Solver Parameters dialog box looks after we have specified all our constraints. Notice that the constraints are listed in alphabetical order, not necessarily in the order in which we defined them.

Figure 18-26 The Solver lists the constraints in alphabetical order and uses defined cell and range names whenever possible.

Notice also that two of the constraints have range references on the left side of the comparison operator. The expression $D$2:$D$7>=$G$15 stipulates that the value of each cell in D2:D7 must be 6 or greater, and the expression $F$2:$F$7<=$G$14 stipulates that the value of each cell in F2:F9 must be no greater than 33.30 percent. Each of these expressions is a shortcut way of stating six separate constraints. If you use this kind of shortcut, the constraint value on the right side of the comparison operator must be a single cell reference, a range of the same dimensions as the range on the left side, or a constant value.

After completing the Solver Parameters dialog box, click Solve. In the advertisement campaign example, the Solver succeeds in finding an optimal value for the objective cell while meeting all the constraints and displays the dialog box shown in Figure 18-27. The values displayed on your worksheet at that time result in the optimal solution. You can leave these values in the worksheet by selecting the Keep Solver Solution option and clicking OK, or you can restore the original values by selecting the Restore Original Values option and clicking OK (or by clicking Cancel). You also have the option of assigning the solution values to a named scenario.

Specifying Integer Constraints

Notice that in Figure 18-27, the Solver arrived at 53.3 for the number of ads placed in Pub4. Unfortunately, because it's not possible to run three-tenths of an advertisement, the solution isn't practical.

To stipulate that your ad-placement variables be restricted to whole numbers, start the Solver, and click the Add button in the Solver Parameters dialog box. In the Add Constraint dialog box, you select the cell reference that holds your ad placement numbers—D2:D7. Click the list in the middle of the dialog box, and select *int*. The Solver inserts the word *integer* in the Constraint box, as shown in Figure 18-28. Click OK to return to the Solver Parameters dialog box.

Chapter 18

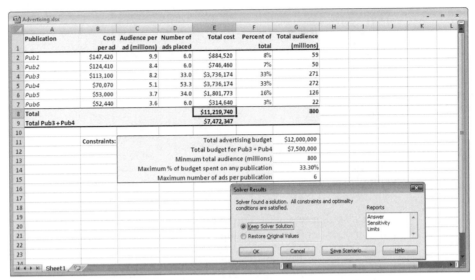

Figure 18-27 When the Solver succeeds, it presents the Solver Results dialog box.

Figure 18-28 To specify an integer constraint, select the item labeled *int*.

Note that when converting numbers to integers, Excel effectively rounds down; the decimal portion of the number is truncated. The integer solution shows that by placing 53 ads in Pub4, you can buy an additional ad in Pub5. For a very small increase in budget, you can reach an additional two million readers.

Determine Whether You Need Integer Constraints

Adding integer constraints to a Solver problem can geometrically increase the problem's complexity, resulting in possibly unacceptable delays. The example discussed in this chapter is relatively simple and does not take an inordinate amount of time to solve, but a more complex problem with integer constraints might pose more of a challenge for the Solver. The Solver can solve certain problems only by using integer constraints. In particular, integer solutions are useful for problems in which variables can assume only two values, such as 1 or 0 (yes or no), but if you're looking for "yes or no" results, you can also use the bin (binary) option in the list in the middle of the Change Constraint dialog box.

Saving and Reusing the Solver Parameters

If you save a workbook after using the Solver, Excel saves all the values you typed in the Solver dialog boxes along with your worksheet data. You do not need to retype the parameters of the problem if you want to continue working with it during a later Excel session.

Each worksheet in a workbook can store one set of Solver parameter values. To store more than one set of Solver parameters with a given worksheet, you must use the Save Model option. To use this option, follow these steps:

1. Click the Solver button on the Data tab.

2. Click the Options button, and then in the Solver Options dialog box, shown in Figure 18-29, click Save Model. Excel prompts you for a cell or range in which to store the Solver parameters on the worksheet.

3. Specify a blank cell by clicking it or typing its reference, and then click OK. The Solver pastes the model beginning at the indicated cell and inserting formulas in as many of the cells below it as necessary. (Be sure that the cells below the indicated cell do not contain data.)

4. To reuse the saved parameters, click Load Model in the Solver Parameters dialog box, and then specify the range in which you stored the Solver parameters.

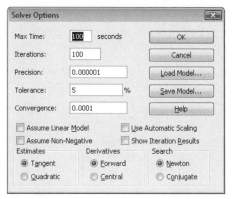

Figure 18-29 Load Model and Save Model in the Solver Options dialog box provide a way to store and retrieve your Solver parameters.

You'll find it easiest to save and reuse Solver parameters if you assign a name to each save model range immediately after you use the Save Model option. You can then specify that name when you use the Load Model option.

For more information about naming, see "Naming Cells and Cell Ranges" on page 441.

Chapter 18

Assigning the Solver Results to Named Scenarios

An even better way to save your Solver parameters is to save them as named scenarios using the Scenario Manager. As you might have noticed, the Solver Results dialog box includes a Save Scenario button. Click this button to assign a scenario name to the current values of your variable cells. This option provides an excellent way to explore and perform further what-if analysis on a variety of possible outcomes.

For more information about scenarios, see "Using the Scenario Manager" on page 588.

Other Solver Options

The Solver Options dialog box contains several options that might need some explanation:

- The Max Time and Iterations boxes tell the Solver, in effect, how hard to work on the solution. If the Solver reaches either the time limit or the number of iterations limit before finding a solution, calculation stops, and Excel asks you whether you want to continue. The default settings are usually sufficient for solving most problems, but if you don't reach a solution with these settings, you can try adjusting them.

- The Solver uses the Precision setting to determine how closely you want values in the constraint cells to match your constraints. The closer this setting is to the value 1, the lower the precision is. If you specify a setting that is less than the default 0.000001, it results in a longer solution time.

- The Tolerance setting applies only to problems that use integer constraints and represents a percentage of error allowed in the solution.

- It's best to leave the Estimates, Derivatives, and Search options at their default settings, unless you understand linear optimization techniques. If you want more information about these options, click Help in the Solver Options dialog box.

Linear Models

A linear optimization problem is one in which the value of the target cell is a linear function of each variable cell; that is, if you plot X Y (scatter) charts of the target cell's value against all meaningful values of each variable cell, your charts are straight lines. If some of your plots produce curves instead of straight lines, the problem is nonlinear.

You can turn on the Assume Linear Model option only for what-if models in which all the relationships are linear. Models that use simple addition and subtraction and worksheet functions, such as SUM, are linear in nature. However, most models are nonlinear. They are generated by multiplying changing cells by other changing cells, by using exponentiation or growth factors, or by using nonlinear worksheet functions, such as PMT.

The Solver can solve linear problems more quickly if you click Options in the Solver Parameters dialog box and then select the Assume Linear Model option. If you select this option for a nonlinear problem and then try to solve the problem, however, the Solver Results dialog box displays the message "The conditions for Assume Linear Model are not satisfied." If you are not sure about the nature of your model, it's best not to use this option.

The Importance of Using Appropriate Starting Values

If your problem is nonlinear, you must be aware of one important detail: Your choice of starting values can affect the solution generated by the Solver. With nonlinear problems, you should always do the following:

- Set your variable cells to reasonable approximations of their optimal values before running the problem.

- Test alternative starting values to see what impact, if any, they have on the Solver solution.

Viewing Iteration Results

If you're interested in exploring many combinations of your variable cells, rather than only the combination that produces the optimal result, you can take advantage of the Show Iteration Results check box in the Solver. Click Options in the Solver Parameters dialog box, and select the Show Iteration Results check box in the Solver Options dialog box. After each iteration, the Show Trial Solution dialog box appears, which allows you to save the scenario and then either stop the trial or continue with the next iteration.

You should be aware that if you use Show Iteration Results, the Solver pauses for solutions that do not meet all your constraints as well as for suboptimal solutions that do.

Generating Reports

In addition to inserting optimal values in your problem's variable cells, the Solver can summarize its results in three reports: Sensitivity, Answer, and Limits. To generate one or more reports, select the names of the reports in the Solver Results dialog box. Select the reports you want, and then click OK. Each report is saved on a separate worksheet in the current workbook.

The Sensitivity Report

The Sensitivity report provides information about how sensitive your target cell is to changes in your constraints. This report has two sections: one for your variable cells and one for your constraints. The right column in each section provides the sensitivity information.

Each changing cell and constraint cell appears in a separate row. The Changing Cell area includes a Reduced Gradient value that indicates how the target cell would be affected by a one-unit increase in the corresponding changing cell. Similarly, the Lagrange Multiplier column in the Constraints area indicates how the target cell would be affected by a one-unit increase in the corresponding constraint value.

The Answer Report

The Answer report lists the target cell, the variable cells, and the constraints. This report also includes information about the status of and slack value for each constraint. The status can be Binding, Not Binding, or Not Satisfied. The *slack value* is the difference between the solution value of the constraint cells and the number that appears on the right side of the constraint formula. A binding constraint is one for which the slack value is 0. A nonbinding constraint is a constraint that was satisfied with a nonzero slack value.

> **Note**
> If you select the Assume Linear Model option in the Solver Options dialog box, the Answer report is the only report that the Solver produces for you (the Limits and Sensitivity reports are not meaningful when using integer constraints).

The Limits Report

The Limits report tells you how much you can increase or decrease the values of your variable cells without breaking the constraints of your problem. For each variable cell, this report lists the optimal value as well as the lowest and highest values that you can use without violating constraints.

TROUBLESHOOTING

The Solver can't solve my problem.

The Solver is powerful but not miraculous. It might not be able to solve every problem you give it. If the Solver can't find the optimal solution to your problem, it presents an unsuccessful completion message in the Solver Results dialog box. The most common unsuccessful completion messages are the following:

- **"Solver could not find a feasible solution."** The Solver is unable to find a solution that satisfies all your constraints. This can happen if the constraints are logically conflicting or if not all the constraints can be satisfied (for example, if you insist that your advertising campaign reach 800 million readers on a $1 million budget). In some cases, the Solver also returns this message if the starting values of your variable cells are too far from their optimal values. If you think your constraints are logically consistent and your problem is solvable, try changing your starting values and rerunning the Solver.

- **"The maximum iteration limit was reached; continue anyway?"** To avoid tying up your computer indefinitely with an unsolvable problem, the Solver is designed to pause and present this message after it has performed its default number of iterations without arriving at a solution. If you see this message, you can resume the search for a solution by clicking Continue, or you can quit by clicking Stop. If you click Continue, the Solver begins solving again and does not stop until it finds a solution, gives up, or reaches its maximum time limit. If your problems frequently exceed the iteration limit, you can increase the default iteration setting by clicking the Solver button on the Data tab, clicking the Options button, and typing a new value in the Iterations box.

- **"The maximum time limit was reached; continue anyway?"** This message is similar to the iteration-limit message. The Solver is designed to pause after a default time period has elapsed. You can increase this default by choosing the Solver command, clicking Options, and modifying the Max Time value.

PART 6
Creating Charts

Basic Charting Techniques

Charting in Microsoft Office Excel 2007 differs dramatically from charting in earlier versions. First, the new Ribbon-based user interface lets you format and customize your charts with fewer mouse clicks and fewer dialog boxes. Second, the current version boasts vastly enhanced presentation capabilities. Now, more than ever, it's easy to turn your spreadsheet numbers into gorgeous graphs. Moreover, because Excel 2007 shares its charting engine with other 2007 Microsoft Office system applications, transporting your charts into Microsoft Office Word 2007 and Microsoft Office PowerPoint 2007 documents is now simpler and more reliable as well.

In this chapter, you'll look at most of the tasks you can perform with charts directly using the Ribbon. In Chapter 20, "Charting Beyond the Ribbon," you'll explore some formatting options that take you into more traditional dialog boxes.

Selecting Data for Your Chart

The first step in creating a chart is to select some data. If you're plotting all the cells in a contiguous block of cells, you don't have to select the entire block; select any cell within the block, and Excel will know what to do. If, on the other hand, you want to plot only certain rows and columns within the range, you'll need to select those rows and columns explicitly.

Under some conditions, it's advantageous to set up your source data as a table (by selecting a cell within it and pressing Ctrl+T or Ctrl+L) before creating a chart from it:

- If you plot data in a table and subsequently add new rows or columns to the table, Excel automatically incorporates those new rows or columns into the chart.

- If you want your chart to focus on particular rows of data within a large block, a table can make that process more convenient. When you convert a range to a table, Excel adds filter controls to each column in the range. You can use these controls to hide the rows in which you're not currently interested. So, for example, you can easily set up a chart that plots the most recent month's numbers in a table of time-related data or the rows that have the top 10 values in some column of interest. Note, however, when you change or remove the filter, Excel adjusts the chart so it always plots the visible rows. To make a permanent plot of particular rows in a range, select those rows explicitly without filtering the range. (You can plot noncontiguous rows by holding down Ctrl while you select each one.)

- If you want your source data and chart to have consistent or complementary formatting characteristics, you can achieve that more easily using table styles and chart styles.

For information about tables, see Chapter 21, "Managing Information in Tables." For information about chart styles, see "Choosing a Chart Style" on page 620.

Choosing a Chart Type

The entry to the charting user interface is via the Insert tab on the Ribbon. When you have selected the data you want to chart (or a single cell within that block of data), click the Insert tab. The Charts group on the Ribbon appears in the center of the Ribbon, presenting you with a selection of available chart types:

Each of the basic chart types shown in the Charts group on the Ribbon includes a large number of subtype options. Clicking a chart-type button reveals the gallery of its subtypes. When you click the Column button, you see the following gallery.

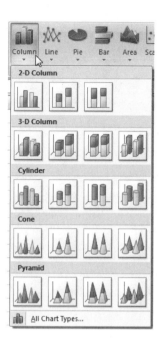

At the bottom of each subtype gallery is an item called All Chart Types. You can click All Chart Types to get a composite gallery of all types and subtypes. (You can also get to that megagallery by clicking the little arrow in the lower-right corner of the Charts group on the Ribbon, right below the Other Charts button.)

> **Note**
>
> The Other Charts button, the rightmost one in the Charts group on the Ribbon, presents a gallery of more exotic chart types, some of which have special data-selection requirements.

To create your new chart, click a chart-type button on the Ribbon, and select the subtype you want from the gallery that descends. Excel responds by displaying a chart object in the center of your screen. A *chart object* is a graphic element that lies atop your worksheet in its own window. You can drag any part of the object's perimeter to move it or drag one of the handles in the corners or midpoints of the sides to change the object's size. As you'll see, you also have the option of turning the chart object into a separate chart sheet.

With the chart object created and selected, Excel adds three tabs to the Ribbon, under Chart Tools, and selects the first of these three, Design. The newly adjusted Ribbon

Chapter 19

looks like this (if you are working at a higher resolution than 1024×768, you will see more items in the Chart Layouts group on the Ribbon):

The Design tab includes all the Ribbon items you're most likely to need first, as you begin working with a newly created chart.

Changing the Chart Type

If you didn't get the chart type you were expecting, click any part of the chart, and click Change Chart Type; this button appears at the left end of the Ribbon when you select the Design tab. The dialog box that appears includes all the Excel chart-type offerings (including all the subtypes), with the current type selected.

> ### Combining Two Chart Types
>
> Sometimes a chart with two or more data series is easiest to understand if one or more of those series is plotted in a chart type that contrasts with the rest of the chart—for example, if one series is plotted in columns and another is plotted as a line. Excel makes it easy to create an "overlay" chart of this kind. First create the chart as though all series were to be plotted in the same type. Then right-click any point or marker in the series you want to change. For example, if you want to change a series plotted as columns so it's plotted as a line instead, right-click one of the columns in that series. On the shortcut menu that appears, choose Change Series Chart Type. This will take you to the gallery of chart types. Select the one you want, and click OK.

Switching Rows and Columns

It would be great if Excel always knew exactly what you wanted and gave you a perfect chart on the first try. Unfortunately, although the program is intelligent, it is not clairvoyant. One of the things it might get wrong on occasion has to do with the assignment of series and data points. For example, suppose you want to plot the following table as a simple two-dimensional column chart:

State	1995	1997	1998	1999	2000	2001	2002	2003
Indiana	1,433	1,636	1,652	1,522	1,932	3,202	1,975	2,445
Washington	1,909	1,851	1,805	1,780	1,871	2,042	2,276	2,288

Source: U.S. Federal Highway Administration, Highway
Statistics, annual. See Internet site
<http://www.fhwa.dot.gov/policy/ohpi/hss/hsspubs.htm>.

If you follow the steps described a few paragraphs ago, Excel gives you this:

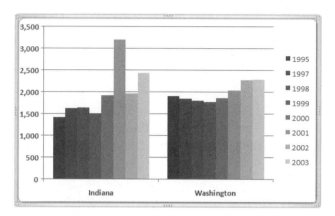

That is, it plots each yearly column in the source range as a data series consisting of two points, Indiana and Washington. If what you actually wanted was two series, Indiana and Washington, each consisting of eight yearly data points, there's an easy fix. Click anywhere in the chart, make sure the Design tab is selected on the Ribbon, and then click Switch Row/Column. Excel flips the chart:

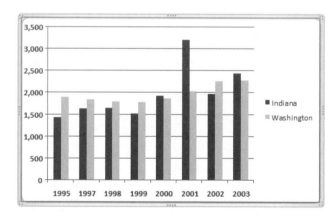

Choosing a Chart Layout

What Excel calls a chart *layout* is a combination of choices affecting such elements as the chart title, legend, axes, axis titles, and gridlines. Each of the program's chart types comes with an assortment of packaged layout options. With the chart selected, you can see the available layouts by clicking the Design tab under Chart Tools on the Ribbon and then opening the Chart Layouts gallery (use the scroll bar or arrows at the right of the gallery to see all the options). These are the available layouts for a line chart:

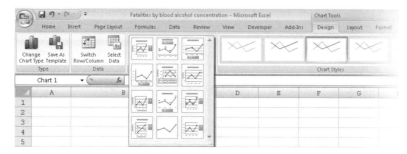

You can experiment with these preconfigured layouts by clicking buttons in the Chart Layouts gallery. If none of them gives you exactly the combination and positioning of chart elements (titles, legend, gridlines, and so on) you're looking for, don't worry. The Layout tab (to the right of Design under Chart Tools) changes the Ribbon so that it provides explicit control over each kind of chart element.

Choosing a Chart Style

A chart *style* is a combination of foreground and background colors designed to coordinate with your cell styles, shape styles, and table styles to give your workbook a consistent, professional, and high-impact appearance. To apply a chart style, select the chart, choose Design under Chart Tools on the Ribbon, and then open the Chart Styles gallery.

The gallery options let you do such things as apply attractive gradient fills to your chart backgrounds, add photorealistic highlighting to bar and column markers, switch line-chart markers from fat to svelte, and so on. The best way to see the wealth of possibilities is to select a chart, open the gallery, and experiment.

Note that cell styles, table styles, and chart styles are all components of the current theme. That is, when you change the theme applied to your workbook (by clicking Page Layout on the Ribbon and opening the Themes gallery at the left side of the Ribbon), your available cell styles, table styles, and chart styles all change as well.

For more information about themes, see "Formatting with Themes" on page 275. For more information about cell styles, see "Formatting with Cell Styles" on page 278. For more information about table styles, see "Formatting Tables" on page 705.

Moving the Chart to a Separate Chart Sheet

If you don't need to have your chart next to the numbers from which it was derived, you might want to consider putting it on its own chart sheet. A *chart sheet* is a separate, special-purpose sheet that gives the maximum amount of screen area to your graph. To move your chart from a worksheet to a chart sheet, right-click it, and choose Move Chart (or select the chart, and click Move Chart, the rightmost item on the Design tab). In the dialog box that appears, select New Sheet, supply a name for the chart sheet (or accept the default name), and then click OK. If you decide to move the chart back to the worksheet, repeat this process, select Object In, type the name of the worksheet you want to move the chart to (or select it from the drop-down list), and then click OK.

> **Note**
>
> You can move a chart object to a chart sheet by selecting the chart and pressing F11. The only disadvantage to this approach is that you don't get to name the chart sheet. (But you can always do that later by double-clicking the sheet tab and changing the default name to something of your choosing.) You can even create a chart on a chart sheet directly from data—by selecting a cell or range and pressing F11. Here the one disadvantage is that Excel uses the current default chart type, which may not be what you want. But you can always switch to a different type by selecting the chart on the chart sheet and clicking Change Chart Type (or, more simply, by right-clicking the chart and choosing Change Type from the shortcut menu).

Adding, Editing, and Removing a Chart Title

If you choose a layout option that includes a title, Excel will provide that for you. If your chart doesn't already have a title, you can add one by selecting any part of your chart, clicking the Layout tab under Chart Tools on the Ribbon, and then clicking Chart Title in the Labels group. On the menu that appears, choose either Centered Overlay Title or Above Chart. The former places the title within the plot area. The latter centers it above the plot area, reducing the size of the plot area to make room. If you need to adjust the position of the title, select it, and drag its bounding rectangle.

However you create the title, you might have to edit its default text. (Except when you're plotting a single data series with an adjacent cell containing text, Excel won't try to pluck a chart's title from the worksheet.) Figure 19-1 shows how your chart might look with a default title and legend. To enter a meaningful title on a chart like this, begin by selecting the default title. Excel responds by enclosing the title in a rectangle with corner handles. The simplest way to enter the text you want is by clicking the formula bar (above the worksheet) and typing. Alternatively, you can select the text you want to replace (*Chart Title*, or whatever else is currently there) and edit it.

> **Note**
>
> To create a multiline title, press Ctrl+Enter at the end of each line.

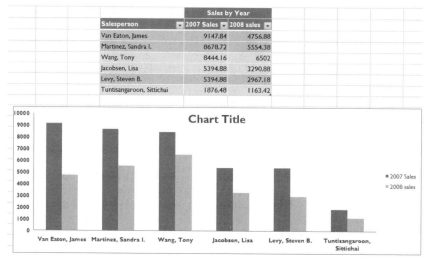

Salesperson	Sales by Year	
	2007 Sales	2008 sales
Van Eaton, James	9147.84	4756.88
Martinez, Sandra I.	8678.72	5554.38
Wang, Tony	8444.16	6502
Jacobsen, Lisa	5394.88	3290.88
Levy, Steven B.	5394.88	2967.18
Tuntisangaroon, Sittichai	1876.48	1163.42

Figure 19-1 If your chart layout includes a title, Excel will create one for you—but you'll probably have to edit the text.

> **Note**
>
> To link a chart title to the contents of a worksheet cell, type a *worksheet-qualified formula* as the title text (that is, a formula that includes the name of the worksheet followed by an exclamation point). For example, suppose you want your chart's title to be the contents of cell A1 on Sheet1. You would type **=sheet1!A1** as your title.

You might think you would be able to edit an existing chart title by selecting it and then editing the contents of the formula bar. Unfortunately, although Excel lets you type text this way, it does not display that text on the formula bar subsequently. To edit an existing title, return to the formula bar, and type your new title entirely. Or click twice—slowly—in the existing title. The first click selects the title object, and the second creates an insertion point, letting you edit in place.

To remove a title, select it, and press Delete. If you see an insertion point in the title when you select it, you can press Esc and then press Delete.

Adding, Editing, and Removing a Legend

If you choose a layout option that includes a legend, a legend you shall have. If you prefer not to use one of the built-in layouts, select your chart, click the Layout tab under Chart Tools on the Ribbon, click Legend in the Labels group, and click one of the available positioning options. The overlay options position the legend within the plot area; the other options put the legend outside the plot, reducing the overall plot area.

Unlike most chart titles, legends get their text from the worksheet. Excel looks for text adjacent to the data series and uses that text for the legend. In many—perhaps most—cases, this works great. In Figure 19-1, for example, Excel has correctly divined that the legend text should be 2007 Sales and 2008 Sales.

If Excel happens to get it wrong or if you want different words in your legend—you can fix matters by altering the text on the worksheet adjacent to your chart data. Alternatively, you can select the chart, click the Design tab, and then click Select Data Source in the Data group. The Select Data Source dialog box appears:

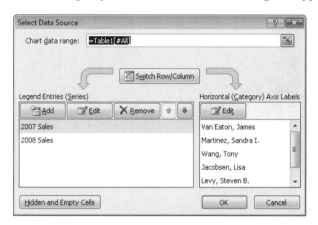

On the left side of this dialog box you see the names of each series in your chart—the names Excel is currently using in the legend. To change a series name, select it in this list, and click Edit. In the Edit Series dialog box that appears, in the Series Name text box, you can either type the text you want directly or point to a worksheet cell containing the desired text. If you do the latter, Excel creates a formula linking the series name to that cell.

> **Note**
>
> If you prefer to type a formula linking a series name to a worksheet cell, you must make the formula worksheet qualified; for example, type **=sheet1!A17**. (It's simpler to point and let Excel create the formula for you.)

If you decide you no longer need a legend, select it, and press Delete.

Adding and Positioning Data Labels

Some of the built-in layout options include data labels—text identifying the value of each point in a data series—but the size of the Ribbon icons doesn't make it easy to discern which do and which don't. You can add data labels to all series in a chart by selecting the chart, clicking the Layout tab, and then clicking Data Labels in the Labels group. A gallery of positioning options will appear. (The available options depend on the chart type.) With some charts you might find a Best Fit option; as Figure 19-2 shows, this option can be handy on pie charts with narrow slices.

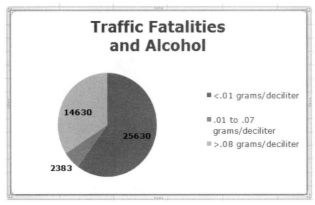

Figure 19-2 Because we chose Best Fit for this chart's data labels, Excel doesn't try to fit the label *2383* into the narrow slice, displaying it outside the pie instead.

To label one particular series in a multiseries chart, select the series, not the entire chart. Handles will appear to confirm that you've selected a series. Then click Data Labels on the Ribbon. To label a single point, rather than an entire series, click once to select the series. Then click a second time on the point you want to label. Again, handles are your guides, confirming the single-point selection. Finally, click Data Labels on the Ribbon.

If you don't like the position of any particular data label, select it, and drag its bounding rectangle.

Adding a Data Table

A *data table* is a copy of your source data, included within the chart. Data tables are useful particularly when the chart and its underlying data are not in close proximity on the worksheet or when you intend to copy the chart to a Word or PowerPoint document. To add a data table, if your chart doesn't already have one, select the chart, click the Layout tab under Chart Tools, and then click Data Table in the Labels group. The options that appear let you choose between having and not having legend keys with your table. The difference is easier discovered than described—and, as you'll see by experimenting, minimal in any case.

Manipulating Axes

If you're not happy with the axes Excel gives you, or if you just want to explore your options, select the chart, click the Layout tab under Chart Tools, and then click Axes in the Axes group. Excel then asks you to specify which axis you want to modify (the number of choices varies by chart type). If you're a veteran of earlier versions, you'll notice that, in this context at least, axes are no longer called *category* and *value*. Instead, Excel uses the more commonplace descriptions *horizontal* and *vertical*. You'll still see axes described as *primary* when there are no secondary axes, but that's because it's possible for a two-axis chart to acquire one or more additional axes (see "Assigning a Series to a Secondary Axis" on page 653). After you have pointed to the axis you want to tailor, the tailoring menu appears. Here, for example, is what you would see for the vertical axis of the chart shown in Figure 19-1:

> **Note**
>
> It's still important to understand the distinction between category and value axes, because those terms remain in use in other parts of the charting interface. A *value* axis is one that is scaled numerically. Value axes are generally vertical (except in bar charts, which are essentially column charts turned 90 degrees), but in an X Y (scatter) chart, both axes are value axes. A *category* axis (horizontal except in the case of bar charts) is delineated either by labels that have no numeric significance or by dates. For more about axes, see "Working with Axes" page 642.

Note that the scaling-factor options (thousands, millions, billions) and the log-scaling option are not mutually exclusive. So, for example, if you choose Show Axis In Thousands and then subsequently choose Show Axis With Log Scale, Excel maintains the scaling by thousands and also switches from an arithmetic to a logarithmic scale.

> **Note**
>
> Other scaling factors are also available. See "Applying a Scaling Factor" page 645.

Axis options for a category axis, such as the horizontal axis in Figure 19-1, are quite different:

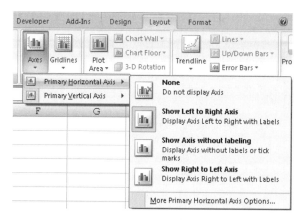

In this case, you can reverse the order of the data points—for example, to show the highest-performing salespeople in Figure 19-1 on the right instead of the left—without changing the sort order of the source data. You also have the option of dispensing with axis labels altogether.

For all axis types—horizontal, vertical, or depth (the third axis on a three-dimensional chart), many more options are available than appear in the drop-down list. For example, you can change the format used for numeric axis labels or restrict an axis to a particular numeric range. If your axis is scaled by units of time, you can change the time interval at which labels appear, and so on. All these additional choices are accessible via the item at the bottom of the axis menu—the one that begins with More (More Primary Axis Options, for example)—and will be discussed in detail in Chapter 20.

Adding Axis Titles

If you have chosen a preconfigured chart layout that includes axis labels, Excel supplies them for you—with default text and alignment. To edit the default (or current) text of a title, begin by selecting the title. You can replace the existing text entirely by typing in the formula bar. Or you can click to position an insertion point within the title and edit that way.

To add an axis title to a chart that doesn't already have one, select the chart, click the Layout tab, and then click Axis Titles in the Labels group. In the submenus for vertical and depth axes you'll find vertical, horizontal, and rotated alignment options. The default alignment is rotated—which means the title reads left to right when you tilt your head 90 degrees to the left. A vertical title uses stacked lettering (not ordinarily suitable for titles consisting of more than a few letters), while a horizontal title reads left to right in the conventional way but reduces the space available for the plot.

Changing the Rotation of Chart Text

To change the rotation of the chart title, an axis title, or the axis labels, start by clicking the Layout tab. Next, click Chart Title (for the chart title), Axis Titles (for an axis title), or Axes (for the axis labels). If you're customizing an axis title or a set of axis labels, continue by selecting the appropriate axis—for example, select Primary Horizontal Axis if you're changing the appearance of your horizontal-axis labels. Click the More option at the bottom of the dialog box that appears—for example, click More Primary Horizontal Axis Options. Finally, select the Alignment category in the formatting dialog box that appears. The Alignment dialog box will look something like this:

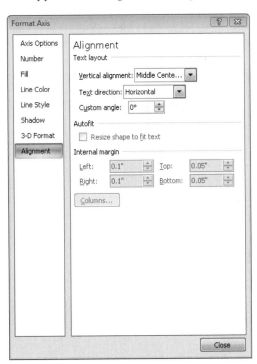

In most cases, the relevant sections of this dialog box are Text Direction and Custom Angle. If Excel has given you angled axis labels for your horizontal axis and you want horizontal ones instead, type 0 in the Custom Angle text box.

Displaying Gridlines

Some of the preconfigured chart layouts in Excel include gridlines, and some do not. You can add or remove gridlines by selecting the chart, clicking the Layout tab under Chart Tools, and clicking Gridlines in the Axes group. In the submenus that appear you'll see the terms *major gridlines* and *minor gridlines*. Major gridlines emerge from axis subdivisions called *major tick marks*. Minor gridlines are drawn from further subdivisions known as *minor tick marks*. Excel determines the positions of these tick marks automatically, but you can override its decisions if your labels or gridlines are not spaced to your satisfaction (see "Adjusting the Spacing Between Gridlines" page 646).

Be aware that major gridlines in certain kinds of three-dimensional charts can make data points appear to have less than their true value. In the following illustration, for example, the data points have exact integer values from 1 to 10, but the gridlines, in combination with the three-dimensional perspective, make each point appear somewhat smaller:

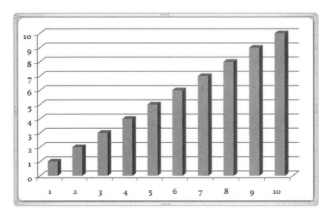

To avoid confusing the viewer in this kind of chart, you might want to consider adding data labels.

Adding Text Annotations

To create a text annotation anywhere on a chart—for example, to provide source information for your chart data or to call attention to a particular chart feature—create a text box on the chart. Click the Layout tab, click Text Box in the Insert group, and then drag a rectangle on the chart. An insertion point will appear in the upper-left corner of the rectangle. Type or paste the text annotation, and then size and position the rectangle as needed.

For more information about using text boxes, see "Working with Text Boxes," page 352.

> **Note**
>
> In earlier versions of Excel, you could create a text annotation on a chart by selecting any part of the chart and typing. Whatever you typed would appear in a text box, and you could size and position the text box as soon as you finished typing. This feature has been "deprecated" in Excel 2007, presumably because usability studies found that users were creating text annotations accidentally.

Changing the Font or Size of Chart Text

Suppose Excel generates a chart with titles, legend, and axis labels all neatly styled in Gill Sans MT—but you'd prefer Goudy Old Style. You can look all over the charting component of the Excel user interface for a command to change the font, but you would look in vain. The Format tab, under Chart Tools, provides access to a fantastic array of fancy text-formatting options. But if all you want is a different font, you need to return to the worksheet component of the user interface. Every tool at your disposal for formatting worksheet text is available there for use with chart text. Select the text you want to modify, click Home on the Ribbon, and then head for the Font group.

With titles and legend text, you can format entire blocks, individual words, or even individual letters. If you need a subscript in your chart title, for example, select the character that needs to be lowered, click Home on the Ribbon, click the Format Cells: Font button (the small rectangle in the lower-right corner of the Font group to the right of the word *Font*), and then, on the Font tab of the Font dialog box, select the Subscript check box. With axis labels—the labels that appear adjacent to a chart axis—it's another story, alas. These you cannot select individually. You must format all the labels for a given axis the same way. If you absolutely require distinct formatting for particular axis labels, you'll need to suppress the normal label display and use text boxes instead.

Applying Shape Styles and WordArt Styles

Now that you have your chart created and laid out with the appropriate chart elements—titles, legends, labels, and so on—it's time to explore the fancy formatting options available via the Format tab. If you select any part of your chart and click the Format tab, you'll find two Ribbon groups of interest: Shape Styles and WordArt Styles. Each of these consists of a gallery plus three dialog box commands. (The WordArt

Styles gallery is available only when you have selected a chart element that includes text—a title, a legend, or an axis.) Here is what you might see when you open the Shape Styles gallery:

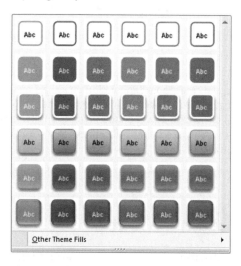

Shape Styles and WordArt Styles are both keyed to the current theme. If you change the theme (by clicking the Page Layout tab on the Ribbon and then clicking Themes), you get different sets of shape styles and WordArt styles. The styles are intended to let you be visually creative (even flamboyant) while maintaining a tasteful degree of consistency across all the elements of your workbook—cells, headings, tables, and charts.

You can apply WordArt styles, as their name suggests, to the textual elements of a chart. You apply shape styles to areas and lines. If you select gridlines, an axis, or a series on a line chart, the Shape Styles gallery displays options for changing the appearance of lines. If you select the chart area, the plot area, a title, a legend, or a data series in a chart type such as column, pie, or bar, you see a Shape Styles gallery that looks more like the one shown previously.

Note

If you're not sure what part of the chart you have selected, look at the Chart Objects list, which appears on the upper-left corner of the Ribbon (right below the word *Home*) when the Format tab is active. In addition to showing you what's selected, this drop-down list also lets you change the selection.

Why would selecting a title produce a gallery of area-oriented shape options? Because titles appear against backgrounds that can be formatted independently of their surrounding areas. When you choose an area option from the Shape Styles gallery, you're determining three factors at once—the color or gradient applied to the area's background, the color of the border around the area (which might be different from the background color), and the color of the text (white against dark backgrounds or black against light ones).

The best way to understand what the Shape Styles and WordArt Styles galleries can do for you is to experiment. Select an element of your chart, open the Shape Styles gallery, rest your pointer on the various options, and notice the effect on your chart. If you don't like what's happening and want to keep the chart looking the way it did before, click somewhere other than the gallery. If you select an option and change your mind, press Ctrl+Z; alternatively, click Reset To Match Style (to the left of the Shape Styles gallery). Experiment similarly with the WordArt Styles gallery.

Further shape-formatting options are available via the three drop-down lists to the right of the Shape Styles gallery. Shape Fill and Shape Outline let you tailor areas and the borders of areas, respectively. The Shape Effects item opens a whole world of other glitzy style choices, including shadows, glows, soft edges, and bevel effects. A similar set of advanced options appears to the right of the WordArt Styles gallery and is available when you select a text element of the chart.

Saving Templates to Make Chart Formats Reusable

If you want to use a particular combination of chart formats repeatedly, it's best to store the formatting information in a template. To do this, first set up a chart that exemplifies the formats you want to reuse. Then select the chart, click the Design tab under Chart Tools, and click Save Template in the Type group. You'll be asked to supply a name. Excel stores your template under that file name in the folder %Appdata%\Microsoft\Templates\Charts, with the extension .crtx. But you don't need to go looking for it there; if you ever need to delete, copy, or rename the template file, select a chart, click the Design tab under Chart Tools, and click Change Chart Type in the Type group. In the Change Chart Type dialog box that appears, click Manage Templates. This opens a Windows Explorer window listing all your templates.

After you have created a template, you can use it the same way you would use any of the built-in chart types. To create a new chart using the template, select your data, click the Insert tab on the Ribbon, click any of the chart-type icons in the Charts group, and then click All Chart Types at the bottom of the gallery that appears. In the Create Chart dialog box, select Templates. As Figure 19-3 shows on the next page, all your defined templates appear (without their file names) in a My Templates gallery.

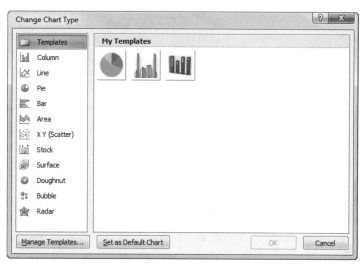

Figure 19-3 Your defined templates appear in their own gallery, accessible by clicking Templates in the Create Chart or Change Chart Type dialog box.

To apply one of your templates to an existing chart, select the chart, click the Design tab under Chart Tools, click Change Chart Type in the Type group, and then select Templates in the Change Chart Type dialog box. Select the template you want to apply, and then click OK.

Charting Beyond the Ribbon

The Ribbon-based user interface in Microsoft Office Excel 2007 provides quick access to a wonderful assortment of chart types, layouts, and styles. With these tools (which you surveyed in Chapter 19, "Basic Charting Techniques") and a few mouse clicks, you can knock out a knockout chart in record time. Chances are, though, that before long you are going to need some of the additional formatting features that are not directly accessible on the Ribbon. You'll learn about these features in this chapter.

Selecting Chart Elements

Just as creating a chart begins with selecting data, applying advanced formatting begins with selecting a chart element—the title, series, area, legend, or whatever—that you want to format.

When you rest your pointer on a chart element, a tip appears telling you which item you're about to select. After you have selected an element, handles appear to confirm the selection—although in some cases these handles might be difficult to see. If you're not sure what you've selected, or if you just want to see what elements are available for formatting, you can open the Chart Objects list. This drop-down list enumerates most of the elements of the current chart that you can format. You can select a chart element directly in the list or simply use the list as a guide. Figure 20-1 shows the Chart Objects list for an example three-dimensional column chart.

To open the Chart Objects list, first select any part of a chart. Then click either the Layout tab or the Format tab on the Ribbon. The Chart Objects list now appears as a drop-down list directly under the Microsoft Office Button in the upper-left corner of the Excel window. Initially you see the name of the object you have selected—Chart Area or Plot Area, for example. To see the entire list of available objects, click the drop-down arrow. As Figure 20-1 shows, the list is tailored to the current chart. Data series within the chart are identified by name.

Figure 20-1 The Chart Objects list enumerates the elements of the current chart that you can format.

Note

If you've used previous versions of Excel, you're probably accustomed to double-clicking a chart element to get to its formatting dialog box. Sadly, this no longer works. Double-clicking the chart simply takes you to the Design tab on the Ribbon. To go directly to a nitty-gritty formatting dialog box for a chart element, try right-clicking the element. Usually, you'll find a relevant Format command on the shortcut menu.

After you have selected an item in the Chart Objects list, you can open its formatting dialog box by clicking Format Selection—directly below the Chart Objects list on the left side of the Ribbon.

Selecting Individual Data Points, Labels, or Legend Entries

The Chart Objects list actually doesn't explicitly list all the elements you can format. Specifically, it doesn't allow you to select individual points in a data series, individual data labels, or individual series names in a legend. You can select and format these items separately from their companions, however. To do so, click the item in question twice (slowly—not a double-click). The first click selects the set, and the second selects the member. After you have refined your selection to an individual item, the Chart Objects list confirms your selection; handles do as well.

Repositioning Chart Elements with the Mouse

You can move the chart title, axis titles, data labels, and legend by dragging them with the mouse. You can also use your mouse to explode a pie slice or doughnut bite. Note, in particular, that you can adjust the positions of individual data labels without moving an entire series of labels; in addition, although Excel creates legends in certain fixed positions, you're free to drag them anywhere you like, even to the middle of the chart.

To restore the default position of an object immediately after you move it, press Ctrl+Z. To restore its initial position later, delete the object, and then re-create it.

Unfortunately, although you can move data labels at will, you have no such freedom with the tick-mark labels that appear along your axes. You can rotate these, but you cannot pick them up and drop them elsewhere. In addition, you cannot do anything with individual axis labels; you can modify them only as a group. Therefore, if you want to change the color of a particular label or move it inside the plot area, you're out of luck. You need to create individual text annotations to serve as axis labels.

For information about rotating axis labels, see "Changing the Rotation of Chart Text" on page 627. For information about adding text annotations, see "Adding Text Annotations" on page 628.

Formatting Lines and Borders

Excel uses lines for axes, line charts, and trendlines. It also uses lines to create borders around a variety of chart elements—the chart area, the plot area, the titles, the legends, the markers on bar and column charts, and so on. Not all of these borders appear by default (for example, chart titles are borderless by default), but all are available if you want them.

The formatting options for all the lines and borders are essentially the same. You can color them, fatten them, change them from solid to dotted or dashed, and so on. (You can also delete them.)

For example, suppose you want to change the color of a series line on a line chart. The element you want to format is called *Series 1* (assuming it's the first data series on the chart). To get to the formatting dialog box for this series, right-click the series, and click Format Data Series. (If that command doesn't appear, you've probably selected some other element. Try again, or select Series 1 in the Chart Objects list. Then click Format Selection, directly below the Chart Objects list on the left side of the Ribbon.) When the Format Data Series dialog box appears, select the Line Color category or the Line Style category. (If you were customizing a border instead of a line, the names of these categories would be Border Color and Border Styles.) Figure 20-2 shows the line-formatting bill of fare.

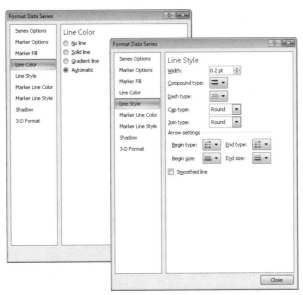

Figure 20-2 When you select Line Color or Line Style, you'll see essentially the same set of options for all the line elements in Excel charts. A similar set of options is available for borders.

The default option in the Line Color category is Automatic—which means "let Excel decide." Usually, that's a good choice, but you have alternatives. If you select Solid Line, the dialog box changes to include a color picker and a Transparency slider. (The default Transparency setting is 0, which means opaque; if your chart has an interesting graphic background, you might want to experiment with making a line element partially transparent.) If you select Gradient Line, several new options appear. For more information about creating gradient lines, see "Filling an Area with a Color Gradient" on page 638. The gradient procedures for lines are essentially the same as for areas.

The Solid Line and Gradient Line options have to do with the line's color, not its substance. Solid Line means the entire line is one color, whether or not the line is broken up into dashes or dots. The Gradient Line option—more commonly used for areas than for lines—lets you apply multiple colors with smooth transitions.

When you select the Line Style category, you can indicate your choice of simple or compound line and unbroken or broken. As the following illustrations show, the Compound Type drop-down list offers four alternatives to a simple line, and the Dash Type drop-down list lets you chop your line in seven different fashions. Whatever you select or don't select in these two drop-down lists, you can vary the weight of your line via the Width drop-down list.

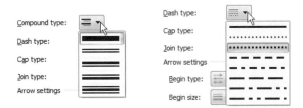

Formatting Areas

Excel 2007 provides a rich set of options for formatting the background areas of your charts—including the plot area, the chart area, and the walls and floors of three-dimensional charts. You can also apply these formatting options to legends, to the background areas of titles and data labels, and to certain kinds of chart markers—including columns, bars, pyramids, cones, cylinders, areas, bubbles, pie slices, and doughnut bites.

To format a chart element's area, right-click the object on your chart, and click the associated Format command. (If you don't see the Format command, select the object in the Chart Objects list, and click Format Selection.) The area-formatting options for a selected chart item appear when you select Fill in the item's formatting dialog box. Figure 20-3 shows the Fill options for the Format Chart Area dialog box. As with line formatting, the default option for area formatting is Automatic, which means "let Excel decide."

Using Transparency to Create a Minimal Chart Display on the Worksheet

As shown in Figure 20-3, the chart area is filled with solid white. This is the default for a new chart displayed on a white worksheet. Note that it is not the same as having no fill; a chart area with no fill is transparent, allowing the underlying worksheet gridlines to shine through.

Making the chart area transparent can be useful at times. If you want to create a worksheet display that minimizes the chart apparatus and simply shows a small graphic to support a set of numbers, using the No Fill option is good way to get there. Eliminate the border around the chart area (see "Formatting Lines and Borders" on page 635), get rid of any chart elements you don't want (the title, legend, or whatever), and assign the No Fill option to your chart and plot areas. Figure 20-4 shows an example of a chart reduced to basics in this way.

Chapter 20

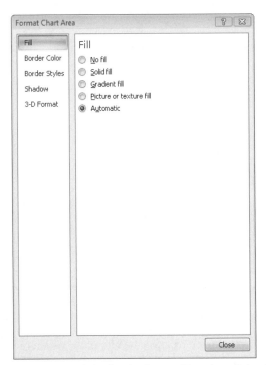

Figure 20-3 Click Fill in the Format Chart Area dialog box to apply solid colors, gradients, pictures, and textures to background areas of your charts.

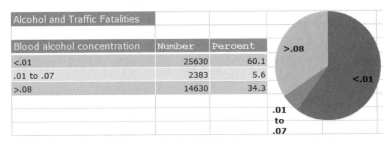

Alcohol and Traffic Fatalities		
Blood alcohol concentration	Number	Percent
<.01	25630	60.1
.01 to .07	2383	5.6
>.08	14630	34.3

Figure 20-4 Less is sometimes more. Applying No Fill to this chart's chart area eliminates distraction.

Filling an Area with a Color Gradient

A *color gradient* is a smooth progression of color tones from one part of an area to another—for example, a transition from bright red at the top of a column marker to black at the bottom. Color gradients can give your chart areas a classy, professional appearance. Of course, depending on how you use them, color gradients can also distract. If you're creating charts that are intended to convince or impress others, it's probably a good idea to exercise a bit of restraint in using gradients. On the other hand, if flamboyance is your style, Excel gives you plenty of ways to express yourself.

Figure 20-5 shows the Fill category of the Format Chart Area dialog box, with the Gradient Fill option selected. The options presented here (which are far more extensive than those of Excel 2003) can be a little bewildering at first. Fortunately, the Excel 2007 Live Preview capability lets you see the effect of a setting on your chart before you leave the dialog box. Experiment on a large region of a chart, such as the plot area of a chart you've moved to a chart sheet, and you'll quickly get an idea of what's possible.

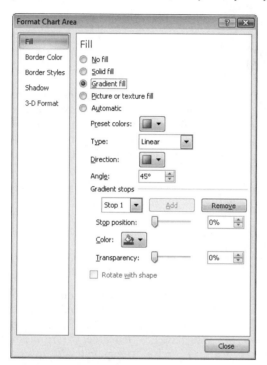

Figure 20-5 The Excel 2007 Gradient Fill options let you select colors, angles, directions, transparency, and more.

A good way to begin your exploration is to open the Preset Colors drop-down list, as shown on the next page:

Chapter 20

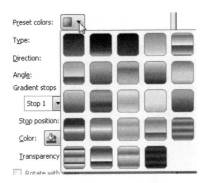

The Preset Colors gallery offers two dozen attractive color gradients. In the gallery, they're all of the same type and direction (moving in a linear fashion from top to bottom), but you can apply other type and direction options to them. Choose one, then choose one of the Direction options, and then open the Direction drop-down list, and you'll see another gallery that looks like this (for the Radial direction):

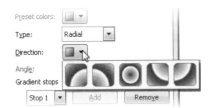

You don't have to stick with the 24 Preset Colors options, of course. With the Gradient Stops, Color, Stop Position, and Transparency controls, you can create any kind of gradient that suits you. *Gradient stops* are boundaries between colors. You can have as many stops and colors as you want. The Stop Position slider determines where the stop occurs. And if you want, you can add a degree of transparency to any or all sections of your gradient.

Filling an Area with a Texture or Picture

If you don't care for solids or gradients, why not fill your background areas or data markers with textures or pictures? You can use images in a wide variety of supported formats, paste in an item from your clip art library (or from Microsoft Office Online), or use one of the 24 texture images supplied by Excel. The latter evoke familiar materials, such as oak, marble, and cloth. For example, Figure 20-6 shows a fish-fossil texture applied to a chart's plot area, with a clip art image applied to the column markers.

To apply a texture or picture, click Picture Or Texture Fill in the format dialog box for the chart element you have selected. Open the Texture drop-down list to choose from the texture gallery, or click the File, Clipboard, or ClipArt buttons to apply a picture. Excel stretches pictures to fit unless you also select the Tile Picture As Texture check box. If you're using a bitmapped image, the stretching is likely to produce distortion, unless the size of the picture is exactly that of the area you're formatting. To avoid distortion, you can shrink the image by moving it away from the left, right, top, and bottom borders of the area—in other words, by setting margins. To do that, set nonzero values in the various Offset text boxes.

If you choose to tile the picture, you get a different set of scaling and offset options. You can also create some interesting mirror effects by experimenting with the Mirror Type drop-down list.

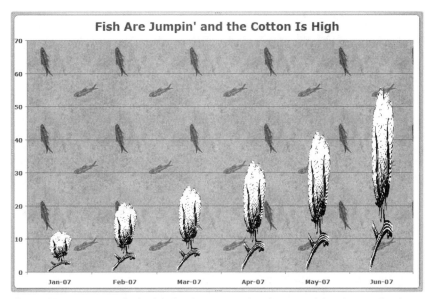

Figure 20-6 We've applied a fish-fossil texture to the plot area of this chart and a clip art image to the column markers.

> **Note**
>
> If you try to drag an image file from Microsoft Windows Explorer onto a chart element, Windows changes your pointer to a plus sign, which generally signifies you're about to perform a drag-and-drop copy. Unfortunately, dragging and dropping has no effect in this context.

Formatting Text

To make simple text-formatting changes—altering the size, font, or style of title text, for example—you need to leave the charting component on the Ribbon and return to the Home tab. Then select the chart text you want to format, and click commands in the Font group on the Ribbon, just as if you were tailoring ordinary worksheet text.

Of course, if you want exotic text formatting, that's another matter. Select your text, click the Format tab (under Chart Tools), and then make your selections from the WordArt Styles group on the Ribbon.

Working with Axes

Excel gives you a great deal of control over the format, position, and scale of your charts' axes. You can specify the line style, color, and weight of the axes, as well as the presence or absence of tick marks and tick labels. You can also override the default scaling and establish the positions at which vertical and horizontal axes intersect.

Specifying the Line Style, Color, and Weight

The default axis is a thin, solid, black line. But you can replace that with broken or compound lines in various colors and weights. For details, see "Formatting Lines and Borders" on page 635. Note that Excel draws your tick marks in the same style as your axis. Therefore, if you choose a heavy red line for the axis, you'll have heavy red tick marks as well—unless, of course, you opt for no tick marks.

Specifying the Position of Tick Marks and Axis Labels

Tick marks are short lines that either cross or abut an axis at regular intervals. Like the lines that mark inches and fractions of inches along a ruler, tick marks help define the scale of a value axis; they separate categories on a category axis. (A *value axis* is one that's numerically scaled; a *category axis* is one that's delineated by text labels. For more information, see "Manipulating Axes" on page 625.) Tick marks come in two degrees, major and minor. Minor tick marks delineate subdivisions between major tick marks. *Axis labels* (which earlier versions of Excel called *tick-mark labels*) are the labels that identify positions along the axis—for example, the month names and numbers in Figure 20-6.

By default, Excel displays major tick marks on the outside of axes and does not display minor tick marks. Excel displays an axis label for each major tick mark, adjacent to the axis. To reposition tick marks or axis labels, right-click the axis, click Format Axis, and select the Axis Options category in the formatting dialog box. The controls you're interested in are in the lower half of the dialog box, labeled Major Tick Mark Type, Minor Tick Mark Type, and Axis Labels.

You will probably want to reposition your axis labels in charts where the horizontal and vertical axes intersect somewhere other than the lower-left corner of the chart. This commonly occurs when the range of the value axis spans negative as well as positive numbers. In such cases, Excel plants the category labels within the plot area unless you visit the Format dialog box, open the Axis Labels drop-down list, and choose Low. Doing so transforms a chart like this:

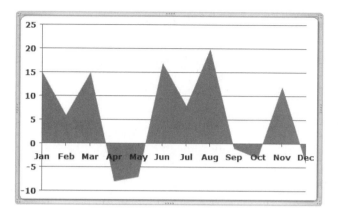

into one like this:

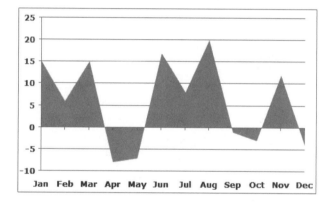

Changing the Numeric Format Used by Axis Labels

When you first create a chart, Excel links the numeric format of your value-axis labels to that of the source data. Create a chart from data with the Currency format, for example, and Excel applies the Currency format to the labels on your value axis. Change the format of the source data, and the labels stay in step.

You can override this linkage by applying a specific numeric format to your axis labels. In the formatting dialog box, select the Number category, and then select the format you want from the list on the right. After you explicitly format your axis labels, Excel no longer copies formatting changes from the source data to the chart. To relink the format of your axis labels with that of the source data, revisit the dialog box, and select the Linked To Source check box.

Changing the Scale of a Value Axis

To override the default scaling of a value axis, right-click it, click Format Axis, and select the Axis Options category in the Format Axis dialog box (see Figure 20-7). Then select the Fixed option to the right of Minimum or Maximum, and in the text box at the far right, type the desired value.

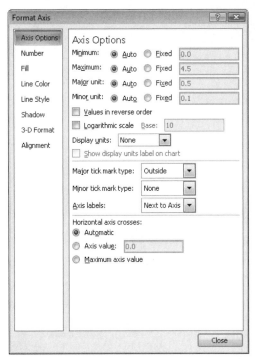

Figure 20-7 By selecting the Fixed option and typing a value in the text box at the right, you can set up your own value-axis scaling.

Changing the Positions of Tick Marks and Gridlines

The Major Unit and Minor Unit values determine the spacing between tick marks—and hence between gridlines. If your axis labels or your gridlines are too close together, select Fixed beside Major Unit, and then in the box at the right, type a larger value. The Minor Unit value is relevant only if you've chosen to display minor tick marks.

Changing the Point Where Axes Intersect

By default, axes intersect at 0 on the value axis. You can move the intersection to a different point by selecting Axis Value below Floor Crosses At and typing a number in the text box at the right. You can also move the intersection to the highest point on the value axis by selecting Maximum Axis Value. On a typical chart with a vertical value axis and a horizontal category axis, that would put the category axis at the top of the chart (unless you also select Values In Reverse Order).

Reversing the Value-Axis Scale

You can turn the value-axis scale upside down so the higher values appear near the bottom of the chart. You might find this option convenient if all your chart values are negative and you're interested primarily in their absolute value. To invert the axis scale, select the Values In Reverse Order check box.

Using Logarithmic Scaling

To use logarithmic scaling, select the Logarithmic Scale check box, and if you want to use a base other than 10, type that base in the box to the right. (The ability to use log scaling on bases other than 10 is new with Office Excel 2007.)

In a logarithmic scale, the lowest value is 1. You cannot plot negative and 0 values. If you apply logarithmic scaling to a chart that includes negative or 0 values, Excel displays an error message and removes the offending values from the chart. You can restore them by returning to linear scaling.

Applying a Scaling Factor

As you saw in Chapter 19, the Axes item on the Ribbon (in the Axes group on the Layout tab) includes three options for assigning a scaling factor to a value axis—thousands, millions, and billions. These choices let you simplify the display of large-numbered labels. Instead of showing 1000000, 2000000, and 3000000, for example, your axis can be marked 1, 2, and 3 and have a label indicating that all values have been reduced by a factor of a million. The Display Units drop-down list in the Format Axis dialog box (see Figure 20-7) offers a few additional scaling options, including hundreds and trillions. Unfortunately, Excel doesn't offer any options for scaling by negative powers of 10.

Changing the Scale of a Text Category Axis

Excel recognizes two kinds of category axes—those that have ordinary text labels and those whose labels are dates. Figure 19-1 on page 622 is an example of a chart with a text category axis. Figure 20-6 is one with a date category axis. (In earlier versions of Excel, date category axes were called *time-scaled*.) Excel 2007 handles the two types of axes somewhat differently. (For more about date category axes, see "Changing the Scale of a Date Category Axis" on page 648.)

Figure 20-8 shows your options for formatting a text category axis.

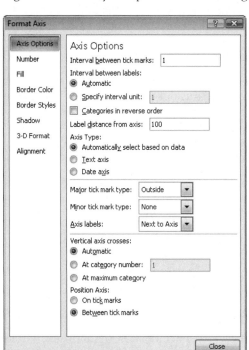

Figure 20-8 The Format Axis dialog box for a text category axis lets you adjust the spacing between gridlines and the position of axis labels, among other things.

Adjusting the Spacing Between Gridlines

Major gridlines are ordinarily drawn from major tick marks, and on a text category axis, a tick mark normally occurs between each axis label (the labels are centered between the tick marks). Because gridlines are most commonly used to help the viewer discern the values of data points, rather than to demarcate categories, Excel leaves category-axis gridlines off by default. If you turn them on and find that you don't want quite as many as Excel gives you, you can have them appear between, say, every other pair of category labels. To modify the frequency at which they appear, increase the Interval Between Tick Marks value. (If you don't display category gridlines, changing this value will still affect the frequency at which axis tick marks appear.)

Note that you don't have any choice about the spacing of minor tick marks. They (and minor gridlines, should you choose to display either) are always evenly spaced between major tick marks and major gridlines.

Curing Label Overlap

Excel displays one category label for each data cluster (or for each data point in a single-series chart). If the chart has many data points, the program sometimes draws the labels vertically or at an angle so they don't overlap. If you coerce the labels into a horizontal posture and you have many labels, you might find them lying atop one another or, at the very least, crowding each other to the point of unreadability. One way to solve the problem is not to display every label. (Other ways include using shorter labels, reducing their font size, increasing the size of the chart, and resigning yourself to angled or vertical labels.)

To display alternate labels, select Specify Interval Unit, and in the text box to the right, type **2**. To display every third label, make that **3**—and so on.

Adjusting the Position of Category Labels

If you display category labels below the axis (the usual placement for a horizontal category axis) and you have a border around the perimeter of the chart, you might find in some cases that Excel draws the labels too close to the border and too far from the axis. You can move them closer to the axis by reducing the number in the Label Distance From Axis text box.

Changing the Intersection of the Value Axis

By default, the value axis crosses the category axis to the left of the first category's data markers. However, you can position its crossing point elsewhere. For example, in a chart comparing two data clusters, such as the one shown in Figure 20-9, you might prefer to position the value axis in the middle instead of at the left.

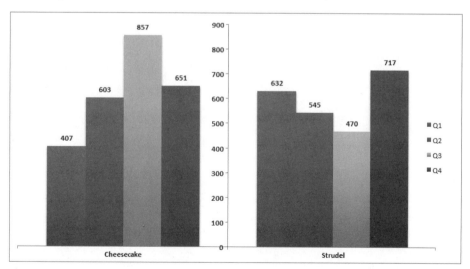

Figure 20-9 When a chart compares two sets of values, it can sometimes be effective to put the value axis between the sets.

To reposition the value axis, select At Category Number (under Vertical Axis Crosses), and in the text box to the right, type a number.

Switching a Category Axis from Text to Date

Excel ordinarily decides whether a category axis should be treated as text or as dates. You can overrule this decision by selecting Date Axis or Text Axis under Axis Type. It wouldn't make sense to have Excel format text labels as dates, but sometimes you might want to treat dates as text. If you have forced a date-oriented axis to be handled as text and then change your mind, you can return it to date status by selecting Date Axis.

Changing the Scale of a Date Category Axis

When a category axis is based on cells containing dates, Excel uses a date scale by default. Your scaling options then are quite different from those available on a text axis. Figure 20-10 shows an example of the formatting options available on a date category axis.

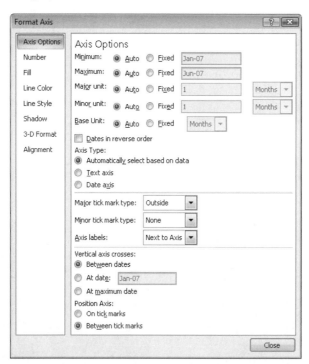

Figure 20-10 You can change the appearance of a time-scaled chart dramatically using the parameters in this dialog box.

Changing the Minimum and Maximum

By default, Excel makes your earliest time value the minimum point on the scale and the latest time value the maximum. By specifying different values for these parameters, you can zoom in on a subset of your data. For example, if your chart plots monthly information from January through December, you can focus on the third quarter by changing the Minimum value to 7/1 of the year in question and the Maximum value to 9/30. Furthermore, if you want to stress that the future is unknown, you can extend the maximum to a date beyond the date of your last data point. Excel then compresses the plot into the left side of the chart, leaving white space on the right.

Changing the Major and Minor Units

The Major Unit setting determines the spacing of major tick marks, axis labels, and major gridlines. To move labels and gridlines farther apart, increase the Major Unit value. The Minor Unit setting determines the spacing of minor tick marks and minor gridlines.

> **Note**
>
> On a time-scaled chart, Excel plots data in chronological order even if it's not sorted by date on the worksheet. We don't recommend randomizing your data, but it's interesting to know that the Excel charting engine doesn't object.

Changing the Base Unit

On charts with date axes, Excel can plot data points only at intervals of the base unit. The available base units are Days, Months, and Years. Excel decides what base unit to use according to the smallest difference in value between points in your source data. In other words, the program usually knows what to do and usually gets it right. You might occasionally find it convenient to overrule, however.

For example, Figure 20-11 plots daily price data, using the automatically determined base unit of Days. Switching the base unit to Months or Years (Figures 20-12 and 20-13) turns the simple daily line chart into an open-high-low-close chart that shows the variation of prices over larger time intervals.

Figure 20-11 With the base unit set to its automatically determined value, Days, Excel generates a simple line chart of daily prices.

Unfortunately, Excel offers only three base unit choices—Days, Months, and Years. Thus, if your data provides, say, hourly price points, you will get a daily open-high-low-close chart regardless. If you'd prefer an ordinary line chart showing hourly price progressions, your recourse is to turn off date scaling in favor of a text category axis. To do that, right-click the category axis, and choose Format Axis. In the Format Axis dialog box (see Figure 20-10), select Text Axis under Axis Type.

Figure 20-12 Changing the base unit to Months creates a monthly open-high-low-close chart.

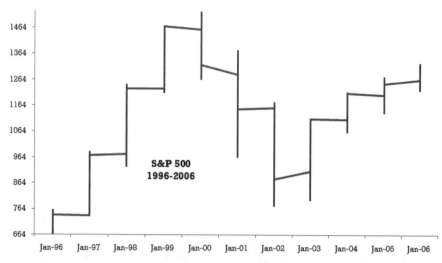

Figure 20-13 Switching the base unit to Years creates yearly bars.

> **Note**
>
> Fiddling with the base unit value is not the only way to get open-high-low-close charts! Excel offers four types of stock charts, including open-high-low-close candlesticks. To see the choices, click the Insert tab on the Ribbon, and then click Other Charts. The stock charts, listed in the gallery under the heading Stock, require that you set up your data in columns—for example, with separate columns for Open, High, Low, and Close. The methods described in this chapter are useful to know about when your data is not arrayed as required for the built-in stock chart types.

Formatting a Depth (Series) Axis

A depth axis (what Excel used to call a *series* axis) appears only in certain charts that use three-dimensional perspective, such as the one shown in Figure 20-14. When each series appears in a separate plane, Excel displays two axes along the floor of the chart and a third axis straight up from the floor. One of the floor axes becomes the usual category axis, and the other becomes the depth axis.

Options for customizing a depth axis are few. You can increase the space between depth gridlines (if you're displaying them) by typing a number greater than one in the Interval Between Tick Marks text box. You can reduce the number of axis labels (labeling every other point, for example) by selecting Specify Interval Unit and typing a number greater than 1 in the text box to the right. And you can reverse the order in which Excel plots the series by selecting the Series In Reverse Order check box. This last option might be useful if the points in your first series obscure those in subsequent series. (You can also deal with that sort of problem by rotating the chart; for information about that approach, see "Changing the Rotation of Chart Text" on page 627.)

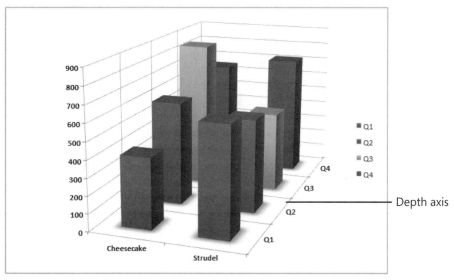

Figure 20-14 This three-dimensional perspective chart has a depth axis as well as the usual value and category axes.

Working with Data Labels

As you saw in Chapter 19, you can add data *labels* (annotations positioned on or near chart markers that indicate the value of data points) by clicking the Layout tab and then clicking Data Labels in the Labels group. The ensuing drop-down lists provide options about where to put the labels—inside or outside column markers, for example. The positioning options vary according to chart type, and in all cases you can adjust a label's position by selecting it individually and then dragging its bounding rectangle.

Additional options concern the content of the data labels. These too vary by chart type (with pie charts, for example, you have the option of putting percentages in the data labels). To see what's available for a chart, right-click its data labels, and click Format Data Labels. Note that content options are not mutually exclusive. You can pack a series name, category name, and value all into the same label, for example.

Labeling Individual Data Points

You don't have to label an entire series at once. To label a single data point, select the series to which it belongs. Pause, and then click the individual data point. With the selection thus refined, right-click, and then click Add Data Labels. You can use a similar method to remove individual data labels. Click a label once to select a set of labels; then pause and click again to refine the selection, and then press Delete.

Labeling with Ad Hoc Text

The standard content options are not your only content options. To put some other text on a data label, create the label in the usual way, select it (click twice to make a single-point selection), and then edit the label the same way you might edit a chart title. To generate a label from the text in a worksheet cell, select the label. Then create a sheet-qualified formula—for example, Sheet2!A2.

Formatting Data Series and Markers

Excel provides plenty of options for formatting the appearance of both entire data series and individual markers within a series. We discussed some of these options earlier in this chapter (see "Formatting Lines and Borders" on page 635 and "Formatting Areas" on page 637). Here you'll look at a couple more.

Assigning a Series to a Secondary Axis

A secondary value axis makes it possible to compare data series that fall within divergent ranges. The secondary axis, positioned on the right, can have a completely different scale from the primary axis. You can assign as many series as you like to the secondary axis.

Figure 20-15 illustrates the use of a secondary axis. The series showing cost per square foot occupies a range so much smaller than that showing median square footage that it's difficult to know how or whether the two series relate to one another. Putting either series on a secondary axis solves the problem.

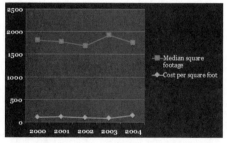 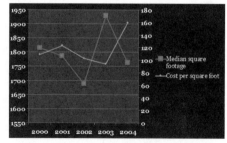

Figure 20-15 Moving either series to a secondary axis makes it easier to see whether and how the two sets of numbers might relate to one another.

To move a series to a secondary axis, right-click it, click Format Data Series, select the Series Options category, and then select Secondary Axis.

Using Two or More Chart Types in the Same Chart

As mentioned in Chapter 19, you can distinguish one or more data series from the rest of a chart by assigning it or them to a contrasting chart type. To do this, right-click a series, and click Change Series Chart Type.

Modifying the Data Source for Your Chart

The simplest way to add new data points to an existing series on a chart is to make the chart's source range a table (select any cell within it, and press Ctrl+T; for more information, see Chapter 21, "Managing Information in Tables") and then add new rows to the table. Excel 2007 incorporates these news rows into the chart without requiring you to do anything further.

If you add a new column immediately to the right of an existing table, Excel expands the table to include the new column. If you've created a chart from such a table, the new column becomes a new data series. That might or might not be desirable, depending on the contents of the new column. If you find yourself with an unwanted new series, you can delete it with the help of the Select Data Source dialog box (see "Modifying Data with the Select Data Source Command" on the next page). Alternatively, and more simply, you can delete a series by selecting it on the chart and pressing the Delete key.

Using the Mouse to Add Data Points

If you choose not to make your source data a table, you can still use your mouse to add data points to an existing chart series. Figure 20-16 shows a candlestick chart that plots data through May 2. Notice that because the chart area is selected, Excel draws two rectangles around the source data. The first rectangle, in column A, outlines the range that the chart is using for its category axis labels. The second, encompassing columns B through E, outlines the four data series. Excel uses magenta for the first rectangle and blue for the second to help you distinguish the two.

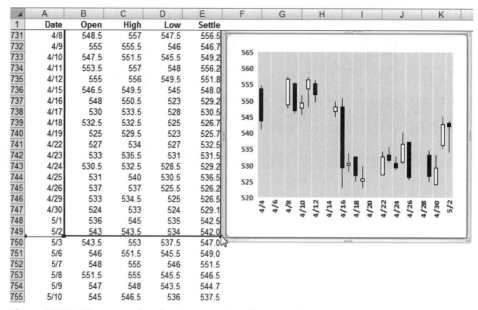

Figure 20-16 When you select the chart area, Excel outlines the source data on your worksheet. You can drag a fill handle to alter the source range.

To extend the chart so it includes the new data in rows 750 through 755, drag the fill handle in the lower-right corner of either rectangle.

Be sure to drag the fill handle, not the bottom of the rectangle if you intend to add data. Dragging the edge of the rectangle moves the data selection without changing its size. Dragging the bottom down five rows in Figure 20-16, for example, would move both the start date and the end date forward.

Modifying Data with the Select Data Source Command

Another simple way to expand or contract a chart is to right-click it and click Select Data. The Chart Data Range box in the Select Data Source dialog box, shown in Figure 20-17, indicates the current extent of the chart's source data. You can edit the reference in place or drag your pointer over the desired range on the worksheet. If your intention is to add or remove an entire series (as opposed to data points within an existing series), you can take advantage of the Add and Remove buttons on the left side of the dialog box. The Remove button is particularly useful if the series you want to excise lies somewhere within the source range rather than at its edge. If the one you want to rid yourself of is the third column of five, for example, it's easiest to select it in the Legend Entries (Series) list and then click Remove.

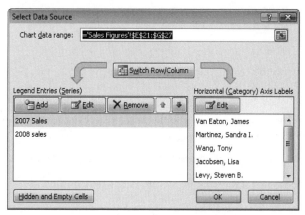

Figure 20-17 You can expand or contract an existing chart by going to the Select Data Source dialog box and modifying the reference in Chart Data Range.

Using Discontiguous Source Ranges

It's not always convenient to set out your source data in a neat, contiguous range. Suppose, for example, that you've downloaded from the United States Department of Agriculture the block of information shown in Figure 20-18. You'd like to whip out a quick column chart comparing turkey production across two states (North Carolina and South Carolina) and three years (2002 through 2004). You could copy the data you need to another part of your worksheet and turn it into a table, but you're in a hurry.

STATE	BROILERS			TURKEYS		
	2002	2003	2004	2002	2003	2004
United States \1	44,059	43,958	45,796	7,495	7,487	7,305
Alabama	5,362	5,405	5,470	(NA)	(NA)	(NA)
Arkansas	5,813	5,843	6,208	522	540	527
California	(NA)	(NA)	(NA)	439	419	414
Delaware	1,544	1,507	1,492	(Z)	(NA)	(NA)
Florida	631	511	463	(NA)	(NA)	(NA)
Georgia	6,453	6,303	6,495	(NA)	(NA)	(NA)
Illinois	(NA)	(NA)	(NA)	90	90	89
Indiana	(NA)	(NA)	(NA)	403	397	410
Iowa	(NA)	(NA)	(NA)	261	268	324
Kentucky	1,404	1,490	1,570	(NA)	(NA)	(NA)
Maryland	1,377	1,374	1,366	16	15	13
Michigan	(NA)	(NA)	(NA)	180	191	188
Minnesota	230	229	232	1,148	1,215	1,228
Mississippi	4,078	4,189	4,387	(NA)	(NA)	(NA)
Missouri	(NA)	(NA)	(NA)	783	724	667
North Carolina	4,411	4,320	4,537	1,160	1,105	1,069
North Dakota	(NA)	(NA)	(NA)	50	35	26
Ohio	215	226	225	219	212	220
Oklahoma	1,141	1,115	1,243	(NA)	(NA)	(NA)
Pennsylvania	706	687	708	234	216	234
South Carolina	1,080	1,145	1,186	369	456	463
South Dakota	(NA)	(NA)	(NA)	159	153	151
Tennessee	895	948	999	(NA)	(NA)	(NA)
Texas	2,882	2,947	3,166	(NA)	(NA)	(NA)
Virginia	1,301	1,299	1,341	446	492	435
West Virginia	359	358	354	89	92	71
Wisconsin	145	155	152	(NA)	(NA)	(NA)

SYMBOLS
NA Not available.
Z Less than 500,000 pounds.
FOOTNOTE
\1 Includes other states not shown separately.

Source: U.S. Department of Agriculture, National Agricultural Statistics Service,
Poultry--Production and Value, annual.

Figure 20-18 Sometimes your source data will arrive in a form that's awkward for plotting.

Here's another way (not better, perhaps, but an alternative):

1. Hold down the Ctrl key, because you're about create a discontiguous selection.

2. Click North Carolina, and then drag the pointer across the three Turkeys numbers for that state.

3. Click South Carolina, and then drag across its Turkeys numbers.

4. With the appropriate data selected, create your chart in the customary way. Excel gives you something like this:

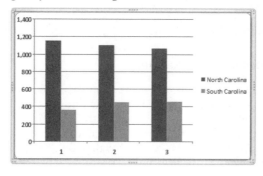

That's an excellent start. Excel has the data markers and legend labels right. But you need to fix the horizontal axis labels.

5. Right-click the chart anywhere, and click Select Data Source (or just click Select Data on the Design tab on the Ribbon). The Select Data Source dialog box appears, with the useless category-axis labels listed in the right side of the dialog box:

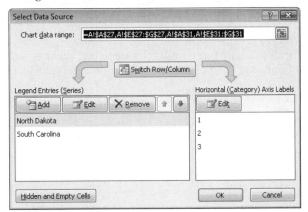

6. On the right side of the dialog box, under Horizontal (Category) Axis Labels, click Edit. The Axis Labels dialog box arrives:

7. Drag the pointer across the worksheet cells containing the appropriate labels—2002, 2003, and 2004. Then click OK.

8. Excel returns you to the Edit Data Source dialog box (in case you have any further duties to perform there). Click OK, and you have your chart:

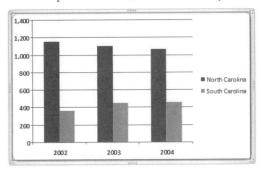

Yet another way to create this chart without copying the desired cells to another part of the worksheet is to hide all the intervening rows and columns in which you're not interested. Excel normally excludes hidden rows and columns within a chart selection, so you'd certainly get the chart you want. The difficulty with this approach is that the moment you reveal those hidden rows and columns, you lose your focused chart.

Changing the Way Excel Plots Empty and Hidden Cells

Excel ordinarily plots empty cells as gaps—that is, it doesn't plot them. It also omits cells in hidden rows and columns. As Figure 20-19 shows, you can change both defaults if you want. The alternatives for empty cells are to plot them as zeros or to fill the gap with a straight line. The latter option is available only in line and X Y (scatter) charts.

Figure 20-19 By default Excel omits missing data in a source range and ignores data in hidden rows and columns.

Hidden and empty cell settings are chart-specific. To modify the behavior for a particular chart, right-click the chart, and click Select Data. Then click Hidden And Empty Cells.

Using Multilevel Categories

Excel lets you categorize your categories. This sounds redundant, but a quick example illustrates the technique. Suppose you want to plot the data shown in Figure 20-20. (Figure 20-21 shows the resulting chart.) The series are months, and the categories are the sales offices located in different cities. The city sales are further classified by state, however. To create this multilevel chart, you simply select the data, including both columns of category information, and plot in the usual manner. Excel recognizes the second category column and creates the appropriate subcategories.

	A	B	C	D	E
1	Salespeople by office				
2					
3			January	February	March
4	Washington	Seattle	13	13	14
5	Washington	Spokane	6	8	10
6	Oregon	Portland	12	12	12
7	Oregon	Eugene	2	2	2
8	California	San Francisco	11	13	15
9	California	Los Angeles	14	18	2
10	California	San Diego	16	16	11

Figure 20-20 This worksheet uses multilevel categories; city sales offices are grouped by state.

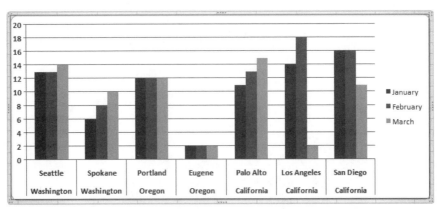

Figure 20-21 A multilevel category chart uses two or more sets of category names to label the category axis.

The capability to create multilevel charts appeared first in Microsoft Excel 97, just before the Excel version that introduced PivotCharts. PivotCharts—charts derived from PivotTables—are a superior alternative to multilevel charts, but they require you to create a PivotTable and that in turn requires you to set your data up in a particular manner. To create a PivotTable from the data shown in Figure 20-20, for example, you need to organize your worksheet like this:

	A	B	C	D
1	State	City	Month	Employees
2	Washington	Seattle	January	13
3	Washington	Seattle	February	13
4	Washington	Seattle	March	14
5	Washington	Spokane	January	6
6	Washington	Spokane	February	8
7	Washington	Spokane	March	10
8	Oregon	Portland	January	12
9	Oregon	Portland	February	12
10	Oregon	Portland	March	12
11	Oregon	Eugene	January	2
12	Oregon	Eugene	February	2
13	Oregon	Eugene	March	2
14	California	San Francisco	January	11
15	California	San Francisco	February	13
16	California	San Francisco	March	15
17	California	Los Angeles	January	14
18	California	Los Angeles	February	18
19	California	Los Angeles	March	2
20	California	San Diego	January	16
21	California	San Diego	February	16
22	California	San Diego	March	11

After creating the PivotTable, you could generate the PivotChart shown in Figure 20-22. If the information you need to plot is relatively simple and you already have it organized in a manner not conducive to PivotTable creation, you're probably better off using the multilevel charting capability.

> **Note**
>
> For more information about creating PivotTables and PivotCharts, see Chapter 22, "Analyzing Data with PivotTable Reports."

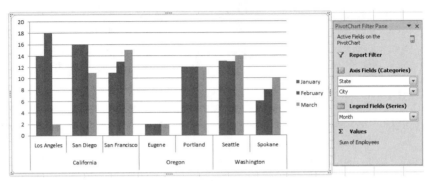

Figure 20-22 PivotCharts like this are an alternative (and in most cases superior) way to plot multi-level data.

Adding Moving Averages and Other Trendlines

A *trendline* is a line that describes the general tendency of a data series. It can be a moving average, a linear-regression line, or a line generated by one of various kinds of non-linear curve-fitting methods.

To add a trendline to a series in an area, bar, column, line, or X Y (scatter) chart, right-click the series, and click Add Trendline. The dialog box shown in Figure 20-23 appears. (Alternatively, you can select any part of the chart, click the Layout tab, and then click Trendline in the Analysis group. The options that descend from the Ribbon when you do this don't cover the full gamut of trendline capabilities, however, and you'll probably want to click More Trendline Options at the bottom of the list—which will take you to the dialog box shown in Figure 20-23. It's simpler to right-click and use the shortcut menu.)

To specify the type of trendline or moving average you want, select one of the six options at the top of the dialog box. If you choose Polynomial, indicate the highest power (from 2 through 6) for the independent variable in the adjacent Order text box. If you select Moving Average, indicate the number of periods Excel should use in its calculations.

After you've chosen the type of trendline you want, you can use the Trendline Name area of the dialog box to customize the name that will appear in the chart's legend. Options under Forecast (not available for moving averages) let you extrapolate the trendline. If you're adding a linear, polynomial, or exponential trendline, you can also set the y-intercept in the Set Intercept box and display the regression equation and R-squared value on the chart.

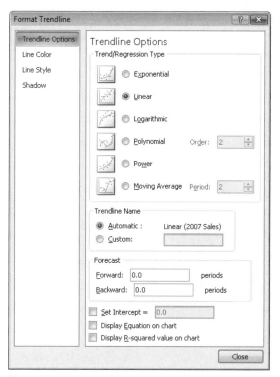

Figure 20-23 Using the Format Trendline dialog box, you can add six different types of trendlines to a data series.

> **Note**
> You can find a more detailed treatment of the Excel trendline features and their use in modeling growth in *Microsoft Office Excel 2007: Data Analysis and Business Modeling*, by Wayne L. Winston (Microsoft Press, April 2007).

Adding Error Bars

When you plot statistical or experimental data, it's often helpful to indicate the confidence level of your data. The Excel error-bar feature makes this easy. To add error bars to a data series in an area, bar, column, line, or X Y (scatter) chart, select the series. Then click the Layout tab, and click Error Bars (the last item on the right side of the Ribbon). As with trendlines, unless your intention is to remove existing error bars (in which case you'll click None), there's little point in resting your pointer on the options that drop down from the Ribbon; instead, click More Error Bars Options to get to the

Chapter 20

dialog box shown in Figure 20-24. Here you can tailor your error bars and specify the range of values you want them to encompass.

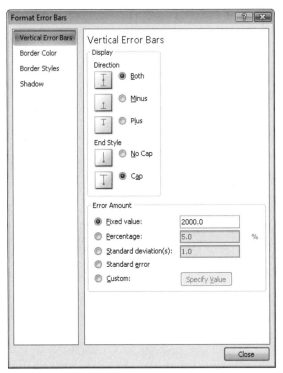

Figure 20-24 You can customize error bars for direction, style, and amount.

Adding High-Low Lines and Up and Down Bars

High-low lines are straight lines that extend between the highest and lowest points in a cluster. You can use them to indicate the range over which a value varies. High-low lines are available only in two-dimensional line charts.

Up and down bars are rectangles drawn between the corresponding points of two line series. Excel fills the bars with one color if the first series is higher than the last (the bars in this case are called *up bars*) and a contrasting color when the opposite is true (in which case they're called *down bars*). Up and down bars are often used in charts that track opening and closing prices of securities or commodities.

You can add either high-low lines or up and down bars (or both) by means of commands in the Analysis group on the Format tab on the Ribbon. You can format these items—for example, customize the colors that Excel uses for up bars and down bars—in the usual way, by right-clicking and then clicking the appropriate format command.

If you have more than two line series in a chart, Excel applies its up bars and down bars to the outer series—the first and fourth in a chart with four series, for example. The high-low lines are always drawn between the highest values in a set and the lowest.

A *candlestick* chart, such as the one shown in Figure 20-16 on page 654, combines high-low lines with up bars and down bars. The high-low lines show the full range over which a price varied in a period, and the up bars and down bars (black for down, white for up in Figure 20-16) show whether the open was above or below the close. Excel offers this chart as one of its built-in stock charts (choose Other Charts on the Ribbon; you'll find it as the second item in the Stock section of the gallery). The candlestick chart requires four series in the order *open*, *high*, *low*, and *close*. (They don't have to have those names, of course, as Figure 20-16 shows.) Excel uses the first and fourth series for its up bars and down bars.

PART 7
Managing Databases and Tables

Managing Information in Tables

Microsoft Office Excel 2007 introduces a whole new set of features for managing information in tables. You'll find these features invaluable for almost any kind of tabular work—whether it be a simple list of names and phone numbers or something much more complex, such as a list of transactions that includes tax or discount calculations, subtotals, and totals. The new features make all the typical tabular manipulations—sorting, filtering, analyzing, formatting, and even generating charts based on tables—easier than they've ever been.

Here are just some of the advances that Office Excel 2007 has made in the area of table management:

- **Autoexpansion** If you add a row directly below the last row of a table or add a column directly to the right of a table, the table expands to incorporate the new row or column. All table styles, conditional formatting, calculations, and data validation rules extend to the new row or column. Charts based on data from the table also are similarly updated. Likewise, if you add a new column adjacent to the table, the new column is automatically incorporated into the table definition.

- **Structured referencing** Formulas that reference elements of a table can use column names and other tags in place of ordinary cell addresses. This kind of referencing, exemplified in Figure 21-1, makes table calculations self-documenting and enhances reliability.

- **Sorting improvements** Older versions of Excel let you sort data on as many as three criteria. In Excel 2007, you can sort on as many criteria as you please. You can also sort data based on the font or fill colors assigned to cells.

- **Filtering improvements** It's easier now to filter a table so you see only the rows in which you're currently interested. You can filter on multiple criteria or on icon sets applied via conditional formatting. You can also use filters based on dynamic date definitions, such as last week or the current quarter.

- **Formula replication** If you add a column to a table that performs calculations based on table data (a column such as the one that generates total scores in Figure 21-1), Excel automatically replicates the calculation formula throughout the column.

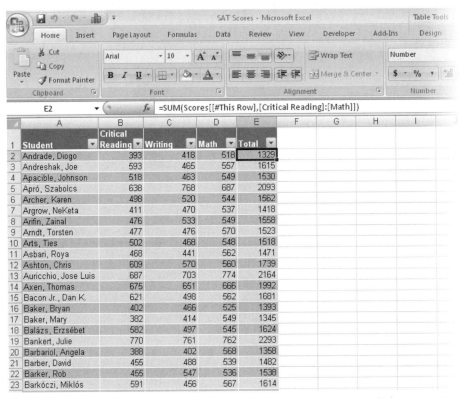

Figure 21-1 Structured referencing, exemplified by the formula in E2, makes calculations easier to understand and less prone to error.

- **Removal of duplicate data** A simple command lets you highlight and (optionally) remove duplicate rows from a table.

- **Table styles** Excel 2007 comes with a large library of styles that you can use to apply gorgeous and consistent formatting to your tables. The styles are intelligent and dynamic. If you use a style that adds *banding* to a table (displaying alternate rows in contrasting colors), the banding adjusts correctly to changes in sorting, filtering, and table dimension. You can also create your own table styles or customize any of the existing styles.

Note

If you used older versions of Excel, you'll notice some terminology changes in Excel 2007. What was formerly called a *list* is now a *table*. (You can still press Ctrl+L to turn a range into a table, but Excel 2007 provides a new shortcut, Ctrl+T. The two shortcuts have the same function.) The term *AutoFilter* has been replaced by the simpler *Filter*. And the AutoFormat command of yore is gone, replaced by *Table Styles*.

How to Organize a Table

In a sense, you can call anything you put in a contiguous block of spreadsheet cells a *table*, but in Excel the term has a more specific meaning. It refers to a block of data organized so that each row refers to an item (a person in an address list, a sale in a transaction log, a product in a product catalog, and so on) and each column contains one piece of information about that item (for example, the postal code of a contact, the date of a sale, or the catalog number of a product). In addition, for a block of data to become a table, you have to designate it as such. (See "Creating a Table" below.)

Typically, the worksheet range defined as a table should have the following characteristics:

- The top row should consist of labels, with each label describing the contents of the column beneath it. Each label should be unique. (The labels row is not mandatory, but if you omit it, Excel will generate one for you using default column names.)

- Each column should contain the same kind of information.

- Each category of information you want to be able to sort by, search on, or otherwise manipulate individually should occupy a separate column.

Creating a Table

After you have some data in a worksheet range, you can designate that range as a table by selecting any cell within it and pressing Ctrl+T or Ctrl+L. That's the easy way. If you want to work a little harder, you can click Table in the Tables group on the Insert tab. Either way, start by selecting a single cell anywhere in the table range before issuing the command. Excel will figure out the dimensions of the table for you and ask for confirmation in the Create Table dialog box:

Unless the program has made some kind of mistake, you can click OK to create your table. If you select more than one cell but less than the entire range before pressing Ctrl+T, Excel will try to create a table out of the specific cells you selected.

Chapter 21

> **Note**
>
> Many new features of Excel tables do not work if your workbook is opened in Compatibility mode. You must convert a workbook you have saved with the type Excel 97–2003 Workbook to an Excel 2007 workbook in order to get the new functionality. See "File Formats" on page 54 for details about converting an existing workbook into native Excel 2007 format.

Overwriting Default Headers

Notice that, in addition to recognizing the size of the table, Excel figures out whether the top row of your range is a header row—a row of column labels. If your range does not include such a row or if for some reason you choose to clear the My Table Has Headers check box in the Create Table dialog box, Excel will create a header row for you using labels such as Column 1, Column 2, and so on. Default headers like these are both ugly and pointless; it's far better to set up your own descriptive headers before creating the table. But if you omit this step, you can always override the defaults later by selecting the header cells and typing over them, just as if they were ordinary worksheet cells. (They're not quite ordinary data, actually; Excel won't let you delete them, and if you try to clear a header, you'll just get the default back.)

Turning a Table Back into an Ordinary Range

If the need arises to turn a table back into an ordinary worksheet range, select any cell or block of cells within the table. Then click Convert To Range in the Tools group on the Design tab. Click Yes to answer the confirmation prompt. Note that after you change a table into a regular range, the formatting turns into regular cell formatting. This can cause unexpected behavior if you ever turn the range back into a table. See the "Formatting Tables section on page 705 for details about managing table and cell formatting.

INSIDE OUT   Check the Ribbon

An easy way to tell whether a range is a table is to select a cell in the range and look at the Ribbon. If you see a Table Tools tab, then the current list has been converted to a table.

Naming a Table

When you designate a range as a table, Excel assigns a name to that table and displays the name in the Properties group on the Design tab:

As this example shows, Excel uses default names (Table1, Table2, and so on) unless you supply your own names. Does the name matter? Perhaps. Formulas that take advantage of structured referencing use the table name, and a descriptive name serves the purpose of self-documentation better than a default name. In the following formula, for example:

```
=SUM(Scores[Math])
```

the word *Scores* is the table's name. (The formula sums the values from the Math column of the Scores table.)

Giving a meaningful name to the table is particularly useful when you have multiple tables on a single worksheet and have formulas that refer to the tables. By using names for the tables, you can instantly tell when looking at a formula which table it is referencing.

It's definitely worthwhile to assign an intelligible name to your table if you think you might at some point record or write a macro that references the table. That way your macro code will be easier to understand (easier for you and easier for anyone else who sees your code). Moreover, if you record a macro that references Table1 and you subsequently name the table SurveyData, your macro will no longer perform as expected and will cause you considerable vexation. It's best to form the habit of naming objects when you create them.

To change a table's current name (default or otherwise), select a cell within the table, and click the Design tab. Then type in the Table Name box in the Properties group.

Expanding a Table

To add a new row to the end of a table, go to the bottom-right cell of the table (ignoring the total row, if there is one), and press Tab. Excel will extend the table for you, no questions asked, copying all formatting and formulas in the process. When you get to the last column in the new row, press Tab to create yet another new row. Thus, after you have created the stub of a table, you can expand it downward by simply typing in the usual way and pressing Tab between cells (or at any rate at the end of each row).

Note that pressing Tab creates a new table row *above* the total row, if your table has a total row. The total row simply moves down one row to accommodate your new data, and Excel updates the formulas appropriately. (For more about the total row, see "Adding Totals to a Table" on the next page.) If you don't have a total row in your table, you can also extend the table by simply typing in the blank row below the bottom row of the table. Using Tab to extend the table works whether you have a total row or not.

Automatic expansion works for columns as well as rows. If you type in any row of the column directly to the right of a table, Excel expands the table to include the new column. If the new data is a formula, the formula is replicated throughout the column.

If you don't want the table to automatically expand or automatically fill columns with formulas, you can turn off the option. Click the Microsoft Office Button, and then click Excel Options. Select the Proofing category, and click AutoCorrect Options. In the Auto-Correct dialog box, shown in Figure 21-2, click the AutoFormat As You Type tab. Clear the Include New Rows And Columns In Table check box to prevent Excel from expanding the table, and clear the Fill Formulas In Tables To Create Calculated Columns check box to prevent Excel from filling entire columns with identical formulas.

Figure 21-2 Use the AutoCorrect dialog box to control table expansion.

If you're not currently displaying a total row with your table, you'll find a minuscule handle in the lower-right corner of the cell occupying the lower-right corner of your table. This handle gives you yet another way to expand your table. Usually, it's easier just to add data and let Excel expand the table. But if you want to add several new rows or columns all at once, the handle is a good way to do it.

Selecting Rows and Columns Within a Table

Excel makes it easy to select rows and columns within a table. If you rest the pointer on the left edge of the first cell in a row, the pointer changes to a solid arrow. Click once, and you've selected the row. If your table happens to begin in column A of the worksheet, be sure you rest the pointer inside the first cell, rather than on the worksheet frame. On the frame, the pointer also changes to a solid arrow, but clicking here will select the entire worksheet row.

To select a column, rest the pointer near the top of the column's heading, and then click. Clicking once selects the column's data, excluding the header and the total (if you have displayed the total row). Clicking a second time selects the entire column—header, data, and total.

To select the entire table, rest the pointer on the upper-left corner of the first column's header. When you see the pointer turn southeast, click. Click once for the data only or twice for everything—data, headers, and totals.

Selecting with the keyboard is even easier, particularly with a large table when the top and left edges are out of sight. Pressing Shift+Spacebar selects the current row, regardless of which cell is selected. Pressing Ctrl+Spacebar selects the current column's data, omitting the header and total. Pressing Shift+Ctrl+Spacebar or Ctrl+A selects all the table's data.

Multiple key presses expand the selection predictably: Pressing Shift+Spacebar twice selects the entire current worksheet row. Pressing Ctrl+Spacebar twice selects the current table column, with the header and total. Pressing Ctrl+Spacebar three times selects the entire current worksheet column. Pressing Shift+Ctrl+Spacebar or Ctrl+A twice gets the entire table, headers, and totals included. Pressing that combination a third time selects all gazillion cells of the worksheet.

Chapter 21

Adding Totals to a Table

To add a total row to your table, select any cell within the table, and then select the Total Row check box in the Table Style Options group on the Designer tab. You can toggle the row on or off by selecting or clearing this check box. Figure 21-3 shows an example of a total row.

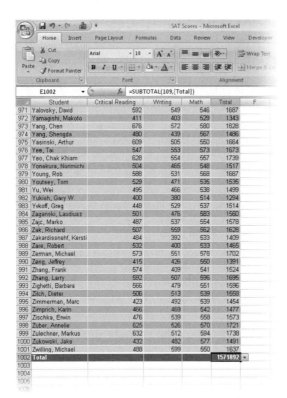

Figure 21-3 The total row uses the SUBTOTAL function to perform summary calculations.

By default, the total row applies the SUBTOTAL function, with a *Function_num* argument of 109, to the rightmost column of the table. (Using 109 in the *Function_num* argument creates a sum that ignores all rows hidden by filters.) That generates a sum in the lower-right corner—which might not be what you want. In Figure 21-3, for example, it would make more sense to show an average in that cell than a sum. It would also be useful to calculate averages in the Critical Reading, Writing, and Math columns, as well as the Total column. All that is quite easy to do. When you click the small arrow at the right edge of a total row cell, a list of alternative functions appears:

You can make the same list appear in any other total row cell (not just the rightmost) by selecting the cell and clicking the arrow that appears. You can also type directly over any of the total row cells. Here's how you might make the total row look if you wanted to replace the sums with averages:

1000	Zukowski, Jake	432	482	577	1491
1001	Zwilling, Michael	488	599	550	1637
1002	Averages	523.7	498.3	549.9	1571.9

Here are a few more points to note about the total row:

- Unlike the total row in an Excel 2003 list, the Excel 2007 total row does not limit you to the commonplace aggregation functions. With the help of the More Functions command in the list, you can create any kind of formulas you want.

- Because the choices in the list—AVERAGE, COUNT, COUNT NUMBERS, and so on—generate formulas based on the SUBTOTAL function (using arguments in the 101–111 range), they ignore rows that are hidden by filters. If you want to aggregate based on all rows except those you manually hide, subtract 100 from the first argument function. For example, change SUBTOTAL(101,column) to SUBTOTAL(1,column). If you want aggregate calculations based on all rows, ignoring the column filter settings, change the formulas to standard aggregate functions. For example, substitute SUM(column) for SUBTOTAL(109,column).

- After you've customized the formulas in the total row, turning the total row off and then back on retains your customized formulas. If you frequently toggle the total row off and on, consider putting the command on your Quick Access Toolbar. (Click the Design tab under Table Tools, right-click the Total Row check box, and select Add To Quick Access Toolbar.)

> **Note**
> You can also add subtotals to your table. Excel still includes the Subtotal command to insert subtotal rows into the middle of a table, but you can achieve the same result more easily in almost all cases by using a PivotTable. See Chapter 22, "Analyzing Data with PivotTable Reports," for information about working with a PivotTable report.

Sorting Tables and Other Ranges

Excel provides numerous ways to sort worksheet ranges. You can use the same techniques to sort both tables and ranges that you have not defined as tables (we'll call the latter *lists*.)

You can sort by column or row, in ascending or descending order, and with capitalization considered or ignored. (When you sort by row, your rows are rearranged, and the columns remain in the same order. When you sort by column, the opposite kind of rearrangement occurs.) You can even define custom sorting sequences so that, for example, your company's division names always appear in a particular order, regardless of their alphabetic sequence. Excel 2007 enhances sorting even more by making it easy to sort by as many fields as you want, not just the three-at-a-time limit of previous versions. And, you can now sort by using the format of the cells, not just the value. Sorting a table is essentially the same as sorting a simple list in the worksheet. Having headings at the top of the range is helpful but not necessary.

Sorting on a Single Column

To sort on a single column—the Last Name column in Figure 21-4, for example—select one cell anywhere within that column. Then either click the Sort A To Z button in the Sort & Filter group on the Data tab (to arrange the column in ascending numeric or alphabetic order) or click the Sort Z To A button (to do the opposite). Excel sorts in the order you want on the column in which the selection resides. If you don't want to switch to the Data tab on the Ribbon, right-click a cell, and then click the appropriate sort command on the Sort menu.

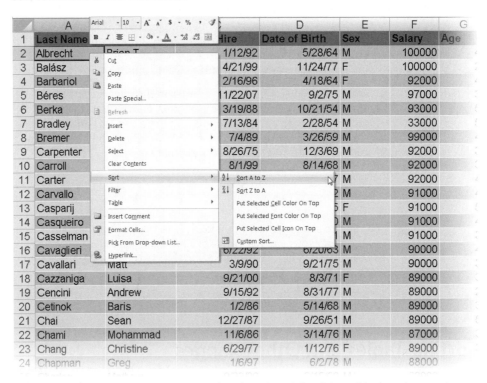

Figure 21-4 One easy way to sort on a single column is to right-click a cell in the column and choose Sort.

 You'll find the Staff.xlsx file in the Sample Files section of the companion CD.

When you click one of the Sort buttons, Excel assumes you want to sort the rows. If you're sorting a table, the table definition determines whether the first row is headers (and should not be sorted) or data (and should be sorted). If you're sorting a list that is not a table, Excel guesses whether the first row is headers or not. If the quick command version doesn't meet your needs, you need to use the Sort dialog box.

To use the Sort dialog box, click the Sort button in the Sort & Filter group on the Data tab. (It's also available when you right-click a cell in the range you want to sort.) If this is the first time you've sorted the current range, the Sort dialog box, shown in Figure 21-5, appears. If you've sorted the range before, the dialog box will display the sort parameters you last used.

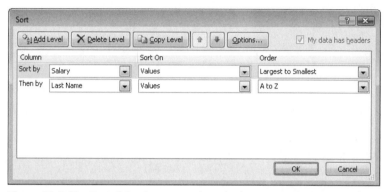

Figure 21-5 The Sort dialog box remembers the last sort settings you used..

If your data includes a header row that should remain in place while the other rows are sorted, Excel usually recognizes that fact and selects the My Data Has Headers check box. If Excel, for some reason, fails to notice a header row or if it detects a header row when one isn't really there, you can correct it before clicking OK.

Sorting on More Than One Column

You can sort on as many columns as you want. To sort on more than one column, click the Add Level button in the Sort dialog box. For example, to sort the staff list shown in Figure 21-4 first in descending order by salary and then in ascending order by last name, you fill out the dialog box as shown in Figure 21-6. Excel then rearranges the list as shown in Figure 21-7.

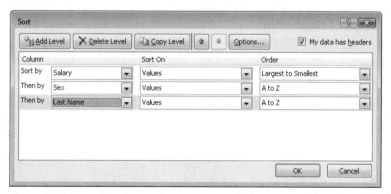

Figure 21-6 To sort on three columns, you supply the names of the column headings in the Sort By and Then By boxes.

	A	B	C	D	E	F	G
1	**Last Name**	**First Name**	**Date of Hire**	**Date of Birth**	**Sex**	**Salary**	**Age**
2	Balász	Erzsébet	4/21/99	11/24/77	F	100000	
3	Hartwig	Doris	11/17/97	3/31/74	F	100000	
4	Holliday	Nicole	11/1/95	6/2/70	F	100000	
5	Lengyel	Attila	7/31/90	9/19/61	F	100000	
6	Lund	Pia	6/30/05	6/16/77	F	100000	
7	Albrecht	Brian T.	1/12/92	5/28/64	M	100000	
8	Nash	Mike	11/20/74	10/17/49	M	100000	
9	Zakardissnehf	Kerstin	3/11/97	8/1/67	F	99000	
10	Bremer	Ted	7/4/89	3/26/59	M	99000	
11	Cochrane	Mark-Stuart	7/23/94	2/28/61	M	99000	
12	Martin	Benjamin	3/27/91	7/20/64	M	99000	
13	Dehenne	Denis	7/12/99	9/20/54	M	98000	
14	Smith	Benjamin	12/4/97	7/30/75	M	98000	
15	Heidemann	Katja	3/30/81	4/18/51	F	97000	
16	Philips	Carol	6/23/00	3/7/64	F	97000	
17	Béres	Kálmán	11/22/07	9/2/75	M	97000	
18	Miller	Frank	5/5/94	6/13/71	M	97000	
19	Pak	Jae B	3/5/97	7/18/68	M	97000	
20	Conroy	Stephanie	7/24/93	5/30/70	F	96000	
21	Schare	Gary	6/17/94	11/29/62	M	96000	
22	Margheim	Diane	4/26/95	6/7/76	F	95000	
23	Cox	Brian	5/3/00	9/22/75	M	95000	
24	Geller	Christa	9/12/92	4/15/70	F	94000	

Figure 21-7 The rows are now arranged in descending order by salary, with rows of common salary arranged first by sex and then by last name.

Sorting Only Part of a List

If you sort a table, Excel always sorts the entire table, regardless of how many cells within the table you initially select. If you want to sort part of a list, make sure it's not a table.

In a regular range, if you select a single cell before sorting, Excel scans the area surrounding the selected cell, highlights the entire contiguous range of cells, and assumes you want to sort that entire range. If you want to sort only part of a range, start by selecting only those rows and columns you want to sort. Then click Data, Sort. To sort rows 10 through 20 in Figure 21-4, for example, you start by selecting A10:G20. If you select one column from something that appears to be a list, Excel will ask you whether you really do want to sort just that one column or whether you want to expand the selection to include the entire list. Most of the time, you'll probably want to sort the entire list, so either convert the list to a table or be sure to select only a single cell before you sort the list.

You can't specify a sort range in the Sort dialog box. You must select the range before you open the dialog box. The dialog box doesn't indicate the range Excel is about to sort. Explore your worksheet immediately after a sort, and use the Undo command if you don't like what you get.

Sorting by Column

Thus far, our examples have involved sorting by row—leaving the columns alone. You also can sort by column, leaving the order of the rows alone. If you have turned the list into a table, you cannot sort by column. This makes sense, because a table is always row oriented. You're more likely to use horizontal sorting with a grid, which doesn't function as a table anyway.

To sort by column, follow these steps:

1. Select the range you want to sort—excluding any row headings that shouldn't be sorted.

2. Click the Sort button in the Sort & Filter group on the Data tab.

3. Click the Options button in the Sort dialog box, and select the Sort Left To Right option, as shown in Figure 21-8.

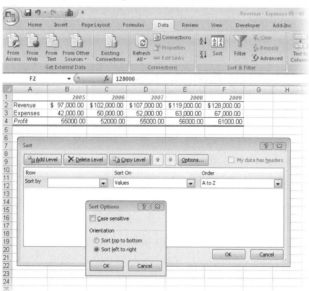

Figure 21-8 Use the Sort Left To Right option to reorder the years into a descending sequence.

4. Click OK to return to the main part of the Sort dialog box.

5. Select the row you want to sort by and the direction of the sort. Add rows to sort by if you need them.

6. Click OK.

Chapter 21

Figure 21-9 shows the result of this left-to-right sort.

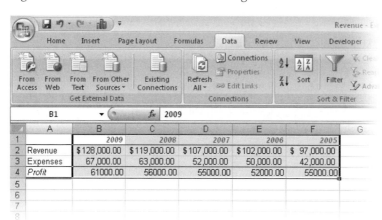

Figure 21-9 The lateral sort specified in Figure 21-8 generates this rearrangement of the data.

Excel doesn't recognize row headings in column-oriented sorts, so it's best to select the range you want to sort, rather than just a single cell, when you're sorting laterally. If you select only one cell, Excel will propose to sort all the contiguous cells, including the labels in your first column.

Sorting Cells That Contain Formulas

You need to exercise caution when sorting cells that contain formulas with cell references. If you sort by row, references to other cells in the same row will be correct after the sort, but references to cells in other rows of the list will no longer be correct.

Similarly, if you sort by column, references to other cells in the same columns will be correct after the sort, but references to cells in other columns will be broken. With either kind of sort, relative references to cells outside the list will be broken by the sort. Relative references from cells outside the sort range will keep referring to the same cells as before—even if the contents of the cell got moved by the sort.

Figure 21-10 demonstrates the hazards of sorting a range that contains formulas. Row 5 of the worksheet calculates the year-to-year change in profit using relative-reference formulas. Cell C5, for example, uses the formula =C4−B4 to calculate the difference between the 2006 profits and the 2005 profits. Each of the other formulas also references the cell directly to its left.

If you include row 5 in the sort range, the formulas get sorted along with the other columns. Each formula in row 5 still references the cell to the left, but B5 now shows an error, because B4 tries to subtract the text *Profit* from the number 61,000.

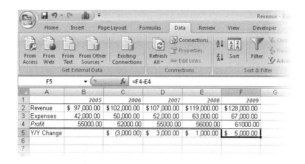

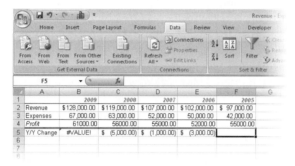

Figure 21-10 Sorting this worksheet laterally has broken the formulas in row 5.

If, on the other hand, you exclude row 5 from the sort range, the formulas keep working, but the meaning of the calculation is different. When the columns were sorted in ascending order, the formulas in row 5 gave the change from the *preceding* year. After you sort the columns in descending order, the formulas in row 5 give the change from the *following* year. Both before and after the sort, the formulas give the change from the previous column.

Sorting is different from cutting and pasting cells. If you pick up each column and move it to its new location, Excel updates the formulas appropriately after each move. If you do it by clicking Sort on the Data tab, Excel doesn't adjust the references.

To avoid the problems associated with sorting ranges containing formulas, observe the following rules:

- In formulas that reference cells outside the sort range, use only absolute references.

- When sorting by row, avoid formulas that reference cells in other rows. If you must use such formulas, reference cells by name, not by address.

- When sorting by column, avoid formulas that reference cells in other columns. If you must use such formulas, reference cells by name, not by address.

Chapter 21

- Cells outside the sort range can make relative references to cells inside the sort range, but they always reference the cell location, not the sorted contents. To exclude the cells from the sort range, insert a blank row or column to separate them from the sorted range.

Understanding the Default Sorting Sequence in Excel

To avoid surprises, you should understand the following points about the way Excel sorts:

- Excel sorts cells according to their underlying values, not their current number formats. This means, for example, that Excel places a date cell formatted as November 16, 2007, ahead of a date cell formatted as 12/27/2007 (because the first date has a lower numeric value), even though if you typed the two dates as text, Excel would reverse their order.

- Excel sorts numeric values ahead of text values. The value 98052 would therefore be sorted ahead of the value 1 Microsoft Way, because the former is a number and the latter is text.

- Logical values are sorted after text, and FALSE is sorted before TRUE.

- Error values (#DIV/0!, #NAME?, #VALUE, #REF!, #N/A, #NUM!, and #NULL!) are sorted after logical values. Excel regards all error values as equivalent; that is, it leaves them in the order it finds them.

- Blanks are placed last, in both ascending and descending sorts.

- The sort order for text depends on many factors, including your current locale settings. If knowing the exact sort order is important for you, type the formula **=CHAR(ROW())** in cell A1. It will return a blank, because the first character in the ANSI character set is not printable. Copy the formula down 255 rows. Convert the formula to values and sort it. That will show you the sort order Excel is using. For reference, here's the current sort order for most Western European characters:

```
'  -  [space]  !  "  #  $  %  &  ( )  *  ,  .  /  :  ;  ?  @  [ \ ]  ^  _  `  { | }
~  ¡  ¦  ¨  ¯  ´  ¸  ¿  `  ´  ¢  £  ¤  ¥  +  <  =  >  ±  «  »  ×  ÷  §  ©  ¬  ®  °  µ  ¶  ·
0  ¼  ½  1  ¹  2  ²  3  ³  ¾  4  5  6  7  8  9  A  a  ª  Á  á  À  à  Â  â  Ä  ä  Ã  ã  Å  å
Æ  æ  B  b  C  c  Ç  ç  D  d  Ð  ð  E  e  É  é  È  è  Ê  ê  Ë  ë  F  f  G  g  H  h  I  i  Í
í  Ì  ì  Î  î  Ï  ï  J  j  K  k  L  l  M  m  N  n  Ñ  ñ  O  o  º  Ó  ó  Ò  ò  Ô  ô  Ö  ö  Õ
õ  Ø  ø  P  p  Q  q  R  r  S  s  ß  T  t  Þ  þ  U  u  Ú  ú  Ù  ù  Û  û  Ü  ü  V  v  W  w  X
x  Y  y  Ý  ý  ÿ  Z  z
```

Note that an apostrophe wins over a hyphen, which wins over a space, and all three come before other letters and numbers. This means they are essentially ignored unless they are the only difference between entries.

Sorting Months, Weekdays, or Custom Lists

Excel ordinarily sorts text in alphabetical order, but it can sort on the basis of any of its custom lists if you want it to do so. The program includes four custom lists by default

(Sun, Mon, Tues, . . .; Sunday, Monday, Tuesday, . . .; Jan, Feb, Mar, . . .; and January, February, March, . . .). If you have a column consisting of these day or month labels, you can sort them in their proper chronological order. If you've created other custom lists, you can sort text fields in the order of those lists as well.

For information about creating and using custom lists, see "Creating Custom Lists" on page 218.

To sort on the basis of a custom list, simply select Custom List in the Order list in the Sort dialog box. The four default custom lists will appear there, along with any others you have created.

You can use a custom list for any sort field you want. You could sort a column of month names using one custom list and a separate column of day names using a separate custom list, all within one sort operation.

Performing a Case-Sensitive Sort

Usually when Excel sorts text, it disregards case variants entirely. In other words, the program regards the letter *A* as equivalent to the letter *a*. You can change this behavior by clicking Options in the Sort dialog box and then selecting the Case Sensitive check box.

If you're familiar with the standard character-encoding systems used by Windows (ANSI or Unicode), you might suppose that selecting the Case Sensitive check box would cause Excel to sort all capital letters before all lowercase letters. That, after all, is how those character-encoding systems are constructed. (The capital alphabet occupies the range 65 through 90 (decimal notation), and the lowercase alphabet resides at 97 through 122.) However, selecting the Case Sensitive check box does not cause Excel to perform a "straight" ANSI or Unicode sort. Instead, it makes the program put lowercase variants ahead of capital variants *of the same letter.*

For example, suppose the range A1:A4 holds the following four text values:

Pine
pine
Tree
tree

If you perform a default (not case-sensitive) ascending sort on these four cells, their order will remain unchanged, because *p* comes before *t* and Excel disregards the variation in case. If you sort again after selecting the Case Sensitive check box, the order becomes

pine
Pine
tree
Tree

because *p* now comes before *P* and because *t* comes before *T*. In a conventional ANSI sort, you'd get

Pine
Tree
pine
tree

because all capitals come before all lowercase letters.

Filtering a List or Table

Filtering a list or table means hiding all the rows except those that meet specified criteria. Excel provides two filtering methods: Simple, which uses lists on the header row, and Advanced, which uses a separate criteria range. The Advanced method can filter in place or extract a subset to another part of the worksheet. You can use both methods with tables and also with standard lists—as long as the lists have header rows.

Using Filters

When you create a table, Excel adds filters to the header row automatically. To turn header row filters on or off, first select any cell in your table. Then click the Filter button in the Sort & Filter group on the Data tab. When you turn on the filter, Excel displays small arrows next to each of the column headings. Clicking the arrow next to any heading reveals a list of the column's unique values, which you can use to specify filtering criteria.

INSIDE OUT   Display Arrows for Selected Columns

Sometimes, you want to apply filtering criteria to only one or two of your columns. If you're working with a standard list—not a table—you can select only the column headings you want to use as filters (the columns must be adjacent to one another). Then click the Filter button. This makes it clear which columns you are using for filtering.

Let's look at an example. Suppose that from the list shown in Figure 21-4 you'd like to see only those rows where the age is 33. To generate this subset, first make sure the filter arrows appear next to the column headings. If they don't, click the Filter button in the Sort & Filter group on the Data tab. Then click the small arrow next to the Age heading. Clear the Select All check box, then select the 33 check box, and finally click OK. The result looks like Figure 21-11.

From the gaps in the row numbers shown in Figure 21-11, you can tell that Excel has hidden the rows that didn't meet the filtering criterion. To remind you that you have filtered your list, Excel also displays the filtered row numbers in a contrasting color.

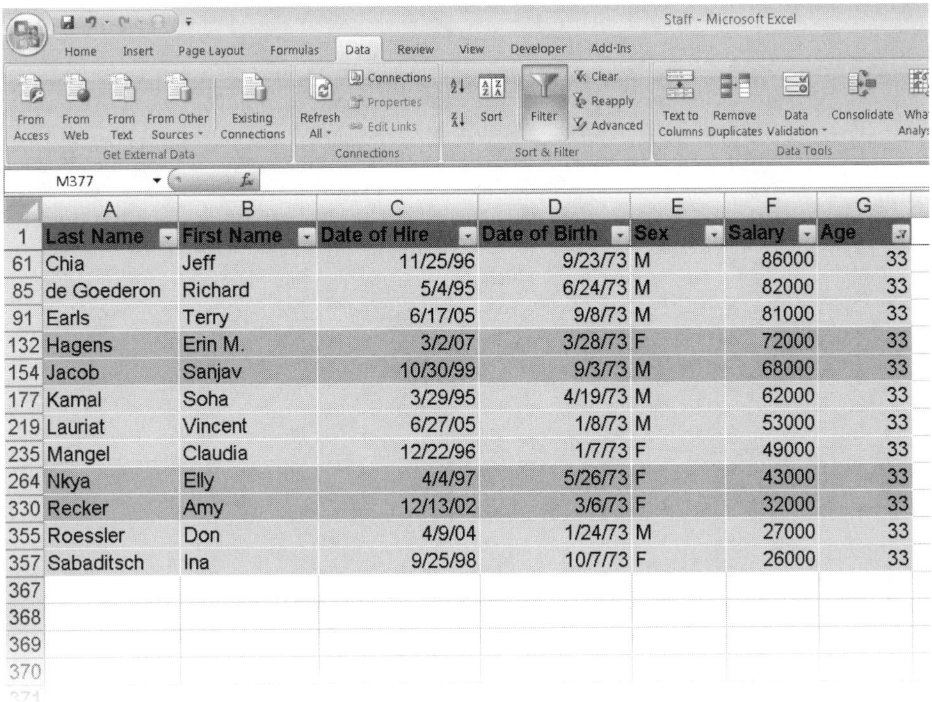

	A	B	C	D	E	F	G
1	Last Name	First Name	Date of Hire	Date of Birth	Sex	Salary	Age
61	Chia	Jeff	11/25/96	9/23/73	M	86000	33
85	de Goederon	Richard	5/4/95	6/24/73	M	82000	33
91	Earls	Terry	6/17/05	9/8/73	M	81000	33
132	Hagens	Erin M.	3/2/07	3/28/73	F	72000	33
154	Jacob	Sanjav	10/30/99	9/3/73	M	68000	33
177	Kamal	Soha	3/29/95	4/19/73	M	62000	33
219	Lauriat	Vincent	6/27/05	1/8/73	M	53000	33
235	Mangel	Claudia	12/22/96	1/7/73	F	49000	33
264	Nkya	Elly	4/4/97	5/26/73	F	43000	33
330	Recker	Amy	12/13/02	3/6/73	F	32000	33
355	Roessler	Don	4/9/04	1/24/73	M	27000	33
357	Sabaditsch	Ina	9/25/98	10/7/73	F	26000	33

Figure 21-11 Use the filter lists to display only those rows in which the age is 33.

As you can see from the selection list, you don't need to select a single item as a filter; you can select as many items from the list as you like. If you can see the item you want to sort by—for example, if you want to see all the rows with the age as 32, and you can see 32 in the list—just right-click the cell you want to match, click Filter, and then click Filter By Selected Cell's Value.

Determining How Many Rows Pass the Filter

Immediately after you add a new filter, Excel displays the number of rows that meet your criteria on the status bar. This information is ephemeral, however. Fortunately, you can use the SUBTOTAL function to arrive at this number. The easiest way to add the SUBTOTAL function is to turn the list into a table. If your list is not already a table, press Ctrl+T, and click OK. Even if you change it back to a range, you want it to be a table long enough to type SUBTOTAL formulas in a total row. After the list is a table, select the Total Row check box on the Design tab to create a total row with a default SUBTOTAL function. The default function displays a sum. To change it to a count, select any cell in the total row, and click the small arrow. Click Count. Otherwise, you can create the Subtotal function yourself.

For more information about the SUBTOTAL function, see "Adding Totals to a Table" on page 673.

Removing a Filter

To remove a filter from a single column, click the small arrow to the right of the column heading, and then click Clear Filter From *Column*. To remove all filters currently in effect, click the Clear button in the Sort & Filter group on the Data tab. To remove the filter arrows, click the Filter button in the Sort & Filter group on the Data tab. This removes the arrows from the header row cells. Converting a table to an ordinary range does automatically turn off the filters, but you can click the Filter button on the Data tab to turn the filters back on without turning the range back into an explicit table.

Using Filter Criteria in More Than One Column

You can specify filter criteria for your list in as many columns as you want. Filter your list on one column, filter the resulting list on another column, and so on. Each successive application of a filter refines the list further so that the result includes only those rows that meet all your criteria.

> **Note**
>
> Basic filter operations always show only the rows that satisfy the criteria for *all* the filtered columns. If you want to see rows that pass either the filter for one column or the filter for another, you need to use the Advanced Filter command.

Using a Filter to Find the Top or Bottom *n* Items

You can use a filter to find the top or bottom *n* items in a numeric column or those items that make up the top or bottom *n* percent of a column's total. Click the arrow for the column, click Number Filters, and then click Top 10. The dialog box shown in Figure 21-12 appears.

Figure 21-12 Use the Top 10 Filter dialog box to zero in on the top or bottom *n* list elements.

The Top 10 Filter dialog box has three boxes. In the first, you can select either Top or Bottom. In the second, you can specify any number from 1 to 500. In the third, you can select either Items or Percent.

Using a Filter to Display Blank Entries

If a column contains blank cells, you find a Blanks check box at the bottom of its filter list. (You open this list by clicking the small arrow to the right of the column header.)

If you want to locate those rows in which a particular column has no entry, select the Blanks check box as your criterion.

Using Filters to Select Dates

Dates can often be frustrating to filter because you usually want to filter based on some kind of grouping. You don't just want March 13, 2008. You want all of March. So in the past, it was usually necessary to create additional columns in the list to calculate just the month or just the year so that you could use those columns as filters. Also, when filtering by dates, you often want to filter by dates that are relative to *now*. For example, you want to see the orders from last month, the plan for next year, or the invoices so far this year. Excel 2007 includes filter capabilities to make all these tasks really simple.

If the column you are filtering by contains dates, the selection list automatically groups the dates into months and years. Click the small arrow for a column that contains dates, and you now see a list of years. You can then expand the years to see months:

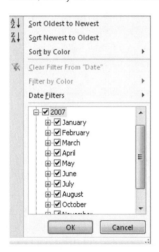

To see individual dates for a month, expand the month heading.

In addition, clicking the Date Filters command in the Filter list gives you many date-specific options, including many that compare the date to the current day—such as Next Month or Last Month.

Using Filters to Specify More Complex Criteria

The example in Figure 21-11 used a single equality comparison for its criterion. That is, we asked Excel to display only those rows in which the Age field was equal to a particular value, 33. Each data type column now has a specialized list of the functions most common to that data type:

- Number filters include comparisons such as Greater Than, Between, and even Above Average.

- Date filters include comparisons such as Yesterday, Next Year, and All Dates In Quarter 1 (regardless of year).

- Text filters include comparisons such as Begins With and Contains.

These data type–specific filtering options can handle most of your basic needs.

Using Custom Filters to Specify Complex Relationships

If you want to get even more complex, you can use the Custom Filter command. To access this command, click the small arrow to the right of a column heading, click the data type–specific menu (such as Number Filter or Data Filter), and then click Custom Filter. The Custom Filter dialog box shown in Figure 21-13 appears. For numeric and date fields, the Custom Filter command is most useful when you use the keyword *or* with two nonequal comparisons in the same column—for example, all the age values less than 25 *or* greater than 65. For text columns, the Custom Filter command lets you create *between* ranges and lets you use sophisticated wildcard comparisons. For example, you might create a filter to find names with *A* as the first letter and *e* as the third letter.

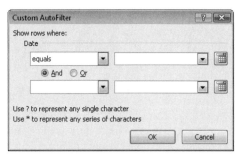

Figure 21-13 Use the Custom Filter dialog box to apply more complex filter criteria to a single column.

You can enter one or two criteria in the Custom Filter dialog box, and you can select from a full range of Excel relational operators. The list boxes on the left side of the dialog box provide a selection of relationships (Equals, Does Not Equal, Is Greater Than, and so on), and the list boxes on the right let you select the values that appear in your list. You can, of course, type directly in the boxes on the right, if you prefer that to fishing through the list for a value.

Suppose, for example, that you want to see all the members of your Staff list with salaries greater than or equal to 90,000 as well as all those with salaries less than or equal to 30,000. After displaying the Custom Filter dialog box for the Salary column, select Is Greater Than Or Equal To in the upper-left box, and type **90000** in the upper-right box. Select the Or option, select Is Less Than Or Equal To in the lower-left box, and type **30000** in the lower-right box. If you neglect to select the Or option, you ask Excel for the names of employees who made both 90,000 or more and 30,000 or less, and you get an empty list.

Finding an Alphabetical Range of Text Values   To find all the text values in a column that fall within a particular range of letters, use the Custom Filter dialog box, and specify two criteria joined by And. For example, to find all last names beginning with B, C, or D, filter the Last Name column, and specify Is Greater Than B and Is Less Than E in the Custom Filter dialog box.

Using Wildcards in Custom Criteria   The Custom Filter dialog box accepts two kinds of wildcard characters. You can use the asterisk (*) to represent any sequence of characters or the question mark (?) to represent any single character. For example, to find all last names starting with B, you can specify Is Equal To B* in the Custom Filter dialog box. To include a literal question mark or asterisk in a filter, precede the ? or * with a tilde (~).

Using the Advanced Filter Command

In contrast to the Filter command, the Advanced Filter command lets you do the following:

- Specify criteria involving two or more columns and the conjunction *OR*.

- Specify three or more criteria for a particular column, where at least one *OR* conjunction is involved.

- Specify computed criteria (for example, all employees whose salaries are more than 25 percent greater than the median salary).

- See in printable form the filters that are applied to the list or table.

In addition, you can use the Advanced Filter command to extract rows from the range, placing copies of those rows in another part of the current worksheet. As with a regular filter, you can use Advanced Filter whether you turn the list into a table or not. Some features—such as showing totals at the bottom—are much easier if you turn the list into a table.

> **TROUBLESHOOTING**
>
> **I can't extract to a separate worksheet.**
>
> You cannot extract rows from a list and place them on a separate worksheet. Your criteria range can be on a different worksheet, but your extract range cannot. After you extract a set of rows, you can, of course, copy or move it to another location.

Specifying a Criteria Range

The Advanced Filter command, unlike the standard filter, requires that you specify filtering criteria in a worksheet range separate from your list or table. Because entire rows are hidden when the filter is executed, it's inadvisable to put the criteria range *alongside* the list. Instead, put it above the list or on a separate worksheet. A criteria range must consist of at least two rows. Type one or more column headings in the top row, and type your filtering criteria in the second and subsequent rows. With the exception of computed criteria, you must spell the headings in your criteria range exactly like those in your list. (Capitalization and formatting don't have to match, but spelling does.) To ensure accuracy, the best way to create these headings is by selecting the column headings in your list and then using the Copy and Paste commands.

Keep in mind that a criteria range does not have to include headings for every column in the list. Columns that are not involved in the selection process don't have to be part of the criteria range.

An Example Using Two Columns Joined by OR

Figure 21-14 shows a list of homes for sale. (The underscored items in column A are hyperlinks to pictures of the houses.) Suppose you're interested in homes with lot size (column H) of at least 2 acres. You'll also consider homes on smaller lots if they're in the elementary-school district U (column O). To filter the list so that homes meeting either criterion are shown, begin by creating the criteria range shown in Figure 21-15. We've created this criteria range above the list, on three newly inserted rows.

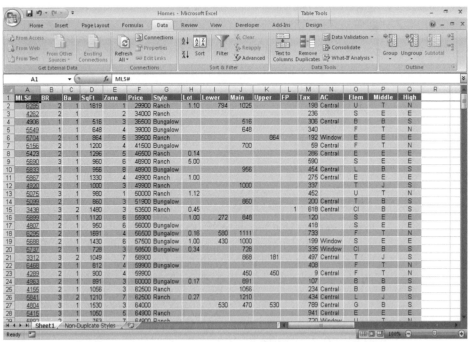

Figure 21-14 Use the Advanced Filter command to locate homes within this list that meet specific criteria.

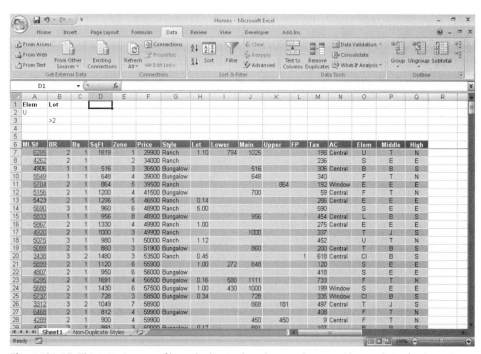

Figure 21-15 This criteria range filters the list to show homes that are either on lots of at least 2 acres or within elementary-school district U.

  You'll find the Homes.xlsx file in the Sample Files section of the companion CD.

You then click Advanced Filter in the Sort & Filter group on the Data tab and fill out the Advanced Filter dialog box, as shown in Figure 21-16. Excel responds by displaying the filtered list shown in Figure 21-17. Some of the Lot fields in that filtered list are blank because the original list didn't include lot-size information about all the homes. Excel treats the blanks as zeros (and therefore less than 2) and includes them only if their Elem fields contain U.

Figure 21-16 In the Advanced Filter dialog box, select Filter The List, In-Place, and specify the addresses of your list and your criteria ranges.

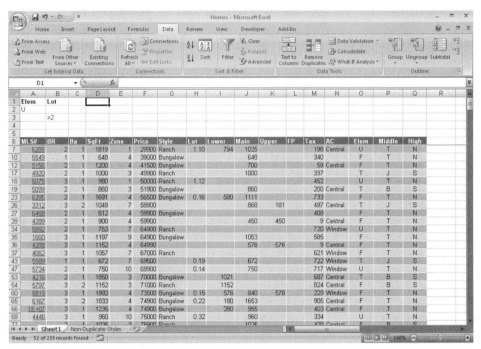

Figure 21-17 Excel responds with a list filtered to show just the homes in which you're interested.

Like a standard filter, the Advanced Filter command hides all rows that don't pass the filter. It also displays the qualifying row numbers in a contrasting color. As with a regular filter, it's worth making the list into a table if you want to add a total row. On the total row, you can easily add a COUNT function to see how many rows passed the filter.

In Figure 21-15, notice that we specified the two criteria on separate lines. This tells Excel to find rows that meet either criterion. If you put the two criteria on the same line, you ask for just those rows that meet both criteria. In other words, criteria on the same line are joined by AND, and criteria on separate lines are joined by OR. You can put as many separate criteria as you like in a criteria range.

We specified both criteria as simple text values. The value U under the Elem heading tells Excel to get any rows with Elem values that begin with the letter *U*. (In other words, there's an implied asterisk wildcard after the U.) If you want the filter to allow only values that match the letter *U* exactly, you type **="=U"**. This clumsy-looking formulation causes the cell to display =U and has the effect of removing the implied asterisk wildcard.

The value >=2 under the Lot heading tells Excel to get rows with Lot values equal to or greater than 2. You can use any of the relational operators >, <, >=, or <= in a numeric criterion. If you want an exact match (all lot sizes of exactly 2 acres, for example), type the number without an operator.

Be aware that a blank cell in a criteria range means "accept any value for this column." If you accidentally include a blank row in the criteria range, you get an unfiltered list.

> **Note**
>
> Provided your criteria range is on the same worksheet as your list, Excel assigns the name Criteria to it immediately after you use it. You can use this behavior as a navigational tool. If you need to return to a criteria range to edit it, you can get there by pressing F5 and selecting Criteria in the Go To dialog box.

An Example Using Three ORs on a Column

Now let's suppose you want to filter the list to show all houses in three elementary-school districts—U, F, and T. You include only the Elem field in the criteria range and type the letters **U**, **F**, and **T** on three separate rows immediately below the heading. The Advanced Filter command then generates the list shown in Figure 21-18.

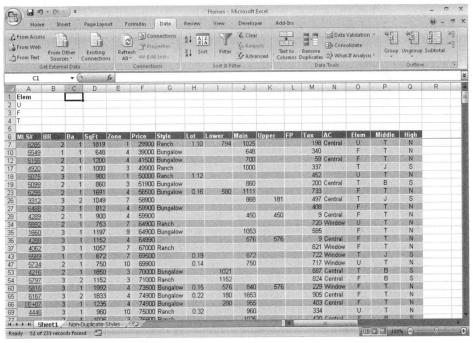

Figure 21-18 Using the criteria range in cells A1:A4 reduces the list to those houses in elementary-school districts U, F, and T.

An Example Using Both OR and AND

If you want to see all houses in middle-school district T or J that are at least 2,000 square feet, you set up the criteria range as in Figure 21-19. The criterion >=2000 appears in cells B2 and B3, because for each of the middle-school districts (T and J), you want to see houses only of 2,000 square feet or more.

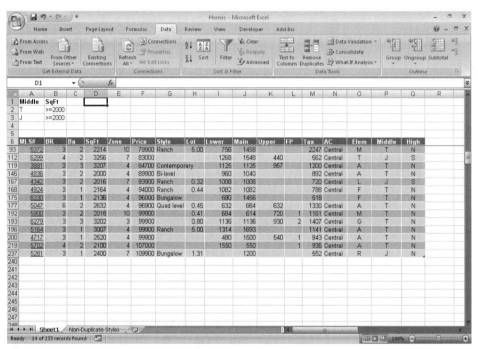

Figure 21-19 To display 2,000-square-foot houses in middle-school districts T and J, repeat the >=2000 criterion in each line of the criteria range.

> **Note**
>
> Each time you use the Advanced Filter command, Excel reexamines the entire list rather than only the rows that passed the most recent filter. Therefore, you don't have to use the Clear command before changing the filter. If you want to refine a filter set—that is, filter the filtrate—add your new criteria to the previous criteria range and filter again.

Applying Multiple Criteria to the Same Column

To apply two or more criteria to the same column, repeat the column in your criteria range. For example, to retrieve rows with Price values from 50,000 to 90,000, your criteria range would look like this:

Price	Price
>=50000	<=90000

To exclude rows with prices in this range but admit everything else, you'd set up this criteria range:

Price	Price
<=50000	>=90000

Using Computed Criteria

Computed criteria involve any test other than a simple comparison of a column's value to a constant. Asking Excel to find houses with prices less than $200,000 does not require a computed criterion. Asking for houses with prices less than the median price of all houses in the list does.

When setting up a computed criterion, observe these rules:

- The column heading above a computed criterion must *not* be a copy of a column heading in the list. This heading can be blank, or it can be anything you want—other than a heading that already appears in the list.

- References to cells outside the list should be absolute.

- References to cells inside the list should be relative—unless you're referencing all the cells in a column.

Let's look at some examples. The next three sections explore referencing cells within the list, referencing a cell outside the list, and referencing all rows in a column.

Referencing Cells Within the List   In cell A2 of Figure 21-20, we used the formula =F6/D6<50 to find all houses with prices per square foot less than $50. Notice that the heading above the criterion (at cell A1) is not a copy of any heading in the list and that the formula uses relative references to fetch values from within the list. F6 and D6 are the relevant values from the first row of the unfiltered list. Excel therefore begins by dividing F6 by D6 and comparing the result to 50. Because the references are relative, it continues by dividing F7 by D7, dividing F8 by D8, and so on.

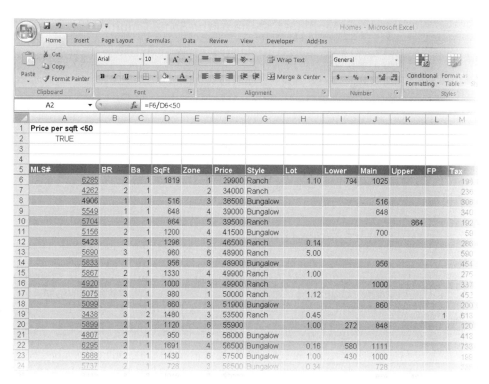

Figure 21-20   The criterion in A2 returns all houses with prices per square foot less than $50.

The formula in A2 happens to return TRUE, because the result of that initial calculation (involving F6 and D6) is TRUE. It doesn't make any difference what that criterion formula returns, however; in fact, as you'll see, it can even return an error value.

In some rows of the unfiltered list, the SqFt column is blank. Dividing by a blank cell always returns the #DIV/0! error constant. This is not a problem. When Excel looks at a row with a blank SqFt value, it compares #DIV/0! with 50, and the result of that comparison is #DIV/0! Because the comparison doesn't yield a TRUE result, the row containing the blank SqFt value is excluded from the filter set—which is, presumably, the outcome you want.

If you've assigned names to the columns of your list, you can use those names instead of first-row cell references in your computed criterion. In other words, with the names SqFt and Price assigned to the appropriate columns, the formula at A2 reads =Price/SqFt<50.

Referencing a Cell Outside the List   The criterion formula in A2 of Figure 21-21 compares prices against the median price, which is stored outside the list, in H1. (The median is calculated with the formula =MEDIAN(price), where price is a name assigned to all cells in the Price column.) The reference to H1 is absolute. If it were not, Excel would compare the price in the first row of the list to H1, the price in the second row to H2, and so on—not what you want.

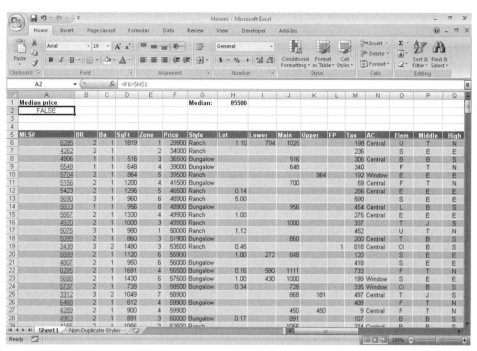

Figure 21-21 This criterion in A2 uses an absolute reference, because the referenced cell, H1, lies outside the list.

Referencing All Rows in a Column   If you change the formula in A2 of Figure 21-21 to =F6>MEDIAN($F$6:$F$238), you get the same set of rows as shown in Figure 21-21. In this case, the MEDIAN function references cells within the list, but the reference has to be absolute. Otherwise, Excel looks at F6:F238 and then at F7:F239, and so on. (You could drop the absolute reference to column F and make the row references absolute. If you use the F4 shortcut to create the absolute references, however, it's just as easy to make the whole reference absolute.)

Extracting Filtered Rows

The Advanced Filter dialog box includes an option for copying the selected rows to another worksheet location, instead of displaying a filtered list. To copy rows rather than display them, select the Copy To Another Location option in the Advanced Filter dialog box, and supply the name or address of the range where you want the information to appear in the Copy To text box.

The easiest way to specify the Copy To range is to click a blank cell in your worksheet where you want the range to start. Be sure the cell has plenty of blank space below and to the right of it. Excel then copies your list's column headings and all the rows that meet the Advanced Filter criteria to the range that begins with the cell you specified. Be careful, though; any data already stored in the selected range will be overwritten.

Alternatively, if you specify a range of cells, Excel copies the rows that pass the filter but stops when the range is full.

If you put the extract range to the side of the source list, be careful not to filter the source list. Filtering the source list hides the entire rows, which will hide rows from your extract range as well. Be sure to either turn off any in-place filters in the source list or put the extract range *below* the source range. Now that Excel 2007 allows a million rows, you should have plenty of room below most lists. The extract range has to be on the same worksheet as the source list, but after you have extracted the list, you can move it to a different worksheet.

> **Note**
>
> When you specify a Copy To range in the Advanced Filter dialog box, Excel assigns the name Extract to that range. You can use this name as a navigational aid. For example, when you need to return to the range to change column headings, select Extract from the Name box to the left of the formula bar.

To copy only certain columns of your list to a new location, create copies of the headings for those columns. Then specify the headings (not only the first cell but the entire set of copied headings) as your Copy To range. Be sure not to select a blank row under the extract headings, or you will get only a single row from the filter.

The Unique Records Only Check Box   The Unique Records Only check box in the Advanced Filter dialog box adds a filter to whatever you specify in your criteria range. It eliminates rows that are duplicates in every respect (not just duplicates in the columns that you happen to be extracting, but duplicates in all columns). The Unique Records Only check box works only in conjunction with the Copy To Another Location option; this option is particularly useful when you are extracting only some of the columns. For example, you could extract only the Price and Style columns. By using the Unique Records Only check box, you would get a list of unique Price/Style combinations from the list.

Removing Duplicate Records

In previous versions of Excel, one reason for using the Unique Records Only check box was to eliminate duplicates from a list. Now that task is much easier, because a special command simply removes duplicate rows from the list. You can use this command in two ways. One way is to simply remove all the duplicate rows—in case there happen to be any. The other way is to select specific columns that you will force to be unique. When you select specific columns, Excel simply chooses the values from all the other columns that happen to be in the first unique combination.

To remove complete row duplicates, select a single cell within the list or table, and click the Remove Duplicates command in the Data Tools group on the Data tab. In the

Remove Duplicates dialog box, leave all the check boxes for the columns selected, and click OK. Excel will tell you how many duplicates it found and how many rows are left.

To remove partial-row duplicates, you will probably want to start by making a copy of the list, because real information will be destroyed in the process. Next, you should sort the list for any columns that you will not include. For example, if you want only one row for each home style but you want that row to be the most expensive home, sort the list in descending order by Price before you execute the Remove Duplicates command.

After you have sorted the list, select a single cell, and click Remove Duplicates. Click the Unselect All button to clear all the check boxes, and then select the check boxes for the few columns in which you want distinct values. For example, you might select only the Style column. Then click OK. You'll end up with a list that contains only the first row for each style—the most expensive, if you sorted the list first.

Using Formulas with Tables

Excel formulas are extremely powerful and useful. They are also extremely cryptic and hard to understand. What exactly does a formula such as =TODAY()–D2 actually mean? Without looking at the worksheet, it's impossible to tell. But what if the formula looked like =TODAY()–[Date of Birth] instead? Just by looking at the formula, you can tell that it calculates the current age in days.

One of the really exciting features of tables in Excel 2007 is the ability to create meaningful formulas in a simple, unambiguous way. One of the most common uses of a formula in a table is to perform a calculation that looks only at values from other rows of the same table. This type of formula is extraordinarily easy.

For example, using traditional formulas, to calculate the (approximate) age in years of each staff member, you would use a formula such as the one in cell G2 in Figure 21-22.

After you change the list to a table, you can edit the formula, and Excel will adjust the reference for you. Just select a cell with the formula, select the cell in the formula with the traditional single-cell reference, and then click the cell you are referring to (in this case, cell D2). Excel automatically replaces the cell address with the name of the table column, as you can see in Figure 21-23.

When you type the formula in the cell, Excel automatically copies the formula to the entire Age column, replacing all the existing formulas.

> **Note**
>
> Excel will automatically replace all the formulas only if they are all equivalent. If you had created an exception formula somewhere in the list, Excel will put the formula into only the one cell, but it adds an AutoCorrect icon that asks whether you want to replace all the formulas in the column with the new formula.

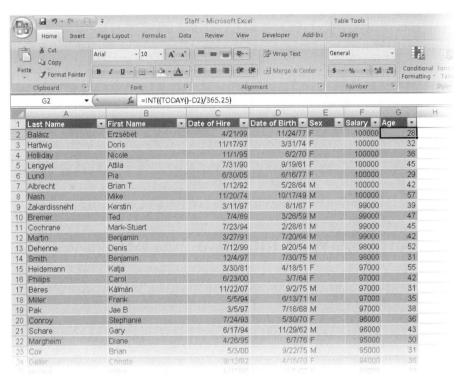

Figure 21-22 The formula in cell G2 uses an ordinary cell reference to D2.

You might wonder about a few characteristics of the formula. First, why did Excel put brackets around the name of the column so it shows up as [Date of Birth]? Well, Excel needs something around the name, because otherwise the spaces in the name could make it hard to tell where the name ends. Simple parentheses wouldn't work well, because they are used in formulas to show calculation order. (Brackets are what Microsoft Office Access 2007 uses to identify column names, and it works pretty well in that application.)

Second, how does the formula know which row to use? In the original formula in cell G2, the reference was D2. When you copy the formula to cell G3, the reference changes to D3. The reference may be a little cryptic, but it's pretty clear the column and the row to which it refers. The reference [Date of Birth] tells which column, but how does Excel know which row? Notice in the traditional reference that the row number in the reference (for example, B2) was always the same as the row number of the cell that contained the formula (for example, G2). The people on the Excel team noticed that in many, many formulas—and especially in formulas in tables—the cell references point to other cells in the *same row*. So they created a rule. If the formula needs a single value (and the minus sign for subtraction needs a single value) and you give it a whole column as the reference, it will pick just the one from the current row. This is called *implicit intersection* because the formula *implicitly* uses the current row to *intersect* the range reference in the formula to get a single cell. (Excel will also implicitly intersect the current column with a horizontal range if necessary, but tables don't have horizontally named rows.)

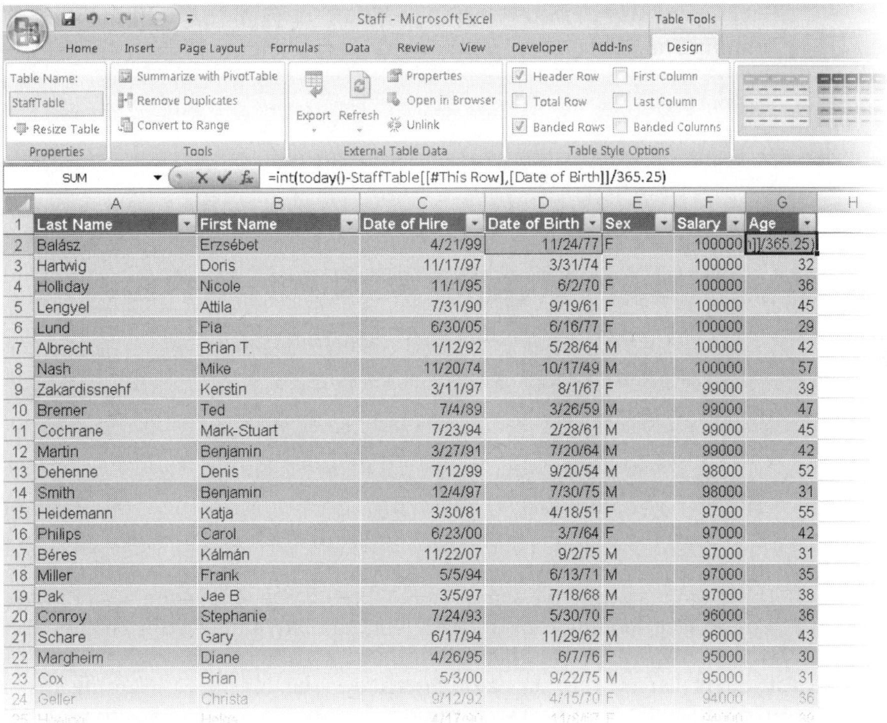

Figure 21-23 By turning the list into a table and editing the formula, we can turn the formula in G2 into something easier to read.

Referencing the Total Row

Sometimes you need to refer to a row that's not the current row. For example, a common calculation in a table involves comparing the current row to the total row. For example, if your table includes sales by regions, you may want to show the percent each region is of the total. Or, because our Staff table example has the age calculated—with the average age in the total row—what if you want to know the age of each staff member compared to the overall average? Excel has a special way to represent the total row in a table formula.

First, type a new heading so Excel will create a new column. Type something like **Versus Avg**. Then, after the new, formatted column appears in the table, select any cell in the column. Type an equal sign to start the formula, and click the Age column for the current row. The formula will say =[Age], showing that it recognizes the Age column. Then type a minus sign (–), and click the cell for the Age column in the total row. (As a keyboard shortcut, press the Left Arrow key to get to the Age column, and then press Ctrl+Down Arrow to jump to the bottom of the table–the total row.) The formula now says =[Age]–TStaff[[#Total],[#Age]]. When you press Enter, Excel inserts the formula into all the cells of the column. You can then apply a number format to the column. The result looks like the worksheet in Figure 21-24.

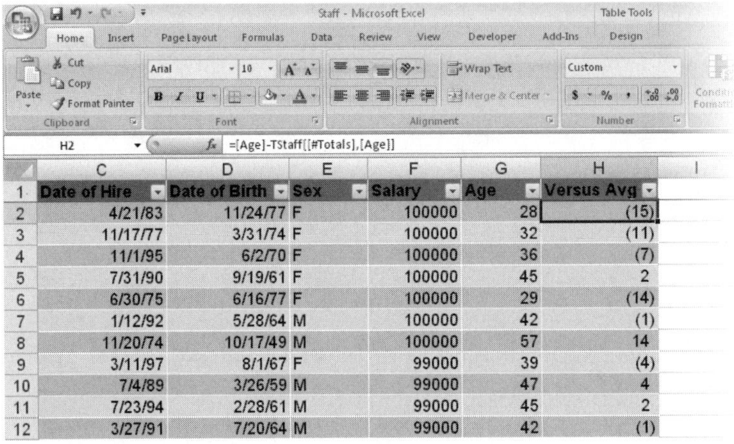

Figure 21-24 This formula uses structured referencing to compare the current row to the total row.

The syntax is a little bit scary, but once you get the hang of it, it's not too bad. The first part, =[Age], should be easy. That's just implicitly intersecting the Age column with the current row. The second part is a little trickier. In the reference TStaff[[#Total],[Age]], TStaff is just an arbitrary name assigned to the table. (See "Naming a Table" on page 671.) [#Total] is a special structured-reference tag that Excel automatically applies to the total row of the table. You can't use the [#Total] tag without first giving the name of the table (Excel wouldn't know which table you meant if you omitted this). So, the full reference has three parts: the name of the table (followed by square brackets), the special structured-reference tag [#Total], and then the column name [Age]. The [#Total] tag and the table column name are separated by a comma.

A structured reference is harder to write than it is to read. Fortunately, Excel will automatically create the structured-reference formula for you as you create new formulas that reference elements of a table.

Explicitly Referencing the Current Row

Implicit intersection lets you use column names in table formulas. It's a great feature and makes formulas much easier to understand and to write. The only time implicit intersection can be a problem is when you use a function that can accept a whole range but you want it to apply to only the current row. Implicit intersection kicks in only when the formula requires a single value–which is typical of arithmetic operations. But functions such as SUM can work just fine with a whole range. Suppose, for example, that you want to sum the scores for different parts of a test—but only for the current student. One way to do this is to simply select each cell separately and use the plus (+) sign to add them. In this way, implicit intersection will work.

But if you have a lot of columns, using a range is easier. Fortunately, Excel has a special structured-reference tag, [#ThisRow], that *explicitly* limits the range to the current row. And Excel automatically adds that special tag when you create a formula that uses a function such as SUM over multiple columns of the current row. Figure 21-25 shows the formula Excel generates when you create a sum of multiple columns in the current row.

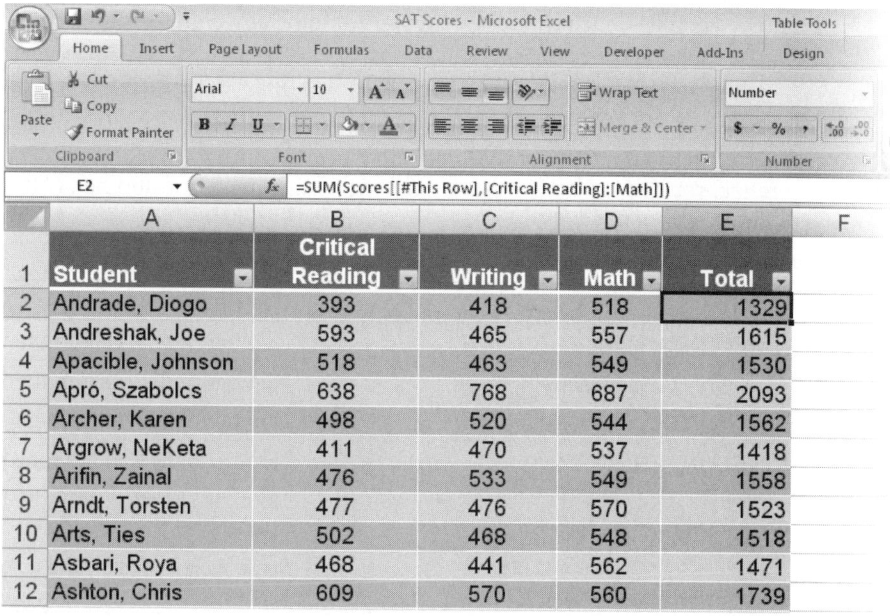

Figure 21-25 The [#This Row] tag tells Excel to total values from the current row only.

The formula =SUM(Scores[[#This Row],[Writing]:[Math]]) includes the standard SUM function. The reference follows the same pattern as when referring to the total row. There's the name of the table, followed by brackets. Within the brackets is the special structured-reference tag [#This Row], followed by a comma. Finally, there is the part that specifies the column. In this case, you're specifying a range of columns, so the formula uses the range (:) operator between two table column names.

Referencing Parts of a Table

In addition to the [#This Row] tag, whose explicit meaning changes depending on the cell containing the formula, Excel has four structured-reference tags for other parts of the table. Table 21-1 lists the tags, along with their meanings.

Table 21-1 **Some Additional Structured-Reference Tags**

Tag	Meaning
#Data	The data region of the table, excluding the header and total rows. If you refer to the table with no qualifier, this is what you get.
#Totals	The total row (if there is one).
#Headers	The header row (if there is one).
#All	The entire table, including headers, data, and totals.

These names are all row oriented. #Totals and #Headers reference single rows, but #Data and #All include all rows. If you combine any of these with a column name, you get the intersection. If you combine multiple row-oriented names, you get the union. For example, [#Headers],[#Data] results in everything *except* the totals.

Table 21-2 provides some example formulas that use the COUNTA function with structured-reference tags. Because each formula returns the total number of cells in a range, you can see how the different tags interact with one another. (All formulas reference a table named Staff.)

Table 21-2 **Some Formulas That Combine Structured-Reference Tags**

Formula	Description
=COUNTA(Staff)	Number of data cells in the table body
=COUNTA(Staff[Salary])	Number of data cells in the Staff column
=COUNTA(Staff[#Headers])	Number of cells in the header row
=COUNTA(Staff[#Totals])	Number of cells in the total row
=COUNTA(Staff[#Data])	Number of data cells in the table (same as referencing the table name alone)
=COUNTA(Staff[[#Data],[Salary]])	Same as referencing the column name alone
=COUNTA(Staff[#All])	Number of cells in the entire table, including the header and total row
=COUNTA(Staff[[#All],[Salary]])	Number of cells in one column, including header and total row
=COUNTA(Staff[[#Headers],[#Data]])	Number of cells in the table, including headers but excluding the total row
=COUNTA(Staff[[#Headers],[#Data],[Salary]])	Number of cells in one column, including headers but excluding the total row

You can use the pointer to generate almost all of these combinations while constructing a formula. To select the #Data portion of the table, rest the pointer on the top-left corner of the table until it changes to a black arrow that points down and to the right, and then click once. To select the #All portion of the table, rest the pointer on the same place, but double-click. To select a column's #Data area, rest the pointer on the top of the column until it turns into a black arrow that points down, and then click once. To select the

#All area for the column, rest the pointer on the same place, but double-click. To select the #Header and #Data combination, you have to manually edit the formula.

When you get used to the brackets, the structured references are much more meaningful than simple cell addresses. And if you change the size of a table, the structured names will automatically adjust. If you change the label in a column heading, any formulas that reference that column will automatically adjust.

> **Note**
>
> How structured reference tags work is a lot more detailed, especially when you include special characters such as & or [in the heading for a column. The details are described in the online Help topic "Using structured references with Excel tables." To find the topic, search for *Structured References*.

Formatting Tables

It is easy in Excel 2007 to make a table look really good. Just select any cell in the table, click the Design tab under Table Tools, and then select a style. The styles have several elements, and you can turn elements on or off at will. To see the full range of elements for the built-in styles, select all the check boxes in the Table Style Options group before selecting a style. The table in Figure 21-26 uses one of the Dark styles—Table Style Dark 6—because it shows the different elements quite clearly.

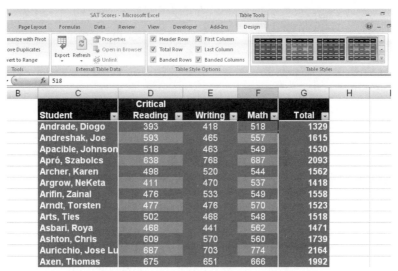

Figure 21-26 This example shows a Dark style, with all six of the Table Style Options selected.

As you clear different check boxes in the Table Style Options group, the appearance of the previews in the Table Styles list change accordingly. The Header Row and Total Row options are different from the other options in that turning them on or off actually changes the structure of the table, not just the format. If you want to have a header row or a total row but don't want a special format for it, you can customize the style, as explained in the next section.

The Banded Rows and Banded Columns options make every other row or column change colors. Including both tends to make the table a little busy. By default, the style definitions alternate one row (or column) dark with one row (or column) light. You can customize the number of rows (or columns in each band). The First Column and Last Column options are like the Header Row and Total Row options but for columns. Many times, as in Figure 21-26, the first column contains names or some other unique label and looks better with a distinct format. It is also often common—again, Figure 21-26 is an example—to have a total column at the right that deserves its own format.

In terms of formatting priority, the header row and total row have priority over any of the columnar formats. Next come the column formats—the First Column, Last Column, and Banded Columns options take precedence over Banded Rows. In cases such as our example, where you can still see banding on the rows even though the Banded Columns option is selected, it means that one of the column bands has no format applied, which lets the lowly row banding show.

> **Note**
>
> If you do not see any changes when you apply a table style, you may have already applied cell formatting to the cells. If that's the case, right-click the Table Styles group on the Ribbon, and click Apply And Clear Formatting. If the format still doesn't work properly—for example, if the font does not change when you change styles—your workbook may have a customized Normal cell style. Make sure the Normal cell font is set to use the current theme's Body font.

Using Themes to Change Style Appearance

Styles are designed to be used with themes. A theme specifies two fonts: Heading and Body. Excel tables use the Body font for all the cells styled with the Table Styles list. Built-in Excel table styles also take advantage of the background/text colors and accent colors defined in the theme. This means you can easily change the look of a table by switching the theme or by changing the font or the colors of the current theme. Excel tables don't use the Effects component of a theme.

To dramatically change the look of a table by switching to a new theme, select any cell in the table, and then click the small arrow below the Themes button in the Themes group on the Page Layout tab. As you rest the pointer on the different themes, you can see the change in the table. Click the theme you like.

To change the color scheme of the current theme without changing the font, click the arrow to the right of the Colors button in the Themes group, and select a new color scheme. To select a new font without changing the colors, click the arrow to the right of the Fonts button in the Themes group. Remember that Excel tables use only the Body font style.

> **Note**
>
> Technically, Excel table styles use the font from the cell style named Normal, and the default font for the Normal cell style is the Body font. If you change the Normal style to use a font that is not the heading or the totals, then the font will not change when you switch themes. If you want the Excel table styles to automatically use the Heading font rather than the Body font, then change the Normal style to use the current Heading font. Changing the Normal style will affect all unformatted cells in the workbook and also the row and column heading labels.

Customizing Table Styles

You can easily create your own style by cloning one of the built-in styles and then modifying its settings. To clone a style, on the Design tab under Table Tools, right-click any style, and click Duplicate. The Modify Table Quick Style dialog box, as shown in Figure 21-27, appears. With this dialog box, you can format individual elements of the style.

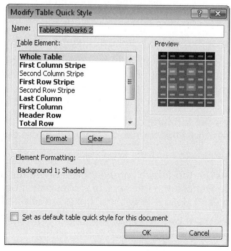

Figure 21-27 You can create your own styles by duplicating and modifying existing ones.

Most of the configurable elements relate directly to the check boxes in the Table Style Options group on the Design tab. If an item in the list is bold, it means that element has a custom format. If the item is not bold, it means the format of the "next layer down" will apply. So, for example, if you clear the formatting for Header Row, then the First Column and Last Column formats will apply to the first and last cells of the header row. (Note: Even if you clear the formatting for header and total rows, a default underlying style consists of the underlying table format plus a bold font; you can't clear that underlying style.)

When you select a modified style element—that is, one that is bold—you can see a brief description of what is different about the element, including the font style, the font theme color, the border definition, and whether there is a background shading.

Table 21-3 describes the table style elements.

Table 21-3 The Elements of a Table Style

Element	Description
Whole Table	Underlying style that applies to everything.
First Column Stripe	Applies only when the Banded Rows check box is selected. Formats the first column and then alternates with the Second Column Stripe format. Set Stripe Size to control how many columns will have this format before cycling to the Second Column Stripe format.
Second Column Stripe	Applies only when the Banded Rows check box is selected. Formats the alternate columns with the First Column Stripe format. Leave it unformatted to show the underlying formatting (including row stripes). Set Stripe Size to control how many columns will have this format before cycling back to the First Column Stripe format.
First Row Stripe	Same as First Column Stripe except applies to row banding.
Second Row Stripe	Same as Second Column Stripe except applies to row banding.
Last Column	Corresponds directly to the Last Column check box.
First Column	Corresponds directly to the First Column check box. Whether First Column is set or not, the First Column Stripe format applies to the same first column. In other words, this format hides the first column of the First Column Stripe format.
Header Row	Controls the formatting of the header row. The check box does not just toggle this format; it completely hides the header row.
Total Row	Corresponds to the Total Row check box.
First Header Cell	Formats the top-left cell of the table—where the header row and the first column intersect. It applies only if both the First Column and Header Row check boxes are selected.
Last Header Cell	Formats the top-right cell of the table if both the Header Row and Last Column check boxes are selected.
First Total Cell	Formats the bottom-left cell of the table if both the Total Row and First Column check boxes are selected.
Last Total Cell	Formats the bottom-right cell of the table if both the Total Row and Last Column check boxes are selected.

After you've created your customized style, it appears at the top of the gallery of styles. You can modify and delete only the styles you've created. After you create a style, you may need to click that style to apply it to the table.

To modify a table style element, right-click the custom style, and click Modify (if you're not already in the Modify Table Quick Style dialog box). Select the element you want to modify, and click Format. Click the tab for the element you want to modify—for example, to change the cell background, click the Fill tab. Select one of the theme colors, and click OK. Then select another element, or click OK to accept the format changes.

When you modify a table style, you cannot choose the font. The table style always uses the font from the Normal cell style (which defaults to the Body theme font). You *can* set the font style, size, and effects. When you modify a table style, it's a good idea to choose theme colors—or their tones and tints, not a custom color. If you choose a custom color, the color won't change when you switch to a new theme.

Chapter 21

A PivotTable report is a special kind of table that summarizes information from selected fields of a data source. The source can be a Microsoft Office Excel 2007 list, a relational database file, an Online Analytical Processing (OLAP) cube, or multiple *consolidation ranges* (multiple ranges containing similar data, which the PivotTable can assemble and summarize). When you create a PivotTable, you specify which fields you're interested in, how you want the table organized, and what kinds of calculations you want the table to perform. After you build the table, you can rearrange it to view your data from alternative perspectives. This ability to "pivot" the dimensions of your table—for example, to transpose column headings to row positions—gives the PivotTable its name and its analytical power.

Introducing PivotTables

PivotTables are linked to the data from which they're derived. If the PivotTable is based on external data (data stored outside Excel), you can choose to have it refreshed at regular time intervals, or you can refresh it whenever you want.

Figure 22-1 shows Books.xlsx, a list of sales figures for a small publishing firm. The list is organized by year, quarter, category, distribution channel, units sold, and sales receipts. The data spans a period of eight quarters (2005 and 2006). The firm publishes six categories of fiction (Mystery, Western, Romance, Sci Fi, Young Adult, and Children) and uses three distribution channels—domestic, international, and mail order. It's difficult to get useful summary information by looking at a list like this, even though the list itself is well organized.

 You'll find the Books.xlsx file in the Sample Files section of the companion CD.

Figure 22-1 It's difficult to see the bottom line in a flat list like this; turning the list into a PivotTable will help.

Figures 22-2 through 22-4 show several ways you can transform this flat table into PivotTables that show summary information at a glance.

The example on the left in Figure 22-2 breaks the data down first by category, second by distribution channel, and finally by year, with the total sales at each level displayed in column B. Looking at this table, you can see (among many other details) that the Children category generated domestic sales of $363,222, with more revenue in 2005 than in 2006.

In the example on the right in Figure 22-2, the per-category data is broken out first by year and then by distribution channel. The data is the same; only the perspective is different.

Left PivotTable

Row Labels	Sum of Sales
Children	420838
Domestic	363222
2005	198675
2006	164547
International	43879
2005	24423
2006	19456
Mail order	13736
2005	6089
2006	7648
Mystery	89346
Domestic	103749
2005	105564
2006	-1815
International	-21474
2005	4274
2006	-25749
Mail order	7072
2005	1825
2006	5247
Romance	928462
Domestic	837227
2005	779354
2006	57873
International	81707
2005	31369
2006	50338

Right PivotTable

Row Labels	Sum of Sales
Children	420838
2005	229186
Domestic	198675
International	24423
Mail order	6089
2006	191651
Domestic	164547
International	19456
Mail order	7648
Mystery	89346
2005	111663
Domestic	105564
International	4274
Mail order	1825
2006	-22317
Domestic	-1815
International	-25749
Mail order	5247
Romance	928462
2005	818721
Domestic	779354
International	31369
Mail order	7999
2006	109740
Domestic	57873
International	50338
Mail order	1530

Figure 22-2 These two PivotTables provide summary views of the information in Figure 22-1.

Both the PivotTables shown in Figure 22-2 are single-axis tables. That is, we've generated a set of row labels (Children, Mystery, Romance, and so on) and set up outline entries below these labels. (And, by default, Office Excel 2007 displays outline controls beside all the headings, so we can collapse or expand the headings to suit our needs.)

Figure 22-3 shows a more elaborate PivotTable that uses two axes. Along the row axis, we have categories broken out by distribution channel. Along the column axis, we have years (2005 and 2006). And we added the quarterly detail (not included in the Figure 22-2 examples) so we can see how each category in each channel did each quarter of each year. With four *dimensions* (category, distribution channel, year, and quarter) and two axes (row and column), we have a lot of choices about how to arrange the furniture. Figure 22-3 shows only one of many possible permutations.

Chapter 22

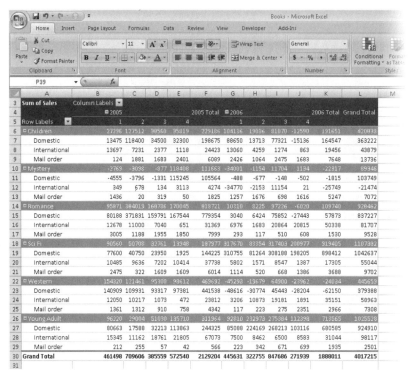

Figure 22-3 In this PivotTable, we've rearranged the data along two axes—rows and columns.

Figure 22-4 presents a different view. Now the distribution channels are arrayed by themselves along the column axis, while the row axis offers years broken out by quarters. The category, meanwhile, has been moved to what you might think of as a page axis. The data has been filtered to show the numbers for a single category, Mystery, but by using the filter control at the right edge of cell B2, we could switch the table to a different category (or combination of categories). Filtering the Category dimension by one category after another would be like flipping through a stack of index cards.

None of these tables required more than a few clicks to generate.

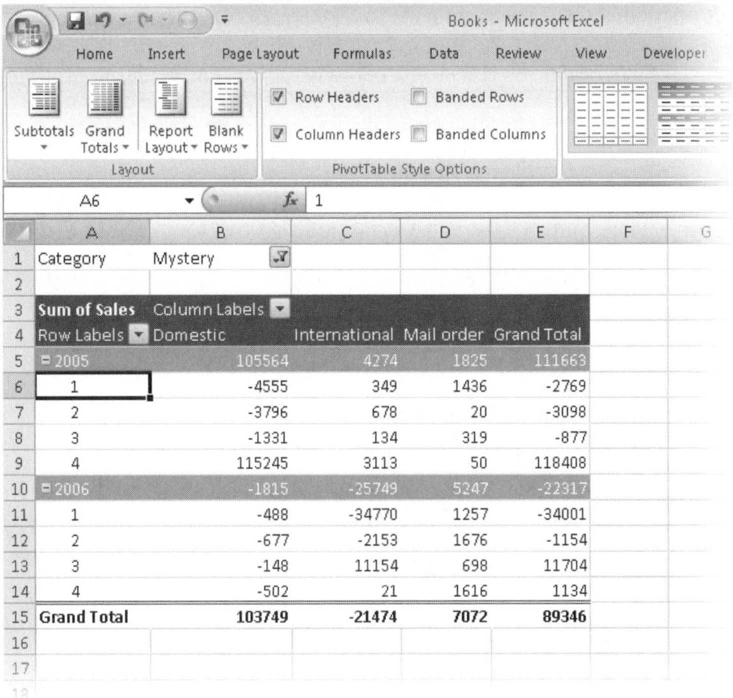

Figure 22-4 This PivotTable presents a "filtered" view, confining the report to a single category.

Creating a PivotTable

You can create a PivotTable from either an Excel range or an external data source. If you're working from an Excel range, your data should meet the criteria for a well-constructed list. That is, it should have column labels at the top (the headings will become field names in the PivotTable), each column should contain a particular kind of data item, and you should not have any blank rows within the range. If the range includes summary formulas (totals, subtotals, or averages, for example), you should omit them from the PivotTable; the PivotTable will perform its own summary calculations.

For information about connecting to and querying external data sources, see Chapter 23, "Working with External Data."

The source range on your Excel worksheet can be a table (as described in Chapter 21, "Managing Information in Tables") or an ordinary list. Starting from a table has the advantage of allowing for expansion. When you create a PivotTable from a table, Excel references your source data by its table name (either a default name, such as Table1, or the name you assign to the table). If you add rows to a table, the table name automatically adjusts to encompass the new data, and hence your PivotTable stays in sync with the expanded source data.

For information about converting a list to a table, see "Creating a Table" on page 669.

To create a PivotTable, select a single cell within the source data and do either of the following:

- Click the Insert tab, and then click PivotTable (in the Tables group).

- If your source data is a table and you're currently on the Design tab under Table Tools, click Summarize With PivotTable (in the Tools group).

Either way, the Create PivotTable dialog box appears. If your source data has a name (we've assigned the name BookSales to the source table in our example), that name appears in the Table/Range box. Otherwise, Excel discerns the extent of your source data and presents a range reference in that box:

By default, your PivotTable arrives on a new worksheet, and that's generally a good arrangement. If you want it elsewhere, specify where in the Location box. After you click OK, Excel generates a blank table layout on the left side of the worksheet and displays the PivotTable Field List window on the right (see Figure 22-5). The PivotTable Field List window is docked at the right by default. You can make it wider or narrower by dragging the split bar on its left edge. You can also undock it or drag it across the worksheet and dock it on the left.

> **Note**
>
> If you want to work with only a subset of items in a field, you can filter the field before you add it to the table. If your data source is large, and particularly if the source is external, you can save some time by filtering in advance. (You can also filter fields after you have created the table, of course.) To filter a field before you add it to the table, select the field name in the PivotTable Field List window, and then click the arrow on the right. For more details, see "Filtering PivotTable Fields" on page 728.

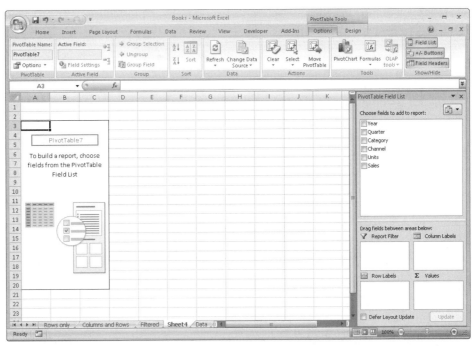

Figure 22-5 As you select the check boxes for fields in the PivotTable Field List window, Excel populates the table layout at the left side of the worksheet.

To put some fields and data on that blank layout, begin by selecting the check boxes for those fields in the Choose Fields To Add To Report area of the PivotTable Field List window. As you select fields, Excel positions them in the four boxes below. These four boxes represent the various components of the table. The Row Labels and Column Labels boxes hold the fields that will appear on the row and column axes. The Report Filter box holds the field (or fields) you want to use to filter the table (comparable to the Category field in Figure 22-4), and the Values box holds the field (or fields) you want to use for calculations—the data you're summarizing (your sales, for example).

Initially, Excel puts selected fields in default table locations that depend on their data types. Most likely you'll want some arrangement other than the one you get by default. That's not a problem, because you can move fields from one location to another easily; just drag them between the various boxes below the PivotTable Field List window. Let's look at an example.

To create the table shown in Figure 22-3, we want to put the Category and Channel fields in the Row Labels box, the Year and Quarter fields in the Column Labels box, and the Sales field in the Values box. When we select the check boxes for those fields, Excel drops the Category and Channel fields in the Row Labels box (because they are text fields) and the Sales field in the Values box (because it's a numeric field). These are all good guesses on the part of Excel—and, in fact, it's just what we want. In addition to putting field headings in the appropriate boxes, Excel begins creating our PivotTable—as Figure 22-6 shows.

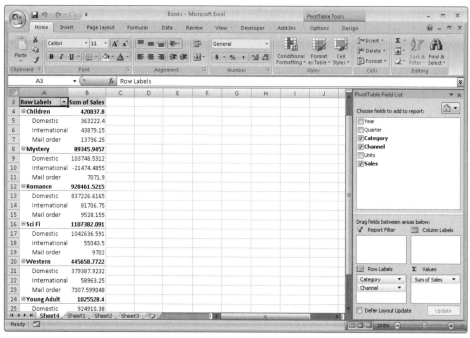

Figure 22-6 Excel builds the table, piece by piece, as you select fields.

So far, so good. The numeric formats aren't right, but we can fix that easily enough.

What remains is to put the Year and Quarter fields into the Column Labels box. Unfortunately, if we simply select their check boxes, Excel drops these fields in the Values box, because the fields are numbers and the program has a predilection for adding numbers. This (see Figure 22-7) is definitely not what we want.

The solution is simple: Select the check boxes for the Year and Quarter fields, and then drag the Sum of Quarter and Sum of Year headings from the Values box to the Column Labels box. (Alternatively, you can make sure your field headings go where you want them by dragging them directly from the Choose Fields To Add To Report box to the appropriate boxes below, disregarding the defaults.)

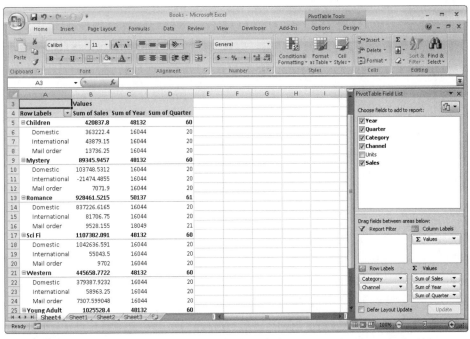

Figure 22-7 By default, Excel puts all numeric fields, including years and quarters, in the Values box. You can fix that by dragging field headings to the appropriate locations.

Rearranging PivotTable Fields

To pivot, or rearrange, a PivotTable, drag one or more field headings from one part of the PivotTable Field List window to another. For example, by using the mouse to change this configuration of the PivotTable Field List window:

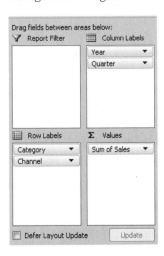

to this one:

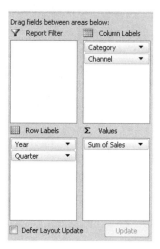

we can change the table from the form shown in Figure 22-3 to this:

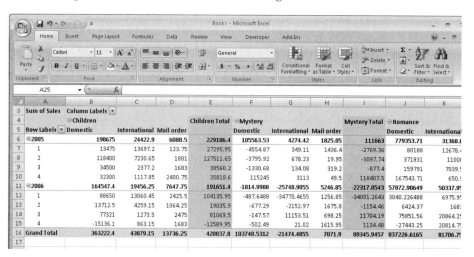

Note

If you don't see the PivotTable Field List window, select a cell in the PivotTable (it disappears when your selection is not within the table). If you still don't see it, click the Options tab under PivotTable Tools on the Ribbon, and then click Field List. This button is a handy way to toggle the field list in and out of view, letting you reduce distraction when you don't need to do any field rearrangement.

INSIDE OUT   Pivot Your Tables the Excel 2003 Way If You Prefer

Earlier versions of Excel let you move fields around by dragging them directly on the table, instead of requiring you to work with the PivotTable Field List window. If you prefer that way of working, right-click any cell in the PivotTable, and click PivotTable Options. In the PivotTable Options dialog box, click the Display tab. Then select the Classic Pivot-Table Layout (Enables Dragging Of Fields In The Grid) check box. Note, however, that this option also changes the appearance of your table from the compact, outline-style pre-sentation of Excel 2007 to the more space-consuming tabular style of earlier versions.

To rearrange fields within the same axis—for example to put Year before Quarter or Channel before Category in Figure 22-3, you can drag field headings from one place to another within the same area of the PivotTable Field List window. Often it's simpler to click the arrow to the right of the field heading you want to move. (For example, you might click the arrow to the right of Category in the Row Labels box.) The menu that appears includes easy-to-use positioning commands:

Refreshing a PivotTable

Because users often generate PivotTables from large volumes of data (and in many cases that data resides on external servers), Excel doesn't automatically update PivotTables when their source data changes. To refresh a PivotTable, right-click any cell within it, and click Refresh. Alternatively, under PivotTable Tools, click the Options tab, and then click Refresh in the Data group. Or, if you like keyboard shortcuts, press Alt+F5.

To ensure that your PivotTable is sorted whenever you open the file, click a cell within the table, click the Options tab under PivotTable Tools, and then click Options in the PivotTable group. In the PivotTable Options dialog box, click the Data tab. Then select the Refresh Data When Opening The File check box, and click OK.

Changing the Numeric Format of PivotTable Data

As Figure 22-6 shows, Excel initially displays numeric PivotTable data in the General format, regardless of how it's formatted in your source range. To fix that, right-click a cell in the field you want to change, and then click Number Format.

Choosing Report Layout Options

PivotTables in Excel 2007, by default, use a more compact presentation style than earlier versions used. This default layout (called Compact) indents inner fields on the row axis beneath their outer fields, letting you see more information at a glance. If you prefer, you can select from two alternative layouts, called Outline and Tabular. To switch from one layout to another, select a cell within the table, click the Design tab under PivotTable Tools, click Report Layout (in the Layout group), and then click one of the displayed layouts (Show In Compact Form, Show In Outline Form, or Show In Tabular Form). Figure 22-8 compares the three layout options.

Note that the layout options affect the row axis only. For example, the outline form simply indents the distribution channels below each category of book.

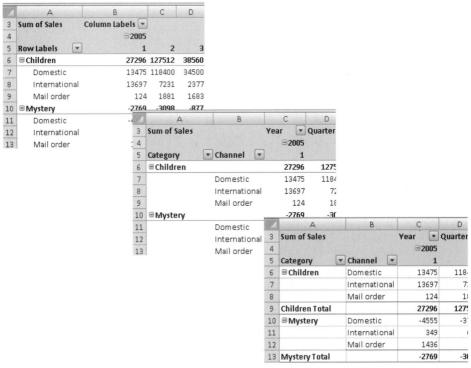

Figure 22-8 Excel offers three PivotTable layout options: Compact (left), Outline (center), and Tabular (right).

Formatting a PivotTable

The Design tab that appears on the Ribbon under PivotTable Tools when you select any part of a PivotTable includes a large selection of professionally designed PivotTable styles. These work just like—and, in fact, are similar to—the styles available with ordinary tables. By choosing from the PivotTable Styles gallery, you can ensure that your PivotTable looks good and uses colors consistent with the rest of your workbook. You can customize the built-in style choices by selecting or clearing the check boxes in the PivotTable Style Options group, and you can add your own designs by clicking New PivotTable Style at the bottom of the PivotTable Styles gallery. To display the PivotTable Styles gallery, click the More button at the bottom of the scroll bar. (This button is a small arrow with a line above it.) For more information about using and customizing built-in styles, see "Formatting Tables" on page 705.

Customizing the Display of Empty or Error Cells

Empty cells in a PivotTable are usually displayed as empty cells. If you prefer, you can have your PivotTable display something else—a text value such as NA, perhaps—in cells that would otherwise be empty. To do this, right-click any cell in the PivotTable, and click PivotTable Options. On the Layout & Format tab in the PivotTable Options dialog box, select the For Empty Cells Show check box, and in the text box type the text or value that you want to see.

If a worksheet formula references a cell containing an error value, that formula returns the same error value. This is usually true in PivotTables as well. Error values in your source data propagate themselves into the PivotTable. If you prefer, you can have error values generate blank cells or text values. To customize this aspect of PivotTable behavior, right-click any cell in the PivotTable, and click PivotTable Options. On the Layout & Format tab in the PivotTable Options dialog box, select the For Error Values Show check box. Then, in the text box, type what you want to see.

Merging and Centering Field Labels

When you have two or more fields stacked either on the column axis or on the row axis of a PivotTable, centering the outer labels over the inner ones can sometimes improve the table's readability. Just right-click a PivotTable cell, click PivotTable Options, and then select the Merge And Center Cells With Labels check box on the Layout & Format tab in the PivotTable Options dialog box. With this option, you can change this kind of presentation:

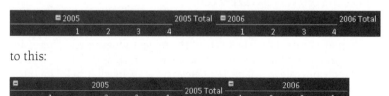

to this:

Hiding Outline Controls

You'll probably find outline controls useful in some contexts and not in others. They're great when you have large or complex PivotTables and you want to be able to switch quickly from a details view to an overview. But if you find they clutter the picture instead of enhancing it, you can banish them easily: Select a PivotTable cell, click the Options tab under PivotTable Tools, and then click the +/– Buttons in the Show/Hide group.

> **Note**
>
> With outline controls suppressed, you can still expand and collapse field headings. Select a heading in the field you're interested in, click the Options tab under PivotTable Tools on the Ribbon, and then click Expand Entire Field or Collapse Entire Field in the Active Field group.

Hiding *Row Labels* and *Column Labels*

The headings *Row Labels* and *Column Labels* that Excel displays near the upper-left corner of your PivotTable may prove distracting at times. You can suppress them by selecting a PivotTable cell, clicking the Options tab under PivotTable Tools, and then clicking Field Headers in the Show/Hide group. Note, however, that removing these labels also removes their associated filter controls—and you might want those controls from time to time (see "Filtering PivotTable Fields" on page 728). The Field Headers command is a toggle. Click it again to restore the headings—and the filter controls.

> **Note**
>
> You can change the name of a PivotTable field or an item within a field by selecting any occurrence of it and typing the name you want. When you change one occurrence, all occurrences in the table change.

Displaying Totals and Subtotals

By default, Excel generates grand totals for all outer fields in your PivotTable using the same summary function as the body of the table. In Figure 22-3, for example, row 30 displays grand totals for each quarter of each year, as well as for the years themselves. Column L, meanwhile, displays per-category totals by channel. The intersection of column L and row 30 displays the grandest of totals, the sum of all sales for the period covered by the table. Because the body of the table uses the SUM function, all these grand totals do as well.

To remove grand totals from a PivotTable, right-click any cell in the table, and click PivotTable Options. On the Totals & Filters tab in the PivotTable Options dialog box, clear the Show Grand Totals For Rows check box, the Show Grand Totals For Columns check box, or both check boxes.

Naturally, PivotTables are not restricted to calculating sums. For other calculation options, see "Changing PivotTable Calculations" on page 731.

Customizing Subtotals

By default, Excel creates subtotals for all but the innermost fields. For example, in Figure 22-3, cell B6 displays the sum of cells B7:B9 (the Children subtotal for Quarter 1 of 2005), cell C10 displays the sum of cells C11:C13 (the Mystery subtotal for Quarter 2 of 2005), and so on. Columns F and K display yearly subtotals. The innermost fields, Channel (for the row axis) and Quarter (for the column axis), do not have subtotals.

To find options affecting all subtotals, select a cell in the PivotTable, click the Design tab under PivotTable Tools, and then click Subtotals on the left edge of the Ribbon:

You can use this menu to turn subtotaling off altogether or to move row-axis subtotals from their default position above the detail items to a position below.

To customize subtotals for a particular field, right-click an item in the field, and then click Field Options. (Alternatively, select an item in the field, click the Options tab under PivotTable Tools, and then click Field Settings in the Active Field group.) Figure 22-9 shows the Field Settings dialog box for the Category field in our example PivotTable.

The Automatic option on the Subtotals & Filters tab in this dialog box means—as Automatic means throughout Excel—you're letting the program decide what to do. In other words, this option gets the default behavior. You can turn off subtotals for the selected field by selecting None. Selecting Custom lets you change the default subtotal calculation, such as from Sum to Average. And, as the text above the function list suggests, you're not limited to one function. You can select as many as you need by holding down Ctrl while you click. Figure 22-10 shows a PivotTable with four subtotaling calculations applied to the Category field. (Note that when you have multiple subtotals for a field, Excel moves them below the detail.)

Figure 22-9 In the Field Settings dialog box, you can override the default subtotaling behavior for a particular field.

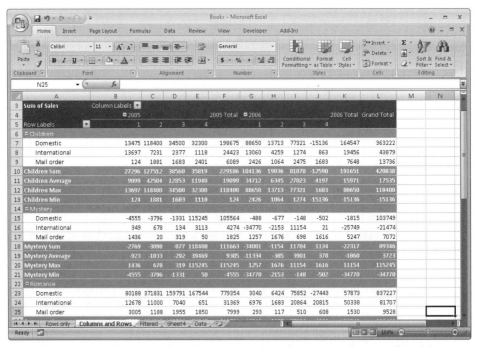

Figure 22-10 You can generate subtotals using more than one summary function; this table uses four for the Category field.

By using the Field Settings dialog box, you can also generate subtotals for innermost fields—subtotals that Excel usually does not display. Such inner subtotals appear at the bottom of the table (just above the grand total row) or at the right side of the table (just to the left of the grand total column). Figure 22-11 shows an example of inner-field subtotaling.

	A	B	C	D	E	F	G	H	I	J	K	L	M
3	Sum of Sales	Column Labels											
4		2005				2005 Total	2006				2006 Total	Grand Total	
5	Row Labels	1	2	3	4		1	2	3	4			
6	Children												
7	Domestic	13475	118400	34500	32300	198675	88650	13713	77321	-15136	164547	363222	
8	International	13697	7231	2377	1118	24423	13060	4259	1274	863	19456	43879	
9	Mail order	124	1881	1683	2401	6089	2426	1064	2475	1683	7648	13736	
10	Mystery												
11	Domestic	-4555	-3796	-1331	115245	105564	-488	-677	-148	-502	-1815	103749	
12	International	349	678	134	3113	4274	-34770	-2153	11154	21	-25749	-21474	
13	Mail order	1436	20	319	50	1825	1257	1676	698	1616	5247	7072	
14	Romance												
15	Domestic	80188	371831	159791	167544	779354	3040	6424	75852	-27443	57873	837227	
16	International	12678	11000	7040	651	31369	6976	1683	20864	20815	50338	81707	
17	Mail order	3005	1188	1955	1850	7999	293	117	510	608	1530	9528	
18	Sci Fi												
19	Domestic	77600	40750	23950	1925	144225	310755	81264	308188	198205	898412	1042637	
20	International	10485	9636	7202	10414	37738	5802	1571	8547	1387	17305	55044	
21	Mail order	2475	322	1609	1609	6014	1114	520	668	1386	3688	9702	
22	Western												
23	Domestic	140909	109931	93317	97381	441538	-48616	-30774	45443	-28204	-62150	379388	
24	International	12050	10217	1073	472	23812	3206	10873	19181	1891	35151	58963	
25	Mail order	1361	1312	910	758	4342	117	223	275	2351	2966	7308	
26	Young Adult												
27	Domestic	80663	17588	32213	113863	244325	85088	224169	268213	103116	680585	924910	
28	International	15345	11162	18761	21805	67073	7500	8462	6500	8583	31044	98117	
29	Mail order	212	255	57	42	566	223	342	671	699	1935	2501	
30	Domestic Sum	388280	654704	342440	528257	1913681	438429	294118	774869	230035	1737452	3651132	
31	International Sum	64605	49925	36587	37573	188689	1773	24694	67519	33560	127546	316235	
32	Mail order Sum	8614	4978	6532	6710	26834	5429	3942	5298	8344	23013	49847	
33	Grand Total	461498	709606	385559	572540	2129204	445631	322755	847686	271939	1888011	4017215	
34													

Figure 22-11 Subtotals for Channel, an inner field, appear in rows 30–32 of this table.

Sorting PivotTable Fields

You can sort a PivotTable field either by its own items (for example, alphabetizing the categories in Figure 22-11) or on the basis of values in the body of the table (for example, sorting categories in descending order of sales totals so the best-selling categories appear at the top). To sort a field, right-click any item in that field, and then click Sort. On the menu that appears, you can click Sort A To Z or Sort Z To A if you want to sort the field by its own items. If you want to sort the field by values in the body of the table, click More Sort Options. You'll see a dialog box similar to the one shown on the next page (with the name of the field you selected in the title of the dialog box).

To sort by values in the table body instead of by items in the selected field, open the Ascending or Descending list. The list will include the available value fields.

> **Note**
> To ensure that Excel retains your sort specification when you update your PivotTable, click More Options in the dialog box shown above. Then select Sort Automatically Every Time The Report Is Updated.

Filtering PivotTable Fields

Filtering a field lets you focus your table on a subset of items in that field. You can filter on the basis of the field's own content (only the Children and Young Adult categories, for example) or on the basis of values associated with the field (for example, the three categories with the best overall sales). You can apply filters either in the PivotTable Field List window or on the PivotTable. If you're working with a large external data source and you need only a subset of the data, you can save yourself some time by filtering in the PivotTable Field List window before you execute the query and create the table.

To filter in the PivotTable Field List window, select the heading for the field you want to filter, and then click the arrow to the right of the field heading. The dialog box that appears includes check boxes for each unique item in the selected field:

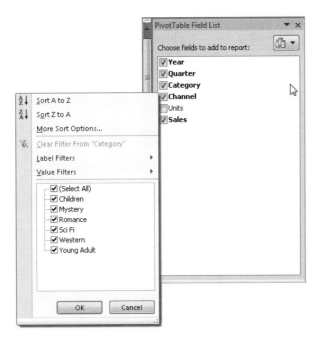

You can use the check boxes to select one or more particular items in your selected field. If your field is more complex than the example here, you might want to click Label Filters, in response to which Excel presents many additional filtering options:

Chapter 22

The options that appear on this menu are tailored for the data type of the selected field. If your field holds dates instead of text, for example, you will see these options:

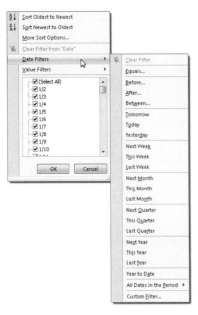

To filter a field on the basis of values associated with that field, click the arrow next to the field heading in the PivotTable Field List window, and then click Value Filters on the menu that appears. For example, to filter the PivotTable in Figure 22-3 so it shows only the three categories with the highest total sales, click the arrow beside Category, and then click Value Filters. In the Value Filters menu:

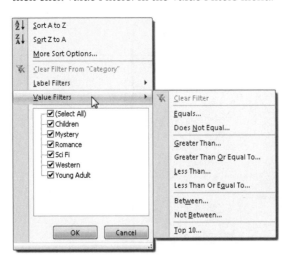

you would click Top 10, which would take you to the Top 10 Filter dialog box:

where you replace the 10 with a 3 and then click OK. Figure 22-12 shows the result.

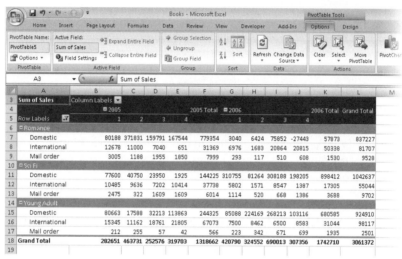

Figure 22-12 We filtered the table to show only the three best-selling categories.

Note that when you apply a value filter to a field, Excel bases its calculations on the current grand total associated with that field. If we wanted to see the three top-selling categories for the year 2005 (in the example shown in Figure 22-3), we would need to filter the Year field as well as the Category field.

Changing PivotTable Calculations

By default, Excel populates the Values area of your PivotTable by applying the SUM function to any numeric field you put there or by applying the COUNT function to any nonnumeric field. But you can choose from many alternative forms of calculation, and you can add your own calculated fields to the table.

Using a Different Summary Function

To switch to a different summary function, right-click any cell in the Values area of your PivotTable, and then click Value Field Settings. (Alternatively, click the Options tab under PivotTable Tools, and then click Field Settings in the Active Field group.) Excel displays the Value Field Settings dialog box, shown in Figure 22-13. Select the function you want from the Summarize Value Field By list, and then click OK.

Chapter 22

Figure 22-13 Using this dialog box, you can change the function applied to a field in the Values area of your PivotTable.

Excel fills in the Custom Name line in this dialog box according to your selection in the Summarize Value Field By list. If you switch from SUM to AVERAGE, for example, the Custom Name line changes to include the word *Average*. You can type whatever you like there, though.

Applying Multiple Summary Functions to the Same Field

You can apply as many summary functions as you want to a value field. To use a second or subsequent function with a field that's already in the Values area of your PivotTable, drag another copy of the field from the PivotTable Field List window into the Values box. Then select a Values area cell, return to the Value Field Settings dialog box, and select the function you want to use. The available functions are SUM, COUNT, AVERAGE, MAX, MIN, PRODUCT, COUNT NUMBERS, STDDEV, STDDEVP, VAR, and VARP.

Using Custom Calculations

In addition to the standard summary functions enumerated in the previous paragraph, Excel also offers a set of custom calculations. With these you can have each item in the Values area of your table report its value as a percentage of the total values in the same row or column, create running totals, or show each value as a percentage of some base value.

To apply a custom calculation, right-click a cell in the Values area, and then click Value Field Settings. Click the Show Values As tab in the Value Field Settings dialog box. Then select a calculation from the Show Values As list. Table 22-1 lists the available options.

When you select a calculation in the Show Values As list, the Base Field and Base Item boxes display choices that are relevant to your calculation. For example, as Figure 22-14 shows, if you select Difference From in our books example, the Base Field box displays Quarter, Category, Channel, and so on. If you select Quarter in this list, the Base

Item box presents the four quarters, along with the self-explanatory items (Previous) and (Next).

Table 22-1 Custom Calculation Options

Difference From	Displays data as a difference from a specified base field and base item
% Of	Displays data as a percentage of the value of a specified base field and base item
% Difference From	Displays data as a percentage difference from a specified base field and base item
Running Total In	Displays data as a running total
% Of Row	Displays each data item as a percentage of the total of the items in its row
% Of Total	Displays each data item as a percentage of the grand total of all items in its field
Index	Uses this formula: ((value in cell) * Grand Total of Grand Totals)) / ((Grand Row Total) * (Grand Column Total))

Figure 22-14 When you choose a calculation such as Difference From, the Base Field and Base Item boxes display relevant options.

Figure 22-15 and Figure 22-16 illustrate some ways you can modify default calculations and Values field names. The table in Figure 22-15 lists 2006–2007 performances at major opera houses around the world by theater, country, opera, composer, and performance date. The PivotTable in Figure 22-16 includes the Date field twice in the Values box. The default summary calculation for date data is Count, and that's fine because we want the number of performances and counting dates is a way to get that. But we used the Custom Name box in the Value Field Settings dialog box (refer to Figure 22-13) to change the name from Count of Date to No. of Performances. When we dragged the second instance of the Date field into the Values box, we used the Value Field Settings dialog box to make the field report the percentage of total. You could use similar techniques with other kinds of polling or survey applications.

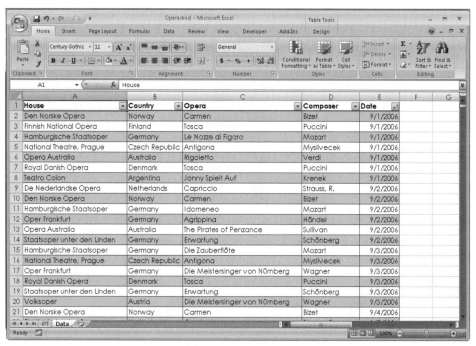

Figure 22-15 From this table, a PivotTable will apply the COUNT function to the Date field to count performances.

You'll find the OperaSked.xlsx file in the Sample Files section of the companion CD.

> **Note**
> If you filter a field, percentage-of-total calculations are based on the data that meets the filter criterion, not the unfiltered data set.

Using Calculated Fields and Items

In case custom calculations don't meet all your analytic needs, Excel lets you add calculated fields and calculated items to your PivotTables. A *calculated field* is a new field, derived from calculations performed on existing fields in your table. A *calculated item* is a new item in an existing field, derived from calculations performed on other items that are already in the field. After you create a custom field or item, Excel makes it available to your table, as though it were part of your data source.

Custom fields and items can apply arithmetic operations to any data already in your PivotTable (including data generated by other custom fields or items), but they cannot reference worksheet data outside the PivotTable.

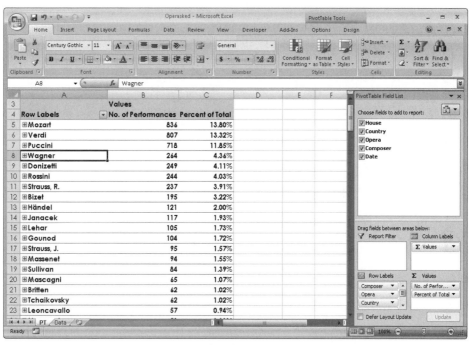

Figure 22-16 The PivotTable uses the Date field from Figure 22-15 twice—once to count performances, a second time to calculate percentage of total.

Creating a Calculated Field

To create a calculated field, select any cell in the PivotTable. Then click the Options tab under PivotTable Tools, and click Formulas in the Tools group. On the Tools menu, click Calculated Field. Figure 22-17 shows the Insert Calculated Field dialog box.

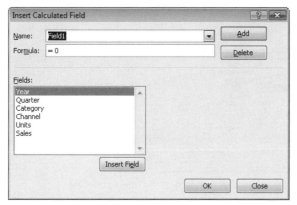

Figure 22-17 Create a calculated field in this dialog box.

Type a name for your calculated field in the Name box. Then type a formula in the Formula box. To enter a field in the formula, select it from the Fields list, and click Insert Field. Figure 22-18 shows an example of a calculated field.

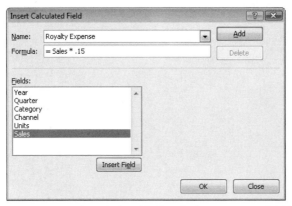

Figure 22-18 This calculated field multiples an existing field by a constant.

Excel adds a new calculated field to your PivotTable when you click either Add or OK. You can then work with the new field using the same techniques you use to work with existing fields.

Creating a Calculated Item

To create a calculated item for a field, select any existing item in the field or the field heading. Then click the Options tab under PivotTable Tools, and click Formulas in the Tools group. On the Formulas menu, click Calculated Item. Excel displays a dialog box comparable to the one in Figure 22-19.

Figure 22-19 Use this dialog box to create a calculated item for a field.

To create a calculated item, type a unique name for the item in the Name box. Then enter a formula in the Formula box. You can select from the Fields and Items lists and click Insert Field and Insert Item to enter field and item names in the formula.

> **Note**
> You cannot create calculated items in fields that have custom subtotals.

Figure 22-20 shows an example of a calculated item. In this case the new item represents domestic sales divided by the sum of international and mail order sales.

Figure 22-20 This calculated item will appear by default whenever you include the Channel field in the PivotTable.

Displaying a List of Calculated Fields and Items

To display a list of your calculated fields and items, along with their formulas, click the Options tab under PivotTable Tools, and then click Formulas in the Tools group. On the Formulas menu, click List Formulas. Excel displays the list on a new worksheet, as shown in Figure 22-21.

As the note in Figure 22-21 indicates, you need to be careful when a cell in your table is affected by more than one calculated field or item. In such cases, the value is set by the formula that's executed last. The Solve Order information in the list of calculated fields and items tells you which formula that is. If you need to change the solve order, select the worksheet that contains the PivotTable, click the Options tab under Pivot-Table Tools, and then click Formulas in the Tools group. On the Formulas menu, click Solve Order.

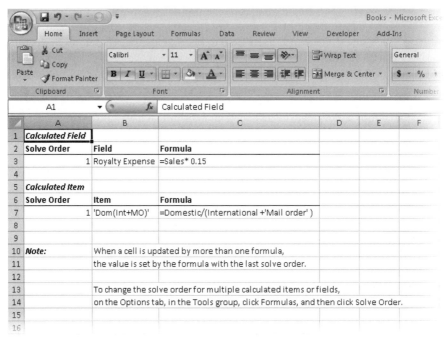

Figure 22-21   Excel lists calculated fields and items on a new worksheet.

Grouping and Ungrouping Data

PivotTables group inner field items under each outer field heading and, if requested, create subtotals for each group of inner field items. You might find it convenient to group items in additional ways—for example, to collect monthly items into quarterly groups or sets of numbers into larger numeric categories. Excel provides several options for grouping items.

Creating Ad Hoc Item Groupings

Suppose that after looking at Figure 22-3 you decide you'd like to see the domestic and international sales figures grouped into a category called Retail. To create this group, select the Domestic and International items anywhere in the table. Then click the Options tab under PivotTable Tools, and click Group Selection in the Group group. Excel creates a new heading called Group1:

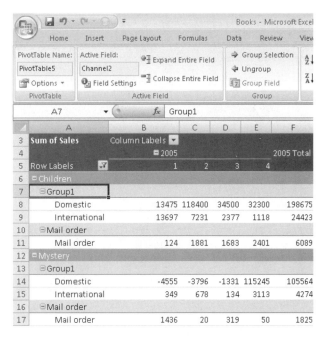

Now you can rename Group1 by simply typing over any instance of it.

Grouping Items in Date or Time Ranges

Figure 22-22 shows a PivotTable that summarizes daily transactions by payee. As you can see, the data in this table is extremely sparse. Most intersections between a day item and a payee item are blank.

You'll find the Transactions.xlsx file in the Sample Files section of the companion CD.

To make this kind of table more meaningful, you can group the date field. To do this, select an item in the field. Then click the Options tab under PivotTable Tools, and click Group Field. Excel responds by displaying the Grouping dialog box, shown in Figure 22-23.

Excel gives you a great deal of flexibility in the way your date and time fields are grouped. In the By list, you can choose any common time interval, from seconds to years, and if the standard intervals don't meet your needs, you can select an arbitrary number of days. You can also create two or more groupings at the same time (hold down Ctrl while you select); the results of grouping by both Quarter and Month are shown in Figure 22-24.

Chapter 22

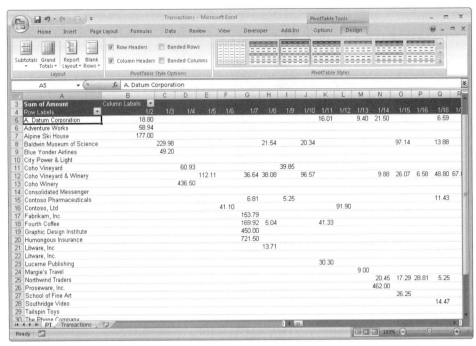

Figure 22-22 To make the data in this table more meaningful, you can group the date field.

Figure 22-23 Excel gives you lots of ways to group by date.

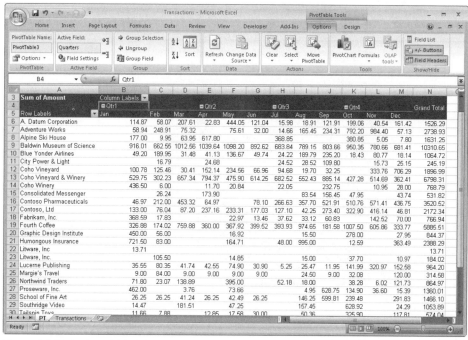

Figure 22-24 In this table, daily data is grouped by months and then by quarters.

Displaying the Details Behind a Data Value

If you double-click any PivotTable value that represents a summary calculation, Excel displays the details behind that calculation on a new worksheet. For example, in Figure 22-24, cell B13 informs us that we spent $529.75 at Coho Vineyard & Winery during the month of January. Double-clicking B13 reveals the details, as shown on the next page.

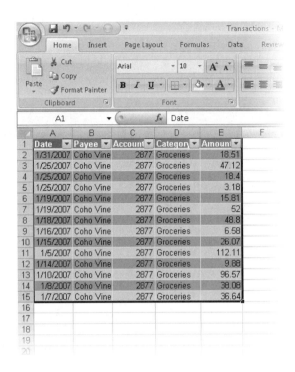

Creating PivotCharts

PivotCharts, like PivotTables, summarize tabular information and allow for easy transposition of fields and axes. They're a great way to study or present elements of your data set.

You can create a PivotChart directly from your source data by selecting a cell in the original data range, clicking the Insert tab, clicking the arrow beneath PivotTable in the Tables group, and then clicking PivotChart. After you specify or confirm your data source and indicate where you want the new PivotChart to reside (in a location either on the existing worksheet or on a new worksheet), Excel presents both a PivotTable layout and a blank chart canvas, along with a PivotChart Filter Pane (see Figure 22-25). Excel creates a PivotTable at the same time it creates a PivotChart—and hence you see a blank table layout. The PivotChart Filter Pane doesn't really add any capability that isn't available via the PivotTable Field List window, so you might want to close one or the other to make more room on the worksheet.

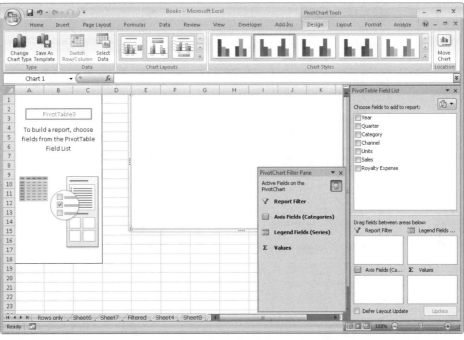

Figure 22-25 When you create a new PivotChart, Excel draws a blank chart canvas as well as a blank table layout. The program creates a PivotTable at the same time it creates the PivotChart.

Figure 22-26 shows a simple PivotChart created from this chapter's Books table. Because charts are generally most effective when applied to a modest amount of data, we've used the Report Filter box to restrict the presentation to a single category (Children), and we've filtered the Channel field to show international and mail order sales only. We've also tidied up a bit by closing the PivotTable Field List window and dragging the PivotChart Filter Pane to a less obtrusive position.

As you can see, when you select a PivotChart, Excel adds a new set of tabs on the Ribbon, under PivotChart Tools. With these tabs, you can manipulate and format your PivotChart the same way you would an ordinary chart. (For details about working with charts, see Chapter 19, "Basic Charting Techniques," and Chapter 20, "Charting Beyond the Ribbon.")

A PivotChart and its associated PivotTable are inextricably linked. You can manipulate fields and axes in either, and the other stays in step.

Chapter 22

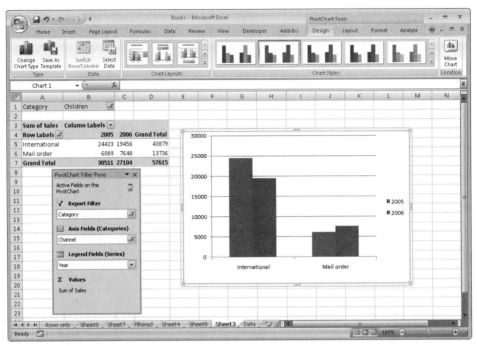

Figure 22-26 We've used a PivotChart to plot two distribution channels for one book category.

In Figures 22-25 and 22-26, we created a PivotChart directly from the source data. You can also create one from an existing PivotTable. Select any cell in the PivotTable, click the Options tab under PivotTable Tools, and then click PivotChart in the Tools group.

Working with External Data

Microsoft Office Excel 2007 is a superb tool for analyzing data, but before you can do any analysis, you have to get the data into Excel. In many cases, the information you need resides somewhere "outside"—on a server, on a Web site, in an XML file, or perhaps in a database program such as Oracle or Microsoft Office Access. Office Excel 2007 supports a wide variety of data formats, including SQL Server (and SQL Server Analysis Services), Access, dBase, FoxPro, Oracle, Paradox, and various kinds of text files. We'll look at some techniques for retrieving external data in this chapter.

Using and Reusing Data Connections

An Office Data Connection (.odc) file is a small XML file that records information about how a workbook connects to an external data source. Such information can include the location and type of the external data, a query specification (if the connection is designed to retrieve a subset of the external source), and details about how to log on to the external server. ODC files are designed to facilitate the reuse of external connections.

Often the simplest way to import data from an external source is to execute an ODC file—a connection that either you or someone else has already established. To see what connections are available, click the Data tab on the Ribbon, and then click Existing Connections in the Get External Data group. A dialog box comparable to the one shown in Figure 23-1 appears.

In Figure 23-1, the Show list, at the top of the dialog box, is set to display all available connection files. You can use this list to restrict the dialog box to connections that are already open on your computer, connections that are already in use in the current workbook, or connections that are available on your network. If a connection file that you're looking for doesn't appear in the Existing Connections dialog box, click Browse For More. This will invoke the Windows Vista search facility, which will gather connection files from various locations on your computer.

Figure 23-1 The Existing Connections dialog box lists connection files that are already established for you.

You can distinguish the various types of connection files that appear in the Existing Connections dialog box by their types of icons. In the examples that follow, we'll assume that you're opening one that looks like Northwind 2007 Customers in Figure 23-1. This connection file enables Excel to import data from an Access database. If you open one of the Web query connections (the three included in Excel 2007 begin with "MSN MoneyCentral Investor"), the dialog boxes you see will be somewhat different from the ones described here. (For more about Web queries, see "Using a Web Query to Return Internet Data" on page 779.)

To open a connection file, double-click it in the Existing Connections dialog box. The Import Data dialog box, shown in Figure 23-2, appears. In this dialog box, you indicate where you want the data to go and whether you want an ordinary table or a PivotTable.

If you accept the default settings, Excel creates a table at the current cell location. (For information about creating a PivotTable, see Chapter 22, "Analyzing Data with Pivot-Table Reports.") The resulting table behaves like any other Excel table (see Chapter 21, "Managing Information in Tables"), except for a crucial difference: The table remains linked to its external source, letting you refresh the data (update it with any changes that have occurred in the external source) on demand or at regular time intervals.

Figure 23-2 By default, Excel renders imported data as a table. Using the Import Data dialog box, you can create a PivotTable (or PivotTable and PivotChart) instead.

Setting Refresh Options

To specify how you want the data refreshed, you can click Properties in the Import Data dialog box (see Figure 23-2). Alternatively, after the table (or PivotTable) has been created, select a cell within it, click the Data tab, and then click Properties. In the External Data Properties dialog box that appears, click the Connection Properties button (to the right of the Name box):

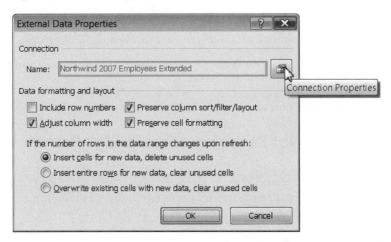

These steps bring you to the Connection Properties dialog box, shown in Figure 23-3. Your refresh options appear on the Usage tab in this dialog box.

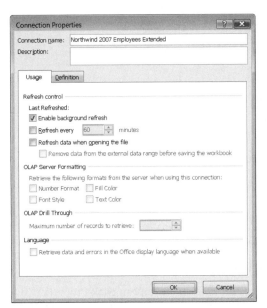

Figure 23-3 You can set your connection to refresh the imported data at regular time intervals.

The check boxes in the Refresh Control area in this dialog box are not mutually exclusive. You can have Excel refresh your data whenever you open the file as well as at regular time intervals. The Enable Background Refresh check box, selected by default, means you can do other work in Excel while the refresh is in progress. Note that this option is not available with online analytical processing (OLAP) queries.

If you select the Refresh Data When Opening The File check box, an additional option to remove the data from your worksheet when you close the file becomes available. You might as well select this check box as well, because Excel is going to refresh the data when you reopen the file anyway.

Requiring or Not Requiring a Password to Refresh

If connecting to your external data requires a password, Excel, by default, will require that you supply the password again whenever you refresh. If that's a burdensome obligation, click the Definition tab in the Connection Properties dialog box. Then clear the Save Password check box.

Refreshing on Demand

In addition to requesting a refresh at regular time intervals, you can refresh the data whenever the need arises. Right-click a cell within the table, and then click Refresh. Alternatively, click the Data tab, click the arrow next to Refresh All, and then click Refresh. (Or simply click Refresh All; this refreshes all connections open in the current workbook.)

Opening an Entire Access Table in Excel

To import an entire table created in Access (as opposed to a specific set of records from that table), click the Data tab, and then click From Access in the Get External Data group. Windows Vista will launch a search for files with the extensions .mdb, .mde, .accdb, and .accde. When you find the Access file you're looking for, select it, and then click Open. You'll be presented with the Select Table dialog box, which is shown in Figure 23-4. (Drag the lower-right corner of the Select Table dialog box if you need to see more of the Description column.)

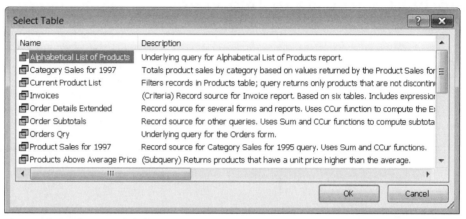

Figure 23-4 When you click the From Access command to open an Access file, the Select Table dialog box asks you to choose which table you want to import.

For information about importing selected records from an Access (or other) database using Microsoft Query, see "Using Microsoft Query to Import Data" on page 759.

The Select Table dialog box actually lists not only tables from your Access file but certain views as well. (The items shown in Figure 23-4, for example, are all views from the Northwind database that Microsoft supplies as a sample file with Access.) If you open any Access view in Excel, you get all the records currently displayed by Access in that view. If you open a table, you import all the records in that table. In either case, the data you import becomes either a table or a PivotTable in Excel, depending on how you complete the Import Data dialog box (see Figure 23-2).

You can set refresh parameters for your imported Access data the same way as for any other data connection. For details, see "Setting Refresh Options" on page 747.

Chapter 23

> **Note**
>
> You can also import an Access table by clicking the Microsoft Office Button, clicking Open, and then selecting Access Databases from the list beside the File Name box. (The resulting table or PivotTable behaves as if you had used the From Access command on the Ribbon.) You cannot save an Excel range as an Access table, however.

Working with Data in Text Files

Excel can read data in fixed-width as well as delimited text files. (A *delimited* file is one that uses some particular character or combination of characters to mark the boundaries between fields. A *fixed-width* file is one that uses space characters—as many as necessary—to achieve field alignment.) You can either open a text file (by clicking the Microsoft Office Button and clicking Open) or import it (by clicking the Data tab and then clicking From Text in the Get External Data group). If you want to be able to maintain a refreshable link to the source file, you need to do the latter.

When you open a comma-separated-values (.csv) file, Excel parses the data immediately into columns. If you open or import any other kind of text file, Excel presents the Text Import Wizard, described next.

> **Note**
>
> When you ask Excel to open or import a text file, the program looks for files with the extensions .prn, .txt, and .csv. If you want a file with a different extension, select All Files in the list to the right of the File Name box. Excel determines a file's type by its content, so it doesn't matter what the extension is.

Using the Text Import Wizard

With the Text Import Wizard, you can show Excel how to parse your text file. You get to tell the program what character or character combination (if any) is used to delimit columns, what kind of data appears in each column, and what character set or language was used to create the original file. You can also use the Text Import Wizard to exclude one or more rows at the top of your file—an option that's particularly useful if your file begins with some kind of noncolumnar descriptive information.

The first page of the wizard, shown in Figure 23-5, presents a preview of the data that Excel is about to import. It also indicates the best estimation of whether your file is delimited or fixed-width. You'll find that the wizard is usually correct with this first guess—but if it's mistaken, you can set it straight. (If you're not sure, just go to the second page. When you get there, you'll know whether the program was wrong, and you can return to the first page to fix the problem.)

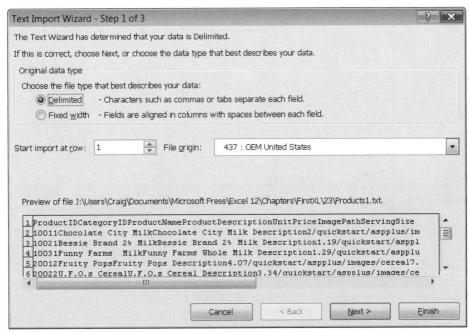

Figure 23-5 You can use the Text Import Wizard to tell Excel how to parse your text file.

While you're still on the first page of the wizard, use the Start Import At Row text box to eliminate any header rows that you can live without in Excel. Header rows make it hard for Excel to parse your file correctly, so you can help the program (and yourself) by lopping them off here. Click Next.

The second page of the Text Import Wizard looks something like either Figure 23-6 or Figure 23-7, depending on whether your file is delimited or fixed-width. In both cases, the vertical lines in the Data Preview section show how Excel proposes to split your file into columns. The Data Preview section regrettably shows a paltry 5 rows at a time and 65 characters per row. You cannot make it show more, but you can look at other parts of the file by using the scroll bars.

If your file is delimited, the second page of the wizard indicates what character Excel regards as the delimiter. In Figure 23-6, for example, the program has correctly divined that the file in question is tab-delimited. Most of the time, Excel gets this right. If it does not in your case, you can select a different check box and see the effect immediately in the Data Preview section. You can also select more than one check box to indicate that your file is delimited by multiple characters. If you select two or more check boxes, Excel breaks to a new column whenever it sees any of your choices.

Chapter 23

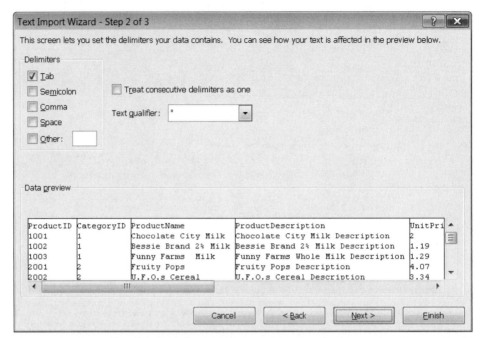

Figure 23-6 If your file is delimited, the second page of the wizard indicates what character Excel has recognized as the delimiter, and the Data Preview section shows how Excel will parse your file.

A separate check box lets you stipulate that Excel should regard consecutive delimiting characters as a single delimiter. You'll find that this option sometimes saves the day with tab-delimited files. The original creator of the file might occasionally have used two or more tabs to skip to the next column when the current column's contents were short. That strategy could disrupt your alignment in Excel unless you tell the program to treat consecutive delimiters as a single delimiter.

Excel is much more likely to introduce errors when trying to parse a fixed-width file. In the file shown in Figure 23-7, for example, the program initially fails to recognize that the first column break should occur between ID and Category to create a Product ID column and a Category ID column. It also erroneously plants a column break in the middle of the Category ID heading. Fortunately, it's easy to fix parsing problems of this sort. (However, if the file is long and the mistakes are many, catching them all is likely to become a trial; if you have a choice between opening a fixed-width file and an equivalent delimited file, by all means go with the latter.)

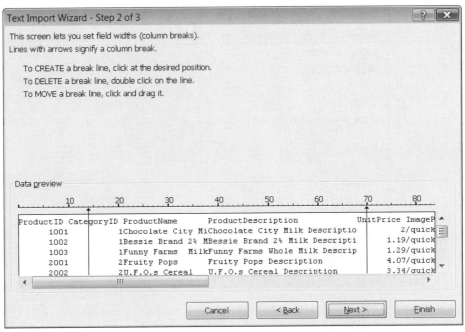

Figure 23-7 If your file is fixed-width, be sure to look at the Data Preview box ; you can fix any mistakes by manipulating the vertical bars.

To fix parsing errors, drag vertical lines to the left or right to reposition the column breaks. To create a column break where one doesn't yet exist, click once at the appropriate place. To remove a column break that shouldn't be there at all, double-click it. When you have finished, click Next.

The third page of the wizard, shown in Figure 23-8, lets you specify the data type of each column. Your choices are limited to General (which treats text as text, numbers as numbers, and dates in recognizable formats as dates), Text (which treats everything as text), Date, and Do Not Import Column (Skip). Excel initially assigns the General description to all columns, and you'll probably want to override that presumption in some cases. For example, if your file happens to have a text field that begins with a hyphen, Excel will regard the hyphen as a minus sign and attempt to turn your text into a formula. You can avoid errors by indicating that the field is Text.

Chapter 23

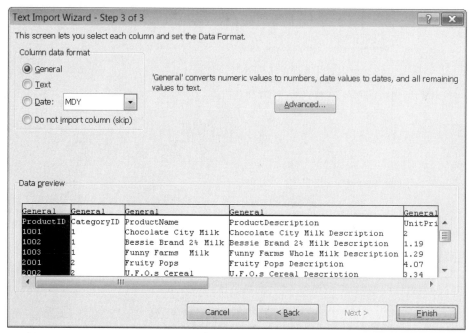

Figure 23-8 You can use the third page of the wizard to control the data type of each column.

Opening dBase Files

Excel no longer gives you the option of saving files in any of the dBase formats, but you can still open such files. To open a dBase file, click the Microsoft Office Button, click Open, and then select dBase Files in the list to the right of the File Name box:

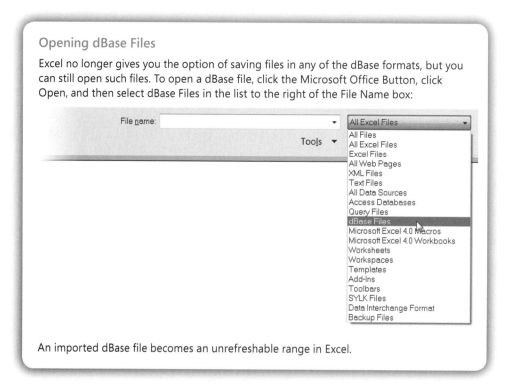

An imported dBase file becomes an unrefreshable range in Excel.

The third page also includes an Advanced button. By clicking it, you can change the way the wizard handles commas and periods in numeric data. By default, Excel uses the settings specified in the Regional And Language Options item of Control Panel. If your text file was created under other assumptions, you'll need to make some adjustments in the Advanced Text Import Settings dialog box. Click OK, click Finish, and then click OK to import the text file.

Parsing Clipboard Text

Occasionally, when working with text data, you might find long text strings that you need to break into separate columns. This can happen, for example, if you paste text into Excel from the Clipboard. To parse such data, select it, click the Data tab, and then click Text To Columns in the Data Tools group.

Working with XML Files

Excel can open, import, and export XML data in any structure. To open a list that has been saved in XML, click the Microsoft Office Button, and click Open—just as you would to open an ordinary Excel workbook. With the Open dialog box set to display all Excel files, your XML files will be included. But if you're having trouble finding the file you want (because of all the other Excel files in the same folder), select XML Files in the list beside the File Name box.

When you open your file, Excel presents the Open XML dialog box, shown in Figure 23-9.

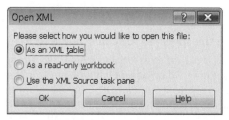

Figure 23-9 When you open an XML data file, Excel presents this dialog box. Choose the first option to open all elements of the XML structure or the third option to work only with particular elements.

As Figure 23-10 shows, the result of opening an XML file using the As An XML Table option is a table that presents each element of the source file, in order, as a table column. All records in the source file are included in the resulting list.

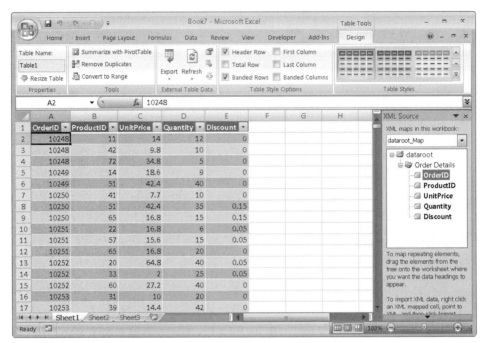

Figure 23-10 Each element of the opened XML file maps to a column in the resulting XML table.

TROUBLESHOOTING

Excel reports a problem with the specified XML or schema source.

When you open an XML file, Excel looks for an associated schema file, which defines the structure of the XML data. If it doesn't find one, or if it finds errors in the associated schema file, you will see an error message. If you click OK, Excel will infer the structure from the data it sees. In many cases, particularly with files that are not particularly complex, this works out fine. You can forget about the error message after you have clicked OK. If Excel can't infer the structure of your file, you will need to fix the schema (or provide one).

After Excel opens the XML file, it can display an XML Source task pane, which shows how the elements of the source file map to columns in the table. If the task pane isn't visible and you want to see it, right-click a cell in the table, click XML, and then click XML Source.

Opening an XML file by the method just described (clicking the Microsoft Office Button and clicking Open) creates a new workbook. If you want to create an XML table on an existing worksheet, click the Data tab, click From Other Sources (in the Get External

Data group), and click From XML Data Import. After you have selected your file in the ensuing dialog box, Excel will ask you where to put the incoming data.

You can refresh an XML table the same way you would an imported text or Access table. For details, see "Setting Refresh Options" on page 747.

Creating an Ad Hoc Mapping of XML Elements to Table Columns

Opening an XML file using the As An XML Table option (see Figure 23-9) might be fine for a relatively simple XML structure. But if your structure is not simple, it's likely you'll be interested in only certain portions of the XML data. In such cases, it's usually more effective to open the file using the third option, Use The XML Source Task Pane. When you do this, Excel presents the XML structure in the XML Source task pane, without creating a table—as shown in Figure 23-11.

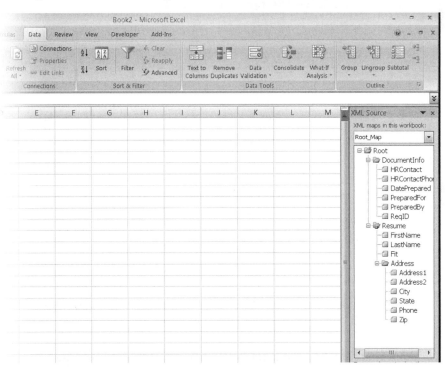

Figure 23-11 When you open an XML file using the XML Structure task pane to map elements to table columns, no data appears until you drag XML elements from the task pane to the worksheet and then refresh.

In the example shown in Figure 23-11, the data file consists of ratings and contact data for a set of job applicants, along with contact information about the human-resources person who conducted each interview. If you're reviewing this data, you might be interested in only the HRContact field from the DocumentInfo element, the LastName and FirstName fields from the Resume element, and perhaps some additional fields pertaining to individual applications. To create a table on your worksheet that displays only the fields you care about, you can Ctrl+click the headings of interest in the XML Structure task pane and then drag the selected set onto the worksheet. (Excel calls this process of associating XML elements with table headings *mapping*.) The result might look like Figure 23-12.

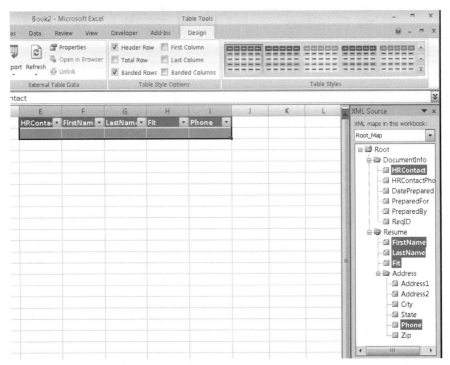

Figure 23-12 You can drag headings from the XML Structure task pane to the worksheet to create a table showing only particular columns.

To populate the table after you have it structured, click a cell in the table header row, click the Data tab (or Design tab), and then click Refresh All. (If you have other tables open and you want to refresh only this one, click the small arrow beneath Refresh All, and then click Refresh.)

Importing XML Data Using an Existing XML Structure

Populating the table by clicking Refresh All, as just described, brings in data from the file whose structure you've imported into the XML Structure task pane. As an alternative, you can right-click a cell in the table header, click XML, and then click Import. You'll then be prompted for the name of an XML data file.

The Import command lets you bring in records from any file whose structure is reflected in the XML Source task pane. Importing is particularly useful when you have a number of identically structured XML files. For example, if each member of your human-resources staff created a separate file of interviewee data with each file built on the same XML schema, you could examine each one in turn with the help of the Import command.

> **Note**
>
> If you perform successive imports of two or more identically structured files, each import replaces the previous one. If instead you want to import several files at once, use the Import procedure as described, and then Ctrl+click each file you want to import.

Using Microsoft Query to Import Data

If you don't have a connection already set up for the data you need, you can create one with the help of Microsoft Query, a versatile querying tool included with the 2007 Microsoft Office system. Query generates statements in SQL and passes those statements to the data source while shielding you from the need to master SQL. If your query is relatively simple, you might not need to interact directly with Query; instead, you can formulate your request by means of a four-step wizard that acts as a front end to Query.

The first step in creating a query is to form a connection to the data source. Click the Data tab, click From Other Sources (in the Get External Data group), and then click From Microsoft Query. The Choose Data Source dialog box, shown in Figure 23-13, appears.

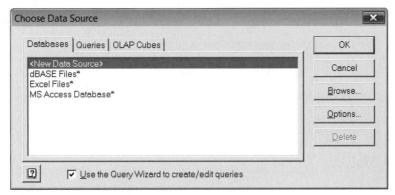

Figure 23-13 The first step in using Microsoft Query is to choose a data source.

You can query a separate Excel file (extracting particular records from a table in that file), a dBase file, or an Access file by selecting one of the options on the Databases tab. To edit an existing query (a .dqy file that has already been created), click the Queries tab. To work with OLAP data, click the OLAP Cubes tab. Otherwise, click

<New Data Source>, and click OK. If you click <New Data Source> and click OK, the Create New Data Source dialog box prompts you to supply a name for the new query, identify the driver for the type of database you are going to query, supply logon information for your connection to the external source, and select the table in the external database you want to use. Click OK to save your changes.

In the following sections, we'll assume for the sake of simplicity that you're going to work with an Access file. After double-clicking MS Access Database in the Choose Data Source dialog box (or selecting that entry and clicking OK), you will see a Select Database dialog box:

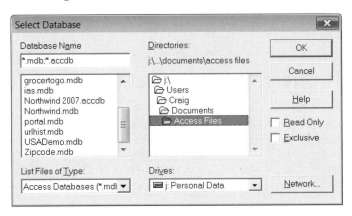

We'll choose the file Northwind.mdb (a sample database that Microsoft included with earlier versions of Access) for this example. After we double-click that file in the Select Database dialog box, the opening page of the Query Wizard, shown in Figure 23-14, appears.

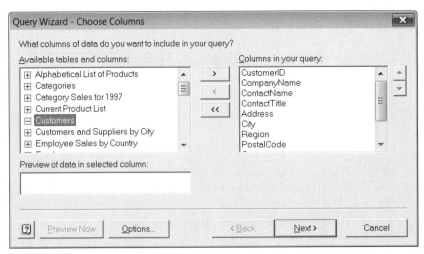

Figure 23-14 The Query Wizard, a friendly front end to Microsoft Query, begins by asking you to choose the columns of data that you want to include in your query.

Choosing Tables and Fields (Columns)

On the first page of the wizard, you see a list of tables on the left and selected fields (Query refers to them as *columns*) on the right. Outline controls (plus signs and minus signs) appear to the left of table names. Your job is to pick the particular fields, from one or more tables, that you want to include in your query.

To add a field to your query, click the plus sign beside the name of the table to which it belongs. This expands the table to reveal its fields. Then select the field, and click the right arrow button to add those fields to your query. (To add all fields from a given table, you can select the table name and click the right arrow button.)

If you add fields from a second or subsequent table to your query, Query performs a *join* operation on the selected tables, if it can. Query joins related tables when it recognizes a primary key field in one table and a field with the same data type (and typically, but not necessarily, the same field name) in the other table. For an example of a query that involves two joined tables, see "Working Directly with Microsoft Query" on page 764.

Filtering Records

After specifying tables and fields and clicking Next, you arrive at the Query Wizard – Filter Data page, shown in Figure 23-15. Here you can specify one or more filter criteria. This is an optional page; if you skip it, Query returns all records from the selected tables.

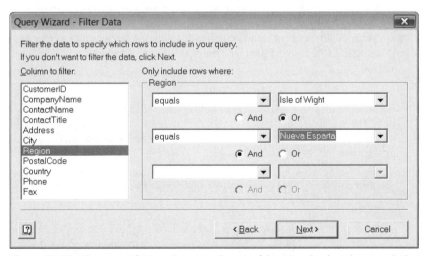

Figure 23-15 Filters, specified on the second page of the wizard, select the records that meet your criteria.

A filter criterion has three components: a field name, a relationship, and a value. You can specify as many as three criteria for each field, connected by And or Or. The list at the left side of the wizard page includes all the names of your selected fields. The lists in the center include available relationships, and the lists at the right include all the available values for the selected field. Figure 23-15 shows how the second page of the wizard would look if you wanted to see only those records in which the Region field equaled either Isle of Wight or Nueva Esparta.

INSIDE OUT   **For More Relationships, Use Microsoft Query Directly**

The Query Wizard offers a long list of relational operators for building filtering criteria. If you use Microsoft Query directly, four additional relationships are available: Is One Of, Is Not One Of, Is Between, and Is Not Between. These additional operators work with two or more values—something the wizard doesn't accommodate. For example, Is Between and Is Not Between both require two values. Is One Of and Is Not One Of can use a list of values. For more information, see "Working Directly with Microsoft Query" on page 764.

TROUBLESHOOTING

The Query Wizard won't let me get rid of a filter.

The Query Wizard is a little clumsy when it comes to letting you remove filters. It doesn't have a Delete button. Clicking Back to return to the previous screen and then clicking Next to return to the Filtering screen doesn't get it done (the previous filter is still there). Clicking Cancel either bails you out of the entire edit process or takes you to Microsoft Query, neither of which is what you probably want. To get rid of a criterion, open its relationship list, and select the blank entry at the top of the list.

If you filter on two more different fields, you'll find that when you select the second field, the wizard removes the first criterion from view. You can tell that you've applied a criterion to a field, however, by looking at the left window on the page. Filtered fields appear there in bold.

Note

Because the wizard accepts up to three criteria per field, you can use it to generate some pretty marvelous filters. But it's a whole lot easier to see what you're doing if you use the full Query interface for multifield filtering. For details, see "Working Directly with Microsoft Query" on page 764.

Sorting Records

After you finish filtering and click Next, the wizard presents its Query Wizard – Sort Order page, shown in Figure 23-16. Sorting is optional, of course. If you decline, Query returns records in the order in which they're stored in the external database field.

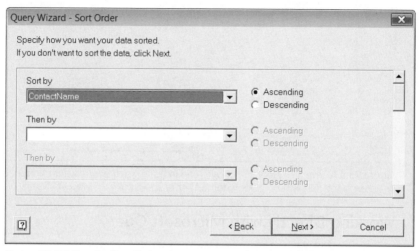

Figure 23-16 Use the Sort Order page to arrange the records that are returned to Excel.

To sort, begin by clicking the Sort By list. There you'll find the name of each field in the table you're querying. Select a field, and then select the Ascending or Descending option to the right of the list. You can sort on as many fields as you want. To remove a sort item, select the blank entry at the top of the list. In Figure 23-16, we've asked for records sorted in ascending order by ContactName. Click Next.

Saving the Query or Moving to Microsoft Query

The Save Query button, on final page of the wizard (see Figure 23-17), lets you name and save your query as a DQY file. The resulting DQY file encapsulates all the selections you've made in the construction of your query—your choice of tables and fields, your filters, and your sorting specifications. Note that this is different from the ODC file you might have made earlier. An ODC file records information required to achieve a connection with an external data source; a DQY file records query specifications.

The View Data Or Edit Query In Microsoft Query option on the last page of the wizard lets you move to the full Microsoft Query for further processing. For information about why you might want to do this and how to use Query, see the following section. If you don't want to move on to Query, select Return Data To Microsoft Office Excel, and click Finish. Click OK in the Import Data dialog box to import the data based on your query.

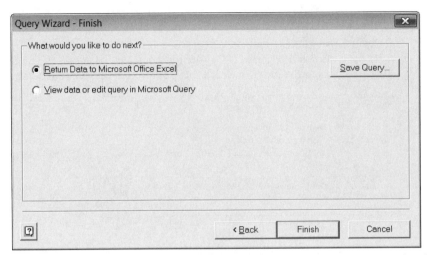

Figure 23-17 Save the query if you want, and indicate whether you want to return directly to Excel or go on to the full Microsoft Query for further processing.

Working Directly with Microsoft Query

The Query Wizard is an ideal tool for creating relatively simple queries, but it doesn't provide access to all the power of Microsoft Query. You'll need to work directly with Query if your query uses criteria involving calculations (other than simple comparisons) or if you want to create a query that prompts the user for one or more parameters when run. Query, but not the Query Wizard, also lets you do the following:

- Filter on the basis of fields that you don't intend to import into Excel—that is, fields that are not included in the *result set*, the records that meet your current criteria.

- Filter using Is One Of, Is Not One Of, Is Between, or Is Not Between.

- Limit the result set to unique entries.

- Perform aggregate calculations, such as totals or averages.

- Create your own joins between tables.

- Edit a query's SQL code.

Getting to Query

If you have already stored the query you want to edit in a DQY file, you can open it in Microsoft Query using either of the following methods:

- Click the Data tab, and then click Existing Connections. Your query will appear in the list, alongside your ODC files, marked by a distinctive icon—two intersecting blue rectangles.

- Click the Data tab, and then click From Other Sources. On the menu that appears, click From Microsoft Query. In the Choose Data Source dialog box, click the Queries tab. Your query should appear there:

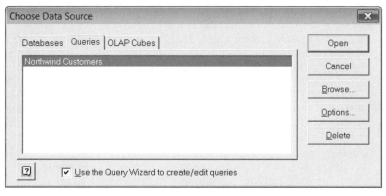

If you have just finished creating your query in the Query Wizard and want to open it in Microsoft Query for further editing, select View Data Or Edit Query In Microsoft Query on the final page of the wizard (see Figure 23-17), and click Finish.

Figure 23-18 shows Query with a query against three tables from Northwind.mdb. The tables are Products, Categories, and Suppliers. The Products table is joined to the Categories table in the CategoryID field and to the Suppliers table in the SupplierID field. The query shows selected fields from these tables, revealing products by category and supplier (CompanyName), along with some price and inventory information.

Chapter 23

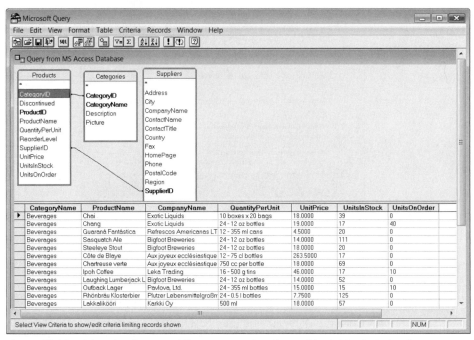

Figure 23-18 We're using Query to edit a query against three tables in Northwind.mdb.

Note that the Query window is divided horizontally into two panes—an upper pane for tables and a lower one for data. The tables pane shows a window for each table that's currently involved in the query. The data pane shows the *result set*—the collection of records that meet the criteria. (At the moment, we haven't defined any filters, so all records in the three tables are included.)

Shortly, you'll see that Query can also accommodate a third pane, in which you specify filtering criteria. All these panes, as well as the individual table windows, are independently sizable and movable. We've bumped the data pane down a bit from its default position to make more room for the Suppliers and Products tables, and we've stretched the windows in which those tables are displayed so that we won't have to scroll to see all their fields. You'll find that Query seldom gives you an ideal window layout when it starts, so you'll want to manipulate it to get the view you need.

Adding and Removing Tables

To add a table to the data pane, click Table, and then click Add Tables. The Add Tables dialog box lists all the tables available in the data source you're using. To add a table, select it, and click Add. You can add as many as you like before closing the Add Tables dialog box. To remove a table, select it in the table pane, and then click Table, Remove Table.

Working with Joins

If Query doesn't already have your tables joined appropriately, you can create your own joins by dragging. If you click a field in one table and then drag to a field in another, Query creates a join based on those fields and draws a line to indicate that it has done so. You can create, inspect, and modify joins by double-clicking any join line or by clicking Table, Joins. Figure 23-19 shows the Joins dialog box for the query shown in Figure 23-18.

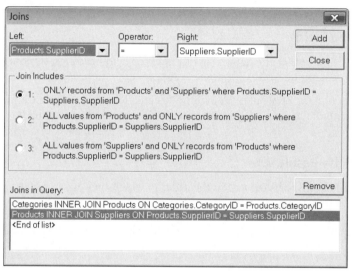

Figure 23-19 The Joins dialog box tells you exactly how your tables are joined and lets you modify the joins or create new ones.

If you're not sure what's joined to what or what the effect of a join is, it's a good idea to visit the Joins dialog box. The Join Includes area in the dialog box provides a pretty clear description of what's happening. By working with the Left, Operator, and Right fields, you can also modify the ways in which your tables are joined.

Adding, Removing, and Moving Fields

To add a field to your data pane, double-click it in a table window. To add all fields to the data pane from a table, double-click the asterisk at the top of the table window.

To remove a field, select its heading (this action selects the entire field), and press Delete. To move a field from its current location, first select its heading, and then drag it to the position you want.

Chapter 23

INSIDE OUT **Hide Selected Fields Without Removing Them from the Query**

If you find yourself scrolling horizontally a lot but don't want to rearrange your fields, you can hide fields that you temporarily don't need to see. Select a field, and then click Format, Hide Columns. To redisplay a hidden field, click Format, Show Columns; select the field in the Show Columns dialog box; and then click Show.

Renaming Fields

By default, Query uses the names of your fields as field headings. If these field names are short and cryptic, you might want to supply different headings.

Select the column you want to change, and then click Records, Edit Column. In the Edit Column dialog box, type a new heading in the Column Heading box, and then click OK.

Sorting the Result Set

Query initially displays records in the order in which they are stored in the external data source. You can change their order by clicking Records, Sort. Figure 23-20 shows the Sort dialog box with the CategoryName field selected. (The dialog box, like others in Query, qualifies field names with the tables to which they belong; it says Categories.CategoryName because the CategoryName field is part of the Categories table.)

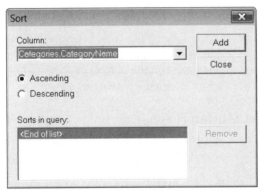

Figure 23-20 The Sort dialog box displays the current sort order and lets you add fields from a list.

The Sorts In Query section in the dialog box indicates what sort specification, if any, is currently in effect. In Figure 23-20, the list is empty, indicating that the result set is currently unsorted. The Column list at the top of the dialog box lists all the table fields available for sorting. When you add a field to the Sorts In Query list, Query performs the sort immediately but leaves the dialog box open in case you want to sort on additional fields. You can sort on as many as you please.

For multiple-field sorts, sort first on the most important sort field. Then sort on your secondary field, and so on. Figure 23-21 shows the result set sorted first by Suppliers.CompanyName and then by Products.ProductName. (The Asc abbreviation in the Sorts In Query list indicates ascending sorts.) The records now are alphabetized by supplier, with records of a common supplier alphabetized by product name.

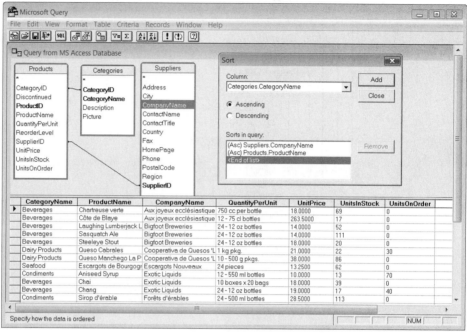

Figure 23-21 We've sorted first by the supplier's company name and then by product name.

When you click Add in the Sort dialog box, Query adds your new sort field above the currently selected field in the Sorts In Query list. If you accidentally add a field in the wrong order, select it, and click Remove. Then add the field in the correct position.

Sorting with the Toolbar   The Sort icons on the Query toolbar work differently from the Sort command on the Ribbon in Excel. You can add a sort to the current list by holding down the Ctrl key when you click a Sort icon. If you do not hold down Ctrl, clicking a Sort icon replaces the current sort with the new one.

Filtering the Result Set

Query provides a variety of methods by which you can filter the result set so that it includes only the records in which you're interested. As with the Query Wizard, you create a filter by specifying one or more criteria—conditions that particular fields must meet.

Chapter 23

Creating Exact-Math Criteria The simplest kind of criterion is one in which you stipulate that a field must exactly equal some value. Query makes it extremely easy to create such criteria:

1. Select a field value that meets your exact-match criterion.

2. Click the Criteria Equals button on the toolbar:

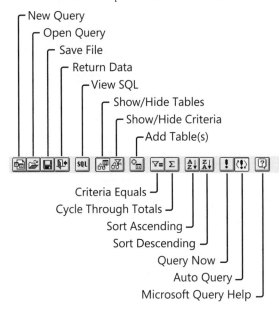

For example, suppose you want to filter the result set shown in Figure 23-21 to include only those records in which the CompanyName field is Bigfoot Breweries. To do this, select any record with the CompanyName field that already equals Bigfoot Breweries, and click the Criteria Equals button. Query responds by displaying the criteria pane (if it's not already displayed) and applying the new filter to the table, as shown in Figure 23-22.

> **Note**
> After you use the Criteria Equals button to specify an exact-match criterion, you can quickly switch to a different match. Type a new value in the criteria pane to replace the current one.

If you have used the Advanced Filter command (see "Using the Advanced Filter Command" on page 689), you'll notice that the criteria pane in Query looks a lot like a criteria range in an Excel worksheet. Field headings appear in the top row, and criteria are stated in subsequent rows. Although you can type new criteria or edit existing ones directly in the criteria pane, it's not necessary, because the Query menu commands take care of entering information in the criteria pane for you. In fact, you don't need to have the criteria pane on your screen at all.

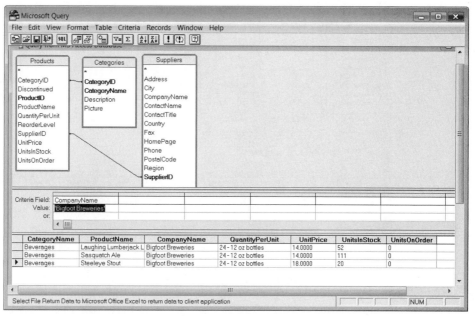

Figure 23-22 When we clicked the Criteria Equals button, Query displayed the criteria pane and applied the filter to the result set.

> **Note**
>
> To remove the criteria pane, click the Show/Hide Criteria button on the toolbar in Query, or click View, Criteria. To remove the tables pane, click Show/Hide Tables, or click View, Tables.

Using Multiple Exact-Match Criteria   To generate a query that uses exact-match criteria in two or more fields, repeat the process just described for the second and each subsequent criterion. For example, to filter the result set in Figure 23-21 to show only those records with CompanyName equal to Exotic Liquids and CategoryName equal to Beverages, select Exotic Liquids in the CompanyName field, click Criteria Equals, then select Beverages in the CategoryName field, and click Criteria Equals again. As Figure 23-23 shows, the criteria pane then shows the two criteria on the same line. Just as with an Excel criteria range, Query treats criteria on the same line as if they are connected by the AND operator.

Chapter 23

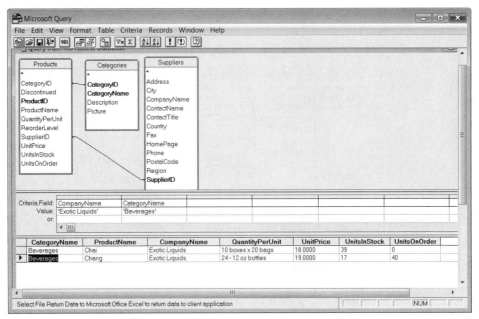

Figure 23-23 When you use the Criteria Equals button in two separate fields, the filter in Query admits only those records that meet both criteria.

Automatic Query vs. Manual Query

By default, Query updates the result set every time you add a new field to the data pane, rearrange the order of the existing fields in the data pane, change a sort specification, or change a filter criterion. (If you're working in the criteria pane, the query is executed as soon as you click away from the current criteria-pane call.) In response to these actions, Query creates a new SQL statement and executes that statement against your data source. (You can see the SQL code—and edit it, if you are inclined—by clicking the View SQL button on the toolbar.) If your data source is particularly large or network traffic is high, Automatic Query can cause annoying delays. You can turn off the Automatic Query feature so that Query executes the current SQL statement only when you ask it to do so.

You can determine whether Automatic Query is on by verifying whether the Auto Query button on the toolbar is selected (has a "pushed in" appearance). To turn the feature off, click the Auto Query button, or click Records, Automatic Query.

To execute the current query in manual mode, click the Query Now button, or click Records, Query Now.

Using Menu Commands to Specify Exact-Match Criteria   If you'd rather use menu commands than toolbar buttons, you can specify an exact-match criterion as follows:

1.   Select a field value that meets your specification.

2.   Click Criteria, Add Criteria. In the Add Criteria dialog box, click Add.

Removing Criteria   The simplest way to remove a filter criterion is to select the criterion's heading in the criteria pane and press Delete. To remove all criteria and restore the unfiltered result set, click Criteria, Remove All Criteria.

Specifying Comparison Criteria   To specify a comparison criterion, follow these steps:

1.   Click Criteria, Add Criteria. You'll see a dialog box similar to the one shown in Figure 23-24.

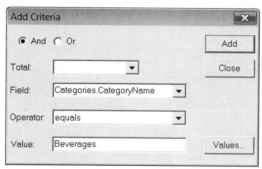

Figure 23-24 The Add Criteria dialog box lets you select fields, comparison operators, and values.

In the Add Criteria dialog box, you can construct your criteria by selecting options from various lists. For example, you can select a field from the Field list and then select an operator, such as Is Greater Than, in the Operator list. You can also enter a value in the Value text box by typing it or clicking the Values button and selecting from the list.

Note

For comparison criteria that don't involve computed fields, be sure the Total field in the Add Criteria dialog box is blank, as it is in Figure 23-24. For more information about the Total field, see "Filtering on Calculated Fields" on page 777.

2.   When you have filled out the Field, Operator, and Value fields, click Add.

Query responds by creating the appropriate entry in the criteria pane and, if Automatic Query is on, executing the new query. The Add Criteria dialog box remains open so you can specify more criteria.

3. To add another criterion, select the And option or the Or option at the top of the dialog box, and then type the information as before.

4. When you've finished typing criteria, click Close.

Filtering on Fields That Are Not in the Result Set   Your filter criteria can be based on fields that are not currently displayed in the result set. The Field list in the Add Criteria dialog box includes all fields in all active tables, not only the fields you plan to return to Excel.

Limiting the Result Set to Unique Entries   To limit the result set to unique entries, click View, Query Properties. In the Query Properties dialog box, select Unique Values Only. You can make this selection before or after you create your filter.

Comparing Fields   Your comparison criteria can compare the value in one field to that in another. For example, to display records where UnitsInStock is less than Reorder-Level, you fill out the Add Criteria dialog box as shown in Figure 23-25. Note that you have to type a field name in the Value box.

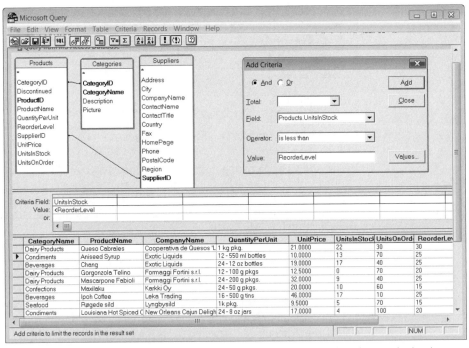

Figure 23-25 This criterion returns records where units on stock are below the reorder level.

Performing Aggregate Calculations

You can analyze your results thoroughly after you get the data back onto the Excel worksheet. If you prefer, however, you can have Query do some of the calculating for you. With Query, you can make aggregate calculations (sums, averages, counts, and so on) the basis of filtering criteria.

Query refers to all calculations as totals, although summing values is only one of the options available. The aggregate functions that are common to all database drivers are AVG (average), COUNT, MIN (minimum), and MAX (maximum). Your driver might support additional functions.

Clicking Through the Totals   One way to perform aggregate calculations is by clicking the Cycle Through Totals button on the toolbar in Query. For example, to find the total of the UnitsOnOrder field, follow these steps:

1. Display the UnitsOnOrder field in the data pane, and remove all filtering criteria from the criteria pane.

2. Select the UnitsOnOrder field, and click the Cycle Through Totals button.

As Figure 23-26 shows, Query responds by displaying the total in the data pane.

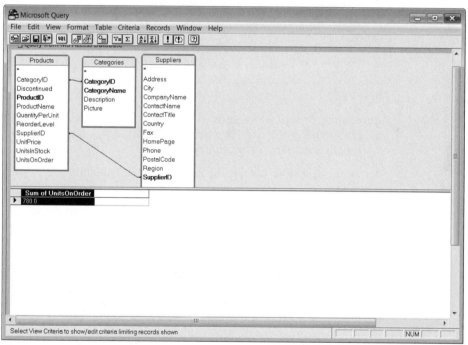

Figure 23-26 We used the Cycle Through Totals button to calculate the total units on order.

Cycling Through the Functions   In the previous example, clicking Cycle Through Totals a second time changes the aggregate function from SUM to AVG, and the number shown in the data pane changes accordingly. Successive clicks on the Cycle Through Totals button result in the count, the minimum, and the maximum. One more click returns the result set to its unaggregated state.

> **Note**
> Not all the aggregate functions are available for every field type.

Using Menu Commands   If you prefer menus to tools, you can use the Edit Column command:

1. Click Records, Edit Column. (Alternatively, double-click the field heading.)

2. In the Edit Column dialog box (see Figure 23-27), select the function you want from the Total list.

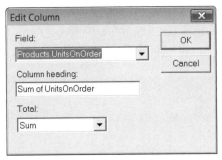

Figure 23-27 Instead of clicking Cycle Through Totals, you can click Records, Edit Column.

Aggregating Groups of Records   In addition to grand totals, you can also calculate totals for groups of records. For example, to find out how many units are on order for each supplier company, do the following:

1. In the data pane, display the CompanyName field followed by the UnitsOnOrder field.

2. Select the UnitsOnOrder field, and click Cycle Through Totals.

As Figure 23-28 shows, Query displays one record for each company and shows the total units on order for each.

Using More Than One Aggregate Field   You can add as many aggregate fields to your result set as you need. To display both sums and averages for a numeric field, for example, you can drag that field to the data pane twice. Click the Cycle Through Totals button to apply the function you want to each copy of the field.

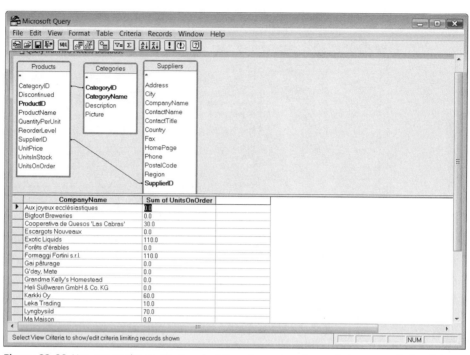

Figure 23-28 You can apply aggregate calculations to groups of records; here we calculated the total units on order per company.

Filtering on Calculated Fields   A field that performs an aggregate calculation is called a *calculated* field. You can use calculated fields as the basis for filtering criteria. To base a criterion on a calculated field in the Add Criteria dialog box, use the Total list to select the function you want. (If you're entering the criterion directly in the criteria pane, type the function name, and enclose the field name in parentheses.) Figure 23-29 shows a criterion that returns the names of companies for whom the total number of products on order is greater than or equal to 20.

Creating a Parameter-Based Query

A *parameter-based* query is one in which a filter criterion is based upon a value supplied by the user when the query is executed. To create such a query, first turn the Automatic Query feature off by clicking the Auto Query button on the toolbar. Then specify a criterion in the usual way—either by using the Add Criteria dialog box or by typing values directly in the criteria pane. Instead of typing a value, though, type a left bracket character, a prompt of your choosing, and a right bracket character. (The prompt must not be identical to the field name, although it can include the field name.) When you execute the query, either from within Query or from within Excel, a dialog box containing your prompt appears. Figure 23-30 shows a parameter-based query.

Chapter 23

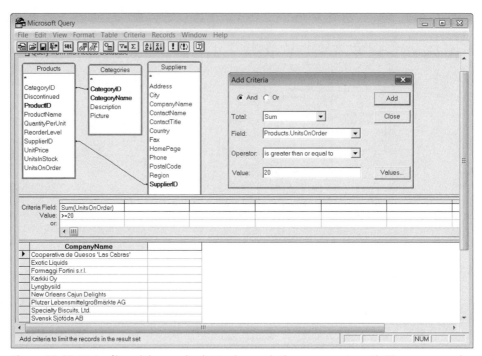

Figure 23-29 We've filtered the supplier list to show only those companies with 20 or more products on order.

Saving a Query

To store your query specification in a reusable DQY file, click File, Save. This step is optional. If you do not save the query, you will still be able to refresh it from the data range that it creates on your Excel worksheet. You will have to re-create it if you want to use it in another workbook, however.

Returning the Result Set to Excel

To return your data to Excel, click File, Return Data To Microsoft Excel. The Import Data dialog box (refer to Figure 23-2) appears, asking you where and how you want the data returned.

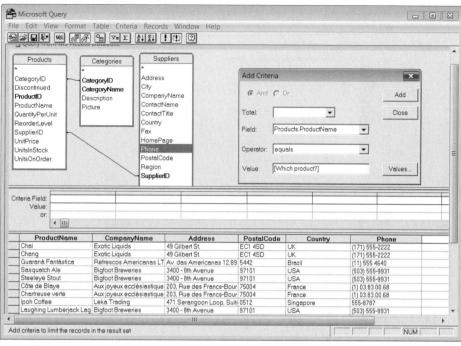

Figure 23-30 When executed, this query will prompt the user for a product name.

Using a Web Query to Return Internet Data

Web queries let you grab specific information, such as stock prices, sports scores, or your company's current sales data, from the Internet or an intranet. You can set up queries to prompt you for the data you want (for stock ticker symbols, for example) or to get the same information every time they're executed. You can try Web queries using a set of sample queries that come with Excel 2007.

The Excel graphical interface for creating Web queries lets you build a query by pointing to the data you want. You can refresh the query at any time or at regular intervals, and you can save the query in an IQY file for reuse in other worksheets. You do not need to understand how the target Web page is built to construct a query to it.

Using an Existing Web Query

To run an existing Web query—one of the samples supplied with Excel or one that you or someone else has already set up—click the Data tab, and click Existing Connections. As Figure 23-31 shows, Web queries are identified in the Existing Connections dialog box by a pair of intersecting blue rectangles and a globe. (The three Web queries supplied with Excel 2007 are all from MSN MoneyCentral Investor.)

Chapter 23

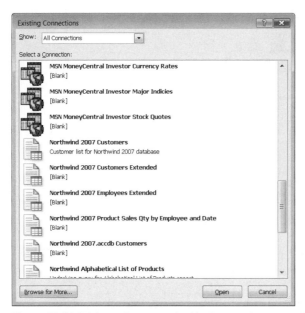

Figure 23-31 Web queries are marked by intersecting rectangles and a globe, and Excel 2007 includes three of them to try.

When you double-click a Web query, Excel prompts you to specify a location for the incoming Web data. Depending on how the query was set up, it might also prompt you for parameters. For example, if you double-click the MSN MoneyCentral Investor Stock Quotes query, after you indicate where you want the data to go, you will see the following dialog box, which prompts you to supply one or more stock symbols:

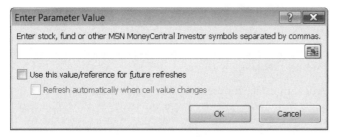

To supply parameters via the Enter Parameter Value dialog box, simply type in the box. If you prefer, you can point to a worksheet range containing your parameters. If you specify a multicell range, Excel parses the range moving across and then down.

If you use a worksheet range to feed parameters to your Web query, you can also stipulate that the query be refreshed automatically anytime the worksheet range changes. To do this, select both check boxes.

Figure 23-32 shows an example of data returned by one of the Web queries supplied with Excel 2007. Note that this query is set up to return the names of market indexes as hyperlinks. Clicking a hyperlink takes you to a relevant page in the MSN MoneyCentral Investor Web site.

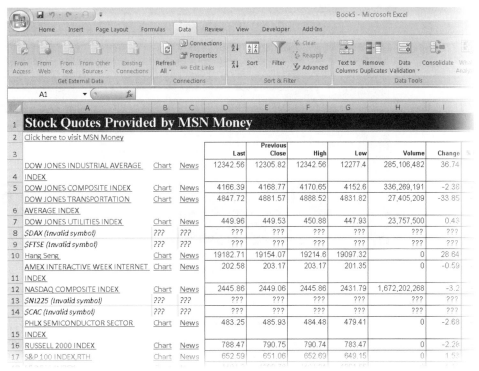

Figure 23-32 Data returned by this Web query includes hyperlinks to the MSN MoneyCentral Investor site.

Creating Your Own Web Query

Excel provides three easy ways to construct a Web query:

- Clicking the Data tab and then clicking From Web

- Copying and pasting information from your Web browser

- Right-clicking in Microsoft Internet Explorer and clicking Export To Microsoft Excel

Using the From Web Command

To create a Web query using the From Web command, follow these steps:

1. Click the Data tab, and then click From Web. The New Web Query form that appears (see Figure 23-33) is a specialized Web browser, and your home page appears in its window.

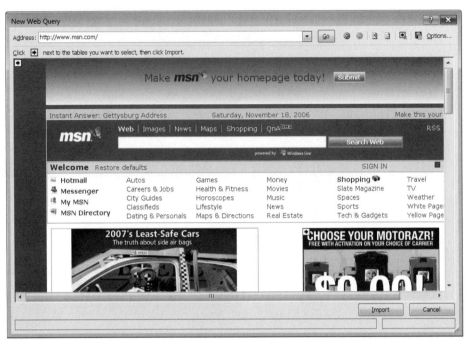

Figure 23-33 The New Web Query form is a specialized Web browser.

2.   If you know the Uniform Resource Locator (URL) of the Web site you want to query, you can type or paste it into the Address field. (Unfortunately, the New Web Query form doesn't include a Favorites menu.)

3.   Click Go; your Web site appears in the main window, as Figure 23-34 shows.

Yellow boxes with arrows appear along the left edge of the window. Each of these boxes represents a section of the Web site that you can import into Excel. As you rest your pointer on any of these yellow boxes, a thick bounding rectangle indicates the section of the site you will be importing if you select the yellow box. You can select any or all yellow boxes.

Saving the IQY File and Setting Formatting Options   After making your selections, you can click Import to transform your selection into a query. But before you do so, you might want to save the query (making it a reusable IQY file) or explore the menu of options. To save the query in its current form, click the Save Query command, directly to the left of the word *Options* on the toolbar in the New Web Query form. To set options, click Options. Figure 23-35 shows the Web Query Options dialog box.

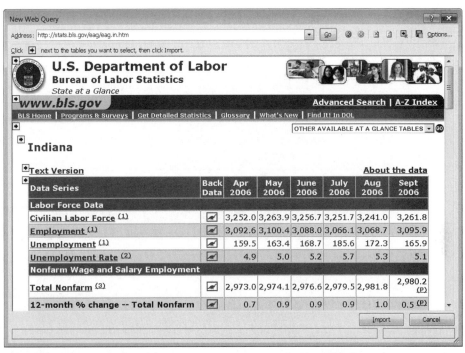

Figure 23-34 We've displayed the site we want to query in the New Web Query form.

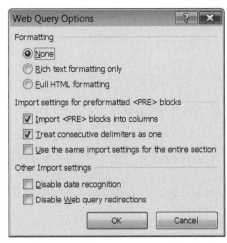

Figure 23-35 In addition to offering other features, the Web Query Options dialog box lets you control how much of the Web site's formatting Excel should preserve.

In the Formatting area of the dialog box, select None to import the data as plain text. Select Rich Text Formatting Only to preserve hyperlinks and merged cells in the Web

Chapter 23

data. Select Full HTML Formatting to retrieve as much as possible of the original Web site's formatting. Figure 23-36 shows a Web site queried with full HTML formatting. Note the inclusion of hyperlinks in the downloaded data.

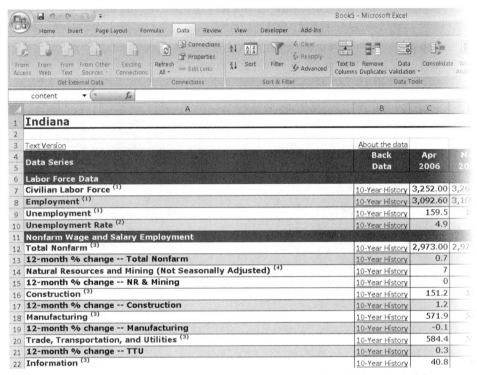

Figure 23-36 Because we queried this site using full HTML formatting, the downloaded data includes active hyperlinks and other welcome formatting characteristics.

Copying and Pasting from the Web Browser

The method for creating a Web query just described is fine if you're starting in Excel and you know the address of the target site. But you can also start from the Web browser. Select the data you want, press Ctrl+C to copy it, open a new Excel worksheet, and press Ctrl+V. You'll see a smart tag near the lower-right corner of the pasted data. Open the menu, shown here, and click Create Refreshable Web Query. Your data selection will appear in the New Web Query form.

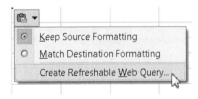

Using the Internet Explorer Export To Microsoft Excel Command

If your Web browser is Internet Explorer, you can also create a Web query by right-clicking a Web page and clicking Export To Microsoft Excel. (If you don't see this command, you probably already have something selected in Internet Explorer. Clear your selection, and try again.) The Export To Microsoft Excel command begins by creating a new instance of Excel (it does this to avoid overwriting Excel data you might already be working with). If you right-clicked something that Internet Explorer recognizes as an HTML table, it transfers that table directly onto Sheet1!A1 as a new Web query. If you clicked anywhere other than an HTML table, the command opens the New Web Query form.

PART 8
Collaborating

Collaborating on a Network or by E-Mail

I n the past, if you wanted to share your worksheets with other people, you copied everything onto floppy disks, carried them down the hall (or flipped them over the partition), and handed them to the person who wanted them. This system (still effective!) was known affectionately as *sneakernet*. The lucky few who worked in large companies might have been connected to a network. These days, small companies and even those who work at home have networks, and everyone can take advantage of the global network known as the Internet. Microsoft Office Excel 2007 makes it easier than ever to get connected and provides easy-to-use tools that can help foster the synergy that is the hallmark of effective collaboration.

Saving and Retrieving Files on Remote Computers

By clicking the Microsoft Office Button and then clicking Save As, you can use the list at the top of the Save As dialog box to save a workbook on any available network drive, on a File Transfer Protocol (FTP) server, in a Web folder on the Internet, or at a Windows SharePoint Services site. The dialog box you see when you click the Microsoft Office Button and then click Open contains a similar list. You can use this list to retrieve workbooks saved on the network or on the Internet.

When you try to open a file that resides on a network drive while another user has the file open, Office Excel 2007 displays the File In Use dialog box, where you can open the file in read-only mode. Figure 24-1 shows the File In Use dialog box that appears when you attempt to open a file that's in use.

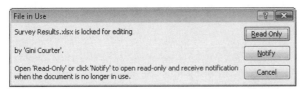

Figure 24-1 The File In Use dialog box appears when you try to open a busy file.

If you click Notify in the File In Use dialog box, Excel opens your file in read-only mode but then alerts you when the file becomes available for read-write access by displaying the File Now Available dialog box shown in Figure 24-2.

Figure 24-2 The File Now Available dialog box alerts you when the file is no longer in use.

Sharing Workbooks on a Network

It has always been possible to share Excel files on a network. You just had to make sure you coordinated your efforts to avoid having more than one person open a file at the same time. With recent versions of Excel, however, two or more people can work on the same workbook simultaneously. In Excel 2007, click the Review tab, and then click Share Workbook in the Changes group on the Ribbon to open the Share Workbook dialog box shown in Figure 24-3.

Figure 24-3 Select the Allow Changes By More Than One User At The Same Time check box to share the workbook.

When you select the Allow Changes By More Than One User At The Same Time check box and click OK, Excel displays a confirmation prompt and then saves the workbook. This is necessary because the workbook must be saved as "sharable" before another user can open it. After you save the workbook, *[Shared]* appears in the title bar whenever anyone opens the workbook, and it remains until you turn off sharing.

Note

To change the name users see in the Share Workbook dialog box when they work with a shared file, click the Microsoft Office Button, and then click the Excel Options button to open the Excel Options dialog box. In the Popular category, edit the User Name box.

Of course, there are inherent risks when people work at the same time in the same file. Conflicts can arise when several people are making changes that affect the same cells. When someone saves changes, Excel not only saves the workbook but also updates it if other users save any changes. A dialog box informs you that Excel has incorporated your changes. After you save, Excel outlines changes that have been made by other people with a colored border and adds a special cell comment to explain who did what when. When you point to the cell, a comment box displays this information, as shown in Figure 24-4. Note that the triangular comment indicator appears in the upper-left corner of the cell instead of in the upper-right corner, as it does for standard cell comments.

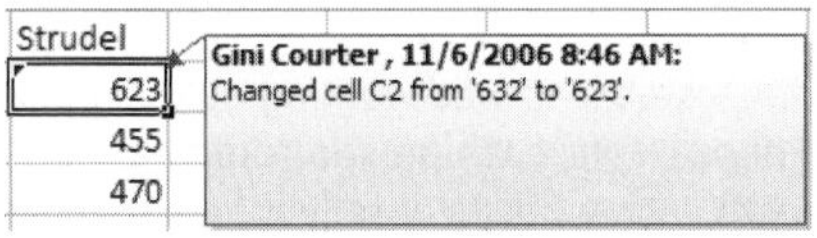

Strudel	Gini Courter , 11/6/2006 8:46 AM:
623	Changed cell C2 from '632' to '623'.
455	
470	

Figure 24-4 Excel outlines cells changed by others in a shared workbook and attaches a comment.

Note

Change tracking, which determines whether outlines and comment boxes appear in your worksheet, is turned on separately. You can control change tracking by clicking the Review tab, clicking Track Changes, and then clicking Highlight Changes. In the Highlight Changes dialog box that appears, select the Track Changes While Editing check box. Make sure this check box is selected before you save the worksheet for sharing if you want to be able to track and review changes later. For more information, see "Tracking Changes" on page 794.

When you save a shared file, Excel looks for conflicts and determines whether any mediation is necessary. Usually, a dialog box appears after you save the file to inform you that Excel has incorporated changes made by other users. However, if others' changes involve any of the same cells you changed, the mediator arrives in the form of the Resolve Conflicts dialog box shown in Figure 24-5.

What You Can and Can't Do with a Shared Workbook

You can edit shared workbooks using Excel 97 and newer versions only. Older versions, such as Microsoft Excel 7 for Windows 95, don't support shared editing.

When you open a workbook for sharing, you can type text and numbers; change cell formatting; edit formulas; and copy, paste, and move data by dragging. You can insert columns and rows, but you can't insert blocks of cells. You can't merge cells, insert charts or other objects, create hyperlinks, assign passwords, insert automatic subtotals, create outlines, or create data tables or PivotTables. You can't do anything with macros except run them, although you can record macros if you store them in a separate, nonshared workbook. The Conditional Formatting, Scenarios, and Data Validation commands are not available for a workbook in shared mode (although you can still see their effects); most of the buttons on the Drawing toolbar aren't available either.

Note

When setting up a multiuser workbook, establish some working guidelines, and design the workbook for maximum safety. For example, each person could have a separate named worksheet in the workbook, with each worksheet reflecting a specific area of responsibility. Then you could create a separate consolidation worksheet that pulls together all the relevant data from the personal worksheets to present it in the necessary format. For more information, see "Consolidating Worksheets" on page 258.

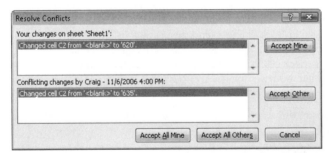

Figure 24-5 If more than one person changes the same cells, the last person to save changes might get to decide which ones to keep.

For each conflict identified, the Resolve Conflicts dialog box specifies the cells involved and lets you decide whose changes to keep. You can resolve conflicts individually or use the buttons at the bottom of the dialog box to accept all the changes entered by you or others. You must resolve the conflicts to save the workbook. If you click Cancel, Excel will not save the workbook.

Chapter 24

Note that conflicts can exist only between the last saved version and the version you are trying to save. If more than two users have made changes to the same cells, each person who saves the workbook gets to decide who wins the conflict of the moment. You can, however, revisit all the conflicts and accept or reject them individually later.

For more information about accepting or rejecting changes individually, see "Reviewing Changes" on page 797.

Using Advanced Sharing Options

You can change some aspects of the default behavior of shared workbooks. To do so, click the Review tab, and then click Share Workbook to open the Share Workbook dialog box. Click the Advanced tab (see Figure 24-6). (The options on this tab are unavailable if you haven't selected the Allow Changes By More Than One User At The Same Time check box on the Editing tab.) Each shared workbook user can set these options individually. Use the first area on the Advanced tab to specify the length of time you want to keep track of changes or whether you want to track them at all. Excel keeps the change history for only the number of days you select. If you need to track changes but are unsure how long you want to track them, set a high number (such as 999 days).

Turning off change tracking detracts from your ability to merge workbooks. For more information, see "Combining Changes Made to Multiple Workbooks" on page 798.

Figure 24-6 Use the Advanced tab to determine the way Excel handles changes.

In the Update Changes area, select when you want updates to occur. Ordinarily when a user saves a file, Excel saves the changes, and it also updates the copy of the workbook with any changes made by others. The Automatically Every option is handy, letting you specify how often updates occur automatically. When you choose automatic updating, the usual procedure is as described previously: Excel saves your changes, and it incorporates changes made by others into your copy. You also can select the Just See Other Users' Changes option, which gives you the ability to hold your changes back until you decide to save them, while at the same time updating your file at regular intervals with any changes recorded by others. This is a good workbook management technique, particularly if your team includes users who aren't in the habit of regularly saving their changes.

As mentioned previously, when conflicts arise, the Resolve Conflicts dialog box shown in Figure 24-5 appears. If you select The Changes Being Saved Win in the Conflicting Changes Between Users area on the Advanced tab in the Share Workbook dialog box, however, Excel essentially resolves all conflicts in favor of the last user to issue the Save command. Click OK to dismiss the Resolve Conflicts dialog box and return to the Share Workbook dialog box.

With the Include In Personal View check boxes, you can change the print settings and any views set using the Filter or Advanced Filter command on the Data tab. With these check boxes selected, each person who has a shared workbook open can have different print and filter settings, which are recalled the next time that person opens the shared workbook.

INSIDE OUT Password-Protect Workbooks Before You Share

You can use the standard Excel password-protection options with shared workbooks, but you must apply the password before sharing. Click the Microsoft Office Button, and then click Save As. Click the small arrow next to Tools, and then click the General Options command. In the File Sharing area, you can type a password for opening the workbook and another password for modifying the workbook. Click OK to save your changes. Then you can disseminate the necessary passwords to members of your workgroup. For more information about file protection, see "Protecting Files" on page 59.

Tracking Changes

Change tracking in Excel is closely linked with shared workbooks. To turn on change tracking, click the Review tab, click Track Changes, and then click Highlight Changes. In the Highlight Changes dialog box, select the Track Changes While Editing check box. Selecting this check box puts your workbook into shared mode and, as the option indicates, saves your workbook (see Figure 24-7)—just as if you had clicked the Share Workbook command. Even if you select the Don't Keep Change History option on the Advanced tab in the Share Workbook dialog box, as shown in Figure 24-6, you can still turn on change tracking by using the Track Changes commands.

INSIDE OUT   Track Changes Without Sharing

You don't have to share a workbook to be able to track the changes you make. Just turn on change tracking and save the workbook in an unshared folder on your own hard disk instead of in a shared network location.

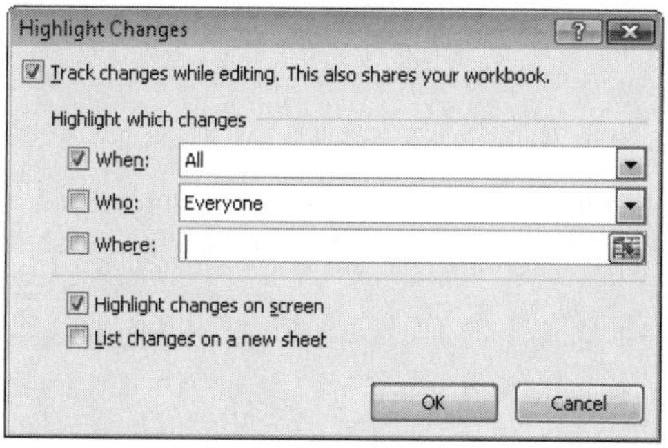

Figure 24-7 Use the Highlight Changes command to show what has been done in a shared workbook.

You control which changes you want highlighted. Use the When list to select whether you want to see all the changes made since the workbook was first shared, only those changes you haven't yet reviewed, those changes that have been made since the last time you saved, or those changes that have been made since a date you specify. The Who options include Everyone, Everyone But Me, and the name of every individual who has made changes to the shared workbook. If you want, you can type a specific cell or range in the Where box. If you select the check box next to the Where option, you can drag to select the cells directly on the worksheet while the dialog box is still open.

Ordinarily, the changes are highlighted on the screen with cell borders and attached cell comments. Clear the Highlight Changes On Screen check box to turn off this option. You can also create a history worksheet detailing all the changes made. To do so, select the List Changes On A New Sheet check box (which is unavailable until you have actually made some changes). The resulting worksheet is inserted after the last worksheet in the workbook, as shown in Figure 24-8.

Action Number	Date	Time	Who	Change	Sheet	Range	New Value	Old Value	Action Type	Losing Action
1	10/17/2006	8:28 AM	Nancy Lawrence	Cell Change	Results	C3	455	545		
2	10/17/2006	8:29 AM	Nancy Lawrence	Cell Change	Results	C4	323	334		
3	10/31/2006	2:12 PM	Gini Courter	Cell Change	Results	B17	40	50		
4	10/31/2006	4:19 PM	Nancy Lawrence	Cell Change	Results	J35	14.2	15.1		
5	11/2/2006	11:13 PM	Gini Courter	Cell Change	Results	C3	455	545		
The history ends with the changes saved on 11/2/2006 at 11:13 PM.										

Figure 24-8 You can choose to create a history worksheet detailing the changes made to a shared workbook.

> **Note**
>
> Formatting changes aren't recorded in the change history.

The *history worksheet* is a special locked worksheet that can be displayed only when a worksheet is in shared mode. The worksheet disappears when you turn off change tracking. If you subsequently restart a shared workbook session, the history starts fresh, and any changes recorded in previous sharing sessions are lost.

> **Note**
>
> To keep track of the change history after discontinuing the sharing session, copy the contents of the locked history worksheet and paste them into another worksheet, or copy the worksheet.

Protecting the Change History

If you want to ensure that Excel records every change made during a sharing session, click the Review tab, and then click Protect Shared Workbook. The Protect Shared Workbook dialog box, shown in Figure 24-9, appears.

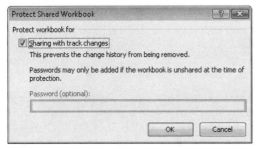

Figure 24-9 You can ensure that change tracking is protected in a shared workbook.

If you select the Sharing With Track Changes check box and then click OK, no one in your workgroup can directly turn off change tracking for the shared workbook. However, anyone can turn off the protection by turning off sharing for the workbook. To eliminate this possibility, you can type a password in the Protect Shared Workbook dialog box. But you must do this when the workbook is *not* in shared mode. Anyone who tries to turn off protection must type the identical, case-sensitive password.

> **Note**
>
> Successfully typing a password to turn off the sharing protection not only turns off protection but also removes the workbook from sharing. Note that this isn't the case unless the workbook has a password. When you remove a workbook from sharing, you cut off anyone else who has the workbook open, and Excel erases the change history.

Reviewing Changes

You can decide at any time to go through each change that users have made to the shared workbook, provided you selected the Track Changes While Editing check box in the Highlight Changes dialog box when you first saved the worksheet for sharing. Clicking the Review tab and then clicking Track Changes, Accept/Reject Changes on the Ribbon saves the workbook and displays the Select Changes To Accept Or Reject dialog box shown in Figure 24-10. The When, Who, and Where lists are similar to those in the Highlight Changes dialog box, except that in the When list, the only options available are Not Yet Reviewed and Since Date.

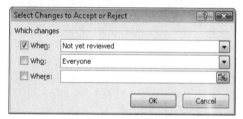

Figure 24-10 Use the Select Changes To Accept Or Reject dialog box to specify which changes you want to review.

When you click OK, the Accept Or Reject Changes dialog box shown in Figure 24-11 appears, and on the worksheet, Excel highlights the first change that meets the criteria you specified in the Select Changes To Accept Or Reject dialog box. (If the cell in question has been changed more than once, Excel lists each change for that cell in the dialog box, and you can select one to accept.) The dialog box describes the change, who made it, and the time it was made. At this point, you can accept or reject the change, or you can accept or reject all the changes. After you have accepted or rejected all the changes, you cannot review them again. You can, however, still display the history worksheet.

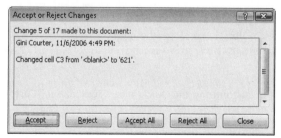

Figure 24-11 Each change is highlighted and described, and you can accept or reject it.

Canceling the Shared Workbook Session

You can discontinue the sharing session at any time by clearing the Allow Changes By More Than One User At The Same Time check box on the Editing tab in the Share Workbook dialog box. (Anyone else using the shared workbook can also do this; no one "owns" the right to enable or disable sharing.) Doing this has several effects. First, the change history is lost. If you subsequently start a new sharing session, the history starts fresh. Second, any other users who still have the shared workbook open won't be able to save their changes to the same file. They'll be in read-only mode, but Excel won't inform them of that until they attempt to save, at which time the Save As dialog box will appear. Even if you turn sharing off and then turn it back on while another person still has the file open, the person won't be able to share the file until they close or reopen it.

You can click the Remove User button on the Editing tab in the Share Workbook dialog box if you want to disconnect someone from the sharing session manually. Doing this maintains the change history for the master workbook. You'll probably want to warn the person you're disconnecting, of course.

Combining Changes Made to Multiple Workbooks

Another way to share a workbook is to make a separate copy of the workbook for each person in your workgroup. This is a good option if not everyone in your group has access to the same network server, if some users need to work on the workbook when they are on the road, or no network or Internet file-sharing options are available to you. In this scenario, after all the distributed copies have been updated with each person's changes, someone collects the copies and merges everyone's work into a master workbook.

You can merge workbooks that were created equal—that is, a set of workbooks created from the same master. When you merge workbooks, all changes made to the merged workbooks are merged into the master workbook. Merging workbooks, like change tracking, is closely linked with the shared workbooks feature; you can merge only workbooks that have been saved with sharing turned on.

The command to merge workbooks, Compare And Merge Workbooks, is well hidden in Excel 2007, but you can easily add it to the Quick Access Toolbar. Click the Microsoft Office Button, and then click the Excel Options button. In the Excel Options dialog box that appears, select the Customize category. In the Choose Commands From list, select Commands Not In The Ribbon. Select Compare And Merge Workbooks in the list of commands, and then click the Add button to add it to the Quick Access Toolbar. In the Customize Quick Access Toolbar list, select whether you want to add the Compare And Merge Workbooks command to the Quick Access Toolbar for all workbooks or just for a specific workbook.

For more information about customizing the Quick Access Toolbar, see "Customizing the Quick Access Toolbar" on page 83.

The following procedure explains how to set up your workbooks for distribution and eventual merging:

1. Open the workbook you want to distribute.

2. Click the Review tab, and then click Share Workbook.

3. On the Editing tab in the Share Workbook dialog box, select the Allow Changes By More Than One User At The Same Time check box.

4. Click the Advanced tab, and make sure a sufficient number of days appears in the Keep Change History For box for all the members of your workgroup to finish their edits and for you to collect and merge the workbooks. If you are unsure about how long to specify, type a large number, such as **999**. If this time limit is exceeded, you will not be able to merge workbooks.

5. Click OK to save the workbook in shared mode.

6. Click the Microsoft Office Button, and then click Save As. Save additional copies of the workbook under different names—one for each person in your distribution list. Save one extra copy to use as a master workbook. Because you have turned on sharing, each copy you save is also in shared mode.

7. Distribute the copies to the members of your group.

After you have prepared, distributed, and collected the edited workbooks, you are ready to merge by following these steps:

1. Open the workbook you want to use as the master workbook. All the changes made to the other workbooks will be replicated in the master workbook. You must have saved this master workbook from the same original shared workbook, just as the workbooks you distributed were.

2. Make sure the other workbooks you want to merge aren't open, and then click Compare And Merge Workbooks on the Quick Access Toolbar to display the Select Files To Merge Into Current Workbook dialog box shown in Figure 24-12.

3. Select the files you want to merge.

> **Note**
>
> Although merging workbooks combines all changes from a set of workbooks, consolidation combines values only from a set of worksheets. (These worksheets can be in different workbooks.) The Consolidate command can assemble information from as many as 255 supporting worksheets into a single master worksheet. For more information about the Consolidate command, see "Consolidating Worksheets" on page 258.

Chapter 24

Excel merges the workbooks you select in the Select Files To Merge Into Current Workbook dialog box one by one, in the order in which they appear in the dialog box. Excel takes all the changes made to the merged workbooks and makes them in the master workbook. You can accept and reject changes and display the history worksheet, just as you can with shared workbooks, as described in "Tracking Changes" on page 794.

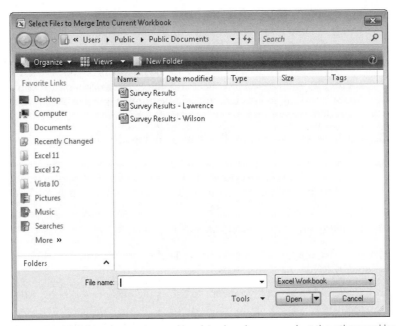

Figure 24-12 When the master workbook is already open, select the other workbooks to merge.

Distributing Workbooks and Worksheets by E-Mail

Provided you have Microsoft Office Outlook 2007 or another compatible e-mail program installed on your system, Excel offers a variety of ways to distribute your work to others via electronic mail. Specifically, you can do the following:

- You can send an entire workbook as an attachment to an e-mail message.

- You can send a workbook out for review.

These options are both accessible by clicking the Microsoft Office Button and then clicking Send. The Send menu also includes an option to send your work to an Internet fax service.

Sending an Entire Workbook as an E-Mail Attachment

To attach the current workbook in its entirety to an e-mail message, click the Microsoft Office Button, click Send, and then click Email. A message appears with the workbook attached. Select recipients, type the subject line and message body, and then click Send to send the workbook to your recipients.

If you're using Outlook 2007 to e-mail a workbook stored in Windows SharePoint Services, you can send the workbook as a shared attachment. Rather than attaching the workbook to the e-mail message, Outlook will attach a link to the workbook's location on a SharePoint site. When you send a workbook from Windows SharePoint Services, Outlook automatically opens the Attachment Options task pane, shown in Figure 24-13. Select Shared Attachments to mail a link to users who have access to the SharePoint site where the document is stored. Select Regular Attachments to send the entire workbook rather than a link.

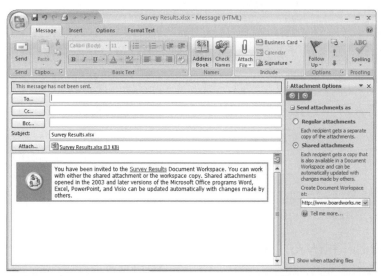

Figure 24-13 When you attach a workbook to an Outlook 2007 e-mail message, the Attachment Options task pane appears. The Shared Attachments option in this task pane helps you create a document workspace on your SharePoint site.

You can also use the Attachment Options task pane to create a document workspace in Windows SharePoint Services, and then you can send a link to the workspace to your recipients. Click the Message tab in the new e-mail message. Click the Dialog Box Launcher in the Include group to open the Attachment Options task pane, shown in Figure 24-13. Select Shared Attachments, and type the uniform resource locator (URL) for your SharePoint document library in the Create Document Workspace text box. (For information about document workspaces, see "Creating a New Document Workspace" on page 816.) If you don't use Windows SharePoint Services, you can safely close the Attachment Options task pane. (Clear the Show When Attaching Files check box to keep the Attachment Options task pane from appearing automatically when you attach a workbook.)

Chapter 24

Naturally, you can also attach a workbook to an e-mail message by working directly in Outlook or another e-mail program. For example, you can do so by creating a new message directly in Outlook, clicking the Insert tab, and then clicking the Attach File command, which has the same effect as the procedure described previously.

Sending a Worksheet or Range by E-Mail

To send one or more worksheets from a workbook but not the entire workbook, copy the worksheets to a new workbook. Select the worksheets, right-click a sheet tab for a selected worksheet, and click Move Or Copy. The Move Or Copy dialog box appears, as shown in Figure 24-14. Select New Book in the Move Selected Sheets To Book list, and select the Create A Copy check box.

Figure 24-14 Use the Move Or Copy dialog box to create a workbook that contains only the worksheets you want to e-mail to the recipient.

To send a range or chart from a worksheet, simply copy the selection in Excel, and then paste it into the body of an Outlook message form.

Sending a Workbook for Review

In previous versions of Excel, the Send For Review command provided an easy way to circulate a workbook for comments and changes by members of your workgroup. When you use this command, Excel attaches the document to an e-mail message and uses "Please review [file name]" as the default subject for your message. To use this command in Excel 2007, you need to add it to your Quick Access Toolbar from the list of commands not on the Ribbon (see "Customizing the Quick Access Toolbar" on page 83).

Ideally, you should use the Send For Review command with workbooks you have set up for sharing. If you apply this command to a workbook that isn't shared, Excel will prompt you to save a shared version. You don't have to share (you can use this command as an alternative way to send any document as an attachment), but your recipients will be able to carry out their reviewing duties more efficiently in a shared workbook.

Controlling Document Access with Information Rights Management

Information Rights Management (IRM) technology, introduced in Microsoft Office 2003, has been improved in the 2007 Microsoft Office system. IRM lets you, the creator of an Excel (or other Office) document, specify which users or groups of users are permitted to read, edit, print, or copy that document. As a means of preventing unauthorized access to or use of your work, it's a more robust mechanism than traditional firewall methods because the access controls remain with your file, even if your file is removed to a different storage medium. It's also both more convenient and more robust than file-level password protection. Rather than distributing passwords to authorized users, you can simply name those users when you set the permissions associated with your document. And you can control the use of your document in a granular fashion, allowing some users to only read, others to read and print, still others to edit (with or without printing permission), and so on.

To set up IRM in your organization, you need to install the Microsoft Windows Rights Management Services (RMS) on a server running Windows Server 2003 and Microsoft Internet Information Services (IIS). This server must be part of a Microsoft Active Directory domain. In addition, you will need a client/server database application such as Microsoft SQL Server 2005.

Before you can apply IRM permissions to a document or use a protected document, you need to have the client-side IRM component installed on your computer. The first time you use IRM in any manner, you'll be prompted to download and install this component (it's free) from a Microsoft site if the component is not already in place. If you're using Windows Live ID authentication, you'll also be prompted (if necessary) to sign on—or to acquire a .NET Passport if you don't already have one.

Full use of IRM requires Office 2003 or newer. Users with older versions can, however, read protected documents for which they have appropriate permission by downloading the free IRM Viewer from *www.microsoft.com*.

Installing IRM

When you open a file that has been protected using IRM, Excel will prompt you to download the RMS client if it is not already installed. But you don't need to wait: You can install the RMS client and use IRM at any time.

Protecting a Document with IRM

To protect a document with IRM, click the Microsoft Office Button, and then click Prepare, Restrict Permission, Restricted Access to open the Permission dialog box shown in Figure 24-15. Select the Restrict Permission To This Workbook check box. In the Read and Change boxes, specify the e-mail addresses of those users to whom you want to grant read and change permissions. (Separate addresses with semicolons.) Alternatively, click the Read and Change buttons, to the left of the boxes, to select names from your address book.

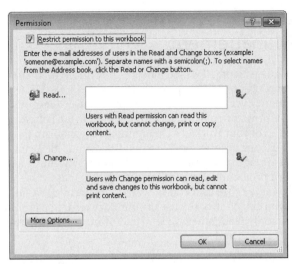

Figure 24-15 Use the Permission dialog box to specify who can read and who can change your file.

The Read and Change options in the dialog box shown in Figure 24-15 apply default settings for those two permissions levels. To refine your permissions settings and to take advantage of additional options, click More Options, and fill out the dialog box shown in Figure 24-16.

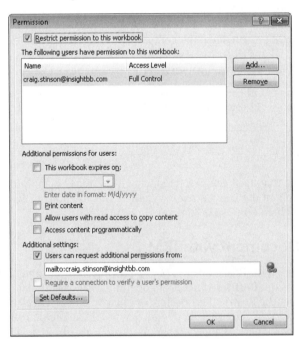

Figure 24-16 Clicking More Options in the Permission dialog box takes you to this dialog box, where you can fine-tune your permissions settings.

The window at the top of this dialog box lists the people to whom you have granted permission to read or change your document. The first address in the list should be your own, and you should set your access level to Full Control. Your address should appear again in the Users Can Request Additional Permissions From box. Users who are denied permission to use your document or who want a higher level of access will be given this link as a means to request an adjustment. You can type a different address in the Users Can Request Additional Permissions From box if you want their appeals to go elsewhere. (You can also clear this check box if you don't want to be bothered with change requests.)

Setting an Expiration Date

If you want your document to be accessible only for a particular period of time, select the This Workbook Expires On check box, and specify a date. No one but you will be allowed to open the document after it has expired.

Allowing Users to Print

Printing is not allowed for any user except you by default. To allow other users to print, select the Print Content check box in the dialog box shown in Figure 24-16. This setting affects both the read and change access levels.

Allowing Users to Click the Copy Command

By default, users with change access are allowed to use the Copy command in your workbook, and users with read access are not. To allow read-only users to click the Copy command, select the Allow Users With Read Access To Copy Content check box. Be aware that allowing users to copy content means those users can replicate formulas and values into unprotected documents. On the other hand, even with the Copy command not available, users can avail themselves of screen-capture utilities to replicate images of your work.

Allowing Programmatic Access

Programmatic access to protected documents—for example, using a Visual Basic for Applications (VBA) macro in another Excel or Office document to read the contents of your protected document—is ordinarily not allowed for anyone but you. To turn on programmatic access (for both the read and change access levels), select the Access Content Programmatically check box.

Making the Current Settings the Default

To make the current settings the default for all future IRM-protected documents, click Set Defaults in the dialog box shown in Figure 24-16. When prompted, click OK to confirm that you want to make your current settings the default settings for IRM.

Adding New Users and Modifying Permissions Settings

To modify the permissions of a document for which you have Full Control access, simply click the Change Permission button above the formula bar. (This button appears
only if you have configured permissions on the workbook.) The dialog box shown in
Figure 24-15 will reappear.

Using a Protected Document

To work with an IRM-protected document, simply open it in the usual manner. If necessary, the IRM client will contact the server to authenticate you, and you might experience a short delay. After the file has opened, if you have only read access, you will find
nearly all of the Excel commands and buttons unavailable on the Ribbon. Attempts to
click the formula bar or press F2 will be met with a beep and an error message, and the
keyboard's alpha keys will be inert. The message above the formula bar notes that this
is a protected document:

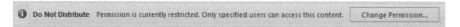

To see what you are permitted to do, click the Permission button at the left end of
the status bar or the Change Permission button above the formula bar. A dialog box
appears listing your permissions. If you need a higher level of access, you can click
Request Additional Permissions.

If you do not have permission to open the workbook, a dialog box will notify you and
ask whether you want to request additional permission. If you click Yes, your default
e-mail program will open a message addressed to the person whose e-mail address is in
the Users Can Request Additional Permissions From box for the workbook.

Alternatively, if you have another Windows Live ID or .NET Passport available to you,
one with higher permissions, you can click Change User and specify the necessary
authentication information. The same recourses are available to you if you try to open a
document while logged on as an unauthorized person.

Collaborating Using the Internet

Chapter 24, "Collaborating on a Network or by E-Mail," surveyed some of the features that Microsoft Office Excel 2007 provides to facilitate file sharing and communication amongst co-workers. This chapter explores additional collaborative features—those that involve the Internet. This chapter will show you how to set up a Microsoft Windows SharePoint Services site, how to transfer your work in Office Excel 2007 to and from the SharePoint site, and how to take advantage of the program's newest collaboration tool, Excel Services.

Using a Windows SharePoint Services Site

Excel 2007, like the other 2007 Microsoft Office system applications, builds on the Office 2003 collaboration features based on Windows SharePoint Services. Office SharePoint Server 2007 offers even tighter integration with Office, and the new Excel Services provide server-side performance for your large Excel workbooks.

If you have access to a SharePoint site, you can use the site as a workgroup document repository. While you and other team members are working on a collaborative project, all the artifacts related to that project—documents, task lists, team-member contact information, deadlines, and links to related materials—can be available for all the team members in a single, centralized location. While you are connected to the site—whether directly by means of your Web browser or by opening a team document in Excel—you can see at a glance which other team members are also online, and you can easily initiate instant messaging conversations with collaborators or send them e-mail.

Downloading and Uploading Documents

Figure 25-1 shows a document library at a SharePoint site, as viewed in Microsoft Internet Explorer. Figure 25-2 shows the same library as viewed in the Open dialog box in Excel. To get to the document library in the Open dialog box, type the site's Uniform Resource Locator (URL) in the Address bar. In the Document Libraries list, double-click the appropriate library to display its files. Double-click the document you want to open.

You can access the shared documents with equal facility from Internet Explorer and from Excel. The one item of information provided on the SharePoint site but not in the Excel Open dialog box is the Windows Messenger icon that appears beside the names of contacts who happen to be online at the moment. You can click that icon to open a menu of actions related to the contact in question—for example, to send the contact an instant message in Windows Live Messenger, to schedule a meeting with the contact, to send e-mail, to place a phone call, or to open the contact's record in Microsoft Office Outlook. As you'll see, this functionality is also available in Excel via the Shared Workspace task pane.

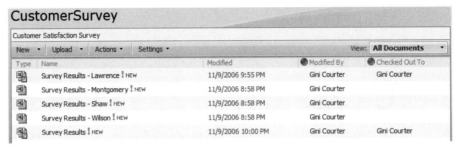

Figure 25-1 You can download a SharePoint document by clicking it in Internet Explorer.

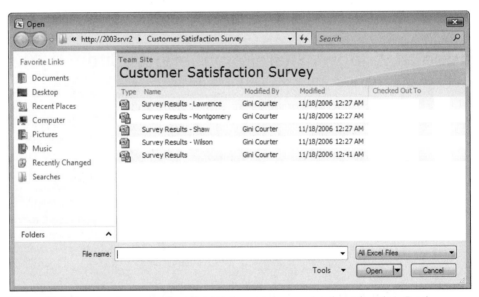

Figure 25-2 You can also access SharePoint documents by opening them directly in Excel.

To download a document from SharePoint to Excel, point to the file and then click the small arrow that appears to the right of the file name, and click Edit In Excel. Alternatively, simply open it from the Open dialog box or the Recent Documents list in Excel.

When you download a SharePoint document from the browser, the document is read-only. However, if another user has not checked out the document, and provided you have Contributor or Administrator privileges for the SharePoint site, you can write changes back to the site without renaming the document. Simply click the Microsoft Office Button, click Save, supply the same file name (and location) as you used to download the document, and click Save. The SharePoint site will accept the modified file without giving you a confirmation prompt, and the read-only designation will disappear.

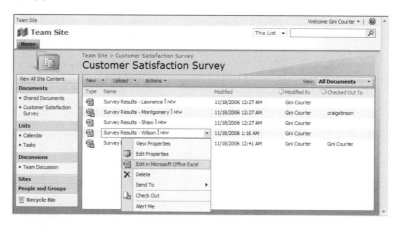

To upload a file to the SharePoint site, you can use the Save command in Excel. Alternatively, from within the document library at the SharePoint site (see Figure 25-1), click Upload, then click Upload Document or Upload Multiple Documents, and finally browse to the file's location on your local storage system. You have must have Contributor or Administrator privileges to upload files.

SharePoint is also a document management server, so you can save an Excel workbook to SharePoint in one more way. Click the Microsoft Office Button, click Publish, and then click Document Management Server to open the Save As dialog box. In the Address bar, type the URL for your SharePoint site. Double-click the document library in which you want to store the document, type a file name, and then click Save.

For information about uploading Excel tables to SharePoint, see "Exporting Excel Tables to SharePoint" on page 818.

Checking Documents In and Out

The SharePoint check-in, check-out mechanism lets users reserve read-write privileges for themselves temporarily while they are editing documents. If you check out a document, only you have read-write privileges. Others can download the document from the site but cannot save changes to it. (They can still save their changes to the document using another name.)

To check a document out, right-click it in SharePoint (in your browser), and click Check Out. To check it back in, save any changes you have made (and want to keep). Then right-click the file name in the browser, and click Check In. SharePoint will present the form shown in Figure 25-3, where you can add comments about the changes you have made.

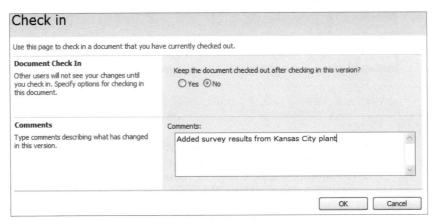

Figure 25-3 When you check a document back in, SharePoint presents this form, letting you append comments to the document.

The site administrator can require document checkout before editing for the entire site or for a specific library. If checkout is required, when you click Edit In Office Excel 2007, you'll see a dialog box, as shown in Figure 25-4, advising you that the file is being checked out and stored in your local drafts folder.

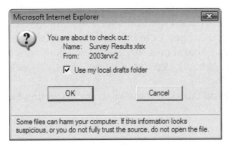

Figure 25-4 With document checkout required, SharePoint automatically checks out the document when you open it for editing in Excel 2007.

The default view in a SharePoint library (see Figure 25-1) includes the Checked Out To column so you can see when a file is locked for editing by another user. In every view, the file icon includes an arrow; if you rest the pointer on the icon, a ScreenTip appears with the name of the user who has checked out the file. Pay attention to whether a file is checked out if you're opening a document for editing. SharePoint will let you open and edit the document, but you will not be able to save your changes with the original file name.

Using the Document Management Task Pane

When you open a SharePoint document in Excel, Excel usually displays the Document Management task pane (shown in Figure 25-5). The Document Management task pane provides, among other things, information about the status of your document and the online availability of your collaborators. (If no task pane or a different task pane is displayed, click the Microsoft Office Button, click Server, and then click Document Management Information.)

Figure 25-5 Document status information, including the status of other team members, appears in the Document Management task pane.

Contacting Team Members

You can see in Figure 25-5 that the current document is accessible to a number of team members. Gini Courter's name appears at the top of the list, above a horizontal rule, because this illustration was captured in her copy of Excel. Craig Stinson (user name craigstinson) is logged on to one of the Microsoft Messenger programs—Windows Live Messenger, Windows Messenger, or MSN Messenger—so he is listed under Online with a green circle in front of his name. The other team members appear under Not Online with gray circles because they are not logged on to any Microsoft Messenger program.

To initiate an instant-messaging conversation with any online Messenger contact (such as Craig Stinson in Figure 25-5), click that person's name. To send e-mail to an offline contact or to a team member who is not a contact, click that person's name. To send mail to all team members, click the Send E-Mail To All Members link near the bottom of the task pane. To perform any other action in relation to a team member, right-click the team member's name, and click the appropriate command.

Getting Document Status Information

Figure 25-5 shows the Members panel of the Document Management task pane. The icons across the top of the pane provide access to other panels. Clicking the Status icon at the left of this array, for example:

opens the Status panel, where you might see something like this:

Note that people named in the Status panel provide access to contact functionality, just as they do in the Members panel. In the previous illustration, for example, you could click Gini Courter's name to launch a Messenger session and ask Gini when she's planning to check in the document.

Assigning and Monitoring Tasks

The Tasks panel lists each task assigned to the current document, along with the name of the person to whom the task has been assigned and the task's deadline. The check box beside each task provides information about the status of that task. A clear check box denotes a task that has not been started. A check mark indicates a completed task.

A square dot within the check box means the task has some other status: in progress, deferred, or "waiting on someone else." In the Tasks panel shown here, for example, Curtis Philips has completed the review, and John Pierce has not started adding scenarios to the workbook:

To add a new task, click Add New Task, at the bottom of the Tasks panel, and then fill out the following form:

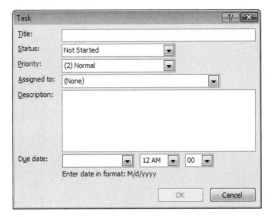

To delete or edit a task (for example, to change its status from Not Started to Completed), click the small arrow to the right of the task, and then click Delete Task or Edit Task as shown on the next page.

To receive an "alert" when the status of a task has changed, click the small arrow to the right of the task, and then click Alert Me About This Task. This action opens a New Alert form in Internet Explorer. (To set an alert for all tasks associated with the current document, click Alert Me About Tasks at the bottom of the Tasks panel.)

Opening Related Documents

The Documents panel, as shown in Figure 25-6, lists all files stored in the current document library—that is, the SharePoint path from which you downloaded the current document. You can open related documents by clicking them in this panel. You can also request change alerts for any or all related documents. To be alerted of changes to a particular document, click the small arrow to the right of the task, and then click Alert Me About This Document. To be notified of changes to any documents or additions or deletions to the current document library, click Alert Me About Documents at the bottom of the Documents panel. You can use the other links at the bottom of the panel to add new documents to the library or to create organizational folders.

Figure 25-6 You can use the Documents panel to open other documents from the same SharePoint library.

Using Links

You can use the Links panel to store and activate links to related Web sites, intranet sites, or off-site documents. To create a link, click Add New Link at the bottom of the panel. For alerts about a particular link, click the small arrow to the right of the task, and then click Alert Me About This Link. For alerts about any link, click Alert Me About Links at the bottom of the panel:

Getting Information About the Current Document

The Document Information panel tells who created the document, who has modified it, and when the last modification took place. Names listed here, as elsewhere, provide access to e-mail and messaging services. An Alert Me About This Document link, at the bottom of the panel, lets you set up or change alerts associated with the current document. If you have the current document checked out, a Check In link at the bottom of the panel gives you an easy way to check it in.

Creating a New Document Workspace

A *document workspace* is a set of documents, along with related task, personnel, and status information, stored at a common SharePoint path. If your SharePoint site includes a library called Shared Documents, for example, that library constitutes a document workspace. You can create new document workspaces as subwebs within your SharePoint Web site that focus on particular projects and are accessible to particular team members. Your new workspace can become, in effect, a semiprivate corner within the overall SharePoint site, with fewer distractions (irrelevant documents and announcements) than the parent site. After your group has finished its work in the new document workspace, you can publish the group's documents to the parent site.

Excel 2007 and SharePoint give you three ways to create a new document workspace:

- By using Excel (or another 2007 Office release application)
- By e-mailing a "shared attachment" to other team members
- By using SharePoint

> **Note**
> To create a document workspace, you must have the Create Subsites permission for the SharePoint site in which you want to create your subsite (subweb).

Creating a Document Workspace from Within Excel

To create a new document workspace from within Excel, follow these steps:

1. In Excel, open the first document you want to include in the document workspace.

2. Be sure the document includes no unsaved changes. (When you create the document workspace, Excel will prompt you to save if you omit this step.)

3. Be sure your SharePoint site is designated as a trusted site in Internet Explorer. To make it a trusted site, open Internet Explorer, and then click Tools, Internet Options to open the Internet Options dialog box. On the Security tab, click the Trusted Sites icon. Then click the Sites button. Type the URL for your site in the Add This Web Site To The Zone box, click Add, click Close, and then click OK.

> **Note**
> By default, the Trusted Sites dialog box has the Require Server Verification (Https:) For All Sites In This Zone check box selected. If your site doesn't use secure Hypertext Transfer Protocol (HTTPS), clear this check box before adding the URL for the SharePoint site.

4. In Excel, click the Microsoft Office Button, click Publish, and then click Create Document Workspace to open the Document Workspace panel:

5. Modify the document workspace name if you want, specify the URL for your SharePoint site in the Location For New Workspace box, and then click the Create button.

The URL for your new document workspace will be the URL of the SharePoint site followed by a slash, which is then followed by your document name. For example, if your site's URL is *http://MySharePointSite* and the document from which you created the document workspace is AnnualReport.xlsx, the address of your new document workspace will be *http://MySharePointSite/AnnualReport*.

Creating a Document Workspace via E-Mail

To create a document workspace using the e-mail services in Microsoft Office Outlook, simply attach an Office document to a message addressed to one or more workspace participants. In the Outlook message window, click the Dialog Box Launcher next to Include to display the Attachment Options task pane (if it isn't already displayed). Then select Shared Attachments, and specify the URL for your SharePoint site.

When you send your message, each recipient will receive an invitation to join the document workspace, along with a link to the site. You will receive e-mail confirmation that the site was created successfully.

For more information about sharing workbooks via e-mail, see "Sending an Entire Workbook as an E-Mail Attachment" on page 801.

Creating a Document Workspace from Within SharePoint

To move a SharePoint document into a new document workspace, click the Documents link on the left side of the SharePoint site, and then click Create. On the Create page, click the Sites And Workspaces link. Use the New SharePoint Site page to define a title, description, URL name, a template for your workspace, permissions and their inheritance, and navigation properties. Then click Create.

Managing a Document Workspace

After you have created a new document workspace, you can add participants or documents either from within SharePoint (using your browser) or from within Excel. To add a document from the browser, navigate to your document workspace subweb, click Documents on the main SharePoint menu, click Shared Documents under the Document Libraries heading, and then click Upload. Browse to select the file you want to upload to your workspace, and then click OK.

To add a new user from within Excel, display a document that's part of your document workspace. Then, on the Members panel in the Document Management task pane, click the Add New Members link.

Exporting Excel Tables to SharePoint

If you have access to a SharePoint site, you can distribute Excel tables by publishing them on the site. When you export an Excel table to the SharePoint site, you can share table data with other users who use the SharePoint site, letting site users update the SharePoint list by opening the list and editing the data. This is a useful strategy for tables that are updated frequently by a number of users, particularly if other users need read-only access to the table data.

You can create a connection from the SharePoint list to the Excel table, or separate the two, depending on whether you want to propagate changes made to the list to the Excel table. If you create a one-way connection to the data in the SharePoint list, changes that are made to the SharePoint list are also made to the Excel table. When you refresh the table data in Excel, the latest data from the SharePoint site overwrites the table data on the worksheet. (Be careful here: This includes any changes you made to the table data.)

If you don't want to keep the Excel table updated with changes from the SharePoint list, you can export the data without any connection to the SharePoint list.

> **Note**
> Unlike in Excel 2003, in Excel 2007 you can no longer create a one-way connection from the Excel workbook to the SharePoint list.

To publish an Excel list in SharePoint, you must first convert the list to a table. Select any cell in the list, and press Ctrl+T or click Table in the Tables group on the Insert tab on the Ribbon. In the Create Table dialog box, verify that the correct range is defined for the table. If your table has headers, select the My Table Has Headers check box, and then click OK. In the External Table Data group on the Design tab under Table Tools, click the arrow below the Export button, and click Export Table To SharePoint List to open the Export Table To SharePoint List dialog box shown in Figure 25-7.

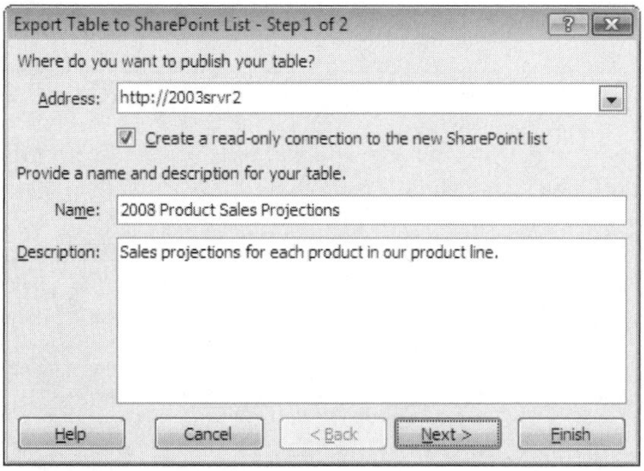

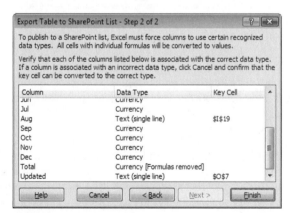

Figure 25-7 Type the URL for your SharePoint site to publish your Excel table as a SharePoint list.

Type your SharePoint site's URL, a name for the SharePoint list, and a brief description. If you want to be able to update the Excel table with changes made on the SharePoint site, select the Create A Read-Only Connection To The New SharePoint List check box. Click Next. The second step of the export, shown in Figure 25-8, shows the column names and data types of the columns that Excel will export to the list. Review the list to make sure the data types are correct.

Figure 25-8 If the data type for a column is incorrect, note the Key Cell address, and correct the contents of the cell.

If a column contains any text values, Excel exports the entire column as text. If a column contains numbers or dates but includes one or more text entries (for example, N/A instead of a number or date), this is your opportunity to clean the data in your table before exporting it. The Key Cell listed is the first cell in a column that contains a text value. For example, in Figure 25-8, the Aug and Updated columns are marked for Excel to export as text because cells I19 and O7 contain text entries. If you need to correct the Excel table, click Cancel to stop the export, fix your data, and then start the export again. When the data types are correct, click Finish to export the Excel table as a SharePoint list. Figure 25-9 shows the example SharePoint list.

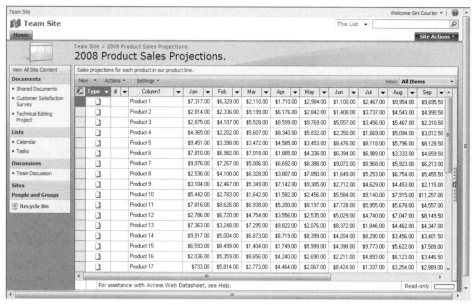

Figure 25-9 User changes to this SharePoint list will be reflected in the Excel table.

Using Excel Services

In every organization, knowledge workers need to analyze increasingly more data more frequently. This version of Excel supports vastly larger worksheets than the prior version to meet these increased demands. The worksheets and workbooks you can create in Excel 2007 are very large. A single workbook can easily contain millions of values—a challenge for a standard desktop or laptop. Although Excel data stores are increasing in size, the number of controls placed on company data is also increasing, particularly for publicly traded companies. Excel Services, new in Office SharePoint Server 2007, is a special server version of the calculation capabilities found in Excel to support and secure Excel workbooks in a multiuser environment by letting other users access all or part of the workbook in their browsers using Office Excel Web Access.

In many organizations, it's difficult to keep track of which version of an Excel workbook represents "the truth." Even when you share a workbook, users create and modify their own copies and then e-mail them to other users. When you save a workbook to Excel Services, the entire workbook is secured on the server. Users cannot open this workbook using Excel, so the workbook stored on the server becomes the "one source of truth." Some workbooks should not be shared, however, because they contain proprietary information or are subject to regulatory constraints such as the Sarbanes-Oxley Act in the United States. By publishing the workbook to Excel Services, you can distribute appropriate information from the workbook and still be able to guarantee compliance with governmental regulations or your company's policies.

Excel Web Access is a visually rich browser client that requires no additional installation. It supports most of the newer formatting options from Excel 2007, including conditional formatting and data visualizations. In addition, Excel Web Access is interactive. Users can filter, apply outlining, and use PivotTables for data analysis. With some planning on your part, Excel Web Access supports what-if analysis using familiar Excel tools such as the goal-seeking feature and the Solver add-in. Users do not need to have Excel 2007 to use Excel Web Access.

You determine which parts of the workbook are displayed in Excel Web Access: specific worksheets, ranges, or charts. You can also use parameters to let users type data in specific cells. (*Parameters* are single cells where users can enter data.) Each parameter must be named.

For information on naming cells, see "Naming Cells and Cell Ranges" on page 441.

Excel Services is a calculation engine that supports most, but not all, of the functionality of Excel. For example, Excel Services does not support XML maps, data validation, or comments. For a complete list of unsupported features, click the Excel Help button, and search for help on Excel Services differences.

Publishing a Workbook to Excel Services

Before publishing the workbook to Excel Services, make sure you have named any cells where you want users to enter data (for example, a starting date and ending date used as report parameters). Then follow these steps to save the workbook to Excel Services:

1. Click the Microsoft Office Button, click Publish, and then click Excel Services to open the Save As dialog box.

2. In the File Name box, type the path to the server with Excel Services and a file name (for example, *http://servername/sitename/filename*).

3. Click the arrow to the right of Save As Type, and select a file type: either Microsoft Office Excel 2007 XML-based file format (.xlsx) or Office Excel 2007 Binary file format (.xlsb).

4. Click the Excel Services Options button to open the Excel Services Options dialog box, shown in Figure 25-10.

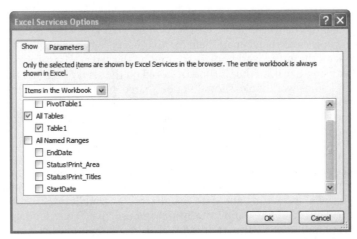

Figure 25-10 Use the Show tab in the Excel Services Options dialog box to show or hide worksheets or items in the workbook.

5. On the Show tab, display the list to select Entire Workbook, Sheets, or Items In The Workbook.

6. If you select Sheets or Items In The Workbook, clear the check boxes for the worksheets or items you do not want to show in Excel Web Access.

7. If you want to define parameters, click the Parameters tab, shown in Figure 25-11.

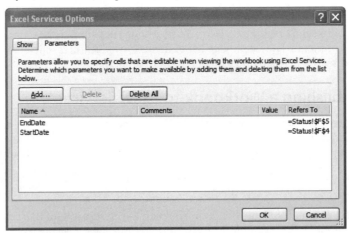

Figure 25-11 Use the Parameters tab in the Excel Services Options dialog box to specify named cells that are user editable.

8. Click the Add button to open the Add Parameters dialog box. Select the check boxes of the parameters you want to add.

9. Click OK to add the parameters. Click OK to close the Excel Services Options dialog box.

10. Click Save to save the workbook to Excel Services.

As the owner of the workbook stored in Excel Services, you can open the workbook in Excel to modify it. When you save the workbook, the changes are automatically reflected in Excel Services and the Excel Web Access client. Excel Web Access users can view the workbook, worksheets, or items you specified. They can edit the values in any cells you set as parameters.

PART 9
Automating Excel

Recording Macros

A *macro* is a set of instructions telling Microsoft Office Excel 2007 (or another application) to perform one or more actions for you. Macros in Office Excel 2007 are like computer programs, but they run completely within Excel. You can use them to automate tedious or frequently repeated tasks.

Macros can carry out sequences of actions much more quickly than you could yourself. For example, you can create a macro that enters a series of dates across one row of a worksheet, centers the date in each cell, and then applies a border format to the row. Or you can create a macro that defines a combination of print settings—margins, orientation, scaling, headers, and footers—that you want to be able to reuse easily in many documents. Macros are great for any task you do repeatedly.

You can create a macro in two ways: You can record it, or you can build it by typing instructions in a module. Either way, your instructions are encoded in the programming language Microsoft Visual Basic for Applications (VBA). (You can also combine the two approaches.)

Even if you're not a programmer and have no intention of becoming one, macros can be a useful addition to your Excel toolkit. Thanks to the macro recorder, you don't have to understand all the ins and outs of VBA to create effective and timesaving macros. And if you're curious about VBA and want to learn to do more with macros than is possible with the recorder alone, you will find the recorder to be an excellent learning tool. You can get a great start on acquiring VBA expertise by examining the code that the recorder generates.

Configuring Macro Security

Macros execute code, and code can serve evil ends as well as good ones. If your system is permitted to run all macros, regardless of their source, you might inadvertently run a macro that will damage your system in some way. Because VBA macros included in Microsoft Office documents (typically attached to e-mail messages) have occasionally served as virus vectors in recent years, Microsoft no longer permits VBA code to run by default. You have to take steps to enable macro execution.

Like other security configuration settings, the settings that permit or deny macro execution are in the Trust Center. To get there, click the Microsoft Office Button, and then click Excel Options. In the Excel Options dialog box, select the Trust Center category, and then click Trust Center Settings.

For more information about the Trust Center, see "The Trust Center" on page 103.

How you configure macro security depends on how you expect to use macros, the degree to which you are concerned about potentially malicious macro code, and perhaps the security policies of your organization. If your organization's IT staff has disabled access to the Trust Center, as well as macro execution, this discussion is moot (unless you can convince someone to relax the rules). Assuming that's not the case, your first stop in the Trust Center should be the Macro Settings category, where you will see something like the following:

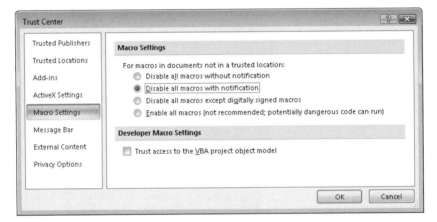

The four options in the Macro Settings area of this dialog box determine how Excel handles macro code in files that are not stored in a trusted location. The default setting disallows such macros but causes a notification bar to appear whenever you open a file that contains a proscribed macro. The notification bar looks like this:

If you know for sure that whatever macros the file might contain are benign, you can overrule the security cop by clicking Options, reading the message that appears, and then selecting Enable This Content. If you use macros regularly, however (for example, if you create them to increase your own productivity), you probably don't want to deal with the notification bar every time you open a workbook containing macros. You might instead be tempted to change the Macro Settings option in the Trust Center to Enable All Macros (Not Recommended, Potentially Dangerous Code Can Run). As the parenthetical comment suggests, however, this is not an ideal approach to macro security.

A better approach is to designate the folders you use regularly, as well as those from which you are likely to open macro-laden files created by trustworthy others, as trusted locations. Excel permits all macro content in files stored in such locations. To configure a trusted location, return to the Trust Center, and select the Trusted Locations category. You will see a list comparable to the following:

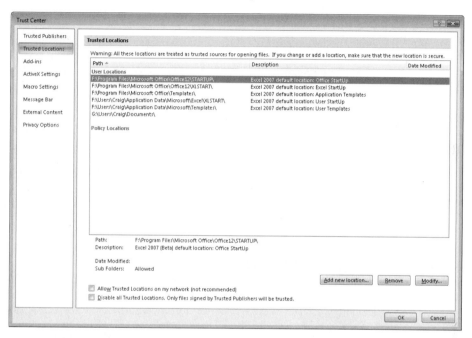

The top area in this dialog box lists trusted locations you create, as well as those provided as defaults by the Microsoft Office Setup program. Below that list, under the heading Policy Locations, you might see additional trusted locations established by your IT staff. To set up a new trusted location, click Add New Location. In the dialog box that appears, you can specify the path of the new location, indicate whether you also want to trust subfolders of that location, and add a description of the location. Excel will provide a date and time stamp for you.

By using the trusted-locations mechanism, you can create no-questions-asked zones for the macros you create and use, without disabling the defenses Excel uses against external threats. If you leave in place the default Macro Settings option—Disable All Macros With Notification—Excel will inform you if you happen to open a file from a nontrusted location that contains a macro. When that occurs, you can make a judgment call about whether to allow the banned content. You can also easily add the new file's folder to your listed of trusted locations by clicking Trust Center in the notification bar.

Having configured the security options to your satisfaction, you still have one more decision to make before you can begin creating your own macros. The Excel default workbook format (.xlsx) does not support macros. To save a workbook containing one or more macros, you need to use one of the following formats:

- Excel Macro-Enabled Workbook (.xlsm)
- Excel Binary Workbook (.xlsb)
- Excel 97–2003 Workbook (.xls)

If you plan to use macros regularly, or even occasionally, you should consider changing the default to one of these macro-supporting formats. To do this, return to the Excel Options dialog box once more (click the Microsoft Office Button, and then click Excel Options), select the Save category, and select a format in the Save Files In This Format drop-down list.

For more information about file format options, see "Understanding the 'XL' Formats" on page 56.

If you prefer not to change the default file format to Excel Macro-Enabled Workbook, you can always save in that format on a case-by-case basis when you create a file that uses a macro. Excel will warn you when you try to save a file with macros in a non-macro-enabled format.

Using the Macro Recorder

To make the macro recorder accessible, you need to display the Developer tab on the Ribbon. Click the Microsoft Office Button, and then click Excel Options. In the Popular category, select the Show Developer Tab In The Ribbon check box, and then click OK. To start the macro recorder, click Record Macro in the Code group on the Developer tab.

> **Note**
> After you have exercised the option to include the Developer tab on the Ribbon, the Record Macro button appears on the status bar next to the word *Ready* as well as in the Code group on the Developer tab. It remains accessible there even if you subsequently clear the Show Developer Tab In The Ribbon check box in the Excel Options dialog box. You'll probably want to keep the Developer tab on your Ribbon, however, because the tab includes numerous other commands useful for working with macros.

To see how the recorder works, try creating a simple macro that inserts a company name and address in a worksheet. Follow these steps:

1. Click Record Macro in the Code group on the Developer tab. Excel displays the Record Macro dialog box shown in Figure 26-1.

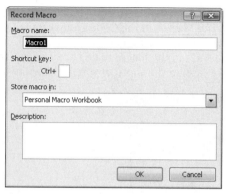

Figure 26-1 In the Record Macro dialog box, you must provide a name and indicate where the macro should be stored. The Shortcut Key and Description fields are optional.

2. Assign a name to the macro. You can accept the suggestion (Macro1) or type your own name. Let's use **CompanyAddress**. (The macro recorder doesn't permit space characters.)

3. Assign a key combination to the macro by typing a letter in the text box. If possible, use something related to the purpose of the macro so you'll remember it later. Let's use uppercase **A**. (The recorder distinguishes capital letters from lowercase ones.)

4. Accept the default of This Workbook for Store Macro In. (We'll discuss the Personal Macro Workbook option later in this chapter.)

5. Type a description for the macro in the Description box. (**Enter company address** will do nicely.)

6. To begin recording, click OK. In the Code group on the Developer tab, the Record Macro button is replaced by a Stop Recording button, as shown in Figure 26-2. (The Stop Recording button also appears on the status bar.)

Figure 26-2 The change from Record Macro to Stop Recording is your only indication that your actions are now being preserved for posterity.

7. Select A6, and type **Coho Winery**. In A7, type **3012 West Beaujolais St.**, and in A8, type **Walla Walla, WA 98765**.

8. In the Code group on the Developer tab, click Stop Recording.

To test the new macro, clear the worksheet, and then press Ctrl+Shift+A. Excel runs the macro and performs the sequence of actions in the same way you recorded them.

Chapter 26

If you forget the keyboard shortcut for a macro or if you didn't bother to assign one, you can run your macro by clicking Macros in the Code group on the Developer tab. In the Macro dialog box that appears, shown in Figure 26-3, you can select a macro and run it. You can also click the Edit button in the Macro dialog box to visit (and alter) the code or click the Options button to assign the shortcut you neglected to assign earlier.

Figure 26-3 The Macro dialog box lets you run macros without keyboard shortcuts.

Recording with Relative References

The macro you just recorded has one serious fault (other than that it doesn't create *your* company address): It always does its business in cells A6:A8. It would be considerably more valuable if you could use it anywhere.

By default, the macro recorder records absolute references. That is, if you're in A6 when you record a cell entry, the action will play back in A6. To make it record relative references instead, click Use Relative References in the Code group on the Developer tab.

The Use Relative References button is a toggle. If you're using relative references and you click this button again, the recorder returns to absolute referencing. You can toggle between the two modes as often as you like while you are recording—which means your recorded macros can contain whatever combination of absolute and relative references suits your purposes.

CAUTION!

When clicked, the Use Relative References command does not change to say *Use Absolute References*, as you might expect. Instead, it appears highlighted on the Ribbon when you're recording (or set to record) relatively, remaining unhighlighted when you're recording absolutely. To avoid disappointment, be sure to verify the state of this toggle when you begin recording.

What to Do When the Macro Recorder Does Not Give You What You Expect

The most likely reason a recorded macro might not generate the expected result is that it was recorded in the wrong relative/absolute state. If output from your macro does not appear in the desired worksheet location, consider the possibility that you recorded it with absolute instead of relative references, and try recording it again.

A second common cause for disappointment is that the macro recorder records completed actions only. An example will illustrate: Suppose you want to record a macro that will place a full date and time stamp in the current cell. You know you can press Ctrl+; to generate the current date and Ctrl+: to generate the current time. But you want the date *and* the time in the same cell, and Excel has no keyboard shortcut for that. A macro can help.

One way to achieve the desired stamp (without a macro) is to type **=NOW()** and then press F9 before pressing Enter. The NOW function returns the full date and time, and pressing F9 before pressing Enter converts the formula to its calculated result.

You might suppose you could turn on the macro recorder, set references to relative, and then record exactly those steps: **=NOW(),F9**. Unfortunately, the result of your work would be a macro that always entered the date and time of its creation, not the current date and time. That's because the macro recorder "sees" a sequence such as this as a single action, even though it might seem like two separate steps to you.

The solution to this problem is to find another way to carry out the action that really does involve discrete steps. You can accomplish that by typing the formula, pressing Enter, selecting the cell in which you typed the formula, copying it to the Clipboard, and then using the Paste Special command and selecting Values in the Paste Special dialog box. That's the long way around when you want to convert a formula to its result immediately, but it works for the macro recorder.

Further troubleshooting of recorded macros requires a rudimentary understanding of VBA. If you like the convenience and enhanced productivity that macros afford, you will probably find it worthwhile to look at the code that the macro recorder generates and learn a bit about how that code works. If you're new to VBA, the following sections will help you get started.

Introducing the Visual Basic Editor

When you clicked OK in the Record Macro dialog box, Excel created a container, called a *module*, for the new VBA code, storing the module in the active workbook. As you carried out the actions for the recorder to record, Excel transcribed those actions into the new module.

The module doesn't appear with the other worksheets and chart sheets in the workbook. To view it, click Visual Basic in the Code group on the Developer tab. This takes you to the Visual Basic Editor. In the upper-left corner of the Visual Basic Editor, you'll find a small window known as the Project Explorer:

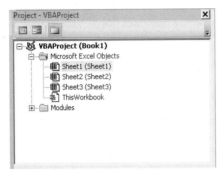

Yours will look different depending on how you've named the current workbook and what other workbooks happen to be open. But in any case, you should see the entry Modules with an outline control (a plus sign) beside it. Click the outline control, and then double-click the entry Module1 that appears. To the right of the Project Explorer, you will see the Code window for Module1, which is displayed in Figure 26-4.

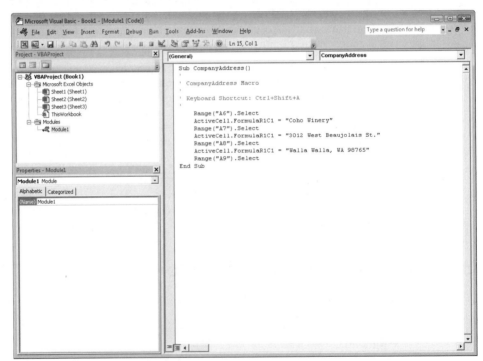

Figure 26-4 Excel stores the VBA code for each action you recorded in the module. You can inspect and edit it in the Visual Basic Editor.

As you can see, a module looks like a window you might see in a word processor. The menu bar above the module includes menus for editing, debugging, and running VBA code. In the module, you can review, type, copy, move, insert, and delete VBA statements and comments, just as you might manipulate text in a word processor. From the Visual Basic Editor, you can switch back to your workbook by clicking the Excel icon at the left edge of the toolbar. From there, you can return to the Visual Basic Editor by clicking Visual Basic in the Code group on the Developer tab. From either place, you can switch to the other by pressing Alt+F11.

The Visual Basic Editor is a big place, full of interesting details, but for now we'll focus only on the code we've recorded. The first and last lines act as the beginning point and the endpoint for the macro. A Sub statement starts the macro and names it, and an End Sub statement ends it. You'll notice that special VBA terms, called *keywords*, appear in dark blue. (You can view and change the colors assigned to various elements of a macro by clicking Tools, Options in the Visual Basic Editor and then clicking the Editor Format tab.)

Below the Sub statement are two comment lines, displayed in green. (If you typed a description for your macro in the Record Macro dialog box, you'll find an additional comment line.) Comment lines begin with the apostrophe character and are ignored when you run the macro. Their only purpose is to help you (or anyone else looking at your code) understand what you've done and why.

The statements following the comments are the meat of the macro—the code that does the (presumably) useful work. Our simple macro includes four lines that select cells and three lines that enter data.

Learning the Basics of Visual Basic

You can get detailed information about a keyword by selecting the word and pressing F1. In Figure 26-4, for example, if you click anywhere within the keyword *Sub* and press F1, the Visual Basic Editor presents a Help screen containing an entry for the Sub statement, as shown in Figure 26-5.

Many Help topics for VBA keywords include one or more examples of the keyword as you might use it in working code. You can copy this code, paste it into a module, and edit the resulting text to meet your needs.

Objects, Methods, and Properties

To VBA, every item in the Excel environment is an *object* rather than an abstract set of data structures or an arrangement of pixels on the screen. Objects can contain other objects. At the top of the hierarchy, the largest object within the Excel *object model* is the Excel application. Objects contained within this largest container include workbooks. Workbooks contain worksheets and chart sheets, worksheets contain ranges (and can also contain chart objects), and so on.

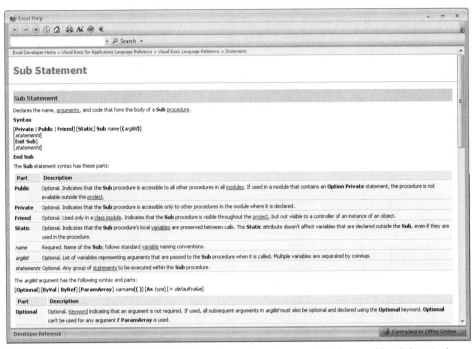

Figure 26-5 You can display detailed Help information about any VBA keyword by clicking in the word and pressing F1.

The first executable (noncomment) statement in the CompanyAddress macro after the Sub statement is the following:

```
Range("A6").Select
```

This line illustrates an important characteristic of VBA code. The syntax of many statements specifies first an object and then an action. An object can be a range, a worksheet, a graphic object, a workbook, or any of the more than 100 types of objects in Excel. Here, we specify a range object (the absolute cell reference A6) and an action (select).

The *behaviors*, or sets of actions, that an object "knows" how to perform are called the *methods* of the object. Methods are like verbs. To understand this concept, imagine you are programming a robotic dog through VBA. To cause the dog to bark, you might use the following statement:

```
Dog.Bark
```

Robotic dogs, however, are (or ought to be) capable of more than just barking. For example, you might want the dog to understand the following statements:

```
Dog.Sit
Dog.RollOver
Dog.Fetch
```

The tricks your robodog can perform, such as barking, rolling over, and fetching, are its methods. The list of methods an object can perform depends on the object. A range object, for example, supports almost 80 different methods that you can use to copy and paste cells, sort, add formatting, and so on.

Like objects in the "real" world, objects in VBA also have properties. If you think of objects as the nouns of VBA and methods as the verbs, then properties are the adjectives. A *property* is a quality, characteristic, or attribute of an object, such as its color or pattern. Characteristics such as your robodog's color, the number of spots on its back, the length of its tail, and the volume of its bark are among its properties.

You set a property by following the name of the property with an equal sign and a value. Continuing the robotic dog example, you could set the length of the dog's tail with the following:

```
Dog.TailLength = 10
```

in which TailLength is a property of the Dog object.

For example, the following executable statement in our CompanyAddress macro:

```
ActiveCell.FormulaR1C1 = "Coho Winery"
```

changes one of the properties, FormulaR1C1, of the active cell, setting that property to the value Coho Winery.

The remaining statements in the CompanyAddress macro consist of two more cell-selection and text-entry couplets. The macro selects cells A7 and A8 and enters text in each cell. (The last line, which selects cell A9, is there only because Excel moves the selection down a row by default after you type something in a cell.)

The Object Browser

You can view the various types of objects, methods, and properties available to Excel by clicking View, Object Browser (or pressing F2) in the Visual Basic Editor. The window displayed on the right of the screen, as shown in Figure 26-6, appears. Select Excel from the drop-down list of libraries at the top of the Object Browser.

On the left is a list of the various classes of objects available to Excel. You can think of a *class* as a template or description for a type of object; a specific chart, for example, would be an object that is an instance of the Chart class. In VBA, classes belong to a project or library. As shown in Figure 26-6, the Object Browser lists the object classes belonging to the library Excel.

If you scroll down the classes and select a class—the Range class, for example—the right pane of the Object Browser lists the properties and methods (called the *members* of the class) belonging to that object. Figure 26-7 shows the members of the Range class.

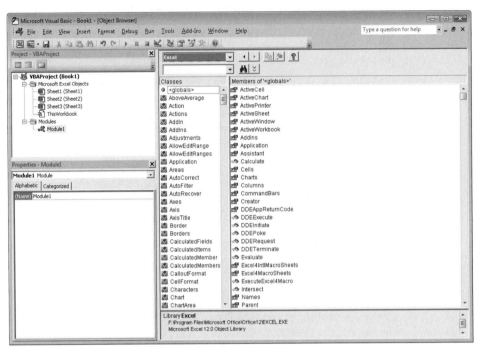

Figure 26-6 The Object Browser displays the classes of objects belonging to the Excel application.

Collections of Objects

You can have more than one instance of the same VBA object. Together, such instances comprise a *collection*. You identify each instance in a collection of objects by either its *index* value (its position within the collection) or its name. For example, the collection of all sheets in a workbook is as follows:

```
Sheets()
```

In addition, a specific instance of a sheet, the third one in the collection, is as follows:

```
Sheets(3)
```

If the third sheet were named Summary, you could also identify it as follows:

```
Sheets("Summary")
```

In VBA, each item in a collection has its own index, but the index numbers for an entire collection are not necessarily consecutive. If you delete one instance of an object in a collection, VBA might not renumber the index values of the remaining instances. For example, if you delete Sheets(3) from a collection of 12 sheets in a workbook, you don't have any guarantee that VBA will renumber Sheets(4) through Sheets(12) to fill the gap.

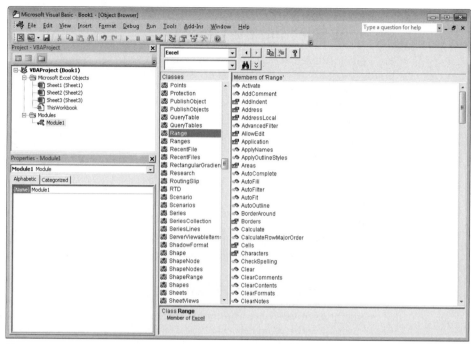

Figure 26-7 Here the Object Browser shows the Range object and some of the Range object's methods and properties.

In other programming languages, you might use a For . . . Next construction such as the following to repeat an operation many times:

```
For n = 1 to 12 ' Activate each sheet
    Sheets(n).Activate
Next n
```

If you run this code in a VBA macro after deleting Sheets(3), VBA displays an error message and stops the macro because Sheets(3) no longer exists. To allow for non-consecutive indexes, VBA offers For Each . . . Next, a control structure that applies a series of statements to each item in a collection, regardless of the index numbers. For example, suppose you'd like to label each sheet in the active workbook by typing the text **Sheet 1**, **Sheet 2**, and so on, in cell A1 of each sheet. Because you won't, in general, know how many sheets any given workbook contains, you might use the following VBA code:

```
Sub EnterSheetNum()
    n = 0
    for Each Sheet In Sheets()
        n = n + 1
        Sheet.Activate
        Range("A1").Select
        ActiveCell.FormulaR1C1 = "Sheet" + Str(n)
    Next
End Sub
```

Chapter 26

Manipulating an Object's Properties Without Selecting the Object

The code just listed activates each sheet in turn, then selects cell A1 on that sheet, and finally assigns a new value to that cell's FormulaR1C1 property. This sequence of steps mimics the steps you would follow if you were working manually. In VBA, everything but the last step in the sequence is unnecessary. That is, you can replace the following instructions:

```
Sheet.Activate
Range("A1").Select
ActiveCell.FormulaR1C1 = "Sheet" + Str(n)
```

with a single instruction:

```
Sheet.Range("A1").FormulaR1C1 = "Sheet" + Str(n)
```

The benefit of this change is that it enables the macro to run faster, because Excel is no longer required to activate sheets and select cells.

Naming Arguments to Methods

Many methods in VBA have arguments that let you specify options for the action to be performed. If the Wag method of the Tail object of our mythical robodog has arguments (for example, WagRate, the number of wags per second; WagTime, the duration of wagging in seconds; and WagArc, the number of degrees of arc in each wag), you can specify them using either of two syntaxes.

In the first syntax, which is often called the *by-name* syntax, you name each argument you use, in any order. For example, the following statement wags the tail three times per second for an hour, over an arc of 180 degrees. (It also assumes that our particular robodog is a member of a collection of such creatures and is named Fido.)

```
Robodogs("Fido").Tail.Wag _
    WagRage := 3, _
    WagTime := 3600, _
    WagArc := 180
```

You assign a value to an argument by using a colon and an equal sign, and you separate arguments with commas.

> **Note**
> The underscore character at the end of the first three lines tells VBA that the line after the underscore is part of the same statement. Using this symbol makes the list of supplied arguments easier to read. You must always precede the underscore with a space character.

In the second syntax, which is often called the *by-position* syntax, you type arguments in a prescribed order. For example, the preceding statement expressed in the by-position syntax looks like this:

```
Robodogs("Fido").Tail.Wag(3,3600,100)
```

Notice that the list of arguments is surrounded by parentheses. The by-position syntax isn't as easy to read as the by-name syntax because you have to remember the order of arguments, and when you review the code later, you won't have the argument names to refresh your memory about their settings.

> **Note**
>
> The macro recorder records arguments by position rather than by name, which can make it more difficult to understand recorded macros than manually created ones in which you've named the arguments. Similarly, when you select a VBA keyword and press F1, the Help topic that appears describes the keyword using by-position syntax.

Adding Code to or Editing Recorded Macros

Suppose you've recorded a macro that enters a series of labels, sets their font, and then draws a border around them. Then you discover that you forgot a step or recorded a step incorrectly—you chose the wrong border format, for example. What do you do?

To add code to an existing macro, you can record actions in a temporary macro and then transfer the code to the macro you want to change. For example, to add to the CompanyAddress macro a step that sets the font options for the company's name to 14-point Cambria Bold Italic, follow these steps:

1. Switch to the worksheet containing the address you typed earlier, and select cell A6, which contains the name of the company.

2. Turn on the macro recorder. In the Record Macro dialog box, type the name **MacroTemp**, and then click OK.

3. Press Ctrl+1 (this is the fastest way to get to the Format Cells dialog box, assuming the current selection is a cell).

4. Click the Font tab, and then select 14-point Cambria Bold Italic. Click OK to apply the formats.

5. Click the Stop Recording button.

6. Click Macros in the Code group on the Developer tab. In the Macro dialog box, select MacroTemp, and click Edit. A window appears containing the original macro you recorded plus the MacroTemp macro, as shown in Figure 26-8.

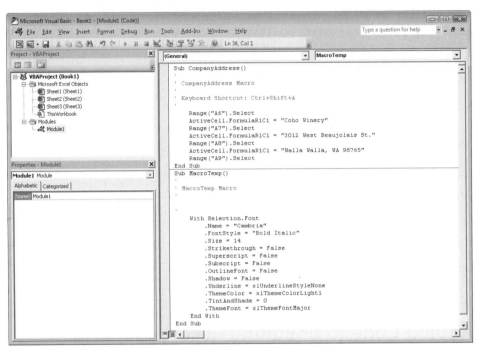

Figure 26-8 The MacroTemp macro contains the formatting code you recorded.

7. Select all the code inside the MacroTemp macro—from the line beginning with *With* through the line beginning with *End With*—and then press Ctrl+C to copy it.

8. Scroll up to display the CompanyAddress macro.

9. Click at the beginning of the line that contains this statement:

```
Range("A7").Select
```

10. Press Enter to create a blank line. Then position the insertion point at the beginning of the blank line.

11. Press Ctrl+V to paste.

12. Scroll down, and delete the entire MacroTemp macro, from the Sub statement to the End Sub statement.

The CompanyAddress macro now looks like this (with the comment lines removed):

```
Sub CompanyAddress()
    Range("A6").Select
    With Selection.Font
        .Name = "Cambria"
        .FontStyle = "Bold Italic"
        .Size = 14
        .Strikethrough = False
```

```
            .Superscript = False
            .Subscript = False
            .OutlineFont = False
            .Shadow = False
            .Underline = xlUnderlineStyleNone
            .ThemeColor = 2
            .TintAndShade = 0
            .ThemeFont = xlThemeFontMajor
        End With
        ActiveCell.FormulaR1C1 = "Coho Winery"
        Range("A7").Select
        ActiveCell.FormulaR1C1 = "3012 West Beaujolais St."
        Range("A8").Select
        ActiveCell.FormulaR1C1 = "Walla Walla, Wa 98765"
        Range("A9").Select
    End Sub
```

To test the macro, return to Excel, clear the company name and address you typed earlier when you recorded the macro, and then press Ctrl+Shift+A.

The With and End With statements that the macro recorder created when you recorded MacroTemp (the statements you subsequently copied into CompanyAddress) specify a group of properties belonging to an object—in this case, the font of the current selection. The With . . . End With construct provides a kind of shorthand for a series of VBA statements that would otherwise look like this, for example:

```
Selection.Font.Name = "Cambria"
Selection.Font.FontStyle = "Bold Italic"
Selection.Font.Size = 14
```

In the CompanyAddress macro, the ActiveCell object and the Selection object both refer to the same range on the worksheet, cell A6. Because you can apply a series of font-formatting options to an entire range, Excel records the action with Selection, rather than with ActiveCell. Enclosing the property assignments within the With . . . End With structure simplifies the code and also makes it run faster.

Using Subroutines in Macros

Suppose you're creating a complex macro and you discover that, among other things, you want the macro to perform a task you've already recorded under a different name. Or suppose you discover that a task you've recorded as part of a macro is something you'd like to use by itself—or in an entirely different macro. In our CompanyAddress macro, for example, it might be convenient if we could quickly and easily apply the font formats of the company name to other items in a worksheet.

With VBA, you can divide large macros into a series of smaller macros, and you can easily string together a series of small macros to create one large macro. A macro procedure that is used by another macro is called a *subroutine*. Subroutines can simplify your macros because you have to write only one set of instructions rather than repeat the instructions over and over. To use a subroutine in another macro, you call the subroutine by using its name in the other macro.

To demonstrate, let's split the CompanyAddress macro into two parts by following these steps:

1. Click Macros in the Code group on the Developer tab. In the Macro dialog box, select CompanyAddress, and click Edit. Then select the statements that format the font of the company's name:

```
With Selection.Font
    .Name = "Cambria"
    .FontStyle = "Bold Italic"
    .Size = 14
    .Strikethrough = False
    .Superscript = False
    .Subscript = False
    .OutlineFont = False
    .Shadow = False
    .Underline = xlUnderlineStyleNone
    .ThemeColor = xlThemeColorLight1
    .TintAndShade = 0
    .ThemeFont = xlThemeFontMajor
End With
```

2. Click Edit, Cut (or press Ctrl+X).

3. Click after the End Sub statement at the end of the CompanyAddress macro, and type **Sub CompanyFont()**.

4. The Visual Basic Editor types an End Sub statement for you. In the blank line between the Sub and End Sub statements, click Edit, Paste (or press Ctrl+V) to insert the font-formatting code.

You've created a new CompanyFont macro by moving the formatting codes from the CompanyAddress macro to the new CompanyFont macro. As mentioned, to run one macro from within another, you must use the name of the second macro in the first. To update the CompanyAddress macro so it uses the CompanyFont macro, follow these steps:

1. Click at the end of this statement, and then press Enter to insert a new line:

```
ActiveCell.FormulaR1C1 = "Coho Winery"
```

2. Type **CompanyFont**.

When you've finished, the two macros should look like the ones in the following listing:

```
Sub CompanyAddress()
    CompanyFont
    Range("A6").Select
    ActiveCell.FormulaR1C1 = "Coho Winery"
    Range("A7").Select
    ActiveCell.FormulaR1C1 = "3012 West Beaujolais St."
```

```
        Range("A8").Select
        ActiveCell.FormulaR1C1 = "Walla Walla, Wa 98765"
        Range("A9").Select
    End Sub

Sub CompanyFont()
    With Selection.Font
        .Name = "Cambria"
        .FontStyle = "Bold Italic"
        .Size = 14
        .Strikethrough = False
        .Superscript = False
        .Subscript = False
        .OutlineFont = False
        .Shadow = False
        .Underline = xlUnderlineStyleNone
        .ThemeColor = xlThemeColorLight1
        .TintAndShade = 0
        .ThemeFont = xlThemeFontMajor
    End With
End Sub
```

When you activate the CompanyAddress macro by pressing Ctrl+Shift+A, Excel runs the first statement in the macro. Because that first statement calls the CompanyFont macro, it switches to the first line of CompanyFont. When Excel reaches the End Sub statement at the end of CompanyFont, it returns to the statement in CompanyAddress immediately after the one that called CompanyFont and continues until it reaches the End Sub statement at the end of CompanyAddress.

Using the Personal Macro Workbook

When you recorded the CompanyAddress macro earlier in this chapter, you placed the macro in a module that belonged to the active workbook. A macro you place in a module is available only when you open the workbook containing the module.

To make a macro available at all times, store it in the Personal Macro Workbook. This workbook is ordinarily hidden; you can unhide it by clicking Unhide in the Window group on the View tab and then selecting PERSONAL in the Unhide dialog box. If the Unhide command is unavailable, you have not yet created a Personal Macro Workbook. To create one, begin recording a macro, as described earlier in this chapter, and then select Personal Macro Workbook in the Store Macro In drop-down list in the Record Macro dialog box. Excel creates the Personal Macro Workbook and places its file (Personal.xlsb) in the XLStart folder. Excel opens Personal.xlsb, as it does any other file in the XLStart folder, each time you start Excel. It's a good place to record macros that you want to be able to use in any workbook.

Going On from Here

In this chapter, you've learned how to create macros with the help of the macro recorder. As you learn more about VBA, you'll notice that the macro recorder often creates more code for a task than you really need. In our CompanyFont macro, for example, the following lines that the recorder generated were unnecessary because all you wanted to do was set the font name, point size, and style:

```
.Strikethrough = False
.Superscript = False
.Subscript = False
.OutlineFont = False
.Shadow = False
.Underline = xlUnderlineStyleNone
.ThemeColor = xlThemeColorLight1
.TintAndShade = 0
.ThemeFont = xlThemeFontMajor
```

The recorder added these lines because it didn't (and couldn't) know they weren't necessary. You can remove them without changing the functionality of the macro.

Earlier in the chapter, you saw that it is possible, using VBA, to change an object's property settings (a cell's font formats, for example) without selecting the object. Nevertheless, the recorder always selects objects before taking actions that affect those objects. It does so because it must mimic everything you do when you create the recording. As you acquire more proficiency with VBA, you'll learn ways to edit the recorder's code to make it more efficient.

As you improve your expertise in VBA, you will probably find yourself creating most of your code directly in the Visual Basic Editor, bypassing the recorder altogether. Chances are, though, you'll still return to the recorder now and then. The Excel object model includes so many objects, methods, properties, and arguments that it's difficult—perhaps pointless—to try to remember them all. When you can't remember what property, object, or method is required in a certain programming situation, one of the easiest ways to get the information you need is by turning on the macro recorder, working through by hand the actions you want to program, and then seeing what code the recorder generates.

Although Microsoft Office Excel 2007 includes a multitude of built-in worksheet functions, chances are it doesn't have a function for every type of calculation you perform. The designers of Excel couldn't possibly anticipate every calculation need of every user. But they do provide you with the ability to create custom functions. In the same way that a macro lets you encapsulate a sequence of actions and then execute that sequence with a single command, a *custom function* lets you encapsulate a sequence of calculations so you can perform those calculations with a single formula.

Custom functions, like macros, use the Visual Basic for Applications (VBA) programming language. They differ from macros in two significant ways. First, they use *function* procedures instead of *sub* procedures. That is, they start with a Function statement instead of a Sub statement and end with End Function instead of End Sub. Second, they perform calculations instead of taking actions. Certain kinds of statements (such as statements that select and format ranges) are excluded from custom functions. In this chapter, you'll learn how to create and use custom functions.

Creating a Simple Custom Function

Suppose your company offers a quantity discount of 10 percent on the sale of a product, provided the order is for more than 100 units. In the following paragraphs, you'll build a function to calculate this discount.

The worksheet in Figure 27-1 shows an order form that lists each item, the quantity, the price, the discount (if any), and the resulting extended price.

You'll find the Treeorders.xlsm file in the Sample Files section of the companion CD. You can use this file for reference or to practice creating your own custom functions.

To create a custom DISCOUNT function in this workbook, follow these steps:

1. Press Alt+F11 to open the Visual Basic Editor, and then click Insert, Module. A new module appears, as shown in Figure 27-2.

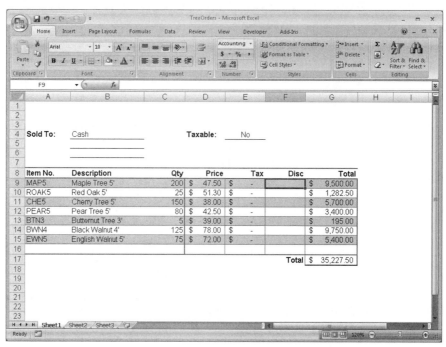

Figure 27-1 In column F, we want to calculate the discount for each item ordered.

2. In the new module, type the following code. To make the code more readable, use the Tab key to indent lines. (The indentation is for your benefit only and is optional. The code will run with or without indentation.) After you type an indented line, the Visual Basic Editor assumes your next line will be similarly indented. To move out (that is, to the left) one tab character, press Shift+Tab.

```
Function Discount(quantity, price)
    If quantity >=100 Then
        Discount = quantity * price * 0.1
    Else
        Discount = 0
    End If
    Discount = Application.Round(Discount, 2)
End Function
```

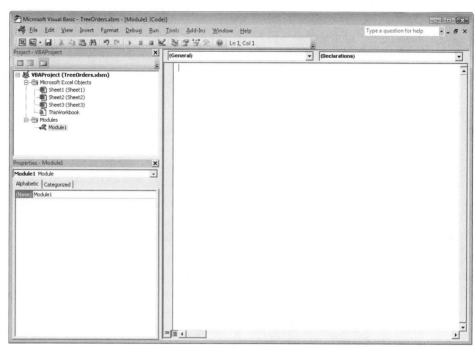

Figure 27-2 Clicking Insert, Module adds a new module to the workbook.

Using Custom Functions

Now you're ready to use the new DISCOUNT function. Press Alt+F11 to switch to the worksheet shown in Figure 27-1. Select cell F9, and type the following:

=DISCOUNT(C9,D9)

Excel calculates the 10 percent discount on 200 units at $47.50 per unit and returns $950.00.

In the first line of your VBA code, Function Discount(quantity, price), you indicated that the DISCOUNT function requires two arguments, *quantity* and *price*. When you call the function in a worksheet cell, you must include those two arguments. In the formula =DISCOUNT(C9,D9), C9 is the *quantity* argument, and D9 is the *price* argument. Now you can copy the DISCOUNT formula to F10:F15 to get the worksheet shown in Figure 27-3.

Let's consider how Excel interprets this function procedure. When you press Enter, Excel looks for the name *DISCOUNT* in the current workbook and finds that it is a procedure in Module1. The argument names enclosed in parentheses—*quantity* and *price*—are placeholders for the values on which the calculation of the discount is based.

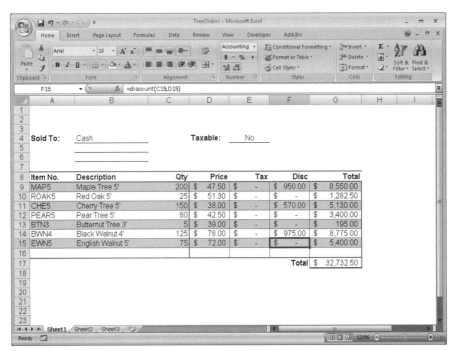

Figure 27-3 This worksheet shows the result of the DISCOUNT custom function.

The If statement in the following block of code examines the *quantity* argument and determines whether the number of items sold is greater than or equal to 100:

```
If quantity >= 100 Then
    Discount = quantity * price * 0.1
Else
    Discount = 0
End If
```

If the number of items sold is greater than or equal to 100, VBA executes the following statement, which multiplies the *quantity* value by the *price* value and then multiplies the result by 0.1:

```
Discount = quantity * price * 0.1
```

The result is stored as the variable *Discount*. A VBA statement that stores a value in a variable is called an *assignment* statement, because it evaluates the expression on the right side of the equal sign and assigns the result to the variable name on the left. Because the variable *Discount* has the same name as the function procedure, the value stored in the variable is returned to the worksheet formula that called the DISCOUNT function.

If *quantity* is less than 100, VBA executes the following statement:

```
Discount = 0
```

Finally, the following statement rounds the value assigned to the *Discount* variable to two decimal places:

```
Discount = Application.Round(Discount, 2)
```

VBA has no ROUND function, but Excel does. Therefore, to use ROUND in this statement, you tell VBA to look for the Round method (function) in the Application object (Excel). You do that by adding the word *Application* before the word *Round*. Use this syntax whenever you need to access an Excel function from a VBA module.

Understanding Custom Function Rules

A custom function must start with a Function statement and end with an End Function statement. In addition to the function name, the Function statement usually specifies one or more arguments. You can, however, create a function with no arguments. Excel includes several built-in functions–RAND and NOW, for example–that don't use arguments. As you'll see later in this chapter, you can also create functions with optional arguments, which are arguments that you can either include or omit when you call the function.

Following the Function statement, a function procedure includes one or more VBA statements that make decisions and perform calculations using the arguments passed to the function. Finally, somewhere in the function procedure, you must include a statement that assigns a value to a variable with the same name as the function. This value is returned to the formula that calls the function.

Using VBA Keywords in Custom Functions

The number of VBA keywords you can use in custom functions is smaller than the number you can use in macros. Custom functions are not allowed to do anything other than return a value to a formula in a worksheet or to an expression used in another VBA macro or function. For example, custom functions cannot resize windows; edit a formula in a cell; or change the font, color, or pattern options for the text in a cell. If you include "action" code of this kind in a function procedure, the function returns the #VALUE! error.

The one action a function procedure can do (apart from performing calculations) is display a dialog box. You can use an InputBox statement in a custom function as a means of getting input from the user executing the function. You can use a MsgBox statement as a means of conveying information to the user. You can also use custom dialog boxes, or UserForms, but that's a subject beyond the scope of this introduction.

Chapter 27

Documenting Macros and Custom Functions

Even simple macros and custom functions can be difficult to read. You can make them easier to understand by typing explanatory text in the form of comments. You add comments by preceding the explanatory text with an apostrophe. For example, Figure 27-4 shows the DISCOUNT function with comments. Adding comments like these makes it easier for you or others to maintain your VBA code as time passes. If you need to make a change to the code in the future, you'll have an easier time understanding what you did originally.

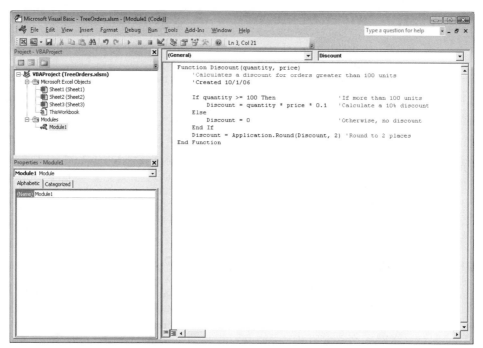

Figure 27-4 The DISCOUNT custom function now includes comments.

An apostrophe tells Excel to ignore everything to the right on the same line, so you can create comments either on lines by themselves or on the right side of lines containing VBA code. You might begin a relatively long block of code with a comment that explains its overall purpose and then use inline comments to document individual statements.

Another way to document your macros and custom functions is to give them descriptive names. For example, rather than name a macro *Labels*, you could name it *Month-Labels* to describe more specifically the purpose the macro serves. Using descriptive names for macros and custom functions is especially helpful when you've created many procedures, particularly if you create procedures that have similar but not identical purposes.

How you document your macros and custom functions is a matter of personal preference. What's important is to adopt some method of documentation and use it consistently.

Creating Custom Functions with Optional Arguments

Some of the built-in Excel functions let you omit certain arguments. For example, if you omit the *type* and *future value* arguments from the PV function, Excel still computes the result because those arguments are optional. Your custom functions can also use optional arguments.

For example, suppose you want to create a custom function called RightTriangle that uses the Pythagorean theorem to compute the length of any side of a right triangle given the lengths of the other two sides. The equation that expresses the Pythagorean theorem is $a^2 + b^2 = c^2$, in which a and b are the short sides and c is the hypotenuse. Given any two sides, you can use this equation to solve for the third side.

In a general-purpose Triangle function, you want to accept three arguments (one for each side of the triangle) but make each argument optional so the user of the function can supply any two arguments and the function will solve for the third argument. The following code does the trick:

```
Function Triangle(Optional side1, Optional side2, _
    Optional hypotenuse)
    If Not (IsMissing(side1)) And Not (IsMissing(side2)) Then
        Triangle = Sqr(side1 ^ 2 + side2 ^ 2)
    Else
        If Not (IsMissing(side1)) And Not (IsMissing(hypotenuse)) Then
            Triangle = Sqr(hypotenuse ^ 2 - side1 ^ 2)
        Else
            If Not (IsMissing(side2)) And Not (IsMissing(hypotenuse)) Then
                Triangle = Sqr(hypotenuse ^ 2 - side2 ^ 2)
            Else
                Triangle = "Please supply two arguments."
            End If
        End If
    End If
End Function
```

The first statement names the custom function and the optional arguments *side1*, *side2*, and *hypotenuse*. The next block of code contains a series of If statements that use the VBA IsMissing function to test whether each possible pair of arguments has been supplied. If *side1* is not missing and *side2* is not missing, Excel computes the square root of the sum of the squares of the two short sides and returns the length of the hypotenuse to the worksheet.

If fewer than two arguments are supplied, the following statement returns a text string to the worksheet:

```
Triangle = "Please supply two arguments."
```

Chapter 27

Now let's see what happens when we use this custom function in a worksheet formula. The formula =Triangle(3,4) returns 5. The *hypotenuse* argument is omitted, so the function returns the square root of $(3^2 + 4^2)$. You could also write the formula =Triangle(3,4,); however, the second comma is not necessary. The formula =Triangle (,4,5) returns 3 because the *side1* argument is omitted. The formula =Triangle(4,,5) also returns 3.

The function as written has at least two flaws. First, if the user supplies all three arguments, the function behaves as though the third argument were omitted. You might prefer to have it return an error message. Second, the function accepts negative and zero arguments even though triangles cannot have sides of negative or zero length.

You can eliminate the first of these defects by adding the following If . . . End If block immediately after the Function statement:

```
If Not (IsMissing(side1)) And Not (IsMissing(side2)) And _
    Not (IsMissing(hypotenuse)) Then
    Triangle = "Please supply only two arguments."
    Exit Function
End If
```

Note that this block includes an Exit Function statement. This saves the function the trouble of searching for missing arguments when it has already discovered that none are missing.

You can use a similar If . . . End If construction to look for arguments less than or equal to zero, returning an appropriate error message and exiting the function if any are found. Note that other kinds of inappropriate arguments (text, for example) will cause the function to return one of the built-in error constants. If you call the function and offer a text argument, the function returns #VALUE! because it attempts to perform arithmetic operations on a nonarithmetic value.

How much error trapping you add to your custom functions depends, of course, on how much work you want to do and how you plan to use the function. If you're writing a function for your personal use, you might not need to deal with every conceivable aberrant use. If you write the function for others, you'll probably want to eliminate all possibility of error—or at least try to do so.

Making Your Custom Functions Available Anywhere

To use a custom function, the workbook containing the module in which you created the function must be open. If that workbook is not open, you get a #NAME? error when you try to use the function. Even if the workbook is open, if you use the function in a different workbook, you must precede the function name with the name of the workbook in which the function resides. For example, if you create a function called DISCOUNT in a workbook called Personal.xlsb and you call that function from another workbook, you must type **=personal.xlsb!discount()**, not simply **=discount()**.

You can save yourself some keystrokes (and possible typing errors) by selecting your custom functions from the Insert Function dialog box. Your custom functions appear in the User Defined category:

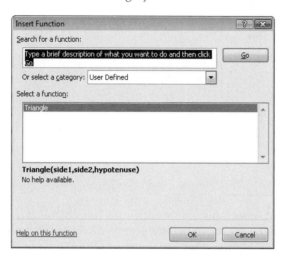

An easier way to make your custom functions available at all times is to store them in a separate workbook and then save that workbook as an add-in. You can then make the add-in available whenever you run Excel. Here's how to do this:

1. After you have created the functions you need, click the Microsoft Office Button, and click Save As.

2. In the Save As dialog box, open the Save As Type drop-down list, and select Excel Add-In. Save the workbook under a recognizable name—such as MyFunctions—in the AddIns folder. (The Save As dialog box will propose that folder, so all you need to do is accept the default location.)

3. After you have saved the workbook, click the Microsoft Office Button, and click Excel Options.

4. In the Excel Options dialog box, click the Add-Ins category.

5. In the Manage drop-down list, select Excel Add-Ins. Then click the Go button.

6. In the Add-Ins dialog box, select the check box beside the name you used to save your workbook, as shown on the next page.

Chapter 27

After you follow these steps, your custom functions will be available each time you run Excel. If you want to add to your function library, press Alt+F11 to return to the Visual Basic Editor. As Figure 27-5 shows, in the Visual Basic Editor Project Explorer under a

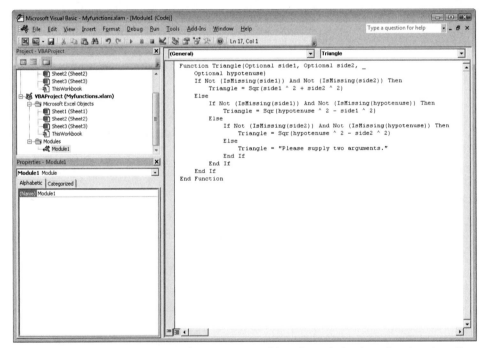

Figure 27-5 If you save your custom functions as an add-in, the code for those functions is available in a module in the Visual Basic Editor, and you can add more functions as the need arises.

VBAProject heading, you will see a module named after your add-in file. (Your add-in will have the extension .xlam.) Double-clicking that module in the Project Explorer causes the Visual Basic Editor to display your function code. To add a new function, position your insertion point after the End Function statement that terminates the last function in the Code window, and begin typing. You can create as many functions as you need in this manner, and they will always be available in the User Defined category in the Insert Function dialog box.

Debugging Macros and Custom Functions

If you made it through the previous two chapters, you now have at least a smattering of Microsoft Visual Basic for Applications (VBA) at your command—as well as, we hope, an appetite for learning more. The best ways to acquire more expertise in this versatile programming language are to read a book on the subject, such as *Microsoft Visual Basic 2005 Step by Step* by Michael Halvorson (Microsoft Press, 2005), and to experiment. As you do your everyday work in Microsoft Office Excel 2007, look for chores that are ripe for automating. When you come across something macro-worthy, record your actions. Then inspect the code generated by the macro recorder. Make sure you understand what the recorder has given you (read the Help text for any statements you don't understand), and see whether you can find ways to make the code more efficient. Eliminate statements that appear unnecessary, and then see whether the code still does what you expect it to do. Look for statements that select ranges or other objects, and see whether you can make your code perform the essential tasks without first selecting those objects.

As you experiment and create larger, more complex macros and functions, you will undoubtedly produce some code that either doesn't run at all or doesn't give you the result you want. Missteps of this kind are an inevitable aspect of programming. Fortunately, the VBA language and the Visual Basic Editor provide tools to help you trap errors and root out bugs. Those tools are the subject of this chapter.

In this chapter, you'll look at two kinds of error-catching tools: those that help you at design time, when you're creating or editing code, and those that work at run time, while the code is running.

Using Design-Time Tools

The Visual Basic Editor design-time error tools let you correct mistakes in VBA syntax and catch misspellings of variable names. They also let you follow the "flow" of a macro or function (seeing each line of code as it is executed) and monitor the values of variables during the course of a procedure's execution.

Catching Syntax Errors

If you type a worksheet formula incorrectly in Excel, Excel alerts you to the error and refuses to accept the entry. The VBA *compiler* (the system component that converts your English-like VBA code into machine language) ordinarily performs the same service for you if you type a VBA expression incorrectly. If you omit a required parenthesis, for example, the compiler beeps as soon as you press Enter. It also presents an error message and displays the offending line of code in a contrasting color (red, by default).

Certain kinds of syntax errors don't become apparent to the compiler until you attempt to run your code. For example, if you write the following:

```
With Selection.Border
    .Weight = xlThin
    .LineStyle = xlAutomatic
```

and attempt to run this code without including an End With statement, you will see this error message:

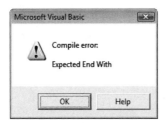

Your procedure will halt, and you will be in *break mode*. (You can tell you're in break mode by the appearance of the word *break* in brackets in the Visual Basic Editor title bar. The line the compiler was attempting to execute will be highlighted—in yellow, by default.) Break mode lets you fix your code and then continue running it. For example, if you omit an End With statement, you can add that statement while in break mode, and then press F5 (or select Run, Continue) to go on with the show. If you want to exit from break mode rather than continue with the execution of your procedure, select Run, Reset.

If you don't like having the compiler complain about obvious syntax errors the moment you commit them, you can turn off that functionality. Click Tools, click Options, click the Editor tab (shown in Figure 28-1), and clear the Auto Syntax Check check box. With automatic syntax checking turned off, your syntax errors will still be flagged when you try to run your code.

 You'll find the files used in this chapter's examples in the Sample Files section of the companion CD.

> **Note**
> You can also use the Options dialog box to change the color the Visual Basic Editor uses to highlight syntax errors. If you don't like red, click the Editor Format tab, select Syntax Error Text in the Code Colors list, and then select a different color.

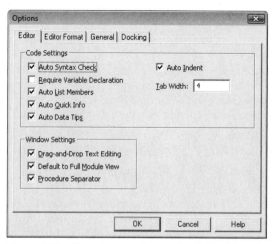

Figure 28-1 Clear the Auto Syntax Check check box if you don't want to know about syntax errors until you run your code.

Auto Syntax Check is on by default. So are three other "auto" options: Auto List Members, Auto Quick Info, and Auto Data Tips. These are all useful, and you should leave them on, especially if you're relatively new to VBA. Auto List Members and Auto Quick Info help you complete a line of VBA code by displaying available options at the current insertion point or the names of arguments required by the function you're currently typing. Auto Data Tips is relevant only in break mode. If you rest your pointer on a variable name in break mode, the Auto Data Tips feature displays the current value of that variable as a ScreenTip.

Catching Misspelled Variable Names

The VBA compiler doesn't care about the capitalization style of your variable names. *MyVar*, *myVar*, and *myvar* are identical names as far as the compiler is concerned. (If you're inconsistent about the capitalization of a variable name, the Visual Basic Editor adjusts all instances of that variable to make them look the same.) If you change the spelling of a variable name in mid-program, however, the compiler creates a new variable—and havoc for your program. An error in programming introduced by a misspelled variable can be especially treacherous because the program might appear to behave normally.

You can virtually eliminate the possibility of inconsistently spelled variable names in a module by adding a single statement at the top of that module (before any Sub or Function statements):

```
Option Explicit
```

The Option Explicit statement forces you to *declare* any variables used in the current module. You declare variables with Dim statements. (For complete details about Dim, type **Dim** in a module, and press F1.) With Option Explicit in place, if you use a variable without first declaring it, you get a Compile Error at run time. If you accidentally

Chapter 28

misspell a variable name somewhere in your program, the compiler will flag the misspelled variable as an undeclared variable, and you'll be able to fix the problem forthwith.

You can add Option Explicit to every new module you create by clicking Tools, Options, the Editor tab, and then selecting the Require Variable Declaration check box. This option is off by default, but it's good programming practice to turn it on. Option Explicit will do more for you than eliminate misspelled variable names. By forcing you to declare your variables, it will also encourage you to think ahead as you work.

Stepping Through Code

The Visual Basic Editor step commands cause the compiler to execute either a single instruction or a limited set of instructions and then pause in break mode, highlighting the next instruction that will be executed. Execution is suspended until you take another action—such as issuing another step command, resuming normal execution, or terminating execution. By issuing step commands repeatedly, you can follow the procedure's execution path. You can see, for example, which way the program branches when it comes to an If statement or which of the alternative paths it takes when it encounters a Select Case structure. (A Select Case structure causes the program to execute one of a set of alternative statements, depending on the value of a particular variable. For details, type **case** in a module, and press F1.) You can also examine the values of variables at each step along the way.

> **Note**
>
> You can monitor the value of variables by displaying the Watch Window or the Quick Watch dialog box or by resting your pointer on particular variables while in break mode. For information about using the Watch Window, see "Using the Watch Window to Monitor Variable Values and Object Properties" on page 865.

You have four step commands at your disposal. You'll find these commands—and their keyboard shortcuts—on the Debug menu:

- **Step Into** Executes the next instruction only.

- **Step Over** Works like Step Into unless the next instruction is a call to another procedure (that is, a subroutine). In that case, Step Into executes the entire called procedure as a unit.

- **Step Out** Executes the remaining steps of the current procedure.

- **Run To Cursor** Executes everything up to the current cursor position.

You can run an entire procedure one step at a time by repeatedly pressing F8 (the keyboard shortcut for Debug, Step Into). To begin stepping through a procedure at a particular instruction, move your cursor to that instruction, and press Ctrl+F8 (the shortcut for Debug, Run To Cursor). Alternatively, you can force the compiler to enter break mode when it reaches a particular instruction, and then you can use any of the step commands.

Setting Breakpoints with the Toggle Breakpoint Command

A *breakpoint* is an instruction that causes the compiler to halt execution and enter break mode. The simplest way to set a breakpoint is to put your cursor where you want the breakpoint and then click Debug, Toggle Breakpoint (or press F9). Click this command sequence a second time to clear a breakpoint. You can set as many breakpoints in a procedure as you like using this method. The Toggle Breakpoint command sets an *unconditional* breakpoint—one that will always occur when execution arrives at the breakpoint. To set a *conditional* breakpoint—one that takes effect under a specified condition only—see the next section.

As Figure 28-2 shows, the Visual Basic Editor highlights a line where you've set a breakpoint in a contrasting color and displays a large bullet in the left margin of the Code window. To customize the highlighting color, click Tools, Options, the Editor Format tab, and then select Breakpoint Text.

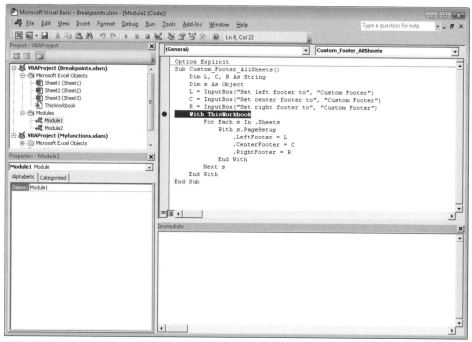

Figure 28-2 The Visual Basic Editor uses highlighting to mark breakpoint lines.

Chapter 28

Setting Conditional Breakpoints Using Debug.Assert

With the Assert method of the Debug object, you can cause the VBA compiler to enter break mode only if a particular expression generates a FALSE result. Figure 28-3 provides a simple example.

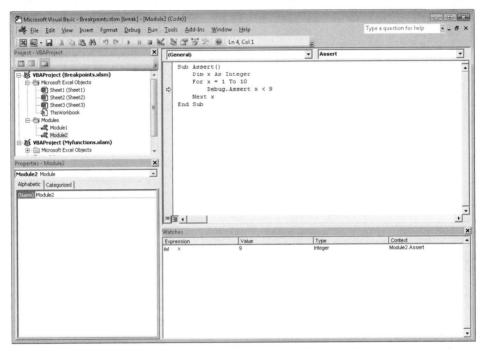

Figure 28-3 This Debug.Assert statement puts the compiler in break mode when the value of *x* equals 9 or greater.

The Debug.Assert statement in this otherwise useless bit of code asserts that *x* is less than 9. As long as that assertion is true, the procedure runs. When it becomes false, the compiler enters break mode. As the Watch Window in Figure 28-3 shows, the compiler enters break mode when *x* is equal to 9. (We'll discuss the Watch Window next.)

> **Note**
>
> You can also use the Watch Window to set conditional breakpoints. See "Setting Conditional Breakpoints with the Watch Window" on the next page.

Using the Watch Window to Monitor Variable Values and Object Properties

The Watch Window shows the current values of selected variables or expressions and the current property settings for selected objects. You can use the Watch Window to monitor the status of variables and objects as you step through a procedure.

To display the Watch Window, click View, Watch Window. (To close the window, click its Close button.) To add a variable or object to the Watch Window, you can select it in the Code window and drag it to the Watch Window. You can add expressions, such as *a + 1*, to the Watch Window in this manner. Alternatively, you can add something to the Watch Window by clicking Debug, Add Watch. In the Expression text box in the Add Watch dialog box (see Figure 28-4), type a variable name or other valid VBA expression.

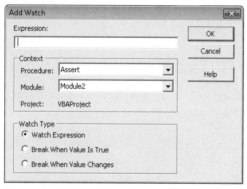

Figure 28-4 You can use the Add Watch dialog box to add a watch variable or to set a conditional breakpoint.

Setting Conditional Breakpoints with the Watch Window

As Figure 28-4 shows, you can use the Add Watch dialog box to set a conditional breakpoint. Click Debug, Add Watch; specify the name of a variable or a VBA expression; and then select either Break When Value Is True or Break When Value Changes. Selecting Break When Value Is True for an expression is comparable to using a Debug.Assert statement to set a conditional breakpoint. The difference is that Debug.Assert causes a break when an expression becomes false, and Break When Value Is True does the opposite.

Using Quick Watch to Monitor a Variable or Add a Watch Item

In break mode, you can select any variable name or expression in your code and click Debug, Quick Watch (or press Shift+F9) to see the current value of the selected item. If you decide you want to monitor that item continuously, you can click Add in the Quick Watch dialog box. The Visual Basic Editor then adds the item to the Watch Window.

Using the Immediate Window

While in break mode or before running a procedure, you can execute any VBA statement in the Immediate window. (If the Immediate window isn't visible, click View, Immediate Window, or press Ctrl+G.) For example, you can discover the value of a variable *x* by typing **Print x** in the Immediate window. (As a shortcut, you can type **?x**. The question mark character is a synonym for Print in VBA.)

You can also use the Immediate window to monitor an action in a procedure while that procedure is running. You do this by inserting Debug.Print statements into the procedure. The statement Debug.Print x, for example, displays the current value of *x* in the Immediate window.

The Immediate window can be a handy place to test VBA statements while you're still wrestling with the syntax of this programming language. If you're not sure a particular statement will have the effect you intend, you can try it in the Immediate window and see what happens.

Dealing with Run-Time Errors

In many cases, run-time errors are caused by factors outside your control. For example, suppose you write the following macro to format the numbers in a selected range using the Indian system of lakhs and crores:

```
Sub LakhsCrores()
    Dim cell As Object
    For Each cell In Selection
        If Abs(cell.Value) > 10000000 Then
            cell.NumberFormat = "#"","""##"","""##"","""###"
        ElseIf Abs(cell.Value) > 100000 Then
            cell.NumberFormat = "##"","""##"","""###"
        End If
    Next cell
End Sub
```

This macro works fine if the person who runs it selects a range containing numbers before running the macro. But if the user selects something else—a chart embedded on the worksheet, for example—VBA displays an error message:

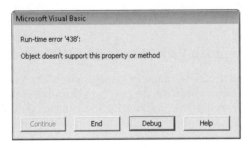

The macro generates a run-time error and enters break mode because the For Each statement has to be applied to a collection or an array, and a chart object is neither. (A range is a collection of cells, so For Each does work with a range.) Even though you can figure out easily enough what the error message means and what you have to do about it (try again with a range selected), the message still might be annoying. If you intend for this macro to be used by someone else, it's definitely impolite to let that other user see such a message.

You can *trap* an error such as this—that is, shield yourself and others from VBA's run-time error messages—by means of an On Error GoTo statement. The statement must appear before the code that might cause a run-time error, and it has the following syntax, in which *label* is a name that identifies an error-handling section elsewhere in your procedure:

```
On Error GoTo label
```

If a run-time error occurs, the On Error GoTo statement transfers execution to the error-handling code. In the case of your LakhsCrores procedure, the macro complete with error handling might look like this:

```
Sub LakhsCrores()
    'Catch run-time error caused by inappropriate selection
    'On Error GoTo ErrorHandler
    Dim cell As Object
    For Each cell In Selection
        If Abs(cell.Value) > 10000000 Then
            cell.NumberFormat = "#""","""##""","""##""","""###"
        ElseIf Abs(cell.Value) > 100000 Then
            cell.NumberFormat = "##""","""##""","""###"
        End If
    Next cell

    'Exit Sub statement keeps execution from entering
    'error handler if no error occurs
    Exit Sub


    'Error Handler
ErrorHandler:
    MsgBox "Please select a worksheet range."
End Sub
```

Notice that the error handler goes at the end of the program, introduced by the label that appeared in the On Error statement. The label must be followed by a colon and must appear on a line by itself. An Exit Sub statement appears before the error handler. This statement terminates the macro when no run-time error occurs; without it, execution would continue into the error handler regardless of whether an error occurred. Now when the user runs the macro after selecting a chart object, the user sees a polite message box instead of a rude run-time error message.

The macro still has a problem, however. The code works fine when the selected range includes numbers, text, or blank cells. However, if it includes a cell containing an Excel error constant, such as #NA, a different run-time error occurs: error 13, Type Mismatch. The message box generated by the error handler shown previously would not be appropriate for this kind of error.

How do you make your code show one message for a nonrange selection and another for a range that includes one or more error values? You use the Number property of the Err object. This property is always set to the most recent run-time error number (or 0, if no procedure is running or if no error has occurred). You can handle both run-time errors (438 and 13) with the following code, for example:

```
ErrorHandler:
If Err.Number=438 Then
    MsgBox "Please select a worksheet range."
ElseIf Err.Number = 13 Then
    MsgBox "Please select a range without error values."
Else
    MsgBox "Sorry! Unknown error!"
End If
```

This isn't particularly elegant, but at least you have all your bases more or less covered.

The foregoing error handler examples assume your program should terminate when a run-time error occurs. The purpose of the error handler is to prevent the jolting VBA message from showing up—and to provide the user with a simple explanation of what went wrong.

In some cases, you'll want your procedure to continue running after a run-time error occurs. In such a case, your error handler needs to return VBA to the appropriate instruction so it can continue executing your program. Use either a Resume statement or a Resume Next statement to do this. A Resume statement causes VBA to reexecute the line that caused the error. A Resume Next statement causes VBA to continue at the line after the line that caused the error.

By combining On Error with Resume Next, you can tell VBA to ignore any run-time errors that might occur and go to the next statement. If you're sure you've anticipated all the kinds of run-time errors that might occur with your program, On Error Resume Next can often be the simplest and most effective way to deal with potential mishaps. In the LakhsCrores macro, for example, you can write the following:

```
Sub LakhsCrores()
    'Tell VBA to ignore all run-time errors
    On Error Resume Next

    Dim cell As Object
    For Each cell In Selection
        If Abs(cell.Value) > 10000000 Then
            cell.NumberFormat = "#""," ""##""," ""##""," ""###"
        ElseIf Abs(cell.Value) > 100000 Then
            cell.NumberFormat = "##""," ""##""," ""###"
        End If
    Next cell
Exit Sub
```

With this code, if the user selects a chart and runs the macro, VBA ignores the run-time error, the program moves on to the For Each block, and nothing happens—because nothing can happen. If the user selects a range containing one or more error values, the program skips over those cells that it can't format and formats the ones it can. In all cases, neither error message nor message box appears, and all is well. This solution works for this particular macro.

Of course, when you use On Error Resume Next, you're disabling the VBA run-time checking altogether. You should do this only when you're sure you've thought of everything that could possibly go awry—and the best way to arrive at that serene certainty is to test, test again, and then test some more.

Integrating Excel with Other Applications

Workbooks seldom live in isolation. The material you manipulate in a Microsoft Office Excel 2007 document is related to other material elsewhere—on the Internet, on a file server, in another Office Excel 2007 document, or perhaps in your collection of digital photography. Just as hyperlinks on Web sites link related information on other Web sites, hyperlinks in your Excel workbooks can connect the various threads of your professional life.

Hyperlinks in Excel can look like text hyperlinks in Web pages. That is, a hyperlink can be a simple word or phrase, underlined and colored to distinguish it from other text in your workbook. After you click such a link, the color ordinarily changes, marking that you've already visited the link's target.

Just as links on Web pages can be attached to graphics as well as text, so can they in Excel. You can assign them to drawing objects or charts, as well as to ordinary worksheet cells.

Here's a short inventory of useful tasks you can perform with hyperlinks in Excel:

- **Link to Web sites** You'll find the ability to link to Web pages particularly useful if you use Excel to generate material on the Web. When you post your Excel document to your Web server, you can already have the appropriate links to related pages in place.

- **Link to other existing documents** Let's say you're a realtor with a worksheet that summarizes your current listings portfolio. You have pictures of each house, but the pictures don't fit neatly into worksheet cells. Create hyperlinks to the pictures instead. You can assign the hyperlinks to cells containing the multiple listing service numbers or street addresses. Or suppose you're looking for a way to catalog your digital photo collection. Although you can use file and folder names to describe photo contents, dates, or locations, Excel limits how much information you can supply in a file name. Consider setting up an Excel table instead, with hyperlinks from descriptive information to individual photo files.

- **Link to a document that doesn't yet exist** Excel will create the document when you click the link.

- **Link to another place in the current document** Perhaps you've built a complete worksheet for someone else to use. You can help that person navigate your document by supplying a table of hyperlinks.

- **Link to an e-message** You can create a contact list in Excel and link each name to the person's e-mail address. When you click the link, Excel launches your default e-mail program, with the message already addressed.

- **Link to a network path** You can make it easy for yourself or other users of your workbooks to connect to a file-server location by entering a UNC path to that location in a worksheet cell. Excel will recognize the address as a network path and create a hyperlink. Clicking the hyperlink opens the network folder in Windows Explorer.

Creating a Hyperlink in a Cell

You can create a hyperlink in a cell by clicking the Insert tab and then clicking Hyperlink. But if you're linking to a Web site and you already know the site's uniform resource locator (URL), you can type the URL directly in the cell. If the URL begins with *www*, Excel assumes it's an HTTP (Web site) URL and creates a hyperlink for you. If the URL doesn't begin with *www*, you need to include the prefix *http://*. (If the URL uses some other prefix, such as *ftp://*, you must, of course, type that.)

As mentioned, you can use the same technique to create a hyperlink to a network path. If the cell contents look like *servername**sharename*, Excel creates a link to the folder *sharename* on the server *servername*.

> **TROUBLESHOOTING**
>
> **Excel doesn't turn my URLs into hyperlinks.**
>
> Excel turns obvious URLs into hyperlinks by default. If it doesn't perform this service for you, click the Microsoft Office Button and then click Excel Options. In the Excel Options dialog box, select the Proofing category, and then click AutoCorrect Options. In the AutoCorrect dialog box, click the AutoFormat As You Type tab. Finally, select the Internet And Network Paths With Hyperlinks check box. Click OK to save your changes.

Turning Ordinary Text into a Hyperlink

To turn text other than a URL or network path into a hyperlink, select the cell that contains the text. Then click the Insert tab, and click Hyperlink. (Alternatively, and more simply, press Ctrl+K.) The Insert Hyperlink dialog box shown in Figure 29-1 appears.

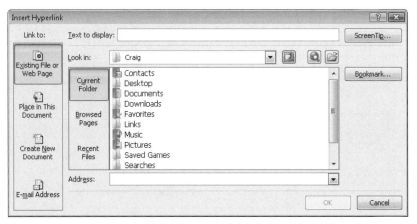

Figure 29-1 You can use the Insert Hyperlink dialog box to link to a file or Web page.

Follow these steps to create a hyperlink in a worksheet cell:

1. In the Address box, type the target of the link (the place to which you'll be taken when you click the link).

2. In the Text To Display box, type the text of the hyperlink. Excel will display this text underlined in your worksheet cell. (Unless you started with an empty cell, this box might already be filled in correctly when you get to the Insert Hyperlink dialog box.)

3. Click ScreenTip to supply the tip that should appear when your pointer rests on the cell. This might be a "friendly" name for a Web site or a description of a file's contents. Click OK to save the tip. If you omit this step, Excel uses a default tip that identifies the target of the link. Click OK to close the Insert Hyperlink dialog box.

> **Note**
>
> Because PivotTable cells move when a PivotTable Report is rearranged, you cannot assign a hyperlink to a cell within a PivotTable.

Linking to a Web Site or Local File

To create a link to a Web site or document in your own file storage, supply the URL or file name in the Address box in the Insert Hyperlink dialog box. If the site or document in which you're interested is one you've visited recently, the dialog box makes this process easy. The most recently used (MRU) list that appears when you click the arrow next to the Address box is identical to the one maintained by Microsoft Internet Explorer. If you don't find what you're looking for in this list, click the Browsed Pages button. That reveals information from the Internet Explorer History bar, sorted so the sites you visited most recently appear at the top of the list. As Figure 29-2 shows, the Browsed Pages list (like the Internet Explorer History bar) also includes the names of files you've recently opened.

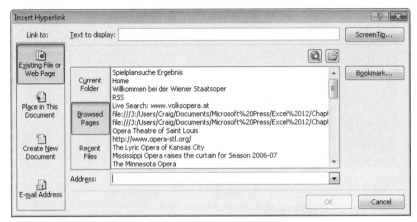

Figure 29-2 Clicking the Browsed Pages button reveals the names of sites you've recently visited and files you've recently opened.

If you don't find your site via the Address list or Browsed Pages—or if you're not sure you've found the right site—click the Browse The Web button (next to the folder icon above the Browsed Pages list). This action launches your Web browser. Use the browser to navigate to the page you want. When you return to Excel, the Insert Hyperlink dialog box will contain the address of that site.

Note that if you're linking to a Web site from your desktop, the Address box must include the appropriate protocol prefix (http:// or ftp://, for example). If you're creating a link that will be used on a Web site, a target address that isn't fully qualified will be assumed to be relative to the current page.

If you're linking to a local document, as opposed to a Web page, you'll probably find that document most easily by clicking the Recent Files button. As Figure 29-3 shows, the Recent Files list includes *only* files from local (and local-area network) storage. If the file you want doesn't appear in the list, click the Browse For File button (above the upper-right corner of the Recent Files list).

TROUBLESHOOTING

I don't want that hyperlink.

Sometimes a URL is just a URL, and you don't want to launch your browser every time you click it. Right-click the cell in question, and click Remove Hyperlink.

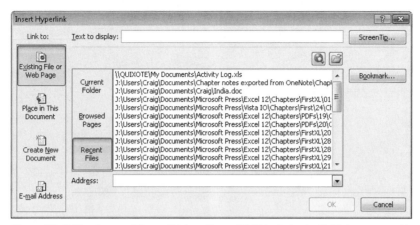

Figure 29-3 The Browsed Pages list (see Figure 29-2) includes both Web pages and local documents. To filter out the Web pages, click Recent Files.

> **Note**
>
> If you're linking to an Excel file, you can also click the Bookmark button to specify a location within that file. You can specify a worksheet name or a named cell or range. Unfortunately, however, you can't use the Bookmark button to link to a bookmark in a Word document.

Linking to a Location in the Current Document

To link to a location in the current document, click Place In This Document in the Insert Hyperlink dialog box. As Figure 29-4 shows, you can link to any worksheet or to a named cell or range. If you select a worksheet name, use the Type The Cell Reference box to identify the cell on that worksheet to which you want to link. Excel links to A1 by default.

Linking to a New File

To create a link to a new file, click Create New Document in the navigation bar at the left side of the Insert Hyperlink dialog box. As Figure 29-5 shows, the dialog box then changes to reveal a pair of buttons. With one, you create the file immediately; with the other, you create the file the first time you click the hyperlink.

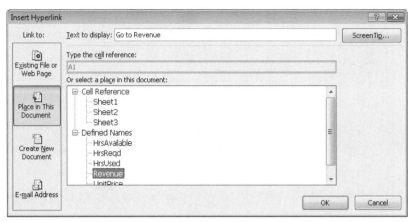

Figure 29-4 You can create a link to any worksheet, named range, or cell on the current worksheet.

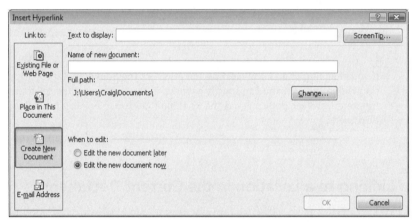

Figure 29-5 You can link to a file that doesn't yet exist—and create it either immediately or the first time you click the hyperlink.

Linking to an E-Mail Message

By clicking the E-Mail Address button in the navigation bar at the left side of the Insert Hyperlink dialog box, you can create a hyperlink that opens your e-mail program and fills out the new message. Figure 29-6 shows how the Insert Hyperlink dialog box appears after you click E-Mail Address. If you use this feature occasionally, the Recently Used E-Mail Addresses portion of the dialog box will list previous addresses, and you can resend to a former recipient by selecting from the list. If the address you want isn't there, though, you have to type it on the E-Mail Address line; Excel won't open your Contacts folder for you.

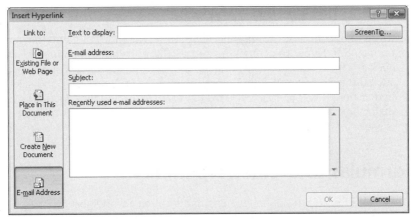

Figure 29-6 You can use this form of the Insert Hyperlink dialog box to create a mailto: link.

Assigning a Hyperlink to a Shape, Image, or Chart

You can assign a hyperlink to a shape, an image, or a chart. To do this, select the object, and press Ctrl+K. (To assign a hyperlink to a chart, you must select the chart area; the easiest way to do this is to click just inside the outer perimeter of the chart.)

> **Note**
>
> The program giveth, and the program taketh away. Because of the redesigned user interface in Excel 2007, you can no longer assign hyperlinks to menu commands or toolbar icons. On the other hand, in earlier versions you were unable to assign hyperlinks to charts.

Selecting a Cell or Object Without Triggering the Hyperlink

To select a cell that contains a hyperlink without activating the hyperlink, click the cell and hold the mouse button down a half second or so. When the pointer changes from a hand to the usual Excel pointer (a white cross), you can release the mouse button.

This click-and-hold procedure does not work for hyperlinks assigned to graphics objects or charts. To select one of these without zooming off to the link target, hold down the Ctrl key while you click.

Editing or Deleting a Hyperlink

If you right-click a cell containing a hyperlink, the shortcut menu that appears includes both an Edit Hyperlink command and a Remove Hyperlink command. If you right-click a graphic object or chart that has a hyperlink attached, typically you'll see no such thing. To edit or delete a hyperlink in this case, press Ctrl, and select the object in question; then press Ctrl+K. This keyboard shortcut takes you to the Edit Hyperlink dialog box, which includes a handy Remove Link button. Click the button, and the link is gone.

Using Formulas to Create Hyperlinks

The HYPERLINK function creates a hyperlink in a worksheet cell, based on two text arguments, one of which is optional. The syntax is as follows:

`=HYPERLINK(link_location,friendly_name)`

In this syntax, *link_location*, a required argument, is a text value that specifies the target of the link, and *friendly_name*, an optional argument, is the text that will appear in the cell. If *friendly_name* is omitted, it is assumed to be the same as *link_location*. Either argument can be a cell reference. Here are two examples:

`=HYPERLINK(http://office.microsoft.com,"Microsoft Office Online")`
`=HYPERLINK("[\\Cervantes\Rocinante\myfile.xlsx\Sheet2!B29")`

The first example displays the text Microsoft Office Online as a hyperlink that connects to *http://office.microsoft.com*. Note that you must include the *http://* prefix in the *link_location* argument. The second example creates a hyperlink that takes you to cell B29 on Sheet2 of Myfile.xlsx, stored on the Rocinante share on the server named Cervantes.

INSIDE OUT **Create Dynamic Links with the HYPERLINK Function**

The most likely use for the HYPERLINK function is to construct a link target from text in another cell. For example, if you want a set of links to jump to different servers at different times, you could type the current server name in a cell and then build HYPERLINK formulas with absolute references to that cell. By changing the cell contents, you could then update all the HYPERLINK formulas at once.

Linking and Embedding

Microsoft long ago stopped using the term *object linking and embedding* (OLE) to describe its technology for creating "compound" documents—that is, documents that integrate data from multiple applications. But the technology is still there, and if you work with the full suite of 2007 Microsoft Office system applications, you will undoubtedly have occasions to take advantage of it.

Part of the reason that OLE has disappeared from Microsoft's formal vocabulary is that linking and embedding capability is nearly universal in major Microsoft Windows applications now, and it ostensibly works so well that you seldom have to think about what you're doing. Nevertheless, it is important to understand the general differences between embedding and linking, to know when it's appropriate to use one form of integration as opposed to the other, and to know how to fix matters in the event that a link becomes broken.

Embedding vs. Linking

When you *embed* another application's data in Microsoft Office Excel 2007, your Excel document stores a complete copy of the source data. Because you have a complete copy (the paragraph from Microsoft Office Word 2007, for example, or the voice annotation you created in a sound-recording program), that information remains intact even if the source is destroyed or becomes otherwise unavailable. But the embedded copy becomes completely independent of the source. The source might change, but the embedded copy does not.

When you *link* your Office Excel 2007 document to some external data, your document records pointers to the source of that data. If the source changes, your workbook can change accordingly.

Whether it changes automatically to match the source, or only when you request an update, depends on options that you set. In any event, your Excel document retains a connection to the source.

If the information you link or embed is text or a graphic, Excel renders it (makes it visible on your worksheet) if it's in a format that Excel recognizes and if you have not explicitly asked for an iconic display. Otherwise, Excel displays an icon that represents the linked or embedded information. When you double-click the icon, Excel renders the information (plays the sound clip or video, for example), provided an application capable of rendering it is available.

In some cases, Excel might display only some of a text document that you link or embed. If you link or embed a multipage Word document, for example, your workbook displays the first page only. To see the rest, double-click that first page.

Because embedding typically records more information in your Excel document than linking does, embedding tends to generate larger files. If minimizing file size matters, you should favor linking over embedding. You should also link if you need to have Excel update your workbook when the source data changes.

On the other hand, if you need to retrieve some information from a document on a network server so you can take it on the road, obviously you'll want to embed it, not link to it. Otherwise, Excel won't be able to find it when you're offline.

Embedding vs. Static Pasting

What's the difference between embedding something and doing an ordinary paste from the Clipboard?

If you paste text into Excel from Notepad (an application that doesn't support embedding), that text arrives as though you typed it directly in the active worksheet cell. (If the text spans multiple lines, Excel delivers each new line to a new cell in the current column.) What you paste, in other words, becomes ordinary worksheet data.

If you embed text from Word (or another word processor that supports embedding), the text appears to land in the cell that was active when you performed the embedding, but in fact it floats above the worksheet cells in an *object layer*. Excel displays the text in an opaque rectangle that's initially aligned with the active cell; you can drag the rectangle to reposition the embedded object. As Figure 30-1 shows, when you select the embedded text, the word *Object*, followed by a number, appears in the name box; white handles appear on the object's bounding rectangle (you can use these to change the size of the rectangle); and an EMBED formula appears on the formula line. You can't do much with this formula, because EMBED isn't a worksheet function, but you can use it as a way of reminding yourself in which program the embedded data originated.

> ## TROUBLESHOOTING
>
> ### How do I get rid of the bounding rectangle?
> To get rid of the bounding rectangle, right-click any part of the embedded item, and select Format Object. Click the Colors And Lines tab in the Format Object dialog box. Below Line, open the Color list, and choose No Line. In the Fill area of the same dialog box, you can make the embedded object transparent by dragging the Transparency slider. (If the embedded object is a picture, right-click it, and select Format Picture instead of Format Object.)

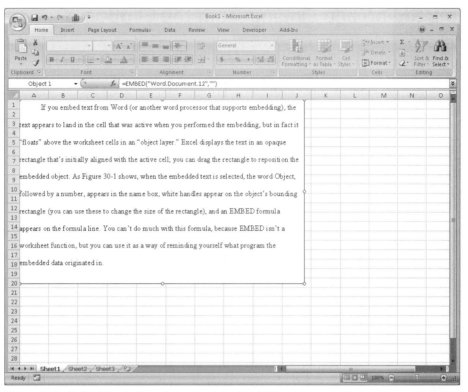

Figure 30-1 Embedding text creates a movable object whose source is identified by an OBJECT formula.

More important, perhaps, if you double-click the embedded object, you can edit it using the application that created it. If you double-click the Word object in Figure 30-1, for example, Excel displays a thick border around the embedded object. The Excel Ribbon is replaced by the Word Ribbon, leaving you with a kind of hybrid user interface. At this point, you are essentially working in Word, although the Excel context remains visible. When you have finished using Word to edit the object, you can click outside it (back on the worksheet), and the Word paraphernalia disappears.

This kind of object editing is called *editing in place*. Not all applications that support embedding offer it. If you double-click an object embedded from an application that doesn't support editing in place, Excel launches a regular copy of that application (although it might include a command on its File menu for updating your Excel document with the changes you make).

In cases where embedding and static pasting are both options, you should favor embedding if you want to retain the ability to edit the material in its native application—or if you want to be able to apply object-formatting commands to the incoming material.

Embedding and Linking from the Clipboard

When you copy data to the Clipboard, the source application typically posts the data to the Clipboard in a variety of formats. When you use the Paste Special command in Excel (or another application, if you're not pasting into Excel), the Paste Special dialog box lists all the available formats that the receiving application knows how to use.

For example, suppose you copy a Microsoft Office PowerPoint 2007 slide. PowerPoint posts the slide to the Clipboard in more than a dozen formats. (If you're using Windows XP, you can see the available formats by opening the Clipbook Viewer application, Clipbrd.exe.) If you right-click a cell on your Excel worksheet and click the Paste Special command, the Paste Special dialog box lists the formats that Excel can accept. In this case, as Figure 30-2 shows, Excel offers a choice of six formats.

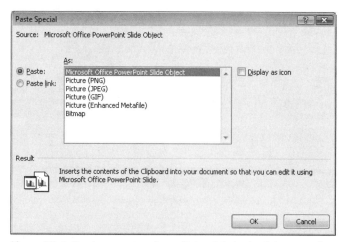

Figure 30-2 Excel can paste a PowerPoint slide in six of the many formats that PowerPoint posts to the Clipboard.

In many cases, the format that appears first in the Paste Special dialog box is the default format—the one that you would get by clicking Paste or pressing Ctrl+V. If the Clipboard data can be embedded, Excel is likely to make the embedding format the default. If you need to be certain, however, you shouldn't depend on these generalizations; use Paste Special instead of Paste.

If the format listed in the Paste Special dialog box includes the word *Object*, choosing that format embeds the Clipboard data. All the other formats produce a static paste. If you're not sure what a format is or does, select it in the Paste Special dialog box, and read the descriptive text below the format list.

As Figure 30-2 shows, the Paste Special dialog box includes two options, Paste and Paste Link. To link your source data, select Paste Link. Excel will render your source data in whatever format you have selected and also create a link to the source.

INSIDE OUT   **Don't Bother Pasting a Bitmap Object**

If you copy a bitmap to the Clipboard, click the Paste Special command in Excel, and then select the Bitmap Image Object format, Excel pastes a picture instead of embedding a bitmap object. (This bug has been around for several versions of Excel.) To embed a bitmap, click Object in the Text group of the Insert tab.

Figure 30-3 shows a block of text paste-linked from Word into Excel. Notice that Excel identifies this as an object (as it does for embedded text). But instead of the EMBED formula you saw with embedded text (refer to Figure 30-1), Excel creates an external-reference formula, similar to the kind of formula it creates if you reference a cell in an external Excel workbook. The linked object also gets a green rotation handle in addition to the usual white handles. You can use the green handle to slant or invert the text block.

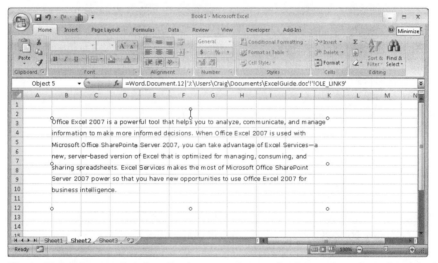

Figure 30-3 When you link data, Excel creates an external-reference formula similar to the formula it would use to reference a cell on another worksheet.

Note

The Paste Link option in the Paste Special dialog box is not available for all the formats that Excel can paste. If it's not available for the data and format you want, try linking by means of the Object command on the Insert tab. For more information, see "Embedding and Linking with the Object Command" on the next page.

As mentioned, if you embed or link a format that Excel cannot render, the incoming data is represented by an icon. In some cases, you can also ask for iconic representation of data that Excel can render. Displaying an icon instead of the rendered data is an excellent choice if you want the user of your Excel document to have access to external information but not be distracted by it. The icon takes up little space on your worksheet, and you can add text beside it to explain its purpose. (An even better choice is a hyperlink; see Chapter 29, "Using Hyperlinks.")

Embedding and Linking with the Object Command

Clicking Object on the Insert tab lets you embed an object that doesn't exist as Clipboard data. As Figure 30-4 shows, the Object dialog box has two tabs, Create New and Create From File. Using the Create New tab, you can create an object from scratch and then embed it. Using the Create From File tab, you can either embed or link an entire file.

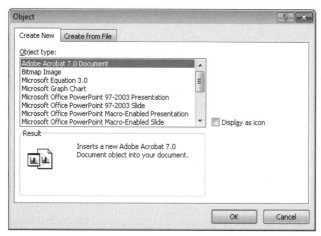

Figure 30-4 By clicking the Object command on the Insert tab, you can create embeddable objects or link or embed entire files.

The list on the Create New tab includes document types that are probably familiar, such as Bitmap Image and Microsoft Office PowerPoint 97–2003 Presentation, as well as the names of OLE server applications on your system—applications that might or might not be familiar. If you select a document type and click OK, Excel launches the application associated with that document type. If the application in question supports editing in place, the Excel user interface is replaced by that of the application, and you will be able to create your object in a window that appears on your Excel worksheet. If the application does not support editing in place, the full application appears in a separate window. After you create your object, you can send the new object to your Excel worksheet by means of a command on the application File menu.

The OLE server names on the Create New tab represent applications whose sole purpose is to create embeddable objects. If you choose Microsoft Equation 3.0, for example, the Microsoft Equation Editor feature appears, letting you create and embed a mathematical, chemical, or other technical expression as an object on your Excel worksheet. As Figure 30-5 shows, the Microsoft Equation Editor is an add-in that supports editing in place. It replaces the Ribbon in Excel and displays its elaborate palette of symbol toolbars.

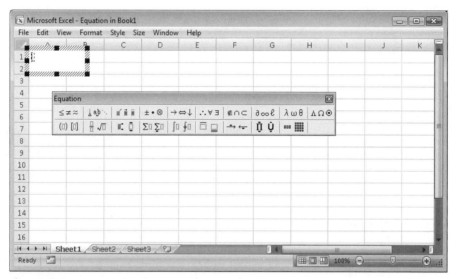

Figure 30-5 You can take advantage of Microsoft Equation Editor and other OLE server add-ins by clicking the Object command on the Insert tab.

On the Create From File tab in the Object dialog box, you can type the name of a file or use the Browse button to locate it. To embed the file, click OK. To create a link to it, select the Link To File check box. To display an embedded or linked object as an icon, select the Display As Icon check box.

Using the Create From File tab in the Object dialog box, you can embed or link any file to your Excel document. If you embed a file type that's not listed on the Create New tab, the resulting formula references the Windows Packager application, as shown in Figure 30-6.

Packager is a "wrapper" that encapsulates the embedded file. When you double-click the object on your worksheet, Packager executes the file, an action equivalent to double-clicking it in Windows Explorer. If the file is not associated with an application, a Run With dialog box appears. In the Run With dialog box, you can choose an application with which to open the file.

Chapter 30

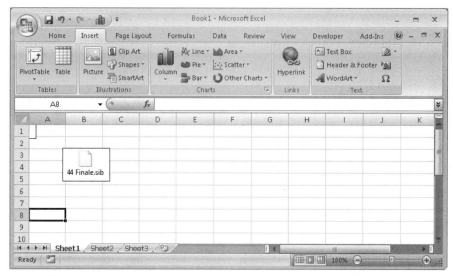

Figure 30-6 You can embed any kind of file in an Excel worksheet. If the file is not associated with an OLE application, Windows encapsulates it using Packager.

Managing Links

If an Excel workbook includes links to other documents, you can use the Edit Links command (in the Connections group on the Data tab) to summon the dialog box shown in Figure 30-7. The Edit Links dialog box lists all the links in the current file, including links created by formula references to cells in other worksheets.

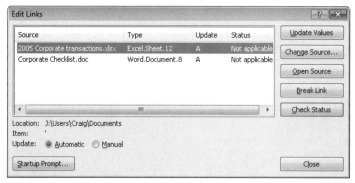

Figure 30-7 To update, alter, or sever a link, click the Data tab, and then click Edit Links (in the Connections group).

Choosing Automatic or Manual Update

The Automatic and Manual options, near the bottom of the dialog box, control the manner in which your links are updated. If you select Automatic (the only choice available for links with other Excel documents), your link is updated whenever the source changes. This automatic updating occurs instantaneously with some source applications and takes a while longer with others. Theoretically, you don't need to concern yourself with refreshing the link; Windows performs that duty for you. If you find that the updating occurs more frequently than you want it to (or if the process intrudes on your concentration in any way), you might want to switch from Automatic to Manual. With updating set to Manual, you can force an update by returning to the Edit Links dialog box and clicking Update Values.

Fixing Broken Links

If Excel tries to update a link and can't find the source file, it presents an error message. This kind of problem occurs most commonly when a file to which you've defined a link is renamed, relocated, or removed. If the source has been renamed or moved and you know its current identity and whereabouts, you can often fix the problem by editing the link formula. Alternatively, revisit the Edit Links dialog box (click Edit Links on the Data tab), and then click the Change Source button. Unfortunately, the Change Links dialog box does not include a file browser, so you'll need to type or edit the file specification manually:

Linking vs. Hyperlinking

Hyperlinks, discussed in Chapter 29, "Using Hyperlinks," are an alternative way to connect an Excel document to an external file. If you want your Excel document to reference supplementary information without making that information obtrusive, you can do it neatly with a hyperlink.

Which method you prefer is likely to be a matter of taste. Most people looking at your Excel document will find a hyperlink self-explanatory, but some might not know immediately how to use an OLE link. On the other hand, an iconic OLE link might more easily grab a viewer's attention. OLE links are also self-repairing—in some cases, at least. (If you rename or move a target of an OLE link, Windows can sometimes update the link information so Excel still finds the linked file.) Hyperlinks are not self-repairing. If you think the target of a link might get renamed or moved, it's safer to use an OLE link.

Chapter 30

Using Excel Data in Word Documents

I ts many presentation features notwithstanding, Microsoft Office Excel 2007 is at heart an analytical tool. When it comes time to organize Office Excel 2007 data and present it in the context of a larger, textual report, you need another stalwart in the 2007 Microsoft Office system suite, Microsoft Office Word 2007. Naturally, Office Word 2007 is designed to work hand-in-glove with Excel, so you can easily do your analysis in Excel and transfer the results to Word when you need to incorporate your tables and charts into a verbal report.

In this chapter, you'll survey the few points you need to know when incorporating your Excel tables and charts into Word. You'll also see how you can use contact lists stored in Excel to generate form letters, mailing labels, and envelopes in Word.

Using Excel Tables in Word Documents

You can create tables directly in Word, of course, but if your tables consist of more than a few rows or columns, you'll probably find it simpler to build them in Excel and then transfer them to your Word documents. You can use either of the following methods to move a worksheet range from Excel into Word:

- Copy the Excel data to the Clipboard, and then use Paste or Paste Special in Word to paste the table in the format of your choice, with or without a link to the source data.

- On the Insert tab in Word, click Object. The Object command in Word works just like its counterpart in Excel. (See "Embedding and Linking with the Object Command" on page 886.)

Pasting an Excel Table from the Clipboard

If you copy an Excel worksheet range to the Clipboard and then paste that range into Word (using either the Paste command or its keyboard shortcut, Ctrl+V), the smart tag menu that appears below the lower-right corner of the pasted data, shown in Figure 31-1, provides quick access to the formatting options you're most likely to want. These options are as follows:

- **Keep Source Formatting** Word receives the data as a block of HTML and creates a table, preserving the fonts, alignment properties, numeric formatting, text color, and shading of your original. In most but not all cases, this option (the default) is an adequate way to create a table in Word that matches the appearance of your Excel data. After you have performed the paste, if you click the pasted data, a Table Tools section appears on the Ribbon in Word, and you can use commands on the Design and Layout tabs to alter the appearance of the table in Word.

- **Match Destination Table Style** The data becomes a table in Word, but Word formats it as if you had created the table directly in Word.

- **Paste As Picture** Word turns the pasted table into a picture and makes picture-formatting functionality available. You might choose this format if you want to add some pizzazz to your numbers—for example, shadows, reflections, borders with rounded corners, and so on.

- **Keep Text Only** If you select this option, Word does not create a table. Instead, it simply pastes each cell's contents in the current default font, separating cells with single tab characters. You might find this option useful if you're simply copying a single column from Excel. Where multiple columns are involved, the Keep Text Only choice sometimes produces a misaligned hash in Word.

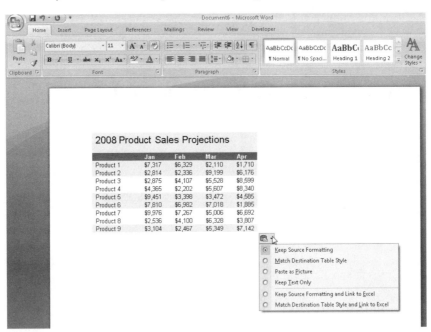

Figure 31-1 Immediately after you paste Excel cells into Word, a smart tag menu gives you access to the formatting options you're most likely to need.

In addition to these four options, the smart tag menu provides commands to link your Word table (in either Excel format or Word format) to its source in Excel. These choices, Keep Source Formatting And Link To Excel and Match Destination Table Style And Link To Excel, are equivalent to selecting Paste Special and selecting the Paste Link option. We discuss these options later in this chapter. (See "Paste-Linking an Excel Table into Word" on page 896.)

> **Note**
>
> Don't close your Excel document before pasting. If you copy data from Excel to the Clipboard and then close the Excel document, your options for pasting into Word are considerably diminished. The default paste format changes from HTML to rich-text format (RTF), and the options to link your Word document to its source in Excel disappear.

Using Paste Special to Control the Format of Your Table

The smart tag menu that appears when you paste Excel data includes only the most commonly used formatting options. These will probably meet your needs in most cases. However, if you are pasting from an Excel document stored in Compatibility mode (that is, saved in the Excel 97–2003 Workbook format), you sometimes might find the HTML badly rendered in Word. (These problems appear to have been solved in the new Excel 2007 formats.)

If your Excel table does arrive with formatting distortions in Word, all is not lost. Erase the pasted data in Word, and then try again using the Paste Special command in Word. (On the Home tab in Word, click the small arrow below Paste, and then click Paste Special.) Figure 31-2 shows this dialog box as it appears when your Excel document is still open. (If you close the Excel document, fewer options are available.)

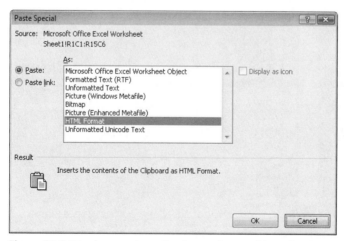

Figure 31-2 Word can paste an Excel range in any of these formats.

With almost any of the formats displayed in the Paste Special dialog box, you can either paste or paste-link. We'll look at the latter operation in a moment in "Paste-Linking an Excel Table into Word" on page 896. The next sections describe the available paste formats:

- Microsoft Office Excel Worksheet Object
- Formatted Text (RTF) and HTML Format
- Unformatted Text and Unformatted Unicode Text
- Picture (Windows Metafile), Bitmap, and Picture (Enhanced Metafile)

Using the Microsoft Office Excel Worksheet Object Format

Pasting the Worksheet Object format provides a completely faithful replication of the appearance of your Excel table—including any graphical elements that happened to be in your Excel selection. It also lets you edit the pasted table using Excel commands and features rather than Word ones. For example, if you want to apply a custom numeric format to your data after pasting it as an object into Word, you can do that by double-clicking the object. When you do this, the user interface of Word temporarily merges with Excel, as shown in Figure 31-3. After you edit the object and click any other part of the Word document, the Excel Ribbon is replaced by the Word Ribbon, and the worksheet column and row headings disappear.

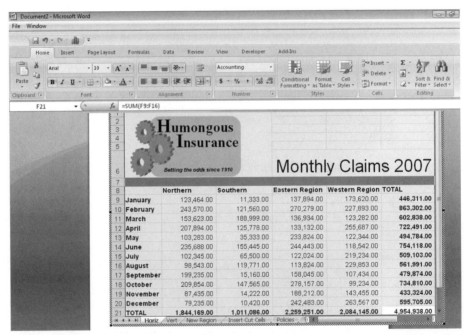

Figure 31-3 When you double-click an embedded Excel object, the Word Ribbon is replaced by the Excel Ribbon, letting you use Excel formatting and editing features to modify the object.

> **Note**
>
> When you double-click an embedded Excel object that includes graphical elements, Word might truncate those elements temporarily. When you return to the regular Word interface, however, Word will fully restore your graphical elements.

An important peculiarity to note about Excel objects embedded in Word documents is that Excel embeds the *entire* workbook, not only the selection you copied to the Clipboard. The sheet tabs at the bottom of Figure 31-3 illustrate this point. Although the editing window that appears in Word when you double-click the Excel object has the same dimensions as the original selection in Excel, you can scroll to any part of the current worksheet and even switch to another worksheet in the same workbook. When you return to Word (by clicking off the embedded object), Word treats any scrolling you do as an edit of the embedded object. If you switch from Sheet1 to Sheet2 while you're editing, you'll see Sheet2 when you return to your Word document.

Using Formatted Text (RTF) and HTML Format

The RTF and HTML formats preserve the font and numeric formatting of your Excel selection. They differ in the way they preserve that formatting. RTF is a method of encoding formatting information that has been available for a long time in Microsoft Office and other kinds of documents. HTML is the default format in Word (the format you get if you press Ctrl+V), a newer technology, and the programming language of the World Wide Web. Both formats generate tables in Word, maintaining the cell alignment you had in Excel and allowing for manipulation via the Table commands in Word. Neither format includes graphical elements that were part of your Excel selection.

HTML is more likely than RTF to render the formatting of your Excel selection accurately. But you might want to experiment to see which format suits your purposes more effectively. If you don't like the results you get, try again with a different format.

Using Unformatted Text and Unformatted Unicode Text

Use Unformatted Text and Unformatted Unicode Text when you do not want your Clipboard data to become a table in Word. Both formats transfer data from the Clipboard as though you had typed it directly into your Word document, using tab characters between the columns of your original Excel selection and return characters at the ends of lines. Ordinarily, the result is that data that was aligned neatly in Excel is no longer aligned in Word. Use the Unicode format if your data includes characters outside the regular ANSI range—for example, characters from non-Latin alphabets. Otherwise, it doesn't matter which of these two formats you use.

Using Picture (Windows Metafile), Bitmap, and Picture (Enhanced Metafile)

Picture (Windows Metafile), Bitmap, and Picture (Enhanced Metafile) formats produce more or less faithful graphical representations of your original Excel selection (including, of course, any graphical elements associated with it). Because the results are pictures, not tables, you can modify them with the picture-formatting features in Word.

Of the three available picture formats, Bitmap usually provides the most faithful replication of original appearances—at the cost of additional file size. For tables not accompanied by graphical elements, however, the Picture (Windows Metafile) format is usually more than adequate. Experiment to see what works best for you.

Paste-Linking an Excel Table into Word

You can paste-link any of the formats shown in Figure 31-2 and described in the preceding sections by selecting Paste Link in the Paste Special dialog box. When you do this, Word creates a field that references the source of your Excel data. The field is a code (comparable to an external-reference formula in Excel) that tells the application how to update the data if you request a manual update. The code also tells the application how to locate the data for editing if you double-click the linked information in your Word document. You can see the code by clicking the Microsoft Office Button in Word, clicking Word Options, selecting the Advanced category, and then selecting the Show Field Codes Instead Of Their Values check box.

Links from Excel into Word are automatic by default, which means that anytime the Excel source is changed, the Word document is automatically adjusted. You can switch to manual linking by going to the Links dialog box, shown in Figure 31-4. To get there, right-click the Excel table in the Word document, click Linked Worksheet Object, and then click Links.

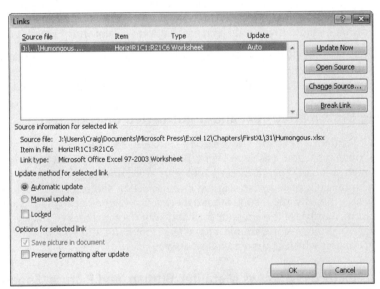

Figure 31-4 In the Links dialog box in Word, you can switch between manual and automatic updating, modify the link specification, or break the connection.

If you're using manual updating, you can also force an update by clicking Update Now in the Links dialog box. A simpler way to update your table is to select it and press F9.

INSIDE OUT   Link to Named Ranges

It is extremely important to make sure Word identifies the source of an Excel link by means of a range name, not by an ordinary range reference. Otherwise, if the source table changes location for any reason (for example, if someone inserts or deletes a few rows), the link will no longer reference the original table. At best, you'll have a blank table in your Word document. At worst, you'll have the *wrong* table.

If the worksheet range has a name at the time you copy it to the Clipboard, Word will reference it by name when you perform your paste-link. If it is not named, Word will reference it by cell address using R1C1 notation. If you subsequently assign a name to the range in Excel and perform a manual update, Word will continue to reference it by address, not by name. If you have inadvertently linked to a range address instead of a range name, the simplest way to fix the problem is to remove the linked data, be sure the source range is named, and then re-create the link.

Linking with Hyperlinks

An alternative way to create a link between a Word document and an Excel document is to use hyperlinks. With an Excel range on the Clipboard, you can click the Home tab in Word, click the arrow below the Paste command, and then click Paste As Hyperlink. As Figure 31-5 shows, Word underlines every character in the pasted range, but the entire block becomes a single hyperlink; clicking any part of it takes you to the source data.

The principal disadvantage of using hyperlinks instead of paste-linking is that hyperlinks don't get updated when the source changes. A hyperlink can make it easy for you or another user to find your way back to the data source, but it provides no assurance that your Word document is faithful to the source.

Using the Object Command

The Clipboard methods just described are fine for importing existing Excel tables into Word documents. If you're creating a table from scratch, you have the option of using an alternative method—by clicking the Object command on the Insert tab in Word. When you do this, the Object dialog box appears. Click the Create New tab, select Microsoft Office Excel Worksheet, and then click OK. Word displays a window into a blank Excel worksheet, as Figure 31-6 shows.

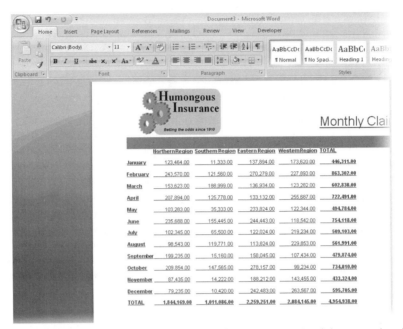

Figure 31-5 Hyperlinks can connect a Word document to an Excel document, but they are not updated when the source changes.

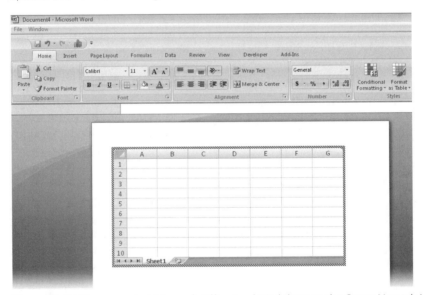

Figure 31-6 When you select Microsoft Office Excel Worksheet on the Create New tab in the Object dialog box in Word, a window into Excel appears in your Word document.

Here you can create your table, taking advantage of all the formatting and calculation tools in Excel. When your table is ready for inclusion in your Word document, click outside the Excel window. The result is an Excel object embedded in your Word file— exactly what you get if you create the table initially in Excel, copy it to the Clipboard, and then choose Microsoft Excel Worksheet Object from the Paste Special dialog box in Word.

The table that Word embeds will have the same row and column dimensions as the Excel window in which you created the table. That is, empty cells will be embedded along with populated ones. If you have to scroll to populate certain cells, some of your Excel table will not be embedded. In short, you need to adjust the size of the Excel window so it includes all the rows and columns you want to see in Word—and no more.

Using Excel Charts in Word Documents

To create a quick chart from scratch in Word, click Chart in the Illustrations group on the Insert tab on the Ribbon in Word. All 2007 Office release applications share a common charting engine, so—provided you're working with a Word 2007 document format (as opposed to a Word 97–2003 document)—you'll be greeted by the same Insert Chart dialog box you might see in Excel:

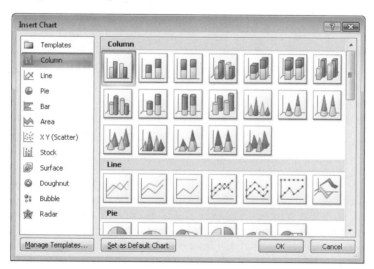

After you select a chart type from this gallery, you will arrive at a worksheet containing dummy data values for your chart (the worksheet will be titled Chart in Microsoft Office Word – Microsoft Excel). Edit those values, and then close the worksheet window. Your chart will then appear in your Word document.

If you're working with the Word 97–2003 format, you won't have the benefit of the familiar 2007 Office release charting engine. Instead, the Insert Chart command will summon a Microsoft Graph window:

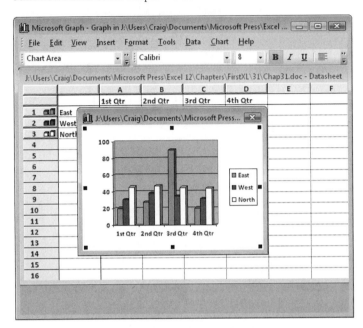

This is a more awkward environment for creating a chart, and we don't recommend it. Instead of using Microsoft Graph, you're better off creating a chart in Excel and then transferring it to your Word document via the Clipboard. Your graph will arrive in Word as a picture, and you'll have the Word picture-formatting options at your disposal.

If you paste an Excel chart into a Word 2007 document, the chart will arrive (by default) as a chart, not a picture, and because Excel 2007 and Word 2007 use a common charting engine, all the formatting tools available to you in Excel will also be available in Word. With the chart selected in your Word document, three new tabs—Design, Layout, and Format—appear on the Ribbon, under Chart Tools. Using these tabs, you can work with the chart in Word exactly as you would in Excel. The chart will, by default, be linked to its source data. With the chart selected, the Design tab includes an Edit Data command and a Refresh Data command. You can use these to return to and modify the source, or to perform a manual update, ensuring that your chart reflects the current numbers in Excel.

If you prefer, you can paste the chart as a picture by using the Paste As Picture command on the smart tag menu that appears right after you paste. If you do this, your chart is no longer linked to the source, but you have the Word picture-formatting tools available for adding shadows, borders, and other visual effects.

An additional command on the smart tag menu lets you embed the source workbook in your Word document. You might want to use this option if you need access to the entire source workbook and you plan to take the Word document offline. Be aware that embedding an Excel workbook means embedding the whole source file, which can add significantly to the size of your Word file.

Using Excel to Supply Mail-Merge Data to Word

Microsoft Word includes a mail-merge feature that facilitates the batch creation of letters, e-mail messages, envelopes, mailing labels, and directories. You can use Excel ranges (as well as many other types of data sources) to supply names, addresses, phone numbers, and so on, for mail-merge use.

Before you merge data from Excel into the mail-merge feature in Word, be sure your Excel worksheet is well structured for this purpose. Your table should meet the following criteria:

- Each column in the first row should be a field name, such as Title, Salutation, First Name, Middle Name, Last Name, Address, and so on.

- Each field name should be unique.

- Every piece of information that you want to be able to manipulate separately in your merge document should be recorded in a separate field. In a form letter, for example, you probably want to work with first and last names separately so you can use both of them in an address block but then use the last name only (with a salutation or title) at the beginning of the letter. Therefore, your Excel table should have separate fields for the first and last names.

- Each row should provide information about a particular item. In a mailing list, for example, each row would include information about a particular recipient.

- Your table should have no blank rows.

To use the mail-merge feature, follow these steps:

1. On the Mailings tab in Word, click the Start Mail Merge command, and then click Step By Step Mail Merge Wizard.

2. The Mail Merge task pane appears and consists of six steps. If you're going to create a mail-merge letter or e-mail message, the third step is the one that involves Excel. When you get there, the Mail Merge task pane will look like the one shown on the following page.

3. To use an Excel table as your data source, select Use An Existing List. Then click Browse. When you browse to your Excel file and then click Open, the Select Table dialog box that appears (see Figure 31-7) will display an entry for each worksheet. Specify the worksheet that contains the records you want to merge, and click OK.

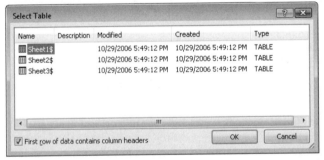

Figure 31-7 In the Select Table dialog box, specify the worksheet that contains the records you want to merge.

4. The Mail Merge Recipients dialog box appears (see Figure 31-8), letting you sort and filter the data source. Initially, the check box to the left of each record is selected, which means all records will be included in your merge. To remove particular items, clear their check boxes.

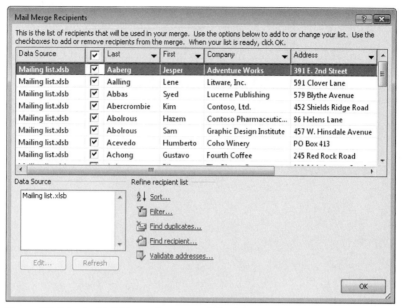

Figure 31-8 In the Mail Merge Recipients dialog box, you can filter and sort the data source.

5. You can use the arrows to the right of each field name for easy filtering. These function like their counterparts in an Excel table. For formulaic filtering—for example, to restrict the list to ZIP codes greater than 9000—click the arrow next to any field (it doesn't matter which), click Advanced, and then fill out the Filter And Sort dialog box shown in Figure 31-9.

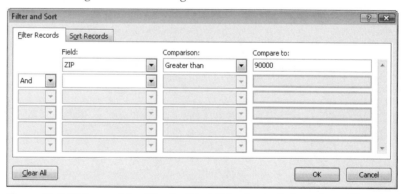

Figure 31-9 We've used the Filter And Sort dialog box to limit our list to ZIP codes that start with 9.

Click the arrow in the Field field and then select the field that will be your filtering criterion. Next, click the arrow in the Comparison field to select a comparison operation, and in the Compare To field, specify a comparison value. If you need more than one filtering criterion, select And or Or by clicking the arrow at the start of the second line, and then continue with more field names, operators, and comparison values.

You can use the Sort Records tab to change the order in which your data will be fed to the mail-merge mechanism. If you're sorting by one field only, however, you'll find it simpler to click the field heading in the Mail Merge Recipients dialog box (refer to Figure 31-8). Click a heading to generate an ascending sort by that heading; a second click turns it into a descending sort.

When you have your data as you want it, click OK to return to the Mail Merge task pane. In the remaining steps, you can create your merge document (the document that uses your data records), preview the results, and then carry out the merge.

Appendixes

Menu to Ribbon Command Reference

This appendix lists the menu commands and major toolbar buttons from Microsoft Excel 2003 and shows you where to find the equivalent functionality in Microsoft Office Excel 2007. In most cases, Microsoft has relocated commands on the new Ribbon structure. In other cases, Excel 2007 has new and better features that replace old functionality using new nomenclature and renamed or repositioned commands. Also, Microsoft has removed a few Excel 2003 commands from Excel 2007. We've organized this appendix to reflect the Excel 2003 menu structure.

This appendix includes commands from all the menus but includes only the Standard and Formatting toolbars, which are usually displayed in Excel 2003. For information about the location of buttons on any of the 19 other toolbars, click the Help button, and type **Excel 2003 commands** in the Search box. Click the Reference topic where you can download a workbook containing lists of all the menu commands and toolbar buttons in Excel 2003 with their 2007 counterparts.

File Menu

Menu	Excel 2003 Location	Excel 2007 Location
File	Menu	Microsoft Office Button
File	New	Microsoft Office Button, New
File	Open	Microsoft Office Button, Open
File	Close	Microsoft Office Button, Close
File	Save	Quick Access Toolbar, Save
File	Save	Microsoft Office Button, Save
File	Save As	Microsoft Office Button, Save As
File	Save As Web Page	Microsoft Office Button, Save As, Save As Type, Web Page
File	Save Workspace	View tab, Window group, Save Workspace command
File	File Search	Windows Start button, Search
File	Permission, Unrestricted Access	Review tab, Changes group, Protect Workbook command, clear the Structure and Windows check boxes under Protect Workbook For
File	Permission, Do Not Distribute	Removed

Menu	Excel 2003 Location	Excel 2007 Location
File	Permission, Restrict Permission As	Review tab, Changes group, Track Changes, Highlight Changes, then specify Who, When, and Where.
File	Check Out	Microsoft Office Button, Server, Check Out
File	Check In	Microsoft Office Button, Server, Check In
File	Version History	Microsoft Office Button, Server, View Version History
File	Web Page Preview	You must add a button to the Quick Access Toolbar for this command: Microsoft Office Button, Excel Options, Customize category, All Commands, Web Page Preview
File	Page Setup	Page Layout tab, Page Setup group, Page Setup Dialog Box Launcher
File	Print Area, Set Print Area	Page Layout tab, Page Setup group, Print Area command, Set Print Area command
File	Print Area, Clear Print Area	Page Layout tab, Page Setup group, Print Area command, Clear Print Area command
File	Print Preview	Microsoft Office Button, Print, Print Preview
File	Print	Microsoft Office Button, Print
File	Print	Microsoft Office Button, Print, Print Preview tab, Print command
File	Send To, Mail Recipient	You must add a button to the Quick Access Toolbar for this command: Microsoft Office Button, Excel Options, Customize category, All Commands, Mail Recipient
File	Send To, Original Sender	Removed
File	Send To, Mail Recipient (For Review)	You must add a button to the Quick Access Toolbar for this command: Microsoft Office Button, Excel Options, Customize category, All Commands, Send For Review
File	Send To, Mail Recipient (As Attachment)	Microsoft Office Button, Send, E-Mail
File	Send To, Routing Recipient	Removed
File	Send To, Exchange Folder	You must add a button to the Quick Access Toolbar for this command: Microsoft Office Button, Excel Options, Customize category, All Commands, Send To Exchange Folder
File	Send To, Online Meeting Participant	Removed

Menu	Excel 2003 Location	Excel 2007 Location
File	Send To, Recipient Using Internet Fax Service	Microsoft Office Button, Send, Internet Fax
File	Properties	Microsoft Office Button, Prepare, Properties
File	Most Recently Used Documents	Microsoft Office Button, Recent Documents
File	Exit	Microsoft Office Button, Exit Excel
File	Sign Out	Removed

Edit Menu

Menu	Excel 2003 Location	Excel 2007 Location
Edit	Undo	Quick Access Toolbar, Undo
Edit	Redo	Quick Access Toolbar, Redo
Edit	Cut	Home tab, Clipboard group, Cut command
Edit	Copy	Home tab, Clipboard group, Copy command
Edit	Office Clipboard	Home tab, Clipboard group, Clipboard Dialog Box Launcher
Edit	Paste	Home tab, Clipboard group, Paste command
Edit	Paste Special	Home tab, Clipboard group, Paste command, Paste Special command
Edit	Paste As Hyperlink	Home tab, Clipboard group, Paste command, Paste As Hyperlink command
Edit	Fill, Down	Home tab, Editing group, Fill command, Down command
Edit	Fill, Right	Home tab, Editing group, Fill command, Right command
Edit	Fill, Up	Home tab, Editing group, Fill command, Up command
Edit	Fill, Left	Home tab, Editing group, Fill command, Left command
Edit	Fill, Across Worksheets	Home tab, Editing group, Fill command, Across Worksheets command
Edit	Fill, Series	Home tab, Editing group, Fill command, Series command
Edit	Fill, Justify	Home tab, Editing group, Fill command, Justify command
Edit	Clear, All	Home tab, Editing group, Clear command, Clear All command

Menu	Excel 2003 Location	Excel 2007 Location
Edit	Clear, Formats	Home tab, Editing group, Clear command, Clear Formats command
Edit	Clear, Contents	Home tab, Editing group, Clear command, Clear Contents command
Edit	Clear, Comments	Home tab, Editing group, Clear command, Clear Comments command
Edit	Delete	Home tab, Cells group, Delete command
Edit	Delete Sheet	Home tab, Cells group, Delete command, Delete Sheet command
Edit	Move Or Copy Sheet	Home tab, Cells group, Format command, Move Or Copy Sheet command
Edit	Find	Home tab, Editing group, Find & Select command, Find command
Edit	Replace	Home tab, Editing group, Find & Select command, Replace command
Edit	Go To	Home tab, Editing group, Find & Select command, Go To command
Edit	Links	You must add a button to the Quick Access Toolbar for this command: Microsoft Office Button, Excel Options, Customize, All Commands, Edit Links
Edit	Object	Select an object to see its associated drawing tools
Edit	Clear, Series	Removed

View Menu

Menu	Excel 2003 Location	Excel 2007 Location
View	Normal	View tab, Workbook Views group, Normal command
View	Page Break Preview	View tab, Workbook Views group, Page Break Preview command
View	Task Pane	In some groups, Dialog Box Launchers will display a task pane instead of a dialog box. For example, Home tab, Clipboard group, Clipboard Dialog Box Launcher.
View	Toolbars, Standard	There is only one toolbar now, but these commands are available on the Home tab and from the Microsoft Office Button.
View	Toolbars, Formatting	There is only one toolbar now, but these commands are available on the Home tab.

Menu	Excel 2003 Location	Excel 2007 Location
View	Toolbars, Borders	There is only one toolbar now, but these commands are available on the Home tab, Font group, Borders command.
View	Toolbars, Chart	There is only one toolbar now, but these commands are available on the Chart Tools tabs when you insert or select a chart.
View	Toolbars, Control Toolbox	There is only one toolbar now, but these commands are available on the Developer tab. To display the Developer tab, click the Microsoft Office Button, click Excel Options, select the Popular category, and then select the Show Developer Tab In The Ribbon check box.
View	Toolbars, Drawing	There is only one toolbar now, but these commands are available on the Drawing Tools tabs when you select or insert a shape.
View	Toolbars, External Data	There is only one toolbar now, but these commands are available on the Data tab.
View	Toolbars, Forms	There is only one toolbar now, but these commands are available on the Developer tab. To display the Developer tab, click the Microsoft Office Button, click Excel Options, select the Popular category, and then select the Show Developer Tab In The Ribbon check box.
View	Toolbars, Formula Auditing	There is only one toolbar now, but these commands are available on the Formulas tab, Formula Auditing group.
View	Toolbars, List	There is only one toolbar now, but the majority of these commands are available on the Table Tools tabs when you select a cell in an Excel table.
View	Toolbars, Picture	There is only one toolbar now, but these commands are available on the Picture Tools tabs when you insert or select a picture.
View	Toolbars, PivotTable	There is only one toolbar now, but these commands are available on the PivotTable Tools tabs when you insert or select a cell in a PivotTable.
View	Toolbars, Protection	There is only one toolbar now, but these commands are available on the Review tab, Changes group
View	Toolbars, Reviewing	There is only one toolbar now, but these commands are available on the Review tab.
View	Toolbars, Task Pane	In some groups, Dialog Box Launchers will display a task pane instead of a dialog box. For example, Home tab, Clipboard group, Dialog Box Launcher.

Menu	Excel 2003 Location	Excel 2007 Location
View	Toolbars, Text To Speech	Removed
View	Toolbars, Visual Basic	There is only one toolbar now, but these commands are available on the Developer tab. To display the Developer Tab, click the Microsoft Office Button, click Excel Options, select the Popular category, and then select the Show Developer Tab In The Ribbon check box.
View	Toolbars, Watch Window	There is only one toolbar now, but these commands are available on the Formulas tab, Formula Auditing group, Watch Window command.
View	Toolbars, Web	There is only one toolbar now, but these commands are available in the Excel Options dialog box. Click the Microsoft Office Button, click Excel Options, select the Customize category, and click All Commands in the Choose Commands From list.
View	Toolbars, WordArt	There is only one toolbar now, but these commands are available on the Drawing Tools tabs when you insert or select WordArt.
View	Toolbars, Customize	Click the Microsoft Office Button, click Excel Options, and select the Customize category.
View	Formula Bar	View tab, Show/Hide group, Formula Bar check box
View	Status Bar	The status bar is always visible by default.
View	Header And Footer	Insert tab, Text group, Header & Footer command
View	Comments	Review tab, Comments group, Show All Comments command
View	Custom Views	View tab, Workbook Views group, Custom Views command
View	Full Screen	View tab, Workbook Views group, Full Screen command
View	Zoom	View tab, Zoom group, Zoom command
View	Sized With Window	Removed
View	Chart Window	Removed

Insert Menu

Menu	Excel 2003 Location	Excel 2007 Location
Insert	Menu	Home tab, Cells group, Insert command
Insert	Rows	Home tab, Cells group, Insert command, Insert Sheet Rows command
Insert	Columns	Home tab, Cells group, Insert command, Insert Sheet Columns command
Insert	Worksheet	Home tab, Cells group, Insert command, Insert Sheet command
Insert	Chart	Insert tab, Charts group
Insert	Symbol	Insert tab, Text group, Symbol command
Insert	Page Break	Page Layout tab, Page Setup group, Breaks command, Insert Page Break command
Insert	Reset All Page Breaks	Page Layout tab, Page Setup group, Breaks command, Reset All Page Breaks command
Insert	Function	Formulas tab, Function Library group, Insert Function command
Insert	Function	Formulas tab, Function Library group, Date & Time command, Insert Function command
Insert	Function	Formulas tab, Function Library group, Math & Trig command, Insert Function command
Insert	Function	Formulas tab, Function Library group, Financial command, Insert Function command
Insert	Function	Formulas tab, Function Library group, Logical command, Insert Function command
Insert	Function	Formulas tab, Function Library group, Lookup & Reference command, Insert Function command
Insert	Function	Formulas tab, Function Library group, Recently Used command, Insert Function command
Insert	Function	Formulas tab, Function Library group, Text command, Insert Function command
Insert	Function	Formulas tab, Function Library group, More Functions command, Cube command, Insert Function command
Insert	Function	Formulas tab, Function Library group, More Functions command, Engineering command, Insert Function command
Insert	Function	Formulas tab, Function Library group, More Functions command, Information command, Insert Function command

Menu	Excel 2003 Location	Excel 2007 Location
Insert	Function	Formulas tab, Function Library group, More Functions command, Statistical command, Insert Function command
Insert	Name, Define	Formulas tab, Defined Names group, Name Manager
Insert	Name, Paste	Formulas tab, Defined Names group, Use In Formula command, Paste Names command
Insert	Name, Create	Formulas tab, Defined Names group, Create From Selection command
Insert	Name, Apply	Formulas tab, Defined Names group, Define Name command, Apply Names command
Insert	Name, Label	Formulas tab, Defined Names group, Define Name command
Insert	Comment	Review tab, Comments group, New Comment command
Insert	Ink Annotations	Review tab, Ink, Start Inking (Tablet PC only)
Insert	Picture, Clip Art	Insert tab, Illustrations group, Clip Art command
Insert	Picture, From File	Insert tab, Illustrations group, Picture command
Insert	Picture, From File	Layout tab under Chart Tools, Insert group, Picture command
Insert	Picture, From File	Layout tab under PivotChart Tools, Insert tab, Picture group
Insert	Picture, From Scanner Or Camera	Removed
Insert	Picture, Ink Drawing And Writing	Review tab, Ink, Start Inking (Tablet PC only)
Insert	Picture, AutoShapes	Insert tab, Illustrations group, Shapes command
Insert	Picture, WordArt	Insert tab, Illustrations group, WordArt command
Insert	Picture, Organization Chart	insert tab, Illustrations group, SmartArt command
Insert	Diagram	Insert tab, Illustrations group, SmartArt command
Insert	Object	Insert tab, Text group, Object command
Insert	Hyperlink	Insert tab, Links group, Hyperlink command

Format Menu

Menu	Excel 2003 Location	Excel 2007 Location
Format	Cells	Home tab, Cells group, Format command, Format Cells command
Format	Row, Height	Home tab, Cells group, Format command, Row Height command
Format	Row, AutoFit	Home tab, Cells group, Format command, AutoFit Row Height command
Format	Row, Hide	Home tab, Cells group, Format command, Hide & Unhide command, Hide Rows command
Format	Row, Unhide	Home tab, Cells group, Format command, Hide & Unhide command, Unhide Rows command
Format	Column, Width	Home tab, Cells group, Format command, Column Width command
Format	Column, AutoFit Selection	Home tab, Cells group, Format command, AutoFit Column Width command
Format	Column, Hide	Home tab, Cells group, Format command, Hide & Unhide command, Hide Columns command
Format	Column, Unhide	Home tab, Cells group, Format command, Hide & Unhide, Unhide Columns command
Format	Column, Standard Width	Home tab, Cells group, Format command, Default Width command
Format	Sheet, Rename	Home tab, Cells group, Format command, Rename Sheet command
Format	Sheet, Hide	Home tab, Cells group, Format command, Hide & Unhide command, Hide Sheet command
Format	Sheet, Unhide	Home tab, Cells group, Format command, Hide & Unhide, Unhide Sheet command
Format	Sheet, Background	Page Layout tab, Page Setup group, Background command
Format	Sheet, Tab Color	Home tab, Cells group, Format command, Tab Color command
Format	AutoFormat	Home tab, Styles group, Format As Table command
Format	Conditional Formatting	Home tab, Styles group, Conditional Formatting command
Format	Style	Home tab, Styles group, Cell Styles command

Tools Menu

Menu	Excel 2003 Location	Excel 2007 Location
Tools	Spelling	Review tab, Proofing group, Spelling command
Tools	Research	Review tab, Proofing group, Research command
Tools	Error Checking	Formulas tab, Formula Auditing group, Error Checking command
Tools	Speech, Show Text To Speech Toolbar	Removed
Tools	Speech	Removed
Tools	Shared Workspace	Microsoft Office Button, Publish, Create Document Workspace
Tools	Share Workbook	Review tab, Changes group, Share Workbook command
Tools	Track Changes, Highlight Changes	Review tab, Changes group, Track Changes command, Highlight Changes command
Tools	Track Changes, Accept Or Reject Changes	Review tab, Changes group, Track Changes command, Accept/Reject Changes command
Tools	Compare And Merge Workbooks	You must add a button to the Quick Access Toolbar for this command: Microsoft Office Button, Excel Options, Customize, All Commands, Compare And Merge Workbooks
Tools	Protection, Protect Sheet	Review tab, Changes group, Protect Sheet command
Tools	Protection, Protect Sheet	Home tab, Cells group, Format command, Protect Sheet command
Tools	Protection, Allow Users To Edit Ranges	Review tab, Changes group, Allow Users To Edit Ranges command
Tools	Protection, Protect Workbook	Review tab, Changes group, Protect Workbook command
Tools	Protection, Protect And Share Workbook	Review tab, Changes group, Protect And Share Workbook command
Tools	Online Collaboration, Meet Now	Removed
Tools	Online Collaboration, Schedule Meeting	Removed
Tools	Online Collaboration, Web Discussions	Removed
Tools	Online Collaboration, End Review	Removed

Menu	Excel 2003 Location	Excel 2007 Location
Tools	Goal Seek	Data tab, Data Tools group, What-If Analysis command, Goal Seek command
Tools	Scenarios	Data tab, Data Tools group, What-If Analysis command, Scenario Manager command
Tools	Formula Auditing, Trace Precedents	Formulas tab, Formula Auditing group, Trace Precedents command
Tools	Formula Auditing, Trace Dependents	Formulas tab, Formula Auditing group, Trace Dependents command
Tools	Formula Auditing, Trace Error	Formulas tab, Formula Auditing group, Error Checking command, Trace Error command
Tools	Formula Auditing, Remove All Arrows	Formulas tab, Formula Auditing group, Remove Arrows command
Tools	Formula Auditing, Evaluate Formula	Formulas tab, Formula Auditing group, Evaluate Formula command
Tools	Formula Auditing, Hide Watch Window	Formulas tab, Formula Auditing group, Watch Window command
Tools	Formula Auditing, Formula Auditing Mode	Formulas tab, Formula Auditing group, Show Formulas command
Tools	Formula Auditing, Show Formula Auditing Toolbar	Formulas tab, Formula Auditing group
Tools	Macro, Macros	Developer tab, Code group, Macros command
Tools	Macro, Macros	View tab, Macros group, Macros command
Tools	Macro, Record New Macro	Developer tab, Code group, Record Macro command
Tools	Macro, Record New Macro	View tab, Macros group, Macros command, Record Macro command
Tools	Macro, Security	Developer tab, Code group, Macro Security command
Tools	Macro, Visual Basic Editor	Developer tab, Code group, Visual Basic command
Tools	Macro, Microsoft Script Editor	Removed
Tools	Add-Ins	Microsoft Office Button, Excel Options, Add-Ins category
Tools	AutoCorrect Options	Microsoft Office Button, Excel Options, Proofing category, AutoCorrect Options
Tools	Customize	Microsoft Office Button, Excel Options, Customize category
Tools	Show Signatures	Microsoft Office Button, Prepare, Add a Digital Signature
Tools	Options	Microsoft Office Button, Excel Options

Appendix A

Data Menu

Menu	Excel 2003 Location	Excel 2007 Location
Data	Sort	Data tab, Sort & Filter group, Sort command
Data	Filter	Data tab, Sort & Filter group, Filter command
Data	Filter, AutoFilter	Home tab, Editing group, Sort & Filter, Filter command
Data	Filter, Show All	Data tab, Sort & Filter group, Clear command
Data	Filter, Show All	Home tab, Editing group, Sort & Filter, Clear command
Data	Filter, Advanced Filter	Data tab, Sort & Filter group, Advanced command
Data	Form	You must add a button to the Quick Access Toolbar for this command: Microsoft Office Button, Excel Options, Customize category, All Commands, Form
Data	Subtotals	Data tab, Outline group, Subtotal command
Data	Validation	Data tab, Data Tools group, Data Validation command
Data	Table	Data tab, Data Tools group, What-If Analysis command, Data Table command
Data	Text To Columns	Data tab, Data Tools group, Convert Text To Table command
Data	Consolidate	Data tab, Data Tools group, Consolidate command
Data	Group And Outline, Hide Detail	Data tab, Outline group, Hide Detail command
Data	Group And Outline, Show Detail	Data tab, Outline group, Show Detail command
Data	Group And Outline, Group	Data tab, Outline group, Group command
Data	Group And Outline, Group	Options tab under PivotTable Tools, Group group
Data	Group And Outline, Ungroup	Data tab, Outline group, Ungroup command
Data	Group And Outline, Ungroup	Options tab under PivotTable Tools, Ungroup command
Data	Group And Outline, Auto Outline	Data tab, Outline group, Group command, Auto Outline command

Menu	Excel 2003 Location	Excel 2007 Location
Data	Group And Outline, Clear Outline	Data tab, Outline group, Ungroup command, Clear Outline command
Data	Group And Outline, Settings	Data tab, Outline group, Dialog Box Launcher button
Data	PivotTable And PivotChart Report	Insert tab, Tables group, PivotTable command, PivotTable/PivotChart command
Data	Import External Data, Import Data	Data tab, Get External Data group
Data	Import External Data, New Web Query	Data tab, Get External Data group, From Web command
Data	Import External Data, New Database Query	Data tab, Get External Data group, From Other Sources command, From Microsoft Query command
Data	Import External Data, Edit Query	You must add a button to the Quick Access Toolbar for this command: Microsoft Office Button, Excel Options, Customize category, All Commands, Edit Query
Data	Import External Data, Data Range Properties	Data tab, Connections group, Properties command
Data	Import External Data, Data Range Properties	Design tab under Table Tools, External Table Data command, Properties command
Data	Import External Data, Parameters	You must add a button to the Quick Access Toolbar for this command: Microsoft Office Button, Excel Options, Customize category, All Commands, Parameters
Data	List, Create List	Insert tab, Tables group, Table command
Data	List, Resize List	Design tab under Table Tools, Properties command, Resize Table command
Data	List, Total Row	Design tab under Table Tools, Table Style Options group, Total Row check box
Data	List, Convert To Range	Design tab under Table Tools, Tools group, Convert To Range command
Data	List, Publish List	Design tab under Table Tools, External Table Data group, Export command, Export Table To SharePoint List command
Data	List, View List On Server	Design tab under Table Tools, External Table Data group, Open In Browser command
Data	List, Unlink List	Design tab under Table Tools, External Table Data group, Unlink command

Appendix A

Menu	Excel 2003 Location	Excel 2007 Location
Data	List, Synchronize List	You must add a button to the Quick Access Toolbar for this command: Microsoft Office Button, Excel Options, Customize category, All Commands, Synchronize List
Data	List, Discard Changes And Refresh	You must add a button to the Quick Access Toolbar for this command: Microsoft Office Button, Excel Options, Customize category, All Commands, Discard Changes And Refresh
Data	List, Hide Border Of Inactive Lists	Removed
Data	XML, Import	Developer tab, XML group, Import command
Data	XML, Export	Developer tab, XML group, Export command
Data	XML, Refresh XML Data	Developer tab, XML group, Refresh Data command
Data	XML, XML Source	Developer tab, XML group, Source command
Data	XML, XML Map Properties	Developer tab, XML group, Map Properties command
Data	XML, Edit Query	Removed
Data	XML, XML Expansion Packs	Developer tab, XML group, Expansion Packs command
Data	Refresh Data	Analyze tab under PivotChart Tools, Data group, Refresh command
Data	Refresh Data	Options tab under PivotTable Tools, Data group, Refresh command
Data	Refresh Data	Design tab under Table Tools, External Table Data group, Refresh command
Data	Refresh Data	Data tab, Connections group, Refresh All command, Refresh command
Data	Refresh Data	Analyze tab under PivotChart Tools, Data group, Refresh command, Refresh command
Data	Refresh Data	Options tab under PivotTable Tools, Data group, Refresh command, Refresh command
Data	Refresh Data	Design tab under Table Tools, External Table Data group, Refresh command, Refresh command

Chart Menu

Menu	Excel 2003 Location	Excel 2007 Location
Chart	Chart Type	Design tab under Chart Tools, Type group, Change Chart Type command
Chart	Select Data	Design tab under Chart Tools, Data group, Select Data command
Chart	Source Data	Design tab under PivotChart Tools, Data group, Select Data command
Chart	Chart Options	Layout tab under Chart Tools
Chart	Location	Design tab under Chart Tools, Location group, Move Chart command
Chart	Location	Design tab under PivotChart Tools, Location group, Move Chart command
Chart	Add Data	Design tab under Chart Tools, Data group, Select Data command
Chart	Add Trendline	Layout under Chart Tools, Analysis group, Trendline command
Chart	3-D View	Layout under Chart Tools, Background group, 3-D View command

Window Menu

Menu	Excel 2003 Location	Excel 2007 Location
Window	New Window	View tab, Window group, New Window command
Window	Arrange All	View tab, Window group, Arrange All command
Window	Compare Side By Side With	View tab, Window group, View Side By Side command
Window	Hide	View tab, Window group, Hide command
Window	Unhide	View tab, Window group, Unhide command
Window	Split	View tab, Window group, Split command
Window	Freeze Panes	View tab, Window group, Freeze Panes command
Window	Currently Open Workbooks	View tab, Window group, Switch Windows command

Appendix A

Help Menu

Menu	Excel 2003 Location	Excel 2007 Location
Help	Menu	Upper Ribbon, Help (the "question mark" button)
Help	Microsoft Office Online	Microsoft Office Button, Excel Options, Resources category, Microsoft Office Online
Help	Contact Us	Microsoft Office Button, Excel Options, Resources category, Contact Us
Help	Check For Updates	Microsoft Office Button, Excel Options, Resources category, Check For Updates
Help	Detect And Repair	Microsoft Office Button, Excel Options, Resources category, Diagnose
Help	Activate Product	Microsoft Office Button, Excel Options, Resources category, Activate
Help	About Microsoft Office Excel	Microsoft Office Button, Excel Options, Resources category, About
Help	Show The Office Assistant	Removed

Standard Toolbar

Menu	Excel 2003 Location	Excel 2007 Location
Standard toolbar	New	Microsoft Office Button, New, Blank Worksheet
Standard toolbar	Open	Microsoft Office Button, Open
Standard toolbar	Save	Quick Access Toolbar, Save
Standard toolbar	Save	Microsoft Office Button, Save
Standard toolbar	Permission	Review tab, Changes group, Track Changes, Highlight Changes, then specify Who, When, and Where
Standard toolbar	Email	Microsoft Office Button, Send, E-Mail
Standard toolbar	Print	Microsoft Office Button, Print, Quick Print
Standard toolbar	Print Preview	Microsoft Office Button, Print, Print Preview
Standard toolbar	Spelling	Review tab, Proofing group, Spelling command
Standard toolbar	Research	Review tab, Proofing group, Research command
Standard toolbar	Cut	Home tab, Clipboard group, Cut command
Standard toolbar	Copy	Home tab, Clipboard group, Copy command

Menu	Excel 2003 Location	Excel 2007 Location
Standard toolbar	Paste	Home tab, Clipboard group, Paste command
Standard toolbar	Format Painter	Home tab, Clipboard group, Format Painter command
Standard toolbar	Undo	Quick Access Toolbar, Undo
Standard toolbar	Redo	Quick Access Toolbar, Redo
Standard toolbar	Ink Annotations	Review tab, Ink, Start Inking (Tablet PC only)
Standard toolbar	Hyperlink	Insert tab, Links group, Hyperlink command
Standard toolbar	AutoSum	Home tab, Editing group, AutoSum command
Standard toolbar	AutoSum	Formulas tab, Function Library group, AutoSum command
Standard toolbar	Sort Ascending	Data tab, Sort & Filter group, Sort A To Z command
Standard toolbar	Sort Descending	Data tab, Sort & Filter group, Sort Z To A command
Standard toolbar	Chart Wizard	Insert tab, Charts group
Standard toolbar	Drawing	These commands are available in the Drawing Tools tabs when you insert or select a shape.
Standard toolbar	Zoom	View tab, Zoom group, Zoom command
Standard toolbar	Microsoft Excel Help	Upper Ribbon, Help
Standard toolbar	PivotTable And PivotChart Report	Insert tab, Tables group, PivotTable command, PivotTable or PivotChart command
Standard toolbar	Comment	Review tab, Comments group, New Comment command
Standard toolbar	AutoFilter	This functionality is now added when you create a table. Otherwise, you must add a button to the Quick Access Toolbar for this command: Microsoft Office Button, Excel Options, Customize category, All Commands, AutoFilter

Formatting Toolbar

Menu	Excel 2003 Location	Excel 2007 Location
Formatting toolbar	Font	Home tab, Font group, Font command
Formatting toolbar	Font Size	Home tab, Font group, Font Size command
Formatting toolbar	Bold	Home tab, Font group, Bold command
Formatting toolbar	Italic	Home tab, Font group, Italic command
Formatting toolbar	Underline	Home tab, Font group, Underline command, Underline command
Formatting toolbar	Align Left	Home tab, Alignment group, Align Left command
Formatting toolbar	Center	Home tab, Alignment group, Center command
Formatting toolbar	Align Right	Home tab, Alignment group, Align Right command
Formatting toolbar	Merge And Center	Home tab, Alignment group, Merge & Center command
Formatting toolbar	Currency Style	Home tab, Number group, Accounting Number Format command
Formatting toolbar	Percent Style	Home tab, Number group, Percent Style command
Formatting toolbar	Comma Style	Home tab, Number group, Comma Style command
Formatting toolbar	Increase Decimal	Home tab, Number group, Increase Decimal command
Formatting toolbar	Decrease Decimal	Home tab, Number group, Decrease Decimal command
Formatting toolbar	Decrease Indent	Home tab, Alignment group, Decrease Indent command
Formatting toolbar	Increase Indent	Home tab, Alignment group, Increase Indent command
Formatting toolbar	Borders	Home tab, Font group, Borders command
Formatting toolbar	Fill Color	Home tab, Font group, Fill Color command
Formatting toolbar	Font Color	Home tab, Font group, Font Color command
Formatting toolbar	Chart, Chart Type	Design tab under Chart Tools, Type group, Change Chart Type command

Menu	Excel 2003 Location	Excel 2007 Location
Formatting toolbar	Chart, Source Data	Design tab under Chart Tools, Data group, Select Data command
Formatting toolbar	Chart, Source Data	Design tab under PivotChart Tools, Data group, Select Data command
Formatting toolbar	Chart, Chart Options	Layout tab under Chart Tools
Formatting toolbar	Chart, Location	Design tab under Chart Tools, Location group, Move Chart command
Formatting toolbar	Chart, Location	Design tab under PivotChart Tools, Location group, Move Chart command
Formatting toolbar	Chart, Add Data	Design tab under Chart Tools, Data group, Select Data command
Formatting toolbar	Chart, Add Trendline	Layout tab under Chart Tools, Analysis group, Trendline command
Formatting toolbar	Chart, 3-D View	Layout tab under Chart Tools, Background group, 3-D View command
Formatting toolbar	AutoFormat	Home tab, Styles group, Format As Table command
Formatting toolbar	Cells	Home tab, Cells group, Format command
Formatting toolbar	Increase Font Size	Home tab, Font group, Increase Font Size command
Formatting toolbar	Decrease Font Size	Home tab, Font group, Decrease Font Size command
Formatting toolbar	Text Direction	Home tab, Alignment group, Orientation command

Keyboard Shortcuts

This appendix lists keyboard-accessible commands and controls in Microsoft Office Excel 2007. Besides being an essential accessibility table, it also provides a glimpse into the depth and breadth of the features available.

Keyboard shortcuts are divided into the following categories in this appendix:

Keyboard Shortcuts by Key

- Function Keys
- Control and Navigation Keys
- Numeric Keys
- Symbols and Keypad
- Alphabet Keys

Keyboard Shortcuts by Task

- Charts and Select Chart Elements
- Dialog Box Edit Boxes
- Dialog Boxes
- Edit Data
- Enter and Calculate Formulas
- Enter Data
- Extend a Selection
- Filter Lists
- Format Cells Dialog Box—Border Tab
- Format Data
- Help
- Help Window
- Insert, Delete, and Copy Cells

- Macros
- Ribbon and Buttons
- Move and Scroll—In End Mode
- Move and Scroll—Worksheets
- Move Within a Selected Range
- Print
- Print Preview
- Select Cells, Rows, Columns, and Objects
- Select Cells with Special Characteristics
- Show, Hide, and Outline Data
- Smart Tags
- Task Panes
- Windows and Office Interface
- Worksheets

Keyboard Shortcuts by Key

This section lists the available keyboard shortcuts according to their position on the keyboard.

Function Keys

Press	To
F1	Display the Help window.
Ctrl+F1	Show/hide the Ribbon.
Alt+F1	Insert a chart as an object.
Shift+Alt+F1	Insert a new worksheet.
Ctrl+Alt+F1	Insert a Microsoft Office Excel 4 macro worksheet.
F2	Toggle Edit and Enter modes.
Shift+F2	Insert/edit a comment.
Alt+F2	Display the Save As dialog box.
Shift+Alt+F2	Save.
Ctrl+Alt+F2	Display the Open dialog box.
Shift+Ctrl+Alt+F2	Display the Print dialog box.

Press	To
F3	Display the Paste Name dialog box.
Shift+F3	Display the Insert Function dialog box.
Ctrl+F3	Display the Name Manager dialog box.
Shift+Ctrl+F3	Display the Create Names From Selection dialog box.
F4	Activate cell A1.
Shift+F4	Find the next (from the most recent search).
Ctrl+F4	Close the workbook.
Alt+F4	Close the application.
Shift+Ctrl+F4	Find the previous (from the most recent search).
Shift+Alt+F4	Close the application.
Ctrl+Alt+F4	Close the application.
Shift+Ctrl+Alt+F4	Close the application.
F5	Display the Go To dialog box.
Shift+F5	Display the Find And Replace dialog box.
Ctrl+F5	Restore the window.
Shift+F6	Display shortcut key pop-ups.
Ctrl+F6	Next window.
Shift+Ctrl+F6	Previous window.
F7	Check spelling.
Ctrl+F7	Move the window.
F8	Extend the selection mode.
Alt+F8	Display the Macro dialog box.
F9	Calculate all, or when a portion of a formula is selected, calculate the selected portion.
Shift+F9	Calculate the active worksheet.
Ctrl+F9	Minimize the active window.
Ctrl+Alt+F9	Calculate all worksheets in all open workbooks, regardless of whether they have changed since the last calculation.
Ctrl+Shift+Alt+F9	Recheck dependent formulas, and then calculate all cells in all open workbooks, including cells not marked as needing to be calculated.
F10	Display shortcut key pop-ups.
Shift+F10	Activate shortcut (context) menus.
Ctrl+F10	Toggle the maximized/restored window.
F11	Insert a chart on a new worksheet.

Appendix B

Press	To
Shift+F11	Create a new worksheet.
Ctrl+F11	Create a new macro worksheet.
Alt+F11	Show the Visual Basic Editor.
F12	Display the Save As dialog box.
Shift+F12	Save.
Ctrl+F12	Display the Open dialog box.
Shift+Ctrl+F12	Display the Print dialog box.

Control and Navigation Keys

Press	To
Backspace	Edit and clear.
Shift+Backspace	Collapse the selection to the active cell.
Ctrl+Backspace	Show the active cell.
Alt+Backspace	Undo.
Delete	Clear.
Shift+Delete	Cut.
Ctrl+Delete	Clear.
End	Toggle End mode.
Shift+End	Toggle End mode (and extend when you press Shift+arrow key).
Ctrl+End	Select the last cell in the worksheet.
Shift+Ctrl+End	Extend the selection to the last cell in the worksheet.
Escape	Cancel (edit, copy, cut, dialog, and so on).
Shift+Escape	Cancel (edit, copy, cut, dialog, and so on).
Ctrl+Escape	Display the Windows Start menu.
Shift+Ctrl+Escape	Display the Windows Task Manager.
Enter	Enter the value, and move down.
Shift+Enter	Enter the value, and move up.
Ctrl+Enter	Fill the value in edited cell into all cells, and do not move.
Alt+Enter	Redo.
Shift+Ctrl+Enter	Fill the value in edited cell into all cells, and do not move.
Home	Select the first cell in the row.
Shift+Home	Extend the selection to the first cell in the row.
Ctrl+Home	Select the first cell in window (or pane).

Press	To
Shift+Ctrl+Home	Extend the selection to the first cell in the window or pane.
Insert	Toggle Overwrite mode in Edit mode.
Shift+Insert	Paste.
Ctrl+Insert	Copy.
Left Arrow	Move left one cell.
Down Arrow	Move down one cell.
Shift+Down Arrow	Extend the selection down one cell.
Ctrl+Down Arrow	Select the last cell in the area down.
Alt+Down Arrow	Open the list (AutoComplete, Filter, Pick From List, or Validation).
Shift+Ctrl+Down Arrow	Extend the selection down to the last cell in the area down.
Shift+Left Arrow	Extend the selection left one cell.
Ctrl+Left Arrow	Select the last cell in the area left.
Shift+Ctrl+Left Arrow	Extend the selection down to the last cell in the area left.
Shift+Alt+Left Arrow	Ungroup.
Ctrl+Alt+Left Arrow	Move the active cell to the previous nonadjacent area within the selection.
Right Arrow	Move right one cell.
Shift+Right Arrow	Extend the selection right one cell.
Ctrl+Right Arrow	Select the last cell in the area right.
Shift+Ctrl+Right Arrow	Extend the selection down to the last cell in the area right.
Shift+Alt+Right Arrow	Group.
Ctrl+Alt+Right Arrow	Move the active cell to the next nonadjacent area within the selection.
Up Arrow	Move up one cell.
Shift+Up Arrow	Extend the selection up one cell.
Ctrl+Up Arrow	Select the cell at the top of the region.
Shift+Ctrl+Up Arrow	Extend the selection up to the end of the region.
Page Down	Scroll down one page.
Shift+Page Down	Extend the selection down one page.
Ctrl+Page Down	Move to the next worksheet.
Alt+Page Down	Scroll one page right.
Shift+Ctrl+Page Down	Extend the selection one worksheet down.
Shift+Alt+Page Down	Extend the selection one page right.
Page Up	Scroll up one page.

Press	To
Shift+Page Up	Extend the selection one page up.
Ctrl+Page Up	Move to the previous worksheet.
Alt+Page Up	Scroll one page left.
Shift+Ctrl+Page Up	Extend the selection one worksheet up.
Shift+Alt+Page Up	Extend the selection one page left.
Return	Enter the value, and move down.
Shift+Return	Enter the value, and move up.
Ctrl+Return	Fill the value in the edited cell into all cells, and do not move.
Alt+Return	Redo.
Shift+Ctrl+Return	Fill the value in the edited cell into all cells, and do not move.
Shift+Space	Select row.
Ctrl+Space	Select column.
Shift+Ctrl+Space	Select all.
Tab	Move to the next cell to the right.
Shift+Tab	Move to the next cell to the left.
Ctrl+Tab	Move to the next window.
Alt+Tab	Move to the next application.
Shift+Ctrl+Tab	Move to the previous window.
Shift+Alt+Tab	Indent.
Ctrl+Alt+Tab	Outdent.

Numeric Keys

Press	To
Ctrl+0	Hide the column.
Ctrl+1	Display the Format Cells dialog box.
Shift+Ctrl+1	Apply the two-decimal-place comma Number format.
Ctrl+2	Toggle the Bold format.
Shift+Ctrl+2	Apply the Time (AM/PM) format.
Ctrl+3	Toggle the Italic format.
Shift+Ctrl+3	Apply the Date format.
Ctrl+4	Toggle the Underline format.
Shift+Ctrl+4	Apply the Currency format.
Ctrl+5	Toggle the Strikethrough format.
Shift+Ctrl+5	Apply the Percentage format.

Press	To
Ctrl+6	Toggle the display of objects.
Shift+Ctrl+6	Apply the two-place Scientific format.
Shift+Ctrl+7	Apply the Outline border format.
Ctrl+8	Toggle the outline symbol display.
Shift+Ctrl+8	Select the current region.
Ctrl+9	Hide the row.
Shift+Ctrl+9	Show the row.

Symbols and Keypad

Press	To
Ctrl+' (apostrophe)	Copy the above cell, and edit.
Alt+' (apostrophe)	Activates the cell style list or dialog box.
Shift+Ctrl+' (apostrophe)	Copy the above cell, and edit.
Ctrl+– (hyphen)	Display the Delete dialog box.
Shift+Ctrl+– (hyphen)	Remove all the borders.
Shift+Ctrl+, (comma)	Fill down.
Ctrl+. (period)	Rotates the active cell through the corners of the selection.
Shift+Ctrl+. (period)	Fill right.
Ctrl+/ (slash)	Select array.
Ctrl+; (semicolon)	Insert the current date.
Shift+Ctrl+; (semicolon)	Insert the current time.
Ctrl+[(open bracket)	Select the direct precedent cells.
Shift+Ctrl+[(open bracket)	Select all the precedent cells.
Ctrl+] (close bracket)	Select the directly dependent cells.
Shift+Ctrl+] (close bracket)	Select all the dependent cells.
Ctrl+Shift+{ (open brace)	Select all the cells directly or indirectly referenced by formulas in the selection.
Ctrl+Shift+} (close brace)	Select cells that contain formulas that directly or indirectly reference the active cell.
Ctrl+` (single left quotation mark)	Display formulas.
Shift+Ctrl+` (single left quotation mark)	Apply the General format.
Ctrl+= (equal sign)	Calculate now.

Press	To
Alt+= (equal sign)	AutoSum.
Shift+Ctrl+= (equal sign)	Display the Insert dialog box.
Ctrl+Add (keypad)	Display the Insert dialog box.
Ctrl+Decimal (keypad)	Rotates the active cell through the corners of the selection.
Ctrl+Divide (keypad)	Select the array.
Ctrl+Multiply (keypad)	Select the current region.
Ctrl+Subtract (keypad)	Display the Delete dialog box.

Alphabet Keys

Press	To
Ctrl+A	Select the current region, or select all.
Shift+Ctrl+A	Insert arguments in the formula.
Ctrl+B	Apply the Bold format.
Ctrl+C	Copy.
Ctrl+D	Fill down.
Ctrl+F	Display the Find And Replace dialog box, Find tab.
Shift+Ctrl+F	Display the Format Cells dialog box, Font tab.
Ctrl+G	Display the Go To dialog box.
Ctrl+H	Display the Find And Replace dialog box, Replace tab.
Ctrl+I	Apply the Italic format.
Ctrl+K	Display the Insert Hyperlink dialog box.
Ctrl+L	Display the Create Table dialog box.
Shift+Ctrl+L	Toggle Filter.
Ctrl+N	Create a new workbook.
Ctrl+O	Display the Open dialog box.
Shift+Ctrl+O	Select the first cell containing a comment.
Ctrl+P	Display the Print dialog box.
Shift+Ctrl+P	Display the Format Cells dialog box, Font tab.
Ctrl+R	Fill right.
Ctrl+S	Save the workbook.
Ctrl+T	Display the Create Table dialog box.
Shift+Ctrl+T	Toggle the total row (when the table is selected).
Ctrl+U	Toggle the Underline format.
Ctrl+V	Paste.

Press	To
Ctrl+W	Close the window.
Ctrl+X	Cut.
Ctrl+Y	Redo.
Ctrl+Z	Undo.

Keyboard Shortcuts by Task

This section lists applicable keyboard shortcuts that are available while performing various types of tasks in Office Excel 2007.

Charts and Select Chart Elements

Press	To
F11	Create a chart of the data in the current range on a new worksheet.
Alt+F1	Create an embedded chart of the data in the current range on the current worksheet.
Down Arrow	Select the previous group of elements in a chart.
Up Arrow	Select the next group of elements in a chart.
Right Arrow	Select the next element within a group.
Left Arrow	Select the previous element within a group.

Dialog Box Text Boxes

Press	To
Home	Move to the beginning of the entry.
End	Move to the end of the entry.
Left Arrow or Right Arrow	Move one character to the left or right.
Ctrl+Left Arrow	Move one word to the left.
Ctrl+Right Arrow	Move one word to the right.
Shift+Left Arrow	Select or deselect one character to the left.
Shift+Right Arrow	Select or deselect one character to the right.
Ctrl+Shift+Left Arrow	Select or deselect one word to the left.
Ctrl+Shift+Right Arrow	Select or deselect one word to the right.
Shift+Home	Select from the insertion point to the beginning of the entry.
Shift+End	Select from the insertion point to the end of the entry.

Dialog Boxes

Press	To
Tab	Move to the next option or option group.
Shift+Tab	Move to the previous option or option group.
Ctrl+Tab or Ctrl+Page Down	Switch to the next tab in a dialog box.
Ctrl+Shift+Tab or Ctrl+Page Up	Switch to the previous tab in a dialog box.
Arrow keys	Move between options in an open list or between options in a group of options.
Spacebar	Perform the action for the selected button, or select or clear the selected check box.
First letter of an option	Open the list if it is closed and in a list, move to that option in the list.
Alt+the underlined letter in an option	Select an option, or select or clear a check box.
Alt+Down Arrow	Open the selected drop-down list.
Enter	Perform the action for the default button in the dialog box (the button with the bold outline, often the OK button).
Esc	Cancel the command, and close the dialog box.

Edit Data

Press	To
F2	Edit the active cell and position the insertion point at the end of the cell contents.
Alt+Enter	Start a new line in the same cell.
Backspace	Edit the active cell and then clear it, or delete the preceding character in the active cell as you edit cell contents.
Delete	Delete the character to the right of the insertion point, or delete the selection.
Ctrl+Delete	Delete text to the end of the line.
F7	Start the spelling checker.
Shift+F2	Edit a cell comment.
Enter	Complete a cell entry, and select the next cell below.
Ctrl+X	Cut the selected cells.
Ctrl+Z	Undo the last action.
Esc	Cancel a cell entry.
Ctrl+Shift+Z	When the AutoCorrect smart tag is displayed, undo or redo the last automatic correction.

Enter and Calculate Formulas

Press	To
= (equal sign)	Start a formula.
F2	Move the insertion point into the formula bar when editing in a cell is turned off.
Backspace	In the formula bar, delete one character to the left.
Enter	Complete a cell entry from the cell or formula bar.
Ctrl+Shift+Enter	Enter a formula as an array formula.
Esc	Cancel an entry in the cell or formula bar.
Shift+F3	Display the Insert Function dialog box.
Ctrl+A	When the insertion point is to the right of a function name in a formula, display the Function Arguments dialog box.
Ctrl+Shift+A	When the insertion point is to the right of a function name in a formula, insert the argument names and parentheses.
F3	Display the Paste Name dialog box.
Alt+= (equal sign)	Insert an AutoSum formula.
Ctrl+Shift+" (quotation mark)	Copy the value from the cell above the active cell into the cell or the formula bar.
Ctrl+' (apostrophe)	Copy a formula from the cell above the active cell into the cell or the formula bar.
Ctrl+` (single left quotation mark)	Alternate between displaying cell values and displaying formulas.
F9	Calculate all worksheets in all open workbooks, or when a portion of a formula is selected, calculate the selected portion.
Shift+F9	Calculate the active worksheet.
Ctrl+Alt+F9	Calculate all worksheets in all open workbooks, regardless of whether they have changed since the last calculation.
Ctrl+Alt+Shift+F9	Recheck dependent formulas, and then calculate all cells in all open workbooks, including cells not marked as needing to be calculated.

Enter Data

Press	To
Enter	Complete a cell entry and select the cell below.
Alt+Enter	Start a new line in the same cell.
Ctrl+Enter	Fill the selected cell range with the current entry.
Shift+Enter	Complete a cell entry, and select the previous cell above.
Tab	Complete a cell entry, and select the next cell to the right.

Press	To
Shift+Tab	Complete a cell entry, and select the previous cell to the left.
Esc	Cancel a cell entry.
Arrow keys	Move one character up, down, left, or right.
Home	Move to the beginning of the line.
F4 or Ctrl+Y	Repeat the last action.
Ctrl+Shift+F3	Create names from row and column labels.
Ctrl+D	Fill down.
Ctrl+R	Fill to the right.
Ctrl+F3	Define a name.
Ctrl+K	Insert a hyperlink.
Ctrl+; (semicolon)	Enter the date.
Ctrl+Shift+: (colon)	Enter the time.
Alt+Down Arrow	Display a drop-down list of the values in the current column of a list if your insertion point is in the cell containing the column name.
Ctrl+Z	Undo the last action.

Extend a Selection

Press	To
F8	Turn on or off extend mode. In extend mode, EXT appears on the status bar, and the arrow keys extend the selection.
Shift+F8	Add another range of cells to the selection, or use the arrow keys to move to the start of the range you want to add, and then press F8 and the arrow keys to select the next range.
Shift+arrow key	Extend the selection by one cell.
Ctrl+Shift+arrow key	Extend the selection to the last nonblank cell in the same column or row as the active cell.
Shift+Home	Extend the selection to the beginning of the row.
Ctrl+Shift+Home	Extend the selection to the beginning of the worksheet.
Ctrl+Shift+End	Extend the selection to the last used cell on the worksheet (lower-right corner).
Shift+Page Down	Extend the selection down one screen.
Shift+Page Up	Extend the selection up one screen.
End, Shift+arrow key	Extend the selection to the last nonblank cell in the same column or row as the active cell.

Press	To
End, Shift+Home	Extend the selection to the last used cell on the worksheet (lower-right corner).
End, Shift+Enter	Extend the selection to the last cell in the current row. This key sequence does not work if you have turned on transition navigation keys (Microsoft Office Button, Excel Options, Advanced category, Lotus Compatibility section).
Scroll Lock+Shift+Home	Extend the selection to the cell in the upper-left corner of the window.
Scroll Lock+Shift+End	Extend the selection to the cell in the lower-right corner of the window.

Filter Lists

Press	To
Alt+Down Arrow	In the cell that contains the arrow, display the Filter list for the current column.
Down Arrow	Select the next item in the Filter list.
Up Arrow	Select the previous item in the Filter list.
Home	Select the first item (Sort Ascending) in the Filter list.
End	Select the last item in the Filter list.
Enter	Filter the list based on the item selected from the Filter list.

Format Cells Dialog Box—Border Tab

Press	To
Alt+T	Apply or remove the top border.
Alt+B	Apply or remove the bottom border.
Alt+L	Apply or remove the left border.
Alt+R	Apply or remove the right border.
Alt+H	If cells in multiple rows are selected, apply or remove the horizontal divider.
Alt+V	If cells in multiple columns are selected, apply or remove the vertical divider.
Alt+D	Apply or remove the downward diagonal border.
Alt+U	Apply or remove the upward diagonal border.

Appendix B

Format Data

Press	To
Alt+' (apostrophe)	Display the Style dialog box.
Ctrl+1	Display the Format Cells dialog box. (Note that you must use the 1 key on the keyboard, not on the keypad.)
Ctrl+Shift+~ (tilde)	Apply the General number format.
Ctrl+Shift+$	Apply the Currency format with two decimal places (negative numbers in parentheses).
Ctrl+Shift+%	Apply the Percentage format with no decimal places.
Ctrl+Shift+^ (caret)	Apply the Exponential number format with two decimal places.
Ctrl+Shift+# (pound)	Apply the Date format with the day, month, and year.
Ctrl+Shift+@	Apply the Time format with the hour and minute and AM or PM.
Ctrl+Shift+! (exclamation point)	Apply the Number format with two decimal places, thousands separator, and minus sign (–) for negative values.
Ctrl+B	Apply or remove bold formatting.
Ctrl+I	Apply or remove italic formatting.
Ctrl+U	Apply or remove underlining.
Ctrl+5	Apply or remove strikethrough.
Ctrl+9	Hide the selected rows.
Ctrl+Shift+((opening parenthesis)	Unhide any hidden rows within the selection.
Ctrl+0 (zero)	Hide the selected columns.
Ctrl+Shift+& (ampersand)	Apply the outline border to the selected cells.
Ctrl+Shift+_ (underscore)	Remove the outline border from the selected cells.

Help

Press	To
F1	Display the Microsoft Excel Help window.

Help Window

Press	To
Tab or Shift+Tab	Select the next or previous hidden text or hyperlink.
Enter	Perform the action for the selected hidden text or hyperlink.
Alt+F4	Close the Help window.
Alt+Left Arrow	Go to the previous Help topic.
Alt+Right Arrow	Go to the next Help topic.
Up Arrow or Down Arrow	Scroll toward the beginning or end of a Help topic.
Page Up or Page Down	Scroll toward the beginning or end of a Help topic in large increments.
Home or End	Go to the beginning or end of a Help topic.
Ctrl+P	Print the current Help topic.
Ctrl+A	Select the entire Help topic.
Ctrl+C	Copy the selected items to the Clipboard.

Insert, Delete, and Copy Cells

Press	To
Ctrl+C	Copy the selected items to the Clipboard.
Ctrl+X	Cut the selected cells.
Ctrl+V	Paste copied cells.
Delete	Clear the contents of the selected cells.
Ctrl+– (hyphen)	Delete the selected row.
Ctrl+Shift++ (plus sign)	Insert a new row.

Macros

Press	To
Alt+F8	Display the Macro dialog box.
Alt+F11	Display the Visual Basic Editor.
Ctrl+F11	Insert a Microsoft Excel 4 macro worksheet.

Ribbon and Buttons

Press	To
F10 or Alt	Display shortcut key pop-ups.
Alt, Tab or Alt, Shift+Tab	Select the next or previous item on the Ribbon.
Enter	Open the selected menu or perform the action for the selected button or command.
Shift+F10	Display the shortcut menu for the selected item.
Alt+Spacebar	Display the Control menu for the Excel window.
Down Arrow or Up Arrow	When a menu or submenu is open, select the next or previous command.
Left Arrow or Right Arrow	Select the menu to the left or right. When a submenu is open, switch between the main menu and the submenu. When the Ribbon is active, select the next or previous tab.
Home or End	Select the first or last command on the menu or submenu.
Esc	Close an open menu. When a submenu is open, close only the submenu.

Move and Scroll—In End Mode

Press	To
End key	Turn on or off End mode. (*End Mode* appears on the status bar.)
End+arrow key	Move by one block of data within a row or column.
End+Home	Move to the last cell on the worksheet in the lowest used row of the rightmost used column.
End+Enter	Move to the rightmost nonblank cell in the current row.

Move and Scroll—Worksheets

Press	To
Arrow keys	Move one cell up, down, left, or right.
Ctrl+arrow key	Move to the edge of the current data region.
Home	Move to the beginning of the row.
Ctrl+Home	Move to the beginning of the worksheet.
Ctrl+End	Move to the last cell on the worksheet in the lowest used row of the rightmost used column.
Page Down	Move down one screen.
Ctrl+Page Down	Select the next worksheet in the workbook.
Ctrl+Page Up	Select the previous worksheet in the workbook.
Page Up	Move up one screen.

Press	To
Alt+Page Down	Move one screen to the right.
Alt+Page Up	Move one screen to the left.
Ctrl+Backspace	Scroll to display the active cell.
F5	Display the Go To dialog box.
Shift+F5	Display the Find And Replace dialog box.
Shift+F4	Repeat the last Find action (same as Find Next).
Tab	Move between unlocked cells on a protected worksheet.

Move Within a Selected Range

Press	To
Enter	Move from top to bottom within the selected range.
Shift+Enter	Move from bottom to top within the selected range.
Tab	Move from left to right within the selected range. If cells in a single column are selected, move down.
Shift+Tab	Move from right to left within the selected range. If cells in a single column are selected, move up.
Ctrl+. (period)	Move clockwise to the next corner of the selected range.
Ctrl+Alt+Right Arrow	In nonadjacent selections, switch to the next selection to the right.
Ctrl+Alt+Left Arrow	Switch to the next nonadjacent selection to the left.

Print

Press	To
Ctrl+P or Ctrl+Shift+F12	Display the Print dialog box.
Alt+F, then press W, then V	Open Print Preview.

Print Preview

Press	To
Arrow keys	Move around the page when zoomed in.
Page Up or Page Down	Move by one page when zoomed out.
Ctrl+Up Arrow or Ctrl+Left Arrow	Move to the first page when zoomed out.
Ctrl+Down Arrow or Ctrl+Right Arrow	Move to the last page when zoomed out.

Appendix B

Select Cells, Rows, Columns, and Objects

Press	To
Ctrl+Spacebar	Select the entire column.
Shift+Spacebar	Select the entire row.
Ctrl+A	Select the entire worksheet.
Shift+Backspace	With multiple cells selected, select only the active cell.
Ctrl+Shift+Spacebar	With an object selected, select all the objects on a worksheet.
Ctrl+6	Toggle the display of objects.

Select Cells with Special Characteristics

Press	To
Ctrl+Shift+* (asterisk)	Select the current region around the active cell (the data area enclosed by blank rows and blank columns). In a PivotTable, select the entire PivotTable.
Ctrl+/ (slash)	Select the array containing the active cell.
Ctrl+Shift+O (the letter O)	Select all cells that contain comments.
Ctrl+[(opening bracket)	Select all cells directly referenced by formulas in the selection.
Ctrl+Shift+{ (opening brace)	Select all cells directly or indirectly referenced by formulas in the selection.
Ctrl+] (closing bracket)	Select cells that contain formulas that directly reference the active cell.
Ctrl+Shift+} (closing brace)	Select cells that contain formulas that directly or indirectly reference the active cell.

Show, Hide, and Outline Data

Press	To
Alt+Shift+Right Arrow	Group rows or columns.
Alt+Shift+Left Arrow	Ungroup rows or columns.
Ctrl+8	Display or hide the outline symbols.
Ctrl+9	Hide the selected rows.
Ctrl+Shift+((opening parenthesis)	Unhide any hidden rows within the selection.
Ctrl+0 (zero)	Hide the selected columns.

Smart Tags

Press	To
Alt+Shift+F10	Display the menu or message for a smart tag. If more than one smart tag is present, switch to the next smart tag, and display its menu or message.
Down Arrow	Select the next item on a smart tag menu.
Up Arrow	Select the previous item on a smart tag menu.
Enter	Perform the action for the selected item on a smart tag menu.
Esc	Close the smart tag menu or message.

Task Panes

Press	To
F6	Move to a task pane from another pane in the program window. (You may need to press F6 more than once.)
Tab or Shift+Tab	When a task pane is active, select the next or previous item in the task pane.
Down Arrow or Up Arrow	Move among choices on a selected submenu, or move among certain options in a group of options.
Spacebar or Enter	Open the selected menu, or perform the action assigned to the selected button.
Home or End	When a menu or submenu is visible, select the first or last command on the menu or submenu.
Page Up or Page Down	Scroll up or down in the selected task pane.
Ctrl+Home or Ctrl+End	Move to the top or bottom of the selected task pane.

Windows and Office Interface

Press	To
Alt+Tab	Switch to the next program.
Alt+Shift+Tab	Switch to the previous program.
Ctrl+Esc	Display the Windows Start menu.
Ctrl+W or Ctrl+F4	Close the selected workbook window.
Ctrl+F6	When more than one workbook window is open, switch to the next workbook window.
Ctrl+Shift+F6	Switch to the previous workbook window.
Ctrl+F9	Minimize a workbook window to an icon.
Ctrl+F10	Maximize or restore the selected workbook window.
Print Screen	Copy a picture of the screen to the Clipboard.
Alt+Print Screen	Copy a picture of the selected window to the Clipboard.

Appendix B

Worksheets

Press	To
Shift+F11 or Alt+Shift+F1	Insert a new worksheet.
Ctrl+Page Down	Move to the next worksheet in the workbook.
Ctrl+Page Up	Move to the previous worksheet in the workbook.
Shift+Ctrl+Page Down	Select the current and next worksheet. To cancel selection of multiple worksheets, press Ctrl+Page Down; to select a different worksheet, press Ctrl+Page Up.
Shift+Ctrl+Page Up	Select the current and previous worksheet.
Alt+O, H, R	Rename the current worksheet.
Alt+E, M	Move or copy the current worksheet.
Alt+E, L	Delete the current worksheet.

Function Reference

This appendix lists all the worksheet functions available in Microsoft Office Excel 2007 in alphabetical order. We include a description, the function syntax, and a description of each argument. Arguments that appear in bold text are required; arguments that do not appear in bold text are optional.

You must type all function arguments in the order shown, and you should not add any spaces between or within arguments. While Excel now generally accepts spaces in functions for readability, when you use spaces within a text argument or a reference argument you must still enclose the entire argument in quotation marks.

Function	Description
ABS	Returns the absolute value of a number and takes the form =ABS(**number**). If a number is negative, this function simply removes the sign, making it a positive number.
ACCRINT	Returns the interest accrued by a security that pays interest on a periodic basis and takes the form =ACCRINT(**issue**, **first interest**, **settlement**, **rate**, par, **frequency**, basis), where *issue* is the issue date of the security; *first interest* is the date of the initial interest payment; *settlement* is the day you pay for the security; *rate* is the interest rate of the security at the issue date; *par* is the par value of the security; *frequency* is the number of coupon payments made per year (1 = annual, 2 = semiannual, 4 = quarterly); and *basis* is the day-count basis of the security (if 0 or omitted = 30/360, if 1 = actual/actual, if 2 = actual/360, if 3 = actual/365, if 4 = European 30/360). See "Analyzing Securities" on page 544.
ACCRINTM	Returns the interest accrued by a maturity security that pays interest at maturity and takes the form =ACCRINTM(**issue**, **maturity**, **rate**, par, basis), where *issue* is the issue date of the security; *maturity* is the security's maturity date; *rate* is the interest rate of the security at the issue date; *par* is the par value of the security; and *basis* is the day-count basis of the security (if 0 or omitted = 30/360, if 1 = actual/actual, if 2 = actual/360, if 3 = actual/365, if 4 = European 30/360). See "Analyzing Securities" on page 544.
ACOS	Returns the arccosine (inverse cosine) of a number in radians and takes the form =ACOS(**number**), in which *number* is the cosine of an angle.
ACOSH	Returns the inverse hyperbolic cosine of a number and takes the form =ACOSH(**number**), in which *number* must be >=1.

Function	Description
ADDRESS	Builds references from numbers and takes the form =ADDRESS(**row_num**, **column_num**, abs_num, a1, sheet_text), in which *row_num* and *column_num* designate the row and column values for the address; *abs_num* determines whether the resulting address uses absolute references (1), mixed (2 means absolute row, relative column, and 3 means relative row, absolute column), or relative (4); *a1* is a logical value (if TRUE, the resulting address is in A1 format; if FALSE, the resulting address is in R1C1 format); and *sheet_text* specifies the name of the sheet. See "Using Selected Lookup and Reference Functions" on page 512.
AMORDEGRC	Returns the depreciation for each accounting period (French accounting system only), including any partial period, and takes the form =AMORDEGRC(**cost**, **date_purchased**, **first_period**, **salvage**, **period**, **rate**, basis), where *cost* is the cost of the asset; *date_purchased* is the date of the purchase; *first_period* is the date of the end of the first period; *salvage* is the salvage value at the end of the life of the asset; *period* is the period for which you want to calculate depreciation; *rate* is the rate of depreciation, and *basis* is the year *basis* to be used (0 = 360 days, 1 = actual, 3 = 365 days, 4 = European 360 days). This function is similar to AMORLINC except a depreciation coefficient is applied, depending on the asset life (1.5 if 3–4 years, 2 if 5–6 years, 2.5 if greater than 6 years).
AMORLINC	Returns the depreciation for each accounting period (French accounting system only), including any partial period. See AMORDEGRC for syntax and arguments.
AND	Helps develop compound conditional test formulas in conjunction with the simple logical operators: =, >, <, >=, <=, and <>. The AND function can have as many as 30 arguments and takes the form =AND(**logical1**, logical2, . . .), where each *logical* can be conditional tests, arrays, or references to cells that contain logical values. See "Using Selected Logical Functions" on page 508.
AREAS	Returns the number of areas in a reference (a cell or block of cells) and takes the form =AREAS(**reference**), where *reference* can be a cell reference, a range reference, or several range references enclosed in parentheses. See "Using Selected Lookup and Reference Functions" on page 512.
ASC	Changes text in double-byte character set languages to single-byte characters and takes the form =ASC(**text**), where *text* is either text or a reference to a cell containing text. Has no effect on single-byte characters.
ASIN	Returns the arcsine of a number in radians and takes the form =ASIN(**number**), where *number* is the sine of the angle you want and must be from –1 to 1.

Function	Description
ASINH	Returns the inverse hyperbolic sine of a number and takes the form =ASINH(**number**).
ATAN	Returns the arctangent of a number and takes the form =ATAN(**number**), where *number* is the tangent of an angle.
ATAN2	Returns the arctangent of the specified x- and y-coordinates, in radians, and takes the form =ATAN2(**x_num**, **y_num**), where *x_num* is the x-coordinate of the point, and *y_num* is the y-coordinate of the point. A positive result represents a counterclockwise angle from the x-axis; a negative result represents a clockwise angle.
ATANH	Returns the inverse hyperbolic tangent of a number and takes the form =ATANH(**number**), where *number* must be between (not including) –1 and 1.
AVEDEV	Returns the average of the absolute deviations of data points from their mean; takes the form =AVEDEV(**number1**, number2, . . .), where the numbers can be names, arrays, or references that resolve to numbers; and accepts up to 30 arguments.
AVERAGE	Returns the arithmetic mean of the specified numbers and takes the form =AVERAGE(**number1**, number2, . . .), where the numbers can be names, arrays, or references that resolve to numbers. Cells containing text, logical values, or empty cells are ignored, but cells containing a zero value are included. See "Using Built-In Statistical Functions" on page 553.
AVERAGEA	Acts like AVERAGE except text and logical values are included in the calculation. See "Using Built-In Statistical Functions" on page 553.
AVERAGEIF	Finds the arithmetic mean cells in the specified range that meet a given criteria and takes the form =AVERAGEIF(**range**, **criteria**, average_range) where *range* is the cells to evaluate; *criteria* is an expression, cell reference, or number used to define which cells to average; and *average_range* is the actual cells to average. Excel uses the top-left cell of *average_range* as the beginning and uses the bottom-left cell of either *average_range* or *range* (whichever is larger) to determine the size of the cell range to be used. If *average_range* is omitted, *range* is used.
AVERAGEIFS	Acts like AVERAGEIF but accepts multiple criteria; takes the form =AVERAGEIFS(**average_range**, **criteria_range1**, **criteria1**, criteria_range2, criteria2, . . .).
BAHTTEXT	Converts a number to Thai text and adds the suffix Baht, using the form =BAHTTEXT(**number**), where *number* can be a reference to a cell containing a number or a formula that resolves to a number.

Function	Description
BESSELI	Returns the modified Bessel function, which is equivalent to the Bessel function evaluated for imaginary arguments, and takes the form =BESSELI(**x**, **n**), where *x* is the value at which to evaluate the function, and *n* is the order of the Bessel function.
BESSELJ	Returns the Bessel function, using the form =BESSELJ(**x**, **n**), where *x* is the value at which to evaluate the function, and *n* is the order of the Bessel function.
BESSELK	Returns the modified Bessel function, which is equivalent to the Bessel function evaluated for imaginary arguments, and takes the form =BESSELK(**x**, **n**), where *x* is the value at which to evaluate the function, and *n* is the order of the Bessel function.
BESSELY	Returns the Bessel function (also called the Weber or Neumann function) and takes the form =BESSELY(**x**, **n**), where *x* is the value at which to evaluate the function, and *n* is the order of the function.
BETADIST	Returns the cumulative beta probability density function and takes the form =BETADIST(**x**, **alpha**, **beta**, A, B), where *x* is the value between A and B at which to evaluate the function, *alpha* is a parameter to the distribution, *beta* is a parameter to the distribution, *A* is an optional lower bound to the interval of *x*, and *B* is an optional upper bound to the interval of *x*.
BETAINV	Returns the inverse of the cumulative beta probability density function and takes the form =BETAINV(**probability**, **alpha**, **beta**, A, B), where *probability* is a probability associated with the beta distribution. For additional argument descriptions, see BETADIST.
BIN2DEC	Converts a binary number to decimal and takes the form =BIN2DEC(**number**), where *number* is the binary integer you want to convert.
BIN2HEX	Converts a binary number to hexadecimal and takes the form =BIN2HEX(**number**, **places**), where *number* is the binary integer you want to convert, and *places* is the number of characters to use. *places* is useful for padding the return value with leading zeros.
BIN2OCT	Converts a binary number to octal and takes the form =BIN2DEC(**number**, places), where *number* is the binary integer you want to convert, and *places* is the number of characters to use. *places* is useful for padding the return value with leading zeros.

Function	Description
BINOMDIST	Returns the individual term binomial distribution probability and takes the form =BINOMDIST(**number_s**, **trials**, **probability_s**, **cumulative**), where *number_s* is the number of successes in trials, *trials* is the number of independent trials, *probability_s* is the probability of success on each trial, and *cumulative* is a logical value that determines the form of the function. If TRUE, it returns the probability that there are at most *number_s* successes; if FALSE, it returns the probability that there are *number_s* successes.
CEILING	Rounds a number up to the nearest given multiple and takes the form =CEILING(**number**, **multiple**), where *number* and *multiple* must be numeric and have the same sign. If they have different signs, Excel returns the #NUM! error value. See "Using the Rounding Functions" on page 500.
CELL	Returns information about the contents, location, or formatting of a cell and takes the form =CELL(**info_type**, reference), where *info_type* specifies the type of information you want, and *reference* is the cell you want information about. *info_type* can be any of the following: *address*, *col* (column #), *color*, *contents*, *filename*, *format*, *parentheses*, *prefix*, *protect*, *row*, *type*, or *width*. See Help for a table of *format* codes returned.
CHAR	Returns the character that corresponds to an ASCII code number and takes the form =CHAR(**number**), where *number* accepts ASCII codes with or without leading zeros. See "Using Selected Text Functions" on page 503.
CHIDIST	Returns the one-tailed probability of the chi-squared distribution (used to compare observed vs. expected values) and takes the form =CHIDIST(**x**, **degrees_freedom**), where *x* is the value at which you want to evaluate the distribution, and *degrees_freedom* is the number of degrees of freedom.
CHIINV	Returns the inverse of CHIDIST (one-tailed probability of the chi-squared distribution) and takes the form =CHIINV(**probability**, **degrees_freedom**), where *probability* is a probability associated with the chi-squared distribution, and *degrees_freedom* is the number of degrees of freedom.
CHITEST	Returns the test for independence and takes the form =CHITEST(**actual_range**, **expected_range**), where *actual_range* is the range of data that contains observations to test against expected values, and *expected_range* is the range of data that contains the ratio of the product of row totals and column totals to the grand total.

Appendix C

Function	Description
CHOOSE	Retrieves an item from a list of values and takes the form =CHOOSE(**index_num**, **value1**, value2, . . .), where *index_num* is the position in the list of the item you want to look up, and the *value* arguments are the elements of the list, which can be values or cell references. Returns the value of the element of the list that occupies the position indicated by *index_num*. See "Using Selected Lookup and Reference Functions" on page 512.
CLEAN	Removes nonprintable characters such as tabs and program-specific codes from a string and takes the form =CLEAN(**text**). See "Using Selected Text Functions" on page 503.
CODE	Returns the ASCII code number for the first character of its argument and takes the form =CODE(**text**). See "Using Selected Text Functions" on page 503.
COLUMN	Returns the column number of the referenced cell or range and takes the form =COLUMN(reference). If *reference* is omitted, the result is the column number of the cell containing the function. If *reference* is a range or a name and the function is entered as an array (by pressing Ctrl+Shift+Enter), the result is an array of the numbers of each of the columns in the range. See "Using Selected Lookup and Reference Functions" on page 512.
COLUMNS	Returns the number of columns in a reference or an array and takes the form =COLUMNS(**array**), where *array* is an array constant, a range reference, or a range name. See "Using Selected Lookup and Reference Functions" on page 512.
COMBIN	Determines the number of possible group combinations that can be derived from a pool of items and takes the form =COMBIN(**number**, **number_chosen**), where *number* is the total items in the pool, and *number_chosen* is the number of items you want in each group. See "Using Selected Mathematical Functions" on page 498.
COMPLEX	Converts real and imaginary coefficients into a complex number of the form $x + yi$ or $x + yj$ and takes the form =COMPLEX(**real_num**, **i_num**, suffix), where *real_num* is the real coefficient of the complex number, *i_num* is the imaginary coefficient of the complex number, and *suffix* is the suffix for the imaginary component of the complex number. If omitted, *suffix* is assumed to be *i*.
CONCATENATE	Assembles larger strings from smaller strings; takes the form =CONCATENATE(**text1**, **text2**, . . .); and accepts up to 30 arguments, which can be text, numbers, or cell references. See "Using the Substring Text Functions" on page 505.

Function	Description
CONFIDENCE	Returns the confidence interval for a population mean and takes the form =CONFIDENCE(**alpha**, **standard_dev**, **size**), where *alpha* is the significance level used to compute the confidence level (an alpha of 0.1 indicates a 90 percent confidence level), *standard_dev* is the population standard deviation for the data range and is assumed to be known, and *size* is the sample size.
CONVERT	Converts a number from one measurement system to another and takes the form =CONVERT(**number**, **from_unit**, **to_unit**), where *number* is the value to convert, *from_unit* is the units for *number*, and *to_unit* is the units for the result. See Help for a table of unit codes.
CORREL	Returns the correlation coefficient of the *array1* and *array2* cell ranges and takes the form =CORREL(**array1**, **array2**), where arrays are ranges of cells containing values.
COS	Returns the cosine of an angle and is the complement of the SIN function. It takes the form =COS(**number**), where *number* is the angle in radians.
COSH	Returns the hyperbolic cosine of a number and takes the form =COSH(**number**), where *number* is any real number.
COUNT	Tells you how many cells in a given range contain numbers, including dates and formulas, that evaluate to numbers; takes the form =COUNT(**number1**, number2, . . .); and accepts up to 30 arguments, ignoring text, error values, and logical values. See "Using Built-In Statistical Functions" on page 553.
COUNTA	Acts like COUNT except text and logical values are included in the calculation. See "Using Built-In Statistical Functions" on page 553.
COUNTBLANK	Counts empty cells in a specified range and takes the form =COUNTBLANK(**range**). See "Using Selected Lookup and Reference Functions" on page 512.
COUNTIF	Counts only those cells that match specified criteria and takes the form =COUNTIF(**range**, **criteria**), where *range* is the range you want to test, and *criteria* is the logical test to be performed on each cell. See "Using Built-In Statistical Functions" on page 553.
COUNTIFS	Acts like COUNTIF but accepts multiple criteria, taking the form =COUNTIFS(**range1**, **criteria1**, range2, criteria2, . . .).

Function	Description
COUPDAYBS	Calculates the number of days from the beginning of the coupon period to the settlement date and takes the form =COUPDAYBS(**settlement**, **maturity**, **frequency**, basis), where *settlement* is the day you pay for the security; *maturity* is the maturity date of the security; *frequency* is the number of coupon payments made per year (1 = annual, 2 = semiannual, 4 = quarterly); and *basis* is the day-count basis of the security (if 0 or omitted = 30/360, if 1 = actual/actual, if 2 = actual/360, if 3 = actual/365, if 4 = European 30/360). See "Analyzing Securities" on page 544.
COUPDAYS	Calculates the number of days in the coupon period that contains the settlement date and takes the form =COUPDAYS(**settlement**, **maturity**, **frequency**, basis). See COUPDAYBS for argument definitions. See "Analyzing Securities" on page 544.
COUPDAYSNC	Calculates the number of days from the settlement date to the next coupon date and takes the form =COUPDAYSNC(**settlement**, **maturity**, **frequency**, basis). See COUPDAYBS for argument definitions. See "Analyzing Securities" on page 544.
COUPNCD	Calculates the next coupon date after the settlement date and takes the form =COUPNCD(**settlement**, **maturity**, **frequency**, basis). See COUPDAYBS for argument definitions. See "Analyzing Securities" on page 544.
COUPNUM	Calculates the number of coupons payable between the settlement date and the maturity date and rounds the result to the nearest whole coupon; takes the form =COUPNUM(**settlement**, **maturity**, **frequency**, basis). See COUPDAYBS for argument definitions. See "Analyzing Securities" on page 544.
COUPPCD	Calculates the coupon date previous to the settlement date and takes the form =COUPPCD(**settlement**, **maturity**, **frequency**, basis). See COUPDAYBS for argument definitions. See "Analyzing Securities" on page 544.
COVAR	Returns covariance, the average of the products of deviations for each data point pair, and takes the form =COVAR(**array1**, **array2**), where *arrays* are cell ranges containing integers.
CRITBINOM	Returns the smallest value for which the cumulative binomial distribution is greater than or equal to a criterion value and takes the form =CRITBINOM(**trials**, **probability_s**, **alpha**), where *trials* is the number of Bernoulli trials, *probability_s* is the probability of a success on each trial, and *alpha* is the criterion value.

Function	Description
CUBEKPIMEMBER	Returns a key performance indicator (KPI) property and returns the name of the KPI. This function takes the form =CUBEKPIMEMBER(**connection**, **kpi_name**, **kpi_property**, caption). *connection* is a text string indicating the name of the cube connection; *kpi_name* is the text name of the KPI; and *kpi_property* is the component of the KPI that is returned (one of KPIValue, KPIGoal, KPIStatus, KPITrend, KPIWeight, or KPICurrentTimeMemeber). This function is supported only when connected to a Microsoft SQL Server 2005 Analysis Services (or later) data source. Cube functions are used with online analytical processing (OLAP) databases, where data structures called *cubes* are used to draw multidimensional relationships among data sets.
CUBEMEMBER	Returns a member or tuple from the cube and takes the form =CUBEMEMBER(**connection, member_expression**, caption). *connection* is a text string indicating the name of the cube connection, *member_expression* is a text string of a multidimensional expression (MDX) that evaluates to a unique number in the cube, and *caption* is a text string to display in the cell instead of the defined caption from the cube. Cube functions are used with online analytical processing (OLAP) databases, where data structures called *cubes* are used to draw multidimensional relationships among data sets.
CUBEMEMBERPROPERTY	Returns the value of a member property from the cube and takes the form =CUBEMEMBERPROPERTY(**connection, member_expression, property**), where *connection* is a text string indicating the name of the cube connection, *member_expression* is a text string of a multidimensional expression (MDX) that evaluates to a unique number in the cube, and *property* is a text string of the property name or a reference to a cell containing a property name. Cube functions are used with online analytical processing (OLAP) databases, where data structures called *cubes* are used to draw multidimensional relationships among data sets.
CUBERANKEDMEMBER	Returns the *N*th (ranked) member in a set and takes the form =CUBERANKEDMEMBER(**connection, set_expression, rank**, caption). *connection* is a text string indicating the name of the cube connection; *set_expression* is a text string indicating a set expression, the CUBESET function, or a reference to a cell containing the CUBESET function; *rank* is an integer specifying the top value to return (1 = top value, 2 = second value, and so on); and *caption* is a text string to be displayed in the cell instead of the caption supplied by the cube. Cube functions are used with online analytical processing (OLAP) databases, where data structures called *cubes* are used to draw multidimensional relationships among data sets.

Function	Description
CUBESET	Returns a calculated set of members or tuples from the cube database and takes the form =CUBESET(**connection**, **set_expression**, caption, sort_order, sort_by), where *connection* is a text string indicating the name of the cube connection; *set_expression* is a text string that returns a set of members or is a reference to a cell range containing a set or members or tuples; *caption* is a text string to be displayed in the cell instead of the caption supplied by the cube; *sort_by* is a text string indicating the value in the set by which you want to sort the results; and *sort_order* is a number specifying the type of sort (0 = none, 1 = ascending, 2 = descending, 3 = alpha ascending, 4 = alpha descending, 5 = natural ascending, and 6 = natural descending). Cube functions are used with online analytical processing (OLAP) databases, where data structures called *cubes* are used to draw multidimensional relationships among data sets.
CUBESETCOUNT	Returns the number of items in a set and takes the form =CUBESETCOUNT(**set**), where *set* is a text string of an expression that evaluates to a set defined by the CUBESET function, the CUBESET function itself, or a reference to a cell containing a CUBESET function. Cube functions are used with online analytical processing (OLAP) databases, where data structures called *cubes* are used to draw multidimensional relationships among data sets.
CUBEVALUE	Returns an aggregated value from a cube and takes the form =CUBEVALUE(**connection**, **member_expression1**, member_expression2, . . .). *connection* is a text string indicating the name of the cube connection, and *member_expression* is a text string of a multidimensional expression (MDX) that evaluates to a unique number in the cube. Cube functions are used with online analytical processing (OLAP) databases, where data structures called *cubes* are used to draw multidimensional relationships among data sets.
CUMIPMT	Returns the cumulative interest paid on a loan between *start_period* and *end_period* and takes the form =CUMIPMT(**rate**, **nper**, **pv**, **start_period**, **end_period**, **type**), where *rate* is the interest rate, *nper* is the total number of payment periods, *pv* is the present value, and *start_period* is the first period in the calculation. Payment periods are numbered beginning with 1; *end_period* is the last period in the calculation, and *type* is the timing of the payment.
CUMPRINC	Returns the cumulative principal paid on a loan between *start_period* and *end_period* and takes the form =CUMPRINC(**rate**, **nper**, **pv**, **start_period**, **end_period**, **type**). For argument descriptions, see CUMIPMT.

Function	Description
DATE	Returns the serial number that represents a particular date and takes the form =DATE(**year**, **month**, **day**), where *year* can be one to four digits from 1 to 9999; *month* is a number representing the month of the year; and *day* is a number representing the day of the month.
DATEVALUE	Translates a date into a serial value and takes the form =DATEVALUE(**date_text**), where *date_text* represents a date entered as text in quotation marks. See "Working with Date and Time Functions" on page 531.
DAVERAGE	Averages the values in a column in a list or database that match conditions you specify and takes the form =DAVERAGE(**database**, **field**, **criteria**), where *database* is the range of cells that make up the list or database and the first row of the list contains labels for each column, *field* indicates which column is used in the function (by label name or by position), and *criteria* is the range of cells that contain the conditions you specify.
DAY	Returns the value of the day portion of a serial date/time value and takes the form =DAY(**serial_number**), where *serial_number* can be a date value, a reference, or text in date format enclosed in quotation marks. See "Working with Date and Time Functions" on page 531.
DAYS360	Returns the number of days between two dates based on a 360-day year (12 months of 30 days each), which is used in some accounting calculations, and takes the form =DAYS360(**start_date**, **end_date**, method), where *start_date* and *end_date* are the two dates between which you want to know the number of days, and *method* is a logical value that specifies whether to use the U.S. or European method in the calculation. If FALSE or omitted, uses U.S. (NASD) method; if TRUE, uses the European method.
DB	Computes fixed declining balance depreciation for a particular period in the asset's life and takes the form =DB(**cost**, **salvage**, **life**, **period**, month), where *cost* is the initial asset cost, *salvage* is the remaining value after the asset is fully depreciated, *life* is the length of depreciation time; *period* is the individual period to be computed, and *month* is the number of months depreciated in the first year (if omitted, it is assumed to be 12). See "Calculating Depreciation" on page 541.
DCOUNT	Counts the cells that contain numbers in a column in a list or database that match conditions you specify and takes the form =DCOUNT(**database**, **field**, **criteria**), where *database* is the range of cells that make up the list or database, *field* indicates which column is used in the function, and *criteria* is the range of cells that contain the conditions you specify.

Appendix C

Function	Description
DCOUNTA	Acts like DCOUNT except it also includes cells containing text, logical values, and error values. See DCOUNT for arguments.
DDB	Computes double-declining balance depreciation and takes the form =DDB(**cost**, **salvage**, **life**, period, factor), where *cost* is the initial asset cost; *salvage* is the remaining value after the asset is fully depreciated; *life* is the length of depreciation time; *period* is the individual period to be computed; and *factor* indicates the method used (2 or omitted indicates double-declining balance, and 3 indicates triple-declining balance). See "Calculating Depreciation" on page 541.
DEC2BIN	Converts a decimal number to binary and takes the form =DEC2BIN(**number**, places), where *number* is the decimal integer you want to convert, and *places* is the number of characters to use. *places* is useful for padding the return value with leading zeros.
DEC2HEX	Converts a decimal number to hexadecimal and takes the same form and arguments as DEC2BIN.
DEC2OCT	Converts a decimal number to octal and takes the same form and arguments as DEC2BIN.
DEGREES	Converts radians to degrees and takes the form =DEGREES(**angle**), where *angle* represents an angle measured in radians.
DELTA	Tests whether two values are equal and takes the form =DELTA(**number1**, **number2**), where *number1* is the first number, and *number2* is the second number (which, if omitted, is assumed to be zero). Returns 1 if *number1* equals *number2*; otherwise, returns 0.
DEVSQ	Returns the sum of squares of deviations of data points from their sample mean; takes the form =DEVSQ(**number1**, **number2**, . . .), where the numbers can be names, arrays, or references that resolve to numbers; and accepts up to 30 arguments.
DGET	Extracts a single value from a column in a list or database that matches conditions you specify and takes the form =DGET(**database**, **field**, **criteria**), where *database* is the range of cells that make up the list or database, *field* indicates which column is used in the function, and *criteria* is the range of cells that contain the conditions you specify.

Function	Description
DISC	Calculates the discount rate for a security and takes the form =DISC(**settlement**, **maturity**, **price**, **redemption**, **basis**), where *settlement* is the day you pay for the security; *maturity* is the maturity date of the security; *price* is the security's price per $100 face value; *redemption* is the value of the security at redemption; and *basis* is the day-count basis of the security (if 0 or omitted = 30/360, if 1 = actual/actual, if 2 = actual/360, if 3 = actual/365, if 4 = European 30/360). See "Analyzing Securities" on page 544.
DMAX	Returns the largest number in a column in a list or database that matches conditions you specify and takes the form =DMAX(**database**, **field**, **criteria**), where *database* is a range that makes up the list or database, *field* indicates which column is used in the function, and *criteria* is the range of cells that contain the conditions you specify.
DMIN	Returns the smallest number in a column in a list or database that matches conditions you specify and takes the same form and arguments as DMAX.
DOLLAR	Converts a number into a string formatted as currency with the specified number of decimal places and takes the form =DOLLAR(**number**, decimals). If you omit *decimals*, the result is rounded to two decimal places. If you use a negative number for *decimals*, the result is rounded to the left of the decimal point. See "Using Selected Text Functions" on page 503.
DOLLARDE	Converts the familiar fractional pricing of securities to decimals and takes the form =DOLLARDE(**fractional dollar**, **fraction**), where *fractional dollar* is the value you want to convert expressed as an integer followed by a decimal point and the numerator of the fraction you want, and *fraction* is an integer indicating the denominator to be used. See "Analyzing Securities" on page 544.
DOLLARFR	Converts a security price expressed in decimals to fractions and takes the form =DOLLARFR(**decimal dollar**, **fraction**), where *decimal dollar* is the value you want to convert expressed as a decimal, and *fraction* is an integer indicating the denominator of the fraction you want. See "Analyzing Securities" on page 544.
DPRODUCT	Multiplies the values in a column in a list or database that match conditions you specify and takes the form =DPRODUCT(**database**, **field**, **criteria**), where *database* is a range that makes up the list or database, *field* indicates which column is used in the function, and *criteria* is the range of cells that contain the conditions you specify.

Appendix C

Function	Description
DSTDEV	Estimates the standard deviation of a population based on a sample, using the numbers in a column in a list or database that match conditions you specify, and takes the same form and arguments as DPRODUCT.
DSTDEVP	Calculates the standard deviation of a population based on the entire population, using the numbers in a column in a list or database that match conditions you specify, and takes the same form and arguments as DPRODUCT.
DSUM	Adds the numbers in a column in a list or database that match conditions you specify and takes the same form and arguments as DPRODUCT.
DURATION	Calculates the weighted average of the present value of the bond's cash flows for a security whose interest payments are made on a periodic basis and takes the form =DURATION(**settlement**, **maturity**, **coupon**, **yield**, **frequency**, basis), where *settlement* is the day you pay for the security; *maturity* is the maturity date of the security; *coupon* is the security's annual coupon rate; *yield* is the annual yield of the security; *frequency* is the number of coupon payments made per year (1 = annual, 2 = semiannual, 4 = quarterly); and *basis* is the day-count basis of the security (if 0 or omitted = 30/360, if 1 = actual/actual, if 2 = actual/360, if 3 = actual/365, if 4 = European 30/360). See "Analyzing Securities" on page 544.
DVAR	Estimates the variance of a population based on a sample, using the numbers in a column in a list or database that match conditions you specify, and takes the form =DVAR(**database**, **field**, **criteria**), where *database* is the range of cells that make up the list or database, *field* indicates which column is used in the function, and *criteria* is the range of cells that contain the conditions you specify.
DVARP	Calculates the variance of a population based on the entire population, using the numbers in a column in a list or database that match conditions you specify, and takes the same form and arguments as DVAR.
EDATE	Returns the exact date that falls an indicated number of months before or after a given date and takes the form =EDATE(**start_date**, **months**), where *start_date* is the date to calculate from, and *months* is the number of months before (negative) or after (positive) the start date. See "Working with Specialized Date Functions" on page 533.
EFFECT	Returns the effective interest rate and takes the form =EFFECT(**nominal_rate**, **npery**). *nominal_rate* is the annual interest rate, and *npery* is the number of annual compounding periods.

Function	Description
EOMONTH	Returns a date that falls on the last day of the month an indicated number of months before or after a given date and takes the form =EOMONTH(**start_date**, **months**), where *start_date* is the date to calculate from, and *months* is the number of months before (negative) or after (positive) the start date. See "Working with Specialized Date Functions" on page 533.
ERF	Returns the error function integrated between *lower_limit* and *upper_limit* and takes the form =ERF(**lower_limit**, upper_limit), where *lower_limit* is the lower bound, and *upper_limit* is the upper bound. If omitted, ERF integrates between zero and *lower_limit*.
ERFC	Returns the complementary ERF function integrated between x and infinity and takes the form =ERFC(**x**), where x is the lower bound for integrating ERF.
ERROR.TYPE	Detects the type of error value in a referenced cell and takes the form =ERROR.TYPE(**error_val**). Returns a code designating the type of error value in the referenced cell: 1 (#NULL!), 2 (#DIV/0!), 3 (#VALUE!), 4 (#REF!), 5 (#NAME!), 6 (#NUM!), and 7 (#N/A). Any other value in the referenced cell returns the error value #N/A. See "Using Selected Lookup and Reference Functions" on page 512.
EUROCONVERT	Converts a number to euros—or converts any EU member currency to euros or any other member currency—and takes the form =EUROCONVERT(**number**, **source**, **target**, full_precision, triangulation_precision), where *number* is the value you want to convert, *source* is the ISO country code for the source currency, *target* is the ISO country code for the currency to which you want to convert, *full_precision* is a logical value that displays all significant digits when TRUE and that uses a currency-specific rounding factor when FALSE, and *triangulation_precision* is an integer equal to 3 or greater that specifies the number of significant digits to use when converting from one EU member currency to another. This function is installed with the Euro Currency Tools add-in. See Help for tables of ISO codes and rounding factors.
EVEN	Rounds a number up to the nearest even integer and takes the form =EVEN(**number**). Negative numbers are correspondingly rounded down. See "Using the Rounding Functions" on page 500.
EXACT	Determines whether two strings match exactly, including uppercase and lowercase letters, not including formatting differences, and takes the form =EXACT(**text1**, **text2**), where both arguments must be either literal strings enclosed in quotation marks or references to cells that contain text. See "Using Selected Text Functions" on page 503.

Appendix C

Function	Description
EXP	Computes the value of the constant *e* (approx. 2.71828183) raised to the power specified by its argument and takes the form =EXP(**number**). The EXP function is the inverse of the LN function.
EXPONDIST	Returns exponential distribution and takes the form =EXPONDIST(**x**, **lambda**, **cumulative**), where *x* is the value of the function; *lambda* is the parameter value; and *cumulative* is a logical value that indicates which form of the exponential function to provide (if TRUE, returns the cumulative distribution function; if FALSE, returns the probability density function).
FACT	Returns the factorial of a number and takes the form =FACT(**number**), where *number* is a positive integer.
FACTDOUBLE	Returns the double factorial of a number and takes the form =FACT(**number**), where *number* is a positive integer.
FALSE	Represents an alternative for the logical condition FALSE, which accepts no arguments and takes the form =FALSE( ). See "Using Selected Logical Functions" on page 508.
FDIST	Returns the F probability distribution and takes the form =FDIST(**x**, **degrees_freedom1**, **degrees_freedom2**), where *x* is the value at which to evaluate the function, *degrees_freedom1* is the numerator degrees of freedom, and *degrees_freedom2* is the denominator.
FIND	Returns the position of specified text within a string and takes the form =FIND(**find_text**, **within_text**, start_num), where *find_text* is the text you want to find (case sensitive), and *within_text* indicates where to look. Both arguments accept either literal text enclosed in quotation marks or cell references. Optional *start_num* specifies the character position in *within_text* where you want to begin the search. You get a #VALUE! error value if *find_text* isn't contained in *within_text*, if *start_num* isn't greater than zero, or if *start_num* is greater than the number of characters in *within_text* or greater than the position of the last occurrence of *find_text*. See "Using the Substring Text Functions" on page 505.
FINDB	Returns the position of specified text within a string based on the number of bytes each character uses from the first character of *within_text*, takes the form =FINDB(**find_text**, **within_text**, start_num), and takes the same arguments as FIND. This function is for use with double-byte characters.
FINV	Returns the inverse of the F probability distribution and takes the form =FINV(**probability**, **degrees_freedom1**, **degrees_freedom2**), where *probability* is a probability associated with the F cumulative distribution, *degrees_freedom1* is the numerator degrees of freedom, and *degrees_freedom2* is the denominator degrees of freedom.

Function	Description
FISHER	Returns the Fisher transformation at *x* and takes the form =FISHER(**x**), where *x* is a value between –1 and 1 (not inclusive).
FISHERINV	Returns the inverse of the Fisher transformation and takes the form =FISHERINV(**y**), where *y* is any numeric value.
FIXED	Rounds a number to the specified number of decimals, formats the number in decimal format using a period and commas, and returns the result as text. This function takes the form =FIXED(**number**, decimals, no_commas), where *number* is the number you want to round and convert to text; *decimals* is the number of digits to the right of the decimal point (assumes 2 if omitted); and *no_commas* is a logical value (if TRUE, prevents commas; if FALSE or omitted, includes commas).
FLOOR	Rounds a number down to the nearest given multiple and takes the form =FLOOR(**number**, **multiple**), where *number* and *multiple* must be numeric and have the same sign. If they have different signs, Excel returns the #NUM! error value. See "Using the Rounding Functions" on page 500.
FORECAST	Returns a single point along a trend line and takes the form =FORECAST(**x**, **known_y's**, **known_x's**). For arguments and usage details, see "The FORECAST Function" on page 564.
FREQUENCY	Returns the number of times that values occur within a population and takes the form =FREQUENCY(**data_array**, **bins_array**). For usage and argument details, see "Analyzing Distribution with the FREQUENCY Function" on page 572.
FTEST	Returns the result of an F-test, the one-tailed probability that the variances in *array1* and *array2* are not significantly different, and takes the form =FTEST(**array1**, **array2**).
FV	Computes the value at a future date of an investment based on periodic, constant payments and a constant interest rate. Takes the form =FV(**rate**, **nper**, **payment**, pv, type), where *rate* is the interest rate, *nper* is the term (periods) of the investment, *payment* is the amount of each periodic payment when individual amounts are the same, *pv* is the investment value today, and *type* indicates when payments are made (0 or omitted = at end of period, 1 = at beginning of period). See "Calculating Investments" on page 535.
FVSCHEDULE	Returns the future value of an initial principal after applying a series of variable compound interest rates and takes the form =FVSCHEDULE(**principal**, **schedule**), where *principal* is the present value, and *schedule* is an array of interest rates to apply.

Appendix C

Function	Description
GAMMADIST	Returns the gamma distribution and takes the form =GAMMADIST(**x**, **alpha**, **beta**, **cumulative**), where *x* is the value at which you want to evaluate the distribution; *alpha* is a parameter to the distribution; *beta* is a parameter to the distribution; and *cumulative* is a logical value that determines the form of the function (if TRUE, returns the cumulative distribution function; if FALSE, returns the probability density function).
GAMMAINV	Returns the inverse of the gamma cumulative distribution and takes the form =GAMMAINV(**probability**, **alpha**, **beta**), where *probability* is the probability associated with the gamma distribution, *alpha* is a parameter to the distribution, and *beta* is a parameter to the distribution.
GAMMALN	Returns the natural logarithm of the gamma function and takes the form =GAMMALN(**x**), where *x* is a positive value.
GCD	Returns the greatest common divisor of two or more integers (the largest integer that divides both *number1* and *number2* without a remainder) and takes the form =GCD(**number1**, number2, . . .), where the *numbers* are 1 to 30 positive integer values.
GEOMEAN	Returns the geometric mean of an array or range of positive data and takes the form =GEOMEAN(**number1**, number2, . . .), where the *numbers* are 1 to 30 positive integer values.
GESTEP	Returns 1 if *number* is greater than or equal to *step*; otherwise, returns 0 (zero) and takes the form =GESTEP(**number**, step), where *number* is the value to test against *step*, and *step* is the threshold value (zero if omitted).
GETPIVOTDATA	Returns data stored in a PivotTable report and takes the form =GETPIVOTDATA(**data_field**, **pivot_table**, field1, item1, field2, item2, . . .), where *data_field* is the name, in quotation marks, for the data field that contains the data you want retrieved; *pivot_table* is a reference to a cell in the PivotTable report that contains the data you want to retrieve; and *fieldx* and *itemx* are 1 to 14 pairs of field names and item names that describe the data you want to retrieve.
GROWTH	Returns values of points that lie along an exponential growth trend line and takes the form =GROWTH(**known_y's**, known_x's, new_x's, const). For arguments and usage details, see "The GROWTH Function" on page 567.
HARMEAN	Returns the harmonic mean of a data set and takes the form =HARMEAN(**number1**, number2, . . .), where the *numbers* are 1 to 30 positive values.

Function	Description
HEX2BIN	Converts a hexadecimal number to binary and takes the form =HEX2BIN(**number**, places), where *number* is the hexadecimal number you want to convert, and *places* is the number of characters to use (useful for padding the return value with leading zeros).
HEX2DEC	Converts a hexadecimal number to decimal and takes the form =HEX2DEC(**number**), where *number* is the hexadecimal number you want to convert.
HEX2OCT	Converts a hexadecimal number to octal and takes the form =HEX2OCT(**number**, places), where *number* is the hexadecimal number you want to convert, and *places* is the number of characters to use (useful for padding the return value with leading zeros).
HLOOKUP	Looks for a specified value in the top row in a table, returns the value in the same column and a specified row, and takes the form =HLOOKUP(**lookup_value**, **table_array**, **row_index_num**, range_lookup), where *lookup_value* is the value to look for; *table_array* is the range containing the lookup and result values sorted in alphabetical order by the top row; *row_index_num* is the row number containing the value you want to find; and *range_lookup* is a logical value, which, if FALSE, forces an exact match. See "Using Selected Lookup and Reference Functions" on page 512.
HOUR	Returns the hour portion of a serial date/time value and takes the form =HOUR(**serial_number**), where *serial_number* can be a time/date value, a reference, or text in time/date format enclosed in quotation marks. See "Working with Date and Time Functions" on page 531.
HYPERLINK	Creates a shortcut or jump that opens a document stored on a network server, an intranet, or the Internet. When you click the cell that contains the HYPERLINK function, Excel opens the file stored at *link_location*. This function takes the form =HYPERLINK(**link_location**, friendly_name), where *link_location* is the path and file name to the document to be opened, and *friendly_name* is the jump text or numeric value that is displayed in the cell.
HYPGEOMDIST	Returns the hypergeometric distribution (the probability of a given number of sample successes, given the size of the sample and population, and the number of population successes) and takes the form =HYPGEOMDIST(**sample_s**, **number_sample**, **population_s**, **number_population**), where *sample_s* is the number of successes in the sample, *number_sample* is the size of the sample, *population_s* is the number of successes in the population, and *number_population* is the population size.

Appendix C

Function	Description
IF	Returns values based on supplied conditional tests and takes the form =IF(**logical_test**, **value_if_true**, value_if_false). You can nest up to seven additional functions within an IF function. If you use text arguments, the match must be exact except for case. See "Using Selected Logical Functions" on page 508.
IFERROR	Returns a specified value when a formula evaluates to an error and takes the form =IFERROR(**value**, **value_if_error**), where *value* refers to the formula you want to check, and *value_if_error* is the value you want to display if *value* returns an error.
IMABS	Returns the absolute value (modulus) of a complex number in x + yi or x + yj text format and takes the form =IMABS(**inumber**), where *inumber* is a complex number for which you want the absolute value.
IMAGINARY	Returns the imaginary coefficient of a complex number in x + yi or x + yj text format and takes the form =IMAGINARY(**inumber**), where *inumber* is a complex number for which you want the imaginary coefficient.
IMARGUMENT	Returns the argument theta, an angle expressed in radians, and takes the form =IMARGUMENT(**inumber**), where *inumber* is a complex number for which you want the argument theta.
IMCONJUGATE	Returns the complex conjugate of a complex number in x + yi or x + yj text format and takes the form =IMCONJUGATE(**inumber**), where *inumber* is a complex number for which you want the conjugate.
IMCOS	Returns the cosine of a complex number in x + yi or x + yj text format and takes the form =IMCOS(**inumber**), where *inumber* is a complex number for which you want the cosine.
IMDIV	Returns the quotient of two complex numbers in x + yi or x + yj text format and takes the form =IMDIV(**inumber1**, **inumber2**), where *inumber1* is the complex numerator or dividend, and *inumber2* is the complex denominator or divisor.
IMEXP	Returns the exponential of a complex number in x + yi or x + yj text format and takes the form =IMEXP(**inumber**), where *inumber* is a complex number for which you want the exponential.
IMLN	Returns the natural logarithm of a complex number in x + yi or x + yj text format and takes the form =IMLN(**inumber**), where *inumber* is a complex number for which you want the natural logarithm.
IMLOG10	Returns the common logarithm (base 10) of a complex number in x + yi or x + yj text format and takes the form =IMLOG10(**inumber**), where *inumber* is a complex number for which you want the common logarithm.

Function	Description
IMLOG2	Returns the base-2 logarithm of a complex number in x + yi or x + yj text format and takes the form =IMLOG2(**inumber**), where *inumber* is a complex number for which you want the base-2 logarithm.
IMPOWER	Returns a complex number in x + yi or x + yj text format raised to a power and takes the form =IMPOWER(**inumber,** **number**), where *inumber* is a complex number you want to raise to a power, and *number* is the power to which you want to raise the complex number.
IMPRODUCT	Returns the product of 2 to 29 complex numbers in x + yi or x + yj text format and takes the form =IMPRODUCT(**inumber1**, inumber2, . . .). The *inumbers* are 1 to 29 complex numbers to multiply.
IMREAL	Returns the real coefficient of a complex number in x + yi or x + yj text format and takes the form =IMREAL(**inumber**), where *inumber* is a complex number for which you want the real coefficient.
IMSIN	Returns the sine of a complex number in x + yi or x + yj text format and takes the form =IMSIN(**inumber**), where *inumber* is a complex number for which you want the sine.
IMSQRT	Returns the square root of a complex number in x + yi or x + yj text format and takes the form =IMSQRT(**inumber**), where *inumber* is a complex number for which you want the square root.
IMSUB	Returns the difference of two complex numbers in x + yi or x + yj text format and takes the form =IMSUB(**inumber1,** **inumber2**), where *inumber1* is the complex number from which to subtract *inumber2*, and *inumber2* is the complex number to subtract from *inumber1*.
IMSUM	Returns the sum of two or more complex numbers in x + yi or x + yj text format and takes the form =IMSUM(**inumber1**, inumber2, . . .), where the *inumbers* are 1 to 29 complex numbers to add.
INDEX	Returns a value or values, or a reference to a cell or range, using one of two forms, *array:* =INDEX(**array**, row_num, column_num) or *reference:* =INDEX(**reference**, row_num, column_num, area_num). The array form works only with array arguments and returns the resulting values located at the intersection of *row_num* and *column_num*. The reference form returns a cell address using similar arguments, where *reference* can be one or more ranges (areas), and *area_num* is needed only if more than one area is included in *reference*. See "Using Selected Lookup and Reference Functions" on page 512.

Function	Description
INDIRECT	Returns the contents of a cell using its reference and takes the form =INDIRECT(**ref_text**, **a1**), where *ref_text* is a reference or a name, and *a1* is a logical value indicating the type of reference used in *ref_text* (FALSE indicates R1C1 format, and TRUE or omitted indicates A1 format). See "Using Selected Lookup and Reference Functions" on page 512.
INFO	Returns information about the current operating environment and takes the form =INFO(**type_text**), where *type_text* is text specifying what type of information you want returned. Information types include *directory*, *memavail*, *memused*, *numfile*, *origin*, *osversion*, *recalc*, *release*, *system*, and *totmem*. See Help for more information.
INT	Rounds numbers down to the nearest integer and takes the form =INT(**number**). When *number* is negative, INT also rounds that number down to the nearest integer. See "Using the Rounding Functions" on page 500.
INTERCEPT	Calculates the point at which a line will intersect the y-axis by using existing x-values and y-values and takes the form =INTERCEPT(**known_y's**, **known_x's**), where *known_y's* is the dependent set of observations or data, and *known_x's* is the independent set of observations or data.
INTRATE	Calculates the rate of interest (discount rate) for a fully invested security and takes the form =INTRATE(**settlement**, **maturity**, **investment**, **redemption**, basis), where *settlement* is the day you pay for the security, *maturity* is the maturity date of the security, *investment* is the amount invested in the security, *redemption* is the amount to be received at maturity, and *basis* is the day-count basis of the security (if 0 or omitted = 30/360, if 1 = actual/actual; if 2 = actual/360, if 3 = actual/365; if 4 = European 30/360). See "Analyzing Securities" on page 544.
IPMT	Computes the interest portion of an individual payment made to repay an amount over a specified time period with constant periodic payments and a constant interest rate and takes the form =IPMT(**rate**, **period**, **nper**, **pv**, fv, type), where *rate* is the interest rate; *period* is the number of an individual periodic payment; *nper* is the term (periods) of the investment; *pv* is the investment value today; *fv* is the investment value at the end of the term; and *type* indicates when payments are made (0 or omitted = at end of period, 1 = at beginning of period). See "Calculating Investments" on page 535.
IRR	Returns the rate that causes the present value of the inflows from an investment to exactly equal the cost of the investment and takes the form =IRR(**values**, guess), where *values* is an array or a reference to a range of cells that contain numbers beginning with the cost expressed as a negative value, and *guess* is an approximate interest rate (assumes 10 percent if omitted). See "Calculating Investments" on page 535.

Function	Description
ISBLANK	Returns TRUE if the referenced cell is empty; otherwise, returns FALSE. Uses the form =ISBLANK(**value**). See "Using the IS Information Functions" on page 511.
ISERR	Returns TRUE if the value contains any error value except #N/A; otherwise, returns FALSE. Uses the form =ISERR(**value**). See "Using the IS Information Functions" on page 511.
ISERROR	Returns TRUE if the value contains any error value (including #N/A); otherwise, returns FALSE. Uses the form =ISERROR(**value**). See "Using the IS Information Functions" on page 511.
ISEVEN	Returns TRUE if the value is an even number; otherwise, returns FALSE. Uses the form =ISEVEN(**value**). See "Using the IS Information Functions" on page 511.
ISLOGICAL	Returns TRUE if the value is a logical value, otherwise, returns FALSE. Uses the form =ISLOGICAL(**value**). See "Using the IS Information Functions" on page 511.
ISNA	Returns TRUE if the value is the #N/A error value; otherwise, returns FALSE. Uses the form =ISNA(**value**). See "Using the IS Information Functions" on page 511.
ISNONTEXT	Returns TRUE if the value is not text; otherwise, returns FALSE. Uses the form =ISNONTEXT(**value**). See "Using the IS Information Functions" on page 511.
ISNUMBER	Returns TRUE if the value is a number; otherwise, returns FALSE. Uses the form =ISNUMBER(**value**). See "Using the IS Information Functions" on page 511.
ISODD	Returns TRUE if the value is an odd number; otherwise, returns FALSE. Uses the form =ISODD(**value**). See "Using the IS Information Functions" on page 511.
ISPMT	Calculates the interest paid during a specific period of an investment. Provided for Lotus 1-2-3 compatibility and takes the form =ISPMT(**rate**, **per**, **nper**, **pv**), where *rate* is the interest rate for the investment, *per* is the period for which you want to find the interest, *nper* is the total number of payment periods for the investment, and *pv* is the present value of the investment (or the loan amount).
ISREF	Returns TRUE if the *value* is a reference; otherwise, returns FALSE. Uses the form =ISREF(**value**). See "Using the IS Information Functions" on page 511.
ISTEXT	Returns TRUE if the value is text; otherwise, returns FALSE. Uses the form =ISTEXT(**value**). See "Using the IS Information Functions" on page 511.

Function	Description
JIS	Changes text in single-byte character set languages to double-byte characters and takes the form =JIS(**text**). *text* is either text or a reference to a cell containing text. Has no effect on double-byte characters.
KURT	Returns the kurtosis of a data set (characterizes the relative "peakedness" or flatness of a distribution compared with the normal distribution), takes the form =KURT(**number1**, number2, . . .), and accepts up to 30 numeric arguments.
LARGE	Returns the *k*th largest value in an input range and takes the form =LARGE(**array**, **k**), where *k* is the position from the largest value in *array* you want to find. See "Functions That Analyze Rank and Percentile" on page 555.
LCM	Returns the least common multiple of integers (the smallest positive integer that is a multiple of all arguments), takes the form =LCM(**number1**, number2, . . .), and accepts up to 29 numeric integer arguments.
LEFT	Returns the leftmost series of characters from a string and takes the form =LEFT(**text**, num_chars), where *num_chars* indicates how many characters you want to extract from the string (1 if omitted). See "Using the Substring Text Functions" on page 505.
LEFTB	Returns the leftmost series of characters from a string, based on the specified number of bytes, and takes the form =LEFT(**text**, num_bytes), where *num_bytes* indicates how many characters you want to extract from the string, based on bytes.
LEN	Returns the number of displayed characters in an entry and takes the form =LEN(**text**), where *text* is a number, a string enclosed in quotation marks, or a reference to a cell. Trailing zeros are ignored, but spaces are counted. See "Using Selected Text Functions" on page 503.
LENB	Returns the number of characters in an entry, expressed in bytes, and takes the form =LENB(**text**). It is otherwise identical to the LEN function. This function is intended for use with double-byte characters.
LINEST	Calculates the statistics for a line using the least squares method to arrive at a slope that best describes the given data and takes the form LINEST(**known_y's**, known_x's, const, stats). For arguments and usage details, see "The LINEST Function" on page 560.
LN	Returns the natural (base e) logarithm of the positive number referred to by its argument and takes the form =LN(**number**). LN is the inverse of the EXP function.
LOG	Returns the logarithm of a positive number using a specified base and takes the form =LOG(**number**, base). If you don't include the base argument, Excel assumes the base is 10.

Function	Description
LOG10	Returns the base-10 logarithm of a number and takes the form =LOG10(**number**), where *number* is a positive real number.
LOGEST	Returns statistics describing known data in terms of an exponential curve and takes the form =LOGEST(**known_y's**, known_x's, const, stats). For arguments and usage details, see "The LOGEST Function" on page 566.
LOGINV	Returns the inverse of the lognormal cumulative distribution function of *x*, where ln(*x*) is usually distributed with parameters *mean* and *standard_dev* and takes the form =LOGINV(**probability**, **mean**, **standard_dev**), where *probability* is a probability associated with the lognormal distribution, *mean* is the mean of ln(*x*), and *standard_dev* is the standard deviation of ln(*x*).
LOGNORMDIST	Returns the cumulative lognormal distribution of *x*, where ln(*x*) is usually distributed with parameters *mean* and *standard_dev*. This function takes the form =LOGNORMDIST(x, **mean**, **standard_dev**), where *x* is the value at which to evaluate the function, *mean* is the mean of ln(*x*), and *standard_dev* is the standard deviation of ln(*x*).
LOOKUP	Looks for a specified value in a one- or two-dimensional range and takes two forms, *vector* or *array*: =LOOKUP(**lookup_value**, **lookup_vector**, **result_vector**) or =LOOKUP(**lookup_value**, **array**), where *lookup_value* is the value to look for, *lookup_ vector* is a one-row or one-column range containing the lookup values sorted in alphabetical order, *result_vector* is a range that contains the result values and must be identical in size to *lookup_vector*, and *array* is a two-dimensional range containing both lookup and result values. The array form of this function works like HLOOPKUP if *array* is wider than it is tall and works like VLOOKUP if *array* is taller than it is wide. See "Using Selected Lookup and Reference Functions" on page 512.
LOWER	Converts a text string to all lowercase letters and takes the form =**LOWER**(text). See "Using Selected Text Functions" on page 503.
MATCH	Returns the position in a list of the item that most closely matches a lookup value and takes the form =MATCH(**lookup_ value**, **lookup_array**, match_type), where *lookup_value* is the value or string to look up, *lookup_array* is the range that contains the sorted values to compare, and *match_type* defines the rules for the search (if 1 or omitted, finds, in a range sorted in ascending order, the largest value that is less than or equal to *lookup_value*; if 0, finds the value that is equal to *lookup_ value*; if –1, finds, in a range sorted in descending order, the smallest value that is greater than or equal to *lookup_value*). See "Using Selected Lookup and Reference Functions" on page 512.

Appendix C

Function	Description
MAX	Returns the largest value in a range; takes the form =MAX(**number1**, number2, . . .); and accepts up to 30 arguments, ignoring text, error values, and logical values. See "Using Built-In Statistical Functions" on page 553.
MAXA	Acts like MAX except text and logical values are included in the calculation. See "Using Built-In Statistical Functions" on page 553.
MDETERM	Returns the matrix determinant of an array and takes the form =MDETERM(**array**), where *array* is a numeric array with an equal number of rows and columns.
MDURATION	Calculates the annual modified duration for a security with interest payments made on a periodic basis, adjusted for market yield per number of coupon payments per year, and takes the form =MDURATION(**settlement**, **maturity**, **coupon**, **yield**, **frequency**, basis), where *settlement* is the day you pay for the security; *maturity* is the maturity date of the security; *coupon* is the security's annual coupon rate; *yield* is the annual yield of the security; *frequency* is the number of coupon payments made per year (1 = annual, 2 = semiannual, 4 = quarterly); and *basis* is the day-count basis of the security (if 0 or omitted = 30/360, if 1 = actual/actual, if 2 = actual/360, if 3 = actual/365, if 4 = European 30/360). See "Analyzing Securities" on page 544.
MEDIAN	Computes the median of a set of numbers; takes the form =MEDIAN(**number1**, number2, . . .); and can accept up to 30 arguments, ignoring text, error values, and logical values. See "Using Built-In Statistical Functions" on page 553.
MID	Extracts a series of characters (substring) from a text string and takes the form =MID(**text**, **start_num**, **num_chars**), where *text* is the string from which you want to extract the substring, *start_num* is the location in the string where the substring begins (counting from the left), and *num_chars* is the number of characters you want to extract. See "Using the Substring Text Functions" on page 505.
MIDB	Extracts a series of characters (substring) from a text string, based on the number of bytes you specify, and takes the form =MID(**text**, **start_num**, **num_bytes**), where *text* is the string from which you want to extract the substring, *start_num* is the location in the string where the substring begins (counting from the left), and *num_bytes* is the number of characters you want to extract, in bytes. This function is for use with double-byte characters.
MIN	Returns the smallest value in a range; takes the form =MIN(**number1**, number2, . . .); and accepts up to 30 arguments, ignoring text, error values, and logical values. See "Using Built-In Statistical Functions" on page 553.

Function	Description
MINA	Acts like MIN except text and logical values are included in the calculation. See "Using Built-In Statistical Functions" on page 553.
MINUTE	Returns the minute portion of a serial date/time value and takes the form =MINUTE(**serial_number**), where *serial_number* can be a time/date value, a reference, or text in time/date format enclosed in quotation marks. See "Working with Date and Time Functions" on page 531.
MINVERSE	Returns the inverse matrix for the matrix stored in an array and takes the form =MINVERSE(**array**), where *array* is a numeric array with an equal number of rows and columns.
MIRR	Calculates the rate of return of an investment, taking into account the cost of borrowed money and assuming resulting cash inflows are reinvested, and takes the form =MIRR(**values**, **finance rate**, **reinvestment rate**), where *values* is an array or a reference to a range of cells that contain numbers beginning with the cost expressed as a negative value, *finance rate* is the rate at which you borrow money, and *reinvestment rate* is the rate at which you reinvest the returns. See "Calculating Investments" on page 535.
MMULT	Returns the matrix product of two arrays (resulting in an array with the same number of rows as *array1* and the same number of columns as *array2*) and takes the form =MMULT(**array1**, **array2**).
MOD	Returns the remainder of a division operation (modulus) and takes the form =MOD(**number**, **divisor**). If *number* is smaller than *divisor*, the result of the function equals *number*. If *number* is exactly divisible by *divisor*, the function returns 0. If *divisor* is 0, MOD returns the #DIV/0! error value. See "Using Selected Mathematical Functions" on page 498.
MODE	Determines which value occurs most frequently in a set of numbers; takes the form =MODE(**number1**, number2, . . .); and accepts up to 30 arguments, ignoring text, error values, and logical values. See "Using Built-In Statistical Functions" on page 553.
MONTH	Returns the value of the month portion of a serial date/time value and takes the form =MONTH(**serial_number**), where *serial_number* can be a date value, a reference, or text in date format enclosed in quotation marks. See "Working with Date and Time Functions" on page 531.
MROUND	Rounds any number to a multiple you specify and takes the form =MROUND(**number**, **multiple**), where *number* and *multiple* must both have the same sign. The function rounds up if the remainder after dividing *number* by *multiple* is at least half the value of *multiple*. See "Using the Flexible MROUND Function" on page 501.

Appendix C

Function	Description
MULTINOMIAL	Returns the ratio of the factorial of a sum of values to the product of factorials and takes the form =MULTINOMIAL(*num1*, *num2*, . . .), where *num*s are up to 29 values for which you want to find the multinomial.
N	Returns a value converted to a number and takes the form =N(**value**), where *value* is the value you want converted. This function is included for compatibility with other spreadsheet programs but is not necessary in Excel.
NA	Represents an alternative for the error value #N/A, which accepts no arguments and takes the form =NA( ).
NEGBINOMDIST	Returns the negative binomial distribution (the probability that there will be *number_f* failures before the *number_s*-th success, when the constant probability of a success is *probability_s*), and takes the form =NEGBINOMDIST(**number_f**, **number_s**, **probability_s**), where *number_f* is the number of failures, *number_s* is the threshold number of successes, and *probability_s* is the probability of a success.
NETWORKDAYS	Returns the number of working days between two given dates and takes the form =NETWORKDAYS(**start_date**, **end_date**, holidays), where *start_date* is the date you want to count from, *end_date* is the date you want to count to, and *holidays* is an array or reference containing any dates you want to exclude. See "Working with Specialized Date Functions" on page 533.
NOMINAL	Returns the nominal annual interest rate and takes the form =NOMINAL(**effect_rate**, **npery**), where *effect_rate* is the effective interest rate, and *npery* is the number of compounding periods per year.
NORMDIST	Returns the normal cumulative distribution for the specified mean and standard deviation and takes the form =NORMDIST(**x**, **mean**, **standard_dev**, **cumulative**), where *x* is the value for which you want the distribution; *mean* is the arithmetic mean of the distribution; *standard_dev* is the standard deviation of the distribution; and *cumulative* is a logical value that determines the form of the function (if TRUE, returns the cumulative distribution function; if FALSE, returns the probability mass function).
NORMINV	Returns the inverse of the normal cumulative distribution for the specified mean and standard deviation and takes the form =NORMINV(**probability**, **mean**, **standard_dev**), where *probability* is a probability corresponding to the normal distribution, *mean* is the arithmetic mean of the distribution, and *standard_dev* is the standard deviation of the distribution.
NORMSDIST	Returns the standard normal cumulative distribution function and takes the form =NORMSDIST(**z**).

Function	Description
NORMSINV	Returns the inverse of the standard normal cumulative distribution (with a mean of zero and a standard deviation of one) and takes the form =NORMSINV(**probability**), where *probability* is a probability corresponding to the normal distribution.
NOT	Helps develop compound conditional test formulas in conjunction with the simple logical operators: =, >, <, >=, <=, and <>. The NOT function has only one argument and takes the form =NOT(**logical**), where *logical* can be a conditional test, an array, or a reference to a cell containing a logical value. See "Using Selected Logical Functions" on page 508.
NOW	Returns the serial value of the current date and time, takes the form =NOW( ), and accepts no arguments. See "Working with Date and Time Functions" on page 531.
NPER	Computes the number of periods required to amortize a loan, given a specified periodic payment, and takes the form =NPER(**rate**, **payment**, **present value**, future value, type), where *rate* is the interest rate, *payment* is the amount of each periodic payment when individual amounts are the same, *present value* is the investment value today, *future value* is the investment value at the end of the term, and *type* indicates when payments are made (0 or omitted = at end of period, 1 = at beginning of period). See "Calculating Investments" on page 535.
NPV	Determines the profitability of an investment and takes the form =NPV(**rate**, **value1**, value2, . . .), where *rate* is the interest rate, and the values represent up to 29 payments (or any size array) when individual amounts differ. See "Calculating Investments" on page 535.
OCT2BIN	Converts an octal number to binary and takes the form =OCT2BIN(**number**, places), where *number* is the octal number you want to convert, and *places* is the number of characters to use (if omitted, uses the minimum number of characters necessary).
OCT2DEC	Converts an octal number to decimal and takes the form =OCT2DEC(**number**), where *number* is the octal number you want to convert.
OCT2HEX	Converts an octal number to hexadecimal and takes the form =OCT2HEX(**number**, places), where *number* is the octal number you want to convert, and *places* is the number of characters to use (if omitted, uses the minimum number of characters necessary).
ODD	Rounds a number up to the nearest odd integer and takes the form =ODD(**number**). Negative numbers are correspondingly rounded down. See "Using the Rounding Functions" on page 500.

Appendix C

Function	Description
ODDFPRICE	Returns the price per $100 of face value for a security having an odd first period and takes the form =ODDFPRICE(**settlement**, **maturity**, **issue**, **first coupon**, **rate**, **yield**, **redemption**, **frequency**, basis), where *settlement* is the day you pay for the security; *maturity* is the maturity date of the security; *issue* is the issue date of the security; *first coupon* is the security's first coupon due date as a serial date value; *rate* is the interest rate of the security at the issue date; *yield* is the annual yield of the security; *redemption* is the value of the security at redemption; *frequency* is the number of coupon payments made per year (1 = annual, 2 = semiannual, 4 = quarterly); and *basis* is the day-count basis of the security (if 0 or omitted = 30/360, if 1 = actual/actual, if 2 = actual/360, if 3 = actual/365, if 4 = European 30/360).
ODDFYIELD	Calculates the yield of a security that has an odd first period and takes the form =ODDFYIELD(**settlement**, **maturity**, **issue**, **first coupon**, **rate**, **price**, **redemption**, **frequency**, basis), where *price* is the security's price. See ODDFPRICE for additional argument definitions.
ODDLPRICE	Calculates the price per $100 face value of a security having an odd last coupon period and takes the form =ODDLPRICE (**settlement**, **maturity**, **last interest**, **rate**, **yield**, **redemption**, **frequency**, basis), where *last interest* is the security's last coupon due date as a serial date value. See ODDFPRICE for additional argument definitions.
ODDLYIELD	Calculates the yield of a security that has an odd last period and takes the form =ODDLYIELD(**settlement**, **maturity**, **last interest**, **rate**, **price**, **redemption**, **frequency**, basis), where *last interest* is the security's last coupon due date, and *price* is the security's price. See ODDFPRICE for additional argument definitions.
OFFSET	Returns a reference of a specified height and width, located at a specified position relative to another specified reference, and takes the form =OFFSET(**reference**, **rows**, **cols**, height, width), where *reference* specifies the position from which the offset is calculated, *rows* and *cols* specify the vertical and horizontal distance from *reference*, and *height* and *width* specify the shape of the reference returned by the function. The *rows* and *cols* arguments can be positive or negative: Positive values specify offsets below and to the right of *reference*; negative values specify offsets above and to the left of *reference*.
OR	Helps develop compound conditional test formulas in conjunction with logical operators and takes the form =OR(**logical1**, logical2, . . .), where the *logicals* can be up to 30 conditional tests, arrays, or references to cells that contain logical values. See "Using Selected Logical Functions" on page 508.

Function	Description
PEARSON	Returns the Pearson product moment correlation coefficient, r, a dimensionless index that ranges from –1 to 1 (inclusive) and reflects the extent of a linear relationship between two data sets. This function takes the form =PEARSON(**array1**, **array2**), where *array1* is a set of independent values, and *array2* is a set of dependent values.
PERCENTILE	Returns the member of an input range that is at a specified percentile ranking and takes the form =PERCENTILE(**array**, **k**), where *array* is the input range, and *k* is the rank you want to find. See "Using Functions That Analyze Rank and Percentile" on page 555.
PERCENTRANK	Returns a percentile ranking for any member of a data set and takes the form =PERCENTRANK(**array**, **x**, significance), where *array* specifies the input range, *x* specifies the value whose rank you want to obtain, and the optional *significance* indicates the number of digits of precision you want. If *significance* is omitted, results are rounded to three digits (0.xxx or xx.x%). See "Using Functions That Analyze Rank and Percentile" on page 555.
PERMUT	Returns the number of permutations for a given number of objects that can be selected from number objects and takes the form =PERMUT(**number**, **number_chosen**), where *number* is an integer that describes the number of objects, and *number_chosen* is an integer that describes the number of objects in each permutation.
PHONETIC	Extracts, in Japanese, Simplified or Traditional Chinese, and Korean, the phonetic (furigana) characters from a referenced cell or range. Takes the form =PHONETIC(**reference**), where *reference* denotes a single cell or range. If *reference* is a range, the function returns phonetic text only from the cell in the upper-left corner.
PI	Returns the value of pi, accurate to 14 decimal places (3.14159265358979), and takes the form =PI( ). It takes no arguments, but you must still type empty parentheses after the function name. To calculate the area of a circle, multiply the square of the circle's radius by the PI function.
PMT	Computes the periodic payment required to amortize a loan over a specified number of periods and takes the form =PMT(**rate**, **nper**, **pv**, fv, type), where *rate* is the interest rate, *nper* is the term (periods) of the investment, *pv* is the investment value today, *fv* is the investment value at the end of the term, and *type* indicates when payments are made (0 or omitted = at end of period, 1 = at beginning of period). See "Calculating Investments" on page 535.

Appendix C

Function	Description
POISSON	Returns the Poisson distribution and takes the form =POISSON(**x**, **mean**, **cumulative**), where *x* is the number of events; *mean* is the expected numeric value; and *cumulative* is a logical value that determines the form of the probability distribution returned (if TRUE, returns the cumulative Poisson probability that the number of random events occurring will be between *zero* and *x* inclusive; if FALSE, returns the Poisson probability mass function that the number of events occurring will be exactly *x*).
POWER	Returns the result of a number raised to a power and takes the form =POWER(**number**, **power**), where *number* is the base number, and *power* is the exponent to which the base number is raised.
PPMT	Computes the principal component of an individual payment made to repay a loan over a specified time period with constant periodic payments and a constant interest rate and takes the form =PPMT(**rate**, **period**, **nper**, **pv**, fv, type), where *rate* is the interest rate, *period* is the number of an individual periodic payment, *nper* is the term (periods) of the investment, *pv* is the investment value today, *fv* is the investment value at the end of the term, and *type* indicates when payments are made (0 or omitted = at end of period, 1 = at beginning of period). See "Calculating Investments" on page 535.
PRICE	Calculates the price per $100 of a security that pays periodic interest and takes the form =PRICE(**settlement**, **maturity**, **rate**, **yield**, **redemption**, **frequency**, basis), where *settlement* is the day you pay for the security; *maturity* is the maturity date of the security; *rate* is the interest rate of the security at the issue date; *yield* is the annual yield of the security; *redemption* is the value of the security at redemption; *frequency* is the number of coupon payments made per year (1 = annual, 2 = semiannual, 4 = quarterly); and *basis* is the day-count basis of the security (if 0 or omitted = 30/360, if 1 = actual/actual, if 2 = actual/360, if 3 = actual/365, if 4 = European 30/360). See "Analyzing Securities" on page 544.
PRICEDISC	Returns the price per $100 of a discounted security and takes the form =PRICEDISC(**settlement**, **maturity**, **discount**, **redemption**, basis), where *settlement* is the day you pay for the security; *maturity* is the maturity date of the security; *discount* is the security's discount rate; *redemption* is the value of the security at redemption; and *basis* is the day-count basis of the security (if 0 or omitted = 30/360, if 1 = actual/actual, if 2 = actual/360, if 3 = actual/365, if 4 = European 30/360). See "Analyzing Securities" on page 544.

Function	Description
PRICEMAT	Returns the price per $100 of a security that pays interest at maturity and takes the form =PRICEMAT(**settlement**, **maturity**, **issue**, **rate**, **yield**, basis), where *settlement* is the day you pay for the security; *maturity* is the maturity date of the security; *issue* is the issue date of the security; *rate* is the interest rate of the security at the issue date; *yield* is the annual yield of the security; and *basis* is the day-count basis of the security (if 0 or omitted = 30/360, if 1 = actual/actual, if 2 = actual/360, if 3 = actual/365, if 4 = European 30/360). See "Analyzing Securities" on page 544.
PROB	Returns the probability that values in a range are between two limits and takes the form =PROB(**x_range**, **prob_range**, **lower_limit**, upper_limit), where *x_range* is the range of numeric values of x with which there are associated probabilities; *prob_range* is a set of probabilities associated with values in *x_range*; *lower_limit* is the lower bound on the value for which you want a probability; and *upper_limit* is the optional upper bound on the value for which you want a probability.
PRODUCT	Multiplies all the numbers referenced by its arguments, takes the form =PRODUCT(**number1**, number2, . . .), and takes as many as 30 arguments. Text, logical values, and blank cells are ignored. See "Using Selected Mathematical Functions" on page 498.
PROPER	Capitalizes the first letter in each word and any other letters in a text string that do not follow another letter—all other letters are converted to lowercase—and takes the form =PROPER(**text**). See "Using Selected Text Functions" on page 503.
PV	Computes the present value of a series of equal periodic payments, or a lump-sum payment, and takes the form =PV(**rate**, **nper**, **payment**, future value, type), where *rate* is the interest rate; *nper* is the term (periods) of the investment; *payment* is the amount of each periodic payment when individual amounts are the same; *future value* is the investment value at the end of the term; and *type* indicates when payments are made (0 or omitted = at end of period, 1 = at beginning of period). See "Calculating Investments" on page 535.
QUARTILE	Returns the value in an input range that represents a specified quarter-percentile and takes the form =QUARTILE(**array**, **quart**). For usage and argument details, see "The PERCENTILE and QUARTILE Functions" on page 557.
QUOTIENT	Returns the integer portion of a division and takes the form =QUOTIENT(numerator, denominator), where *numerator* is the dividend and *denominator* is the divisor.

Appendix C

Function	Description
RADIANS	Converts degrees to radians and takes the form =RADIANS(**angle**). *angle* represents an angle measured in degrees.
RAND	Generates a random number between 0 and 1 and takes the form =RAND() with no arguments, but you must still type empty parentheses after the function name. The result changes with each sheet recalculation. See "Using Selected Mathematical Functions" on page 498.
RANDBETWEEN	Generates random integer values between a specified range of numbers and takes the form =RANDBETWEEN(**bottom**, **top**), where *bottom* is the smallest, and *top* is the largest integer you want to use, inclusive. See "Using Selected Mathematical Functions" on page 498.
RANK	Returns the ranked position of a particular number within a set of numbers and takes the form =RANK(**number**, **ref**, order). For usage and argument details, see "The RANK Function" on page 557.
RATE	Calculates the rate of return of an investment that generates a series of equal periodic payments or a single lump-sum payment and takes the form =RATE(**nper**, **payment**, **present value**, future value, type, guess), where *nper* is the term (periods) of the investment; *payment* is the amount of each periodic payment when individual amounts are the same; *present value* is the investment value today; *future value* is the investment value at the end of the term; *type* indicates when payments are made (0 or omitted = at end of period, 1 = at beginning of period); and *guess* is an approximate interest rate (assumes 10 percent if omitted). See "Calculating Investments" on page 535.
RECEIVED	Calculates the amount received at maturity for a fully invested security and takes the form =RECEIVED(**settlement**, **maturity**, **investment**, **discount**, basis), where *settlement* is the day you pay for the security; *maturity* is the maturity date of the security; *investment* is the amount invested in the security; *discount* is the security's discount rate; and *basis* is the day-count basis of the security (if 0 or omitted = 30/360, if 1 = actual/actual, if 2 = actual/360, if 3 = actual/365, if 4 = European 30/360). See "Analyzing Securities" on page 544.
REPLACE	Substitutes one string of characters with another string and takes the form =REPLACE(**old_text**, **start_num**, **num_chars**, **new_text**), where *old_text* is the text string where you want to replace characters, *start_num* specifies the starting character to replace, *num_chars* specifies the number of characters to replace (counting from the left), and *new_text* specifies the text string to insert. See "Using the Substring Text Functions" on page 505.

Function	Description
REPLACEB	Substitutes one string of characters with another string and takes the form =REPLACEB(**old_text**, **start_num**, **num_bytes**, **new_text**), where *old_text* is the text string in which you want to replace characters, *start_num* specifies the starting character to replace, *num_bytes* specifies the number of bytes to replace, and *new_text* specifies the text string to insert. This function is for use with double-byte characters.
REPT	Fills a cell with a string of characters repeated a specified number of times and takes the form =REPT(**text**, **number_times**), where *text* specifies a string in double quotation marks, and *number_times* specifies how many times to repeat *text*. The result of the function cannot exceed 32,767 characters.
RIGHT	Returns the rightmost series of characters from a string and takes the form =RIGHT(**text**, num_chars), where *num_chars* indicates how many characters you want to extract from the string (1, if omitted). Blank spaces count as characters. See "Using the Substring Text Functions" on page 505.
RIGHTB	Returns the rightmost series of characters from a string, based on the number of bytes you specify, and takes the form =RIGHTB(**text**, num_bytes), where *num_bytes* indicates how many characters you want to extract from the string, based on bytes. This function is for use with double-byte characters.
ROMAN	Converts an Arabic numeral to Roman numerals, as text, and takes the form =ROMAN(**number**, form), where *number* is the Arabic numeral you want converted, and *form* is a number specifying the type of Roman numeral you want (1, 2, or 3 = more concise notation; 4 or FALSE = simplified notation; TRUE = classic notation).
ROUND	Rounds numbers to a specified number of decimal places and takes the form =ROUND(**number**, **num_digits**), where *number* can be a number, a reference to a cell that contains a number, or a formula that results in a number. *num_digits* can be any positive or negative integer and determines the number of decimal places. Type a negative *num_digits* to round to the left of the decimal; type zero to round to the nearest integer. See "Using the Rounding Functions" on page 500.
ROUNDDOWN	Rounds numbers down to a specified number of decimal places and takes the same form and arguments as ROUND. See "Using the Rounding Functions" on page 500.
ROUNDUP	Rounds numbers up to a specified number of decimal places and takes the same form and arguments as ROUND. See "Using the Rounding Functions" on page 500.

Appendix C

Function	Description
ROW	Returns the row number of the referenced cell or range and takes the form =ROW(reference). If *reference* is omitted, the result is the row number of the cell containing the function. If *reference* is a range or a name and the function is entered as an array (by pressing Ctrl+Shift+Enter), the result is an array of the numbers of each of the rows or columns in the range. See "Using Selected Lookup and Reference Functions" on page 512.
ROWS	Returns the number of rows in a reference or an array and takes the form =ROWS(**array**), where *array* is an array constant, a range reference, or a range name. See "Using Selected Lookup and Reference Functions" on page 512.
RSQ	Returns the square of the Pearson product moment correlation coefficient through data points in the arrays *known_y's* and *known_x's* and takes the form =RSQ(**known_y's**, **known_x's**).
RTD	Returns real-time data from a program that supports COM automation and takes the form =RTD(**progID**, server, topic1, topic2, . . .), where *progID* is the program identifier (enclosed in quotation marks) for a registered COM automation add-in that has been installed on the local computer, *server* is the name of the server where the add-in should be run (if other than the local computer), and *topics* are up to 28 parameters describing the real-time data you want.
SEARCH	Returns the position of specified text within a string and takes the form =SEARCH(**find_text**, **within_text**, start_num), where *find_text* is the text you want to find, *within_text* indicates where to look, and *start_num* specifies the character position in *within_text* where you want to begin the search. See "Using the Substring Text Functions" on page 505.
SEARCHB	Returns the position of specified text within a string, expressed in bytes; takes the form =SEARCHB(**find_text**, **within_text**, start_num); and is otherwise identical to SEARCH.
SECOND	Returns the seconds portion of a serial date/time value and takes the form =SECOND(**serial_number**), where *serial_ number* can be a time/date value, a reference, or text in time/ date format enclosed in quotation marks. See "Working with Date and Time Functions" on page 531.
SERIESSUM	Returns the sum of a power series and takes the form =SERIESSUM(**x, n, m, coefficients**), where *x* is the input value to the power series, *n* is the initial power to which you want to raise *x, m* is the step by which to increase *n* for each term in the series, and *coefficients* is a set of coefficients by which each successive power of *x* is multiplied. The number of values in coefficients determines the number of terms in the power series.

Function	Description
SIGN	Determines the sign of a number. Returns 1 if the number is positive, zero (0) if the number is 0, and –1 if the number is negative; takes the form =SIGN(**number**), where *number* is any real number.
SIN	Returns the sine of an angle. The complement of the COS function, it takes the form =SIN(**number**), where *number* is the angle in radians.
SINH	Returns the hyperbolic sine of a number and takes the form =SINH(**number**), where *number* is any real number.
SKEW	Returns the skew of a distribution (the degree of asymmetry of a distribution around its mean), takes the form =SKEW(**number1**, number2, . . .), and accepts up to 30 arguments.
SLN	Returns straight-line depreciation for an asset for a single period and takes the form =SLN(**cost**, **salvage**, **life**), where *cost* is the initial asset cost, *salvage* is the remaining value after asset is fully depreciated, and *life* is the length of depreciation time. See "Calculating Depreciation" on page 541.
SLOPE	Returns the slope of a linear regression line and takes the form =SLOPE(**known_y's**, **known_x's**). For arguments and usage details, see "The SLOPE Function" on page 565.
SMALL	Returns the *k*th smallest value in an input range and takes the form =SMALL(**array**, **k**), where *k* is the position from the smallest value in *array* you want to find. See "Using Functions That Analyze Rank and Percentile" on page 555.
SQRT	Returns the positive square root of a number and takes the form =SQRT(**number**).
SQRTPI	Returns the square root of (number * pi) and takes the form =SQRTPI(**number**).
STANDARDIZE	Returns a normalized value from a distribution characterized by *mean* and *standard_dev* and takes the form =STANDARDIZE(**x**, **mean**, **standard_dev**), where *x* is the value you want to normalize, *mean* is the arithmetic mean of the distribution, and *standard_dev* is the standard deviation of the distribution.
STDEV	Computes standard deviation, assuming that the arguments represent only a sample of the total population, and takes the form =STDEV(**number1**, number2, . . .), accepting up to 30 arguments. See "Using Sample and Population Statistical Functions" on page 558.
STDEVA	Acts like STDEV except text and logical values are included in the calculation. See "Using Sample and Population Statistical Functions" on page 558.

Function	Description
STDEVP	Computes the standard deviation, assuming that the arguments represent the total population, and takes the form =STDEVP(**number1**, number2, . . .). See "Using Sample and Population Statistical Functions" on page 558.
STDEVPA	Acts like STDEVP except that text and logical values are included in the calculation. See "Using Sample and Population Statistical Functions" on page 558.
STEYX	Calculates the standard error of a regression and takes the form =STEYX(**known_y's**, **known_x's**). For arguments and usage details, see "The SLOPE Function" on page 565.
SUBSTITUTE	Replaces specified text with new text within a specified string and takes the form =SUBSTITUTE(**text**, **old_text**, **new_text**, instance_num), where *text* is the string you want to work on; *old_text* is the text to be replaced; *new_text* is the text to substitute; and *instance_num* is optional, indicating a specific occurrence of *old_text* within *text*. See "Using the Substring Text Functions" on page 505.
SUBTOTAL	Returns a subtotal in a list or database and takes the form =SUBTOTAL(**function_num**, **ref1**, ref2, . . .), where *function_num* is a number that specifies which function to use in calculating subtotals (1=AVERAGE, 2=COUNT, 3=COUNTA, 4=MAX, 5=MIN, 6=PRODUCT, 7=STDEV, 8=STDEVP, 9=SUM, 10=VAR, 11=VARP), and the *refs* are 1 to 29 ranges or references for which you want the subtotal.
SUM	Totals a series of numbers and takes the form =SUM(**num1**, num2, . . .), where the *nums* (max 30) can be numbers, formulas, ranges, or cell references. Ignores arguments that refer to text values, logical values, or blank cells. See "Using the SUM Function" on page 497.
SUMIF	Tests each cell in a range before adding it to the total and takes the form =SUMIF(**range**, **criteria**, sum_range), where *range* is the range you want to test, *criteria* is the logical test to be performed on each cell, and *sum_range* specifies the cells to be totaled. See "Using Built-In Statistical Functions" on page 553.
SUMIFS	Tests each cell in a range using multiple criteria before adding it to the total and takes the form =SUMIFS(**sum_range**, **criteria_range1**, **criteria1**, criteria_range2, criteria2, . . .), where *sum_range* is the range containing values you want to sum, *criteria_rangeX* is a cell range containing data to be evaluated, and *criteriaX* is a cell range containing values, expressions, references, or text that define which cells will be added to the total.

Function	Description
SUMPRODUCT	Multiplies the value in each cell in a specified range by the corresponding cell in another equal-sized range and then adds the results. It takes the form =SUMPRODUCT (**array1**, **array2**, array3, . . .) and can include up to 30 arrays. Nonnumeric entries are treated as zero. See "Using Selected Mathematical Functions" on page 498.
SUMSQ	Returns the sum of the squares of each specified value in a specified range, takes the form =SUMSQ(**number1**, **number2**, . . .), and takes up to 30 arguments or a single array or array reference.
SUMX2MY2	Calculates the sum of the differences of the squares of the corresponding values in *x* and *y* and takes the form =SUMX2MY2(**array_x**, **array_y**), where *x* and *y* are arrays that contain the same number of elements.
SUMX2PY2	Calculates the sum of the sum of the squares of the corresponding values in *x* and *y* and takes the form =SUMX2PY2(**array_x**, **array_y**), where *x* and *y* are arrays that contain the same number of elements.
SUMXMY2	Calculates the sum of the squares of the differences of the corresponding values in *x* and *y* and takes the form =SUMXMY2(**array_x**, **array_y**), where *x* and *y* are arrays that contain the same number of elements.
SYD	Computes depreciation for a specific time period with the sum-of-the-years'-digits method and takes the form =SYD(**cost**, **salvage**, **life**, **period**), where *cost* is the initial asset cost, *salvage* is the remaining value after the asset is fully depreciated, *life* is the length of depreciation time, and *period* is the individual period to be computed. See "Calculating Depreciation" on page 541.
T	Returns the text referred to by value and takes the form =T(**value**), where *value* is the value you want to test. This function is included for compatibility with other spreadsheet programs but is not necessary in Excel.
TAN	Returns the tangent of an angle and takes the form =TAN(**number**), where *number* is the angle in radians.
TANH	Returns the hyperbolic tangent of a number and takes the form =TANH(**number**), where *number* is any real number.
TBILLEQ	Calculates the bond-equivalent yield for a U.S. Treasury bill and takes the form =TBILLEQ(**settlement**, **maturity**, **discount**), where *settlement* is the day you pay for the security, *maturity* is the maturity date of the security, and *discount* is the discount rate of the security. See "Analyzing Securities" on page 544.

Appendix C

Function	Description
TBILLPRICE	Calculates the price per $100 of face value for a U.S. Treasury bill and takes the form =TBILLPRICE(**settlement**, **maturity**, **discount**), where *settlement* is the day you pay for the security, *maturity* is the maturity date of the security, and *discount* is the discount rate of the security. See "Analyzing Securities" on page 544.
TBILLYIELD	Calculates a U.S. Treasury bill's yield and takes the form =TBILLYIELD(**settlement**, **maturity**, **price**), where *settlement* is the day you pay for the security, *maturity* is the maturity date of the security, and *price* is the security's price. See "Analyzing Securities" on page 544.
TDIST	Returns the percentage points (probability) for the student t-distribution, where a numeric value (x) is a calculated value of *t* for which the percentage points are to be computed. This function takes the form =TDIST(**x**, **degrees_freedom**, **tails**), where *x* is the numeric value at which to evaluate the distribution; *degrees_freedom* is an integer indicating the number of degrees of freedom; and *tails* specifies the number of distribution tails to return (if 1, returns the one-tailed distribution; if 2, returns the two-tailed distribution).
TEXT	Converts a number into a text string using a specified format and takes the form =TEXT(**value**, **format_text**), where *value* can be any number, formula, or cell reference, and *format_text* specifies the format using built-in custom formatting symbols. See "Using Selected Text Functions" on page 503.
TIME	Returns the decimal number for a particular time and takes the form =TIME(**hour**, **minute**, **second**), where *hour* is a number from 0 (zero) to 23 representing the hour, *minute* is a number from 0 to 59 representing the minute, and *second* is a number from 0 to 59 representing the second.
TIMEVALUE	Translates a time into a decimal value and takes the form =TIMEVALUE(**time_text**), where *time_text* represents a time entered as text in quotation marks. See "Working with Date and Time Functions" on page 531.
TINV	Returns the t-value of the student's t-distribution as a function of the probability and the degrees of freedom and takes the form =TINV(**probability**, **degrees_freedom**), where *probability* is the probability associated with the two-tailed student's t-distribution, and *degrees_freedom* is the number of degrees of freedom to characterize the distribution.
TODAY	Returns the serial value of the current date, takes the form =TODAY( ), and accepts no arguments. See "Working with Date and Time Functions" on page 531.

Function	Description
TRANSPOSE	Changes the horizontal or vertical orientation of an array and takes the form =TRANSPOSE(**array**). If *array* is vertical, the result is horizontal, and vice versa. Must be entered as an array formula by pressing Ctrl+Shift+Enter, with a range selected with the same proportions as *array*. See "Using Selected Lookup and Reference Functions" on page 512.
TREND	Returns values of points that lie along a linear trendline and takes the form =TREND(**known_y's**, known_x's, new_x's, const). For arguments and usage details, see "The TREND Function" on page 564.
TRIM	Removes leading, trailing, and extra blank characters from a string, leaving single spaces between words, and takes the form =TRIM(**text**). See "Using Selected Text Functions" on page 503.
TRIMMEAN	Returns the mean of the interior of a data set (the mean taken by excluding a percentage of data points from the top and bottom tails of a data set). This function takes the form =TRIMMEAN(**array**, **percent**), where *array* is the array or range of values to trim and average, and *percent* is the fractional number of data points to exclude from the calculation.
TRUE	Represents an alternative for the logical condition TRUE, which accepts no arguments, and takes the form =TRUE( ). See "Using Selected Logical Functions" on page 508.
TRUNC	Truncates everything to the right of the decimal point, regardless of its sign, and takes the form =TRUNC(**number**, num_digits). Truncates everything after the specified *num_digits* to the right of the decimal point. See "Using the Rounding Functions" on page 500.
TTEST	Returns the probability associated with a student's t-test and takes the form =TTEST(**array1**, **array2**, **tails**, **type**), where *array1* is the first data set; *array2* is the second data set; *tails* specifies the number of distribution tails (if 1, uses the one-tailed distribution; if 2, uses the two-tailed distribution); and *type* is the kind of t-test to perform (1 = paired, 2 = two-sample equal variance, 3 = two-sample unequal variance).
TYPE	Determines the type of value a cell contains and takes the form =TYPE(**value**). The result is one of the following numeric codes: 1 (number), 2 (text), 4 (logical value), 16 (error value), or 64 (array). See "Using Selected Lookup and Reference Functions" on page 512.
UPPER	Converts a text string to all uppercase letters and takes the form =UPPER(**text**). See "Using Selected Text Functions" on page 503.

Appendix C

Function	Description
VALUE	Converts a text string that represents a number to a number and takes the form =VALUE(**text**), where *text* is the text enclosed in quotation marks or a reference to a cell containing the text you want to convert. This function is included for compatibility with other spreadsheet programs but is not necessary in Excel.
VAR	Computes variance, assuming that the arguments represent only a sample of the total population, and takes the form =VAR(**number1**, number2, . . .), accepting up to 30 arguments. See "Using Sample and Population Statistical Functions" on page 558.
VARA	Acts like VAR except text and logical values are included in the calculation. See "Using Sample and Population Statistical Functions" on page 558.
VARP	Computes variance, assuming that the arguments represent the total population, and takes the form =VARP(**number1**, number2, . . .). See "Using Sample and Population Statistical Functions" on page 558.
VARPA	Acts like VARP except text and logical values are included in the calculation. See "Using Sample and Population Statistical Functions" on page 558.
VDB	Calculates depreciation for any complete or partial period, using either double-declining balance or a specified accelerated-depreciation factor, and takes the form =VDB(**cost**, **salvage**, **life**, **start_period**, **end_period**, factor, no_switch), where *cost* is the initial asset cost, *salvage* is the remaining value after the asset is fully depreciated, *life* is the length of depreciation time, *start_period* is the period number after which depreciation begins, *end_period* is the last period calculated, *factor* is the rate at which the balance declines, and *no_switch* turns off the default switch to straight-line depreciation when it becomes greater than the declining balance. See "Calculating Depreciation" on page 541.
VLOOKUP	Looks for a specified value in the leftmost column in a table, returns the value in the same row and a specified column, and takes the form =VLOOKUP(**lookup_value**, **table_array**, **col_index_num**, range_lookup), where *lookup_value* is the value to look for; *table_array* is the range containing the lookup and result values sorted in alphabetical order by the leftmost column; *col_index_num* is the column number containing the value you want to find; and *range_lookup* is a logical value, which, if false, forces an exact match. See "Using Selected Lookup and Reference Functions" on page 512.

Function	Description
WEEKDAY	Returns a number value representing the day of the week for a specified date and takes the form =WEEKDAY(**serial_number**, return_type), where *serial_number* is a date value, a reference, or text in date form enclosed in quotation marks, and *return_type* determines the way the result is represented (if 1 or omitted, Sunday is day 1, if 2, Monday is day 1, if 3, Monday is day 0). See "Working with Date and Time Functions" on page 531.
WEEKNUM	Returns a number that indicates where the week falls numerically within a year and takes the form =WEEKNUM(**serial_num**, return_type), where *serial_num* is a date within the week, and *return_type* is a number that determines the day on which the week begins (1 or omitted = week begins on Sunday, 2 = week begins on Monday).
WEIBULL	Returns the Weibull distribution and takes the form =WEIBULL(**x**, **alpha**, **beta**, **cumulative**), where *x* is the value at which to evaluate the function, *alpha* is a parameter to the distribution, *beta* is a parameter to the distribution, and *cumulative* determines the form of the function.
WORKDAY	Returns a date that is a specified number of working days before or after a given date and takes the form =WORKDAY(**start_date**, **days**, holidays), where *start_date* is the date you want to count from; *days* is the number of workdays before or after the start date, excluding weekends and holidays; and *holidays* is an array or reference containing any dates you want to exclude. See "Working with Specialized Date Functions" on page 533.
XIRR	Returns the internal rate of return for a schedule of cash flows that is not necessarily periodic and takes the form =XIRR(**values**, **dates**, guess), where *values* is a series of cash flows that corresponds to a schedule of payments in dates, *dates* is a schedule of payment dates that corresponds to the cash flow payments, and *guess* is a number you think is close to the result.
XNPV	Returns the net present value for a schedule of cash flows that is not necessarily periodic and takes the form =XNPV(**rate**, **values**, **dates**), where *rate* is the discount rate to apply to the cash flows, *values* is a series of cash flows that corresponds to a schedule of payments in dates, and *dates* is a schedule of payment dates that corresponds to the cash flow payments.
YEAR	Returns the value of the year portion of a serial date/time value and takes the form =YEAR(**serial_number**), where *serial_number* can be a date value, a reference, or text in date format enclosed in quotation marks. See "Working with Date and Time Functions" on page 531.

Appendix C

Function	Description
YEARFRAC	Returns a decimal number that represents the portion of a year that falls between two given dates and takes the form =YEARFRAC(**start_date**, **end_date**, basis), where *start_date* and *end_date* specify the span you want to convert to a decimal, and *basis* is the type of day count (0 or omitted = 30/360, 1 = actual/actual, 2 = actual/360, 3 = actual/365, 4 = European 30/360). See "Working with Specialized Date Functions" on page 531.
YIELD	Determines the annual yield for a security that pays interest on a periodic basis and takes the form =YIELD(**settlement**, **maturity**, **rate**, **price**, **redemption**, **frequency**, basis), where *settlement* is the day you pay for the security; *maturity* is the maturity date of the security; *rate* is the interest rate of the security at the issue date; *price* is the security's price; *redemption* is the value of the security at redemption; *frequency* is the number of coupon payments made per year (1 = annual, 2 = semiannual, 4 = quarterly); and *basis* is the day-count basis of the security (if 0 or omitted = 30/360, if 1 = actual/actual, if 2 = actual/360, if 3 = actual/365, if 4 = European 30/360). See "Analyzing Securities" on page 544.
YIELDDISC	Calculates the annual yield for a discounted security and takes the form =YIELDDISC(**settlement**, **maturity**, **price**, **redemption**, basis), where *settlement* is the day you pay for the security; *maturity* is the maturity date of the security; *price* is the security's price; *redemption* is the value of the security at redemption; and *basis* is the day-count basis of the security (if 0 or omitted = 30/360, if 1 = actual/actual, if 2 = actual/360, if 3 = actual/365, if 4 = European 30/360). See "Analyzing Securities" on page 544.
YIELDMAT	Calculates the annual yield for a security that pays its interest at maturity and takes the form =YIELDMAT(**settlement**, **maturity**, **issue**, **rate**, **price**, basis), where *settlement* is the day you pay for the security; *maturity* is the maturity date of the security; *issue* is the issue date of the security; *rate* is the interest rate of the security at the issue date; *price* is the security's price; and *basis* is the day-count basis of the security (if 0 or omitted = 30/360, if 1 = actual/actual, if 2 = actual/360, if 3 = actual/365, if 4 = European 30/360). See "Analyzing Securities" on page 544.
ZTEST	Returns the two-tailed P-value of a Z-test (generates a standard score for *x* with respect to the data set, *array*, and returns the two-tailed probability for the normal distribution). This function takes the form =ZTEST(**array**, **x**, sigma), where *array* is the array or range of data against which to test *x*, *x* is the value to test, and *sigma* is the known population's standard deviation.

Index to Troubleshooting Topics

Error	Description	Page
Advanced Filter	I can't extract to a separate worksheet.	689
Context tabs	Did your Design tab disappear?	271
Date formats	Concatenated dates become serial numbers.	507
Fit to page	My manual page breaks don't work.	421
Formatting codes	Decimal points in my Currency formats don't line up.	314
Hidden window	Nothing happens when you try to open a workbook.	176
Hyperlinking	Excel doesn't turn my URLs into hyperlinks.	874
Hyperlinking	I don't want that hyperlink.	876
Incorrect sum	Inserted cells are not included in formulas.	435
Input cells	The results in my two-input data table are wrong.	587
Input values	The Solver can't solve my problem.	611
Intersection	My IS function returns unexpected results.	511
Matching units	The PMT function produces unrealistic results.	539
Names	My old worksheet-level names have changed.	445
Negative time	Excel displays my time as #####.	531
OLE	How do I get rid of the bounding rectangle?	882
Queries	The Query Wizard won't let me get rid of a filter.	762
Rounding	My formulas don't add numbers correctly.	140
Rounding	Rounded values in my worksheet don't add up.	467
Time formats	I can't enter a number of hours greater than 9999.	530
Typing functions	I get a #NAME? error.	494
Volatile functions	Random numbers keep changing.	575
XML	Excel reports a problem with the specified XML or schema source.	756

Index

Symbols and Numbers

& (ampersand), 436–437, 458
' (apostrophe, single quote), 142–143, 458, 835, 852
* (asterisk, multiplication sign), 225, 427, 458, 689
\ (backslash), 142–143
{ } (braces), 458, 469, 471
[ ] (brackets)
   Query, 777–778
   structured references, 457, 458, 704–705
   time and date notations, 529
   time codes, 528
^ (caret), 142–143, 458
: (colon), 458, 840
, (comma)
   array constants, 471, 472
   formatting while typing, 297–298
   imported data, 755
   separating arguments, 491, 840
   structured references, 457, 458
   styles of, 298
© (copyright symbol), 228
/ (division sign, slash)
   data entry, 139
   formatting while typing, 297–298
   keyboard command activation, 40
   operator precedence, 427
   structured references, 458
$ (dollar sign)
   cell references, 429–430
   data entry, 138
   formatting while typing, 297–298
   structured references, 458
= (equal sign), 427, 458, 478, 840
> = (greater than or equal to operator), 478
> (greater than operator), 458, 478
- (hyphen), 753
< = (less than or equal to operator), 478
< (less than operator), 458, 478
– (minus sign), 138, 256, 427, 458

< > (not equal to), 478
( ) (parentheses)
   argument syntax, 841
   functions and, 438, 490
   negative numbers, 138
   operator precedence and, 427
. (period), 458, 755
% (percent sign), 139, 297–298
+ (plus sign), 138, 256, 427, 458
# (pound sign)
   ##### error display, 531
   expand cell indicator, 140
   structured references, 458
? (question mark), 225, 689
" (quotation mark), 142–143, 458
; (semicolon), 471, 472
~ (tilde), 225, 689
_ (underscore character), 840
1-dimensional arrays, 468–469
1-variable data tables, 583–586
2-dimensional arrays, 470
2-variable data tables, 586–587
3-dimensional arrays, 470
3-dimensional cell references, 448–449
3-dimensional chart axes, 651–652
3-dimensional formulas, 453–454
3-dimensional graphic effects, 378–381
3-dimensional rotation, 370, 371
4-part formats, 312
12- and 24-hour clocks, 523, 528
12/31/29 magic crossover date, 523
1900 and 1904 date system, 522
2008 New Projects.xlsx, 151
2008 Projections.xlsx file, 412

A

A functions, 556
A status link indicator, 475
A1 reference style, 431–432

Z